The Irish Franciscans, 1534–1990

D1570318

The Irish Franciscans
1534–1990

Edel Bhreathnach, Joseph MacMahon OFM
& John McCafferty

EDITORS

FOUR COURTS PRESS

Typeset in 10.5 pt on 13.5 pt AGaramond by
Carrigboy Typesetting Services for
FOUR COURTS PRESS LTD
7 Malpas Street, Dublin 8, Ireland
www.fourcourtspress.ie
and in North America for
FOUR COURTS PRESS
c/o ISBS, 920 NE 58th Avenue, Suite 300, Portland, OR 97213.

A catalogue record for this title is available
from the British Library.

ISBN 978–1–84682–209–4 hbk
978–1–84682–210–0 pbk

Printed in England
by MPG Books, Bodmin, Cornwall.

Contents

PART II: THE LEGACY OF THE IRISH FRANCISCANS

Illustrations

PLATES

appear between pp 302 and 303

Contributors and editors

CONTRIBUTORS

Fr Patrick Conlan OFM, Franciscan Friary, Merchants' Quay, Dublin 2

Dr Bernadette Cunningham, Deputy Librarian, Royal Irish Academy

Professor Mary E. Daly, College Principal, UCD College of Arts and Celtic Studies

Fr Ignatius Fennessy OFM, Librarian, Franciscan Library Killiney

Professor Raymond Gillespie, Department of History, NUI Maynooth

Dr Małgorzata Krasnodębska-D'Aughton, Department of History, University College Cork

Professor Colm Lennon, Department of History, NUI Maynooth

Dr Mary Ann Lyons, History Department, St Patrick's College, Drumcondra

An tOllamh Mícheál Mac Craith OFM, Scoil na Gaeilge, Ollscoil Éireann, Gaillimh

Dr Joseph MacMahon OFM, Secretary, Irish Franciscan Province

Dr Michael O'Neill, Architectural Historian and Consultant, Dublin

Professor (Emeritus) Pádraig Ó Riain, Department of Early and Medieval Irish, University College Cork

Professor Salvador Ryan, St Patrick's College, Maynooth

Professor M.W.F. Stone, De Wulf-Mansion Centre for Ancient, Medieval and Renaissance Philosophy, Katholieke Universiteit Leuven

EDITORS

Dr Edel Bhreathnach, Academic Project Manager, UCD Mícheál Ó Cléirigh Institute

Dr Joseph MacMahon OFM, Secretary, Irish Franciscan Province

Dr John McCafferty, Director, UCD Mícheál Ó Cléirigh Institute

Foreword

CAOIMHÍN Ó LAOIDE OFM
Minister Provincial, Franciscan Province of Ireland

As a Franciscan in 2009, this volume cannot be received with any calm detachment or cool objectivity. Instead, the long awaited achievement of a complete history of the Irish Franciscans is cause for great delight and gratitude. It is also an occasion for the singular consolation and challenge that comes with immersion in the story of our forebears. Consolation – in that however difficult our own times are, there have been worse periods from which the Franciscans emerged with life and vitality. Challenge – in that the Franciscans faced a variety of trials and opportunities with verve and creativity, but also with their opposites.

The words of Chief Rabbi Jonathan Sacks come to my mind:

> History is what happened to someone else. Memory is what happened to me. Memory is history internalised, the past made present to those who relive it. Through personal identification with the great moments of the past, they become part of what makes us who we are. We become characters in a continuing story which began before we were born and will continue after we have ceased to be.

> Without memory, there is no identity, and without identity we are cast adrift into a sea of chance, without compass, map or destination.

Commemoration is something we Christians learned from the Jewish people – we know that our identity is incrementally marked and deepened by a succession of commemorative experiences, which is why histories and historians are honoured as custodians of identity.

The year 2009 marks a very significant commemoration for Franciscans and so the publication of this history comes at a beautifully apposite moment. Eight hundred years ago, in 1209, St Francis of Assisi walked to Rome with a few companions to ask the most powerful pope of the age, Innocent III, to approve his rule, or way of life. Against all the odds, this sophisticated Pontiff saw the Holy Spirit at work in the ragged group of young men led by the drop-out son of a *nouveau riche* cloth merchant. The lives of the men and women described in this volume were touched by a call similar to that of St Francis, and were shaped by the rule which Innocent approved so long ago.

A team of collaborators has been at work over many months in the production and editing of this history. My deep and sincere gratitude goes to the Mícheál Ó Cléirigh Institute at UCD which has been at the heart of this achievement. The partnership between the Franciscan Province of Ireland (OFM) and UCD has been mutually enriching to a degree which could not have been anticipated at its beginnings. The history of the Irish Franciscans is simply the latest in a succession of wonderful events and enterprises and we can look forward to many more. My congratulations to the editors, Drs Edel Bhreathnach and John McCafferty from UCD who have worked with Joseph MacMahon OFM, not solely as academic colleagues, but as friends with a shared appreciation and reverence for the Franciscan Tradition.

Do chum glóire Dé agus onóra na hÉireann.

Introduction

Irish Franciscans have made history and Irish Franciscans have written history. This present volume was inspired by two anniversaries – the 400th of St Anthony's College, Louvain in 2007 and the 800th of St Francis' journey to Rome to seek approval of the rule from Pope Innocent III in 1209. In the wake of a well-received summer school in Leuven during May 2007 the editors decided that a single volume history of Irish Franciscanism covering the period 1534–1990 could be realized before the close of the eighth centenary in 2009. Anniversaries apart there are a number of good reasons why the first decade of the twenty-first century is an appropriate time to undertake such a project. In his 1995 reflection on fifty years of Dún Mhuire, Killiney, Monsignor Patrick Corish remarked: 'the manuscripts, of course, are an unalienable Franciscan inheritance. The library too was assembled by Franciscans for Franciscan purposes, and it does seem unthinkable that it should be broken up or pass out of Franciscan control'.[1] Corish's estimation presents a stark choice between Franciscan continuity and alienation or closure. Yet there was a somewhat different future in store. In 1997 and then again in 2000 the friars signed partnership agreements with University College Dublin. In consequence many books and manuscipts have changed their physical location from Killiney to the repositories of the university. Ownership, though, has remained unaltered and the partnership arrangement has, over time, transformed notions of control and use. Both UCD's long tradition of Celtic studies and Irish history and the friars' venerable commitment to Ireland's culture and history have been reinvigorated by a working relationship energized by mutual respect. Dún Mhuire had been founded as a house of studies one of whose central aims was to be the production of a history of the Irish Franciscan province. While the friar scholars of the house made very distinguished and fundamental contributions to that work (as the bibliography of this book shows) they did not bring it to completion. This volume attempts that history in very changed circumstances. Some of the contributors are friars but most of them are not. In part this reflects the overall spirit of partnership fostered by the Mícheál Ó Cléirigh Institute. More vitally it bears witness to the way in which the story of the friars, Poor Clares and the Third Order has begun to attract the attention of scholars across a very wide range of disciplines. In turn, the variety of contributors moves the volume outside of the Franciscan *familia* and, hopefully, ensures a

---

1 Millett & Lynch, *Dún Mhuire* (1995), p. 7.

richly contextualized and collaborative understanding of just under five hundred
years of religious, social and economic life of Irish people at home and abroad.

    While very consciously evoking the Killiney project this history does not begin
with the arrival of the first friars in the thirteenth century. Francis Cotter's *The
friars minor in Ireland from their arrival to 1400* (1994) and Colmán Ó Clabaigh's
The Franciscans in Ireland 1400–1534 (2002) offer between them a recent narrative
and thematic treatment of the first three centuries. In any event English state-
sponsored reformation changed the shape of Irish Franciscanism in ways that are
traceable right down to the era of Vatican II. That council altered both the
language and structure of the liturgy partly in a bid to make it more engaging for
more people. The editors and contributors to this work also hope to engage the
reader by combining scholarly rigour with an awareness of the linguistic, physical,
spiritual, theological and intellectual environment within which Franciscans lived
and worked from the sixteenth to twentieth centuries. Michael O'Neill's chapter
in this book is unlike all of the others as it is mainly concerned with the middle
ages in describing the architecture and layout of the pre-reformation houses. The
network of ruined friaries is still striking today but in the centuries immediately
after their destruction they were not only imposing landscape features but
also appear to have had a particular hold on the friars and their supporters.
Franciscans repeatedly returned to, or lingered near, the places where their
predecessors had been. Many nineteenth- and twentieth-century friaries were
located near where houses had been before the mid-sixteenth century. Donagh
Mooney's early seventeenth-century history of the province offered not only an
early martyrology for Irish Franciscans but also a gazeteer of foundations which
could still find expression in the anonymous nineteenth-century frescoes in the
refectory at St Isidore's Rome or on the home page of the website of today's
province.[2] Such a deliberate recapitulation of the medieval past is not unique to
Irish Franciscans but it has certainly been very marked. Many of the chapters in
this volume show that evocation of the past was intimately bound up with a
ceaseless process of decline and reform. For example, amongst the friars minor
overall numbers have fallen to about one hundred or below at least once in every
century since 1500 with the sole exception of the last century. Periods of decline
have brought both abuse and determination and periods of reform have brought
both abundance and disarray. Through the centuries Franciscans have been
courageous and cowardly, generous and greedy, humble and haughty, poor and
prideful, smart and silly but, as every contribution here shows, always of
significance in Irish life.

2 www.franciscans.ie, accessed 11 February 2009.

While this volume gathers together many of those involved in the study of Irish Franciscan history it is far from being definitive. The UCD–OFM partnership and its institutional manifestation – the Mícheál Ó Cléirigh Institute – are dedicated to ensuring that the book and manuscript heritage of the friars becomes easily accessible to interested researchers. Without conservation, digitization and fieldwork already undertaken in the last decade a number of the essays which follow could never have been written. Małgorzata Krasnodębska-D'Aughton's work on silver plate is just one example and points to the potential of this vast archive to open up, in future, brand new areas of enquiry. This history, like Dún Mhuire, and like the Mícheál Ó Cléirigh Institute, aims to encourage others to join us in our work and in extending our appreciation of the archive as an expression of the Franciscan experience in Ireland. Here the signs are most encouraging, as Martin Stone's researches into the rich intellectual deposits left by Irish Franciscan Scotists show. Because of 2007 and because of the current vigour of studies in the early modern period in both the English and Irish languages this volume has a lot to say about the sixteenth and seventeenth centuries in the contributions by Colm Lennon, Mary Ann Lyons, Mícheál Mac Craith, Ray Gillespie, Pádraig Ó Riain, Salvador Ryan, Bernadette Cunningham and Ignatius Fennessy. But as the ground-breaking chapters by Joseph MacMahon, Patrick Conlan and Mary Daly show, much remains to be done on the eighteenth, nineteenth and twentieth centuries. Happily, as with the remarkable exile efflorescence of the seventeenth century, the sources are not lacking and offer an abundance for new generations of scholars.

Edel Bhreathnach
Joseph MacMahon OFM
John McCafferty
Editors
March 2009

Acknowledgments

We wish to thank the following individuals for assistance with this volume: Martin Fanning, Four Courts Press, Colmán Ó Clabaigh OSB, Glenstal Abbey, Raghnall Ó Floinn, National Museum of Ireland, Anthony Corns of the Discovery Programme, Anthony Lynch and Julitta Clancy who compiled the index. Much support for this work emanated from the UCD-OFM partnership and we also thank Elizabeth Dawson, Evelyn Flanagan, Seamus Helferty, Rena Lohan and Margaret Purcell for their work in the transfer of many of the books and manuscripts consulted by our contributors from Killiney to UCD. Without the assistance of the Departments of the Taoiseach and Arts, Sports and Tourism, the Irish embassy to Belgium and the Irish Franciscan Province, neither this volume nor the Louvain 400 commemorations would have been possible. We also would like to record our gratitude to Louis Brennan OFM, Caoimhín Ó Laoide OFM and Ulic Troy OFM. We gratefully acknowledge the award of a grant in aid of publication from the Senate of the National University of Ireland.

The greatest thanks are due to our contributors who not only wrote the scholarly articles but also gave generously of their time and expertise in a host of different ways.

PART I

The Irish Franciscans, 1534–1990

The dissolution to the foundation of St Anthony's College, Louvain, 1534–1607

COLM LENNON

At the time of the dissolution of the monasteries in Ireland in the late 1530s the Franciscans appeared to be in a stronger position to face the challenge of the Reformation than most of their counterpart orders. Not only had there been a rapid expansion in the number of Franciscan friaries in the previous century, but a strong internal reforming spirit had animated most sections of the order. Many of the new foundations made since the mid-fifteenth century had been for the movement of strict Observance, while several existing houses transferred from the traditional Conventuals to the Observant vicariate. Moreover, the same period had witnessed the phenomenal rise of the Third Order regular and secular of St Francis throughout much of the country, with almost fifty houses of regular Tertiaries being established between 1440 and 1540. On an organizational level, the rise of Observantism in particular was characterized by enthusiasm on the part of Irish friars for full participation in the national and international constitutional structures of the Franciscans, thereby opening them to new ideas and making them *au courant* with contemporary events on the Continent and in England. Pastorally, the friars in late medieval Ireland had established their reputation for inspirational preaching and effective ministry, at a time perhaps when clerical zeal in general was languishing, at least according to the well-known report of 1515 that none of the clergy preached the gospel in Ireland, 'saving the poor friars beggars'.[1] The close ties between the Franciscan order and their lay patrons and associates, especially outside the Pale, elicited a reciprocal system of support in town and countryside.[2]

This survey of Franciscan history in Ireland between the 1530s and the 1600s examines how the strengths of the order in the late middle ages were drawn upon in the face of ecclesiastical disruption and religious uncertainty. An impressive network of up to 100 houses of Observants, Conventuals and Tertiaries, accommodating between 500 and 1,000 persons and embracing the entire island, lent an air of ubiquity to the presence of the friars in the Reformation and early Counter-Reformation periods, notwithstanding the closure of a significant number of friaries from the late 1530s onwards. Their attunement to many of the theological

---

1 'State of Ireland and plan for its reformation', *c.*1515 in *State Papers, Henry VIII*, ii, 15.   2 For an excellent survey of the order in late medieval Ireland, see Ó Clabaigh, *Franciscans in Ireland*.

and jurisdictional points at issue between the Protestant reformers and the defenders of the Catholic position thrust them into a prominent role in countering the innovations in religious practice and organisation under Henry VIII, Edward VI and Elizabeth I. The nexus between the friars and their lay protectors allowed for the survival of many houses against the odds, and ensured that there was a vocal clerical element preaching against the reforms, and teaching the norms of Catholic orthodoxy throughout the later sixteenth century. A leadership role was guaranteed to the friars, given the prestige of their order among the elites of Gaelic society particularly, but also at points of interface between the two ethnicities of late medieval Ireland. This was buttressed by their strong engagement with Gaelic cultural forms in the communication of their message of renewal. Inurement in the vibrant Counter-Reformation milieu of their continental *confrères* also brought a strand of militancy into the missionary work of a minority of the friars, a number of whom were executed for their religious beliefs.

ROYAL SUPREMACY AND THE DISSOLUTION OF RELIGIOUS HOUSES, 1539–60

By the time the mechanisms for the systematic dissolution of the religious houses, including the friaries, were applied in Ireland in 1539–40 under the aegis of royal ecclesiastical management, opposition to the king's supremacy had assumed very much a Franciscan focus. Indeed, even before the Irish parliament passed the Act of Supremacy and other Reformation statutes in 1536, there are indications that Irish Observants were fully aware of the issues involved in Henry VIII's break with Rome. Francis Faber, the French-born visitor of the Irish houses of strict Observance in 1534, had, during his provincialate in England the previous year, come under the influence of strong Observant antipathy there to the king's supremacy.[3] On his departure for Ireland, Eustace Chapuys, the imperial ambassador in London, reported to Charles V that Faber 'would brew up there all he could for the preservation of the holy see'.[4] Opining that the visitor 'may do wonderful service' in this respect because of the friars' influence, Chapuys explained to his master that 'especially among the wild Irish ... these Cordeliers [Observants] are feared, obeyed and almost adored not only by the peasants but also by the lords who hold them in such reverence as to endure from them blows from a stick'.[5] When the campaign to promulgate the royal supremacy began officially in Ireland under the English-born archbishop of Dublin, George

---

3 Ó Clabaigh, *Franciscans in Ireland*, pp 77–8; P. Rogers, 'The Irish Franciscan Observants and the royal supremacy' (1935), p. 204.   4 Ó Clabaigh, *Franciscans in Ireland*, p. 78.   5 Ibid.

Browne, a former Augustinian friar, the most vociferous opponents were among the Observant Franciscans. Browne found that he could 'neither make them swear [to the supremacy] nor yet preach amongst us, so little they regard mine authority',[6] while Thomas Aagarde in his frustration berated the Observants in 1538 as 'false and crafty bloodsuckers', who considered that there was 'more virtue in one of their coats and knotted girdles than ever was in Christ and his passion'.[7] Dr Saul, an Observant at Waterford, was one such antagonist who preached against the supremacy in March 1538, for which offence he was imprisoned in Dublin castle.[8] No doubt the news of the execution of the Observant friar, John Forest, in London that year not only steeled the resolve of his Irish *confrères*, but also raised the stakes, the Englishman's case centring on substantive issues of doctrine rather than merely on the question of schism within the Henrician church.[9]

Archbishop Browne made an attempt to subsume the Observant Franciscans within the more malleable Conventuals, as he had done successfully in England, but, apart from the expedient of 'naming them conventuals', nothing was accomplished.[10] The danger that they posed to another aspect of the royal reforms of late medieval religion, the dismantling of shrines and removal of sacred images in 1539, was articulated by the chancellor, John Alen, who feared that the campaign might be undermined by 'the enticement and conduct of our friars obstinates [sic]'.[11] By that stage, however, news was percolating of the wholesale dissolution of the religious houses in England, and the likelihood of a similar programme being initiated in Ireland occasioned a flurry of precautionary moves on the part of religious communities. Unlike the monasteries and nunneries, the friaries had little real estate, the Conventuals perhaps being slightly better endowed than the Observants. The commission for suppression of the monasteries was issued in April 1539, and the work of closing the houses and pensioning off the occupants began in the late autumn of that year. By late 1540 the intensive phase of disbandment of communities, including the mendicants, had been completed in the zone of English jurisdiction in the Pale, Wexford and Ormond, within which the campaign of dissolution was initially effected. Further suppressions of individual houses in the north-east, south and west of the country followed before the death of Henry VIII in 1547, resulting in an overall closure rate of about forty per cent of the mendicant orders' friaries and priories.[12]

The rate of attrition among the Franciscan Conventuals and Observants was broadly in line with this national trend. Also, three-quarters of the two dozen

6 Rogers, 'The Irish Franciscan Observants and the royal supremacy', p. 210.   7 Thomas Aagarde to Thomas Cromwell, 5 April 1538 (*State Papers, Henry VIII*, ii, 570).   8 Ibid., ii, p. 562; Conlan, *FI*, p. 27.   9 P. Marshall, 'Papist as heretic: the burning of John Forest, 1538' (1998).   10 B. Bradshaw, *The dissolution of the religious orders* (1974), pp 95–6.   11 Ibid., p. 211.   12 Ibid., pp 206–7.

Franciscan houses that were officially suppressed during the Henrician period were affiliated to the Observants, demonstrating the deep penetration through foundation or conversion of the strict observance into the regions of Ireland that lay mostly under English jurisdiction. These included friaries in the towns and cities of Carrickfergus, Cork, Drogheda, Dublin, Limerick and Waterford, only Kilkenny facing suppression as a Conventual house. Of the larger towns, including Cashel, Clonmel, Ennis, Trim, Wexford and Youghal, only Dundalk, Buttevant and New Ross had Conventual friaries at the dissolution. Two of the houses in the south-western marches of the Pale, Castledermot and Clane, remained Conventual at their closures, but the suppressed houses of Kildare, Kilcullen and Enniscorthy were Observant. Of the more rural friaries that were affected, Carrickbeg and Muckross were Conventual, Galbally and Multyfarnham belonging to the Observant movement. Most of the Franciscan closures took place in the 1539–40 phase of the dissolutions, only a few falling in the follow-up campaign of Sir Anthony St Leger during the 1540s. Of the three dozen remaining houses of the First Order located outside the zone of English jurisdiction that were unaffected by the Henrician suppressions, up to two-thirds were affiliated to the Observants, while the vast majority of the four dozen or so houses of regular Tertiaries were similarly untouched during that period.[13]

Notwithstanding the decimation of the order's structures within the anglicized zone of Ireland, the friars retained a significant presence therein. In the major urban centres, the friary buildings were decommissioned and mostly lost to the religious sphere. Some fell to demolition, but most were turned to secular purposes. The friary in Waterford, for example, became a hospital, in Limerick a court-house and in Dublin a private residence.[14] The civic authorities in Kilkenny, Drogheda, Clonmel and Waterford benefited by receiving grants of the town premises of the Franciscans, which normally comprised only a couple of acres at most.[15] In many places, however, there are indications that the friars continued to live communally in close proximity to their former domiciles, perhaps not without municipal connivance. Whereas in Dublin, Kilkenny and Cork, the Franciscan communities appear to have dispersed soon after 1540, at Waterford, Youghal, Wexford, Limerick and Dundalk, they remained on for at least a number of years, in the last-mentioned town, for instance, occupying 'a small cottage nearby'.[16] Several communities of Franciscans even persisted in occupying their officially closed friaries, particularly in places at some remove from the English heartland. Cashel, Clane, Claregalway, Ennis, Enniscorthy, Galbally and

---

13 The statistical information is based on Donatus Mooney, 'Brussels MS. 3947'; *MRH*, pp 240–62. 14 *MRH*, pp 254, 260; H. Clarke (ed.), *Dublin, part I: to 1610* (2002), p. 19.   15 Bradshaw, *Dissolution of the religious orders*, p. 143.   16 L.P. Murray, 'The Franciscan monasteries after the dissolution' (1935), p. 278.

Kilcullen were among the centres in which friars seem to have remained in possession in spite of their official suppression, in some instances for several decades.

To understand this intermittent pattern of continuity, a number of factors may be adduced. Some instances of the survival of communal Franciscan living were very brief, but others lasted for periods of from seven-to-ten years up to half-a-century. Relative proximity to the seat of government power exercised an influence, those houses located in border and peripheral regions that underwent formal suppression managing to endure the longer. Cities, which had more of the character of quasi-autonomous enclaves the farther they were removed from Dublin, offered the possibility of institutional protection or concerted communal intervention. Larger and smaller towns, which were usually under the sway of powerful noble families, could be supportive of the friars' continuation in their midst. Some premises proved to be more suitable than others for continued occupation, selected friaries being precluded from religious use either through dilapidation or else through their prime utility for secular purposes. Above all, the supportiveness of local potentates, institutions and communities was crucial, a corollary to the pervading spiritual influence of the Observants, as attested by contemporary observers. The mutuality of the bond between the friars and the laity, forged through generations of familial and communal interplay, is captured in the intricate interweaving of names of founders and Franciscan houses in the list provided by Francis O'Mahony in his brief history of the Irish province.[17] Thus, it is no surprise that the full dissolution of Ennis friary, an O'Brien foundation of the thirteenth century and burial place of family members, should have been delayed by several decades through the protection of the clan in the mid-sixteenth century, nor that the MacCarthys, the Fitzgeralds of Desmond and the Barrys should have performed a similar role in relation to their respective foundations and family burial places at Muckross, Youghal and Buttevant.[18] In order to understand the quality of the connections thus elicited, three important examples of noble and civic patronage securing the survival of Franciscan activity at Multyfarnham, Slane and Limerick – those of the Nugents, Flemings and the local citizenry respectively – are worthy of observation.

That Multyfarnham friary continued as a place of sanctuary for religious until the early seventeenth century was due to the protection of the Nugent family of Delvin. When the commissioners for the suppression of the monasteries visited Multyfarnham in 1540, they found a compact and well-repaired set of buildings, and a small island 'near a lake'. A year later, visitors found evidence of continuing

---

17 'Brevis synopsis', pp 144–68. **18** *MRH*, p. 250; Conlan, *FI*, pp 134–5; 'Brussels MS. 3947', pp 72–3; P. Conlan, 'The Franciscans at Buttevant' (2002), pp 196–7.

habitation, the church standing, the buildings well maintained and the furniture and books unconfiscated. In this almost-exceptional case of the preservation not only of the property but also the chattels of a friary, the 'protecting hand of the lord of Delvin' has been detected.[19] The Franciscans withdrew from the friary to the island, called 'friars' island', for some time after 1540, but were re-established in their house at Multyfarnham under Nugent patronage by the 1550s. The castle of the barons of Delvin at Clonyn lay just twelve miles away from the friary, which had been heavily patronized by the Nugents since its foundation. The friary had become the necropolis of the family, its church containing very ornate stone table-tombs several commemorating family members. Multyfarnham was the centre for the patronal festivals of the entire sept of the Nugents who gathered there annually for several days of ceremony and feasting. It was also a place of learning, its library housing a copy of the famous twelfth-century saga *Cogadh Gaedhel re Gallaibh.* From the 1560s the friary came under the protection of Christopher Nugent, baron of Delvin, who became notable as a vociferous opponent of state political and religious reforms. Among his acts of defiance of the regime was the harbouring of the Franciscan bishop of Kilmore, Richard Brady, at Multyfarnham in the 1580s and 1590s. During the climactic years of the Nine Years War, it was a source of deep embarrassment to crown officials that a friary be 'suffered to stand untouched' in 'the heart of the English Pale'. Eventually action was taken by Sir Francis Shane in 1601 against 'the nursery of all mischievous practices', which seriously disrupted communal life, but the friars continued to regroup in and around the pole of Multyfarnham.[20]

Another example of long-standing associations between layfolk and the Franciscans helping a foundation to continue, occurred at Slane, Co. Meath, in the case of the Third Order house there. In 1512, Christopher Fleming, the baron of Slane, and his wife, Elizabeth Stuckley, had granted the hermitage of St Erc, in the grounds of Slane Castle, to members of the Third Order, including Fr Malachy O'Bryen and Br Donagh O'Bryen, who were already living there.[21] With it was associated a college for twelve clerics, established in the same location.[22] Institutional life in this complex of buildings was formally ended at the dissolution in 1540, with the confiscation of the premises, garden and closes.[23] In 1543, the properties and goods attached to the 'friary' were granted by the crown to the then-baron, James Fleming.[24] During the later Tudor period, the Flemings, who retained the ecclesiastical perquisites of advowson, tithes and rentals of Slane

19 Bradshaw, *Dissolution of the religious orders*, p. 141.   **20** For an analysis of the Delvin family's role as patrons of the church, see C. Lennon, 'The Nugent family and the diocese of Kilmore' (2001). **21** Ó Clabaigh, *Franciscans in Ireland*, p. 99; *MRH*, p. 274.   **22** A. Cogan, *The diocese of Meath: ancient and modern* (1862–70), i, p. 286; O.C. Curran, *History of the diocese of Meath, 1860–1993* (1995), p. 1041; *MRH*, p. 361.   **23** *MRH*, p. 274.   **24** Ibid.

college and parish, were protectors of Roman Catholic bishops and several friars. They acted as intermediaries for the mission of the Counter-Reformation clergy in the region, using the resources of the older corporate system of devotion to support the Catholic renewal, and thus playing a role similar to that of the Nugent family of Delvin in their protection of the Franciscans at Multyfarnham. To underscore the closeness of the ties between the patronal family and the order, the example of a baron of Slane becoming a Tertiary may be adduced. According to Mooney, a member of the family took on the habit of a penitent in the hermitage of Slane, living within earshot of the church where Mass was celebrated, separating himself from the secular world until his pious death.[25]

At Limerick, where there was an interface between English and Gaelic cultures, a network of supporters of both ethnic backgrounds came forward to assist the Observant Franciscan community in the transitional phase after it had been ordered to dissolve in 1542. In what appears to have been a systematic but benevolent stripping of assets, up to twenty of these abettors of varying social rank divided the possessions and lands of the friars among them. In the case of the sacral objects, such as silver chalices, brass candlesticks, books and vestments, local merchants and tradesmen were reported to have held them in pledge: John McSheedy, a tailor of Limerick, for example, held 'a book of the friars in gage for 8*d*.'. Similarly, the gardens of the friary, some within the precincts, were being leased by people from long-established Limerick families, such as Creagh, Rice, Harrold, Stritch, and Comyn, for sums ranging from eight shillings to sixteen pence. Stephen Harrold's rental of the churchyard yielded the most significant amount, he being committed to paying £16 per annum.[26] This minute dismemberment of the friars' property might in other circumstances smack of opportunism,[27] but the friary was granted to the local entrepreneur, Edmund Sexton, who had also acquired other monastic lands.[28] What is suggested by the citizens' involvement is rather a scheme for the retention of the community in the vicinity of the dissolved friary, possibly with contributions to their welfare, by securing the holy objects for worship and also the small property portfolio for income. If such was the intention, the plan was successful in the short-term, as the Observants remained in being as a community until 1548, when their dispersal took place. This protective network of well-wishers, probably with the backing of the O'Briens of Thomond and the Fitzgeralds of Desmond, ensured the shepherding of the resources of the old order to be channeled eventually into a Counter-

---

25 'Brussels MS. 3947', p. 104.   26 BL Add. MS 19,865, ff 68–9.   27 See, for example, the case of Cork, where the local citizenry dismembered the friars' possessions very soon after the closure of the friary: H.A. Jefferies, *Cork: historical perspectives* (2004), p. 109; see also Bradshaw, *Dissolution of the religious orders*, pp 153–5.   28 Bradshaw, *Dissolution of the religious orders*, p. 152.

Reformation organization, in which the Franciscans were to play a prominent part. Even Edmund Sexton, the grantee of the friary, reflecting the general mood, was reprimanded for releasing from prison a friar who had preached against the king's supremacy while he was mayor of the city.[29]

The force of the initial onslaught of officialdom against the Franciscan friaries in the 1540s was thus frequently vitiated through the intervention of local powers. Continuity depended not only on the strength of these leaders, however, but also on the strategic location of the foundations in the context of the expansion of English civil jurisdiction in the later Tudor period. Multyfarnham and Slane, for example, were cushioned from its effects by a vibrant gentry ascendancy in the western Pale, but Limerick, along with its counterpart-boroughs in the south and south-west, gradually became more enmeshed in the government's assertion of control through the provincial presidencies. This was especially so after the adoption of Protestantism as the state religion on the accession of Edward VI in 1547. In these circumstances, any public vestiges of communal living on the part of the mendicants in boroughs such as Kilkenny and Waterford, as well as Limerick, were precluded, the religious affiliations of the citizens notwithstanding.[30] A similar effect may be witnessed in respect of the Franciscan houses in the southern part of the Pale, south Leinster and east Munster, regions in which the outreach of central government was felt during the 1550s and 1560s. The friars at Kildare, Kilcullen and Clane were driven out of their houses during the years 1547 to 1550, before the restoration of the Fitzgeralds of Kildare to their earldom.[31] At New Ross the expulsion of the friars came in 1549–50, though they may have reoccupied their house briefly under Queen Mary before the final destruction in 1558.[32] The friary at Cashel was forced to close in 1550, while that at Nenagh lasted longer, eventually falling to destruction in the Elizabethan period after 1558.[33] The path of English politico-religious reform may thus be traced in the pattern of delayed closures in the southern half of the country, though the relocation of the friars out of the public eye was undoubtedly a feature in many places.

During the reign of Queen Mary, which witnessed the restoration of Roman Catholicism in England and Ireland, comparatively few Franciscan survivals are recorded in the zone of crown control. Appeals made to the queen and Cardinal Pole, her papal legate, for the re-establishment of the religious communities in their traditional locations were fraught with difficulty, as the properties had in many cases been granted to lay occupants and, in some cases, been demolished.[34]

---

29 Ibid.   **30** *MRH*, pp 253, 254, 260; 'Brussels MS. 3947', pp 62–3, 80–1, 82–3.   **31** *MRH*, pp 245, 252; 'Brussels MS. 3947', pp 85, 86.   **32** *MRH*, p. 257; 'Brussels MS. 3947', pp 81–2.   **33** *MRH*, pp 244, 257; 'Brussels MS. 3947', pp 75, 76–8.   **34** For the context of the vexed issue of the retention of ecclesiastical property by the laity, see F. Heal, *Reformation in Britain and Ireland* (2003), pp 177–8.

In all, seven houses of Observants were mentioned as either possible targets for revival of communal living, or else as having in fact undergone renewal *in situ*.[35] In the former category are Kilcullen, Trim and Enniscorthy, in the latter are Dundalk, Waterford and Kilkenny, while Multyfarnham certainly continued as a centre of mendicant living. It is in the entreaty of the friars of Kilcullen, two of whom went to London to put the case to Queen Mary and Cardinal Pole, that the movement towards restoration is attested.[36] They asked for the recovery of the friary of Kilcullen itself, which was held by Roland Eustace, Viscount Baltinglass, Trim, which had been granted to the town's citizens, Enniscorthy, which Richard Butler held 'without title', and Multyfarnham, which its purchaser, Thomas Cusack, was reported as willing to give back.[37] In all of these cases, apparently, the premises were available for repossession, and the lay grantees perhaps not averse to the friars' re-entry. By contrast, according to the emissaries, some houses were beyond recovery, especially Carrickfergus in which English soldiers had stabled their horses.[38] Revived communities may also have appeared in Dundalk, Kilkenny and Wexford during the Marian period, but none survived beyond the first five years of the reign of Queen Elizabeth I.[39] The fate of the friars without a protected base is plaintively attested in the words of the emissaries from Kilcullen *c*.1554: 'we have all been living in the mountains since the suppression'.[40]

THE ELIZABETHAN PERIOD

As the early phase of the Reformation concluded with the re-imposition of Protestantism under Queen Elizabeth in 1560, the frontline of Franciscan continuity lay along the borders of north Munster (along with its extreme south-west), Connacht and Ulster. The expansion of the state's administrative apparatus into these regions during the subsequent decades brought with it the closure of two or three dozen houses, thus far untouched, the most intensive period of new dissolutions taking place in the 1580s, when at least twelve friaries were suppressed. Yet the piecemeal and haphazard nature of the Elizabethan campaign gave a breathing-space to the occupants, allowing them to prepare for a phased withdrawal. More generally, the Observant friars were enabled to marshal their considerable practical and moral resources to forge a counter-reformation, which drew upon a network of bases abroad as well as in Ireland. As most places that survived were located in areas of Gaelic culture, the articulation of much of that spiritual programme was in the Irish language, through the medium of which a

35 Bradshaw, *Dissolution of the religious orders*, p. 144.   **36** Conlan, *FI*, p. 29.   **37** For the text of the appeal of the friars of Kilcullen, see T.F. Mayer (ed.), *The correspondence of Reginald Pole* (2003), ii, pp 398–9. **38** Ibid., p. 399.   **39** *MRH*, pp 249, 253, 261.   **40** Mayer, *The correspondence of Reginald Pole*, ii, p. 399.

rich inheritance of Franciscan learning and literature had been bequeathed from the medieval period. The interpenetration of the two ethnic communities of the late middle ages, however, ensured a vibrant hybridism, especially in some of the larger towns to which the friars returned after an absence in the late sixteenth century. In an era characterized by militant action in support of politico-religious principles, it is not surprising that some Franciscan friars became enmeshed in the thralls of campaigns of the various rulers of Gaelic and Anglo-Ireland. Accordingly, the friars' self-assertion in the Counter-Reformation and the struggle for an Irish Catholic polity down to the early seventeenth century were, to a large extent, reciprocal movements.[41]

The survival of the Irish province

Fundamental to the successful survival of the Observant Franciscans in the later sixteenth century was the robustness of the administrative structures under-pinning the order. The legacy of a strong independent provincialate from the fifteenth century fostered self-confidence and, as necessary, self-reliance in the face of adversity.[42] Throughout the period, Irish vicars provincial continued to be elected, some twenty individuals holding office down to the incumbency of Flaithrí Ó Maoil Chonaire [Florence Conry] in 1606–9.[43] Provincial chapters were held consistently in functioning friaries such as Askeaton and Donegal. Only in the most difficult circumstances was the meeting not convened, as in 1605 in the wake of the government proclamation expelling seminary priests and Jesuits from Ireland.[44] Participation in the international administration of the Observantine Franciscans provided a vital lifeline to the world of Tridentine Catholic renewal which eventually took firm root in Ireland. Visitors were appointed by the order in Rome to preside at provincial chapters and report back on conditions obtaining in the country. Attendance by Irish Franciscan leaders at international chapters appears also to have continued from the early Reformation onwards. In 1540 the Irish vicar provincial had journeyed to Rome, taking the opportunity to brief the Holy Roman Emperor on events in Ireland *en route*.[45] Contact was also made with the general chapter of the Capuchin order, with a view to introducing into Ireland this new reformed group within the Franciscan family.[46] Although naturally subject to periodic dislocation, this efficient administration helped to bolster morale at home, and also served to provide a valuable support network abroad, especially when the necessity arose for friars to seek refuge in continental Franciscan houses for reasons of education or security.

41 See M. Mac Craith, 'Creideamh agus athartha: idéolaíochta agus aos léinn na Gaeilge' (1996).   **42** F.X. Martin, 'The Irish friars and the Observant movement of the fifteenth century' (1960).   **43** 'Brevis synopsis', pp 169–71.   **44** Conlan, *FI*, p. 35.   **45** Ibid., p. 27; Bradshaw, *Dissolution of the religious orders*, p. 208.   **46** Bradshaw, *Dissolution of the religious orders*, p. 208.

For example, when Teige O'Daly was arrested in late 1577 or early 1578, he was found to have in his possession a letter of recommendation to the provincial of Portugal, presumably from his Irish superior for use in his impending flight from Ireland.[47]

The contrasting fate of the Conventual Franciscans during the period points up the value of strong pre-existing structures, capable of withstanding the reformers' pressures. At the time of the closures there were twenty-two Conventual houses, mainly located in the zone of English jurisdiction. Most were suppressed and some of those that survived, such as Monaghan, for example, joined the Observants. In that case, the superior, Fr Raymond MacMahon, attached himself to the friary of Multyfarnham.[48] The brief Marian interlude down to 1558 may have raised hopes of a revival for Conventuals and Observants alike, but the subsequent decade witnessed the almost total subsuming of the Conventuals within the Observant ranks. As part of his assertion of political paramountcy in Ulster, Shane O'Neill, acting as protector of the Conventuals, tried to break the pattern of the Irish province being governed through the medium of commissaries general appointed from abroad. An attempt to elect an Irish provincial failed in 1564, however, and an Italian, Girolamo Fiorati, was installed instead.[49] In 1566–7, agreement was reached that all the Conventuals should join the Observants, ensuring for all practical purposes the end of the Conventual province in Ireland in the early modern period,[50] but, as late as 1569, there was a proposal that a new provincial for the Conventuals should be appointed.[51] Individual Conventuals may have remained on in the vicinity of their houses, as is clear from the case of the friar of Roscrea who was in the company of Teige O'Daly, an Observant, on his capture there.[52] A slow changeover, begun in Armagh in 1567,[53] was still in the process of taking place as late as 1577–8.

The education of the Irish friars
Another vital resource that bore upon the continuing health of the Franciscan order in Ireland was the maintenance of access to education, both at home and through migration to places abroad.[54] For a vital twenty-year period into the

---

47 PRO SP 63/60/25, 'Sir William Drury to the Irish privy council', 24 March 1578; 'Brussels MS. 3947', p. 76. 48 Conlan, *FI*, p. 26. 49 Ibid. 50 'Brussels MS. 3947', p. 19. 51 When Miler Magrath, bishop of Down and Connor, was returning to Ireland from Rome in 1569, he was given letters by the Conventual Franciscans to whom he belonged, entrusting him with the task of appointing a new provincial in succession to Fiorati: Archives of the Conventual Franciscans, Rome: Regestis Ordinis, f. 51; H. Sbaralea, *Minoritanea Ecclesiae Synopsis*, MS C188, f. 210 (I am grateful to Revd Patrick Ryan, C.S.Sp., for these references). 52 'Brussels MS. 3947', p. 76. 53 Ibid., p. 36. 54 For the context, see H. Hammerstein, 'Aspects of the continental education of Irish students' (1971). See Stone, 'The theological and philosophical accomplishments of the Irish Franciscans' in this volume.

Elizabethan era, a network of houses was intact, including some of the traditional places of training for novices in the order. In the north-west, for example, Dromahair and Donegal remained as important centres for the novitiate until the late 1580s, as did Moyne in the west, and Kilcrea and Timoleague in the south.[55] Of course, Multyfarnham continued to flourish under Nugent patronage, the indications being that, exceptionally, its impressive *studium*-style library was preserved after the general confiscation of monastic chattels. Until well into the second half of the sixteenth century, then, it was possible for young novices to train in Ireland under Franciscan professors, such as John McGrath and Maurice O'Fihely of the Conventuals, and Raymund Burke, an Observant.[56] As part of a general educational tendency in mid- to later Elizabethan Ireland, however, those seeking a Franciscan training were increasingly directed towards academies abroad (where Irish friars had already resorted to gain degrees in the late middle ages).[57] Patrick O'Healy was one of the first of a new wave, studying at Cuenca and later at Alcalá de Henares.[58] O'Healy's companion in martyrdom, Conn O'Rourke, was a friend of Seán Ó Cathasaigh (John Casey), who was also named among the Irish studying for the priesthood at Paris in 1580, and one Tadhg Ó Súilleabháin attended Bologna university.[59] By the close of the century, a number of Franciscans in positions of leadership within the order and the Catholic church in Ireland were products of an academic training in continental universities, including Louvain. Flaithrí Ó Maoil Chonaire studied at Salamanca in the 1590s. That Franciscans were highly regarded as teachers is attested by the entrusting of the education of his sons, Henry and Hugh Óg, by Hugh O'Neill, earl of Tyrone, to Peter Nangle and Aodh Mac Aingil [Hugh MacCaughwell], who became a friar and guardian of St Anthony's College, Louvain.[60]

The pastoral care for which the Franciscans were so notable in the late medieval period appears to have continued during the transitional phase, leading into the Counter-Reformation. Evidence suggests that Franciscan preachers were just as active in the last decades of the sixteenth century as they had been formerly.[61] Among those who were known for their homilies were Patrick O'Healy, Tadhg Mac Domhnaill and William Ó Cearnaigh, all of whom suffered death for their religious beliefs.[62] Eoghan Ó Dubhthaigh [Eoghan O'Duffy], who was provincial from 1580 to 1583, was famous as a preacher. His sermons were lent drama through his preaching with his eyes closed, and he concluded them with Irish verses containing the nub of his lesson. Ó Dubhthaigh's personal saintliness

55 B. Millett, 'The Irish Franciscans and education' (2001), p. 18. 56 Ibid., pp 16–17. 57 Ó Clabaigh, *Franciscans in Ireland*, pp 128–9. 58 B. Millett, 'Patrick O'Healy, O.F.M., and Conn O'Rourke, O.F.M.' (1999), pp 55–6. 59 Millett, 'Irish Franciscans and education', pp 18–19. 60 Ibid., p. 20. 61 See C. Ó Clabaigh, 'Preaching in late medieval Ireland: the Franciscan contribution' (2001). 62 Millett, 'Irish Franciscans and education', p. 20.

and austerity, travelling barefoot as he did, added to the inspirational appeal of his mission.[63] The administration of the sacraments continued in spite of the difficulties of the ministry: Fr John O'Dowd, for example, was killed after hearing confessions at his friary of Moyne in 1579. Whether the country missions of the Observants in the vicinity of towns, such as the one that took place in the vicinity of Kilkenny in 1537,[64] continued on into the late sixteenth century is uncertain, but Lenten missions such as the one conducted by Donatus Mooney at Monahincha near Roscrea where he reconciled an apostate Conventual friar about 1611 certainly did.[65]

The Third Order

The phenomenal success of the Tertiary movement of St Francis in late medieval Ireland, which saw the founding of up to four dozen houses of the Third Order regular by 1540, contributed to the strong Franciscan presence in the late sixteenth century. While only tenuous evidence remains of the activity of secular or lay Tertiaries who lived out in the community in the later fifteenth and early sixteenth centuries, solid testimony to the vibrancy of the regular Tertiaries is provided by the large numbers of houses, mostly in Connacht and Ulster, which were built to accommodate mostly men, but also women, who opted to live conventually.[66] The Third Order secular and regular were an expression of a strong, penitential spirituality pervading late medieval Christianity, the members, whether lay or clerical, committing themselves to lives of austerity and prayer. Both were under supervision of the friars of the First Order, to which they may have been adjuncts, but by the later fifteenth century the regular Tertiaries at least had forged an independent standing for themselves. In 1457 one of their own brothers had been appointed visitor of all the houses instead of a friar of the First Order, ostensibly due to the 'distance of places' and the 'dangers of roads'.[67] While internationally the friars of the First Order reasserted their jurisdictional rights over the regular Tertiaries under the auspices of the bull, *Inter coetera*, of 1521, it appears that the Irish province of the Third Order retained much of its autonomy, and, as late as 1600, was still governed by its own provincial superior, who in that year was one Donatus Cossaeus.[68]

The first waves of monastic dissolutions may have accounted for the demise of about an eighth of the total number of houses of regular Tertiaries, mainly located in the marches of the Pale or the isolated crown territories of north Munster and

63 'Brussels MS. 3947', pp 49–50. See also Mac Craith: '"Collegium S. Antonii Lovanii"' in this volume. **64** Bradshaw, *Dissolution of the religious orders*, p. 12; Ó Clabaigh, *Franciscans in Ireland*, pp 141–2. **65** 'Brussels MS. 3947', p. 76. **66** The best recent account of the Franciscan Third Order in late medieval Ireland is in Ó Clabaigh, *Franciscans in Ireland*, pp 80–105. See Conlan, 'The Secular Franciscans' in this volume. **67** *CPL 1455–64*, xi, p. 140. **68** *MRH*, p. 266. See Conlan, 'The Secular Franciscans'.

east Ulster. About a further quarter of the communities of Tertiaries followed that course to suppression in the earlier Elizabethan period, while, of the remaining sixty per cent, almost half survived until the early years of the seventeenth century, the vast bulk of them situated in Ulster. As long as they continued to operate, these communities of Third Order Franciscans were available to complement the work of the friars of the First Order. It appears that numbers of secular clergy had been increasingly drawn to the Third Order regular in order to fulfil their need for a reformed priestly lifestyle, without their committing to the friars minor of the First Order. As their associates in devotion and piety, however, the Tertiaries were a popular and influential force in the provision of a pastoral ministry, although they may not have had the preaching skills that characterized their friar-*confrères*.[69] Their very presence was a reflection of the impulse towards corporate Christianity that elsewhere in Europe (and Anglo-Ireland) manifested itself in the foundation of colleges, religious fraternities and guilds, and may have provided a platform for the post-Tridentine Catholic renewal.[70] Also faintly attested is an important educational role played by the Tertiaries: Donatus Mooney asserted that many of the Third Order houses were engaged in 'conducting schools for the education of boys of the district'. According to him, a portion of their monasteries was set aside for pedagogy, a function commem-orated in the appellation, 'the schoolhouse', for that part of the buildings down to his time in the early seventeenth century.[71] Given the distribution of the last cohort of houses of Tertiaries that persisted into the 1600s – in Donegal, Derry and Tyrone – it is likely that the Third Order was an important source of reinforcement for the politico-religious position of the notable families of the region, such as O'Donnells, O'Neills and MacSweeneys, who had patronized their foundation.[72]

Irish Franciscan bishops

Due to the near-intact network of friaries in the northern and western parts of Ireland, members of the Franciscan First Order were frequently available for appointment to bishoprics within the region in the second half of the sixteenth century.[73] A dozen Irish Franciscan episcopal nominees, both Conventual and Observant, served in dioceses in the provinces of Tuam, Armagh and Cashel in the decades from the 1550s to the 1600s. They provided ecclesiastical and pastoral leadership, as well as, in some cases, support for militant campaigns for the official restoration of Catholicism. Academic standards among them seem to have

---

69 Ó Clabaigh, *Franciscans in Ireland*, pp 101–2.   **70** Ibid., p. 105.   **71** 'Brussels MS. 3947', p. 102.
72 These houses were at Balleeghan, Ballymacswiney, Ballynasaggart (in Tyrone and Donegal), Corickmore, Killybegs, Killydonnell, Kilmacrenan, Magherabeg, Omagh, Pubble and Scarvagherin.
73 B. Millett, 'Conor O'Devany, O.F.M., and Patrick O'Loughran' (1988), p. 437.

been high: John MacGrath, who became bishop of Lismore in 1550, and Raymond Burke, appointed to the diocese of Emly in 1551, were both described as professors, as was Maurice O'Fihely, bishop of Ross from 1554 to 1559.[74] Most of those who became bishops from the 1560s and 1570s onwards appear to have been educated on the Continent. Patrick O'Healy, bishop of Mayo from 1576, studied at Cuenca and Alcalá de Henares in Spain, and Seán Ó Cathasaigh, bishop of Killala from 1580, studied in Paris,[75] while Miler Magrath, appointed to Down and Connor in 1565, and Richard Brady, bishop successively of Ardagh and Kilmore from 1576, were likewise probably graduates of continental seminaries.[76] At least two of these bishops – O'Healy and Magrath, as well as Conor O'Devany, bishop of Down and Connor from 1582 – were present in Rome for their consecrations, indicating the close ties being forged between the Irish episcopate and the Counter-Reformation papacy.

In these post-Tridentine years, a premium was being set on the appointment of bishops of a high calibre in terms of personal piety and organizational skills. Notwithstanding his later being thoroughly discredited, Miler Magrath was at the time of his appointment regarded as a virtuous and worthy man, capable of 'good works that will be to the utmost benefit in promoting the church', and furthermore noted for his understanding of how ecclesiastical bureaucracy functioned.[77] In spite of the dangers entailed in carrying out episcopal functions on the ground, the Elizabethan bishops attempted to promulgate the decrees of the Council of Trent in their dioceses. Conor O'Devany, for example, was one of six bishops who, in 1587, with a large number of priests, met somewhere in Clogher to promulgate the decrees of the Council of Trent.[78] Earlier, on St Francis's Day, 1572, Donat O'Gallagher, bishop of Killala from 1570, had convened an assembly of friars in the abbey of Galway, which had emboldened them 'to go about ten, fourteen, sixteen, yea twenty in a company', and to determine to meet in councils in Donegal and Adare.[79] The perils entailed in exercising a papally-sanctioned mission as bishop elicited traits of character ranging from endurance to weakness. Bishop Richard Brady's last years as fugitive bishop of Clogher in the 1600s were overshadowed by captivity and deprivation

74 Millett, 'Irish Franciscans and education', pp 16–17. 75 Millett, 'Patrick O'Healy, O.F.M., and Conn O'Rourke, O.F.M.', p. 56, idem, 'Irish Franciscans and education', pp 18–19. 76 While there is no substantial evidence for Miler's having been educated on the Continent, his familiarity with the administrative machinery of the curia in Rome suggests that he may have studied in that city, perhaps at the *studium generale* of the Conventuals at the basilica of the Holy Apostles: see John Polanco, SJ, to Richard Creagh, 2 Dec. 1565 (Archivum Romanum Societatis Iesu [ARSI], Germ. 106, ff 44–5); on Richard Brady, see I. Fennessy, 'Richard Brady OFM, bishop of Kilmore' (2000), p. 229. 77 See John Polanco, SJ, to Richard Creagh, 2 Dec. 1565 (Archivum Romanum Societatis Iesu, Germ. 106, ff 44–5). 78 L.F. Renehan, *Collections on Irish church history* (1861–73), i, p. 435. 79 M.V. Ronan, *Reformation in Ireland under Elizabeth* (1930), p. 421.

which he bore with fortitude.[80] Bishop Conor O'Devany's imprisonment in the late 1580s under the threat of a charge of *praemunire* sharpened his political skills, as his exploitation of governmental feuds leading to his release in 1590 demonstrates, and he thereafter eschewed involvement in the Nine Years War.[81] On the other hand, the harshness of Miler Magrath's incarceration in London in the late 1560s led to his apostatizing, and his eventual appointment as Church of Ireland bishop of Down and Connor, and later Cashel.[82]

Irish Franciscan martyrs

As with the generality of the population, the Franciscan experience of conflicting loyalties between religious and political allegiances in late sixteenth-century Ireland was to evoke a variety of passive and active responses, not least among the bishops. Archbishop Richard Creagh of Armagh, who was close to the Franciscans, and contemplated becoming a friar minor, even after his consecration in 1564,[83] came under pressure, while imprisoned in London, through the agency of Miler Magrath to follow his course of conversion to Anglicanism. Creagh refused, committed strongly as he was to his papal warrant, though professing his loyalty to Queen Elizabeth in the political sphere.[84] When the bishop of Mayo, Patrick O'Healy was arrested, along with his companion, Conn O'Rourke in 1579, he was charged with a traitorous attachment to the campaign of James Fitzmaurice for the restitution of the old politico-religious order in Munster. He refused an offer of preferment within the Church of Ireland, and claimed to be pursuing purely religious ends. Both men were executed at Kilmallock in March 1579, condemned by court martial for treachery.[85] Conor O'Devany, having survived his prison ordeal in the late 1580s, appears to have had no involvement in the appeal of several Catholic bishops and political leaders to King Philip II of Spain in 1593 for military assistance for a campaign against English incursions into Ulster. Yet he was a victim of the collapse of the confederates' war and the imposition of a new regime after 1607. Arrested and charged with conspiring with Hugh O'Neill, earl of Tyrone, O'Devany and a priest, Patrick O'Loughran, were publicly executed in Dublin in 1612.[86]

Counterpointing this lack of political involvement was the militancy of Bishop Donat O'Gallagher. Appointed to the diocese of Killala in 1570, O'Gallagher was a member of the embassy of Archbishop Maurice Fitzgibbon of Cashel to Madrid in the early 1570s in pursuance of a papal transfer of the sovereignty of Ireland to

---

80 Fennessy, 'Richard Brady OFM, bishop of Kilmore' (2000).   **81** Petition of Conor O'Devany to Lord Deputy Fitzwilliam, 11 November 1590 (PRO SP 63/166/59 i).   **82** L. Ó Mearáin, 'The apostasy of Miler MacGrath' (1958).   **83** C. Lennon, *An Irish prisoner of conscience of the Tudor era* (2000), pp 40, 71.   **84** Ibid., p. 96.   **85** Millett, 'Patrick O'Healy, O.F.M., and Conn O'Rourke, O.F.M.', pp 64–78.   **86** Millett, 'Conor O'Devany, O.F.M., and Patrick O'Loughran', pp 446–69.

Philip II. Furthermore, he was engaged in canvassing for aid for the rebellion of the zealous Catholic, James Fitzmaurice.[87] On his return to Ireland in 1572, O'Gallagher threw himself into the organization of his own order and the wider Catholic community in the west of Ireland.[88] When Fitzmaurice was mustering support in Italy and Spain in the late 1570s for a renewal of his crusade, O'Gallagher travelled to Rome and the Iberian peninsula, where he was joined by a *confrère*-bishop, Conor O'Mulryan of Killaloe. Both bishops expressed their mistrust of Thomas Stucley, the renegade adventurer who hijacked a fleet assembled earlier, bound for Ireland in 1578.[89] O'Gallagher joined Fitzmaurice in Lisbon and sailed with his expedition, which also included at least two Franciscan friars, Shane O'Farrell of Askeaton and James O'Hea of Youghal.[90] As a landing was made at Dingle in 1579 and a religious banner unfurled, Bishop O'Gallagher appeared, dressed in episcopal attire.[91]

There is no doubt that O'Gallagher's habituation in a counter-reformation milieu in Spain and Italy influenced his attitude towards the issues at stake in the revolts in Munster. As a member of Fitzmaurice's entourage, he would have identified with the characterization of the war in the province as a religious one, in which the ideology of the French Leaguers against the Huguenots became manifest. Within a very short time of its occurrence, the massacre of French Protestants on St Bartholomew's Day, 1572, was known of in the west of Ireland, as O'Gallagher convened his assembly of friars, and talk of a Spanish-style inquisition was current.[92] Three friars who attended the Donegal meeting late that year travelled to France whence they returned to Galway.[93] Such constant intercourse with the European regions where the Catholic renewal entailed countering Protestantism steeled the resolve of many of the Irish Franciscans to the point of supporting military action to restore the Roman church as the official state religion in Ireland.

The perception that some of their *confrères* had suffered martyrdom undoubtedly served to deepen the certitude about the rightness of the campaign for the defence of the Roman church on the part of Irish Franciscans. At least two dozen priests and brothers of the First and Third Orders were killed in the Elizabethan period on the grounds of their commitment to their order and their faith. Unlike the high profile Bishop Patrick O'Healy, who paid with his life for his association with the Desmond rebels, most of the others who died in violent circumstances were caught in their friaries, as the agents of government fanned out into the north, west and south. Some, such as Fr John O'Dowd, for example,

---

87 Ronan, *Reformation in Ireland under Elizabeth*, pp 405, 407–8, 501.   88 Ibid., pp 420–1.   89 Ibid., pp 579–80.   90 Millett, 'Patrick O'Healy, O.F.M., and Conn O'Rourke, O.F.M.', p. 65.   91 Ronan, *Reformation in Ireland under Elizabeth*, p. 610.   92 Ibid., pp 420–1.   93 Ibid., p. 421.

who was killed after hearing confessions at his friary of Moyne in 1579, were engaged in their round of pastoral duties.[94] Others either failed to escape when their friaries were raided or else stayed to take the consequences. Teige O'Daly, who died at Limerick in 1578, had migrated from Askeaton to the former Conventual friary of Roscrea, which had been absorbed within the Observantine movement in the late 1560s. When the soldiers came, he took flight towards his former friary in the company of a Conventual friar. Captured, he spent nine weeks in prison in Limerick before being hanged, drawn and quartered in March 1578.[95] Brother Felim O'Hara of Moyne was elderly when a raid was made on the friary in 1582 by the soldiers of the president of Connacht, Sir Nicholas Malby. The provincial of the order, Eoghan Ó Dubhthaigh, who had been staying there, escaped by boat with all of the members of the community, except O'Hara, who was bayoneted to death in front of the high altar.[96] A famous preacher, Tadhg Mac Domhnaill, was captured by soldiers at Bantry friary in 1580 and drowned with a companion.[97] In the same year, a friar named Donal O'Neylan suffered an excruciating ordeal at the hands of executioners in Youghal where he was apprehended.[98]

These episodes of cruelty on the part of state agents were atypical of the prevailing religious regime which inclined naturally towards leniency under Elizabeth. Yet all manifested a deepening contrariety between officials and friars that was shaped by the circumstances of resistance to reform in the latter half of the queen's reign. Most of the deaths of Franciscans took place in areas that had become flashpoints in the Desmond and other revolts of the 1570s and 1580s, and were preceded by raids on friaries by parties of troops. The reputation of the order for confirming the Catholicism of the populace in these and other places perhaps explains the targeting of the friaries. Moreover, as the religious component of political opposition to the government's policies crystallized, the role of Catholic bishops and priests, including friars, became increasingly suspect. The threat of military intervention from the Continent was very real, especially after the landing of a Catholic force at Smerwick in 1580, occasioning a rigorous response on the part of the secular authorities to the perceived sources of succour for the invaders. Most of the Franciscan victims of this punitive campaign were dispatched by martial law, and the haphazard manner of many of the deaths bespeaks a lack of purposeful planning. For those who suffered, however, there was a compelling clarity about the reasons for their deaths. Some, including Patrick O'Healy, Conn O'Rourke, Teige O'Daly and Donal O'Neylan, were made an offer of having their lives spared if they would renounce their

---

94 'Brevis synopsis', pp 174–5.   95 'Brussels MS. 3947', p. 76.   96 Ibid., p. 52.   97 Millett, 'Irish Franciscans and education', p. 20.   98 'Brussels MS. 3947', p. 73.

Catholicism. With the exception of the Conventual companion of Teige O'Daly, who apostatized, all refused, Bishop O'Healy turning down the promise of preferment within the Church of Ireland prelacy.[99] Some are reported as having explicitly professed articles of their faith at their trials and executions, and many were killed wearing their religious habits, having expressed that preference when offered a choice.

The reputation of those Franciscans who were perceived to have suffered martyrdom was spread almost contemporaneously at home and abroad through oral communication and literary testimony. The latter included the genre of martyrologies composed both by *confrères* of the victims and non-Franciscan writers. Minorite accounts of the holy deaths of Irish members of the order began with the work of the English Franciscan, Thomas Bourchier, whose *Historia ecclesiastica de martyrio fratrum ordinis divi Francisci* was published in Paris in 1582. Containing pen-portraits of Patrick O'Healy and Conn O'Rourke, the work was translated into Spanish by Juan Campoy, who had known O'Healy well. In 1587 Francesco Gonzaga, minister general of the Observant Franciscans, published his history of the order, *De origine seraphicae religionis Franciscanae*, in which he wrote a lengthy account of the martyrdom of O'Healy and O'Rourke. Through the work of Gonzaga, the narrative of these early Irish Franciscan martyrs was subsumed within the general minorite martyrological tradition. The most important Irish Franciscan sources were Donatus Mooney and Francis O'Mahony whose histories of the Irish Franciscan province written in the early seventeenth century contained information on a large number of martyrs of the First and Third Orders. Again, their work, especially Mooney's, was informed by eye-witness testimony, including that of the Conventual friar, then an old man, who informed Mooney in 1611 of the circumstances of Teige O'Daly's killing at a time when he himself (the witness) had apostatized.[1] Upon these sources were based the later listings of Franciscans in a martyrological context compiled by the friars minor, Luke Wadding, Maurice Conry, Anthony Bruodin, and Arthur du Monstier. Conor O'Devany, himself ultimately a Franciscan victim of the state regime in 1612, compiled a list, 'Index martyrialis', which contained the names and circumstances of each death as noted by him during the course of his thirty-year career as bishop of Down and Connor. Although it has not survived, the work was used by the leading seventeenth-century martyrologist, David Rothe.

Among the non-Franciscan writers who commemorated the lives of the martyred ones, perhaps the most important was John Howlin, whose 'Perbreve compendium' was composed *c*.1590.[2] He included accounts of the deaths of the

---

99 Millett, 'Patrick O'Healy, O.F.M., and Conn O'Rourke, O.F.M.', pp 65–75.   **1** 'Brussels MS. 3947', p. 52.   **2** Edited and published in P.F. Moran, *Spicilegium Ossoriense* (1874–84), i, pp 82–109.

Franciscans, Patrick O'Healy and Conn O'Rourke, Teige O'Daly and Donal O'Neylan in his impeccably accurate history, which was informed at certain key points by his own and others' eye-witness observation of events. Through Howlin, these early lives and hallowed deaths were passed on in the Irish martyrological tradition that contained in the works of Henry Fitzsimon, David Rothe, Philip O'Sullivan Beare and many others.[3] Irish Franciscan martyrs also figure among the martyrological catalogues of European writers, such as Richard Verstegan, the English *émigré* publisher. His *Theatrum crudelitatum haereticorum nostri temporis*, printed in Antwerp in 1587, contained an account of the deaths of Patrick O'Healy and Conn O'Rourke, as well as that of Archbishop Dermot O'Hurley, three years earlier, which was accompanied by an illustration of the ordeal by torture and hanging of the three men. Thus were the Franciscan martyrs subsumed as icons of Catholic resistance to a Protestant regime within the ideology of the Counter-Reformation.

The martyrological writings were significant in a number of ways in both reflecting the cult of the martyrs and helping to burnish it. The works bore testimony to the lively *fama martyrii* that was current among their fellow-countrypeople. Verstegan's illustration of the hanging of Patrick O'Healy and Conn O'Rourke, for example, depicts the popular story that the wolves and other wild beasts refused to devour their venerable corpses. The saintly deaths of the martyrs, as perceived by the martyrologists, not only commemorated their steadfastness, but also pointed up, for some, the political element in the struggle for the restoration of Catholicism. This was especially the case when the correlation was made between the nascent national sentiment of rebels such as James Fitzmaurice and Hugh O'Neill and the sacrifice of O'Healy, O'Rourke, O'Neylan and others, who were done to death in the white heat of insurgency. Moreover, as evidenced by the absorption of the Franciscan and other martyrs within the martyrological mainstream, their ordeals were located within a broader Counter-Reformation milieu of battling Protestantism, and this contributed to Catholic activism in Ireland. Within the Franciscan community, the nearly-contemporaneous circulation of accounts of deaths that found their way into print suggests a fervid pattern of exchange of information among members at home and abroad, in centres such as Paris, Brussels, Rome, Madrid, Lisbon and elsewhere. It also serves further to highlight the extent of the diaspora of the Irish Franciscans in the late sixteenth century. And the transposition of the story of the Irish martyrs into the culture of the printed word and illustration copperfastened

---

3 See Henry Fitzsimon, *Catalogus praecipuorum sanctorum Hiberniae* (Liège, 1619); David Rothe, *De processu martyriali quorundam fidei pugilum in Hibernia, pro complemento Sacrorum Analectorum* (Cologne, 1619); and Philip O'Sullivan Beare, *Historiae Catholicae Iberniae compendium* (Lisbon, 1621).

the links between the Irish Franciscans and the literary efflorescence of the European Catholic renewal to which they themselves became notable contributors.

The Irish friars and the Gaelic tradition

In laying the foundations of a highly successful religio-cultural project that blossomed with the foundation of Louvain in 1607, the Irish Franciscans drew heavily upon the minorite tradition of engagement with Gaelic literature and learning. From their initial establishment in Ireland, the friars had engaged very effectively with the modes of communication of the *aos dána* (the learned class).[4] Indeed there had been a history of the recruitment of Gaelic friars from among the hereditary bardic families, as in the case of the Observant Philip Bocht Ó hUiginn, the fifteenth-century poet-friar.[5] His work had displayed the adaptability of the bardic tradition to continental devotional themes and motifs.[6] A salient feature of Franciscan spirituality in the late middle ages was the making available of Irish translations of popular works of European devotion and hagiography.[7] Included in this genre were a great many texts suitable for the sermons used by the Irish friars during the middle ages.[8] These works were instructional and practical, and adapted to the needs of laymen and women. Continuity with the period during which the Reformation was introduced is provided by the activities of Friar Brian MacGrath of Donegal, noted for his prophetic powers, as well as his exemplary piety, who preached to popular acclaim in Gaelic and Anglo-Ireland down to his death in 1549.[9] That preaching techniques remained attuned to vernacular culture down to the age of the Catholic renewal is attested by the popularity of Eoghan Ó Dubhthaigh, the noted homilist and poet, who was minister provincial of the order in the early 1580s. He used to conclude his sermons, which sometimes lasted three hours, with Irish language verses, containing the essence of what he had taught.[10]

A strong interlinking of the Gaelic language and the Catholic renewal after Trent, fostered by the Franciscans, aided the acculturation of the Counter-Reformation in Ireland by the early seventeenth century.[11] Besides his use of verse as an evangelical aid in his sermons, Eoghan Ó Dubhthaigh also composed poems, such as *'Léig dod chomhmórtas dúinn'* and *'A bhanba, is truagh do chor!,'* which are redolent of the polemical discourse of the confessionalized Europe of the late sixteenth century.[12] The field was left open for the primacy of Irish in the

---

4 C. Mooney, 'Scríbhneoirí Gaeilge Oird San Froinsias' (1995).   5 Ó Clabaigh, *Franciscans in Ireland*, p. 141.   6 Ibid., p. 115   7 B. Millett, 'Translation work of the Irish Franciscans' (1996–7), pp 1–6. 8 Ó Clabaigh, 'Preaching in late medieval Ireland'.   9 Ó Clabaigh, *Franciscans in Ireland*, pp 63, 107, 141. 10 Ó Clabaigh, *Franciscans in Ireland*, p. 144.   11 M. Caball, *Poets and politic* (1998), p. 106.   12 Ibid., pp 78–9. See Mac Craith, '"Collegium S. Antonii Lovanii"' in this volume.

evangelical context because of the widespread rejection of the almost exclusively anglicizing trend within the state-sponsored Reformation in Ireland. A key battleground was the printing-press, and control thereby of the means of catechesis. Ironically, it was a poem by the Franciscan, Philip Bocht Ó hUiginn, *'Tuar Ferge Fighide'*, which had the distinction of being the first ever work printed in a Gaelic Irish typeface in 1571 – as part of a Protestant project.[13] The work was a trial piece printed on one side of a broadsheet at a press in the home of Alderman John Ussher of Dublin, which also produced a Protestant primer.[14] This initiative was not followed through with more printing for Anglicanism in the Irish language until the seventeenth century, however, and even then the font of Irish type was used very sparingly. Instead the battle for Irish language was ultimately won by the Franciscans in their publication programme of devotional and catechetical writings from 1611 onwards. By contrast with the overall failure of the royal policy of using the press to foster Protestant evangelisation through the medium of Irish, Franciscan writers such as Flaithrí Ó Maoil Chonaire and Bonaventure Ó hEodhasa produced in print at Louvain a series of spiritual works designed for the Counter-Reformation mission in Ireland and abroad.

CONCLUSION

It remains finally to draw together some of the other cultural elements that fused to create the broader Irish Catholic *mentalité* underpinning the foundation of St Anthony's College, Louvain, in 1607. Although becoming associated principally with old Irish religion and scholarship,[15] the college benefited from its being able to draw upon a cultural rapprochement between Gaelic and Old English elements in interface areas such as the southern cities of Ireland and the Pale borders. In this respect the Franciscans were to the fore, being inured in the traditions of Hiberno-English usage that had been used in previous ages to fashion hymns, as well as fostering Gaelic literary forms.[16] In Limerick, the future archbishop, Richard Creagh (who was something of a Franciscan *manqué*),[17] composed the first post-Tridentine catechism for use in Ireland as he conducted a school in the city down to 1562. The work, in Irish and English, with Latin explanations, was entitled *Epitome officii hominis Christiani*, and predated the first Irish catechism, set in print at Louvain in 1611, by fifty years.[18] In the Pale

13 E.W. Lynam, *The Irish character in print* (1968), pp 5–7.   14 N. Williams, *I bprionta i leabhar: na Protastúin agus prós na Gaeilge* (1986), p. 22.   15 P.J. Corish, 'Dún Mhuire: fifty years' (1995) p. 1. 16 Ó Clabaigh, *Franciscans in Ireland*, p. 140.   17 Although not a member of the order, Creagh strove to follow the Franciscan rule, and had a minorite breviary with him in the Tower of London in 1564: Lennon, *An Irish prisoner of conscience of the Tudor era*, pp 40, 71.   18 Ibid., pp 44, 135.   19 H. Coburn Walshe,

marches, where Multyfarnham friary continued as a flourishing religious community down to 1601, William Nugent, brother of Christopher, the baron of Delvin who protected the friars, was a poet in the Irish language. He was also a militant recusant, leading a rebellion of disaffected Old English and Gaelic against the crown in 1581 and later campaigning on the Continent for assistance for the Catholic cause.[19] In a poem such as *'Fada i n-éagmais inse Fáil'*, which reflected his experience of missing Ireland while in England, Nugent articulated his patriotism in terms of an attachment to a cultural milieu that was shared by the Gall, or Anglo-Norman, and Gaoidheal, and characterized by its Catholicism, or metonymically, 'her masses' and 'her religious orders'.[20]

While drawing heavily upon native Gaelic and English springs in the formulation of their mission in the 1600s, the Irish Franciscan friars were also attuned in the *fin de siècle* period to the revived Catholic spirituality emanating from the Continent, and indeed were contributors to its diffusion. The educational migration of members of the Irish order to European schools and academics (and away from the English universities) in the later sixteenth century, which has already been alluded to, accustomed them to the latest fashions in post-Tridentine intellectual life in Spain, the Spanish Netherlands, Italy, Portugal and France. Among the graduates of colleges in the last-mentioned country, for example, were the Franciscans, Seán Ó Cathasaigh, Denis Molan, Edmund Mullarkey and Cornelius Desmond.[21] While involved perhaps in a tangential way in the world of print through the researching of martyrologies of Irish Catholics, for example, engagement with continental manuscript sources for catechetical and other works in the late sixteenth century is suggested by the work of Flaithrí Ó Maoil Chonaire. Educated at Salamanca, the future founder of St Anthony's, Louvain, translated from the Spanish into Irish a small catechism of Jeronimo de Ripalda in 1593 and sent it to Ireland in 1598.[22] He also prepared for the printing press an Irish translation of an early sixteenth-century Catalan devotional tract under the title *Sgáthán an Chrábhaidh*, or *Desiderius*.[23] Aodh Mac Aingil, who became archbishop of Armagh just before his death in 1626, was a distinguished poet of bardic family background and tutor to Hugh O'Neill's sons.[24] Having studied at Salamanca and joined the Franciscans, he was closely associated with the early phase of St Anthony's College where he became professor of philosophy and theology. His devotional work, *Sgáthán shacramuinte na hAithridhe*, was

'The rebellion of William Nugent, 1581' (1990).   **20** Caball, *Poets and politics*, pp 66–7; V. Carey, '"Neither good English nor good Irish": bi-lingualism and identity formation' (1999), pp 55–6, 60–1.   **21** C. Mooney, *Irish Franciscan relations with France* (1951), pp 21–2.   **22** Millett, 'Translation work of the Irish Franciscans', p. 6.   **23** The work was published at Louvain in 1616. For more on this subject see the contributions by M.W.F. Stone, Salvador Ryan and Mícheál Mac Craith to this volume.   **24** Millett, 'Irish Franciscans and education', p. 20.

published in Louvain in 1618.[25] Mac Aingil is a bridging figure between the Gaelic cultural milieu of Ulster and the academic environment of the Counter-Reformation which he graced with his theological scholarship.

Thus, there was only a very brief hiatus between the forcible closure of the friary of Multyfarnham in 1601 and the new foundation of St Anthony's at Louvain in 1607. That it should have been the Franciscans who bridged the temporal and cultural gap is hardly surprising given their leading role in the marshalling of the resources of the Irish Catholic church between the first impact of the monastic closures and the establishment of a fully-blown Counter-Reformation mission. The mutual link between the laity and the friars was critical to ensuring the survival of a strong network of functioning friaries, particularly in the south, west and north of the country. At a time of dislocation of most other ecclesiastical structures, an organizational and training regime was maintained intact by the Franciscan Observants (with their associated Tertiaries) that allowed for the continuation of pastoral and devotional traditions. Links to the continental Catholic regions had been strengthened by the educational migration of a generation of young friars, and through their immersion in the Tridentine renewal a counter-reformation sensibility was formed. A confessionalized aware-ness of the contrariety of Protestantism and Catholicism which could give rise to persecution and martyrdom was elicited, and an ideological commitment, developed thereby on the part of some, countenanced the use of militant means for the official restoration of Catholicism. These sentiments, when transposed onto their home country, especially by those Franciscans who assumed leadership responsibilities, resulted in the forging of the certainty that Ireland was a Catholic nation, nourished culturally by Gaelic hereditary learning and scholarship, and sanctified by the deaths of the holy martyrs.[26] The fraternity of founders of St Anthony's, Louvain, were witnesses to the continuity of a vibrant Irish Catholic culture within an increasingly cosmopolitan counter-reformation world.

---

25 For the intellectual context, see B. Cunningham, 'The culture and ideology of Irish Franciscan historians at Louvain' (1991). 26 See J. Bossy, 'Catholicity and nationality in the north European Counter-Reformation' (1982).

The role of St Anthony's College, Louvain in establishing the Irish Franciscan college network, 1607–60

MARY ANN LYONS

During the first quarter of the seventeenth century, Flaithrí Ó Maoil Chonaire (d. 1629) and Luke Wadding (d. 1657), highly influential figures in Franciscan circles on the Continent and in Ireland, established two dedicated colleges for the education of their Irish *confrères*, St Anthony's in Louvain and St Isidore's in Rome, which became the linchpins in the formation of an Irish Franciscan network that evolved along two axes, the first across northern Europe and the second around Rome. This chapter focuses specifically on the role played by St Anthony's in spearheading the construction of that flank of the network which extended from Paris to Wielun in Poland during the first sixty years of the seventeenth century. Key to the Irish Franciscans' success in establishing their colleges and outlying friaries was the support they drew from local secular rulers, from dominant elements within the local Franciscan province, and from particularly influential members of the ecclesiastical hierarchy. The importance of these factors has long been duly acknowledged by historians.[1] However, more recently, scholars including Gráinne Henry, Jan Pařez, David Worthington and Mícheál Mac Craith have highlighted the intimate connections that existed between these nascent Irish Franciscan foundations and locally-based Irish émigré groups, and have detailed the extent of the Franciscans' dependence on their compatriots for material support.[2] The following overview of the construction of this northern branch in the Irish Franciscan network, radiating outwards from St Anthony's, draws these strands of scholarship together to examine the fortunes of individual foundations within the wider context of the contemporaneous establishment of a permanent Irish émigré presence in Europe during the early decades of the seventeenth century.

---

1 See G. Cleary, *Father Luke Wadding and St Isidore's College Rome* (1925); idem (ed.), *Ireland's tribute to St Francis* (1928); B. Jennings, 'The Irish Franciscans in Prague' (1939); C. Mooney, 'The golden age of the Irish Franciscans' (1944); B. Jennings (ed.), 'The Irish Franciscans in Poland' (1957); *Luke Wadding commemorative volume* (1957); Millett, *Irish Franciscans* (1964); C. Mooney, *Irish Franciscans and France* (1964); Jennings, *Louvain papers*, p. v.   2 G. Henry, *Irish military community* (1992); idem, 'Ulster exiles in Europe' (1993); J. Pařez & H. Kuchařová, *Hiberni v Praze – Éireannaigh i Prág* (2001); J. Pařez, 'The Irish Franciscans in seventeenth- and eighteenth-century Prague' (2003); M. Mac Craith & D. Worthington, 'The literary activity of the Irish Franciscans in Prague' (2003).

A brief overview of the wider context within which the Irish Franciscan college network evolved in this period is useful in contextualizing the scale and significance of the order's presence and influence on the Continent. Of the approximately forty-five Irish secular and religious houses established on the Continent between 1578 and the end of the seventeenth century, just under sixty per cent were founded by male and female religious orders to train men and women for the Irish mission. Among these, the Franciscan foundations were in the majority, numbering seven in total, the most prestigious being the three colleges: St Anthony's in Louvain, founded in 1607, St Isidore's in Rome, established in 1625, and the College of the Immaculate Conception in Prague, founded in 1629. Other less high profile Irish Franciscan houses were to follow, including a friary in Wielun, Poland (1645), a residence in Paris (1653), a novitiate at Capranica near Sutrin in Italy (1656), and a refuge at Boulay near Metz which opened at the end of the century. By comparison, the Capuchins had six houses, the Dominicans four (one of which was a convent); the Cistercians two, and the Augustinians, Jesuits and Benedictines had one each.[3]

ST ANTHONY'S COLLEGE, LOUVAIN

Dissatisfaction with the admission policy at Christopher Cusack's secular Irish colleges in the Spanish Netherlands, combined with growing unease at the level of Jesuit dominance in the Spanish universities, prompted the Connacht-born Flaithrí Ó Maoil Chonaire[4] to found a dedicated Irish Franciscan college in Louvain, devoted to ensuring theological orthodoxy and high standards of pastoral practice on the Irish mission. As early as September 1606, he was endeavouring to raise funds for Irish students studying in Louvain.[5] In many vital respects, conditions in the Spanish Netherlands during the early 1600s were especially conducive to Ó Maoil Chonaire's foundation of St Anthony's College at Louvain, even if in its early years it did struggle to survive. Key to his success was the material and legal support provided by the Spanish crown, the papacy, the University of Louvain, the Franciscan order, various members of the local secular ecclesiastical establishment, and the Irish military community in Spanish Flanders.

In September 1606 King Philip III of Spain (r. 1598–1621) made provision for the college to receive a yearly grant of 1,000 crowns, the first payment of which the fledgling community received on 3 April 1607. On that day, Pope Paul V

3 J.J. Silke, 'The Irish abroad, 1534–1691' in *NHI* iii, p. 616. For the most recent surveys of the foundation of the Irish continental college network see T. O'Connor, 'The Irish College, Rome' (2003), pp 13–32; idem, *Irish Jansenists* (2008). 4 For Flaithrí Ó Maoil Chonaire see *ODNB*, vol. 12, pp 996–8. 5 Jennings, *Louvain papers*, p. 1.

(1605–21) also granted the Bull of foundation which stipulated that the purpose of the college was to train Franciscans to combat heresy in Ireland.[6] By June 1607 the Faculty of Arts at the University allowed the friars to celebrate Mass in its chapel of St Anthony the Abbot on Montagne St Antoine. The faculty later facilitated the Irish community's construction of a covered passage joining the chapel to their house. The Archduke Albert of Austria (1559–1621), viceroy of the Spanish Netherlands, demonstrated his support by bestowing his *placet* on the college in August, and on 19 September the community were authorized by the minister general of the Franciscan order to receive novices, the first five of whom were duly received on 1 November. Archduke Albert and his wife, Isabella, lent further support to the foundation, granting the Irish Franciscans permission in September 1610 to purchase a house near the church of Sint Jacobus where they remained until 1618. Within a year of the friars having purchased a piece of land outside the town's inner gate and on the bank of the river Dyle in May 1616, the Archdukes laid the foundation stone for a new house (capable of accommodating forty men) and a chapel, construction of which was apparently complete by 1618.[7]

Meanwhile Ó Maoil Chonaire's cultivation of close ties with leading figures within the Catholic church hierarchy in the region proved significant in facilitating St Anthony's integration into the church in Spanish Flanders. The first sign of his success was in April 1609 when the *placet* of the archdiocese of Mechelen (Malines) was bestowed on St Anthony's.[8] The high regard in which Ó Maoil Chonaire was held within the church in Flanders was publicly acknowledged in May 1620, when at the request of the vicariate, Ó Maoil Chonaire exercised the *pontificilia* in Mechelen following the death of Archbishop Mathias Hovius (1596–1620).[9] He also developed a good relationship with Hovius's successor and former bishop of Ghent, Jacob Boonen (1573–1655). Significantly, in November 1620 the first theological thesis to emerge from St Anthony's, defended by John Barnewall and presided over by Aodh Mac Aingil, was dedicated to Boonen. The archbishop also presided at the consecrations of several Irish bishops in Spanish Flanders, including William Tirry of Cork and Thomas Fleming of Dublin. As Thomas O'Connor's recent study of Irish Jansenists has shown, Ó Maoil Chonaire's connections with the ecclesiastical establishment in Spanish Flanders also proved vital in enabling scholars from St Anthony's to integrate with the rigorist, anti-Jesuit theological tendency of which he was a strong advocate. Under Ó Maoil Chonaire's direction, in the 1620s St Anthony's backed the University of Louvain's efforts to maintain its degree-granting monopoly against the Jesuits. The Irish Franciscan reputation for strict Augustinianism and

---

6 Ibid., pp v, 4–7; Millett, *Irish Franciscans*, p. 106; O'Connor, *Irish Jansenists*. **7** Jennings, *Louvain papers*, p. v. **8** Ibid., p. 20. **9** B. Jennings, 'Irish names in the Malines ordination registers' (1951), p. 149.

opposition to Jesuit influence was also significant in shaping the fortunes of their later foundations in Rome and Prague.[10]

It is difficult to overestimate the dependence of this fledgling college on the nascent Irish émigré military community in Spanish Flanders. The symbiotic relationship that existed between these two émigré groupings was particularly manifest in the early 1640s when the Franciscan and the military agendas for shaping Ireland's future very publicly interwined.[11] Undoubtedly the most iconic demonstration of this fusion of the two groups' identities and agendas was the career of Owen Roe O'Neill (*c.*1583–1649). The nephew of Hugh O'Neill (*c.*1550–1616), earl of Tyrone, Owen Roe had joined the Irish regiment in Spanish Flanders and by 1633 was commander of his own regiment. After the outbreak of rebellion in Ireland in 1641, he returned to Ireland where he was the Catholic confederacy's most successful general. When O'Neill sailed from Ostend for Ireland in late June 1642, it was aboard a frigate called the *St Francis*, which had been purchased for him through the good offices of the Franciscan order, and he had the support of Luke Wadding. O'Neill's interment in the Franciscan friary in Cavan further testified to his close affinity with the friars.[12] The intimacy of the connection between the two communities was also demonstrated in Aodh Mac Aingil's dual appointment as chief chaplain of the Irish regiment in 1606 and as guardian of St Anthony's College in 1607.[13]

Gráinne Henry has uncovered substantial archival evidence of various forms of financial support provided by the Irish regiment in Spanish Flanders to the community of St Anthony's in its formative years. In addition to individual private donations such as Cornelius O'Reilly's gift of 120 *escudos* to the 'Irish Franciscans at Louvain' in 1616, Hugh O'Neill's son, Henry (d. 1610), colonel of the Irish regiment and Captain James Gernon (Garland) organized major collections within their regiment and company respectively in order to contribute towards the construction of college buildings and a chapel. The strength of ordinary, rank-and-file soldiers' attachment to the Franciscans in Louvain is clearly apparent from Gernon's collection to which the majority (112) each donated the equivalent of one month's salary. A total of 850 *escudos* was raised –

10 See O'Connor, *Irish Jansenists*. **11** C. Mooney, 'The Irish sword and the Franciscan cowl' (1949–53); R.A. Stradling, *The Spanish monarchy and Irish mercenaries* (1994), pp 134–6. **12** Mooney, 'Irish sword', p. 84; Jennings, *Wild Geese*, pp 590–1; J.I. Casway, 'Owen Roe O'Neill's return to Ireland in 1642' (1969); idem, *Owen Roe O'Neill and the struggle for Catholic Ireland* (1984); Stradling, *The Spanish monarchy and Irish mercenaries*, p. 135; for Owen Roe O'Neill see *ODNB*, vol. 41, pp 851–6. For a very useful overview of the state of the Catholic church in seventeenth-century Ireland, see P.J. Corish, *The Irish Catholic experience* (1986 repr.), chap. 4, and an excellent recent case study of the Irish Franciscans in Ulster in B. Mac Cuarta's *Catholic revival in the north of Ireland* (2007), esp. pp 79, 83–5, 127–9. **13** Henry, *Irish military community*, p. 102; idem, 'Ulster exiles in Europe', p. 55.

almost the annual salary of a captain in the Army of Flanders. Ties between the
two communities were consolidated by clerical students serving as soldiers in Irish
companies in order to finance their studies at St Anthony's: indeed, certain
individual priests, including Flaithrí Ó Maoil Chonaire, received 'pay out of the
army', but never actually worked directly with the soldiers. More generally close
family connections existed between the two groups, as a large proportion of men
serving in the Army of Flanders had brothers or near kin in St Anthony's as well
as in other Irish colleges and religious institutions in that region. In the period
1600–10, only five of the twenty-eight Irish clerical students listed for the
archdiocese of Mechelen did not have a brother or a close relative serving in the
Irish regiment. So strong were these family and kin connections that by the 1620s,
the Franciscans had established a monopoly as padres to the Irish regiments.[14] The
view of one contemporary that Bonaventure Ó hEodhasa's Irish-language
catechism, *An Teagasg Criosdaidhe* (first published in Antwerp in 1611 and later by
the Irish press at St Anthony's in 1614) was conceived 'for the instruction of Irish
soldiers in the doctrine of Trent', if accurate, further testifies to the close
relationship between the Franciscans at Louvain and the Irish soldiers serving in
the Spanish Army.[15]

Apart from ministering to the émigré military community, the Franciscans in
Louvain, like many other Irish religious and secular communities on the
Continent, also fulfilled several important practical functions for the soldiers and,
as a consequence, even had an input in shaping the structure and organization of
the Irish infantry. The friars' comparatively superior literacy and their intimate
knowledge of genealogies and social divisions in Ireland proved invaluable in
assisting Irish soldiers as they lobbied for pensions, promotions and honorary
titles. So significant was the role of the friars that in 1607 an English agent
reported in exaggerated terms that 'no man can get a pension' without Flaithrí
Ó Maoil Chonaire's recommendation.[16] Certain Irish officers developed a
particularly strong affinity with the Louvain community. Before the foundation
of the college in Prague (1629) figures such as Captain Somhairle Mac Domhnaill
[Sorley MacDonnell] (d. 1632), who had been based in Spanish Flanders before
serving in the imperial forces in Bohemia during the Thirty Years War,
maintained close ties with St Anthony's. Mac Domhnaill, who was probably the
greatest émigré collector of Irish Franciscan literature generated on the
Continent, arrived at Dunkirk in 1616, and subsequently fought in the imperial
army at the Battle of the White Mountain (1620), just outside Prague. His ties

14 Henry, *Irish military community*, pp 70, 104, 105, 108, 186. **15** Ibid., pp 102, 135; Henry, 'Ulster exiles in
Europe', p. 53; Jennings, *Wild Geese*, p. 552; on Bonaventure Ó hEodhasa see *ODNB*, vol. 41 (2004), p. 634;
see also T. O'Connor, 'Religious change, 1550–1800' (2006), pp 178–9. **16** Henry, *Irish military*

1 St Anthony's College, Louvain in the eighteenth century.

with the Louvain community were familial and scholarly: two of his cousins were community members and his *Duanaire Finn*, among other documents, passed into the possession of St Anthony's soon after his death. His personal attachment to St Anthony's is also borne out by the fact that his last two company chaplains, Bernard Conny and Hugh Ward [Aodh Mac an Bhaird], were Franciscan academics from Louvain and by his interment in the cloister of St Anthony's (see figure 1).[17]

THE IRISH FRANCISCANS IN PARIS

Although the Louvain community was struggling to overcome serious and ongoing financial difficulties in 1613, Flaithrí Ó Maoil Chonaire and several others were soon investigating the possibility of opening another permanent Irish residence in northern Europe. Initially they set their sights on extending St Anthony's sphere of influence into France and specifically Paris in the hope that by establishing a permanent residence for Irish Franciscans, they might challenge Thomas Messingham's monopoly position as rector of the secular Irish college

community, pp 105–6. **17** H. McDonnell, *Wild Geese of the Antrim MacDonnells* (1996); idem, 'Responses of the MacDonnell clan to change' (2003); Mac Craith & Worthington, 'Literary activity of the Irish

there. However, strong opposition from local religious orders, including the Franciscans, ensured that successive concerted attempts to achieve this goal ended in failure. The first of these initiatives came in 1617 when Donatus Mooney, the Irish Franciscan provincial, based in Louvain, engaged the assistance of the French queen, Marie de Medicis (d. 1642), to acquire a residence in Paris for young Irish friars attending university there. However, Mooney's initiative was quickly stymied by an alliance of local Franciscans and the *parlement* of Paris, who made much of the Irish Franciscans' reputation for being sympathetic towards the Spanish. Thereafter, successive attempts by the Louvain community to establish a residence in the French capital were obstructed in a similar fashion. In 1621, at the intermediate general chapter, permission was granted to the Irish province to dispatch suitable friars to Paris and Aodh Mac Aingil, definitor general, made arrangements for some of these to be accommodated in rented rooms in the Collège des Bons Enfants.[18] Although a small Irish Franciscan community lived in Paris in March 1621, once again objections from local Franciscans stifled plans for a permanent Irish residence for them.

However, the following year, a significant breakthrough seemed imminent when several influential figures within the order, along with members of the Catholic hierarchy in Paris, demonstrated active support for the proposal. After the Cardinal de Retz, archbishop of Paris, granted permission for the Irish friars to attend the University of Paris and reside in some college, seminary, or house within the university, the minister general of the order, Benignus of Genoa (d. 1625), authorized the guardian of St Anthony's, Louvain to send Irish friars to the Grand Couvent (Franciscan college) in Paris. They were to attend the University and to live, with a suitable friar as superior, in the kind of residence stipulated by the archbishop. St Anthony's was to retain its close supervisory role: Benignus decreed that no member of the Irish province was to be sent to, or recalled from, Paris except by the minister provincial of Ireland or the guardian of St Anthony's.[19] Aodh Mac Aingil was appointed superior of this new community. Both he and Flaithrí Ó Maoil Chonaire were instrumental in orchestrating this initiative. Mac Aingil had served Benignus as commissary visitor in Aquitaine in 1621 and in the adoption of a stricter discipline code at the Grand Couvent. For his part, Ó Maoil Chonaire persuaded his correspondent Cornelius Jansen (1585–1638) to request the Abbé de Saint-Cyran's support for the foundation of a dedicated college for Irish Franciscans in Paris.[20] Yet in spite of the influential figures involved, opposition from Parisian religious, including the Cordeliers of the Grand Couvent, ensured that this plan, like those before it, failed to

Franciscans in Prague', pp 119–21. **18** O'Connor, *Irish Jansenists.* **19** Millett, *Irish Franciscans*, pp 184–5, n. 2. **20** Mooney, *Irish Franciscans and France*, p. 27; Millett, *Irish Franciscans*, p. 185, n. 2.

materialize. Thus, in 1627, although a number of Irish Franciscans continued to reside in the rented rooms set aside for them in the Collège des Bons Enfants, they made it clear to the royal council in Paris that they did still not have a religious house.[21]

In the 1640s, the Irish provincial Bernard Conny's lobbying of Cardinal Jules Mazarin (d. 1661) to permit the establishment of an Irish friary in the city again proved fruitless. It was only in the 1650s, with the backing of the exiled Stuart court, that an Old-English element within the Irish Franciscans, led by Fr George Dillon, succeeded in establishing a residence in Paris. The upshot of all this obstruction was the deferred foundation of a permanent, dedicated house of study for the Irish Franciscans in Paris until 1666 when a breakthrough finally came. In June of that year, the superior and discreets of St Anthony's (with which the Irish foundation in Paris was intimately connected) appointed a member of their own community, who at the time was lecturing theology in St Anthony's, as president of the Paris residence. In addition, they dispatched two lectors of philosophy and several students of philosophy in order to form a college community.[22]

ST ISIDORE'S COLLEGE, ROME AND OUR LADY OF THE PLAIN, CAPRANICA

While local opposition frustrated the Louvain community's plans for expansion into Paris, in Rome in 1625 Fr Luke Wadding, a Waterford-born Franciscan, who was educated in Portugal and Spain and intimately connected with the Spanish embassy in the eternal city, took charge of an unfinished and debt-laden friary and church on the Pincian Hill and established St Isidore's house of studies and recollection for Irish Franciscans (see figure 2). Supported by Pope Urban VIII, and by the minister general of the Franciscan order, Benignus of Genoa, Wadding's foundation, initially comprised of two faculty and three students, went on to produce generations of students who defended theses in philosophy and theology, many of whom lectured on Scotist philosophy and theology in Franciscan and other schools throughout Europe. In 1627, in a drive to consolidate the Irish Franciscan advantage in Rome, Wadding persuaded Cardinal Ludovico Ludovisi (d. 1632), protector of Ireland, to rent a house near St Isidore's for the formation of Irish secular students whom he undertook to supervise. The first students arrived in the Irish College on 1 January of the following year. However, Wadding's initial progress in extending Irish Franciscan control ended

---

21 Millett, *Irish Franciscans*, p. 185, n. 23.   **22** Mooney, *Irish Franciscans and France*, p. 29.

2 1661 map of Rome depicting St Isidore's College.

abruptly when, just three years after Ludovisi's death in 1632, the Jesuits took over the Irish College. Wadding continued as guardian of St Isidore's down to 1649[23] but in the early 1650s, he had become concerned that the Cromwellian regime was preventing men professed in Ireland from going to St Isidore's. As an expedient, Wadding received novices at his college but simultaneously petitioned the pope, Alexander VII, to grant him permission to open another friary which would operate as a dedicated novitiate for the Irish mission. In 1656, just a year before Wadding's death, papal approval was granted for his second foundation, the friary of Our Lady of the Plain (*La Madonna del Piano*) outside the town of Capranica, thirty-five miles north of Rome.[24]

COLLEGE OF THE IMMACULATE CONCEPTION, PRAGUE

While Wadding consolidated Irish Franciscan influence in Rome and personally grew in stature with the Holy Office and the Congregation for the Propagation of the Faith, by the late 1620s St Anthony's had become overcrowded and its

---

23 On Luke Wadding see *ODNB*, vol. 56, pp 643–9; O'Connor, 'The Irish College, Rome', pp 16–21; idem, *Irish Jansenists*. **24** Millett, *Irish Franciscans*, pp 195–8; *ODNB*, vol. 56, p. 645.

finances strained to the point that the community was compelled to look beyond Paris and consider possibilities for setting up another college elsewhere in northern Europe. Jan Pařez contends that the original idea of establishing a Franciscan college in Prague, which would serve as a refuge for Irish Franciscans and a training centre for those destined for service on the Irish mission, is likely to have originated with Luke Wadding. If indeed this was the case, it is clear that responsibility for the realization of that idea fell squarely on the shoulders of the Louvain community, and specifically Malachy Fallon (d. 1651).[25]

Some time before January 1629, Fallon was dispatched from Louvain to Vienna to investigate the possibilities for opening a house within the Empire. He was supported by letters of commendation from the Archduchess Clara Eugenia addressed to the Emperor Ferdinand II (r. 1619–37), the electors, the princes and prelates of the Empire. In mid-March, Fallon wrote to Hugh Ward, guardian of St Anthony's, telling him he was hopeful of success. Significantly, whilst in Vienna, Fallon also met with and received encouragement from the archbishop of Prague, Cardinal Ernst Adalbert von Harrach (1598–1667). By mid-November 1629, both Harrach and the emperor had granted permission for the foundation of the Irish Franciscan College of the Immaculate Conception, in recently re-Catholicized Prague. When the Irish first arrived in Prague, they were accommodated by the local Franciscan province in a nearby friary (Our Lady of the Snows) until construction of the Irish college on the site of the former monastery of St Ambrose was completed in 1631. In return for their *confrères'* hospitality, the Irish taught philosophy and theology in the Prague friary. Having overseen the construction of the college, Patrick Fleming (d. 1631), formerly the first lector in philosophy at St Isidore's and then lector at St Anthony's, was appointed first guardian and secured a grant of further property from the city authorities. In April 1631 the Irish were ceremonially installed in their own convent in the presence of Cardinal Harrach.

Almost immediately, in marked contrast with their Louvain *confrères*, the barely-established Prague community encountered obstacles that threatened its very survival. Firstly, soon after the formal opening of the college, Fleming became aware of the Austrian Franciscans' opposition to the Irish foundation on the grounds that it threatened their interests. The Bohemian Capuchins, too, strongly disapproved: having recently purchased a site for a new monastery immediately adjacent to the College of the Immaculate Conception, they asserted their priority of right over the Irish. Faced with this dilemma, Fleming made representations to Luke Wadding in Rome. However, the Irish college suffered an even more severe blow when, in a new phase in the Thirty Years War (1618–48),

25 Pařez, 'Irish Franciscans', p. 105.

the Saxon occupation of Bohemia in 1631 compelled them, along with other religious, to flee the city. Their guardian, Patrick Fleming, and another friar, Mathew Hore, were murdered by a group of Czech peasants and the house was reduced to a ruinous state. The following summer, Fleming's successor as guardian, Gerald Fitzgerald, returned to Prague and set about restoring the premises before he received orders from the Nuncio in Vienna not to proceed with the repairs until the next general chapter of the Franciscans should give its formal approbation. At this point, Luke Wadding's mediation in Rome proved crucial in ensuring the survival of the Prague college. He procured fresh letters of commendation addressed to the queen of Hungary, the Spanish agent at the imperial court in Vienna, and Cardinal Harrach, and he personally interceded with the Nuncio.[26] According to Brendan Jennings, it was thanks to Wadding's representations that the new Franciscan general promptly silenced all opposition within the order and took the Irish college under his own immediate jurisdiction. When Cardinal Harrach received Gerald Fitzgerald in Prague in early October 1632, he promised to be a patron and protector of the Irish community. Soon after, an amicable compromise was reached with the Bohemian Capuchins. Repairs to the house were completed by the following November, and the community settled into a normal, if materially precarious, existence.[27]

These formidable obstacles notwithstanding, the timing of the friars' arrival in Prague was, in other respects, fortuitous. The Irish Franciscans' reputation for strict Augustinianism and aversion to Jesuit influence followed them from Louvain to Prague, as did their associated appeal to opponents of the Jesuits. In the 1630s and 1640s, while their patron, Cardinal Harrach was intent upon countering Jesuit influence at both the imperial court and the University of Prague, he used the Irish Franciscans, among other orders, as a counterweight both to the Jesuits and their supporter, the emperor. Although their preoccupation with stabilizing the Prague foundation and with supplying friars for the Irish mission made them reluctant to become embroiled in Czech ecclesiastical politics, the Irish friars were gradually drawn into this local dispute. Just as in Louvain, their anti-Jesuit stance worked to their advantage because the cardinal appointed several members of the community, among them former lecturers at St Anthony's, to teaching posts in his *Collegium Adalbertinum* or archiepiscopal seminary (est. 1635), and made Malachy Fallon *professor primarius*. As members of faculty in Harrach's seminary, the Irish Franciscans were thus brought into close contact with the secular clergy of the diocese of Prague and with the regular clergy of prestigious monasteries including Strahoff and Monserrat. The long-

---

26 Jennings, 'Irish Franciscans in Prague', pp 211–14; Pařez & H. Kuchařová, *Hiberni v Praze – Éireannaigh i Prág*; Pařez, 'Irish Franciscans', pp 105–7.   **27** Jennings, 'Irish Franciscans in Prague', p. 215.

term value of these contacts became apparent when, for instance, an address, sent on behalf of the Irish community to Rome in 1651, had the backing of thirty-six of Bohemia's most eminent diocesan and abbatial dignitaries.[28]

The expansion of the Franciscan network eastwards from St Anthony's followed and reflected the steady extension of the Irish military émigré presence beyond Spanish Flanders as growing number of Irish soldiers fought in the imperial army during the Thirty Years War. Like St Anthony's, the fledgling Franciscan community in Prague enjoyed vital generous support from this sizeable émigré population. In its early years, the Prague community was often obliged to go without food for three or four days at a time. What supplies the friars had appear to have been furnished by Irish soldiers in the imperial service who were quartered in or near Prague. On one occasion, these soldiers invited Brother Francis Magennis and Fr Francis Wolverston to their quarters at Misnia where they gave their guests alms to the value of 200 crowns, along with 22 cows, 40 sheep, and several horses. Among the most prominent figures within this community were Colonel Walter Butler (d. 1634), Lieutenant-colonel Robert Geraldin, Captain Walter Devereoux, Captain Edmund de Burgo and Lieutenant Walter Gall. Crucially, the Emperor Ferdinand II lavishly rewarded their service in the imperial army, and his favour and pensions allowed these Irish officers to acquire substantial estates throughout Bohemia, which, in turn, permitted the more pious to support the Irish Franciscan college in Prague through provision for Masses, donations and bequests.[29] Colonel Walter Butler was a particularly enthusiastic supporter and a generous benefactor of the new Franciscan foun-dation, presenting gifts of horses, carriages, pictures, clocks and furniture for their house.[30] He established regular correspondence with the community and paid several visits. When he died, he left 30,000 florins in his will to the Irish Franciscans in Prague, along with instructions that his remains were to be transferred for interment in their church. Patrick Taaffe, a member of the Prague community and Butler's regimental chaplain, received the colonel's widow, Countess Anna Maria von Dohna, into the Catholic church, and she in turn donated 16,000 florins to the Franciscan community between 1658 and 1666.[31] It is significant that although Irish men were members of local Augustinian and Jesuit communities, the Irish nobility in Bohemia showed a distinct preference for patronizing this dedicated Irish community of Franciscans. This is evidenced from the many references made in mid-seventeenth-century wills and other

28 Ibid., p. 219; Pařez, 'Irish Franciscans', pp 106–7.   **29** Jennings, 'Irish Franciscans in Prague', p. 216; Mooney, 'Irish sword', p. 85; Pařez, 'Irish Franciscans', pp 107, 112–13.   **30** On Walter Butler see *ODNB*, vol. 9, pp 231–3.   **31** Jennings, 'Irish Franciscans in Prague', p. 216; Millett, *Irish Franciscans*, p. 147; Pařez, 'Irish Franciscans', pp 123–4; Mac Craith & Worthington, 'Literary activity of the Irish Franciscans in

sources to the burial of Irish nobles at the Irish college. It was this noble support that permitted construction of the new college chapel in 1652.[32]

The Franciscan college in Prague, like St Anthony's and several Irish secular colleges elsewhere, played a very significant role in the lives of these Irish noble and military émigrés as the friars represented a real spiritual, cultural and political point of connection with Ireland. On a more immediate level, the college also offered a range of practical services to soldiers. It served as a banking facility where Irishmen could deposit and withdraw their savings and legal documen-tation. For instance, in 1650 the Franciscans released a passport that had been issued to a Captain Denis Kavanagh by Emperor Ferdinand III (r. 1637–57), authorizing his return to Ireland. Like their Louvain *confrères*, the Prague community also assisted Irish soldiers employed in imperial service in drafting petitions and requests for payment of salaries, pensions, promotions and so on.

The Prague community was fortunate to enjoy the ongoing support of two emperors in its formative years, receiving financial assistance for the construction of a new convent and chapel and along with regular consignments of wood, fish, butter and corn. This privileged relationship was copperfastened in August 1654 when the Emperor Ferdinand III took the Irish college and all its possessions under his own protection and became its patron. Thereafter Leopold I (1659), Charles VI (1718) and Maria Theresa (1746) confirmed and continued that privilege.[33]

LOUVAIN, ROME AND PRAGUE: AN IRISH FRANCISCAN NETWORK

By the beginning of the 1630s, then, the three pivotal institutions within the Irish Franciscan network on the Continent were established. Thereafter, connections and contacts (positive and occasionally negative) between staff and students of St Anthony's, St Isidore's and the College of the Immaculate Conception in Prague quickly intensified. Among these was John Punch (d. 1672/3), a native of Cork, who entered the order at St Anthony's before proceeding to study and subsequently lecture at St Isidore's.[34] Several of Wadding's students took up teaching posts in Louvain, notably Bonaventure Delahoyde and Bernardine Barry. Indeed, both men, along with another of Wadding's students, Bonaventure Mihan (Mahony), served as guardians of St Anthony's in the 1630s, 40s and early 50s. Others, such as Anthony O'Brien, Daniel Brouder, Brandon (Bonaventure)

Prague', pp 123–4; *ODNB*, vol. 9, pp 231–3.   **32** Pařez, 'Irish Franciscans', pp 113–14.   **33** Jennings, 'Irish Franciscans in Prague', pp 217–18; Pařez, 'Irish Franciscans', p. 114.   **34** Cleary, *Father Luke Wadding and St Isidore's College Rome*, pp 83–6; on John Punch see *ODNB*, vol. 45, pp 561–2. See also Fennessy, 'A select prosopography of some Irish Franciscans on the Continent' in this volume.

O'Connor, and John Brady, who either studied or taught at St Isidore's, went on to teach in Cardinal Harrach's archiepiscopal seminary in Prague.[35] The intimacy of the connection between the three colleges is also borne out by the fact that several Irish Franciscans studied and taught in all three institutions over the course of their careers. Patrick Fleming, from Co. Louth, entered the order at St Anthony's in Louvain in 1617, and proceeded to become lector of philosophy at St Isidore's in 1625. He subsequently returned to Louvain and, from there, was dispatched to oversee the foundation of the new Irish Franciscan college in Prague.[36] Francis Tarpy began as a student at St Isidore's before holding the chair of philosophy in Louvain and later, that of theology at Prague.[37] Significantly many of these Franciscans spent sojourns back in Ireland in the course of their careers, thereby increasing connectivity between the order's networks at home and abroad.

Just how tight-knit that network was can be gleaned from a letter, dated 6 March 1641, in which the Irish friars at Prague protested to the provincial in Ireland about allegations made against them by some of their *confrères* at Louvain. They complained about reports that their house in Prague was a den of drunkenness, that the only religious service observed there was that of raising glasses, and that all visiting brothers were being advised to avoid their company, least they should fall prey to the leprosy of intoxication. The friars feared the damage these defamatory comments would cause to their community as they knew this news would spread like wildfire. As they put it, there was neither a rumour nor a fable that started in Ireland that was not heard without delay in the entire province, thanks to the eager tongues of those who preferred to note the smallest fault rather than acknowledge the greatest good.[38] In light of the particular circumstances which gave rise to this *communiqué*, such comments cannot be interpreted too literally. Nonetheless, the episode is illuminating in two telling respects. First, it shows that the Prague community believed their Louvain *confrères* looked down on them, and second, it testifies to the efficacy of the Franciscan network for conveying information throughout the entire Franciscan province.

The leading role played by the Irish Franciscan colleges, and specifically St Anthony's, in maintaining the momentum for Irish historical, hagiographical and controversial theological scholarship, certainly until the 1660s, is widely acknowledged and is dealt with in detail elsewhere in this volume.[39] Similarly, St

35 Cleary, *Father Luke Wadding and St Isidore's College Rome*, pp 102–4, 123, 128–9, 132, 134–6, 139.
36 Ibid., pp 141–2; Pařez, 'Irish Franciscans', p. 107; Mac Craith & Worthington, 'Literary activity of the Irish Franciscans in Prague', p. 121.   37 Cleary, *Father Luke Wadding and St Isidore's College Rome*, p. 124.
38 Mac Craith & Worthington, 'Literary activity of the Irish Franciscans in Prague', pp 127–8.   39 For general surveys of the scholarly output of Irish Franciscans on the Continent during this period see

Isidore's scholars, especially Luke Wadding and his two nephews, Francis Harold (d. 1685) and Bonaventure Baron (d. 1696), were the dominant Irish contributors to Catholic church history in general. While the output of the Prague college never matched that of either St Anthony's or St Isidore's, members of that community did make significant contributions to contemporary Catholic philosophy and theology, especially in the field of Scotist studies, and they played an important complementary role in fostering the Irish language and the study of Irish history and hagiography.[40] Their first guardian, Patrick Fleming, was an accomplished scholar, who had been actively involved in the great hagiographical enterprise spearheaded at St Anthony's. Following his lead, a handful of writers in Prague produced scholarly works, most of which remain in manuscript form since the college does not appear to have had a printing press. When Philip O'Reilly, who lectured in both Louvain and Prague before being appointed guardian of the Prague College in 1650, produced a translation into Irish of St Francis de Sales' *Introduction to the devout life*, he apparently hoped to have published in Louvain.[41] Furthermore, members of the Prague and Louvain colleges occasionally presented a common front in criticizing books on Ireland or Irish history which they both deemed misleading, erroneous or offensive. In 1640 two members of the Prague community, Patrick Relachan and Francis Farell (d. 1663?), wrote to the Tipperary-born historian, Thomas Carew (d. *c*.1672), who served as chaplain to both Colonel Walter Butler and his successor Walter Deveroux's Irish regiment, objecting to his portrayal of Ulster and Connacht men as barbarous and uncouth in his famous *Itinerarium*, published in 1639.[42]

EXTENDING THE IRISH FRANCISCAN NETWORK: WIELUN, POLAND

The College of the Immaculate Conception, Prague quickly became the largest of the Irish province's continental houses: in 1642, the community numbered 30; by 1650–2, it had grown to 44 and by Spring 1654, there were 51 friars in residence, though not all of these were Irish.[43] By that time, plans were once again afoot at St

---

B. Millett, 'Irish literature in Latin, 1550–1700' in *NHI* iii, pp 561–86, and, more recently, M.A. Lyons, 'Foreign language books, 1550–1700' (2006) and O'Connor, 'Religious change, 1550–1800' (2006); E. Bhreathnach & B. Cunningham, *Writing Irish history: the Four Masters and their world* (2007); N. Ó Muraíle (ed.), *Mícheál Ó Cléirigh, his associates and St Anthony's College* (2008). See Cunningham, 'The Louvain achievment I: the Annals of the Four Masters', Ó Riain, 'The Louvain achievement II: hagiography' and Stone, 'The theological and philosophical accomplishment of the Irish Franciscans' all in this volume. **40** Cleary, *Father Luke Wadding and St Isidore's College Rome*, pp 88–100, 108–12; on Francis Harold see *ODNB*, vol. 25, p. 362; on Bonaventure Baron see *ODNB*, vol. 4, pp 13–14. **41** Mac Craith & Worthington, 'Literary activity of the Irish Franciscans in Prague', pp 128–9. **42** Ibid., pp 125–7, 130; on Thomas Carew see *ODNB*, vol. 10, pp 64–5. **43** Millett, *Irish Franciscans*, pp 135–6.

Anthony's to extend the Irish Franciscan chain of foundations into north-eastern Europe. However, the failed outcome to successive initiatives highlights the challenges that Irish orders in general experienced in endeavouring to establish a presence in areas of Europe where they could not rely on support from the local province, or from secular rulers, and where (crucially) a significant Irish émigré presence, such as existed in Spanish Flanders and Prague, had not yet been established.

The stance adopted by the local Franciscan province has been stressed as an important factor which determined whether plans for Irish foundations reached fruition, as in Louvain, Rome and Prague, or repeatedly failed, as in Paris. In the mid-1640s and early 1650s, when overcrowding at the Prague college precipitated attempts to establish new foundations in Namslav, Würzburg, and Wielun, opposition from local provinces effectively stifled the Irish plans. When in 1653 the Irish friars opened a house in Namslav in Silesia, they failed to show due deference to the local province. The Bohemian Franciscans, who had a friary in Bratislava, viewed the Irish initiative as setting a dangerous precedent, and a violation of their jurisdiction. Their minister provincial, Constantine Dubsky, complained vigorously to Luke Wadding about the insatiable ambition of certain friars within the Prague community. While he overtly promised stiff opposition to the Irish, Dubsky stated that Bohemians were confident that Wadding would put a stop to his compatriots' self-aggrandising plans. The Bohemian Franciscans also brought the matter to the notice of the order's commissary general at Vienna, and petitioned Emperor Ferdinand III. According to Benignus Millett, the Prague community had attempted this new foundation without either the knowledge or the approval of Wadding or the major superiors of the Irish Franciscans. In the end, their Bohemian *confrères* successfully thwarted the planned expansion. The Prague community's effort to open a house in the German city of Würzburg had a similar end.[44]

When in 1645 St Anthony's College tried once again to meet the increasing needs of the apostolate in the Irish province as well as in Scotland and England by opening a fourth continental foundation for the formation of Irish students in Poland, it encountered serious difficulties.[45] The impetus for the foundation at Wielun (in south central Poland) appears to have come directly from Louvain in July of that year when Fr Peter Marchant (d. 1661), commissary for the *Natio Germano-Belgica*, which included St Anthony's in Louvain, dispatched Fr James MacCaughwell and several others to set up a house in Poland. The first obstacle they encountered was King Ladislaus IV's (r. 1632–48) adamant refusal to permit any such new foundation in his realm. By contrast, the Polish Franciscan minister

44 Ibid., pp 137–9.   45 Ibid., p. 167; C. Giblin (ed.), *Irish Franciscan mission to Scotland* (1964).

provincial, Fr Bonaventure Koletzin, and his advisors, took pity on their foreign *confrères* and granted the Irish temporary use of their friary of the Annunciation in Wielun. Notwithstanding his initial rebuff to the Irish, in mid-July King Ladislaus formally consented to this transfer of the Wielun friary, gave the friars permission to remain in his kingdom, and took them under his special protection and patronage. At the same time, the Polish provincial wrote to Peter Marchant, warmly praising the Irish Franciscans, and offering assurances that he would do all in his power to ensure that the community at Wielun wanted for nothing. He also promised to do his utmost to acquire a new foundation for them in one of their preferred locations – Poznan or Gdansk. Meanwhile, in June 1646, the Franciscan minister general, Giovanni di Napoli, confirmed the grant of Wielun friary to the Irish, and forbade any disturbance of the Irish community. Eight months later, James MacCaughwell, guardian of Wielun, informed Luke Wadding that the Irish were willing to wait a while for papal confirmation of the grant of the friary since their Polish *confrères* were still doing their best to secure a premise on their behalf at one of the alternative sites.

Despite these promising signs, by Spring 1653, the attitude towards the Irish within the local Franciscan province had changed significantly. A new provincial had been elected and, feeling no compunction to honour the commitment made to the Irish in 1645, he moved to repossess Wielun friary. Mindful of the high regard in which Luke Wadding was held in Rome, and conscious of the trouble that he was likely to cause when appraised of their planned revocation of the transfer of Wielun friary, the Polish Franciscan superiors launched a campaign to discredit the Irish, whom they accused of ingratitude for the kindness shown them by their hosts. The Irish protested at their treatment, but the Polish authorities' intervention proved decisive in forcing them to leave Wielun in July or August 1653. Disadvantaged by the absence of an Irish military émigré population in their vicinity, they subsequently scattered across communities at Prague, Namslav in Silesia, and St Anthony's in Louvain. A subsequent plan by St Anthony's College to erect a church and friary for an Irish community in the Polish town of Jablonow, detailed in a deed dated 11 November 1654, apparently failed to materialize.[46]

CONCLUSION

In just over twenty years (1607–29) the Irish Franciscans succeeded in establishing three prestigious colleges in Louvain, Prague, and Rome; the first two continued to function down to the late eighteenth century and the third, St Isidore's,

---

46 Jennings, 'Irish Franciscans in Poland'; Millett, *Irish Franciscans*, pp 166–83.

continues to have an Irish presence. Together, these foundations provided the Irish province with generations of well-educated missionary priests and religious, and supplied many continental colleges and universities with lectors in philosophy and theology, as well as making significant contributions to theological, philosophical, historical and hagiographical scholarship. While Luke Wadding's very considerable influence over the affairs of the Irish Franciscan province, at home and abroad, should not be underestimated, it was St Anthony's in Louvain which spearheaded the expansion of the Irish Franciscan presence across northern Europe during the first sixty years of the seventeenth century. Having founded three colleges in quick succession, the Franciscans' advance slowed dramatically and decisively as failure to secure the support of local provincial superiors, and the absence of established and supportive Irish emigré populations, delayed their progress in establishing a permanent presence in Paris and limited their expansion beyond the borders of Bohemia.

The Irish Franciscans, 1600–1700

RAYMOND GILLESPIE

At the centre of the history of the Irish Franciscans in the seventeenth century lies an enigma. On the one hand archival survival for a reconstruction of the history of the order is remarkable and a great deal has been published on the subject. On the other hand there has been little attempt to realize the potential of this material by drawing it into a survey of the Franciscan experience across the entire century. The evidence has been mined for studies of individual friaries or examinations of short periods but the broader picture continues to be elusive. One reason for this is that the seventeenth-century experience of the Irish Franciscans was so diverse that a single overarching theme cannot hope to contain it. Previous attempts have characterized the early part of that century as a 'golden age' but that understanding could hardly apply to the latter part of the century with its political machinations and recriminations against members of the order for their activities in the 1640s and 1660s.[1] Ultimately the fractiousness of the 1660s and 1670s calmed towards the end of the century providing a very different tenor to Franciscan history by the 1690s. Perhaps rather than unifying the changes over a century in a grand synthesis the way to view the Irish Franciscan experience in the seventeenth century is through the lens of generational change. In the years between 1600 and 1700 roughly three generations of Irishmen passed through the order and each of those generations had its own priorities to achieve and problems to resolve. How they did that shaped the order to create a tradition that one historian has described as being 'distinctively Irish as well as being distinctively Franciscan'.[2]

THE IRISH PROVINCE IN THE EARLY SEVENTEENTH CENTURY

The situation in Ireland

In 1603 the most pressing problem that a new generation of Irish Franciscans faced was the rebuilding of a community shattered by war and persecution during the 1590s. In the first decade of the seventeenth century the friars concentrated on re-establishing a support network that had been broken by the Nine Years War and the flight of the Ulster nobility in 1607.[3] The account of the province written

---

1 For the 'golden age' see Mooney, 'The golden age of the Irish Franciscans' (1944).   2 Corish, 'Dún Mhuire: fifty years' (1995), p. 1.   3 Mac Cuarta, *Catholic revival in the north of Ireland*, pp 18–19.

by the provincial, Donatus Mooney, in Louvain in 1617–18 reveals the slow re-establishment of Franciscan houses near their former locations in the years after 1612.[4] When the Irish provincial chapter met in 1612 only the friaries of Donegal, (at Bundrowes) Armagh and Multyfarnham had regular communities and the number of guardians appointed for the province was eight. Smaller houses must have existed, however, since the office of 'president' was introduced presumably to oversee these communities. Only two of the eight houses were in Ulster (Donegal and Armagh) while two were in Connacht, one in Leinster and the remainder in Munster. By 1613 the position is somewhat clearer. A list of priests, mainly in Munster, for that year provides some evidence for Franciscan activity but since it was provided by an informer it probably understates the numbers.[5] While the list names fifty-six Franciscans another report of the same year states there were actually 130 members of the order in Ireland.[6] On the basis of the 1613 list the greatest concentration of Franciscans lay across the counties of the south and west coast of Ireland with nine in Cork, five in Waterford, four in Limerick and six in Clare. In Cork most of the friars appear to have been in the city where Mooney claimed that they lived in lodgings, but in practice some must have lived in the surrounding countryside, although Mooney says nothing about established communities outside Cork.[7] Some communities had certainly existed a decade earlier, as at Buttevant where Lord Barry acted a protector to Franciscans who openly wore their habits.[8] In Co. Waterford the high recorded number of Franciscans was due to the inclusion in this figure of the friary at Clonmel, where two friars (one 'a great preacher') were named. Mooney was inclined to attribute the survival of Clonmel to local popular support, noting that the church was much frequented by the town dwellers, both magistrates and people, who met with great devotion on Sundays and festivals for stations (*stationesque*) at which they made offerings for the church and the poor. This, Mooney claimed, was an old custom and the reluctance to break the well-established link between civic identity and the Franciscans may well explain the survival of the order at Clonmel.[9] Survival through inertia was common. In 1611 the need for a statute to expel friars 'out of their dissolved houses where, for the most part, they still keep and hover' was considered and a report on the state of Catholicism in 1613 noted that in some parts of the country where Dublin's authority was weak friars continued their lives as before.[10] Thus the 1613 list described the Clare Franciscans as 'simple friars and very old' and further north an account of the diocese of Elphin in 1631 also described parishes being cared for by old Franciscans; signs of

---

4 'Brussels MS. 3947', pp 120–4.   5 TCD MS 567, ff 35–5v.   6 Hagan, 'Miscellanae Vaticano-Hibernica, 1580–1631', p. 301.   7 For the identification of the friars see B. Egan, *Friars of Broad Lane* (1977), pp 37–8. 8 *Cal. S.P. Ire., 1606–8*, pp 132–3.   9 'Brussels MS. 3947', p. 78.   10 *Cal. S.P. Ire., 1611–14*, p. 189; Hagan,

continuity rather than of a new mission.[11] In inland regions the position was much less favourable. Tipperary could boast only one friar and Kilkenny three. Clearly in this situation conventual life was impossible and according to one note in the 1613 list for Kilkenny 'Malachy Ragged [Ragget], a Franciscan friar, innkeeper usually with his father Richard Ragged of this city, alderman'. Donatus Mooney claimed there were five or six friars in the city who lived in lodgings.[12] In central Ireland the greatest concentration of friars was in Westmeath with seven Franciscans, reflecting the importance of Multyfarnham as a community that had weathered the storms of the 1590s, protected by the Nugent family who provided accommodation for the friars near the site of the old friary. By 1617 it had become something of a national centre for the order.[13] Outside Munster and Leinster the situation appeared less promising. For Connacht the 1613 list records only five friars in Galway and three in Mayo. According to Mooney in 1617–18 there were six members of the community at Moyne, a community that, at its peak in the late medieval period, had fifty members.[14] These figures are understatements. The friars of Kinaleghin, near Portumna, Co. Galway, on the other hand, were protected by the Clanricard family and their building had been restored for them by the family yet it does not appear in the 1613 list.[15] Nevertheless this position represents a considerable retreat for the order given that this had been the heartland of late medieval Observant activity. No figures appear in the 1613 list for Ulster but Mooney's evidence suggests that the Donegal and Armagh communities were functioning. Both had been protected by O'Donnell and O'Neill respectively in the years after the war of the 1590s and had been provided with places of safety. More significantly for the future by Mooney's time the guardian of Armagh had been educated in the new Irish Franciscan house in Louvain and two of the community had studied in Louvain and Paris.[16] These areas clearly had direct links with Louvain and they may have organized the Franciscan preaching campaigns in Ulster after 1610.[17]

Communication with this wider world was made easier by the presence of Franciscan houses at Drogheda, represented by six friars in Louth on the 1613 list, and, after 1616, at Dundalk.[18] The Drogheda community had been re-established about 1610 and by Mooney's time there was a community of four with their own chapel, fixed altar and pulpit. The friars wore their habit within the community.[19] This provides a contrast to the communities of Cork or Clonmel that were more traditional in their outlook.

'Miscellanea Vaticano-Hibernica, 1580–1631', p. 301. **11** Ibid., p. 363. **12** 'Brussels MS. 3947', p 83. **13** Ibid., pp 92–3. **14** Ibid., p. 52. **15** J.P. Dalton, 'The abbey of Kilnalahan' (1909–10), pp 195–202. **16** 'Brussels MS. 3947', pp 36–7. **17** Mac Cuarta, *Catholic revival in the north of Ireland*, pp 83–4. **18** 'Brussels MS. 3947', pp 35. **19** Ibid., p. 32.

The evidence of the 1613 list and of Donatus Mooney's 1617–18 account suggests that some progress was being made in reconstructing the Franciscan province, including the formation of new communities. Nodes which might act as centres of mission were clear at traditional centres in Cork, Clonmel and Multyfarnham as well as more modern ones such as Armagh and Drogheda. On the strength of this Paul V granted very extensive missionary faculties to the order in Ireland in 1612, the extent of which was later to be a cause of concern for some diocesan bishops.[20]

The mission from Louvain

It was obvious from even a brief glance at the state of the Irish Franciscan province that it was not be possible for the friars to transform it from within. The training of clergy for the Irish mission to the standards envisaged by the Council of Trent, and the provision of an infrastructure for that mission, could not be organized in Ireland. As a result during the first half of the seventeenth century an Irish Franciscan infrastructure was established on the Continent to train the order's clergy and to develop its strategy for the Irish mission. Initially the order recruited from the students of the already established colleges and by 1622 some fifty-two students of the college at Douai and four from Bordeaux had joined the Irish Franciscans.[21] The earliest Franciscan foundation was St Anthony's College in Louvain in 1607, followed in 1625 by St Isidore's, Rome. Each of these produced offshoots, from Louvain a college was founded in Prague in 1629 and from Rome Capranica was established to the north of the city in 1656. In addition the Irish Franciscans had a university residence in Paris from 1622 to 1670 and friaries at Wielun in Poland (1645–53) and at Boulay in Lorraine in the late seventeenth century. The choice of Louvain for the establishment of the oldest Irish Franciscan house was not accidental. Within Spain the Irish colleges had fallen under the control of the Jesuits. While the Louvain foundation was not like Salamanca, in that it did not envision lay students, the Jesuit educational monopoly within Spain may have led the Franciscans to look elsewhere. Moreover, as described by Mary Ann Lyons in this volume,[22] Louvain had a substantial Irish community created by the army of Spanish Flanders in which many Irishmen served and they required pastoral services. As a result there were often kinship connections between those training as friars and those serving in the army.[23]

From its inception the house at Louvain encountered difficulties. While the conception of a house to further the Irish mission was straightforward the

20 B. Jennings (ed.), 'Miscellaneous documents – I 1588–1634' (1946), pp 173–5.   21 Mooney, *Irish Franciscans and France*, pp 19, 113–14.   22 See Lyons, 'The role of St Anthony's College, Louvain in establishing the Irish Franciscan College network' in this volume.   23 Henry, *Irish military community*, pp 104–5.

execution of the idea was not. The strategies of mission organized from Louvain were clearly rather ad hoc ones. The Louvain Franciscans vacillated between alternatives. They became involved with the pastoral care of the Irish serving in the armies of Spain in the Low Countries partly because of the close connections between the community and those forces. The influence of the founder of the college, Flaithrí Ó Maoil Chonaire, also pressed them into a mission to Scotland that consumed scarce resources. The scholarly activities engaged in by the Louvain community were directed as much at the Irish in Spanish Flanders as towards the Irish at home. Nor was it clear what the strategies of mission would be and a number of innovations were adopted but all for short periods. The community invested in a font of Irish type early in its history but its influence in Spanish Flanders and in Ireland, a culture largely unused to print and based on manuscript and oral transmission, is difficult to assess. The earliest product using that font, Bonaventure Ó hEodhasa's *An Teagasg Críosdaidhe* may not have been intended for Ireland but for the Irish-speaking soldiers of Spanish Flanders.[24] The second edition of *c.*1614 may have had a different market in mind. Whereas the 1611 edition had been produced by an Antwerp printer whose book had a formal title page with printer's device and imprint the second edition lacks this formal layout. The first edition had used Roman type for approbations and marginal notes while the second edition used Irish type. In all, the second edition, which lacks a title page, looks better adapted to a manuscript culture and therefore more suitable to use in Ireland. By 1618 the Franciscans ceased publishing works that could be in any sense described as devotional and they did not resume again until the 1640s.

This stop-go strategy is also characteristic of the hagiographical project conceived by Hugh Ward and carried out by John Colgan. On Colgan's death the project lapsed following the publication of two scholarly volumes of saints' lives. No one in Louvain seems to have considered the pastoral possibilities of this material although some in Ireland did, and in Kilkenny William Swayne, parish priest of Gowran, printed translations of parts of Colgan's work that were of local interest.[25] In Paris the Franciscan Robert Rochford saw the pastoral possibilities of saints' lives and his lives of Patrick, Brigit and Colmcille, reprinted at St Omer in 1625, were shipped into Ireland.[26]

Not all these discontinuities of approach can be blamed on a lack of strategic thought. At least some of the problems lay with the Louvain community's perennial financial difficulties. The newly founded college had four sources of

---

24 For the first edition in the hands of Irish soldiers in Flanders see *Cal. S.P. Ire., 1611–14*, p. 185. **25** B. Cunningham & R. Gillespie, 'The cult of St David in Ireland before 1700' (1999), pp 37–9. **26** B.B [Robert Rochford], *The life of the glorious bishop S. Patrick* (1625).

funding: an annual grant from Philip III of Spain, the right to collect alms in the area around the college, fundraising in Ireland itself and finally, and most importantly, there were the contributions of the most immediate patrons of the order, the Irish regiment in Spanish Flanders under the command of Henry O'Neill.[27] Most of the potential patrons of the Franciscans in Louvain were of Old Irish backgrounds, and particularly from the Ulster worlds of O'Neill and O'Donnell.[28] For such patrons their emphasis was on the native Irish cultural inheritance, especially with an Ulster focus, and this tended to influence the college's understanding of its role. By contrast the student body in Louvain was much more mixed. According to a list of the novices admitted to St Anthony's in the ten years from 1607 sixteen came from Ulster dioceses, but thirteen came from Connacht, fourteen from Munster and twenty-two from Leinster, including Meath.[29] The Irish language, for instance, played a large part in the ethos of the college because in the early part of the seventeenth century many of the friars in Louvain had originated in the learned families of Gaelic Ireland. Some had less skill. Aodh Mac Aingil, for instance, learned to read and write Irish at Louvain, taught by Bonaventure Ó hEodhasa and Ó hEodhasa's early seventeenth-century Irish grammar may have been composed to teach Irish to those needing the language to carry out the Irish mission.[30] Again the exploration of Irish language sources for history and hagiography came to be a central feature of the college's intellectual life. Indeed so powerful was the link between the college and Irish language and culture it was seen by some as the guardian of that tradition. As far as the secular priest John Lynch, in the 1660s, was concerned it was 'the labours of the Rev. Fathers of St Francis in Louvain College [that] would once more revive the Irish language' through their exploration of 'the more abstruse vernacular documents', translating them into Latin and preparing an Irish dictionary, which it appears was never published.[31] The college showed enthusiasm for gathering contemporary material in Irish and about Ireland. While Tadhg Ó Cianáin's account of the Flight of the Earls was written in Rome in 1608 or 1609, Louvain acquired the manuscript soon after his death.[32] Donatus Mooney's Latin account of the history of the Irish province written in 1617–18 may well be linked to the building of the new college in 1617 so that the new institution would remember its inheritance.[33] Both documents serve to link the Irish-speaking community of Louvain and the Irish Franciscan community into the

27 See also Lyons in this volume. 28 Ibid. 29 Jennings, *Louvain papers*, pp 54–8. 30 C. Ó Maonaigh (ed.), *Sgáthán shacramuinte na hAithridhe* (1952), p. 94. For the grammar P. Mac Aogáin (ed.), *Graiméir ghaeilge na mBráthar Mionúr* (1968), pp ix–xi, 3–108. 31 M. Kelly (ed.) *Cambrensis eversus* (1850), ii, p. 379. 32 N. Ó Muraíle (ed.), *Turas na dtaoiseach nUltach as Éirinn* (2007), pp 18–19. See Mac Craith, '"Collegium S. Antonii Lovanii"' in this volume. 33 Jennings, *Louvain papers*, pp 43–4.

developments of contemporary Europe and they were supplemented by the Irish language manuscript material collected by Mícheál Ó Cléirigh during his period in Ireland in the 1620s and 1630s.[34] This was a reputation that the college was concerned to protect. In 1640 the Louvain community fell into a dispute with the Irish Franciscan house in Prague over their depiction of the Ulster Irish and this was to sour relations between the two colleges for some years.[35]

While the history of the Franciscan house in Louvain is relatively easy to construct it is more difficult to measure its interaction with Ireland. It is certainly possible to trace a flow of ideas and artefacts from Ireland to Louvain in the early seventeenth century. Among the books in John Colgan's room at Louvain at the time of his death a number had come from the friary at Donegal, possibly brought back by Mícheál Ó Cléirigh when he returned from Ireland with his manuscript material in the 1630s.[36] Liturgical items from Ireland made their way to Louvain. The vestments from the friary of Kilconnell, for instance, were in Louvain by 1654.[37] It is more difficult to trace ideas and people moving from Louvain to Ireland. While many friars were undoubtedly trained in Louvain it is very unclear how many returned to Ireland as opposed to becoming part of the European mission. However, it is possible to trace a trail of items from Louvain into Ireland from the 1630s. One manuscript copy of Bonaventure Ó hEodhasa's *Rudimenta grammaticae Hibernicae* made by Fr Anthony Hally at Louvain in 1634 was, according to a note at the beginning, made for the community at Limerick.[38] The same manuscript contains an Irish summary of the Rule of St Francis, already printed in Louvain, a biblical work and a number of printed items from the Low Countries. It may be that Hally put this entire compilation together at Louvain as a resource for the Limerick community. Again in 1632 the clergy of Cashel complained that Franciscans returning there from Spanish Flanders were bringing printed images of St Francis, presumably made in Louvain, bearing promises that no one wearing the Franciscan habit would have an unhappy death and that persecutors of the order would be punished.[39] Since these items were in Latin and English rather than Irish they were, presumably, not the product of the friars' press at Louvain but standard broadsheets of a kind generally available to confraternities throughout Europe.

34 See the essays by B. Cunningham and P. Ó Riain on the Louvain achievement in this volume.   **35** Mac Craith and Worthington, 'The literary activity of the Irish Franciscans in Prague', pp 127–8.   **36** I. Fennessy (ed.), 'Printed books in St Anthony's College, Louvain, 1673' (1996), pp 93–6.   **37** P. Walsh, *Gleanings from Irish manuscripts*, (1933), p. 65.   **38** Marsh's Library, Dublin, MS Z3.5.3.   **39** B. Millett, 'Calendar of volume 1 of the *Scritture riferite nei congressi, Irlanda*' (1963–4), p. 47.

REVIVAL IN PEACE, 1620–40

The success of the Irish Franciscan recovery strategy did not lie with the order
alone but was bound up with the environment in which it was executed. In the
early 1620s that environment began to change. The removal of the hard-line
Protestant Arthur Chichester from the Irish lord deputyship together with wider
political considerations, including the war with Spain in the mid-1620s, resulted
in a more relaxed attitude towards Catholicism although some remained wary of
the Franciscans because of their close Spanish links.[40] The political episode of the
Graces in the late 1620s suggested that there might even be the possibility of some
form of quasi-legal recognition for Catholicism. Apart from a brief interlude in
the early 1630s the decades of the 1620s and 1630s provided an easier context for
the consolidation of the order. Friars became more visible, sometimes wearing
their habits in public whereas previously they had been worn under normal dress,
and the number of communities grew.[41] Novitiates were re-founded and schools
for the teaching of humanities, theology and philosophy were established at a
number of Irish locations.[42] Chapters could also be held in public and celebrations of the feast of St Francis at Multyfarnham attracted large attendances.[43]
Estimates of the numbers of Franciscans in the Irish province can only be guessed
but in 1617–18 Donatus Mooney reckoned that there were 120 friars in Ireland
and in 1623 the Franciscan archbishop of Dublin thought there were about 200,
another contemporary estimate putting about ninety of these in the northern
ecclesiastical province of Armagh.[44] The first surviving chapter bill, that for 1629,
lists thirty-two houses to which superiors could now be appointed as opposed to
eight in 1612. The geography of this is revealing on a number of grounds (map 1).
First, it highlights the importance of the major port towns, all of which had
communities established in them by 1629. Drogheda and Waterford, for instance,
were particularly important in this regard and in 1629 Thomas Strange, the
guardian of Waterford, noted that he was staying in the city 'to see our friars on
shipboard'.[45] This reflects the importance of sea links with the European colleges
as the sources of manpower and pastoral resources. Louvain certainly kept in
touch with events in Ireland with letters passing to the college at least every three
months.[46] Secondly, however, what the distribution of the 1629 houses suggests is
the continuity between the location of pre-reformation friaries and that of the

40 For instance *Cal. S.P. Ire., 1615–25*, p. 534–7.   **41** For an Ulster case study see Mac Cuarta, *Catholic
revival in the north of Ireland*, pp 127–9.   **42** Jennings, 'Miscellaneous documents – I: 1588–1634', p. 100;
'Brevis synopsis', p. 163. For the case of Multyfarnham see T. O Donnell, *Franciscan abbey of Multyfarnham*
(1951), pp 58–9.   **43** *Cal. S.P. Ire., 1625–32*, pp 163–4.   **44** 'Brussels MS. 3947', p. 18; Moran, *History of the
Catholic archbishops of Dublin* (1864), i, p. 290; Jennings, *Wadding papers*, p. 37.   **45** *Merchants' Quay
Report* (1906), p. 12.   **46** *Cal. S.P. Ire., 1615–25*, p. 90.

Map 1: Franciscan houses in 1629, compiled by Raymond Gillespie, drawn by Anthony Corns. Source: Cathaldus Giblin (ed.), *Liber Lovaniensis* (Dublin, 1956), pp 4–6.

Map 2: Franciscan houses in 1647, compiled by Raymond Gillespie, drawn by Anthony Corns. Source: Giblin (ed.), *Liber Lovaniensis*, pp 13–17.

new communities. Clearly the new houses were not in the same buildings as
before, or even on the same sites, but the newly established 'houses of refuge'
were as close as possible to those of the pre-existing communities. This was
necessary to ensure that the connections between the new communities and the
old patronage networks was maintained. The survival of the emergent Franciscan
community depended on lay support and the friars' pastoral style was well suited
to this situation. According to a report on the state of Irish the church in 1613 the
Franciscans were held '*in grandissme veneratione*' and mention was made of one
Munster friar in 1611 'who for his birth and qualities is much esteemed by the
people'.[47] The developing reciprocity between the laity and the friars can be
charted in the gifts of chalices made by laypeople to Franciscan communities. The
number of surviving chalices donated to friaries by laymen and women rose from
six in the second decade of the seventeenth century to eleven in the 1620s and
seventeen in the 1630s.[48] Such tangible evidence provides clear indications not
only of reviving Franciscan fortunes but of the support base that helped to sustain
that revival.

Disputes in the Catholic community

The benefits of this resurgence in Franciscan fortunes were mixed. Increased
numbers, revitalized convents and renewed lay support all created tensions within
the wider Catholic community over the distribution of scarce resources and the
disposition of authority. Franciscans clashed with other religious orders over the
establishment of confraternities, developed as one of the ways of organizing and
motivating supporters. Such groups promised spiritual benefits for their members,
usually derived from the power of their patrons. Most convents maintained a
mortuary book, listing the names of the patrons and dates of their death so that
they could be remembered in anniversary Masses.[49] In the 1630s Franciscans
circulated printed sheets in the diocese of Cashel extolling the spiritual benefits of
St Francis and indulgences granted to the order were noted in the friars'
catechisms.[50] In Limerick conflict over the spiritual power of patrons broke out
into open warfare in 1634 during a dispute between the Franciscans and the
Dominicans and Jesuits. Two Franciscans were held to have preached, against the
orders of the vicar general,

---

47 Hagan, 'Miscellanea Vaticano-Hibernica, 1580–1631', p. 301; *Cal. S.P. Ire., 1611–14*, p. 372. **48** See M.
Krasnodębska-D'Aughton, 'Franciscan chalices, 1600–50' in this volume. **49** None of these have survived
but for notes from Galway see M.J. Blake, 'The obituary book of the Franciscan monastery at Galway'
(1910). The later Meelick obituary has survived. See I. Fennessy (ed.), 'The Meelick obituary and chronicle'
(2006–7). **50** For instance Ó Maonaigh, *Sgáthán shacramuinte na hAithridhe*, pp 198–200; A. Ó Fachtna,
Antoin Gearnon, Parrthas an Anma (1953), p. 112.

to the great prejudice of the other orders that St Francis once a year upon his anniversary day descended from heaven into purgatory and delivered from thence the souls of all the Franciscans that he found there, which say the priests, is a greater heresy than ever Luther or Calvin taught.[51]

The Limerick case may have been dramatic but it was far from unusual. There was continual low-level tension between religious orders competing for resources. In 1629 when a proclamation was being prepared to banish Catholic clergy, advice offered included that 'the Jesuits and Franciscans each said that the other were deserving of repression but that they were humble, poor souls who might have been exempted from the proclamation'.[52] Such disputes often turned on the number of religious communities depending on alms and the capacity of local towns or parishes to support them. Historical claims as to who had established themselves first in a particular area became important. In Dundalk the appearance in the early 1630s of the Discalced Carmelites where the Franciscans were already well established led to an order by the vicar general of Armagh that the Carmelites should leave. An appeal to Rome followed and a full hearing of the case before the archbishop of Armagh was ordered in 1634 but the ruling remained the same. The Carmelites decamped to Ardee only to encounter the same problems there and an appeal to Rome brought no better result in that case.[53]

Even more intense were the disputes between Franciscans and the secular clergy. Here the issues were more complex. As early as 1613 the newly appointed Franciscan archbishop of Tuam, Flaithrí Ó Maoil Chonaire, turned his attention to this problem since he regarded disputes between seculars and regulars as providing an occasion for criticism by Protestants. In an attempt to resolve the problem he reviewed the decrees of the Council of Trent and conceded that secular bishops did indeed have rights over regular clergy.[54] In some cases finance played a significant part as secular clergy resented the provision of pastoral services by Franciscans with a resulting loss of fees to the parish clergy. The problem was not a new one. Donatus Mooney had noted in 1617–18 that secular clergy complained about the administration of the sacraments by friars, which had resulted in the Franciscans in Cork being placed under interdict and for that reason the practice had been curtailed.[55] There was also the issue of the control of the local bishop over the Franciscans. The Council of Trent had ruled on this

51 HMC: *Report on the manuscripts of R.R. Hastings* (1928–47), iv, p. 60. **52** *Cal. S.P. Ire., 1625–32*, p. 446. For other anti-Jesuit comments by Franciscans see *Cal. S.P. Ire., 1611–14*, p. 372. **53** Jennings, *Wadding papers*, p. 256; Moran, *Spicilegium Ossoriense* i, pp 195–7; L.P. Murray, 'Will of James Hussey of Smarmore, Co. Louth' (1936), pp 317–18. **54** B. Hazard, 'The public career of Florence Conry, c.1560–1629' (2008), pp 115–18. **55** 'Brussels MS. 3947', p 84; Jennings, *Wadding papers*, pp 10–11.

matter by making religious orders subject to the diocesan bishop in pastoral matters but implementing that decision was more difficult. In Cork in 1640, for instance, relations between the bishop and the friars were strained over this issue.[56] In addition ethnic clashes between Old English secular clergy and Franciscans and their native Irish counterparts were not unknown. In 1623 a plan was developed to split the Irish Franciscan province into two parts. Ulster and Connacht were to be assigned to the Gaelic Irish and Munster and Leinster to the Old English. The matter raised itself again at the provincial chapter at Athlone in 1644 and a formal division was approved at the general chapter at Toledo in 1645 but never implemented.[57]

Hardly surprisingly relationships fractured in particular places and in specific circumstances. Personality clashes and local jurisdictional disputes undoubtedly worsened particular situations. In Drogheda between 1618 and 1625 there was a long running dispute between the Franciscans and the vicar general, Balthazar Delahoyde. The reasons underlying the dispute were complex but what lay at the heart of the problem was Delahoyde's favouring of the Jesuits over the Franciscans in establishing confraternities. This clearly had important economic implications since it deprived the Franciscans of a key strategy for maintaining supporters in the town. The dispute quickly developed into wider arguments about the relationship between secular and regular clergy. Much of this oratorical violence was inspired by the two main protagonists, Delahoyde and the Franciscan Donatus Mooney, and their deaths took much of the heat from the local situation but did not resolve the issues raised in the debate.[58] In the late 1620s these issues exploded again in Dublin as the resentment of the secular clergy, led by Paul Harris and Patrick Cahill, against the Franciscans spilled over into direct action. The 1613 clergy list records only one Franciscan in Dublin and Mooney's account of the province does not mention any but by 1629 there was at least one well-established friary in the capital, in Cook Street, which was destroyed in an attempt by the government to close it down. Within a few years Franciscans were again in the city in some numbers at a time when economic conditions were unfavourable for supporting a large clerical body.[59] Harris and others resented this revival by what he described as men 'who are now become R[everend] Fathers though neither learned or civil men' and he began preaching against them. He levelled accusations of favouritism against the archbishop of Dublin, then a Franciscan.[60] The resentment is perhaps understandable. Certainly

56 Egan, *Friars of Broad Lane*, pp 41–2.   **57** C. Giblin, 'A 17th century idea: two Franciscan provinces in Ireland' (1951).   **58** For the details of the dispute see B. Jackson, 'Sectarianism: division and dissent in Irish Catholicism' (2005).   **59** Jennings, *Wadding papers*, pp 330, 333, 337, 344, 353; Sheffield Archives, Wentworth Wodehouse Muniments, Strafford Letter Books, vol. 20, no. 175.   **60** Paul Harris, *The excommunication published by the L. archbishop of Dublin, Thomas Fleming* (1633), p. 42.

in Elphin the Franciscan bishop, Boetius Egan, tended to favour Franciscans, presenting the Elphin convent with a chalice in 1634 and donating a copy of John Colgan's hagiographical work to the convent at Kilconnell in 1649.[61] The situation in Dublin developed into a complex theological dispute that would have repercussions beyond Ireland as the university of Paris and the Vatican were drawn into the debate.[62] In Munster bishops tried to forestall such a dispute by placing severe limitations on the pastoral activities of the Franciscans to some effect.[63]

The state of the Irish province by 1640

By 1640 what is striking about the Irish Franciscans is how much had been achieved in recreating the structure of the province. By 1639 there were some 574 friars in the Irish province, a substantial increase from the 200 estimated in 1623.[64] What is even more impressive is the relationship that they fostered with those among whom they lived and worked. Henry Piers in the 1680s remembered Multyfarnham before 1640 as a place of 'great splendour' and 'they had their church in good repair, the quire adorned with pictures, images, relics and organs and the cloister and apartments neatly furnished'.[65] In Dublin the 1629 attempt to close the city's religious houses, including that of the Franciscans, demonstrated that the government knew exactly where such convents were located but rarely moved against them.[66] Perhaps most revealing is the fact that Protestants deposing in the wake of the 1641 rising showed themselves familiar with the Franciscans in their neighbourhood. One man in Kildare was able to name the guardian of the Franciscans and several friars in the Kildare community while others were able to name the guardian of Castledermot and friars from other communities.[67] Even those well established in the world knew friars. Editha Gardner, a wife of a soldier serving the lord president of Connacht in 1641 was well acquainted with a friar at Rosserk and the nephew of another friar, Paul Molloy, was a clerk in the court of king's bench.[68] All this suggests that some forms of accommodation had been made with all those who lived in Ireland but those accommodations were not to last.

POLITICS AND WAR, 1640–60

By the 1640s the generation that had shaped the outlook of the Irish Franciscans and established them in their Louvain home was passing. In 1629 Flaithrí Ó

61 The volume is now in Marsh's library, see M. McCarthy, *Marsh's Library, Dublin* (2003), pp 59–60. **62** For the details of this see O'Connor, *Irish Jansenists*, pp 129–70.   **63** Jennings, *Wadding papers*, pp 341, 440–1, 447–50.   **64** Millett, *The Irish Franciscans*, p. 96.   **65** TCD MS 883/2, p. 43.   **66** For this see M. Ní Mhurchadha, *Early modern Dubliners* (2008), pp 92–101.   **67** TCD MS 813, f. 260, 335, MS 814, f. 47, 59, MS 831, ff 67v 151v, 239.   **68** TCD MS 831 f. 271, MS 814, f. 164v.

Maoil Chonaire, who had been instrumental in establishing the college and shaping its early years, died. He was predeceased in 1626 by Aodh Mac Aingil, who had reached the top of the ecclesiastical tree as archbishop of Armagh. Six years later, in 1635, Hugh Ward, the man who had done much to establish the study of hagiography at Louvain, died. By 1643 Mícheál Ó Cléirigh, the college's link with the older learned orders in Ireland was also dead. It seemed clear that the order in Louvain now had to rely on a new generation.

The war of 1641

The most immediate problem facing the order was the outbreak of war in Ireland at the end of October 1641. As the country slid towards what many contemporaries regarded as anarchy friars responded in a number of ways. Some actively supported the rising and Thomas McKiernan, guardian of Dundalk, had been involved in its planning.[69] One friar in Laois favoured 'banishing the English' from Ireland. Another at Portumna claimed that the rising was 'grounded upon a national quarrel and inveterate malice which the Irish had to the English' and claimed that the pope would send arms. When the guardian of Strade, Stephen Lynch, was asked if it was lawful to kill a man because he would not go to Mass he allegedly replied 'that it was as lawful for them to kill this deponent as to kill a sheep or a dog'.[70] Others appeared to revel in sectarian violence. One friar 'in a trumpeting and rejoicing manner' it was alleged 'said it was brave sport to see the young men [meaning the sons of the English slain] defending themselves on every side and their two eyes burning in their heads'.[71] Such sentiments are hardly surprising since the University of Louvain, where at least some of the Irish friars had been educated by 1641, was one of the prominent centres of Counter-Reformation ideology in Europe. Such confessional division was the stuff of debate there and can be detected in the early seventeenth-century devotional texts from Louvain and the Irish language poetry composed by friars. Hugh Burke, the commissary of the Irish Franciscans in Germany and Belgium, and based in Louvain, described the rising in Ireland as 'the hour of our deliverance now come' and added 'this is a war waged solely for God and the defence of the Catholic church, the kingdom and monarchy of Christ's vicar on earth'.[72] For Burke in the safety of Louvain there was none of the messiness created by the realities of social and political relationships in Ireland itself. These realities caused some Franciscans to take a different view. William Lynch FitzPatrick a friar present at the massacre at Shrule attempted to save some of the English Protestants and help them escape. Another friar, Richard Burke, also attempted to save settlers but without success.[73]

69 J.T. Gilbert (ed.), *A contemporary history of affairs in Ireland* (1879), i, pp 498, 531.   **70** TCD MS 815, f. 108v; MS 814, f. 108; MS 831, f. 151v.   **71** TCD MS 830, f. 140.   **72** *Merchants' Quay Report*, pp 110, 112.   **73** TCD MS 831, ff 75, 239, 273.

This mentality is perhaps best accounted for by fear of divine judgment rather than humanitarian concern. Fear of acting unjustly might just provoke divine retribution. Laurence Geoghan, the guardian of Castledermot, for instance, fell sick 'his mouth was drawn up to his ear on one side, his tongue … out. His eyes were still open after his death'. This was widely believed to be God's punishment for his actions against settlers in the early weeks of the rising.[74] One final possibility was to remain as neutral as possible without betraying one's origins. The diary kept by the Franciscan Tuarlach Ó Mealláin during the Ulster campaigns of the 1640s is as remarkable for what it does not say as for what it records. Ó Mealláin is very circumspect, recording what he was involved in but making few comments on it almost to the point of trying to remain neutral as the world collapsed around him.[75] Such diverse possibilities regarding how to behave in this new world were to pose problems for the Irish Franciscans in the later 1640s.

While the rising prompted diverse moral responses it did have one significant advantage for the Franciscans. As the power of the Dublin administration waned Catholicism became the de facto established religion over most of Ireland and this allowed the Franciscans to expand openly their network of houses. The expansion in the number of houses is clear from the chapter bill of 1647, by which time the network had reached its greatest extent (see map 2). The bill listed some sixty-one houses as opposed to thirty-two recorded on the bill for 1629.[76] In addition by 1645 chapter bills record that schools of philosophy, theology and humanities were being run by the order. It is difficult to reconstruct what these new houses may have looked like. In some cases, as at Limerick, the older medieval house was reoccupied. In other cases the hurried erection of buildings may have given them a rather flimsy appearance. In 1645 Msgr Massari, the chaplain to the papal nuncio, described the newly occupied Franciscan house near Cavan as being 'a marvellous structure in the Ulster fashion, the church, cells, refectory and all the other apartments being of wood, roofed with sods. I was accommodated with a room well plastered with mud on the outside and full of branches of odoriferous shrubs and rushes'.[77] This account finds a parallel in another of Multyfarnham in the 1680s that described the house as composed of 'thatched cabins'. Such apparently insubstantial structures may have been typical of Franciscan convents of the mid- seventeenth century. How many people such friaries accommodated is unknown. In some cases communities expanded significantly. Waterford, for instance grew from fifteen friars in 1642 to thirty in 1649.[78] In Kilkenny there were forty in 1649, up from seven or eight in 1635.[79] In the case of Multyfarnham

---

74 TCD MS 813, ff 1, 307; MS 814, ff 47, 157.   **75** C. Dillon (ed.), 'Cin lae Uí Mhealláin' (2000).
76 Giblin, *Liber Lovaniensis*, pp 4–6, 20–9.   **77** M. Massari, 'My Irish campaign' (1917), pp 248–9.
78 *Merchants' Quay Report*, p. 236; B. Jennings, 'Sint-Truiden: Irish Franciscan documents' (1962), p. 22.
79 Hagan, 'Miscellanae Vaticano-Hibernica', p. 91; Jennings, 'Sint-Truiden', p. 22.

in 1646 there were some thirty Franciscans as well as some novices – a significant increase from the seven that made up the community in 1613.[80] Some of the newer communities were much smaller. Enniscorthy, for instance, had only five friars in 1642.[81] One estimate by the provincial in 1648 reckoned the number of friars in Ireland at about 400.[82] Allowing for this being an underestimate and for friars of the Irish province who were abroad this might suggest a total strength of over 600 friars. If that were so it would suggest that numerically the order had not expanded significantly since the late 1630s despite the politically favourable circumstances. One explanation for this apparent paradox may be the depressed economic condition of Ireland in the 1640s, which left little surplus income in the hands of the traditional supporters of the Franciscans for their upkeep. As Thomas Strange, the guardian of Waterford, commented in 1642 'wars have impoverished all our benefactors' and two years later it was also observed that 'the convents are so poor that we cannot continue studies and the country and our benefactors so poor that they cannot relieve us'.[83] Such economic conditions certainly restricted the potential expansion of the order in the 1640s.

The Franciscans and the Catholic Confederation

Reconstructing the Franciscan network of houses and intensifying the mission was one of the most obvious features of the history of the order in the 1640s but that decade had a much more profound effect in drawing the order into a larger political debate. In the years before the 1640s the Franciscans had succeeded in restructuring themselves by adopting a low-key political position akin to that of the more conservative Old English. This conservative political position was set out by Bonaventure Ó hEodhasa in his *An Teagasg Críosdaidhe*. As he put it in his commentary on the fourth commandment (on honouring parents) 'Not only are we bound to honour our fathers and mothers but we are likewise bound to give the same honour to every superior either of church or state'.[84] One outworking of that was that Mícheál Ó Cléirigh was happy to date the completion his annals by the regnal year of the then king, Charles I. In the 1640s, however, Franciscans found themselves catapulted into more public political roles. As the Irish hierarchy was reconstructed from the 1620s Franciscans carved out a prominent niche for themselves. Of the thirty-seven bishops consecrated for Irish dioceses between 1620 and 1648 eight, or rather over a fifth, were Franciscans. All had been trained in Louvain. The rationale for their appointment was clear, they were the sons of landed gentry and hence could exist with little or no diocesan income.[85]

---

80 Massari, 'My Irish campaign', pp 113–14.   **81** *Merchants' Quay Report*, p. 215.   **82** *Comment. Rinucc.*, iii, p. 560.   **83** *Merchants' Quay Report*, pp 192, 235; Jennings, *Louvain papers*, p. 151.   **84** F. Mac Raghnaill (ed.), *Bonabhentura Ó hEodhasa, An Teagasg Críosdaidhe* (1976), p. 67.   **85** D. Cregan, 'The social and cultural

With the establishment of the Catholic Confederation in 1642 these men found themselves thrust into the public world of political organization. Between 1642 and 1646, for instance, Thomas Fleming, archbishop of Dublin, was one of those who from the Supreme Council dictated confederate policy in Ireland. At lower levels Franciscans also found themselves in leadership roles. Peter Nugent, a Franciscan, was a member of the local confederate council for Westmeath in the early 1640s.[86]

Entry into this political world inevitably brought choices and those choices became more difficult and more pressing when after 1643 the Confederation of Kilkenny and the crown tried to formulate a peace that would accommodate all parties to the dispute in Ireland. In 1646 a treaty was agreed between the Confederation and the king. While there were some concessions to Irish Catholics they were limited and some of the most crucial issues were left unresolved. As far as the papal nuncio, Giovanni Battista Rinuccini, was concerned it was an unacceptable agreement and he purged the General Assembly of those who did not support him, excommunicating his opponents. What seemed to some to be an unacceptable use of papal authority by the nuncio created divisions in the Irish Franciscan community that would last for almost forty years. One of the first to oppose Rinuccini was the Franciscan friar Peter Walsh, then based in Kilkenny. In 1647 he preached a series of sermons supporting the Confederation's position on monarchy and opposing Rinuccini's view of papal authority. This cost him his position but gained him the support of David Rothe, the local bishop. In 1648, with Rothe's support, he drafted the reply to Rinuccini's excommunications of those who supported the peace in *Queries concerning the lawfulness of the present cessation.* On the other side of the argument was the provincial, Thomas McKiernan, who exiled Walsh to the convent of Castledermot until he escaped to London and thence to Madrid. McKiernan was not alone and could count on considerable support, indeed probably the majority of Irish Franciscans, including Thomas Fleming (Franciscan archbishop of Dublin), Anthony Geoghan (Franciscan bishop of Clonmacnoise), and Boethius Egan (Franciscan bishop of Ross). The debate that Walsh initiated on the acceptability of Rinuccini's excommunications, since they interfered with the rights of conscience, continued into the 1650s with Irish Franciscans abroad taking both sides. In Paris John Punch (Ponce) defended Rinuccini's actions with Redmond Caron in Ghent and Antwerp arguing a more strongly Royalist case, such as would have been espoused by Peter Walsh's patron, the earl (later duke) of Ormond. Indeed Caron, as visitor of the friars in Ireland, with Patrick Plunkett, guardian of Mellifont, had

background of a counter-reformation episcopate' (1979).   **86** TCD MS 817, f. 68v.

unsuccessfully proposed at the general chapter in Kilkenny in 1649 a division of the province into two parts to accommodate the different positions of the friars.[87]

In the 1640s the most important role played by the Irish Franciscans was not in Ireland but in continental Europe. In Rome the Franciscan Luke Wadding acted as Irish political emissary for the Confederation. St Anthony's in Louvain also played a central role in shaping a positive image of Ireland in Europe during the wars. This function of upholder of Ireland's status can be traced back into the early seventeenth century when the decision by Hugh Ward set in train the collecting and editing of saints' lives by the Louvain Franciscans. That scheme culminated in the 1645 with the publication of John Colgan's monumental *Acta Sanctorum*. It contained a preface by Colgan that spoke to the times.[88] Colgan argued that Ireland, the land of saints, had developed as a result of a series golden ages and times of crises which were resolved from outside.[89] The coming of the British holy man Patrick had produced the first golden age of the Irish church, revealed clearly in the lives of the saints that had been collected by Mícheál Ó Cléirigh, and which Colgan was now editing. This world had been shattered by the coming of the Vikings but the church was again revitalized by the twelfth century reform under the guidance of the holy man St Malachy (who had close links with the European reformer St Bernard of Clairvaux) that again produced the golden age of the medieval church. This was, in turn, brought to an end by Henry VIII. While Colgan did not explicitly say so, he probably believed the church would again be renewed by holy men from abroad in the seventeenth century and there is little doubt that it was himself and his colleagues, the Louvain Franciscans, who were to be cast in this role.

Colgan's view of the history of Ireland reveals a great deal of his understanding of Ireland's position in Europe. First, it explained to the Irish what their links with Europe were. Spiritual regeneration had come from outside the country, whether through St Patrick or St Bernard's disciple Malachy, and hence Ireland belonged to a wider christendom. The early Irish church had provided missionaries who had evangelized Britain and Europe in the early middle ages in a way that Rome had not. Colum Cille, the stories of whose life, together with those of Patrick and Brigit, were collected by Colgan in a volume entitled *Triadis Thamaturgae* in 1647, was the quintessential missionary monk. Thus Irish and European ideas and experiences were firmly intertwined. Secondly, Colgan was intent on explaining to Europeans the significance of the Irish people. Colgan's works were issued in Latin from the press in Louvain. They were large folio

---

87 Gilbert (ed.), *Contemporary history*, ii, p. 34; Jennings, 'Sint-Truiden', pp 19–22; O'Connor, *Irish Jansenists*, pp 275–305. 88 Colgan, *AS*, sig a3-a6. 89 For the use of the phrase 'land of saints' see *Merchants' Quay Report*, pp 216–17, Jennings, *Louvain papers*, pp 143–4.

volumes intended for scholarly rather than devotional reading. There are a number of contexts for these publications. In 1588 the Sacred Congregation of Rites and Ceremonies had been established which was responsible for formal canonization and the recognition of saints. Processes became increasingly rigorous with new regulations in 1629 and 1634. Neither Patrick, Brigit, Colum Cille nor almost any other Irish saint had ever had papal approval. Colgan's work was therefore intended, in part, to explain to European scholars and Roman reformers the world of Irish sanctity and the validity of its national saints. Colgan's preface clarified the nature of the Franciscan mission from Louvain and provided a central role for the friars in the reshaping of Catholic Ireland in a new golden age, which appeared to be under way in the 1640s. In particular it explained how a college founded in the culture of defeat after the Flight of the Earls would have a central role in the restoration of an old order.

These issues, important as they were in the political ferment of the 1640s when many options for the political organization of Ireland emerged, were quickly sidelined by the implosion of the Irish Catholic cause in the late 1640s. The Cromwellian re-conquest of Ireland in 1649–50 changed both the religious and political context within which the friars worked. The 1650s saw a breaking of the structures that had been established in the early seventeenth century although the evidence for the detail of this is thin. Friaries were destroyed by the war and the Cromwellian clampdown that followed it.[90] The provincial chapter of 1658, for instance, listed at least twelve vacant friaries outside Munster with many more in that province empty.[91] The number of friars also probably fell sharply as a result of the killings of friars and their exile from the country after an act of banishment of priests in 1653.[92] Indeed the friars may have been singled out since a view current in the 1650s believed that they had been instrumental in the planning of the rising of 1641, orchestrated from Multyfarnham.[93] It is difficult to quantify the impact of this in any meaningful way but by 1663 the number of friars in Ireland stood at about 200, or about where it was in the early 1620s.[94] Most of what had been achieved before 1640 was undone by the Cromwellian years.

REMONSTRANCE, RESTORATION AND NEW INTERESTS, 1660–98

The Remonstrance and political disputes

The 1640s and 1650s left a deep imprint on those who were involved in Irish Franciscan life after the Restoration. The debates between supporters of the lord

90 Moran, *Spicilegium Ossoriense*, i, pp 415–16; Millett, *Irish Franciscans*, pp 73–88.   **91** Giblin, *Liber Lovaniensis*, p. 54.   **92** For a discussion of this see Millett, *Irish Franciscans*, pp 96–105.   **93** For this question see O Donnell, *Franciscan abbey of Multyfarnham*, pp 62–4.   **94** Millett, *Irish Franciscans*, p. 97.

lieutenant, the earl of Ormond, and of Rinuccini continued to reverberate in Ireland as many who had debated these issues in the 1640s returned to the fray. In particular Peter Walsh, who had opposed the papal centralism of Rinuccini in the 1640s, emerged as one of the leaders in the Irish political nation worried about the relationship of the Protestant monarch and state, to which they wished to be loyal and receive regrants of their lands lost in the 1650s, and the Catholic church to which they wanted to remain faithful. As a solution to this dilemma Walsh and others proposed a Loyal Formulary or Remonstrance of 1661 which suggested an oath of loyalty to the king while recognising papal jurisdiction in spiritual matters. Fifteen Franciscans signed the original document, including Redmond Caron, Walsh's erstwhile ally from the 1640s, George Dillon and Anthony Gearnon, the author of the devotional work *Parrthas an anma*.[95] The king approved the Remonstrance and Walsh's political patron, the duke of Ormond (then lord lieutenant), thought it a useful tool to separate the politically loyal from those who gave their allegiance to a foreign power. The subsequent debate split the Franciscans as the debate about the censures in the 1640s had done. Theologians at the University of Louvain condemned the proposal for its limitations on papal power although those in the Sorbonne seemed well disposed. However, Walsh's abrasive personality did not help in promoting the cause. Matters came to a head in 1666 with a national synod rejecting the Remonstrance and proposing an alternative oath that was not found acceptable by Ormond or Walsh.[96]

By 1666 the debate over the Remonstrance, and any political hopes that Walsh may have harboured, were dead. Some Franciscans who had supported the cause claimed they were persecuted. Some recanted and others were excommunicated.[97] Walsh remained in Ireland until his death in 1688 and his political position, and the patronage of Ormond, meant that his voice continued to be listened to in government circles despite marginalization in the church. However, the debate on the Remonstrance scarred the order for most of the rest of the century. John Brennan, bishop of Waterford in the 1670s and 1680s, claimed that the divisions that the debates had produced undermined both morale and discipline. According to Bishop Brennan in 1674 Franciscans were 'refusing obedience to their superior and these also go about the country giving great disedification'.[98] There were even some conversions to Protestantism from among the friars, including the highly dramatic conversion sermon by Anthony Egan.[99] One

Another estimate concurs roughly with the number of preachers in the 1663 report see B. Jennings, 'The religious orders in Ireland in the seventeenth century' (1937), p. 80. **95** *Cal. S.P. Ire., 1660–2*, p. 504. **96** Walsh and his circle are discussed in Millett, *Irish Franciscans*, pp 418–63 and the politics of the Remonstrance in A. Creighton, 'The Remonstrance of December 1661 and Catholic politics in Restoration Ireland' (2004–5). **97** *Cal. S.P. Ire., 1669–70*, pp 98–101; Bodleian Library, Oxford, Carte MS 118, f. 138, Carte MS 60, f. 400. **98** P. Power (ed.), *A bishop of the penal times* (1932), p. 39. **99** Ibid., pp 38–9; A.

manifestation of the lack of discipline was the re-emergence in 1672 of the proposal of the 1640s to split the Irish province into two parts. Bishop Brennan of Waterford saw the hand of Francis Coppinger, a supporter of Walsh, behind this move although he, and Oliver Plunkett (archbishop of Armagh), also saw merits in the suggestion. Rome refused to sanction the change.[1]

Louvain and Rome in the late seventeenth century

What is striking about both the political debates within the order and the consolidation of the Franciscans in the late seventeenth century is the limited role that the house in Louvain played in those processes. The death of John Colgan in 1658 removed the last of the major scholars from the house. The catechetical projects did not proceed any further and the hagiographical project ground to a halt after Colgan's death. Louvain's change in orientation from an intellectual powerhouse for Irish learning to a more restrained seminary is indicated by the type of Irish-interest manuscripts that were generated there. These were not new pastoral works or scholarly editions of texts but finding aids to the existing manuscript collections.[2]

Louvain Franciscan intellectual endeavour moved into other areas of activity, related more to wider European intellectual debates. From the middle of the seventeenth century the Louvain Franciscans became increasingly interested in the academic elucidation of the structure of the Irish language. Ó Cléirigh's dictionary appeared in 1643, as a spin off from his historical work, and the following year the friar Maurice Conroy from Louvain received permission to publish an Irish–Latin dictionary.[3] By 1659 another grammar existed, being copied for the Franciscan Patrick Plunkett in Madrid, a work that was frequently recopied.[4] In 1662 Richard Plunkett, from the Franciscan house at Trim, produced a manuscript Irish–Latin dictionary and in 1667 Francis O'Molloy published his *Grammatica Latino-Hibernica* in Rome. By 1706 the Dublin friar Francis Walsh had produced an Irish-Irish dictionary and by 1712 he had begun a Latin–English–Irish dictionary. In 1713 he had completed a 'Grammatica Anglo–Hibernia'. Finally, in 1728 Hugh McCurtain produced his *Elements of the Irish language.* While McCurtain was not a Franciscan his work was published by the press in Louvain and was accompanied by a Franciscan devotional work of 1663 by John Dowley. All this marks a change in attitudes toward the Irish language. It was no longer simply a tool for mission but a subject for study in

Egan, *The Franciscan convert* (1673).   **1** Power, *A bishop of the penal times*, pp 35, 39; J. Hanly (ed.), *The letters of Saint Oliver Plunkett* (1979), pp 318–9. 322, 332.   **2** UCD-OFM, A34 for instance; P.A. Breatnach, 'Repertoria manuscriptorum Collegii S. Antoni' (2007).   **3** S. Ua Súilleabháin, 'The lost has been found: the earliest surviving bilingual Irish dictionary' (2004), pp 392–405.   **4** TCD MS 1431, Mac Aogáin,

itself rather than the focus on hagiography or history that had characterized the
early seventeenth-century Louvain experience. The effect of this was to situate
Louvain intellectual activity in the midst of the contemporary European interest
in language and translation and also the Europeanisation of the Irish language.[5]

As Louvain's interest in hagiography and history scholarship waned others
developed scholarly interests. The Irish Franciscan community in Prague had
been caught up in disputes in the early seventeenth century but in the years after
1650 intellectual interests asserted themselves again.[6] More importantly, the Irish
Franciscan college of St Isidore's in Rome developed a scholarly role for itself. St
Isidore's had moved along a different intellectual trajectory to that of Louvain in
the early seventeenth century. Its existence was not ensured by a network of native
Irish patrons that had supported Louvain but, under the influence of the Old
English friar Luke Wadding, it carved out a role for itself in the scholastic
philosophical system flourishing in Europe based on the works of John Duns
Scotus. At the time of his death in 1657 Wadding had produced some thirty-three
works, including a fifteen-volume edition of the works of Scotus and an eight-
volume history of the Franciscans. All these works were published in the centres
of the seventeenth-century book trade in Rome, Lyon or Antwerp in contrast to
the locally published works of the Louvain college. The influence of this project
was felt across Europe as those trained by Wadding spread out across the
Continent as teachers and scholars.[7] After Wadding's death the college in Rome
briefly considered the problem of the provision of materials for the pastoral
mission in Ireland. In 1638 the Roman Congregation Propaganda Fide had
sanctioned the casting of type for the production of books in Irish but nothing
was produced until 1676. In that year the Propaganda type was used to produce
Francis Molloy's Irish language catechism *Lucerna fidelium* and an Irish grammar
by Molloy followed in 1677.[8] The excursus by the Rome Franciscans into this sort
of work was brief since the type was not used again until 1707 when Bonaventure
Ó hEodhasa's *An Teagasg Críosdaidhe* was reprinted in Rome. However brief, the
interest in the use of the Irish language and the work of Louvain was serious and
the scriptural text in the Irish language inscribed above the entrance of the
Theological Hall in St Isidore's dates from this period as do the portraits of the
Rome and Louvain Franciscans by Fra Emanuele da Como.

Graiméir ghaeilge na mBráthar Mionúr, pp xix–xxv, 109–42.   **5** J. de Clercq & P. Swiggers, 'The Hibernian
connection: Irish grammatography in Louvain' (1990).   **6** Mac Craith & Worthington, 'Literary activity
of the Irish Franciscans in Prague', pp 126–32.   **7** For a sample see Cleary, *Father Luke Wadding and St
Isidore's College Rome*, p. 156.   **8** D. McGuinne, *Irish type design* (1992), pp 37–8; P. Ó Súilleabháin (ed.),
Froinsias Ó Maolmhuaidh, Lucerna fidelium (1962), pp ix–xii.

The Irish province in the late seventeenth century

What may have driven Roman interest in producing pastoral materials for the Irish mission was the solid progress that was made in the later seventeenth century in rebuilding and consolidating the Franciscan presence in Ireland in the aftermath of the Cromwellian regime. Friaries were reoccupied in the wake of the Restoration and by the time of the middle chapter of 1672 only six were listed as vacant.[9] Some of the these friaries were older conventual houses now absorbed into the reform movement but significantly friaries were founded in places such as Strabane and Derry where there had been no medieval presence. This marks a shift in the Franciscans' understanding of their role as they began to move out from their traditional areas of influence into new missionary areas. The number of Franciscan convents can only be a rough guide to the strength of the order in Ireland if only because, as Archbishop Oliver Plunkett alleged, they might be kept open with small numbers so that visitation fees could be collected.[10] It is difficult to make estimates of the size of the province but in 1663 the minister provincial reckoned that there were some 200 friars in Ireland, excluding Irish friars in the colleges abroad.[11] Numbers rose in the years after 1660, although probably in rather fitful bursts as periods of toleration alternated with anti-Catholic reaction. In 1673, for instance, Catholic bishops and regular clergy were banished from Ireland by proclamation and, despite attempts by Ormond to calm the situation, the aftermath of the popish plot was felt in Ireland with a 1678 proclamation again banishing Catholic bishops and regular clergy. More detailed local evidence suggests that these proclamations did not have a dramatic impact on Franciscan numbers. In the diocese of Waterford Bishop Brennan reported that the number of Franciscans at Waterford, Carrick-on-Suir and Clonmel changed only slightly from eleven priests in 1672 to ten in 1675 and nine in 1678. In Armagh the changes were more marked as numbers of friars in Dundalk, Drogheda and Armagh fell from twenty-four in 1671 to about eighteen in 1678.[12]

There are indications that during this period the Franciscans in Ireland were moving in new directions. Episcopal reports stress their traditional role as confessors and preachers but they were also assuming new roles. The Franciscan relationship with the printed word at Louvain had been uncertain and such books, especially catechisms, that were produced there were probably intended more for the training of clergy than day-to-day use by most laypeople. However, in the years after 1660 copies of some of the devotional works originally produced by the Louvain press appear in Ireland not as printed books but as part of the manuscript tradition. This was especially true for Anthony Gearnon's *Parrthas an*

9 Giblin, *Liber Lovaniensis*, p. 118.   **10** Hanly, *Letters of Saint Oliver Plunkett*, p. 512.   **11** Millett, *Irish Franciscans*, p. 97.   **12** Power, *A bishop of the penal times*, pp 31, 46, 64; Hanly, *Letters of Saint Oliver*

anma (1645). Two, or possibly three copies, of this tract (or extracts from it) were made in the years after 1660. One of these manuscripts also contains poems by the early seventeenth-century Franciscan Bonaventure Ó hEodhasa and at least two others contain part of his 1611 catechism.[13] Of even more interest is the copy of Aodh Mac Aingil's 1618 work on penance, *Sgáthán Shacramuinte na hAithridhe*, made for Brian Maguire of Fermanagh in 1701–2.[14] This work was intended for use by clergy rather than laity and its strong emphasis on the spiritual dimension of repentance marks it out as a strongly Tridentine text. The acquisition of such a text by a layman points to the achievement of the Franciscans in introducing such ideas to a wide community. By the early eighteenth century even more interest was being shown in a much wider range of Franciscan works by Tadhg Ó Neachtain and his circle in Dublin.[15] Both of the seventeenth-century manuscripts were written by laymen, one in Fermanagh and the second in Dublin and this suggests that what had begun as books for the clergy were filtering down into lay hands. Unfortunately there is very little evidence to suggest how these manuscripts were read but those who advocated the spiritualized world of Trent were clear that reading was better than hearing or reciting. Reading provided time for meditation and meditation led to a deepening of religious experience. To this end the percolation of the written word into the hands of laypeople in the late seventeenth century might be seen as a significant achievement by the Irish Franciscans.[16]

In addition to traditional methods of spreading the devotional message of Tridentine spirituality the friars became involved in other new activities. In 1632 they assumed responsibility for the penitential pilgrimage site of St Patrick's Purgatory in Lough Derg, Co. Donegal. They had shown an interest in the importance of this site as early as 1611 when it had been depicted as a frontispiece in Ó hEodhasa's *An Teagasg Críosdaidhe*.[17] In the short term the Franciscans could achieve little here since the pilgrimage was closed in the 1630s and during the 1650s when the site was sacked. The mission was taken up again in the late seventeenth century but in a rather halting fashion as political developments, such as the anti-Catholic scare of the early 1680s, interrupted progress. One commentator observed in 1683 that 'lately the friars began to build therein [St Patrick's Purgatory] and penitents resorted thither in great numbers until about

Plunkett, pp 237, 512. **13** BL Sloane MS 3567 (1664–5), BL Egerton MS 196 (1688) and possibly RIA MSS 24 L 28 (undated); 23 L 19 (seventeenth century); C iv 1, pp 497–518 (seventeenth century). **14** Cambridge University Library Add. MS 4205, ff 3–90v. **15** In particular BL Egerton MS 198 and RIA MS 23 I 9. There was at least one Franciscan in this circle in Dublin who may well have supplied exemplars. See MacMahon, 'The silent century, 1698–1829' in this volume. **16** See Ryan, 'A wooden key to open Heaven's door' in this volume. **17** B. Cunningham & R. Gillespie, '"The most adaptable of saints": the cult of St Patrick in the seventeenth century' (1995), pp 94–6.

three years ago the duke of Ormond, lord lieutenant of Ireland, and the privy council ordered certain gentlemen to see it demolished again which was done accordingly'.[18] It is clear that the pilgrimage did not remain closed for long. By the early eighteenth century the pilgrimage had again become an important religious event but it had been reshaped by the Franciscans. According to an admittedly hostile witness, John Richardson, efforts were made to transform the pilgrimage from a set of popular rituals into an interior spiritual experience. Pilgrims were provided with instructions, printed in modern form, that urged them not simply to perform the rituals but pointed out the biblical significance attached to them and urged them to meditate on their actions, turning the ritual into an example of Tridentine interiority. In the same way as Franciscan printed devotional works made their way into lay society to promote spiritual reflection, ritual was similarly treated. Such was the triumph of Franciscan reform.[19]

The consolidation of the position of the Franciscans in the 1670s and 1680s, as in the 1620s and 1630s, brought its own problems. The unresolved jurisdictional issues from the early seventeenth century, with their economic implications, continued to plague the friars. As in the 1620s and 1630s local and personal issues continued to play an important role in the way in which those tensions were played out. Perhaps the most dramatic example of this was the aftermath of the appointment of Oliver Plunkett as archbishop of Armagh in 1669. From the outset of his episcopate Plunkett realized that the Franciscans were a powerful force. In a survey of his archdiocese in 1671 he reckoned that there were over ninety friars in the area, strongest in counties Donegal and Armagh with eighteen and fourteen friars each, or probably half the strength of the Irish province.[20] Plunkett considered that the Franciscans had failed to adhere to the discipline of the decrees of the Council of Trent, and in particular to submit themselves to his authority. Some such as John Brady or Phelim O'Neill were deliberately undermining his episcopal authority by undertaking pastoral functions without his permission.[21] Moreover he maintained that convents were often empty, had inadequate communities and lacked regular observances.[22] These problems were magnified by the Franciscans' own inadequate arrangements for the training of their novices. Plunkett complained that there were too many novitiates and that novices were admitted with no selection, were not trained or disciplined so that, as he put it, they 'sow thistles and it will be difficult for them to harvest melons'.[23] None of this was particularly unusual. From Waterford Plunkett's contemporary John Brennan echoed the same problems. Franciscans used customs and rituals

---

18 TCD MS 883/1, p. 215. **19** John Richardson, *The great folly, superstition and idolatry of pilgrimage in Ireland* (1724), pp 52–61. **20** Hanly, *Letters of Saint Oliver Plunkett*, pp 237–8. **21** Ibid., p. 440. **22** Ibid., pp 512–13, 522. **23** Ibid., pp 238, 362, 368, 373, 380, 460–1, 469, 472.

that were counter to normal practice decreed by diocesan synods and, as in Armagh novices were 'rough and uninstructed', there being too many inadequate novitiates.[24] However Plunkett highlighted one other problem that proved to be much more contentious: the right to quest or beg for alms after mass. In the late seventeenth century the other main order of friars, the Dominicans, began to reoccupy the locales of their older houses as a result of which competition developed between the Franciscans and Dominicans for the right to beg for alms.[25] The Franciscans appealed to Rome to confirm their rights and privileges since the Dominicans had previously abandoned the areas and this matter was remitted to Plunkett. The most powerful Franciscan card was their local support and petitions with the names of hundreds of supporters were prepared as part of the case.[26] Nevertheless, Plunkett duly decided in favour of the Dominicans in 1671 and the Franciscans appealed both to the Irish government in 1674 and to Rome but Propaganda Fide recognized the rights of the Dominicans in 1678.[27] As Plunkett rightly realized this was a crucial moment as local loyalties and Franciscan sensibilities coalesced in an explosive mixture. As the archbishop himself noted the only gain from his decision 'would be the hatred of one or the other'.[28] The local discontents that grew out of his decision were to prove fatal for Oliver Plunkett.

In this fraught ecclesiastical world discontent over one issue could easily be mobilized for other ends. Rumours of a Catholic conspiracy in England in the late 1670s inevitably had an impact on Ireland and, despite the duke of Ormond's attempts to maintain calm, fears of a Catholic plot here too led to the arrest of Oliver Plunkett on a charge of conspiring with France. In these circumstances the Franciscan strategy was to maintain a low public profile until the crisis had passed and at Multyfarnham, for instance, it was noted that during this crisis the community 'upon proclamation issued by the state they dispersed' apparently willingly.[29] However, among those who informed against Plunkett were a number of south Ulster Franciscans including John Mac Moyer, George Croddan and Anthony Daly. Croddan was typical of those Franciscans that Plunkett had condemned. While a professed Franciscan he did not live in a community and had been previously involved in other accusations against secular clergy.[30] Mac Moyer and Daly were more conventional figures. Daly was motivated by a genuine concern

---

24 Power, *A bishop of the penal times*, pp 32, 39, 46–7.   **25** Here were also disputes between Franciscan friaries as to the territory over which they could quest but much less evidence on this has survived. For an example of such a dispute see Dalton, 'The abbey of Kilnalahan', pp 213–16.   **26** C. Giblin, 'The Franciscan mission in the diocese of Clogher' (1970), pp 193–203; P.J. Campbell, 'The Franciscan petition lists: diocese of Armagh, 1670–71' (1992–3).   **27** Hanly, *Letters of Saint Oliver Plunkett*, pp 413–14; B. Jennings, 'An appeal of the Ulster Franciscans against Blessed Oliver Plunkett' (1956).   **28** Hanly, *Letters of Saint Oliver Plunkett*, p. 114.   **29** TCD MS 883/2, p. 43.   **30** Hanly, *Letters of Saint Oliver Plunkett*, pp 87, 359, 560, 574; Cuthbert Mhág Craith (ed.), *Dán na nBráthar Mionúr* (1967–80), i, pp 237–8.

for the Franciscan order which he felt was under attack by Plunkett. He lodged formal complaints with Rome about Plunkett's actions and may have attempted to have him assassinated by tories (as Plunkett believed) before turning to the civil power.[31] Mac Moyer's hatred of Plunkett stemmed from the decision of Plunkett on questing in 1671 and perhaps to an even greater extent the social disruption consequent on the archbishop's attempts to stamp out banditry or toryism in Armagh in the 1670s.[32] Protection of their own way of life led these men to become instrumental in the execution of the man they saw as a threat at Tyburn in July 1681.

While the problems of the Franciscans were not solved by the execution of Oliver Plunkett an important flash point had been removed. Tensions between bishops and orders in their dioceses and secular and regular clergy still existed and in 1684 the secular clergy who made up the chapter of the collegiate church at Galway thought it necessary to pass an act that no friar would ever be admitted to the living of St Nicholas or any parish attached to it in Galway.[33] It would, however, be wrong to overstress the significance of this low-level tension in the life of many of the friars. While education in Louvain certainly brought some friars, and probably a growing number, into the world of administrative, political or theological disputes there were also many who had little interest in these matters or were not equipped to deal with them. According to Bishop Brennan in 1678 there were only three Franciscan priests in Waterford (as opposed to thirty in 1649) only one of whom was 'learned' and at Carrick-on-Suir none of the Franciscans preached 'being deficient both in talent and in learning; however they lead an edifying life'.[34] Such locally trained friars may have lacked the academic polish of some such as Peter Walsh but they were central to maintaining the Franciscan community in late seventeenth-century Ireland.

The accession of the Catholic James II to the throne in 1685 and the beginnings of a Catholicization of Irish government and the army from 1687 should have brought changes for the Irish Franciscans. Indeed there were some very visible changes. Most obviously they could now wear the habit in public, and hence were more recognizable, and in Cashel they openly established a school.[35] However the evidence for the activities of the order under the Irish Catholic revanche is rather ambiguous. According to the chapter bills of 1689 and 1690 almost as many convents still remained vacant as in the 1660s (map 3).[36] Some evidence for limited expansion in the late 1680s is provided by the histories of

31 C. Mooney, 'Accusations against Oliver Plunkett' (1956–7), pp 120–6; Hanly, *Letters of Saint Oliver Plunkett*, p. 542. **32** T. Ó Fiaich, 'The fall and return of John Mac Moyer' (1958–9). **33** E. MacLysaght, 'Report on the documents relating to the wardenship of Galway' (1944), p. 36. **34** Power, *A bishop of the penal times*, p. 64. **35** Ibid., pp 85, 88, 94. **36** Giblin, *Liber Lovaniensis*, pp 188, 194.

individual convents. The numbers of friars in Waterford between 1672 and 1687 rose from four to five but at Carrick-on-Suir they fell from three to two and only Clonmel saw significant growth with numbers rising from four to six over the period.[37] In Limerick the old convent was leased from its new owner and the friars reoccupied it.[38] At Meelick, Co. Galway, in 1685 consideration was being given to rebuilding the old friary and in 1686 a new roof was constructed, funded by donations from a number of local residents.[39] It seems likely that at Kilconnell work was done to the building in the 1680s as in 1709 Thomas Molyneux on a journey to Connacht noted 'this abbey was in repair an inhabited by friars in King James's time so that the woodwork, the wainscot and ordinary painting still remains'.[40] In Cashel too work was done on the newly reclaimed friary and a new chapel was constructed by 1687.[41] The Jacobite regime may not, however, have lasted long enough to allow any major infrastructural improvement. Yet such building projects point to the ability to fundraise and construct a support base, that had been one of the Franciscans' strengths in the seventeenth century. At Meelick the community built around itself a support network focused on the confraternity of the cord of St Francis to which a number of prominent local residents belonged.[42] Such arrangements were not unusual. The Franciscans in Waterford had a confraternity in 1678 at which there was 'a considerable attendance of both sexes at the monthly meeting'.[43] The existence of this support base allowed other projects to be undertaken through the raising of finance and in particular the repair of friaries.

In the years after the battle of the Boyne in 1690 Franciscan concerns changed again. The generation who had fought and re-fought the wars of the 1640s were dying out. Peter Walsh died in 1688. Most of his supporters had predeceased him: John Punch in 1673, Valentine Browne in 1672 and Anthony Gearnon in 1677. New problems now faced the Irish Franciscan province. The immediate reaction to the collapse of the Catholic regime of James II appears to have been muted. The provincial chapters of 1693 and 1697 were held in Dublin, apparently with little or no fear of discovery or persecution. Nor is there any evidence in the chapter bills that convents were being left vacant. Indeed fewer were vacant in 1697 than in 1689.[44] By 1700 there are even hints of expansion. According to the chapter bill of 1700 (map 4) new convents had been established in the previous decade. Numbers too had expanded. According to a list of 1700 the Irish Franciscan province contained 567 professed members, with the inclusion of

37 Power, *A bishop of the penal times*, pp 31, 72. 38 B. Egan, *Franciscan Limerick* (1971), p. 21. 39 C. Giblin, 'Papers relating to Meelick friary, 1644–1731' (1973), pp 64–76. 40 A. Smith (ed.), 'Journey to Connaught' (1846), p. 168. 41 Power, *A bishop of the penal times*, p. 85. 42 Fennessy, 'The Meelick obituary and chronicle (1623–1873)' (2006–7). 43 Power, *A bishop of the penal times*, p. 64. 44 Giblin, *Liber Lovaniensis*, nos. 66, 67.

Map 3: Franciscan houses in 1684, compiled by Raymond Gillespie, drawn by Anthony Corns. Source: Giblin (ed.), *Liber Lovaniensis*, pp 166–9.

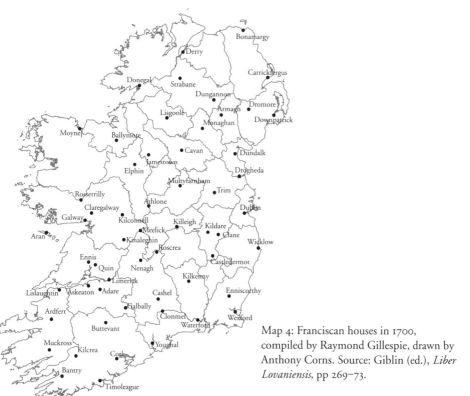

Map 4: Franciscan houses in 1700, compiled by Raymond Gillespie, drawn by Anthony Corns. Source: Giblin (ed.), *Liber Lovaniensis*, pp 269–73.

novices this rises to 583.[45] In effect the strength of the Irish province was now slightly greater than what it had been in 1639; the community had succeeded in rebuilding itself despite the internal political problems of the late seventeenth century. However, after 1697 a change in attitude toward their place in the world is clear among the Irish Franciscan community. The middle chapter of 1699 and the provincial chapter 1700 were held in St Anthony's College, Louvain.[46] The immediate occasion of this move appears to have been the passage of the 1697 Bishops' Banishment Act by the Irish parliament. This required all regular clergy and all bishops as well as those exercising ecclesiastical jurisdiction to leave Ireland by 1 May 1698. Franciscan superiors advised that the act should be obeyed and in 1698 an Irish Franciscan college was set up in Boulay, near Metz, as an additional house of refuge. The community at Kilconnell divided up their grain and dispersed.[47] Other friaries felt themselves immediately under threat and began to take measures to ensure that their possessions would be protected in the event of their being dissolved. At Meelick chalices and books were consigned to the care of friends of the house who were required to return them to the guardian of the convent when requested.[48] Much of what had been achieved in the course of the seventeenth century appeared under threat.

Despite the increase in the administrative documentation available for the Franciscans in the late seventeenth century it is difficult to reconstruct the particular influences at work on most of the friars. In one case, however, a brief glimpse into the world of one Franciscan is possible. Of the life of Cormac MacPharlane we know little apart from the fact that he left Ireland for Spain in the late 1690s, possibly in the wake of the Bishops' Banishment Act.[49] However, in 1697–8, before he left Ireland, he compiled a commonplace book that provides some insights into his world.[50] What this reveals is a friar fluent in Latin, English and Irish. A good deal of the volume is made up of secular verse in Irish including a poem on doctors and advice on a marriage. Political concerns surface in a poem on a casualty of the battle of the Boyne. There are also a few devotional items in Irish including a poem on the Annunciation. In English too there is a good deal of secular verse but among the English works is a transcript of a printed religious work entitled *A net for the fishers of men*, which MacPharlane describes as a 'small and profitable treatise', published at Douai in 1685 but available in the Dublin stationery shop of William Weston in 1688.[51] MacPharlane's interest in print did

---

45 C. Giblin, 'A list of the personnel of the Franciscan province of Ireland' (1965).   **46** Giblin, *Liber Lovaniensis*, nos. 81, 103.   **47** W.P. Burke, *The Irish priests in the penal times* (1914), pp 129–30.   **48** Giblin, 'Meelick friary', pp 68–73. See Krasnodębska-D'Aughton, 'Franciscan chalices, 1600–50', in this volume.   **49** Mhág Craith (ed.), *Dán na mBráthar Mionúr*, i, pp 260–1.   **50** TCD MS 1375.   **51** R. Gillespie, *Reading Ireland: print, reading and social change* (2005), p. 149.

not end with devotional works. Another item copied into his notebook was a London printed broadsheet on the Treaty of Ryswick entitled *The proposal of a general [peace] between France, Germany, Lorraine, Holland and Liege* (1697). Finally, the Latin works are again a mixture of secular and devotional works with epitaphs on Sarsfield, Owen Roe O'Neill and Constantine Maguire, killed at the Boyne, Latin verses on three of the provinces of Ireland, charms, recipes and astrological notes. Again there are Latin prayers, including a prayer to St Anthony, and religious verse. The Cormac MacPharlane who compiled this commonplace book may be the same man who owned an older manuscript, British Library Egerton MS 136, probably originally written in the 1630s. This contains religious works in Irish, of the sort that were well known in late fifteenth-century Irish sources, usually in translation from Latin. Taken together these two manuscripts suggest a friar deeply attached to traditional religion as exemplified in late medieval devotional works but equally at home with works of a Tridentine devotional hue such as *A net for the fishers of men*. It also suggests a friar who had interests wider than simply religious ones, especially in verse. His political interests both in Ireland and in continental Europe are clear. All this reveals a man at home in many linguistic communities and able to move between the worlds of manuscript and print culture. These were important attributes of the seventeenth-century Franciscan friars and they demonstrate the ability of the order to move in and between many spheres, understanding not only the religious but also the secular concerns of those over whom they exercised pastoral care.

CONCLUSION

By the end of the seventeenth century the Franciscan order in Ireland had undergone a dramatic transformation. In 1600 it had been a small, fragmented organization but by 1700 it was a well-established body with almost 600 members. Not all of that transformation was due to the friars themselves. External circumstances had helped them to implement their strategies for survival and growth. However the success of the order was in large measure due to their vision of themselves as distinctively Irish and distinctively Franciscan. The main feature of this vision was the close link that the Franciscans fostered with their lay supporters. This was not always an easy strategy since the Franciscans spanned religious and ethnic worlds and lived off the sometimes limited surplus generated by their supporters.[52] Many Franciscans were trained in the ways of Tridentine

---

52 See, for instance, the dispute between a friar and Dáibhí Ó Bruadair over some cloth in J. Mac Erlean (ed.), *Duanaire Dháibhidh Uí Bhruadair* (1910–17), ii, pp 206–15.

Europe, which sometimes had only a tangential link with the traditional religion of parts of Ireland. As one Franciscan in the 1690s at Shrule, Co. Mayo, put it to a visitor from Spanish Flanders, who complained of the lack of knowledge of the catechism among the native Irish, although they 'knew not as much as they do in other countries they know enough to be saved'.[53] The genius of the Franciscan order in seventeenth-century Ireland was not its enforcement of a programme of Tridentine reform. Rather, it was its ability to recognize the changing needs of successive generations of seventeenth-century Irish people and to maintain support from the ethnically diverse groups that the order served in that changing world. In that the Franciscans were more than equal to their task.

---

[53] Bodleian Library Oxford, Rawlinson MS C439, f. 6.

The silent century, 1698–1829

JOSEPH MAC MAHON OFM

In studies of Irish Franciscan history the voices of the seventeenth-century friars are distinct and familiar while those of the eighteenth century are largely silent and receive less attention, perhaps because their achievements were more modest and the documentary remains are fewer. The present chapter aims to provide an outline of the history of the Irish Franciscans during that century and beyond up to Catholic Emancipation in 1829. Part I is a short chronological survey of the period under consideration and Part II considers the period in a thematic way by looking at the main features of the life and ministry of the friars.

PART I: OVERVIEW

The Irish province, 1697–1751

Faced with the choice of either exile or persecution at home, the Irish Franciscan authorities met in February 1698 and advised the friars to comply with the Banishment Act by leaving the country before 1 May 1698.[1] Each house was to draw up an inventory of its goods which were to be entrusted to benefactors for safekeeping.[2] A list of Irish Franciscans compiled in 1700[3], showed that there were 567 professed members and 16 novices, but probably about 100 of these were resident in the four continental colleges of Louvain, Prague, St Isidore's, and Capranica, leaving roughly 460 friars attached to the 62 Irish houses listed in the bill of appointments of the provincial chapter of 1697.[4] How many of these left the country by the deadline is difficult say and estimates vary, but it was certainly in excess of the 214 Irish friars in France who received charitable grants from the Holy See in 1699.[5] In sum, however, there were enough of them active on the Continent to alarm the minister general.[6]

The sudden influx of so many friars put a severe strain on the continental colleges and the friars at Louvain found it almost impossible to support their Irish guests.[7] Resources in Prague were clearly over-stretched, with friars living three to

---

1 Giblin, *Liber Lovaniensis*, pp 225–6. (Henceforth the term 'friars' will be used to designate 'Franciscans'.)
2 Giblin, 'Meelick friary, 1644–1731' (1973), pp 69–73; B. Egan (ed.), 'Inventory of articles belonging to the friary of Donegal, 1698' (1952); B. Jennings, 'The chalices and books of Kilconnell Abbey' (1944).
3 Giblin, 'Personnel of the Franciscan province of Ireland, 1700' (1965).   4 Giblin, *Liber Lovaniensis*, pp 200–3.   5 Moran, *Spicilegium Ossoriense*, ii, p. 347.   6 Jennings, *Louvain papers*, pp 321–2.   7 C. Giblin (ed.), 'Catalogue of material of Irish interest in the collection Nunziatura di Fiandra, Vatican archives'

a room and reduced to iron rations by February 1700.[8] Such cramped living conditions doubtlessly induced the friars to extend the college in 1704[9] and to acquire a building at Boulay in Lorraine in 1699. Many were forced to seek refuge elsewhere. In May 1700, Bonaventure Conolan sailed from France to Cadiz looking for a home and found six Irish friars already in residence in the friary there while two more arrived the following week obliging him to move to the friary at Huelva.[10] Tired of travelling he sought permission to remain there and serve as a chaplain to catholic immigrants.[11] Some of the exiles would eventually return home but others would settle down and end their days on the Continent. The number of friars who remained in Ireland after the deadline is unknown but between one hundred and two hundred seem to have continued to live there. A few enlisted under the Registration Act of 1703 and disguised themselves as secular priests but most did not and risked capture and exile. Indeed as early as February 1700, friars were already beginning to return to Ireland.[12]

It is difficult to find precise details of the friars' whereabouts during these early years and even as late as 1731 the authorities had to admit that 'as soon as they perceive themselves to be discovered, [they] remove to some distant place where it is hardly possible to find them out.'[13] It was not until after 1745 that the friars began to emerge more fully from the shadowy world in which they had been living. Not surprisingly, life in the province was seriously disrupted. The regular chapter of 1700 was held at Louvain[14] and that of 1714 was cancelled, both for safety reasons.[15] Even though the friars remained constantly vigilant, some were captured by the authorities, among them Anthony Molloy and Bonaventure Murphy who were found guilty in 1699 of continuing to remain in the country and were ordered to be transported.[16] Anthony French, writing from Galway in 1710, described 'the storm of persecution' then raging which had obliged him to go into hiding.[17] James Kilkenny was fortunate in being rescued 'in a riotous manner' by a group of supporters in November 1715 as he was being taken to Roscommon gaol and in spite of substantial rewards offered for his recapture he contrived to remain free.[18] Following a tip-off the friary in Dublin was raided on a Sunday morning in June 1718 and two of the friars were arrested, tried and found guilty.[19] A sketchy picture emerges from state documents of the presence

(1961), pp 68–9 (henceforth cited as 'Nunziatura'). **8** FLK *Prague Transcripts*, x (1662–1702), 15 February 1700. **9** Jennings, 'Irish Franciscans in Prague', p. 217. A further wing was added in 1739. **10** FLK MS E2.39. **11** FLK MS E2.40. **12** Giblin, 'Nunziatura' (1970), pp 74–5. **13** 'Report on the state of popery, Ireland, 1731' (1914), p. 125; (1915), p. 138 (henceforth cited as 'State of popery'); see Burke, *Irish priests in the penal times*, pp 407–8 for reports of friars in Clare living in locations scattered about the county in 1715. **14** FLK MS C118. **15** Giblin, *Liber Lovaniensis*, pp 330–1. **16** Burke, *Irish priests in penal times*, pp 310–11. **17** Giblin, 'Nunziatura' (1962), p. 21. **18** Ibid., p. 451; see also pp 400, 408 for other similar cases. **19** Burke, *Irish priests in penal times*, pp 303–4; Anthony Bryan OFM, registered as a priest of Rathfarnham,

and movement of the regulars and gives the impression of a precarious and scattered existence. When Sir Thomas Molyneux visited Kilconnell in 1709 he was told that all that remained of the community there were two elderly friars 'blind with age' who were living in a little cabin less than half a mile from the friary. They were unable to beg and employed an individual to collect alms for them.[20] Thady O'Rourke, bishop of Killala (1707–36), who had himself been secretly ordained bishop in Newgate gaol by the incarcerated Bishop Donnelly of Dromore,[21] was seen at different times in 1712 travelling about the counties of Mayo and Sligo, using the pseudonyms of Fielding and Fitzgerald and frequenting 'the Convent of Milic as much as possible where he generally ordains priests.'[22] The Dublin authorities were informed that the community of Muckross was scattered in 1714, with the guardian, an old man, living five miles outside Killarney.[23] Others continued to move about and the same source shows David Fitzgerald of Askeaton having crossed the Shannon to Co. Clare with the river in fact proving to be a useful escape route for friars fleeing from the authorities in both directions. Perhaps the most striking feature about the friars that emerges during these years is their mobility. In the *Report on the state of popery* of 1731, there are constant references to 'strolling', 'vagrant', 'vagabond' friars who go about among the poor, begging and celebrating mass, preaching, and confirming them in 'their old Idolatry and Superstition' and their aversion to Protestantism,[24] and indeed causing 'much mischief'.[25]

Following the years of upheaval, a measure of cautious normality began to prevail though there were occasional alarms as in 1719 when David Kery, guardian of Boulay, was advised to delay his trip to Ireland because the friars were 'very uneasy upon the Spanish and Scoth's account, so far that they cannot meet or travaille.'[26] Nonetheless, they had begun to return to their traditional locations, especially in Connacht, and by 1715 they were back in Kilconnell, Meelick and Kinaleghin.[27] Even as early as 1708 they were settled in Galway, as an inscribed chalice from that year indicates.[28] In 1724 they repaired their chapel there and celebrated mass publicly, an act of defiance which led to four of them being arrested and charged with high treason though, embarrassingly for the authorities, they were acquitted. Already at this early stage a clear pattern was beginning to emerge of some friars dwelling together in community and others living in isolation.[29]

was arrested at the same time. See K. MacGrath, 'John Garzia. A noted priest-catcher and his activities' (1949) for a full account of the arrests and trials.   **20** F.J. Bigger, *The Franciscan friary of Kilconnell* (1900–1). **21** J.A. MacNamee, *History of the diocese of Ardagh* (1954), p. 228. **22** Burke, *Irish priests in penal times*, pp 214, 227, 433–5. **23** Ibid., pp 213–14. **24** 'State of popery' (1913), p. 143. **25** Ibid., p. 127. **26** Jennings, 'The Irish Franciscans at Boulay', p. 149. **27** J. Hardiman, *The history of the town and county of the town of Galway* (1820), p. 255, n. 3. **28** B. Jennings, 'The abbey of St Francis, Galway' (1946). **29** 'State of popery' (1915), p. 173. See H. Fenning, 'Some problems of the Irish mission' (1965), p. 86 for

On the one hand, the Meelick chronicle records an almost normal pattern of life and activity for the community well before 1731 with the friars in residence, rebuilding the church with the support of generous benefactors and serving the people pastorally.[30] The friars of Trim found refuge north of the town where they continued their pastoral work and *c*.1720 built a residence at Courtown, Co. Meath, where they remained until *c*.1826.[31] On the other hand, the names of eight friars were laid before the Grand Jury sitting at Carrick-on-Shannon in July 1714 accused of exercising their 'fryars function in and about the County Leitrim'.[32] Each assisted in a parish in the county and none lived in community.

Decline, 1751–90

The regulars were dealt a major blow in 1751 when Propaganda Fide in Rome among other decrees on the Irish church, forbade religious superiors to receive novices in Ireland although they could continue to receive them in the continental colleges.[33] One can measure the feelings of the friars from a letter they sent from the chapter of 1753 to the minister general who was a Spaniard.[34] Appealing to his national pride by referring to the tradition that the first Franciscans in Ireland had come from Spain and describing themselves as 'quasi-orphans', they sought his help against the 'false brothers', those bishops and their allies who had requested the decree. In truth, however, before 1751 numbers had already begun to decline and traditional locations were being abandoned but the decree certainly accelerated the process. Perhaps symbolic of the decline was the remark made by the mayor of Youghal in 1744 that a friar 'at times sculkd about the town'; it was as if he were a ghost haunting a once familiar but now abandoned place.[35] The decree had an immediate impact. The friars of St Isidore's complained in 1754 that the normal rhythm of community life and of studies was difficult to maintain.[36] Louvain fared better but within a few years it was clear to the friars that the closure of the home novitiates, the gradual loss of privileges and subjection to the bishops made their future quite uncertain.[37]

The decree not only depressed the numbers but also the friars themselves. In June 1763, the provincial, Christopher French, in declining Propaganda Fide's appeal for missionaries to be sent to Scotland, wrote of the province 'hastening towards its final destruction'.[38] Two years later, French's successor, James

---

James MacDonnell's description of the situation in 1766.   **30** Fennessy, 'Meelick obituary and chronicle'. **31** Cogan, *The ecclesiastical history of the diocese of Meath*, i, p. 121.   **32** Burke, *Irish priests in penal times*, p. 443.   **33** See H. Fenning, *Undoing of the friars of Ireland* (1972), pp 154–236 for an extended treatment of events leading up to this.   **34** FLK MS C118.   **35** Burke, *Irish priests in penal times*, p. 381.   **36** St Isidore's College, *Liber Discretorialis Coll. S. Isidori 1741–1878*.   **37** Burke, *Irish priests in penal times*, p. 319. Curiously the bishop of Ferns was under the impression that the number of friars had increased considerably, whereas the reverse was the case.   **38** H. Fenning, 'Documents of Irish interest in the *Fondo Missioni*' (1995), p. 17.

MacDonnell, outlined the situation facing the friars in similarly sombre terms.[39] Dublin had nine friars but three were sick, five were over sixty years old and three others served in parishes, while Ennis did not have a fixed residence and its eight friars were dispersed throughout the locality. Most places had but two or three friars and Galway boasted the largest community with thirteen though ten of these were old. In all, forty-one locations are listed as either vacant or 'without residence, dispersed about the district'. It was a declining and aging province and MacDonnell complained bitterly in April 1766 that 'the decrees against regulars will soon extinguish what was long attempted, and yet the heaviest stroke is from Propaganda which will effectually annihilate what they ought to promote.' Besides this, he added, the bishops were coveting, even compelling the best regulars to engage in parish ministry thereby further weakening them.

Propaganda Fide relented in 1773 and allowed the Franciscans to receive up to forty novices every three years.[40] Nine locations were approved as novitiates but only three of them appear to have functioned, which shows how debilitated the province had become in reality and that there were too few new men to make up for the losses of the previous decades.[41] Three years later they numbered only 185, a drop of 215 in twenty-five years, and during Anthony French's term of office, 1772–6, 66 friars alone had died.[42] The decline would continue over the following decades and they would disappear from many of their traditional strongholds. For example, Elphin is emblematic of the collapse. In 1766 nine friars were attached to the community, yet by 1787 there remained only one old bed-ridden man, although it would not be until 1835 that Franciscans would disappear entirely from the area.[43]

The continental colleges

The province was struck further severe blows by political events on the Continent. The religious reforms of Emperor Joseph II affected the friars in Louvain and resulted in the community enduring some years of acrimonious unrest.[44] While Louvain was spared for the sake of the mission, the emperor saw no reason why Prague should continue and it was confiscated in 1786.[45] The emperor's meddling was but a prelude to the massive upheaval caused by the French Revolution. Boulay was suppressed in 1790 although it was not until

---

39 Fenning, 'Some problems of the Irish mission', pp 84–7.   **40** Fenning, *Undoing of the friars of Ireland*, pp 314–15 for the terms of the decree. See FLK MS C105 for permission granted by Propaganda to open a novitiate in Wexford in July 1773.   **41** See ibid., pp 322–3.   **42** Ibid., p. 339.   **43** C. Giblin, 'The Franciscans in Elphin' (1988).   **44** P. Conlan, 'Declaration of Emperor Joseph II on the Irish and English Franciscans and Dominicans' (1992–3), pp 121–5; see Fenning, *Undoing of the friars in Ireland*, pp 357–60 for a succinct account of this; A.A. Wijffels, 'Calendar of documents relating to St Anthony's College, Louvain, 1782–5' (1982); also FLK MS C14.   **45** Jennings, 'Irish Franciscans in Prague', pp 221–2.

September 1792 that the friars were dislodged and their goods confiscated.[46] Louvain was the next college to fall when it was taken over in January, 1793.[47] Three years later the friars were forced to leave and were given refuge at Tildonck by Baron Snoy et d'Oppuers whose family had been benefactors for many years.[48] James Cowan, the guardian, managed to buy back the college when it was put up for sale in 1797[49] and over the next two decades it was used for various purposes. It was a trying time for Cowan and he was finally forced to conclude that the survival of St Isidore's was all that could be retrieved.[50] As provincial he set about winding up the college's affairs and in July 1822 St Anthony's, Louvain was sold.[51]

St Isidore's, Rome and Capranica fared better than the northern colleges, but precariously. When foreigners were ordered to leave Rome in 1798, the guardian of St Isidore's, James MacCormick, and three other friars remained behind to protect the building and its archives.[52] The books were moved to Propaganda Fide and other libraries while the manuscripts were sent to Paris.[53] Finally, when papal control of Rome was restored in 1814, St Isidore's was returned to the friars. During the 1790s Capranica had functioned as a novitiate for St Isidore's but all that ceased in 1798 when the French army invaded the Papal States.[54] Richard Walsh, superior of the community, volunteered to remain as a caretaker but by 1808/9 his tolerance for the place had been exhausted and the friary was abandoned until it was restored to the friars in August 1815.[55]

What had befallen the continental colleges was symptomatic of what was taking place in the province. As early as 1730, Anthony French, the commissary visitor, had found the province 'in a languishing condition'[56] and by 1800 it had only about 120 friars.[57] It is little wonder then that the decline in numbers, the continuing withdrawal from traditional locations, the loss of the continental colleges and the internal indiscipline began to turn minds to the possible causes of its deteriorating condition. From a merely statistical point of view, the main reason for the closure of many houses was the decline in personnel for it was clearly impossible to keep more than sixty houses open and pastorally viable with a number that had fallen to about a quarter of what it was at the beginning of the century. And from an economic point of view, friaries in larger urban areas were more likely to survive than those in rural districts. Turning to the deeper causes, there is little doubt that the spirit of the age was a factor. Laurence Callanan

46 Jennings, 'Irish Franciscans in Boulay', p 151; see Mooney, *Irish Franciscans and France*, pp 73–81 for an account of the confused events of these years at Boulay.   47 See Jennings, *Louvain papers*, pp 497–500 for an account of the confiscation.   48 FLK MS E4.8.   49 Jennings, *Louvain papers*, pp 512–14.   50 Ibid., p. 636.   51 Ibid., pp 641–8.   52 FLK MS E11.28.   53 St Isidore's College, 'Libro maestro dell intrate ed uscite del convento de S. Isidoro delli religiosi Franciscani Irlandesi a Roma, 1787–1860'.   54 See P. Conlan, *St Isidore's College Rome*, (1982), pp 113–15 for an account of this period in Capranica.   55 Jennings, *Louvain papers*, p. 593.   56 Giblin, 'Meelick friary', p. 85.   57 K. MacGrath, 'Sidelights on

blamed 'the growing corruption of morals … modern and impious maxims, and the utter overthrow of evangelical principles' for the malaise.[58] The sustained anti-regular campaign that had been a feature of Enlightenment thinking on the Continent was pervasive in Ireland and was quite widespread, as Fr Charles O'Connor, parish priest of Castlerea and a friend to the friars, complained, 'Thus do the maxims of modern France prevail even among the clergy of Ireland …'[59]

But others believed that the friars themselves were the cause of the decline. Even though accusations of laxity are far more likely to be recorded than faithful observance, there are enough complaints of lack of discipline in visitators' reports on the colleges throughout the century to raise serious questions and it undoubtedly contributed to the decline of the province. It manifested itself in various guises. Writing in September 1802, the provincial, Anthony Coen, deplored what he called 'the degenerate lifestyle – scenes that would disgrace a public bagnio or brothel' that he had found at Meelick.[60] In James Cowan's view, the province was 'tumbling into annihilation' because some friars were putting their own interests and those of their family before the good of the province in choosing where they would minister and to whom they would bequeath their goods and money.[61] Likewise, community life was being undermined by the large number of friars living outside the provincial structures. When James Doyle OSA, became bishop of Kildare and Leighlin in 1819, there were at least four friars scattered about his diocese, one of whom, John Donovan, was a source of annoyance to the local parish priest because of his independent ways. The bishop believed that such behaviour was giving regulars a bad name and was anxious to prevent it because strolling friars had neither religious discipline nor a useful ministry.[62] In his official report written in June 1828, the visitator, Daniel Healy, summed up some of the difficulties he had encountered: vagrant friars creating havoc in the friaries in which they had settled; ambitious men seeking power and position; others acting independently in the name of religion and the Connacht friars refusing to agree to his plan to abandon the traditional rotational system of electing provincials.[63] To make matters worse, the outgoing provincial, Joseph Murphy, was unanimously deemed to be unworthy of exercising an active voice in the province after being charged with embezzlement by the civil authorities. 'Now or never is the time to re-establish our almost extinct Order', was the verdict of William O'Meara in 1815.[64] By contrast, however, there were also signs

---

the Irish Franciscans, 1798–1850' (1952), p. 81.   **58** Jennings, *Louvain papers*, p. 527.   **59** Fenning, *Undoing of the friars in Ireland*, p. 351.   **60** FLK MS E4.56.   **61** Jennings, *Louvain papers*, p. 634, writing in January 1817.   **62** T. McGrath, *Religious renewal and reform in the pastoral ministry of bishop James Doyle* (1999), pp 101–2.   **63** FLK MS E16.33. A system of rotating the office of provincial, with each *plaga* or region holding it for three years, was in operation from about 1621 to the 1830s.   **64** FLK MS E18.27.

of new life. Candidates were still presenting themselves for entry to the order, St Isidore's had reopened its doors[65] and there was new building under way at home.

Internal organization

Organizationally the Irish province belonged to the Recollect branch of the Stricter Observance reform of the order. The Recollects were friars who sought to live the rule in the way they believed Francis and his followers did before papal dispensations allowed for a more modified interpretation of it.[66] In 1526 the Recollect movement was divided into three 'nations' or areas – Spain, France and Germany – with the last one eventually embracing the provinces of Germany, Belgium, England, Scotland and, by 1630, Ireland. The German–Belgian Nation, as it was called, was governed on behalf of the minister general by a commissary general though his governance of the Irish province was conditioned by its remoteness, the special privileges it enjoyed and because it had its own representatives who managed business on its behalf in Rome and at the courts of catholic monarchs.[67] The Irish could have recourse to the minister general and were not reluctant to do so. Besides the commissary, the visitators appointed to carry out the triennial visitation of the province were invariably Irish friars and not outsiders as would normally be the case. Each of the continental colleges had its own particular statutes.[68]

The province itself was divided into four *plagae* or regions, more-or-less corresponding to the four civil provinces, and generally a friar lived and worked within his own *plaga*. Hence a strong provincialism was a characteristic feature among the friars and one that undermined the unity of the body as a whole and prevented it from being able to adapt to changing circumstances. Provincial rivalries flared up from time to time and could be quite bitter, as evidenced by the dispute that broke out in 1746 when the provincial definitory appointed a Munster friar as guardian of Dublin. It raged for ten years, generating a large volume of correspondence that involved the friars and church authorities in

65 See FLK MS E4; by February 1821 there were eighteen students at St Isidore's. **66** See M. Carmody, *The Leonine union* (1994), pp 5–28; P. Yates, *Recollect Franciscan poverty* (2005), pp 25–81 for a short history of the Recollects. **67** See Millett, *Irish Franciscans*, pp 3–7 on provincial chapters and appointments; pp 55–7 on the seven privileges granted to the Irish province relating to exemptions from the general statutes; pp 205–9 on the role of the commissary general in relation to the Irish province; pp 60–5 on the role of the procurators in the seventeenth century. Also FLK MS C30, 'Natio Germano-Belgica' for the minutes of the meetings of the provincials of the nation; the guardian of St Anthony's, Louvain or his nominee represented the Irish provincial at these meetings. **68** See FLK MS C26 for the statutes of Prague; St Isidore's College, 'Visitation book', pp 14–26 for the statutes of St Isidore's.

Ireland, Brussels and Rome.[69] Although it raised fundamental issues about the rights of the provincial vis-à-vis the privileges of each region it changed nothing. The *plaga* system also extended to the continental colleges in that each region had its own lecturer in residence.

At times the friars could be contentious and some were not above anonymously making false claims about the conduct of a provincial chapter, as happened in 1706[70], while others were overly concerned about their personal status in an age when such things mattered.[71] A more serious dispute arose in 1710 with the minister general, who abolished the customary right of ex-provincials from voting at meetings of the provincial definitory. In response, the province submitted a lengthy document to the papal authorities defending the tradition[72] and even had recourse to the Queen of Spain requesting her help against the general.[73] They won their case and continued the ancient practice.

Formation

Prior to 1751 it was usual for candidates to complete the novitiate year in their local friaries, a system that raises questions about the standards of entry, the level of education and the quality of formation. From the Meelick chronicle it appears that candidates could range in age from 16 to the early 30s though they were more likely to be nearer the canonical age of 25 required for ordination to the priesthood.[74] On completing the year the novices took final vows and most were ordained to the priesthood, a measure that was determined by the financial impoverishment of the colleges, before continuing their studies on the Continent. Such was the large number of candidates entering in the early years that the colleges were unable to accommodate them all and some were advised to join other provinces.[75] Occasionally the commissary general would send Irish friars to different Spanish provinces for studies.[76]

The continental colleges observed all the austere demands of regular life, as well as a full programme of studies. [77] However, it is not surprising that the indiscriminate acceptance of candidates should lead to visitation reports revealing critical shortcomings at times. Charges of indiscipline were levelled against the friars at St Isidore's and there are recurring admonitions made to correct the deficiencies.[78] Some of these are listed in an undated memo written by Francis O'Higgins as the decline of discipline and doctrine, lectors eating and drinking outside the house, breach of the cloister, hurried recitation of the office and

69 See FLK MS E58.   **70** Giblin, *Liber Lovaniensis*, pp 306–10.   **71** FLK MS E64, 115–32; see MS C42 for a resolution to a similar dispute in 1716.   **72** UCD-OFM MS D1, pp 919–30.   **73** FLK MS C118. **74** See Fennessy, 'Meelick obituary and chronicle', passim.   **75** Giblin, 'Meelick friary', pp 71–2. **76** Giblin, 'Nunziatura' (1958), p. 66.   **77** See for instance FLK MS C26 'Ex libro memorabilium, Statuta domestica' (Prague), pp 9–48.   **78** See St Isidore's College, 'Visitation Book' for these.

absence from prayer.[79] Even more serious charges of falling standards were levelled against the friars in Prague by the visitor in 1744.[80]

The normal course of studies consisted of two years of philosophy and three years of theology though this was extended later. The writings of John Duns Scotus were the subject matter for teaching and study in all the colleges. A list of theses defended by Irish Franciscans in the University of Louvain from 1639 to 1769 confirms this pattern though a rare one follows St Bonaventure and a few are commentaries on biblical texts.[81] The theses also reveal that friars in the eighteenth century were unequivocally opposed to Jansenism.[82] A number of text-books and class notes survive, including a two-volume work by Anthony Murphy, composed at Prague in 1753. Its very title, *Theologica dogmatica adversus atheos, libertinos, judaeos, caeterosque infideles, hetherodoxos tam veteres, quam recentiores,* proclaims its defensive stance while its content reveals its strongly orthodox teaching. Lecturers were exhorted to provide solid theological material based on scripture, patristic writings and the church councils and to avoid unnecessary speculation.[83] They were free to use their own method of teaching but they were obliged to uphold the teaching of Scotus. At least one former student, Bishop James O'Donel of Newfoundland, was sceptical of the value of the courses he followed:

> Tis true I spent 7 years of my precious time dealing by wholesail [sic] and retail, in categories, precisions, quiddities and entities, universal *a parte rei, & mentis* and such other useful stuff; at which I got such a surfeit as never to wish any friend of mine to employ any great part of his time on the refinement of trumpery of the kind; however it is absolutely necessary that he should pay strict attention to the rules of just reasoning.[84]

Lifestyle of the friars

The lifestyle of the Irish Franciscans differed quite significantly from that of their continental *confrères* of the Recollect movement. A papal indult of July 1701 exempted them from observing particular requirements of the rule: fasting, wearing the religious habit, the prohibition on receiving money and riding on horseback.[85] Given the unsettled nature of their lives it would have been impossible for them to observe the statutes fully. By this time they were accustomed to possess money and bequeath their goods to the friary or family

79 FLK MS E26.21 (probably written in 1760).   **80** Fenning, *Undoing of the friars in Ireland*, pp 73–4 for a brief account of the visitations of 1737 and 1744.   **81** E. Reusens, *Documents relatifs a l'histoire de l'université de Louvain* (1889–92), iii, pp 424–77.   **82** See also FLK MS E66.1–25.   **83** FLK MS C26 'Statuta domestica' (Prague), p. 12.   **84** C.J. Byrne (ed.), *Gentlemen-bishops and faction fighters* (1984), pp 171–2.   **85** FLK MS E54.1; these concessions were renewed in June 1774; see also FLK MSS E54.2, p. 26.

members, practices that were strictly disallowed by the rule. However, the making of wills by individual friars became necessary because of legal constraints on regulars. In 1773, the provincial, Anthony French, got the friars to agree to bequeath one half of their possessions to their own community with the other half being applied to masses for their repose[86] but this arrangement was not universally respected and some friars continued to leave money and livestock to their families.[87] Communities rarely purchased books for the friary library and depended instead on acquiring the personal libraries of friars on their deaths.[88]

Each house was entitled to quest or beg for alms in a defined area. This was an important source of income as well as being a means of associating with people and even of recruiting to the order.[89] The Galway friars quested in the countryside for potatoes, grain, wool and meat and this was supplemented by stipends they received from chaplaincies, funerals, masses for the dead, candle money and annual collections.[90] Questing could lead to abuses. In 1729 James Byrne turned up in Roscrea and announced that he would henceforth carry out the quest of the area to the exclusion of the Meelick friars who had inherited the right since the departure of their Roscrea *confrères*.[91] Questing rights were often a cause of contention between seculars and regulars and it was also the source of the few disagreements that occurred between the regulars themselves.[92] The generosity and protection of prosperous patrons could mean the difference between comfort and misery. The Kinaleghin friars were given free-rental accommodation and the use of eight acres of land by a local landowner, and were sufficiently well-off to be able to build a large, well-slated chapel.[93]

The surviving account books show that while the friars were not in want they still had to be prudent. The end of year accounts of Wexford for 1750 show that they were just about managing to keep out of debt though they still had to pay off the cost of the journey of the previous guardian to the chapter and the grinding of malt and the brewing of hops.[94] The Cork accounts reveal that church collections from 1764 to 1779 averaged about £60 per annum and this was supplemented by questing in the city and county.[95] Other sources of revenue were occasional alms and rent receipts, but the total income was not enough to meet their needs and at times they were obliged to borrow money.[96] They lived simply but took a liberty on the feast of St Francis in 1764 in buying 'an apple pie for dinner'.[97] In keeping with their rule, they looked after their sick well. Having the

86 P. Ó Súilleabháin, 'Documents relating to Wexford friary and parish' (1965), pp 123–4.   **87** FLK MS E3.38.   **88** See Ó Súilleabháin, 'Documents relating to Wexford friary and parish', p. 128.   **89** FLK MS E42.33.   **90** Hardiman, *History of Galway*, p. 268.   **91** Giblin 'Meelick friary', p. 83; also I. Murphy, *The diocese of Killaloe in the eighteenth century* (1991), pp 98–9.   **92** H. Fenning, *The Irish Dominican province, 1698–1797* (1990), pp 155–8, 231, fn 84, 475–7.   **93** Burke, *Irish priests in penal times*, p. 253.   **94** FLK MS C105.   **95** W. O'Connell, 'Cork Franciscan Records, 1764–1831' (1942), pp 6–7.   **96** Ibid., p. 8.   **97** Ibid., p. 16.

provincial residing in the house could be a costly affair since the community had to cover his postal and travel expenses, including trips to the general chapter.[98] Houses in the larger urban areas were sufficiently well supported by generous benefactors to allow them to carry out new building or extensive refurbishment. The Dublin community was able to refurbish its chapel in 1749 and purchase a site at Merchants' Quay seven years later to serve as the new friary.[99]

Friars responsible for running parishes lived a less structured form of community life or little or none at all if they were scattered. Those at Multyfarnham, Meelick and Courtown managed to live in community while ministering in a parish but it was becoming the more usual practice for 'parish' friars to live separately, as in the case of those at Askeaton who ministered in neighbouring parishes in the 1750s and 1760s.[1] Similarly in the diocese of Raphoe, the Franciscans had no fixed or formed houses from the early 1780s until they faded away in the early years of the nineteenth century.[2] The degree of community living of these men varied from occasional gatherings to little contact with each other. Likewise their lifestyle also varied: some lived simply and were noted for their holiness while others were worldly in dress and manners. Tomás Ó Gliasáin had the latter in mind when he penned his critical comments on friars who ceased to imitate their founder and desired to be fashionable instead.[3]

If the life and activity of eighteenth-century Franciscans is obscure, then that of the lay friars is virtually lost from view entirely. There is no Brother Mícheál Ó Cléirigh among them! The 1700 list of personnel reveals that there were fifty eight lay friars or ten per cent of the entire group. Of these perhaps twenty-five were Irish, judging by their surnames, and the rest foreigners.[4] The latter were concentrated in the continental colleges since it was the practice there to recruit lay friars locally as it made sense for locals to carry out the quest. Lay friars also performed the domestic chores of the community but they did not have the right to vote in elections and be appointed to positions of authority at provincial and local levels.

Spirituality and devotional practices
Inevitably the friars of the eighteenth century were affected by the less religiously intense and more secular spirit of the age, especially following the collapse of the structures which had sheltered them from such influences. Even on the Continent where these structures remained intact the spirit among the clergy and

98 Ibid., p. 5. **99** N. Donnelly, *Roman Catholics. State and condition of Roman Catholic chapels in Dublin* (1904), p. 36; P. Fagan, *An Irish bishop in penal times* (1993), p. 39. **1** J. Begley, *The diocese of Limerick* (1938), pp 601, 625, 638. **2** C. Giblin (ed.), *The diocese of Raphoe* (1980), pp 38, 193; C. Mooney, 'The friars and friary of Donegal' (1952), p. 24. **3** Mhág Craith, *Dán na mBráthar Mionúr*, i, p. 348. **4** Giblin,

religious in general could be described as more easygoing.[5] The urbane Sylvester Lloyd was at ease with the age and others, such as Nioclás Ó Dómhnaill, display something of the same spirit on a lesser scale. This does not imply that they were less devotional than their predecessors but they were less intense.

The evidence clearly suggests that the friars practised and promoted a spiritual and devotional life that was continuous with that of their late medieval *confrères*.[6] It was centred on Jesus Christ, with particular emphasis on his passion, and devotion to the Virgin Mary, both of which are presented in an affective and embodied manner. A moving example of this is the sermonized version of the dialogue between Jesus and Mary on the eve of the passion, based on *Meditationes Vitae Christi*, a thirteenth-century Franciscan work.[7] Jesus prepares his mother by revealing to her the necessity of his passion and she responds with a series of affectionate expressions and, encouraged by him, accepts the Father's will. The short sermon is simple and is intended to move the hearers to sympathize with mother and son, to imitate their virtues and join their own suffering with theirs.[8] Since the cross was a central theme it is not surprising to find Francis Fleming in his commentary on the Third Order rule written in 1759 encouraging members to become 'Disciples of the Cross'.[9] Likewise the way of the cross (*via crucis*), which only Franciscans were permitted to erect, was actively promoted by them and in 1746–7 a set was installed in the chapel at Wexford.[10] The *via crucis* proved to be a popular devotion if publication of aids to its practice is a measure of this. One such was published by Christopher Fleming, the renowned preacher.[11]

The portiuncula indulgence[12] was another important Franciscan devotion which appealed to the popular mind and even lingered in the memory long after the departure of the friars. The indulgence was granted annually on 2 August, the feast of St Mary of the Angels. In the course of his tour of Kerry in 1788, the Revd David Beaufort was informed by the caretaker of Muckross friary that on the feast 'Mass is celebrated here on a temporary altar with great pomp … when 4 or

'Personnel of the Franciscan province of Ireland, 1700', pp 47–57.   **5** See O. Chadwick, *The popes and European revolution* (1981) for a description of the religious atmosphere during the period.   **6** See C. Ó Clabaigh, 'The cult of St Francis' (2006), pp 142–62.   **7** See C. Ó Maonigh (eag.), *Smaointe beatha Chríost* (1944), caibidil 53.   **8** C. Ó Maonaigh (eag.), 'Agalladh Iosa agus Mhuire aige triall chum na páise' (1965). The authorship of this collection of sermons is unknown but internal evidence strongly suggests that it comes from a Franciscan milieu; Fr James Pulleine, dean of Dromore diocese, is also credited with being the author of these sermons: see D. Ó Doibhlin, 'Penal days' (2000), p. 169.   **9** FLK MS B110. **10** Ó Súilleabháin, 'Documents relating to Wexford friary and parish', pp 121–2; there is also an early reference to the erection of the *via crucis* in Galway friary chapel: see C. Mooney, *Devotional writings of the Irish Franciscans* (1952), p. 27.   **11** Christopher Fleming, *Meditations and prayers adapted to the stations of the holy way of the cross* (1795); see H. Fenning, 'Dublin imprints of Catholic interest 1790–1795' (2004–5), p. 135; this was the 3rd edition.   **12** This plenary indulgence was originally granted by Pope Honorius III at the request of St Francis to those who visit the Portiuncula chapel in Assisi on 2 August; it was later

5 other friars attend and all the country come here to confess and do penance.'[13] Lough Derg also had a 'portiuncula' chapel dedicated to 'ye BVM of the Angels' from about 1763 when Anthony O'Doherty appears to have built a house on the island for the use of the friars.[14] Devotion to the Immaculate Conception, St Francis of Assisi and St Anthony of Padua and others was well established long before this.[15] In a poem lamenting the pursuit and exile of the clergy and friars written in 1713, the help of a number of saints, including St Francis and St Louis, is invoked.[16] A poetic version of *Si quaeris miracula,* a hymn to St Anthony, was composed in Irish by Tadhg Ó Neachtain in 1717[17] and the protection of the saint was invoked on Sylvester Lloyd on his return to Ireland from Paris in 1723 by the same poet.[18] Ó Neachtain also translated a life of the saint in 1718.[19]

The pastoral ministry of the friars

During the early years of the century the ministry of the friars was largely hidden and was conducted in both private houses and, where possible, in chapels.[20] Services were certainly being conducted in the friary chapel at Cook Street Dublin when it was raided in 1718. Apart from celebrating the liturgy, the friars catered for the spiritual and devotional needs of the faithful by preaching, teaching and catechizing.[21] Those living in urban areas, though not directly responsible for the administration of parishes, were frequently called upon to administer the sacraments and preach where a need arose.[22]

The Franciscans had a long tradition of ministering to pilgrims at Lough Derg since the early 1630s[23] and continued there until *c.*1782.[24] When Bishop Hugh McMahon of Clogher visited the island in 1714 he was impressed by their ministry and wrote that the Franciscans 'beyond all other ecclesiastics who came there, labour the most strenuously'.[25] Irish Franciscans had worked as missionaries in Scotland during the first half of the previous century and returned once again in the early years of the eighteenth century, remaining there until at least 1743.[26] In July 1706 the lay friar, John Fraser was granted permission to go on the Scottish mission as '*socius et catechista*'[27] to join five Irish friars who were already serving there.[28]

extended to all Franciscan churches.   **13** G. Lyne, 'Rev. Daniel A. Beaufort's Tour of Kerry' (1985), p. 188. **14** D. O'Connor, *Lough Derg and its pilgrimages* (1879), pp 152, 172.   **15** See Ó Clabaigh, 'The cult of St Francis'.   **16** Mhág Craith, *Dán na mBráthar Mionúr,* i, pp 282–3; ii, p. 258. Mhág Craith identifies St Louis with King Louis IX of France who was patron of the lay Franciscans but the saint in question could also be St Louis of Toulouse who enjoyed a cult in late medieval Ireland.   **17** Mhág Craith, *Dán na mBráthar mionúr,* i, pp 283–5.   **18** Ibid., pp 280–2.   **19** P. Ó Súilleabháin (eag.), *Beatha Naoimh Antoine ó Phadua,* (1957).   **20** Giblin, 'Nunziatura' (1961), pp 113–15.   **21** Burke, *Irish priests in penal times,* pp 12–13. **22** See for instance P.J. Corish (ed.), 'Bishop Caulfield's *Relatio status,* 1796' (1966), p. iii on the role of regulars in the diocese of Ferns.   **23** Mooney, 'The friars and friary of Donegal', pp 32–3.   **24** O'Connor, *Lough Derg and its pilgrimages,* p. 138.   **25** Ibid., pp 142–4.   **26** See C. Giblin (ed.), *Irish Franciscan mission to Scotland* (1964) for an account of the earlier mission.   **27** FLK MS E16.1.   **28** J.F.S. Gordon,

A large number of Franciscans also served as chaplains in foreign armed services, particularly in the French service.[29] Those employed by the French were attached to the Louvain community which benefited from their income. Other friars served as chaplains in less violent environments, either to wealthy families, both at home and abroad, or attached to embassies. Peter MacNamara worked out of the Sardinian embassy in London 'in the spiritual service of the Poor Roman Catholics' of the city,[30] and Patrick Connell was chaplain at Naples for several years to 'our country people' and to French and German speakers.[31] In the 1740s Thomas Mahon ministered to Irish-speaking catholics in London and was attached to the Lincoln's Inn Fields meeting houses which during the harvest season would be thronged on Sundays and where he would hear ten confessions in Irish for every one in English.[32] Indeed friars had to be proficient in the language, even in Dublin, according to Anthony Fitzsimons.[33] Other friars found positions for themselves in continental provinces and even dioceses and appear to have had little trouble settling.

There is ample evidence that the friars were engaged in educational activities.[34] Anthony Hedegane was reported to have established 'a popish seminary or ffriery' near Crusheen, Co. Clare in 1714[35] and there are other references to popish schools being run by friars though these may be no more than novitiates.[36] But it was during the second half of the century that catholic schools began to flourish and the friars established academies in Clonmel, Athlone, Carrick-on-Suir, Multyfarnham, Dalkey, Donegal, Limerick, Killarney, Wexford and Dromnaquoil in Co. Down. Fr Henry Young invited the friars at Adam & Eve's in 1820 to run 'a day, evening, and Sunday free school for the poor male children of Milltown and the neighbouring villages', the Sunday school being for the mill workers.[37] During the later part of the period the friars established and supported social aid organizations, mainly orphanages. The Patrician Orphan Society was founded by them in the late 1770s or early 1780s after a number of foundlings had been left at the door of Adam & Eve's.[38] Other similar societies were set up at Merchants' Quay during the severe fevers of 1817–19.[39] Societies of a more spiritual nature were also founded and directed by the friars. The arch-confraternity of the Cordbearers of St Francis, a kind of auxiliary branch of the Third Order that had

The Catholic church in Scotland (1869), pp 2–4, 629–36.   **29** For a list of friars who served with the French, see Mooney, *Irish Franciscans and France*, pp 110–12.   **30** P. Fagan (ed.), *Ireland in the Stuart papers* (1996), i, note on p. 326.   **31** Ibid., ii, pp 38, 94.   **32** C. Giblin, 'Ten documents relating to Irish diocesan affairs 1740–84' (1978), pp 73–4.   **33** P. Mac Cana, *Collège des Irlandais* (2001), p. 33.   **34** See C. Giblin, 'Franciscan teachers in Ireland' (1947) for an account of the teaching activity of the friars.   **35** Burke, *Irish priests in penal times*, pp 407–8.   **36** See 'State of Popery' (1914), iii, p. 144 on the Kilmacshalgan refuge of the Moyne friars where one of these schools was in operation.   **37** M.V. Ronan, *An apostle of catholic Dublin* (1944), p. 99.   **38** Ibid., p. 54.   **39** FLK MS C87 and Ronan, *An apostle of catholic Dublin*, p. 100.

been in existence in Ireland since the early seventeenth century, may have been revived *c*.1712.[40] The Third Order itself was revived in Dublin by Francis Fleming in 1759.[41] Limerick friary could boast of two confraternities founded in the first quarter of the nineteenth century.[42] The province produced some notable preachers during the period. The finest preacher of his age was reputed to be Christopher Fleming of whom it was said by a non-catholic in 1769 that in sixty years of listening to preachers in Britain and Ireland he had never heard Fleming's equal.[43] Such was his renown that many Protestants came to listen to him. A glimpse of the style and content of the friars' preaching in the rural areas can be gleaned from a collection of sermons put together during the first half of the eighteenth century, possibly by a friar.[44] The author wrote simple and clear explanations of sin, confession, fasting, almsgiving and prayer and special prominence is given to almsgiving and works of mercy. Unfortunately, few traces remain of the topics of the friars' preaching, apart from the above and a volume of Fleming's sermons.[45]

A fuller picture of the pastoral style of the friars is revealed in the Irish poetry of the period. The quality most commonly associated with them is their 'gentleness'. In Tadhg Ó Neachtain's opinion it was not Sylvester Lloyd's style to be stern but gentle like his founder, St Francis.[46] Similarly, an anonymous poet referred to Ambrose Cassidy, who served as a parish priest in Co. Leitrim, as '*úr-chroí*' and '*dea-chroí*'[47] and other friars spoken of in similar terms and with esteem and affection include Tadhg O'Rourke, Pól MacAogáin, Francis Walsh, James O'Sheil and Felim O'Hanlon.[48] Turlough O'Carolan described Felim O'Neill, noted for his hospitality, as '*sagart geanamhuil, barramhuil, cráfach, suairc*'.[49] The southern friar-poet, Nioclás Ó Domhnaill, was clearly held in respect and affection by his fellow Cois Máigh poets, not only for his poetic talents but also because of his generosity, graciousness and conviviality.[50]

Regulars and seculars

Tension between the regulars and the secular clergy occurred periodically over the century as it had during previous centuries. Its causes could vary from differing theological views to simple human factors.[51] An obvious cause was financial:

---

40 See I. Fennessy, 'Guardians and staff of St Anthony's College, Louvain' (2000), p. 232; see Fennessy, 'Meelick obituary and chronicle', pp 326–435 for accounts of people receiving the cord throughout the period. 41 FLK MS B110. 42 FLK MSS C177–9. 43 P. Ó Súilleabháin, 'A celebrated eighteenth-century preacher in Dublin' (1966), p. 106. 44 Ó Maonaigh, *Seanmónta Chúige Uladh*, pp x–xi. 45 Christopher Fleming, *Sermons on different subjects, both of faith and morals* (1822–3). 46 Mhág Craith, *Dán na mBráthar Mionúr*, i, pp 280–1. 47 Ibid., p. 323. 48 Ibid., passim. 49 Ibid., p. 306. 50 Ibid., p. 350. 51 For an excellent explanation of these causes see Fenning, *Undoing of the friars in Ireland*, pp 47–53; see Giblin, 'Nunziatura' (1961), pp 113–15 for an example of the tension in 1707.

regulars and seculars were competing for scarce financial resources. In Galway there was a long-running dispute between the two groups over funeral stipends which began in 1712 and flared up from time to time over the next century.[52] Questing rights were another source of potential conflict.[53]

The regulars regarded themselves as orthodox and loyal to the papacy and thought some of the seculars less sound on these matters.[54] Some took it upon themselves to inform Rome of theological deviancy among the seculars, as in the case of Bishop Dunne of Kildare whose pastoral letter of 1726 they judged unorthodox, if not worse,[55] and supplied the Congregation of Religious with lists of books they regarded as tainted with Jansenist and Gallican views.[56] The civil authorities, like their European counterparts, had long been hostile to the regulars and on occasion dangled the prospect of their suppression before the eyes of the secular clergy as the price for emancipation.[57] A small influential body of seculars were certainly political 'gallicans' in that they thought this was a price worth paying and were willing to concede the rights and privileges of the regulars as part of the bargain. Tensions between the parties often arose from lack of clarity regarding their respective roles. Understandably the bishops were anxious to implement the reforms of the Council of Trent and impose a tighter discipline which hampered the free-ranging style of the regulars who had been accustomed to move about and minister to the people in their own way. The bishops were aided by the policy of Pope Benedict XIV (1740–58), who in 1746 granted them control over regulars living outside their communities.[58] But the really serious problem for the friars was that they did not quite know what their purpose was in the changing circumstances. Matters were made worse by some bishops who were equally ignorant of their role vis-à-vis regulars and who overstepped the mark. Some indeed barely tolerated the regulars, as was revealed in an abstract of an examination by the authorities of Patrick Fitzsimons, later archbishop of Dublin, in 1751, 'Does not encourage them but cannot prevent them'.[59] Bishop Sweetman of Ferns made repeated efforts to control the friars by curbing their educational and devotional activities[60] and Archbishop Lincoln of Dublin and Bishop Plunkett of Meath also tried their hands at restraining the regulars.[61] Restrictions

52 M. Coen, *The wardenship of Galway* (1984), p. 24 and passim.   **53** See N. Donnelly, *Short history of Dublin parishes* (1915), xv, pp 58, 80.   **54** See Fenning, 'Some problems of the Irish mission', pp 64–7 for an explicit expression of this in a letter to the Cardinal Protector in 1735.   **55** Giblin, 'Nunziatura' (1971), pp 40–5.   **56** Fenning, 'Some problems of the Irish mission', p. 65, n. 12; see Fenning, 'Documents of Irish interest in the *Fondo Missioni*', p. 46 for the views of Bishop John T. Troy OP, then bishop of Ossory, on the unorthodox views of some of his episcopal colleagues in 1786.   **57** Cogan, *The ecclesiastical history of the diocese of Meath*, iii, p. 61.   **58** See Fenning, *Undoing of the friars in Ireland*, pp 123–35 on the views of Benedict and the Roman background to the conflict.   **59** Burke, *Irish priests in penal times*, p. 307.   **60** Giblin, 'Franciscan teachers in Ireland', p. 39; also Ó Súilleabháin, 'Documents relating to Wexford friary and parish', p. 115.   **61** See Fenning, *The Irish Dominican province*, pp 275–88 for an account of this

were placed on the establishment of sodalities, questing, faculties for hearing confessions and jurisdiction over the Poor Clares. The decree of 1750 prohibiting novitiates in Ireland was considered by regulars as a major effort to curb and even destroy them and this view was still common in 1815 when the Wexford friar Richard Hayes, provoked by what he called 'the universal system of episcopal coercion', claimed that the aim of the anti-regular bishops was 'to make us *die a natural death*'.[62]

However, it would be mistaken to think that the relationship between regulars and seculars was one of constant conflict. There are too many examples of correct and even amiable relations to conclude otherwise. Father John Wickham, parish priest in Co. Wexford, bequeathed his considerable book collection to the friars at Wexford in 1777;[63] several young men were directed towards a Franciscan vocation by secular clergy;[64] and good relationships existed between the regulars and the bishops of Connacht throughout the period. In 1822 William O'Meara, was recommended as coadjutor bishop of Limerick by the great majority of the local clergy.[65] And it was common practice in many places for the clergy to call upon the assistance of the friars in time of need.

Relations with other regulars were good, even cordial, especially as the threat against them grew. One friar who made a notable contribution to the development of other religious congregations was Laurence Callanan (1739–1818). He was a constant supporter of Nano Nagle and her companions in their work for the education of the poor and in the foundation of the Presentation Sisters.[66] Callanan drew up the constitutions of the new congregation and was instrumental in giving the institute its name.[67] He was also an influential figure in the establishment of the Ursuline Sisters in Ireland and, according to Nano Nagle's biographer, T.J. Walsh, 'Few names recur more frequently in the early pages of the Ursuline and Presentation annals'.[68]

Political allegiances

Given their past history, it comes as no surprise to learn that some friars were deeply involved in political affairs. As early as 1697 two members of the Louvain fraternity were arrested on charges of spying for the French against William of Orange but were later released.[69] Three Irish friars, Bonaventure de Burgo,

dispute; see Cogan, *The ecclesiastical history of the diocese of Meath*, ii, pp 190, 193 for Plunkett's part. **62** C. Giblin (ed.), 'Papers of Richard Joachim Hayes, O.F.M.' (1979–80), p. 110; Hayes's italics; see pp 82–6 for a biographical note on Hayes (henceforth cited as 'Hayes papers'). **63** P. Ó Súilleabháin, 'The library of a priest of the penal days' (1963–4). **64** FLK MS E3.53. Fr John Grogan recommended some young men from his parish near Multyfarnham as candidates for the Order in 1815. **65** Begley, *Diocese of Limerick*, pp 468–9. **66** T.J. Walsh, *Nano Nagle and the Presentation Sisters* (1959), p. 21. **67** Ibid., p. 102. **68** Ibid., p. 139. **69** Giblin, 'Nunziatura' (1970), pp 65–6; the Pope was at this time an ally of William.

Francis Mellaghlin and Paul Ward were among a group of envoys who sought to influence European leaders to bring pressure to bear unsuccessfully on the London authorities on behalf of Irish Catholics on the eve of the Peace of Utrecht in 1713.[70]

The friars unanimously supported the Stuart cause and some were actively engaged in its promotion, none more so than Sylvester Lloyd and Ambrose O'Callaghan who were held in high esteem by James III and his officials.[71] Lloyd was sent to Paris by the Irish regulars in 1723 to lobby the French court against the Irish Parliament's Popery Bill which sought to introduce additional repressive measures against Catholics. Whether or not he was responsible for the eventual quashing of the bill, Lloyd certainly claimed the credit for it.[72] O'Callaghan was delegated by the Irish bishops to lobby the emperor in Vienna when it was feared that the same bill would be reactivated in 1725 and three years later he held a watching brief for the Pretender at the Congress of Soissons.[73] O'Callaghan summed up the feelings of his *confrères* when he wrote of 'his passionate inclination for what concerns his [James's] service', 'for whom I'd sacrifice more than I can expect in this world'.[74] Both he and Lloyd were rewarded for their loyalty and efforts. The former was appointed bishop of Ferns in 1729[75] a year following Lloyd's appointment as bishop of Killaloe on the nomination of James who, writing to the latter, understood the move as to 'enable you to be useful to religion and my service ...' a clear indication that, in his mind, the Catholic and Stuart causes were virtually identical.[76] James went on to remind Lloyd that his promotion was 'a proof of my regard for your order, which I am sure will always continue to deserve well of me.' The Pretender's regard was shown by the fact that of the thirteen Franciscans who were appointed bishops to Irish dioceses during the century, all but two were nominated by him. While there was an element of self-promotion in the loyalty of such men, nonetheless they were genuinely loyal to the cause and were willing to suffer for it and did so in 1734 when they had to go into hiding[77] and again in 1744 when possibly the strain caused the death of O'Callaghan in August that year while Lloyd had to flee to France.[78] During this last outbreak of Jacobite insurgency other friars also suffered. Thirteen regulars, including four friars, were summoned to appear at the assizes at Drogheda in 1744 but instead went into hiding.[79] Bishop Patrick French and the entire community at Athlone also managed to escape arrest.[80] The only

70 C. Giblin, 'Vatican archives: Lettere di particolari' (1973), p. 118.   71 Fagan, *Stuart papers*, i, p. 209.
72 See Mhág Craith, *Dán na mBráthar Mionúr*, i, pp 280–2 for Tadhg Ó Neachtain's poem lauding Lloyd's achievements; also Fagan, *Sylvester Lloyd*, p. 63.   73 See Fagan, *Sylvester Lloyd*, pp 56–7.
74 Fagan, *Stuart papers*, i, p. 47; see also i, p. 91 for Lloyd's expressions of loyalty.   75 Ibid., i, p. 189.
76 Ibid., i, p. 126.   77 Ibid., i, p. 195.   78 Burke, *Irish priests in penal times*, p. 369.   79 J. Brady (ed.),
Catholics and catholicism in the eighteenth-century press (1965), pp 66–7.   80 Burke, *Irish priests in penal*

friar who was actively involved in the events of 1745 was John Cruise of St
Isidore's who crossed to England and incurred heavy debts for the cause which
James later paid off.[81] Loyalty to the Stuarts began to waver in the 1760s. Prior to
1760 the beneficiaries of the customary prayer for the royal family added to
provincial chapter bills were always the Stuarts but from then until 1781, when
King George III and his family were explicitly mentioned for the first time, there
is a deliberate ambiguity to cater for the changing allegiances of the friars.[82]
Certainly by 1774 the friars at Dublin, Galway, Cork, Wexford and Rosserrilly
had concluded that the time had arrived to recognize political reality and together
with other clergy and laity proceeded to swear the Oath of Allegiance in that year
and the later one of 1782.[83]

The outbreak of the French Revolution dealt a heavy blow to the Irish
Franciscans. The loss of Boulay and Louvain and the ill-treatment the friars
suffered at the hands of the revolutionaries over the following twenty-five years
were enough to dampen their partiality towards the French. James Connolly and
Daniel Kelly both died as a result of ill-treatment, the former in Rochefort in
1794[84] and the latter in 1811–12.[85] As a student at Louvain, Richard Power later
recounted how he was forced to flee along with others before the invading
French. He was taken prisoner several times but eventually managed to make his
way to Antwerp and from thence to England.[86]

Few friars were classified as 'democrats' or sympathizers of the United
Irishmen and the 1798 rising by the authorities. Francis Higgins, the Castle agent,
identified John Connolly, parish priest of Booterstown, as one and Fr John
Martin OSA, following his capture, confessed that he had been recruited into the
United Irishmen by James MacCartan of Drogheda and Patrick Duffy of
Monaghan, both Franciscans.[87] Ambrose Cassidy aided the French after their
landing at Killala and was imprisoned as a result.[88] But most friars seemed to have
followed the lead of the bishops in opposing revolution. And Peter Moran of
Adam & Eve's even assisted the authorities by supplying Higgins with 'most
interesting intelligence', in return for which Moran hoped the authorities might
recommend him to the archbishop for 'a scanty living near Loughlinstown.'[89] On
the outbreak of the rebellion the Dublin community publicly declared its

times, pp 332, 451.   **81** Fagan, *Stuart papers*, ii, pp 95, 137.   **82** Faulkner, *Liber Dubliniensis*, pp xiii–xiv for
the changing formula.   **83** R. Walsh, 'A list of ecclesiastics that took the oath of allegiance' (1912).   **84** C.
Mooney, 'A Leitrim victim of the French Revolution' (1964), pp 332–52.   **85** A. Faulkner (ed.), 'Letters of
Charles Bonaventure Maguire, O.F.M.' (1981), p. 286.   **86** K. MacGrath, 'Sidelights on the Irish
Franciscans' (1952), p. 85.   **87** M.V. Ronan, 'Priests in the Independence movement, 1796–8' (1946), p. 96.
Following his arrest Duffy was found to be carrying 'treasonable' literature.   **88** R. Hayes, 'Priests in the
Independence movement of '98' (1945), p. 262; for more information on Cassidy see Mhág Craith, *Dán na
mBráthar Mionúr*, ii, p. 283.   **89** T. Bartlett (ed.), *Revolutionary Dublin, 1795–1801* (2004), p. 307.

3 Richard Hayes OFM (d. 1824), campaigner for the anti-veto cause during the
Catholic Emancipation debate.

allegiance 'to the best of Kings'[90] and the Wexford brethren condemned the conduct of 'a drunken and inebriated rabble', as they described the rebels.[91] There are references to friars intervening to save lives. Anthony Dunne, a curate in Cloone, Co. Leitrim, interceded successfully with General Humbert to spare the house of a prominent Protestant, and tried to persuade the invaders of the hopelessness of their cause.[92] When about a hundred pikemen arrived the next day to join the French, Dunne convinced them to return home. In Multyfarnham Thomas Moran succeeded in saving the life of the warden of Wilson's Hospital, when the school was occupied by the insurgents in September 1798.[93]

When the government sought a qualified veto which would allow it the right to block a candidate for episcopal office on the grounds of suspect loyalty, in return for emancipation, the bishops rejected the measure. In 1814 when the Holy See announced that it favoured granting the crown its request,[94] there was instant opposition and it galvanized the Wexford friar, Richard J. Hayes, into action (see figure 3). Hayes foresaw the most disastrous effects if the battle on the veto question were to be lost: 'the destruction of the Catholic religion and of the little freedom Ireland enjoys.'[95] He was appointed delegate of the Catholic laity in September 1815 to present the anti-veto case to the Pope and he conducted such a trenchant and undiplomatic campaign against making any concessions whatsoever to the British government that he was expelled from the papal states in July 1817.[96] Yet, he agitated so forcibly and was so rarely out of the news that he kept the anti-veto campaign alive and ultimately succeeded though he did not live to see it as he died in 1824. Daniel O'Connell, who was a friend of the friars, believed he had done his work well and regretted that he had not been adequately supported.[97]

Intellectual and cultural interests

Unlike the seventeenth century no significant intellectual figures stand out among the Franciscans during the period under consideration, partly because their writings have not yet been studied.[98] Bishop Peter Archdekin of Killala published *A short view of the practice of giving money at interest* in 1734 with the purpose, as he put it in the extended title, 'to make easy the conscience of such as

---

90 MacGrath, 'Sidelights on the Irish Franciscans', p. 86. **91** K. Whelan, 'The role of the Catholic priest in the 1798 rebellion in county Wexford' (1987), p. 311. **92** MacNamee, *History of the diocese of Ardagh*, pp 594–5; also C. Mooney, 'St Anthony's College Louvain' (1969), pp 44–5 on Dunne's experience in the French army. **93** K.M.G. [Kevin MacGrath], 'Multyfarnham in '98' (1948), p. 101. **94** See M.J. Brenan, *An ecclesiastical history of Ireland* (1864), ii, pp 441–8 for a translation of the documents. **95** Giblin, 'Papers of Richard Joachim Hayes, O.F.M.' (1979–80), p. 131. **96** Giblin, 'Papers of Richard Joachim Hayes, O.F.M.' (1983), pp 115, 191. James MacCormick was unimpressed by Hayes's 'imprudence in political affairs' and believed he should have confined himself to following instructions he was getting from Ireland; see FLK MSS E13.227, 229. **97** Giblin, 'Papers of Richard Joachim Hayes, O.F.M.' (1988), p. 66. **98** See C. Giblin, *Irish exiles in Catholic Europe* (1971), iv, pp 33–4 where some of these are mentioned.

give their money at interest … when they do not require extravagant, or unusual interest or gain; and do only take what by the custom and laws of the land, is allowed and taxed.'[99] However, the learned work failed to ease the conscience of Bishop James Gallagher of Raphoe who wrote to the nuncio at Brussels in 1736 seeking his opinion on the soundness of the book's views which were quite new and liberal and which should have been welcome to Irish Catholics who had few opportunities for making money because of the legal restrictions imposed on them.[1]

Other friars turned their attention to the translation of continental theological and devotional literature. Felim O'Neill, guardian of Dungannon in 1735, may well have been the author of *Seanmónta Chúige Uladh* and translator of *De imitatione Christi*.[2] Walter Kelly translated a work of bible history in four volumes into Irish.[3] A translation of the Italian *Specchio Spirituale*, which included among other topics, speculation on the origins of St Patrick's Purgatory and its history, was made by Thomas Magauran, a Cavan friar, about 1704 under the title *Sgáthán Spioradálta*.[4] Sylvester Lloyd's translation of the *Montpellier Catechism* from French was a popular textbook but it caused him trouble for a time when the original French text was placed on the Index of Prohibited Books in 1721 because of its perceived Jansenist leanings.[5] Years later, in 1738, Lloyd published a bilingual catechism for the use of the clergy and people of Killaloe of which he was then bishop.[6] Some friars were prominent figures in the Irish literary circles of the early part of the century. In the poetry they are no longer the furtive figures of the civil documents but reveal clearer personalities as they move in a freer and safer environment. One of these was Francis Walsh who had published his *Grammatica Anglo-Hibernica; or, A Brief Introduction to the Irish Language* in 1713, thus continuing the tradition of the Louvain Franciscans in the study of language and grammar.[7] He may have been the author of *The antediluvium world; or, A new theory of the earth*, published in 1744. Tadhg Ó Neachtain, a prominent member of the Irish language circle, mentions Walsh in one of his poems as well as another friar, Pól Mac Aogáin, who was a close friend of the poet's father, Seán.[8] Ó Neachtain senior and Mac Aogáin conducted a poetic dialogue during

99 See H. Fenning, 'Dublin imprints of Catholic interest: 1701–1739' (1997–8), p. 149. Fenning suggests that Archdekin may have been addressing the problem of those Catholics who were lending money to landowners though they themselves were forbidden to invest in land.   **1** Giblin, 'Nunziatura' (1966), pp 69–70.   **2** A. Faulkner, 'Tóruidheacht na bhfíreun air lorg Chríosda' (1973–4).   **3** M. Ní Mhuirgheasa (eag.), *Stair an Bhíobla* (1941–5), which was largely based on Sieur de Royaumont's *L'histoire du vieux et du nouveau testament* (1670).   **4** A. Faulkner, 'Thomas Magauran, O.F.M. (*c.*1640–1715)' (1970).   **5** See Fagan, *Sylvester Lloyd*, pp 20–32 for an account of the controversy.   **6** Sylvester Lloyd, *The Doway catechism in Irish and English* (1738); see Fagan, *Sylvester Lloyd*, pp 154–6 for comments on this work; also P. Ó Súilleabháin, 'Roinnt caiticeasmaí gaeilge' (1964–5), p. 114.   **7** On this see A. Harrison, *Ag cruinniú meala. Anthony Raymond (1675–1726)* (1988), pp 32–5, 67–8.   **8** Ibid., pp 135–7 for Ó Neachtain's poem; Mac

the latter's imprisonment in the notorious 'Black Dog' prison.[9] Perhaps the most colourful character among the literary friars was Denis Taaffe who left the order two years after returning to Ireland from Prague in 1788. He never strayed far from his Irish Franciscan heritage though and in the early years of the nineteenth century he wrote *An introduction to the Irish language* and was the first secretary of the Gaelic Society, founded in Dublin in 1806.[10] His best known work, *Impartial history of Ireland* in four volumes, published in 1808, had, in the view of one reviewer, 'a boldness of view that many characterize as rash and imprudent'.[11]

Whatever about the quality of the literary activity of the eighteenth-century friars, there is no doubt that many were 'bookish' men.[12] In spite of the difficulties of acquiring and keeping books, the friars did remarkably well and demonstrated that books were precious to them. The early lists from Meelick and Kilconnell libraries reveal that they had relatively small libraries – not more than fifty books – which covered scripture, patrology, systematic theology, the lives of Irish saints, Franciscan authors, mainly Duns Scotus, but also Irish Franciscan writers such as Baron, Punch and O'Molloy. Most of the works, as one would expect, are theological but later lists from Wexford (500 titles) and Cork (600) show a wider selection. Not surprisingly, the libraries of the continental colleges far surpassed those on home territory.[13] When the rationalist thinker, John Toland, visited the college at Prague in 1708, he was received warmly and found the friars there 'easy and well-bred' and was well pleased with the 'courteous behaviour and good literature' of Francis O'Devlin, one of the resident friars.[14]

CONCLUSION

In surviving the penal period the friars had shown much resourcefulness and had continued to contribute to the life of the church and the people. Paradoxically

---

Aogáin and Walsh are the first two members of the 'scolairí Gaeilge' mentioned, in verses 2 and 3 respectively (p. 135). **9** Mhág Craith, *Dán na mBráthar Mionúr*, i, pp 262–79. **10** T. O'Donnell, 'A Gaelic grammarian' (1952). **11** R.S. O'Duffy, 'Rev Denis Taaffe: the patriot historian', undated, MS article in FLK MS E42.33. **12** For a list of some of the contents of Meelick, Donegal and Kilconnell libraries see n. 2 above. Also K. MacGrath, 'The Irish Franciscan Library at Prague' (1951), pp 29–33 (MS 1791 in Prague University Library contains a catalogue of the contents of the Franciscan library); T. Wall, 'Days of reading and a sermon to the books at Multyfarnham' (1949), pp 13–17; T. Wall, 'Some Franciscan "ex libris" from Multyfarnham library' (1951) (some of the books came from Jamestown and Trim friaries); W. Crowley, 'Gleanings of past years: our library' (1985); I. Fennessy, 'Books in the Franciscan friary, Cork' (2004–5); P. Ó Súilleabháin, 'The library of a parish priest for the penal days'; I. Fennessy, 'Books listed in Wexford friary shortly before 1798' (2002–3). **13** See I. Fennessy, 'Alphabetical indexes for Irish Franciscan incunabula in Rome and Dublin' (2001); idem, 'An alphabetical index for some manuscripts in St Isidore's College, Rome' (2001). **14** Quoted in Mac Craith & Worthington, 'Aspects of the literary activity of the Irish Franciscans in Prague', p. 132.

they seemed to have been most resilient during the first half of the century when conditions were least favourable but as soon as these began to improve their decline is more clearly visible. From the mid-century onwards it is easy to see how James Cowan, writing in 1817, could describe the province as 'tumbling into annihilation'. Numbers had dropped drastically and many locations had been abandoned, a phenomenon that was mirrored in Europe where the order was facing extinction.[15] Many external factors – the penal legislation, the prohibition on receiving novices and the assault on the colleges – had a detrimental impact on them but the main cause of their decline was the fact that they did not have a clear vision of their identity and mission. They gave the impression of drifting helplessly through choppy and unfamiliar waters not knowing when, and where they would land, if ever. And even had they known the course to follow, the structure of governance in the province was far too fragile to allow them take it. The provincial's term of office was only three years and his authority was seriously impaired by the divisive provincial mentality and the *plaga* system. The imprudence of accepting mediocre candidates into the province only made matters worse. On the other hand, the evidence also shows that in many quiet ways the friars did achieve much and left behind them memories of a grateful people and a legacy that would survive.

---

15 See D. Vorreaux & A. Pembleton, *A short history of the Franciscan family* (1989), pp 82–9 for a brief account of the fortunes of the European Franciscans in the eighteenth century.

Reforming and seeking an identity, 1829–1918

PATRICK CONLAN OFM

THE FRANCISCANS IN 1800

In Europe

The Irish Franciscan province spent the nineteenth century searching for an identity. The persecutions of earlier centuries, the consequent disruption of their life and ministry and the adaptations this necessitated resulted in a confused notion among the Irish friars of who they were and what they ought to be doing as Franciscans.[1] But their weakened state during the early decades of the nineteenth century could not compare with the trauma and disintegration suffered by their *confrères* on the Continent. Whatever hopes these and other religious had of an ecclesiastical and religious restoration in 1815 were short-lived as the suppressions and the dispersal of religious continued and intensified over the century, not only in Europe but also in Latin America.[2] Many provinces of the order disappeared, with fifty-nine alone vanishing between 1861 and 1880, more than forty of them in Italy. The general administration of the order thus faced a gargantuan task in trying to restore the basic structures which supported community life and the ministry of the friars. This turned out to be a very slow process. For instance, the friars began to return once again to France in the 1840s and it was only in 1860 that they were able to establish a new province. Indeed many friars had a weakened sense of their Franciscan identity; basic values such as community life and poverty had been lost, standards of education had dropped and the future of the order must have seemed uncertain.

Efforts to rebuild the order concentrated on a return to living the regular life with an emphasis on the strict observance of external forms and rites, such as the wearing of the habit and observing the rule of cloister. Legislative measures were adopted and imposed but these were obsolete in many cases and more realistic steps were needed urgently. Not alone were the restoration and the reform of the order absolutely essential but the authorities judged that now was the opportune moment to attempt the reunification of the various branches of the Observant family. But given the confusing structure of the different branches and the hostility to the idea of unification among the friars they believed that it would be nothing short of a miracle if this were achieved.

---

1 See MacMahon, 'The silent century, 1698–1829', in this volume. 2 L. Iriarte de Aspurz, *Franciscan history: the three orders of St Francis of Assisi* (1983), pp 375–96; H. Holzapfel, *Manuale Historiae Ordinis*

In Ireland

It is against this background that efforts made to reform the Irish province and restore the full discipline of the regular life, need to be understood. Although they did not experience the same degree of destruction as did their continental *confrères*, they were under serious threat during the introduction of Catholic Emancipation when they faced possible extinction. It was clear to some of them at least that they were in need of reform as their Franciscan identity was diluted following the havoc of the previous centuries. Furthermore, the rise of a diocesan clergy after 1800 forced them out of parish work which had been one of their main ministries, especially in rural areas. Working for so long in parish ministry had changed both their lifestyle and their identity and therefore its loss reinforced their sense of disorientation. While reluctantly they were willing to admit that reform was necessary, the question was: what kind of reform? Most friars, however, saw little need to change and were satisfied that their way of life was authentically Franciscan. The continental friars were scandalized by the lifestyle of the Irish friars and tried to impose their ideals on a comfortable Irish province during the second half of the nineteenth century. This chapter relates the history of the struggle to reform the province from outside and reactions to it from inside.

The life and organization of the Irish Franciscans in the early nineteenth century
A nineteenth-century Irish friary generally consisted of three or four priests with a perpetual tertiary (a male member of the Third Order in vows), a housekeeper/ cook and servants.[3] The friars lived like priests in a presbytery rather than as religious in a community. They dressed like secular clergy and prayer was said in private. Income came from mass stipends and collections. They were popular among the people and served them by celebrating mass, preaching (sermons were adapted from books), hearing confessions, blessing the sick, conducting popular devotions and offering spiritual advice.

The province continued to hold its chapter every three years with the permission of the minister general who approved the decisions and appointments. In the year of a chapter the outgoing definitory (council of the province), the guardians and some senior friars met around the feast of St Bonaventure in July, to hold elections, discuss the state of the province and pass legislation.[4] The new definitory appointed guardians and published their names in a chapter bill.[5] The

Fratrum Minorum (1909), pp 327–30; 373–80; M. Carmody, *The Leonine union* (1994), pp 26–35. **3** Conlan, *Franciscan Ireland*, pp 53–60; MacGrath, 'Sidelights on the Irish Franciscans 1798–1850' (1952); account books in FLK; P. Conlan, 'The Franciscans in Clonmel' (1999), p. 99. **4** Faulkner, *Liber Dubliniensis*, pp 210–333; on the internal organization of the province see MacMahon, 'The silent century, 1698–1829', in this volume. **5** Between them *Liber Dubliniensis* and *Liber Killiniensis* contain the chapter

minister provincial continued to live where he had hitherto ministered: for example, Anthony Garrahan continued as parish priest of Elphin and William O'Meara remained in Cork friary.[6] During his three-year term he visited the friaries to monitor the life and activities of the friars and encourage them.[7] With due permission, he convened a mid-chapter or intermediate chapter, which was a meeting of the definitory, senior friars and ex-provincials held between the regular provincial chapters.

In 1800 there were 120 friars, declining to 65 by 1850 and rising to 130 by 1900.[8] There were thirty-eight friaries in Ireland in 1800 but many of these would close during the course of the century as their occupants died: Dungannon (1816–17), Quin (1820), Timoleague and Buttevant (1822), Jamestown and Kinaleghin (1824–5), Edgeworthstown (1828), Elphin (1835), Meelick (1848), Claregalway (1847) and Aglish (1862). The provincial closed Ross in 1832 and Thurles in 1891. By 1900 there were but twelve friaries still functioning: Dublin, Wexford, Athlone, Limerick, Galway, Multyfarnham, Waterford, Clonmel, Cork, Ennis, Carrickbeg and Drogheda. St Isidore's in Rome and Our Lady's in Capranica were the continental colleges.

Candidates to the order normally stayed in a friary before spending a year in the novitiate and then taking solemn vows.[9] In the early years of the century until 1823 the novitiate was in Cork or Wexford. From then until 1831 candidates did their novitiate in Spain or in an Italian friary, after which St Isidore's became the sole novitiate until it was transferred to Drogheda in 1860. The newly-professed were ordained nine months after completing novitiate but this was increased to two years in 1838 and to four years in 1856. Clerics studied under Italian friars at St Isidore's and paid a hundred pounds for their education.

The pastoral ministry of the friars

In their pastoral ministry the friars continued to encounter obstacles created by some bishops who sought to impose their authority over religious orders. Bishop Murphy of Cork and the regulars fell out in 1815 when the bishop asked them to preach in the North Chapel for free on Sundays.[10] Rome issued a decree in the same year that favoured the regulars and eased the difficulty, at least for the moment. When an enthusiastic young priest, John (Thomas) Mullock, arrived in Ennis in 1830 and found the friary in a ruinous condition, he opened a new

bills for the nineteenth century.   **6** B. Egan, 'An eminent Franciscan of the emancipation era' (1971); B. Egan, 'An annotated calendar of the O'Meara Papers' (1975).   **7** The Clonmel account book for the period, FLK C220, records visitations in 1802, 1803, 1804, 1808, 1810, 1811, 1813, 1814, 1817, 1821 and two in 1823.   **8** P. Conlan, 'Vocations to the Irish Franciscans 1800–1980' (1987); for individual friars see *Liber Killiniensis* pp 230–341, or the annual edition of *The Irish Catholic Directory* from 1838.   **9** Conlan, *St Isidore's College Rome*, pp 161–3.   **10** P. Conlan, 'Will they ever stop fighting?' (forthcoming); DPA, Russell

chapel and stopped ministering in the parish chapel.[11] Bishop Mac Mahon objected arguing that this made the pastoral care of the people more difficult. Mullock, however, replied that the friars had a right to a public church and were merely restoring a way of life that had been interrupted by persecution. Once again Rome decided in favour of the regulars.

A similar dispute broke out in the Waterford diocese.[12] In 1828 the friars in Clonmel withdrew from parish ministry and were refused faculties by the bishop. Similarly when a new guardian in Carrick-on-Suir began ministering independently of the parish priest in 1831 the bishop also refused him faculties. The matter went to Rome and remained unresolved until both the bishop and the guardian died in 1837. The friars in Waterford had worked in St John's parish for years but in 1830 they began building a new church and friary. When the guardian asked the bishop in 1833 for permission to open the church he refused and the matter was referred to Propaganda Fide. Following an investigation, Rome recommended that the church should open but Bishop Abraham held out. The dispute remained deadlocked until the bishop died and his successor was told to solve the problem. The church was in use by October 1839. Similar conflicts in other dioceses continued on and off during the century. When the Maynooth Statutes were published in 1875 there was an immediate reaction from the friars because their rights of questing (seeking alms) and of admitting laity to the Franciscan Third Order were restricted. They argued that the bishops had no jurisdiction in these matters. The upshot of these disputes was that the friars and regulars in general began to shape a particular form and style of ministry centred on their own churches which consisted principally in the celebration of masses, hearing confessions, conducting popular devotions, the blessing of the sick and needy and providing spiritual counsel.

Catholic Emancipation 1829

The regulars faced a more serious problem in 1829 when the British government decided to grant Catholic Emancipation. In order to get the bill through a suspicious Commons, a bigoted House of Lords and a scrupulous George IV, it was resolved to sacrifice the major religious orders and limit the power of the forty-shilling freeholders at elections.[13] The bill allowed for the prohibition and

Papers.   **11** P. Conlan, *Franciscan Ennis* (1984), pp 34–5; I. Murphy, *The diocese of Killaloe, 1800–1850* (1992), pp 136–9.   **12** APF, *Acta* 198 (1835) ff 62–78; *SOCG* 950 (1835) ff 191–202, 243–60, 267–89; APF, *Acta* 200 (1837) ff 153–63; *SOCG* 952 (1837.1) pp 318–35, 340–50, 365–70; Henry Hughes, provincial, to Cardinal Lambruschini, cardinal protector, undated, in AGFM, *Hibernia 1*, pp 131–2, *Collectanea Hibernica* (1976–7), p. 144.   **13** R. Walsh, 'A list of the regulars registered in Ireland' (1914), pp 34–48; P. Hughes, *The Catholic question, 1688–1829* (1929), pp 306–10; W.J. Fitzpatrick, *The life, times and correspondence of the Right Reverend Dr Doyle, bishop of Kildare* (1861), ii, pp 115–34; W.S. Lilly & J. Wallis, *A manual of law*

final suppression of Jesuits and members of other religious orders bound by monastic or religious vows. All religious had to register within six months and those found living illegally within the kingdom would be banished. Those who had been trained elsewhere were forbidden to return to Ireland and at the same time the training of novices was prohibited within the kingdom. Since formation took place in Rome friars would automatically became outlaws on returning to Ireland. Less serious was the banning of the public wearing of the religious habit, the ringing of church bells and other restrictions. The friars sought the counsel of Daniel O'Connell who advised that the anti-religious parts of the bill would be unworkable, in his view.[14] With that hopeful outcome the Franciscans registered as required by law.[15]

EARLY ATTEMPTS AT REFORM, 1829–79

Early attempts at reform from outside the province began in 1819 when Pope Pius VII commanded in the decree *Felicis recordationi* that the system of rotating the office of provincial, whereby each civil province held it for three years, be ended.[16] In spite of the prohibition the provincial and other officers continued to be elected following the customary system for another twenty years. Within the province itself, following repeated calls for change, minor reforms were introduced after the 1828 chapter.[17] Six years later the chapter held in Waterford passed statutes that continued in force until 1872.[18] Henry Hughes, who was provincial from 1837 until he was appointed vicar apostolic of Gibraltar in 1839, obeyed the orders of the minister general to put the statutes of 1834 into effect during the visitation of the friaries.[19] He looked at how the divine office, meditation, prayers with servants, prayers for benefactors and other devotional practices as well as the making of wills were being implemented.[20] John Mullock's diary of 1838 describes progress in the province.[21] Fifty friars were active in the ministry and new churches had opened in Aglish, Athlone, Carrick-on-Suir, Clonmel, Cork, Drogheda, Dublin, Ennis, Galway, Limerick, and Waterford. The minister general ordered that rotation of offices should stop to facilitate the election of good superiors at the 1839 chapter.[22] In spite of this apparent progress not enough

specially affecting Catholics (1893), pp 46–8.   **14** O'Connell to W. O'Meara, O.F.M., 18 March 1829 in FLK MS J/1/29, edited in *Irish Ecclesiastical Record* (1895), p. 494; C. Giblin, 'Daniel O'Connell and the Irish Franciscans' (1950).   **15** P. Conlan, 'The outlaw friars of Athlone' (1978).   **16** APF, *SC Irlanda* xxvii, (1839), f. 230.   **17** Dardis Diary, f. 4, FLK C669/2.   **18** Faulkner, *Liber Dubliniensis*, pp 240–4.   **19** M. Ó Huallacháin, 'Some papers of Henry Hughes, O.F.M.' (1997–8).   **20** Letter and visitation details in any friary account book in FLK, e.g. Carrick-on-Suir, MS C345.   **21** Mullock Diary, FLK MS M-F1, pp 40–3.   **22** Minister general to Walsh 11 July 1839, FLK MS C120; APF, *SC Irlanda* xxvii (1839), ff 182–5, 227–32 & 244–5.

had been done and more fundamental reforms were needed. The urgency of this was highlighted by Joseph Killian's attempts to have himself re-elected as provincial by delaying the chapter of 1843 and by depriving some friars of their right to vote. This chapter turned out to be a tumultuous affair and the following one, at which Patrick (Anthony) McCabe was elected as provincial, was regarded as illegal but was allowed to stand for the good of the province.[23]

Apart from having to contend with factionalism in the province during these years, the friars faced other serious problems. Coping with the famine then raging in Ireland was one such major preoccupation. The Meelick community ran into financial problems as it tried to feed the needy.[24] Bishop Henry Hughes sent a hundred pounds from Gibraltar in 1847 to aid the victims.[25] Shortage of personnel was also a pressing problem. When asking permission for the chapter in 1849, McCabe reported that there were forty-two priests for fourteen friaries and that he was unable to accede to the minister general's request to send a friar to work in Jerusalem because he did not have enough friars to carry on the ministry at home.[26] The new definitory, elected that year, tried to improve regular discipline by issuing decrees on tighter control over local administration and finances and the recitation of the divine office in community. Furthermore, no candidates for the order were to be accepted without proper examination and approval by persons appointed for the purpose.[27] A brief description of the way of life of the Galway friars in 1850 by Michael Jennings, a member of the fraternity, reveals that they were living in community and were praying the divine office together. They rose at 6a.m. and their prayer programme consisted of meditation and the recitation of the Small Hours of the Divine Office early in the morning; Vespers and Compline were recited at 2p.m. with Matins and Lauds at 4p.m.; the rosary was said at 10p.m. followed by spiritual reading and night prayers with the servants. A theological discussion for the friar-priests was held on Mondays and the annual retreat took place before Pentecost.[28] From this it would appear that the reform was making some progress.

23 Mullock Diary p. 60; Michael Malone, O.F.M., to Propaganda, 30 June 1847, and Luigi Flamini da Loreto, minister general, to Propaganda, 29 July 1847, in APF, *SC Irlanda* xxix (1847–8), ff 138–9, 223; Alessandro Barnabo, pro-secretary of Propaganda Fide, to minister general, 28 July 1847, in AGFM, *Propaganda* (1816–68), f. 345, *Collectanea Hibernica* (1978), p. 109.   **24** P. MacFhinn, *Mílic* (1943), pp 19–21.   **25** Letter of 18 March 1847 in DAA, Murray Papers, 32/3/76, calendared in *Archivium Hibernicum* (1985), p. 46.   **26** McCabe to Luigi Flamini da Loreto, minister general, 21 February 1849 and reply of same 12 March 1849 in AGFM, *Hibernia 1*, ff 111–14, *Collectanea Hibernica* (1976–7), pp 142–3.   **27** Faulkner, *Liber Dubliniensis*, pp 275–6.   **28** AGFM, *Hibernia 1*, pp 104–5, *Collectanea Hibernica* (1976–7) p. 141.

Cardinal Cullen and reform

The mid-century witnessed further moves to accelerate the rate of reform. In a meeting with a number of superiors general in January 1851 Pope Pius IX informed them that he wanted each religious institute's way of life to be observed, at least in novitiates and houses of study. [29] Following this, the new minister general, Venanzio da Celano, wrote to the friars in 1851 putting the pope's wishes in a Franciscan context. In Ireland, Paul Cullen, who became archbishop of Armagh in 1849 and moved to Dublin in 1852, was appointed Apostolic Visitor of the Regulars of Ireland in 1850, a duty he took very seriously.[30] Cullen suggested Limerick as the first Irish Redemptorist foundation hoping that their presence might lead to the renewal of the Dominicans and Franciscans.[31] He maintained that the Franciscans needed reform more than any other religious institute in Ireland and, having spent many years in Rome and being in a position to judge, he believed that this should start with a proper course of studies at St Isidore's College. Both he and the minister general recommended a special visitation of the province before the 1852 chapter.[32] Peter (Francis) O'Farrell (1809–75), guardian of Drogheda, was Cullen's choice as visitor.[33] As he visited each friary, O'Farrell attempted to impose the observance of his own statutes. These covered both the proper care of the friary church and the administration of the community finances as well as stressing the importance of mental prayer, the recitation of divine office in choir and the wearing of the habit in the friary and the church.[34] Except for the decree on the habit, O'Farrell's statutes summarized existing provincial legislation. Using his authority as apostolic visitor, Cullen intervened by asking O'Farrell to request Propaganda Fide to nominate the definitory rather than follow the customary practice of the chapter electing it.[35] O'Farrell complied and forwarded the names to Rome including that of Anthony Dardis for the position of provincial. These names were approved and the chapter went ahead.[36] However over the following two years the resentment of the friars, including members of the new definitory, towards O'Farrell was clearly manifest. They claimed that O'Farrell was overbearing, had exceeded his authority and had ignored the fact that wearing the habit was against civil law since 1829. In spite of

29 M. Carmody, 'Pius IX and the reform of religious life' (draft article in FLK).   **30** P. MacSuibhne, *Paul Cullen and his contemporaries* (1961), i, pp 1–71.   **31** J. Sharp, *Reapers of the harvest: the Redemptorists in Great Britain and Ireland* (1989), p. 21.   **32** Carmody, 'Pius IX and the reform of religious life', p. 3.   **33** P. Conlan, 'Father Peter Francis O'Farrell, O.F.M.' (1984), pp 28–35.   **34** Carmody, 'Pius IX and the reform of religious life', pp 6–7; Athlone friary archives, account book under 15 May 1852.   **35** Carmody, 'Pius IX and the reform of religious life', p. 8; AGFM, *Australia 1* (1852–98), ff 316–19, *Collectanea Hibernica* (1978), pp 131–2, O'Farrell to Venanzio da Celano, minister general, 1 July 1852.   **36** Carmody, 'Pius IX and the reform of religious life', pp 8–9; AGFM, *Hibernia 1*, 136, *Collectanea Hibernica* (1976–7), p. 145, Venanzio da Celano to Propaganda; the decree is in *Liber Dubliniensis* pp 338–9; APF, *SC Irlanda* xxxi (1852–53), ff 252–3, Cullen to Giacomo Fransoni, Cardinal Prefect of Propaganda, 4 October 1852; f 436, same to same,

Cullen's support, O'Farrell's appeals were rejected and he was removed as guardian in Drogheda.[37] He went to Australia in 1854 where he collected funds for a permanent Franciscan foundation before his death in 1875.

Matters seemed to be improving when the provincial, Edmund Hogan, reported to the general chapter in 1856 that there were now fifty-five friars living in sixteen friaries.[38] It was at this general chapter that Bernard van Loo, then provincial of the Recollect Belgian province, made his celebrated call for the four branches of the Observant family to drop their distinctive names and instead become 'true friars minor'.[39] The Irish would hear more of both van Loo and unification before long. Hogan also reported that outside the country there were five Irish friars in Australia and one in Boston, while Bishops Hughes and Mullock served respectively in Gibraltar and Newfoundland. There were seven priests, ten clerics and four brothers at St Isidore's and three Italian friars in Capranica. On the one hand, the optimism of the friars appeared to be justified as new churches and friaries were opened or existing ones renovated during the second half of the century: Ennis (new church and friary in 1855 and extended in 1888); a new friary in Dublin (1856); Wexford (the church renovated in 1857); Athlone (new friary in 1869); Limerick (a new church in 1879 and a friary within a decade of this); Clonmel (a new church in 1886 followed by the friary in 1892) and a new friary opened in Carrick-on-Suir in 1896. On the other hand, however, most of this progress was of a material and structural nature and, while some progress had been made on the internal reforms, the fundamental issues had not been addressed, at least in the eyes of the continental reformers.

Reform from Belgium: Bernard van Loo

The appointment of Bernard van Loo (1818–85) as general visitor to Ireland was a new departure since hitherto visitors were invariably Irish and the change of practice indicated a determination on the part of the order's superiors to accelerate reform. But more important than being from a different province was the fact that van Loo was also a figure of some significance within the order, a leading member of the group pushing for reform and unification. He was the first of the major visitors from the Recollect branch of the order, to which Ireland belonged, to attempt to tackle the reform of the Irish friars. The Recollect branch

18 April 1853. **37** Carmody, 'Pius IX and the reform of religious life', pp 10–15; various documents in AGFM, *Australia 1* (1852–98), ff 320–5, *Collectanea Hibernica* (1978), pp 132–3; APF, *SC Irlanda* xxxii (1854–56), ff 146–7, Venanzio da Celano, minister general, to Giacomo Fransoni, Cardinal Prefect of Propaganda, 8 April 1854. **38** AGFM, *Hibernia 5*, ff 77–80, *Collectanea Hibernica* (1985–6), pp 200–2; the number of friaries varies from one report to another and is therefore confusing; there were twelve well-established ones and others, such as Thurles and Claregalway, are included because the friars still had a tenuous link with them. **39** Carmody, *Leonine union*, p. 33.

was noted for its rigorous life of asceticism, contemplation, study, preaching and missionary life, all of this protected by strict rules of cloister. It also favoured drawing up detailed statutes covering all elements of daily life so that the individual would be left in little doubt on what was expected of him.

At the 1856 general chapter van Loo was elected procurator general of the Recollects and Alcantarines (the Spanish wing of the Observants which had a strong presence in Latin America and Asia) and was also charged by his province to investigate the possibility of re-founding the English province which was on the brink of extinction.[40] While travelling to Ireland as visitor in 1857,[41] he sought suitable sites in England for Belgian foundations, the first one being founded in Cornwall in 1858, followed by another in Gorey, Co. Wexford, the same year. The Gorey venture did not work out as the Belgians had hoped and they opted to move to Killarney instead in 1860. Two Belgians were sent to Drogheda friary to learn English.

Van Loo believed that regular observance in Ireland would improve through the example of the Belgians. Not surprisingly, he emphasized the need for reform and believed that there was nothing in the rule that could not be observed in Ireland with the possible exception of the wearing of the habit. As part of his reform programme he sought to provide the Irish friars with adequate legislation and to this end he published an Irish edition of the 1852 statutes of the Dutch Recollects.[42] He summarized the minimum obligations consistent with Franciscan life and spelt out the demands of regular observance as found in the much-respected Gaudentius van den Kerckhove's commentary on the general statutes of the order. He wanted the statutes to be taken in their obvious sense and not analyzed to extinction.[43] He also believed that the problem of friars leaving the order to look after needy parents must be tackled.[44] Van Loo was not over-impressed by the changes undertaken thus far nor was he hopeful about future efforts at reform. He reported that he had done his best to persuade the Irish to accept reform and had given them much needed legislation but unfortunately

40 S. Dirks, *Histoire litteraire et bibliographique des Frères Mineurs de l'Observance de St François* (1885) pp 421–4; obituary in *Acta Ordinis Minorum* 4 (1885), pp 47–8; Carmody, *Leonine union*, pp 33–4.   **41** APF, *SC Irlanda* xxxiii (1857), ff 162 & 242 contains letters from the minister general requesting faculties for van Loo to conduct the visitation; the letter from van Loo may be found in FLK MS E3.   **42** *Ordinationes pro Conventibus Missionariorum Pr[ovinciae] Hib[erniae] O.F.M. S[ancti] F[rancisc]i* (1857); copies in FLK, AGFM *Hibernia* 1 f 162 & APF, *SC Irlanda* xxxiii (1857–60), f. 942; G. van den Kerckhove, *Commentarii in generalia statuta Ordinis S. Francisci Minorum provinciis nationis Germano-Belgicae* (1700) was a standard commentary on the statutes of the German-Belgian nation.   **43** FLK MS E3 Van Loo to Hogan, 25 September 1857.   **44** P. Conlan, 'Vocations to the Irish Franciscans 1800–1980' (1987), p. 34; idem, 'Irish Franciscans and Australia' (1983), pp 8–10; see the difficulties with the will of Charles A. Dalton in APF, *SC Irlanda* xxxv (1865–7), ff 933–46 and related material in AGFM, *Propaganda*, ff 461–4, 478–81 & 484–5, *Collectanea Hibernica* (1978), pp 117–19.

goodwill was lacking.[45] There were some good men in the province and van Loo suggested that these should be gathered into a designated house of strict observance to be joined by young friars as they returned to Ireland from Rome on completing their studies.[46] However the minister general rejected the suggestion and opted instead to keep up the pressure for the reform of the entire province. Van Loo's suggestion is highly significant because it is not dissimilar to the strategy finally adopted at the end of the century in introducing the reform to the province. Other avenues towards reform were also proposed, including one by Emmanuel Kenners, a Belgian friar studying English in Drogheda friary, who suggested that a novitiate staffed by Belgians be established near Dublin, that Irish houses be placed under Belgian control and the Irish provincial become a member of the Belgian definitory.[47] However, none of these came to anything. As part of his reform, van Loo sought permission to appoint the definitory and at his suggestion Laurence Gregory Cosgrove was appointed provincial in 1858 and reminded of his overriding obligation to promote reform.[48] Kenners reported from Drogheda that the Irish friars were not happy with the appointments being imposed on them and were plotting to have them nullified, unsuccessfully, as it transpired.[49] The minister general conveyed van Loo's far from optimistic conclusions to Propaganda Fide that friars were living like secular clergy and saw no need to change.[50]

Cosgrove set to work immediately by getting the general definitory to agree that the Irish friars could continue to accept and use money in accordance with the dispensations allowed them in penal times, a mitigation of the strict prohibition on the use of money.[51] Following visitation of the friaries in 1859 Cosgrove reported that buildings were in good repair, that the friars were popular with the people and that preaching was done to his satisfaction but he had to admit that van Loo's statutes were not being observed.[52] Shortage of priests made

45 Van Loo to Bernardino Trionfetti da Montefranco, 20 September 1857, in AGFM, *Hibernia 1* ff 168–9, *Collectanea Hibernica* (1976–7), pp 147–8 and *Regestrum … Germano-Belgicae 5* (1844–85) ff 279–80, *Collectanea Hibernica* (1978), p. 127; same to same 17 October 1857 in AGFM, *Hibernia 1* ff 170–1, *Collectanea Hibernica* (1976–7), p. 148. **46** APF, *SC Irlanda* xxxiii (1857–60), ff 436–8; Gaetano Bedini, secretary of Propaganda Fide, to Bernardino Trionfetti da Montefranco, minister general, 25 September 1857, in AGFM *Propaganda* (1816–68), ff 354–6, *Collectanea Hibernica* (1978), p. 110. **47** Kenners to van Loo and Dardis to same, both 10 February 1858, in AGFM, *Regestrum … Germano-Belgicae 5* (1844–85), ff 116–17B, *Collectanea Hibernica* (1978), pp 120–1. **48** Faulkner, *Liber Dubliniensis*, pp 340–1; Cosgrove to general in AGFM, *Hibernia 1* ff 1801, *Collectanea Hibernica* (1976–7), p. 150. **49** FLK MS E3 for the general's letter of 17 May 1858; Kenners to van Loo, 25 April 1858, in AGFM, *Regestrum … Germano-Belgicae 5* (1844–85), ff 172–3, *Collectanea Hibernica* (1978), p. 122. **50** APF, *SC Irlanda* xxxiii (1857–60) ff 436–8; Gaetano Bedini, secretary of Propaganda Fide, to Bernardino Trionfetti da Montefranco, minister general, 25 September 1857, in AGFM, *Propaganda* (1816–68), ff 354–6, *Collectanea Hibernica* (1978), p. 110. **51** AGFM, *Consultationes generales*, I (1856–68) n. 103, *Collectanea Hibernica* (1985–6), p. 190. **52** Cosgrove to the general in AGFM, *Hibernia 1,* ff 189–90, *Collectanea Hibernica* (1976–7), p. 151.

it impossible to fulfil the minister general's wish that the definitors ought to reside in Dublin.[53] Attention was also given to improving the formation system. New statutes for students at St Isidore's were approved in 1856.[54] A temporary novitiate opened in Capranica in 1859 and was transferred to Drogheda in 1860 on condition that perfect common life and regular discipline be observed.[55] A note of resentment is discernible at the presence of Belgian friars in Ireland and Cosgrove wanted them removed from the country claiming that the Irish friars were as edifying as they were but his request was refused.

There was a flurry of correspondence in 1861 between Archbishop Cullen, Cardinal Barnabo at Propaganda Fide and Bernardino Trionfetti, minister general, before it was decided to re-appoint the definitory for another term so that the reform of the province might not be impeded.[56] The reform continued to advance slowly. Following his visit to the houses in 1861 Cosgrove was able to inform the minister general that common life was fairly well observed with a greater sense of poverty and that the divine office and meditation were now being carried out in choir.[57] This improvement of common life was also reported to the general chapter the following year as well as the statistical state of the province.[58] Outside Ireland there were three friars in Australia and one each in the US, the Holy Land and the Papal States. There was a bishop in Newfoundland and another in Australia. The intermediate chapter in 1863 designated Waterford as the friary where young priests could live a life of regular observance. Financially, it was proving difficult to make ends meet and many houses could not pay the annual tax for the upkeep of St Isidore's.[59] The provincial sent £300 each year to the college, a practice that led to the creation of provincial accounts and eventually evolved into the present system of centralized financial administration.

While the standard of regular observance had improved somewhat it was thought better to continue appointing the definitory. Another Belgian, Emmanuel Kenners (1825–94), who had studied English in Drogheda and worked in

53 AGFM *Hibernia 1*, ff 228–9, *Collectanea Hibernica* (1976–7), p. 153.   54 AGFM, *Hibernia 1*, ff 142–53, *Collectanea Hibernica* (1976–7), p. 146.   55 AGFM, *Hibernia 1*, ff 180–1, *Collectanea Hibernica* (1976–7), p. 150; Conlan, *St Isidore's College Rome*, p. 117; Cosgrove, provincial, to Bernardino Trionfetti, general, June and 30 November 1860 AGFM, *Hibernia 1*, f. 240 & 241–2, *Collectanea Hibernica* (1976–7), p. 154; P. Conlan, *The Franciscans in Drogheda* (1987), pp 42–6.   56 Cullen to Barnabo, 5 February 1861 in APF, *SC Irlanda* xxxiv (1861–4), ff 28–30; edited in MacSuibhne, *Paul Cullen* (1974), iv, p. 87; Gaetano Bedini, secretary of Propaganda, to Trionfetti, 18 February 1861 in AGFM, *Propaganda* (1816–68), f. 371, *Collectanea Hibernica* (1978), p. 112; Trionfetti to Propaganda 7 February 1861, APF, *SC Irlanda* above, f. 31; the minutes of the chapter are in FLK MS C841.   57 Cosgrove to Trionfetti, 12 May and 10 July 1861 in AGFM, *Hibernia 1*, f. 253–6, *Collectanea Hibernica* (1976–7), pp 155–6.   58 AGFM, *Hibernia 1*, f. 265–7, *Collectanea Hibernica* (1976–7), pp 156–7.   59 Cosgrove to Raffaele Lippi da Montecchio, minister general, 13 March 1863, in AGFM, *Propaganda* (1816–68), f. 403–4, *Collectanea Hibernica* (1978), p. 113; Filippo da Castellare OFM, to Bernardino dal Vago, general, 10 May 1870 in AGFM, *Hibernia 2*, ff 20–1, *Collectanea Hibernica* (1979–80), p. 163.

England, was appointed visitor.[60] On his visit to the friaries, Kenners found a situation ranging from excellent, as in the novitiate community in Drogheda, to seriously deficient in most places in that the common life was not being observed, the friars were providing little pastoral service to the people and the decree of 1858 restricting the use of money was not being observed. He also believed that a house of studies for philosophy and the humanities was needed in Ireland. The minister general decided that the reform had not advanced to the point where the Irish could elect the provincial and definitory. Kenners and Cullen suggested Peter Hanrahan as provincial but the minister general opted instead for Aloysius Cavanagh with Hanrahan as vicar-provincial. The general definitory also decided that the provincial should live in Dublin near Cullen and that Dublin friary would be an example of common life and regular observance for the rest of the country. The statutes of van Loo and the decree of the general definitory on money should be implemented[61] and women working in friaries be replaced. The definitory met in 1864 and sent their decisions to all the friars.[62] Cloth for habits would be ordered through one manufacturer to ensure proper colour and quality. A drop in vocations in Italy made it difficult to find local friars for Capranica and lecturers for both St Isidore's and Capranica, which was now the house for philosophy.

During the next decade matters continued to improve slowly as Isidore da Boscomare, a lecturer at St Isidore's, who was appointed visitor for the 1867, 1870 and 1876 chapters, acknowledged. During his first visit he found that regular observance had changed for the better though there was room for improvement, a view that was echoed by Cardinal Cullen.[63] The chapter of 1870 was called the Great Chapter because it was the last time that titular guardians were allowed to be present at a chapter, a decision the Irish friars tried unsuccessfully to overturn since it had been the practice since 1612.[64] The chapter was also noteworthy in that the right to elect the provincial was restored to the Irish friars, though this was not necessarily a sign that Rome was satisfied with progress, as subsequent events would reveal.

The visit of the minister general

A noteworthy event was the visit of Bernardino dal Vago da Portugruano, minister general, to Dublin to meet the definitory in October 1872, the first visit

60 The visitation documents on are in AGFM, *Hibernia 1*, ff 327–68, *Collectanea Hibernica* (1979–80), pp 161–8; other material is in APF, *SC Irlanda* xxxiv (1861–4) ff 1147, 1310–13, 1334. **61** Kenners had both printed in the form of a four-page leaflet; copies in FLK MS E3. **62** Copy in FLK MS E3. **63** Details of the visitation are in AGFM, *Hibernia 1*, ff 436–84, *Collectanea Hibernica* (1979–80), pp 173–7. **64** Petition to renew the Rescript and its abolition by Propaganda; both documents are in *Liber Dubliniensis*, pp 342–3; on the history, see, 'Brussels MS. 3947', p. 121. The chapter of 1876 was occasionally also called the

of a minister general since the thirteenth century.[65] While the visit as such might not have had the desired impact on the Irish friars, nevertheless, on the broader scene, it was important because it indicated clearly that transforming the Irish province was but part of a wider scheme of reform. Dal Vago had been appointed general by Pope Pius IX and, owing to the impossibility of holding general chapters due to the disturbed political conditions in Italy, he would continue in office for the next twenty years.[66] The Holy See was eager to transform the diverse branches of the order into a strong centralized and reformed body. Dal Vago was the pivotal figure in bringing about this policy and worked tirelessly at it.[67] He had set out a clear and ambitious programme of reform which aimed at improving communication between the central government and the periphery. To this end he visited as many provinces as possible in order to understand the situation of the order world-wide and how it could be reformed and unified. He established the *Acta ordinis minorum* in 1882, still the official organ of the general curia. He enacted much needed new legislation and also understood that a key element of his programme must be to restore and improve education and learning in the order. For this purpose, he constantly exhorted the provinces to set up minor seminaries (known as seraphic colleges) in which young men hoping to join the order might be educated to a sufficiently high standard so as to undertake higher studies, established St Bonaventure's College, a centre for research at Quaracchi, near Florence, designed to rediscover the intellectual tradition of the order and founded the Antonianum in Rome, a higher institute of education for young friars, to which the Irish province contributed.[68] Among his associates were two friars who worked to reform the Irish province, the Belgian Bernard van Loo and Gregor Janknecht of the province of Saxony.

During these years the location of the novitiate at Drogheda was a matter of much debate. The friary was regarded as unsatisfactory because it was too small and there was discussion on whether it ought to be transferred to an existing house, such as Dublin or Multyfarnham, or should a new location be found for it. Local Protestant opposition had killed plans for a novitiate at Ballywaltrim, near Bray, and, in a letter indicating that he was fed up with the vacillation, the minister general ordered that the novitiate remain in Drogheda.[69] However, the

capitulum magnum because sixty ballots failed to elect a provincial.   **65** Address by Kehoe in AGFM, *Hibernia* 2, ff 238–9, *Collectanea Hibernica* (1979–80), p. 175; details of the meeting in FLK MS E37. **66** I. Beschin, *Vita del servo di Dio P. Bernardino dal Vago da Portugruaro* (1927).   **67** See Carmody, *Leonine union*, pp 4–5, 36–41 for dal Vago's programme of reform.   **68** The centre at Quaracchi was transferred to Grottaferrata, near Rome, in the 1970s and, at the end of 2008, it moved into St Isidore's College. The centre specializes in producing critical editions of the works of Franciscan authors. **69** Richard Hill, custos, to Cosgrove, provincial, 20 August 1874, Cosgrove to the minister general, 5 August 1874 & 25 August 1874, general to Cosgrove, 2 September 1874, in AGFM, *Hibernia* 2, ff 433–8, 452–4, *Collectanea Hibernica* (1979–80), pp 189–90.

mid-chapter of 1875 decided to move it to Ennis instead but permission was only granted in 1877.[70] This chapter also decided to establish a foundation in Sydney and the first two friars set out for the mission in March 1879.[71]

MORE RADICAL REFORMS, 1879–97

Reform from Saxony: Gregor Janknecht

Gregor Janknecht of the province of Saxony (1829–96) was appointed visitor in 1879, a decision that indicated clearly the high priority the minister general placed on the reform of the Irish province.[72] Janknecht's work for the reform of the order was impressive. He served as a definitor general in 1862–9 and co-operated with his friend Bernard van Loo in supporting the minister general in reforming the order. He re-erected the Custody of St Elizabeth in Thuringia and responded to the *Kulturkampf* by moving formation to Holland and the US where his friars founded the Province of the Sacred Heart in 1879. He revived two provinces in Brazil before his death in 1896.

Janknecht turned his attention to the reform of the Irish province and over the next decade was the mastermind behind the more concerted efforts to impose change. Writing to the minister general prior to the chapter, he reported that regular observance and religious discipline were totally lacking although there was a semblance of common life in five communities. Among the shortcomings he listed were the fact that women were working in friaries, that there were opposing factions among the friars, that some were wont to drink whiskey with the laity, that only one of the four friars recently returned from finishing studies in Rome was living in a house where the common life was observed and concluded that it would be better to suppress the Irish province rather than let it continue as it was. He went on to recommend that community life should be introduced to every friary and silence observed, that clerics should study the humanities and philosophy in a house in Ireland before going to Rome for further studies and that only those friars who observed the common life should be appointed as superiors. Following the chapter of 1879 at which the level of regular observance required in the friaries and the problem of friars addicted to alcohol were debated

---

70 The relevant documents are in AGFM, *Hibernia 2,* ff 469–71 & 493–6, *Collectanea Hibernica* (1979–80), pp 191–2; Conlan, *Franciscan Ennis,* pp 44–8. **71** Kehoe to Bernardino dal Vago, 22 August 1877, in AGFM, *Hibernia 3,* ff 139–40, *Collectanea Hibernica* (1982), pp 97–8. **72** The visitation documents are in AGFM, *Hibernia 3,* ff 194–5, 208–50, *Collectanea Hibernica* (1982), pp 101–7; documents on Australia are in AGFM, *Australia 1,* ff 411–19, 429–58, *Collectanea Hibernica* (1978), pp 139–41; short biography of Janknecht in *Acta Ordinis Minorum* xcviii (1979), pp 362–4; draft biography by K. Rakemann in FLK; letters between him and van Loo in AGFM, *Regestrum … Germano-Belgicae 5* (1844–85).

at length, Janknecht was a little more hopeful in his final report. The Irish province could learn from seeing the lifestyle of their brethren in Belgium, Holland and Saxony.

In his endeavour to promote higher standards of education, the minister general conducted a personal visitation of St Isidore's college in 1880.[73] He expressed satisfaction with Luke Carey as guardian though both Carey and his provincial, Richard Hill, were aware of the criticism of the standard of studies, especially in philosophy, at St Isidore's. Dal Vago took up one of his favourite themes and encouraged the creation of a seraphic college and suggested that clerics study the humanities and possibly philosophy in Ireland. The provincial, Richard A. Hill, pointed out, however, that resources in Ireland were limited though he was pleased to announce to the general the decision of the intermediate chapter of 1881 that clerics would spend a year in Ireland studying Latin and English before proceeding to Rome. It would take another ten years, when pressure for reform was irresistible, before the friars finally set up a seraphic college at Capranica.

The reformers take over formation

The minister general was keen for the Irish to train some of their own as lecturers in philosophy and theology and not have to depend on Italian friars for this purpose. While the definitory decided in 1883 to do this, the problem of finding a lecturer urgently for St Isidore's became critical. Dal Vago found a suitable friar in Bernard Doebbing (1855–1916) of the province of Saxony, who was approved by Janknecht and Carey, and appointed him as instructor of those in formation at St Isidore's, a title that enabled him to act as lecturer and master of students. Doebbing joined the friars in 1872 and studied in the US. He was ordained in 1879 and taught in Cleveland before joining the Franciscan researchers at St Bonaventure's College at Quaracchi. From the reformers' point of view, Doebbing's appointment was providential and was to have major significance for the course of the history of the Irish province over the following century.

The pressure on the Irish to reform would intensify noticeably from now on. In a letter written to dal Vago in 1883, Gregor Janknecht outlined a plan of campaign to reform the Irish by taking control of the entire formation system and renewing it in the Franciscan spirit.[74] He had come to the conclusion that the Franciscan tradition had been lost in Ireland and that to recover it novices and tertiaries should be formed in another province, such as Belgium, and then proceed to a properly reformed college at Capranica before moving to an equally

73 Memorandum by Bernardino dal Vago, 25 July 1880, and Hill to same 6 July 1889, in AGFM, *Hibernia* 3, ff 285–6, 289–90, *Collectanea Hibernica* (1982), p. 109.   74 AGFM, *Hibernia* 3, ff 453–6, *Collectanea*

reformed St Isidore's college for theology. From subsequent decisions taken by the general administration of the order, it seems clear that this plan was adopted as official policy and a far tougher line towards the Irish was now the order of the day. Doebbing's appointment was the first step in implementing the new policy but it was not the only one. When concern about the new formation regime at the college was expressed at the intermediate chapter of 1884, the minister general strongly rejected any interference from the Irish, pointing out that the college was now under his immediate jurisdiction and the Irish definitory had no rights there.[75] Doebbing set about his task with diligence by reviewing the timetable and imposing a more disciplined regime with an emphasis on silence, reading during meals and recitation of the divine office.[76] He enrolled the students at the College of Propaganda Fide but they were unable to cope and lectures resumed at St Isidore's, a clear vindication of the reformers' view that young Irish friars were inadequately prepared for such studies. By inviting four German brothers, followed by three Dutch and six German clerics to St Isidore's, Doebbing had enough friars for full community life. Public theological disputations were re-introduced as academic acts, this being represented as a return to the spirit of the founder, Luke Wadding.

The appointment of another significant Recollect figure, Aloysius Lauer (1833–1901), a general definitor, as visitor for the 1885 chapter was clearly intended to increase the pressure on the province to take the reform seriously.[77] He was elected procurator general for the Recollect branch of the order in 1889 and was later appointed minister general of the unified order by Pope Leo XIII in 1897. A further indication of the tougher stance was demonstrated when it became known that the Irish were being stripped of their rights at St Isidore's. Since its foundation it had been the practice for the Irish definitory to forward a list of three names of Irish friars to the minister general for him to choose one for the position of guardian of St Isidore's. Now, however, this right was suspended and instead the visitor was given the right to name the guardian, a departure that did not please the Irish friars.

At the 1885 chapter the friars reluctantly agreed to the wishes of the minister general to send the novices to Harreveld, in Holland, belonging to the province of Saxony until the friary in Ennis was ready. Lauer hammered home the familiar exhortations to the friars.[78] A seraphic college must be set up for educating

Hibernica (1983), p. 182. **75** Documents are in AGFM, *Hibernia 3,* ff 460–7, *Collectanea Hibernica* (1983), pp 182–3; the intermediate congregation minutes are in FLK MS C841. **76** Earlier documents in FLK, MS C841; Doebbing in AGFM, *Hibernia 3,* ff 442–3, *Collectanea Hibernica* (1983), pp 180–1; on his appointment see Conlan, *St Isidore's College Rome*, pp 187–9. **77** Documents are in AGFM, *Hibernia 3,* ff 490, 509–15, 524–8, 539–51, *Collectanea Hibernica* (1983), pp 185–91 and *Australia 1,* 508–11 *Collectanea Hibernica* (1978), pp 144–5; the chapter minutes are in FLK MS C841. **78** AGFM, *Hibernia 3,* ff 550–1,

potential candidates to the order; brothers or tertiaries had to replace women in friaries; consumption of whiskey, brandy or gin was strictly forbidden before lunch; attention was to be paid to the proper celebration of mass and the office; the third order should be encouraged and fostered; and friars should show prudence in visiting the houses of laypeople. In August the following year, the minister general instructed the provincial, Alphonsus Jackman, that novices would continue to be sent to Harreveld and that the newly professed friars would remain there studying the humanities until they had reached a proper standard that would enable them to follow a course of philosophy.[79] Then they would go to Rome for further studies. Candidates for the brotherhood should also go to Holland.

Since the reforms had been opposed by many members of the province, the minister general made his views absolutely clear prior to the mid-chapter of 1887.[80] The seed for the reform of the province had been sown at St Isidore's with the appointment of Bernard Doebbing. Regular discipline would now be restored over the entire province. The discipline in Rome would be extended to Capranica and there would be no excuses for the Irish not training their own lecturers. Young friars could not return to lax houses and one Irish friary had to be designated for full regular observance for them. In case they were not clear on what full observance meant he proceeded to spell it out: proper observance of the cloister; prohibition on the personal use of money; the wearing of both habit and tonsure, the full choral recitation of the divine office and community meditation in choir. The young priests would remain at St Isidore's until this house was ready and the novices would remain in the novitiate at Harreveld until the minister general decided otherwise. He insisted that a seraphic college be established and in the meantime young men could be sent to the college at Harreveld, which would remain a training centre for Irish friars. Tertiaries or brothers must replace women in friaries. If the Irish played their part, the situation would be tolerable. The mid-chapter met in 1887 and named Ennis as the house of regular observance for young priests.

Janknecht and the Reform Decree of 1888

The pace of reform in Ireland was still far too slow to satisfy the authorities in Rome and more drastic measures were needed. Students at St Isidore's wrote to the minister general appealing to him to continue the reform despite opposition to it in the province.[81] Doebbing agreed with the students and stressed that the

Collectanea Hibernica (1983), p. 191.   **79** The letters are in AGFM, *Hibernia 3*, ff 574–6, 584–5, 589–90, *Collectanea Hibernica* (1983), pp 193–4.   **80** The mid-chapter documents are in AGFM, *Hibernia 3*, ff 593–4, 597, 603–8, 618–21, 628–9, *Collectanea Hibernica* (1983), pp 194–7; the minutes are in FLK MS C841. **81** The letters are in AGFM, *Hibernia 3*, ff 655–76 & 683–6, *Collectanea Hibernica* (1983), pp 199–201; letter

old and the new must to be kept apart while Aloysius Lauer reluctantly agreed that the Irish were unable or unwilling to reform. The way forward lay with the new men and he supported issuing a special decree on the reform of the Irish province. Janknecht once again proved that he was the mastermind behind the reform of the province when he suggested the way forward.[82] The general definitory should request authorization from the Holy See to nominate the provincial superiors of the province, appoint non-Irish friars as superiors in St Isidore's and Capranica, and send candidates for the province to be educated by the friars of Saxony. While the last point had been decided and was already in operation, the other two were new, but what made the plan more drastic was the fact that the weight of the Holy See would now be thrown firmly behind the reform. The minister general would appoint the provincial and give the friars a last chance to reform. Janknecht was appointed visitor and was empowered to hold a chapter or suspend it if unsuitable friars were elected.

Janknecht found the province in a poor state and concluded that issuing and implementing the minister general's decree was the only way forward. At the chapter of 1888, he unveiled the decree which had been approved by Propaganda Fide.[83] Novices would not be received in Ireland for six years and instead the province of Saxony would train them with Peter Begley, an Irish friar of the reform, as assistant master. New priests would return to Ireland only when there were enough of them to take over two houses, one as the novitiate. Once this happened, formation could then begin again in Ireland with a seraphic college, a novitiate and a house for the study of the humanities and philosophy. Theology would remain in Rome, where lay friars also would receive proper training.

This plan of action would unfold slowly over the following decades. The seraphic college opened in Capranica in 1891 and was transferred to Multyfarnham in 1899 once it had been taken over by the reformed friars. The novitiate returned to Ennis for a few years before moving to Killarney in 1902. The clerics studied the humanities and philosophy there. Later, after a brief period at University College Cork, the friars settled on University College Galway for the humanities and philosophy in 1932. Theology would remain in Rome and novices and students would no longer pay their own expenses.

of January 29 in FLK MS E34. **82** Pre-chapter documents are in AGFM, *Hibernia 3*, ff 701–63, *Collectanea Hibernica* (1983), pp 205; the decision of the general definitory is in AGFM, *Consultationes ii* (1869–91), f. 826, *Collectanea Hibernica* (1985–6), p. 191; the letter of 14 June 1888 is in AGFM, *Hibernia 6*, ff 2–5, *Collectanea Hibernica* (1992–3), p. 191; Janknecht's letter of 30 June 1888 is in FLK MS E 37; for an example of the spirituality of the reform see P. Conlan, *A true Franciscan, Br Paschal* (1978). **83** The chapter minutes are in FLK MS C841; related documents are in AGFM, *Hibernia 3*, ff 770–3, 776–80, *Collectanea Hibernica* (1983), pp 205–6; the approval of the acts in AGFM, *Consultationes ii* (1869–91), f. 843, *Collectanea Hibernica* (1985–6), p. 192; approval by Propaganda Fide in AGFM, *Hibernia 6*, ff 2–5,

Irish reaction to the Reform Decree

The reform decree mobilized the Irish into action and they sent a delegation to Rome to explain their objections.[84] Among other arguments they pointed out that appointing the Germans as presidents of St Isidore's and Capranica could arouse fears in Ireland of a German takeover. The minister general mounted a robust defence of his decisions pointing out that the reform had been going on for thirty years and despite promises little had happened. The story of the 'oppression' of the Irish friars by the Germans surfaced in the *Boston Pilot* of 7 December 1888, followed by an editorial in the *Freeman's Journal* of 9 February 1889 about the rumoured transfer of St Isidore's to the German friars.[85] Following pressure from Propaganda Fide, Archbishop William Walsh of Dublin issued a pastoral letter on February 15 saying that there was no question of taking over ancient Irish property. Nicholas Dillon, then in St Isidore's and brother of the politician John Dillon, kept Walsh informed and he in turn kept Cardinal Manning of Westminster abreast of the affair. Waterford Borough Council petitioned Propaganda Fide about the fate of the colleges that had been founded by the Waterford-born Luke Wadding. The appointment of a non-Irish friar as superior of St Isidore's, would continue to raise concerns in Ireland over the next few years.[86] The mayor of Waterford wrote to Propaganda Fide in June 1895 objecting to the appointment and the aldermen and burgesses of Clonmel wrote in the same vein in July, followed by those in Drogheda and Cork. But the minister general reminded Propaganda that the matter had been decided in 1889 and Propaganda informed the mayor of Waterford that appointing an Irish superior was not in the best interests of the Irish friars at the moment. The Irish continued their attempts to annul the decree of the minister general or at least modify it by requesting Propaganda Fide to review the case and the congregation, having done so, decided that the decree must be observed and Leo XIII confirmed the decision.[87] In fact, the Irish lost further ground when the case was reviewed a second time and the right of the Irish provincial to receive novices was transferred to a friar of the reform designated by the minister general. A seraphic

Collectanea Hibernica (1992–3), p. 191. **84** Documents opposing the decree in AGFM, *Hibernia* 3, ff 777–809, *Collectanea Hibernica* (1983), pp 206–8; AGFM, *Consultationes ii* (1869–91), f. 852, *Collectanea Hibernica* (1985–6), p. 192; FLK MSS C841 (definitory meetings) & E34 (letters). **85** Related documents in AGFM, *Hibernia 4*, ff 56–9, 113, *Collectanea Hibernica* (1984), pp 100, 105; the general's letter of 17 February 1889 is in FLK MS E34; Archbishop Walsh's public letter is in APF, *SC Irlanda*, xivl (1889–90), ff 58–9; his letter of 26 February is in DAA, Walsh Papers, 347/6. **86** APF, N.S., 126 (1898), ff 527–57; related documents in AGFM, *Hibernia 5*, ff 73–4, 134–5, *Collectanea Hibernica* (1985–6), pp 200, 207. **87** Related documents in APF, *Acta* 259 (1889) numbers 8 (1 April 1889) & 45 (16 December 1889), ff 237–45, 807–10; APF, *SOCG* 1031, ff 418–68; APF, *SC Irlanda*, xivl (1889–90), ff158–9, 255–67, 275–6; copy of documents in FLK MS E64; others in AGFM, *Hibernia 4*, ff 3–18, 33–43, 73–82, 91–8, 114–39, *Collectanea Hibernica* (1984), pp 96–106; AGFM, *Hibernia 6*, ff 6–63, *Collectanea Hibernica* (1992–3), pp 191–3.

4 A black friar, 'Fr Slattery osf' *c.*1870 (FLK).

college for young Irishmen aspiring to be friars was opened in Capranica in 1891. The novitiate was moved to Rome the same year and Peter Begley went to Ireland seeking vocations for the reform.

The 'Black' friars continue their campaign[88]

The replies of the Irish definitory to a questionnaire on the implementation of the reforms failed to convince the new minister general, Luigi da Canali da Parma, in April 1891 and, as a result, he postponed the provincial chapter until early 1892.[89] Aidan McCarthy, a native of Manchester and a definitor of the new province of England, was appointed visitor.[90] He reported that there were many positive things in the province and that the friars tried to lead a common life in the larger houses. The chapter of 1892 approved a series of new regulations: limitations on the amount of money a local superior could spend; prohibition on the involvement of friars in political affairs (this was the height of the Parnell crisis); the mandatory holding of regular theological discussions; and obliging priests to wear the tonsure and sandals.

When Gregor Janknecht wrote an account to commemorate Doebbing's ten years at St Isidore's in 1893, little did he think that it would provoke such a storm of protest and reveal the deep divisions within the reformist camp.[91] Luke Carey felt that his role was neglected and that he was open to charges of falsifying the house accounts and demanded a commission of inquiry. The minister general prevaricated and a split opened between strict reformers supporting Doebbing, and moderate reformers backing Carey. The row rumbled on until 1918 and would have damaging consequences for the reform and the province at large.[92]

The Irish continued to mount a dogged opposition to the reform campaign. Prior to the general chapter of 1895 which was to discuss and decide on the unification of the different branches within the order,[93] the definitory wrote to the minister general requesting that full rights be restored to the Irish province and strongly objecting to the reform decree.[94] But the reformers were not for

---

88 The unreformed friars were known as 'Black' friars because they dressed like clergymen, while the new breed of reformed friars formed by the Germans were known as 'Brown' friars because they wore the habit. **89** The memorandum and replies are in AGFM, *Hibernia* 4, ff 260–75, *Collectanea Hibernica* (1984), pp 113–15. **90** The visitation and chapter documents are in AGFM, *Hibernia* 4, ff 316–22, 334–44, *Collectanea Hibernica* (1984), pp 117–19; also *Hibernia* 6, ff 130–4, *Collectanea Hibernica* (1992–3), pp 194–5; the letters from the general are in FLK MS E38; the chapter minutes are in FLK, MS C841. **91** *Memoria initii et progressus reformationis almae Provinciae Hiberniae O.S.F., 1883–1893*; Conlan, *St Isidore's College Rome*, pp 204–5. **92** When Benignus Gannon, a moderate reformer, was elected provincial in 1904 he ordered Janknecht's book to be destroyed. Carey's version of events was published in 1909, *Epistola circa instaurationem Collegii S. Isidori de Urbe ad Rev. P. Lucam Carey, O.F.M., eiusdem Collegii quondam guardianum et huius responsio*. **93** Carmody, *Leonine union*, pp 127–50. **94** AGFM, *Irlanda* box; letters of the general in FLK MSS E37 and E39; AGFM, *Hibernia* 5, ff 81–2, 105–7, *Collectanea*

turning and Luigi da Parma responded publicly at the chapter by declaring that all seven Recollect provinces were flourishing with the sole exception of Ireland but the young friars in formation at St Isidore's would restore the glorious tradition of that province. When David Fleming was appointed visitor to the province in 1895 he was told not to hold a chapter but, ignoring the instruction, he went ahead with the chapter which elected an opponent of the reform, Alphonsus Jackman, as provincial.[95] The general definitory reprimanded Fleming but reluctantly approved the acts of the chapter including new statutes.[96] Fleming, however, was far more hopeful and justified his actions by reporting that there was a good spirit among the friars.[97] Most communities observed the common life and regular discipline. Furthermore he believed that the time had come to mollify the Irish and hopes began to rise that the reformed friars would soon return to Ireland. The *discretorium* or house council at St Isidore's discussed this possibility in January 1896.[98] It recommended that Ennis be rejected in favour of Multyfarnham as the place to house the first group of reformers. The community there could easily move elsewhere and few people would disturb the friars with pastoral calls. New communities should be under the jurisdiction of a commissary general and since Athlone was centrally located it could serve as a novitiate.

The first 'Brown' friars return to Ireland

There were now sufficient young reformed friars in Rome for the next stage of the reform to be put into action. Peter Begley returned to Ireland in May 1896 as delegate general and negotiated with the provincial about the return of the 'brown' friars.[99] Jackman protested to the minister general about the takeover of Multyfarnham and in response the general definitory sought special faculties from Propaganda Fide to proceed and place it under the control of the general. Still Jackman objected and Propaganda threatened to suspend him from all ecclesial offices if he did not comply and requested the local bishop and Archbishop Walsh of Dublin to persuade the provincial to obey.[1] Jackman capitulated and the

Hibernica (1985–6), pp 202–4 and *Hibernia 6,* ff 321–2, *Collectanea Hibernica* (1992–3), p. 203. **95** Relevant documents in AGFM, *Hibernia 5,* ff 120–67, *Collectanea Hibernica* (1985–6), pp 205–12; letters from the general are in FLK MS E39; chapter minutes are in FLK MS C841; the decisions of the general definitory in AGFM, *Consultationes…, iii (1891–1903),* nn 210, 220, 235, *Collectanea Hibernica* (1985–6), pp 192–3. **96** *Staututa Provincialia almae provinciae S. Patricii Fratrum Minorum Hiberniae, condita in capitulo provinciali eiusdem Provinciae habito Dublinii in nostro conventu ad Immaculata Conceptionem B. V. M. die 7a Augusti a.d. 1895* (1895); see AGFM, *Hibernia 6,* ff 334–47, *Collectanea Hibernica* (1992–3), p. 203. **97** AGFM, *Hibernia 5,* ff 149–54, *Collectanea Hibernica* (1985–6), pp 209–10; part of the report has been re-arranged in *Liber Killiniensis,* pp 228–9; letters from Fleming to the provincial are in FLK MS E39. **98** AGFM, *Hibernia 6,* ff 367–70 & 381–2, *Collectanea Hibernica* (1992–3), pp 204–6. **99** AGFM, *Hibernia 5,* ff 193–6, *Collectanea Hibernica* (1985–6), pp 214–15; *Consultationes …, iii (1891–1903),* n. 325, *Collectanea Hibernica* (1985–6), p. 193. **1** From here on see AGFM, *Hibernia 6,* ff 387–98, 423–38,

reformers, Frs Nicholas Dillon, Patrick Cahill and Lawrence O'Neill with Brs Felix Steppler and Didacus McNamara, moved into Multyfarnham on 11 December 1896, the first step in re-possessing the province, a process that would take over thirty years to complete.[2] The minister general nominated Begley as guardian and Dillon as vicar. Begley set to work immediately by beginning the construction of a new wing so that the seraphic college could be transferred to Multyfarnham.[3] The first boys arrived in October 1899. It operated as a normal boarding school with fees of twenty pounds paid in advance. Those thinking of joining the friars would spend five years there and sit the matriculation examination.

The 'black' friars realized that there was no way back and that their era was over. Some left and joined dioceses. The others faded away over the next few decades, remembered with affection by the people near their friaries. Not surprisingly the mid-chapter in 1897 was a sombre affair.[4] The minister general forbade the provincial to come to Rome. Leo XIII issued the Bull *Felicitate quadam* on 4 October 1897 by which the four families of the Order of Saint Francis (OSF) became the Order of Friars Minor (OFM).[5] The pope nominated Aloysius Lauer as minister general with David Fleming as a general definitor. The Irish definitory congratulated Lauer, recalled what he had done for them in the past and hoped that he would remember their troubles. The provincial of Saxony informed Lauer that they wanted to cease their Irish venture in favour of their missions in Brazil.[6] Four German lay-friars opted to join the Irish province and the remaining ones withdrew when Doebbing resigned as vice-regent and president of St Isidore's in 1898. The Irish were in control of St Isidore's once more, but now they were reformed Irish friars. A new era was opening for the Irish Franciscans.

APPLYING REFORMS IN THE IRISH PROVINCE, 1897–1918

The 'brown' friars take over the provincial administration

With permission from the Holy See, the minister general appointed Peter Begley as provincial and Bernard Cooney as vicar in 1899.[7] The latter would represent the

Collectanea Hibernica (1992–3), pp 206–8; letters from the general on September 20 & 26 are in FLK MS E37.   **2** Conlan, *St Isidore's College Rome*, p. 206; F. Steppler, 'A college is founded' (1947), p. 93.   **3** 'Over half a century', *Franciscan College Annual* (1956); [A. Wogan], 'Recollections' (1948); C. Moriarty, 'A corner of memory' (1949).   **4** AGFM, *Hibernia* 5, ff 225–7, *Collectanea Hibernica* (1985–6), p. 217; minutes in FLK MS C841; permit and letter of approval in FLK MS E38.   **5** Carmody, *Leonine union*, pp 149–79; definitory minutes in FLK MS C841.   **6** AGFM, *Saxonia S. Crucis 3*, ff 218–9, *Collectanea Hibernica* (1985–6), pp 230–1; on Doebbing and related events, AGFM, *Hibernia* 5, ff 329–69, *Collectanea Hibernica* (1985–6), pp 224–6; Conlan, *St Isidore's College Rome*, pp 206–7.   **7** AGFM, *Hibernia* 5, ff 311, 383–5, *Collectanea Hibernica*

'black' friars until his death in 1907. It was decreed that the new general constitutions must be observed in all the friaries while taking into account the needs of the 'black' friars. Only friars dedicated to perfect observance could be appointed superiors and those who did not wish to follow the new way should live in designated friaries. Houses should be chosen for a seraphic college, a novitiate and a house of studies.

The plan was to appoint guardians only to those houses taken over by the reformers so that when the new definitory met it named guardians for Multyfarnham and Ennis and presidents or superiors for the other communities.[8] At the request of the reformers, Propaganda Fide confirmed the title of the 'Province of St Patrick' on 22 August 1899 and this lasted until 1921 when the traditional title of the 'Province of Ireland' was restored. Cork friary was set aside for 'black' friars living the full common life. A commission was appointed to draft new statutes which were approved in 1899,[9] though a revised version was commissioned by the 1902 chapter. Ennis, the second reformed house, became the novitiate once again in August 1899 and would remain so until 1902.[10] At the mid-chapter in 1900, Athlone was added to the list of guardianates thus making it the third reformed house. A commission was set up to resolve many minor problems about regular observance. All sorts of minutiae such as the use of pocket or wristwatches, what papers different friars might read and the quality of various foods were clarified. The pastoral services traditionally offered to the people by the 'black' friars did not change when the 'brown' friars took over.[11]

When the general, Aloysius Lauer, died in 1901, David Fleming was elected to replace him until the next general chapter in 1903. Continuing the process of implementing the unification of the order, the general definitory set about correcting the anomaly of having French houses in England and an English house in Ireland.[12] Thus, it was decreed that houses belonging to the French friars in England should transfer to the English province and likewise Killarney should pass to the Irish province. The Irish paid £3,000 for Killarney and the novitiate was moved there from Ennis in 1902. The outgoing superior, Alphonsus Bulens, another priest and a brother changed provinces in order to remain in Killarney. The French moves brought a few friars into the Irish province, one of them being Brendan Jennings from Leamington Spa, who had joined the French friars in England in 1900. The general definitory also decided early in 1903 that the superior of St Isidore's and by implication of Capranica, would be appointed by

(1985–6), p. 227.   **8** Related documents in AGFM, *Hibernia* 5, ff 390–3, *Collectanea Hibernica* (1985–6), p. 228; the minutes are in FLK MS C841.   **9** P. Begley, *Puncta Disciplinae pro Provincia Hiberniae S. Patritii O.F.M.* (1899).   **10** Conlan, *Franciscan Ennis*, pp 52–3.   **11** See note 15 below; details for 1925 are taken from the *Irish Franciscan Directory* of that year.   **12** Conlan, 'The Franciscan friary, Killarney' (1977), pp 108–10.

the Irish definitory, an entirely new departure, which indicated satisfaction with the progress of the reform.

A major priority of the reform was improving the formation and education of young friars. Now that the seraphic college and the novitiate were firmly established in Multyfarnham and Killarney respectively, the provincial authorities moved to set up the remaining elements of the system. In 1906 permission was sought from Archbishop Walsh of Dublin for a house of studies at Finglas and when this was refused they turned to Cork.[13] Sir Bertram Windle, president of University College Cork, a convert and a Franciscan tertiary, saw a need for a Catholic hall of residence and when he learned of the interest of the friars, he arranged for the purchase of the derelict Protestant Berkeley Hall and suggested that it be renamed St Anthony's Hall.[14] It was inaugurated as a Franciscan student house and a Catholic hall of residence on 17 February 1909. Long-running tensions between the moderate and strict reformers crystallized around the new hall with the latter expressing their doubts about the decision. They were not opposed to an improved system of education but were definitely hostile to its taking place in a non-ecclesiastical institution where young friars would have to mingle with lay students, thereby risking involvement in worldly affairs which was contrary to their spirituality. Benignus Gannon, a moderate and provincial since 1905, identified Nicholas Dillon as the source of these objections. The minister general contacted Gannon, who believed that the matter had been cleared in Rome. The building was large, but the friars hoped for increased vocations. Both Archbishop Fennelly of Cashel and Dr Windle had asked that part of the building would be used as a residence for secular students. The official opening took place on 6 October 1909 and Francis Maher was appointed dean of residence at the university.

The strict reformers mounted a campaign against Gannon who did his best to address accusations of laxity levelled against him. When writing to the friars in 1910 about certain abuses he left himself open to attack by mentioning that wearing the habit in public was against the civil law and ordered the friars not to do so where this might be seen as a provocation.[15] This applied particularly in Dublin where Archbishop Walsh had spoken against it in 1906. The wearing of the habit was regarded as a litmus test of conscientious orthodoxy by the strict reformers and three members of the definitory complained to the minister general about the growing number of abuses in the province, particularly the

---

13 DAA 1905, 372/7, and 1906, 374/6; B. Egan, 'The Friars Minor and the Honan Hostel', (1980).   14 P. Conlan, 'Berkeley Hall – St Anthony's Hall – Honan Hostel' (1995); for documents see Egan, 'The Friars Minor and the Honan Hostel'.   15 *Epistola de Quibusdam Abusibus eliminandis* (1910); the reaction to the letter is in AGFM, *Irlanda*, as well as FLK MS E88.

wearing of clerical garb instead of the habit and the use of bicycles. The minister general reminded Gannon of what previous generals had done for the good of the Irish province and recommended that regular observance be strictly observed. Dissatisfaction with the policy being pursued by Gannon surfaced when four definitors informed the minister general that they were morally certain that further relaxation would follow if the chapter were to take place.[16] But Alfred McLaughlin, the general visitor, found no evidence of relaxation and provided a detailed account of the state of the province.[17] Admittedly, the situation in Carrickbeg was poor and that in Clonmel hopeless but he was satisfied with most houses while twenty-three pupils attended the seraphic college at Multyfarnham and there were great hopes for St Anthony's Hall. Despite attempts to exclude him from the office of provincial in 1908, John Capistran Hanrahan, another moderate, succeeded Gannon as provincial in 1911.[18] However, events in Italy were to cast a long shadow over Ireland.

Victory of the strict reformers

Dionysius Schuler, elected minister general in 1903, continued the process of amalgamating the Italian provinces, a measure that infuriated the Italians and led to Pope Pius X deciding in 1911, for the good of the order in Italy, to replace the general administration.[19] None other than Bernard Doebbing, now bishop of Nepi and Sutri since 1902, gathered as many friars as possible in the church at the general curia, summoned Schuler and promulgated the document replacing the general definitory with a new one to serve until the 1915 chapter. Pacificus Monza was named minister general with Peter Begley among the six definitors general. Begley was now in a powerful position to influence affairs in Ireland, a development that was welcomed by the leader of the strict reformers at home, Nicholas Dillon.[20] Dillon set out to get rid of the entire definitory as well as the guardians in Cork and Rome and the president at St Anthony's Hall as soon as possible. With the aid of Begley and possibly Doebbing, Dillon launched his attack by persuading the Spanish Capuchin, Cardinal Vives y Tutó, prefect of the Congregation for Religious, to follow the Roman example by replacing the Irish definitory in 1912 because of its purported relaxed attitude to reform. Dillon himself was appointed provincial.[21] Gannon, Baldwin and Jackman objected, claiming that they had not been given a chance to defend themselves. Because of the outbreak of World War I, no provincial chapter was held between 1911 and 1918, thus allowing Dillon a free hand to implement his notion of the reform.

16 All letters in this section are in AGFM, MS *Irlanda*.　**17** The report is in AGFM, MS *Irlanda*. **18** Minutes are in FLK MS C841 as well as old enumeration MS P46 and AGFM, MS *Irlanda*. **19** Carmody, *Leonine union*, pp 211–16.　**20** Egan, 'The Friars Minor and the Honan Hostel', pp 658–9. **21** Fennessy, *Liber Killiniensis*, pp 56–7.

Dillon was set on having St Anthony's Hall shut down and travelled to Rome where he met the Franciscan Cardinal Diomede Falconio and the secretary of state, Cardinal Merry del Val.[22] Dillon told the former that the emerging laxity should have been prevented at the 1911 chapter. He held that all studies could be conducted in the safe environment of Rome and later claimed that the cardinal was opposed to St Anthony's Hall. The interviews with Cardinal Merry del Val centred on the hall of residence and Dillon's efforts to have David Fleming removed from St Isidore's because he considered him a supporter of the moderate wing in the province. As a result, Fleming was told to leave St Isidore's. The cardinal interpreted the Holy See's 1909 approval of St Anthony's Hall as an expression of hope for its success that need not stop the superiors from closing it if they wished.[23] According to Dillon, the clerics had consorted with lay students, especially women, while attending the university. Gannon and Windle appealed to Merry del Val. The matter returned to the Congregation for Religious but Dillon was determined to get rid of the hall and announced its sale. Windle and Bishop O'Callaghan of Cork, however, found a way to keep it open as a university residence by applying the residue of the Honan estate to buy the hall and thus it became the Honan Hostel. The Franciscan students moved to Ennis.

The minister general issued a decree following the changes in 1912.[24] In a reversal of reform practice the new definitory would elect presidents for all friaries and a year later would elect guardians for reform houses. No clerics could attend secular universities. All 'brown' friars were strictly bound to wear the habit inside and outside their houses. Two lists of friars were prepared: one of those who stood for the faithful observance of the rule and the other of those who supported a less faithful observance. The latter were deprived of active and passive voice. Since good superiors might be few in number they could be re-elected to office with a dispensation. The visitor general to the Irish province must not be from the English province but from one where regular observance, particularly the wearing of the habit in public, was in force. Dillon had triumphed.

The minutes of the definitory meetings held during these years reveal some of the thinking of the strict reformers and the measures they introduced.[25] For instance, many elements of Franciscan life in Ireland were discussed at a long meeting in Multyfarnham in August 1913. Practical matters such as a fair price for St Anthony's Hall, setting up a holiday house for the friars near Moyne in Mayo and land problems in Multyfarnham, were discussed as well as matters of principle such as whether or not the new confessionals in Drogheda were in line

---

22 Fennessy, 'Repercussions of reform' (2004–5), pp 282–5.   **23** Conlan, 'Berkeley Hall – St Anthony's Hall – Honan Hostel', pp 24–8.   **24** FLK MS E13.   **25** Minutes of these meetings are in FLK MS C841, Provincial definitory minutebook, pp 367–413; changes in personnel in 1913–16 in *Liber Killiniensis*, pp 58–60.

with poverty. During its time in office Dillon and his definitory paid much attention to detail and tried to cover all contingencies and thus ensure that every friar would know what was expected of him at any moment of every day. For instance, it decided that guardians could permit brothers to have watches provided these were of mediocre quality and that they could read selected Catholic papers.

The First World War and the Easter Rising

These years were momentous ones both nationally and internationally. The province provided its fair share of chaplains to the British forces during the Great War even though some media reports had suggested that Ireland was not playing its part and that Franciscans could not serve as chaplains because this would involve giving up the habit.[26] The friars served in many theatres of the war. Both Bonaventure Bradley and Raphael McAuliffe served on the Western Front, where the former was wounded during the Battle of Loos and the latter was honoured with a full military funeral in Limerick when he died while visiting his sick mother.[27] Xavier Power saw service in Scotland and Belgium. Elsewhere John Chrysostom Dore was awarded the Military Cross for his dedication during the Monastir offensive in Salonika and Leo Sheehan entered Jerusalem in 1917 with the Camel Corps under General Allenby. Friars also served in the Royal Navy. Laurence O'Neill was nicknamed 'The Admiral' after serving with the Royal Navy in the Mediterranean while another naval chaplain, Benedict Coffey, served in the Adriatic. There were casualties among the friar-chaplains. Isidore O'Meehan was accidentally shot dead in Mesopotamia in 1919 and Francis Maher was invalided home from Egypt and died in 1918. Alfred Clarke was with the Australian Imperial Force on the Western Front and was also invalided back to Ireland before the end of the war. Denis O'Callaghan suffered from chronic nervous problems after his war experiences. At its meetings in 1915 the Irish definitory agreed to contribute £200 to their needy Belgian brethren.

The provincial authorities were more circumspect on political issues nearer home. Easter Week 1916 was not mentioned at definitory meetings, perhaps because of a desire to maintain peace between friars with opposing loyalties. On the republican side was Mícheál Ó Conghaile and on the other side stood Nicholas Dillon, who came from a prominent nationalist family and had been a barrister before he joined the friars. Like Dillon, most friars were constitutional nationalists but there were also republican supporters among them, such as

26 T. Johnstone & J. Hagerty, The cross on the sword (1966); I. Fennessy, 'Father Peter B. Bradley and Irish Franciscan chaplains in World Wars I and II' (2003). 27 B. Egan, 'A West Limerick chaplain of World War I' (1982).

Patrick (Fidelis) Kavanagh, author of the popular history on the insurrection of 1798, who had inspired republicans. The Irish Volunteers trained and fundraised in a hall attached to the friary in Dublin while the Cork Volunteers used St Francis Hall belonging to the friary, forming up and marching from there as a gesture in 1916. Fidelis Griffin must have had a hint of the Rising when he heard the confessions of the volunteers in Athlone and gave each of them a medal on Holy Saturday of 1916.[28] Later two 1916 veterans joined the Franciscans: Joseph Corcoran as Br Louis and James Gartlan as Br Leo. Two others had relatives in the order: Gearóid Ó hUallacháin had four sons while Joseph Timmons had a brother and two sons.

Even at this relatively late stage the friars were reminded that their status was illegal when a dispute about rates came to a head in early 1916.[29] Five years earlier, the friars in Ennis, in keeping with their reformed views on strict poverty, decided not to pay rates on the grounds that they lived on charitable alms and did not own the buildings in which they lived. But they lost their case two years later on appeal to the King's Bench because the Franciscan order was an illegal organization under the Emancipation Act of 1829. In a similar case in Athlone, the local Urban District Council wrote off the friary rates for 1913–14 as a bad debt but in response the local government board auditor surcharged the members of the council to pay the friary rates. The whole country was enraged. One angry man wrote that 'some in-bred brat had the cheek … to declare the Franciscans outlaws'. The notion that the friars were outlaws gained much media coverage. In response the government introduced the Religious Orders Relief Bill but there were more demanding Irish items when parliament returned after the Easter recess in 1916 and the bill was quietly withdrawn.

The return of the moderate reformers

Alfred McLaughlin, visitor general at the chapter of 1911, was re-appointed in 1917, the decree forbidding the appointment of an English friar as visitor being set aside because of the war. He was instructed to forward the details needed by the minister general to appoint a new Irish definitory.[30] Having conducted a comprehensive visitation checking on the level of reform in the various houses, he sent three lists of friars to Rome: the first gave those who would take a strict line and cause the province to break-up; the second contained those who, through laxity, would overturn the progress of thirty years; and the final list named friars

---

28 M. Mitchell, *The man with the long hair* (1993), p. 25; personal communication from Joseph Timmons, who was out in Dublin in 1916; Cork friary chronicle.   **29** Conlan, 'The outlaw friars of Athlone'. **30** FLK MS E46; the report of his visitation is in AGFM, MS *Irlanda*.

who would promote reform while exercising common sense. The general accepted this last list of moderate reformers.

On the foot of this report, Seraphin Cimino, the general since 1915, wrote to the province on 26 January 1918 laying down clear norms.[31] He imposed the wearing of the habit inside and outside the friaries with the exception of Ulster. Money could be used outside the friary if it was deemed necessary by the provincial or local superior. Friars professed before 1887 who did not wish to obey these laws should be assigned to some houses under the authority of the provincial and be deprived of active and passive voice. The letter ended naming the new definitory. John Capistran Hanrahan, who had been deposed in 1912 and replaced by Dillon, was re-appointed as provincial and only two of the outgoing definitory, including Dillon, were retained. The rigorist approach of Dillon had failed. It was too strict and divisive. Hanrahan was perceived as having the ability to move the reform forward while maintaining unity among the friars. The more moderate policy was clearly revealed when guardians were appointed to eight houses and presidents to the remaining seven, the division being made on the basis of size of the community rather than 'brown' or 'black' houses.[32]

The process of reform moved on as three more houses were claimed in rapid succession: Wexford was taken over on 15 April 1918, Clonmel on 16 April and Galway on 19 April and these were later followed by Dublin in April 1921, Carrick-on-Suir on 25 July 1924 and Drogheda on 6 August 1924. The remaining 'black' friars were confined to Waterford. As 'black' houses were taken over, Vincent O'Grady moved from Wexford to Carrickbeg and finally to Waterford. He died in 1926 and is popularly remembered as the last of the 'black' friars. If the 'brown' friars had hoped for a surge in vocations as an immediate result of the reform they were disappointed for this did not happen until the 1920s.[33] In 1920 there were 140 members of the province, including those on the missions: 85 priests, 16 clerics, 21 brothers, 9 novices and 9 tertiaries.

John Capistran Hanrahan died in 1920 and was succeeded as provincial by Dominic Enright. Hubert Quinn became provincial in 1924. A friar of vision, he began several projects that would lead to major developments within the province. The nineteenth century had been about finding the right way to follow St Francis. The coming of Quinn and his vision began an apparent second golden age for the Irish Franciscans in the twentieth century.

31 Fennessy, *Liber Killiniensis*, pp 61–2.   **32** Minutes in FLK MS C841.   **33** P. Conlan, 'Vocations to the Irish Franciscans 1800–1980' (1987).

A second golden age: the Irish
Franciscans, 1918–63

MARY E. DALY

... It is hoped that what he has recorded will be sufficient to give a
fair idea to any intelligent reader of events and developments in the
province. He only wishes he had at hand similar records for each
year from 1224 to his own time. May what he has written, save
some future historian at least some of his time.

Canice Mooney, *Provincial Chronicle*, 31 December 1948.

In the half-century or so after the end of the Great War, the Irish Franciscan
community re-established itself as a significant pastoral and intellectual force in a
newly independent Ireland. The cultural history of the Irish Free State has often
been dismissed as insular and sterile. In reality this was a period when the Irish
people re-discovered and re-claimed a cultural heritage that had been lost or
hidden for many centuries. These years also marked the high point of what US
historian Emmet Larkin has dubbed, 'the devotional revolution', a revolution
which began *c.*1850 when Irish Catholicism, no longer constrained by the penal
laws, became much more evident. It set about erecting churches and other
religious buildings and introducing new forms of public ceremonial and rituals
that reflected post-tridentine Rome rather than pre-famine peasant Catholicism.
The early years of the new state were also a time when catholic clergy played a
major role as public intellectuals, seeking to guide public opinion on important
social questions such as poverty, social and medical services and emigration.
While the prominent role assumed by the catholic clergy is often seen as
indicating a wish to control key elements of Irish society, it also reflects the reality
that the clergy accounted for a significant proportion of the educated elite of
nationalist Ireland. Furthermore, religious orders such as the Irish Franciscans
who had houses in Rome, Capranica, Louvain, Australia, India, China and
southern Africa and close links with Franciscans throughout the world had a
much more international perspective than the majority of the Irish people. While
various friars contributed to debates on topics such as late marriage and the
decline of rural Ireland,[1] their major contribution to the cultural and intellectual

---

1 Felim Ó Briain was probably the major contributor on these topics.

formation of the new Irish state was made through the study of Irish history and culture in an international context.

By 1918 when Nicholas Dillon's six-year term as minister provincial came to an end, the transfer of friaries from 'Black' Friars to 'Brown' Friars was well advanced.[2] Wexford and Galway were transferred in 1918. Dublin in 1921, Drogheda in 1923, Carrick-on-Suir in 1924 and the process was completed with the transfer of Waterford in 1927.[3] While Conlan suggests that many Irish people were sad to see the supplanting of the 'Black' Friars with a new reformed order, the evidence indicates that the friars continued to have a strong place in the affections of the Irish people. When Fr Columba Hanrahan died in Athlone in 1943 'all houses in the town were closed in mourning. The coffin had to be guarded perpetually to prevent people stripping off bits of his habit and chord as relics'. Large crowds travelled from a distance to attend his funeral despite wartime travel restrictions.[4] Affection and support for the order is also evident in rising vocations and the friars' capacity to fund a number of ambitious new activities.

VOCATIONS AND FUNDING NEW BUILDINGS

The first half of the twentieth century saw a steady increase in the numbers entering religious life, and the Irish Franciscans formed part of this wider trend. The number of friars increased from 110 in 1900, to 150 by 1920, 250 by 1945 and 400 by 1960, peaking at 430 by 1965.[5] When Canice Mooney reviewed a list of new novices in 1946 he noted that they came from counties Leitrim, Cork, Kerry, Limerick Roscommon, Mayo, Derry and Tyrone, but there were none from the east. He also noted 'the presence of so many old Franciscan names'.[6] The growth in vocations made it possible to open new houses, and to commit a significant number of friars to full-time scholarship. At the same time a steady stream of friars were dispatched to missions in China, India and South Africa.[7] More centralized control, introduced as part of the reforms, made it possible to make the most effective use of the talents and resources of the province. There was an extensive programme of building and improvement. New houses were opened and existing convents were extended and embellished. Although the early 1920s were a very difficult period economically and many other institutions in Ireland found themselves with significantly reduced incomes due to wartime inflation

2 See Conlan, 'Reforming and seeking an identity, 1829–1918' in this volume.   3 Conlan, *FI*, p. 67. See also Conlan, 'Reforming and seeking identity' in this volume.   4 Mooney, *Chronicle of the Province of the Friars Minor 1939–63* (henceforth *Chronicle II*), 16 March 1943, pp 24–5. (The *Chronicle* is the diary of events in the province; each house kept a chronicle of local events.)   5 Conlan, *FI*, pp 67–8.   6 *Chronicle II*, 17 May 1946, p. 53.   7 See also Conlan, 'Reforming and seeking identity' in this volume.

and taxation, in 1923 the Franciscan Provincial Chronicle recorded that the finances of all houses except Drogheda were '*in optimo*'.[8] During these years most houses were upgraded with proper plumbing and heating and new kitchens. In 1929 it was decided that electricity would be installed in all houses that wanted it. The church in Ennis acquired new stained glass windows and a new organ was installed in Killarney. In 1927 plans were drawn up for a new church in Limerick at a cost of £40,000[9]. The foundation stone was laid for a new church (St Anthony's) in Athlone at a cost of £35,000 in 1929.[10] This church was consecrated on 10 June 1932.[11] In October 1932 the definitory was told that the debt outstanding on the Limerick church had been almost liquidated and the debt on the church in Athlone stood at £3,000. A new convent in Waterford had been completed and the church was undergoing major alterations. Again the level of debt was modest.[12] These substantial investments were financed by bequests, donations and other fundraising efforts such as bazaars and sweepstakes. In October 1932, it was agreed that the proceeds of the next sweepstake would go to finance the new house of studies in Galway. St Anthony's pools emerged as a major fund-raising venture during the 1950s.

THE FRIARS AND POLITICS, 1914–39

Although the Provincial Chronicle makes no mention of the formation of the Irish Free State in 1922, or any of the other momentous events, such as the Easter Rising, the Anglo-Irish war and the civil war, they undoubtedly had a major impact on the province. A number of friars served as chaplains to the British forces during the 1914–18 war. Nicholas Dillon, who served as provincial from 1912 to 1918, was the brother of John Dillon MP, the last leader of the Irish parliamentary party at Westminster. In October 1921 Mairead Gavan Duffy, writing from Rome, claimed that all the Irish clergy in that city, with the exception of the Irish College, had 'telegraphed their horror' when the Easter Rising broke out, but by 1921 St Isidore's and San Clemente (the house of the Irish Dominicans) had changed their opinion.[13] In Ireland a number of friars had close ties with leading republicans, most notably Limerick's Fr Philip Murphy, chaplain to the lords mayor of Limerick, who was forced to leave the city when the police raided the friary in March 1921 following the murder of the incumbent mayor George Clancy and former mayor Michael O'Callaghan.[14] According to

8 FLK MS C841 *Chronicle*, 22–23 August, p. 495. (MS C841, henceforth *Chronicle I*, provides an account to August 1939).   **9** *Chronicle I*, 23–26 August, pp 464–5.   **10** Ibid., 4 June 1929, p. 475.   **11** *Irish Catholic Directory*, p. 597.   **12** *Chronicle II*, 19 October 1932, p. 595.   **13** *Documents on Irish foreign policy* [*DIFP*], I, doc. no. III, p. 199 (11 October 1921).   **14** Conlan, *FI*, p. 69. For information on the murders see D.

Patrick Murray, most republican activity on the part of the Irish Franciscans ended with the Treaty. The majority supported the Irish Free State and the government of W.T. Cosgrave and whatever political tensions existed within the Irish Franciscans during the 1920s were generally between those who supported the Irish Free State and those who remained faithful to the Anglo-Irish tradition. In 1924 the Provincial Chronicle recorded a decision to invest £3,000 in the Irish Free State National Loan.[15] In the uncertain financial circumstances surrounding the new state this should be regarded as a gesture of support. Yet Murray also notes that a number of Irish Franciscans ministered to anti-Treaty republicans and played a key role in reconciling excommunicated republicans to the catholic church, and when Eamon de Valera, leader of anti-Treaty Sinn Féin visited Ennis in February 1922, the only priest to greet him publicly was Fr Leopold O'Neill OFM.[16] In 1929 Joseph Walshe, secretary of the Department of External Affairs, described Fr Pacificus, guardian of St Isidore's as 'a little Republican'.[17] Fr Michael O'Flanagan, formerly attached to the diocese of Elphin and one-time secretary of Sinn Féin who remained loyal to the anti-Treaty cause, stipulated in his will that his funeral should take place in the church of Adam & Eves, Merchants' Quay, where it took place in August 1942. This incident is further evidence of the diverse political opinions that were tolerated by the order. Nevertheless when St Isidore's was threatened with the loss of its garden in 1926 because Mussolini was planning to embark on a major road-widening programme in the area, the Chronicle records that the Irish Franciscans invoked the assistance of the British Minister in Rome, Sir William Tyrell and the British Foreign Secretary Sir Austen Chamberlain. This could be interpreted either as evidence of residual ties to the British government, or alternatively as a pragmatic determination to invoke all possible means of support. The Chronicle also notes that a request was made to all Irish archbishops and bishops and university heads to sign a letter of support.[18] When the threatened road scheme re-emerged in 1931, W.T. Cosgrave, president of the executive council of the Irish Free State appealed to Mussolini,[19] and this appeal appears to have been successful. For his efforts he was accorded the rare honour of becoming a lay member of the First Order of St Francis.

The appointment of the Irish-American Paschal Robinson OFM as the first papal nuncio to Ireland in 1929 also served to strengthen relations between the order and the new state. The Irish government had pressed hard for the appointment of a nuncio, against the evident wishes of the Irish hierarchy.[20] The

Macardle, *The Irish Republic* (London, 1968 edition), p. 496.   **15** *Chronicle I*, 23 July 1924, p. 516. **16** P. Murray, *Oracles of God* (2000), pp 170–1.   **17** *DIFP*, III, 1926–32, no. 228: Joseph P. Walshe to Patrick McGilligan, p. 322 (19 June 1929).   **18** *Chronicle I*, p 539.   **19** *DIFP* III, no. 520: W.T. Cosgrave to Benito Mussolini, p. 742 (24 February 1931).   **20** D. Keogh, *Ireland and the Vatican* (1995), pp 36–67.

Irish Catholic Directory described Dr Robinson's appointment as one that 'confers honour not only on Ireland but also on the illustrious Order of St Francis'.[21] When Paschal Robinson died in Dublin in 1948 he received the last rites from the Franciscan Provincial. Dr Robinson left written instructions concerning his funeral: he wished to be buried in the Franciscan habit, without any insignia of his archepiscopal rank; only a simple Requiem Mass should be celebrated, and he wished to be buried in a cemetery used by the Franciscan order. The Irish government was keen to give Dr Robinson a state funeral, and in deference to his wishes they asked the Franciscan order to act as pallbearers in place of the usual military officers. The order agreed that Dr Robinson's remains would be carried in a hearse rather than a gun carriage. The *Irish Catholic Directory* described the funeral service in the Pro-Cathedral as 'the essence of simplicity'; business was 'completely suspended' along the route of the funeral cortege and the streets were lined with 'dense crowds' despite a steady drizzle.[22]

THE FRIARS AND IRISH CULTURE

Margaret O'Callaghan has observed that an enthusiasm for Irish language and culture was something that united those who were divided by the civil war, and that the early years after independence saw a sustained drive to gaelicize Ireland and to reconnect with Ireland's history and heritage.[23] The friars participated actively in this process. In November 1922, when the civil war was still underway and the new Irish Free State had not yet come into existence, a petition supported by all friars present at the definitory was sent to the procurator, asking that the order re-establish a foundation in Donegal.[24] Despite overwhelming support the Franciscan house at Rossnowlagh on the shores of Donegal Bay did not re-open until after the Second World War. However, the petition to re-open a house in Donegal, close to the reputed location of Mícheál Ó Cléirigh's birthplace at Kilbarron and the area where he and his collaborators had compiled the Annals of the Four Masters, reflected a strong desire to reclaim the order's Irish heritage. The new church of St Anthony's at Athlone, which opened in 1932, was dedicated to the Four Masters. In August 1923 a petition from friars wishing to spend time in an Irish College at either Ring or Spiddal was granted unanimously.[25] On 26 May 1929 the first high mass since penal times was said in the ruins of Muckross Abbey (formerly a Franciscan friary) in Killarney. An estimated 2,800 Franciscan

21 *Irish Catholic Directory 1931*, 1 December 1929, p. 560.   22 *Irish Catholic Directory 1949*, pp 729–32. 23 M. O'Callaghan, 'Language, nationality and cultural identity' (1984).   24 *Chronicle I*, 29 November 1922, p. 483.   25 *Chronicle I*, 23 August 1923, p. 497.   26 *Irish Catholic Directory 1930*, 26 May 1929, p. 604.

tertiaries from Cork, Tralee and Killarney marched in procession from Killarney to the grounds of the abbey.[26] Some weeks later, as part of the celebrations for the centenary of the granting of Catholic Emancipation in 1829, the province organized the first mass said at the Rock of Cashel for over three centuries.[27] In August 1930 mass was celebrated in the ruins of another medieval Franciscan foundation – Askeaton Abbey – when an estimated 2,000 Franciscan tertiaries arrived by special trains in Limerick City and then processed to Askeaton to the sound of hymns played by the Boherbuoy marching band.[28] These pilgrimages to sites that were prominent in Ireland's Christian heritage attracted considerable support that transcended the divisions of the Irish civil war. When Fr Antonine Kelly OFM gave the oration at the first national pilgrimage to Faughart, the reputed birth-place of St Brigid, on 1 July 1934, the attendance included Eamon de Valera (president of the executive council), four government ministers – Frank Aiken, P.J. Little, Joseph Connelly and Frank Fahy – as well as W.T. Cosgrave, the Lord Mayor and members of Dublin corporation in their robes, and representatives of Dundalk urban district council and Louth County Council.[29] On 17 March 1935 Fr Fintan Russell OFM gave the sermon at the dedication of the National Memorial Church of St Patrick in Donegal. This church, a parochial church, dedicated to the 'magnificent Four Masters' stood near the ruins of the ancient friary on the edge of Donegal Bay.[30] Anniversaries of the foundation of ancient Franciscan foundations were also celebrated. Despite wartime stringencies and travel restrictions, the 600th anniversary of the founding of Muckross Abbey and the 700th anniversary of the coming of the order to Wexford were celebrated in 1940. Both events received widespread coverage in the newspapers, although Canice Mooney believed that the Wexford festivities anticipated the arrival of the friars in that town by twenty years![31] He did not query the ceremonies held at Ballymote in November 1942 to mark the arrival of the friars there in 1442, which was celebrated with a year-long programme of events.

THE RE-ESTABLISHMENT OF ST ANTHONY'S COLLEGE, LOUVAIN

The most significant testimony to the order's commitment to reclaiming its heritage was the re-opening of St Anthony's College in Louvain. The college which closed during the French Revolution,[32] had for many centuries been the home in exile of the Irish Franciscans and the intellectual base for the

---

27 *Irish Catholic Directory 1930*, 30 June 1929, p. 590.   **28** *Irish Catholic Directory, 1931*, 10 August 1930, p. 624.   **29** *Irish Catholic Directory 1935*, 1 July 1934, pp 601–2.   **30** *Irish Catholic Directory 1936*, 17 March 1935, pp 618–19.   **31** *Chronicle II*, 8 December 1940, p. 12.   **32** See MacMahon, 'The silent century, 1698–1829' in this volume.

5 Eamon de Valera being received by Canice Mooney OFM, at Merchants' Quay
on the occasion of a Solemn Mass in the early 1940s (FLK).

conservation and transmission of the history and culture of Gaelic Ireland. The
decision taken by the congress definitory on 27 November 1922 was ratified by
the order on 21 November 1923. The re-opening of St Anthony's proved to be a
sensitive operation that required the agreement of the Belgian Franciscans and
Cardinal Mercier, archbishop of Mechlen (Malines). The Irish friars were to be
attached to the convent of St Anthony's. They undertook not to establish a
seraphic college (a minor seminary), a novitiate, or a branch of the Third Order
without the permission of the Belgian provincial. They also undertook to observe
the regulations of the Belgian province with respect to clerical dress and carrying
money. Six Irish friars were nominated to return to the re-founded college at
Louvain: Dominic Enright, Fidelis Griffin, Fridolin Fehilly, Flannán Ó Néill,
Roger Moloney and Barnabas McGahan. The Irish province agreed to provide
£8,000 for the re-building of the college. Dublin, St Isidore's in Rome and the
provincial each provided £1,000, with the balance coming from the remaining
Irish houses. [33] Fr Brendan Jennings, a distinguished historian, formerly a member
of the English province was appointed as the first guardian of St Anthony's
College, Louvain. The formal re-opening took place in 1927, which was the 310th
anniversary of the laying of the college's foundation stone by Archdukes Albert

33 *Chronicle I*, 21 November 1923, pp 491–4.

and Isabella in 1617 and the 500th anniversary of the founding of the University of Louvain in 1425. On 29 June 1927 the King and Queen of the Belgians and a distinguished group of cardinals and other clergy celebrated the 500th anniversary of the founding of the University of Louvain. The formal re-opening of St Anthony's College took place on the following day. The attendance included Cardinal O'Donnell, archbishop of Armagh, Cardinal Bourne, archbishop of Westminster, Mgr Ladeuze, rector of the university, and a number of American bishops. The Revd Hubert Quinn, the Irish provincial, remarked that it was very appropriate that the college should be re-opened by Cardinal O'Donnell, given the close links between the O'Donnell family and the founders of St Anthony's College.[34]

Louvain rapidly became an integral part of the scholarly formation of the Irish Franciscans. The junior seminary or seraphic college remained at Multyfarnham. By the late 1920s students there were sitting the Leaving Certificate and it was decided to permit the appointment of lay professors where necessary. The province made bursaries available to the seraphic college for students whose families could not meet the expense.[35] In 1937 a decision was taken to provide ten free places for boys aged 14–16 to be educated at the seraphic college with a view to becoming missionaries.[36] Novices entering the order initially went to Killarney where they were professed. In 1924 it was agreed that in future theology students would either go to St Anthony's where they would attend classes at the Catholic university at Louvain, or to St Isidore's, in which case they would study at the Gregorian university in Rome. In 1930 approval was given for a handball alley at Louvain '*pro pile manuali lusoria*'.[37] However the question of where or whether Franciscan students should take courses in the humanities remained unresolved. In 1909 the province opened St Anthony's Hostel in Cork to enable students to attend courses at University College Cork, but this experiment came to end when Nicholas Dillon became provincial. In 1926 approval was given for Finian Cronin to study at UCD. In February 1927 Eugene Hoade was permitted to go to Galway to take an arts degree. In November 1930 the Visitator General reported that the Franciscans had been invited '*alla Universita Cattolica di Galway*' and the following October it was decided to establish a student house in Galway, either in the Franciscan convent or an adjoining house, where young Franciscans could live and continue their theological studies while taking degrees at UCG. A call went out to all Irish Franciscan houses to send any books that could be spared from their libraries to supply the new student house.[38] When St Anthony's College,

34 *Irish Catholic Directory 1928*, 30 June 1927, pp 589–90.   **35** *Chronicle I*, 30 January 1929, p. 570.   **36** *Chronicle II*, 6–7 January 1937 definitory, p. 624.   **37** Ibid., 28 February 1930, p. 577.   **38** Ibid., 11 October 1931, p. 593.

Galway opened in the autumn of 1932 the pattern for the intellectual formation was now established: following a period of novitiate in Killarney, students would take philosophy or arts degrees at UCG before proceeding to Rome or Louvain for theological studies. Students who took an arts degree at UCG had to do a two-year course in philosophy before moving on to Rome. By the late 1930s a growing number of friars were taking post-graduate courses either at UCG, UCD or Louvain in disciplines such as mathematics, economics, philosophy, psychology, history and Celtic studies. St Anthony's, Louvain and St Isidore's, Rome allowed members of the province to have access to an international scholarly education and major research libraries, facilities that were all too scarce in the hard-pressed circumstances of the newly independent state. It is therefore not surprising that a growing number of Franciscans were appointed to academic posts in Irish universities from the late 1930s, beginning in 1936 with Felim Ó Briain as professor of philosophy at UCG.

THE SECOND WORLD WAR

The Second World War was a particularly difficult time for the province, given their extensive international connections. Restrictions on transferring money outside the state, imposed following the outbreak of war, meant that it was no longer possible to provide financial support for St Isidore's or St Anthony's. In September 1939 it was decided that no young students should be sent to Louvain or Rome and that all students in Louvain should move to Rome. St Anthony's College, Galway now assumed a critical role, as the base for students taking degrees at UCG, and a theological college substituting for Louvain and Rome.[39] The college was extended during the war to cope with the additional number of students. When German troops invaded Belgium in May 1940 there were four members of the Irish community in Louvain: Sylvester O'Brien, Hyacinth Nolan, Luke Burke and Didacus Connery. On 17 May Irish newspapers reported that they were among the refugees who landed in England and that the college was left in the charge of a Belgian servant and was later taken over by the university.

The Irish Franciscans who were studying in Rome when war broke out continued their studies and were ordained there, sending a blessing to their families in Ireland after their ordinations via Vatican Radio. In October 1941 Canice Mooney reported that the first of that year's ordinands had managed to reach Ireland after a journey that took them to Lisbon, Gibraltar and Liverpool. The remainder had arrived safely by the end of that month. In July 1942

---

39 Ibid., 3 September 1939, p. 4.

ordinations took place in Rome and in St Anthony's College, Galway. According to the *Irish Press* 'with few exceptions' this was the only group of Irish Franciscans to be ordained in Ireland since the destruction of Donegal Abbey at the beginning of the seventeenth century.[40] A number of friars became RAF chaplains. One, who had American citizenship by virtue of being born there, became a chaplain to the US army. Two members of the Irish province went on temporary transfer to England, where the province was under serious pressure because of the number who had enlisted as military chaplains. In November 1944 rumours reached Ireland that St Anthony's College, Louvain had been damaged in the conflict, but more re-assuring news came in February 1945 when Frs Cyril O'Mahony and Cyprian Davidson (both RAF chaplains), visited Louvain and reported that the college was in good condition. The Irish friars returned to Louvain in March 1946. In November 1942 press reports reached Ireland that the Franciscan missionaries in China were well and were carrying on their work unmolested by the Japanese. However a letter from China that reached Dublin in February 1945 reported that one Irish missionary was in Chinese-controlled territory. The remainder were positioned behind Japanese lines and most of the churches and mission property had been destroyed in the fighting.

Neutral Ireland was less disrupted by the war, although in June 1940 it was decided to move manuscripts, paintings and rare books from Merchants' Quay to Multyfarnham 'as the war is now next door to us'.[41] They were brought back in February 1945. In 1941, a dark period during the war, the province decided to ask the archbishop of Dublin for permission to open a new house of studies close to Dublin. The decision to embark on this project is a remarkable testimony to the order's resilience and faith in a brighter future.

Post-war renewal was active and focused. In June 1946 the Irish Provincial ordered each community to appoint someone who would be responsible for encouraging vocations. His message pointed out that the province had heavy commitments: a new mission in South Africa, where it was taking over from the Bavarian Franciscan community, plans for expanding its mission in China, and to act on the re-opening of a Franciscan house in Donegal. At the definitory meeting it was reported that approximately forty friars had volunteered to serve on the missions.[42] The decade following the ending of war saw many friars depart for South Africa. However, the mission to China ended following the communist victory. During the 1950s a number of Irish friars were sent on loan to Franciscan communities in the US. Fundraising in the US was used to finance Irish Franciscan missionary activities and a number of projects in Ireland, such as the new house at Rossnowlagh.

40 Ibid., 14 July 1942, pp 19–20. 41 Ibid., 29 June, 19 July 1940, p. 10. 42 Ibid., 29 June 1946, p. 56.

In December 1951 Canice Mooney reflected on the condition of the Irish province and concluded that

> It continues to progress in most domains. The building of the churches at Rossnowlagh and Cork proceeds apace. Many booklets and articles by friars have appeared in the course of the year and several broadcasts were given … Perhaps the domain that leaves most room for improvement is the important one of preaching. There is no outstanding preacher at present, though there are several who are good, some for missions some for retreats. Fr Athanasius Giblin is doing good work lecturing to workers in Limerick and Fr Felim Ó Briain is organizing study circles in Co. Mayo. Good examination results. Many Irish Franciscans are doing valuable education work abroad in South Africa, USA Australia and Near East. Fr Ivo O'Sullivan is in the Far East. Our Chinese mission is in a sorry plight. Fr Stephen White is the only missionary there now.[43]

GORMANSTON

The 1950s saw the province taking on a much more prominent role in Irish secondary education at a time when the numbers attending secondary schools were rising. The Irish province bought Gormanston Castle in the late 1940s – the novelist Evelyn Waugh had considered buying the property. Although the possibility of moving the secondary school to Gormanston was first discussed in 1949, the decision to erect a large secondary school catering for up to 400 boys at Gormanston was not taken until 1955. Multyfarnham had long been regarded as too small for the province's needs. The purpose-built modern school building attracted widespread media interest for its modern facilities. Gormanston soon became established, not simply as a premier boarding school, but as the location for many summer schools and study groups in Ireland of the 1960s. In 1956 a Limerick TD suggested that the order open an Irish-speaking secondary school in Foynes, an approach that was probably inspired by favourable reports about Gormanston. The suggestion was apparently referred to the provincial but did not go any further. In 1959 the order was asked to consider opening a school in Killiney, but again there is no indication that the suggestion was given serious consideration. Multyfarnham was transformed into an agricultural college, a decision that reflects the province's awareness of the importance that the government attached to agricultural education at the time. The appropriately

---

43 Ibid., 19 December 1951, pp 103–4.

named St Isidore's agricultural college (St Isidore is the patron saint of farmers) was officially opened in November 1956 by Minister for Agriculture James Dillon, the nephew of Fr Nicholas Dillon, who spent his last years in Multyfarnham. The Multyfarnham property was substantially extended the following year with the acquisition of Donore House and 600–700 acres of land, formerly owned by Sir Walter Nugent, member of an old Anglo-Norman catholic family and loyal patrons of the friars in the seventeenth century.

PASTORAL AND MISSIONARY WORK

The first half of the twentieth century marked the peak of formal observance of catholic religious practices in Ireland. This was not simply a matter of attendance at Sunday mass, Easter duties or other religious observances required by the church. The numbers engaged in non-mandatory observances such as pilgrimages, missions, membership of sodalities and other lay organizations reached an all-time high, and these events were widely reported in local and national newspapers. These formalized religious observances were most developed in cities and the larger towns, which were often the locations of important Franciscan houses. In 1944 an estimated 40–50,000 attended the annual blessing of throats on the feast of St Blaise (3 February), at Merchants' Quay.[44] Although the large turnout may have been boosted by a wartime rise in diphtheria cases, the numbers attending continued to rise long after this threat had passed. In 1956 newspapers reported that Merchants' Quay attracted 100,000 for the blessing of throats.[45] Other indulgences and feast days, such as the Portiuncula indulgence (celebrated on 3 August) attracted thousands to Multyfarnham and Merchants' Quay. The Third Order of St Francis had thousands of members in the cities and towns with Franciscan houses, providing the friars an extensive network of connections throughout Irish society. Similarly the sodalities and branches of St Vincent de Paul Society hosted by various Franciscan churches extended their network among the wider public. When the general election of January 1948 brought to an end sixteen years of Fianna Fáil governments, Canice Mooney noted that the new Taoiseach, John A. Costello was a member of the St Vincent de Paul conference attached to Merchants' Quay. Indeed one of the most striking features of Irish life during this period are the close personal relationships that existed between the order, and Ireland's political, business and cultural elite. The President and Taoiseach, together with other political leaders often attended landmark events such as the formal opening and dedication of Rossnowlagh on 29 June 1952.[46] The

44 Ibid., 4 February 1944, p. 30.   45 Ibid, 3 February 1956, p. 153.   46 *Irish Catholic Directory 1953*, 29

order's close connections with the first and second chairmen of CIE – Teddy Courtney the second chairman was a Franciscan tertiary – guaranteed the company's support for the sodality based at Merchants' Quay which was established in 1947 and which recruited CIE workers. This sodality published its own periodical, *Terminus* in which many scholarly historical articles were published by friars such as Canice Mooney. In 1956 the same sodality donated a large statue of the Virgin Mary, which was erected on the roof in Merchants' Quay. Merchants' Quay also hosted a sodality for hotel and catering workers, and for many years it supplied a chaplain to the Dublin Stage Guild, a connection which meant that the proceeds from many film premieres of the time, including *The Student Prince* (1955), *Interrupted Melody* (1956) and *South Pacific* (1958), went to support the Merchants' Quay building fund. In 1951, Fr Sylvester O'Brien the chaplain to the Dublin Stage Guild arranged for the rosary to be recited backstage in several Dublin theatres during the month of May.

Retreats and missions also formed a major part of the pastoral work of the friars. Pilgrimages were expressions of popular religious devotion, and opportunities for travel and sociability. The Third Order established especially close links with Knock where the pilgrimage season generally opened with the annual Third Order pilgrimage, which attracted crowds in excess of 8,000 during the mid-1950s. The Third Order also ran pilgrimages to Lough Derg, compensating for the dietary privations on the island by holding a reunion breakfast after the event. After the Second World War pilgrimages to Rome, Assisi, and Lourdes became regular features in Franciscan calendars. The Holy Year of 1950 was marked by a series of pilgrimages to Rome, some of which included visits to the Oberammergau passion play.

Members of the order were also actively in movements that promoted catholic social teaching, such as Muintir na Tíre rural weeks,[47] *An Rioghacht*, and wider public debates on issues such as education, late marriages and rural decline. The order also produced popular religious works for sale and distribution to the Irish laity. They included short biographies of Franciscan saints – SS Anthony and Francis – as well as a short biography of Paschal Robinson the first Irish papal nuncio. Fr Lucius McClean, who was based at Merchants' Quay became nationally known for his religious columns in the *Sunday Independent*. Members of the province frequently broadcast on Radio Éireann, most commonly on historical and cultural topics, but also on religious matters.

June 1952, p. 649.   **47** *Chronicle II*, August 10 1942, p. 20. Fergus Barrett speaking on rural education, *Standard*, 16 April 1943.

CELTIC STUDIES

By the 1940s the Irish Franciscans were increasingly identified with the study and transmission of the Irish language and Irish history. This was a remarkable achievement, because the order's scholarly work in these disciplines only resumed during the 1930s. Although St Anthony's College, Louvain was responsible for rescuing and preserving Irish history and culture throughout the seventeenth and eighteenth centuries, this intellectual tradition appears to have disappeared by the early nineteenth century. In 1819 Richard F. Walsh, who was responsible for rescuing the library at Louvain, lamented the loss of the tradition of scholarship in the Irish province. The Louvain manuscripts returned to Ireland in 1872, but although their importance was sufficiently recognized for them to be surveyed by the Historical Manuscripts Commission in 1906,[48] there is no evidence that members of the province were engaged in studying the manuscripts at this time, and no Irish Franciscan figures among the leading names in the revival of the Irish language at the beginning of the twentieth century.

The 1920s provide ample evidence, however, of the order's renewed interest in its historical and cultural heritage, best seen in the re-opening of St Anthony's College, Louvain and demands by the friars to attend Irish colleges in the Gaeltacht. The strong emphasis placed in the newly independent state on the recovery of Ireland's Gaelic heritage highlighted the importance of books and manuscripts held by the Irish Franciscans and the order's role as their custodian. In 1930 a decision was taken to conserve the manuscripts held in Merchants' Quay and plans were approved for *Analecta Franciscana Hibernica*, an edition of devotional texts written in the Irish language by Irish Franciscans in the seventeenth and eighteenth centuries.[49] It is hardly a coincidence that around the same time the definitory approved plans to open a house of studies in Galway, which would enable members of the province to take degrees at UCG, thus opening the way for future friars to become fluent in the Irish language since the university taught many of its degree programmes through Irish. A significant number of the Franciscan students who attended UCG took degrees in Celtic studies and Irish history with distinction, many advancing to master's and doctorates, either in UCG or at UCD. Within a remarkably short period the Irish Franciscans had re-established their tradition of scholarship in Irish history, language and culture, which had been lost for more than a century, and reclaimed their status as the religious order most closely identified with Gaelic Ireland. The key figures behind these developments were the provincial Fr Hubert Quinn, who had graduated with a degree in Christian archaeology in Rome, Fr Brendan

---

48 Corish, 'Dún Mhuire: fifty years' (1995), p. 2.   **49** *Chronicle II*, 28 February 1930, p. 577.

Jennings the first guardian of St Anthony's, Louvain in 1927, and Fr Felim
Ó Briain, who was the driving force behind *Analecta Franciscana Hibernica.*[50]
Felim Ó Briain, a native of Co. Mayo joined the Franciscan order at the age of 21,
apparently without any formal secondary schooling, after a number of years spent
'working hard on the land and on the bogs'. An obituary note by Canice Mooney
ranked him 'among the most outstanding members the Irish Franciscan province
has produced for the last hundred or two hundred years'. According to Canice
Mooney, Felim O'Brien planned to specialize in Irish ecclesiastical history and
editing *Analecta Franciscana Hibernica,* and to this end in the early 1930s he
embarked on a doctorate at Louvain. His thesis was a study of St Brigid. Before it
was complete he was recalled to Ireland to compete for the vacant chair of
philosophy at UCG, a post that he held for the next twenty years. Although he
was a fluent Irish speaker, he had no professional training in either old or modern
Irish, which handicapped his efforts to finish his planned book on St Brigid and
his edition of Bonaventure Ó hEodhasa catechism.[51] Yet his long presence in St
Anthony's, Galway, where he served for many years as master of students, enabled
him to promote Franciscan scholarship in these disciplines.

By the 1940s the order was increasingly identified with the Irish language.
Friars were in demand to preach in Irish and to act as chaplains for Irish summer
colleges. In 1943 Canice Mooney was among the speakers in the Mansion House
at an official commemoration of the Golden Jubilee of the founding of the Gaelic
League. Fergus Barrett became chairman of Comdháil Náisiunta na Gaeilge, a
new Irish language group in the same year. In 1940 the community at Merchants'
Quay organized an Irish-speaking pilgrimage by train to Knock where participants
included An Seabhac and Pádraig Óg Ó Conaire, civil servants, gardaí, university
lecturers and students. Radio Éireann gave extensive coverage to the pilgrimage,
broadcasting the Stations of the Cross in Irish, which were recited from the train, a
rendering of Caoineadh na dTrí Mhuire, and benediction in Irish from the shrine.

The scholarly credentials of the friars in history and Celtic studies were
increasingly being recognized with the appointment of Fr Brendan Jennings to
the Irish Manuscripts Commission and growing requests for lectures by members
of the province at Oireachtas na Gaeilge, the Irish Historical Society and local
historical societies. Members of the order were ubiquitous at the historical
commemorations throughout Ireland during these years, such as the centenary of
the death of Daniel O'Connell, marked in Derrynane, or in Cavan to mark the
tricentenary of the death of Owen Roe O'Neill. Felim Ó Briain officiated at a
mass at Tara to mark the 150th anniversary of the 1798 Rising there.

50 *Analecta Franciscana Hibernica, Antonianum,* 5 (1930), pp 396–400. **51** *Chronicle II,* 24 January 1957,
pp 172–5.

6 Seán T. Ó Ceallaigh and Brendan Jennings OFM (FLK).

The celebrations marking the 300th anniversary of the death of Mícheál Ó Cléirigh in 1943–4 gave prominent public recognition to the part played by the Irish Franciscans in recording and transmitting the history and culture of Gaelic Ireland. The commemorative events included the issuing of a commemorative stamp, various lectures and articles, including radio talks. Celebrations culminated in the weekend of 24–5 June 1944, with a commemorative mass, a banquet in the Gresham Hotel organized by the Donegal Men's Association, and a special concert in the Gaiety Theatre (lent free for the occasion by proprietor Louis Ellman because of the friars' close links with the Dublin Stage Guild). A packed house listened to premieres of three works in honour of the Four Masters, which were composed for the occasion by Aloys Fleichmann, Eamon Ó Gallachóir and Reamon Ó Frighil. These pieces were performed by the Radio Éireann orchestra and the new Radio Éireann choir, which was making its first public appearance. The speakers included Taoiseach Eamon de Valera, Professor Eoin Mac Neill and the provincial, Fr Evangelist MacBride. The evening's programme was broadcast live on Radio Éireann from 8p.m. to 11p.m. with an interval talk by Canice Mooney on Mícheál Ó Cléirigh. Canice Mooney claimed that 'Everybody was very pleased – except those who failed to secure tickets, and those who received worse tickets than they had expected!', although a letter appeared in the *Evening*

Mail some days later complaining about the large number of cars parked outside the theatre – at a time when there was an acute shortage of petrol![52]

The widespread national recognition of the significance of Mícheál Ó Cléirigh and the Four Masters highlighted the role of the friars in researching and promoting Gaelic scholarship. With the ending of the war in Europe, new scholarly opportunities were emerging. In 1945 Canice Mooney was dispatched to Spain on behalf of the National Library to investigate and copy manuscript holdings in Spanish libraries relating to the Irish overseas. The archives in Rome were also scoured for evidence relating to the history of the Irish Franciscans and the Irish overseas by several members of the order over the next ten years. In April 1946 Dr McQuaid, archbishop of Dublin, gave the Irish province permission to open what the *Irish Catholic Directory* described as 'a hostel', which would be used as 'a School of Celtic Studies by members of the order, and a permanent home of the valuable manuscripts held in Merchants Quay'. According to the *Irish Catholic Directory* the house in Killiney, re-named Dún Mhuire was 'in congenial surroundings, and will be adjacent to the city centre for the convenience of the student Fathers who wish to attend the university, the Dublin Institute for Advanced Studies or consult city libraries'.[53] The order had first sought permission for a house of study in the neighbourhood of 1941, when the provincial Fr Augustine O'Neill applied to the archdiocese of Dublin, only to be rejected by the diocesan chapter.[54] By the spring of 1946 Canice Mooney, Pádraig Ó Súilleabháin, Cuthbert McGrath and Br Matthew Taylor had moved to Killiney from Merchants' Quay, and they were soon joined by Bartholomew Egan, Anselm Faulkner and Cathaldus Giblin. Three of the group, Bartholomew Egan, Cuthbert McGrath and Anselm Faulkner, had been conferred with PhDs at UCG earlier in that year, and Canice Mooney had just been appointed as an assistant professor at the Dublin Institute for Advanced Studies. Irish was the common language at Dún Mhuire. Indeed, shortly after the new community assembled, a *seanchaí*, Pádraig Liam Mac Donnchada, alias Paddy Willy, was invited to join them for a week 'in order to improve our Irish'. In April 1947 Canice Mooney reflected on the new house where he and other members of the community had been in residence for two months:

> so far everything about the future, exact status, plan of studies policy for
> this house remains still vague and undetermined … It partakes of the
> nature of a residence for the minister provincial, a centre for various
> activities of individual friars, a holiday home, a convalescence home and a

---

52 Ibid., 24–25 June 1944, pp 32–3.   **53** *Irish Catholic Directory 1946.* diary 18 April 1945, p. 683.
54 *Chronicle II*, 11 July 1941, pp 15–16.

house of studies. Only the future can foretell which it will eventually become, or whether it will be found possible or advisable to combine these distinct aspects. Nor is it certain whether as a house of studies it is destined solely for those engaged on Irish language, literature and history, (as a recently erected plaque in the oratory implied, though using the not-too-happy expression Litterae Celticae) or whether those fathers engaged in various other totally different spheres of study will also be stationed here (as certain other facts would seem to suggest). It was thought that Irish would be the normal and official language of the community. To a degree that is still the position, but here, too, it is found that throughout force of circumstances, English frequently pushes Irish into the background – or down to one of the side tables.

Here is a case in which the contemporary chronicler remains less well-informed than the historian will be![55]

In the summer of 1947 Canice Mooney spent several weeks travelling in Roscommon, Leitrim, Kerry and Limerick collecting folklore about the friars. He also visited sites associated with the friars, including the reputed site of the first Irish Franciscan convent in Youghal and 'one of the most recent, the tragic St Anthony's Hall Cork, now the Honan hostel'. Reflecting on these entries, he went on to note that:

> This chronicle is growing rather egoistic, but it may have some provincial or historic interest to put on record that contact is being maintained with the old sites and some effort made to gather information about the friars of the penal days and their places of refuge and to find out how much information is available in the different friary archives for the history of the Irish Franciscans during the eighteenth and nineteenth centuries – a period that so far has been almost completely neglected.[56]

The scholarship produced at Dún Mhuire has already been documented in a commemorative volume published in 1995.[57] While centred on the historical and cultural contributions of the Irish Franciscans, it extended much more widely to include many aspects of Irish history and culture, and religious writings. The year 1958 saw the first issue of *Collectanea Hibernica*, an annual scholarly publication of collections of documents on Irish ecclesiastical history under the general

55 Ibid., 22 April 1946, p. 50. **56** Ibid., 19 August 1946, pp 58–9. **57** Millett & Lynch, *Dún Mhuire*, (1995) includes a comprehensive bibliography of works published by members of the Dún Mhuire

editorship of Benignus Millett.[58] Members of the order were very active in the Irish Catholic Historical Society, and in 1958 Canice Mooney, Cathaldus Giblin and Benignus Millett were asked to contribute to a projected three-volume *History of Irish Catholicism*, which with the approval of the Irish hierarchy was placed under the general editorship of Revd Patrick Corish, Maynooth. Canice Mooney was appointed as a member of the editorial committee.[59]

The celebrations in 1957 to mark the tercentenary of the death of Luke Wadding exceeded the commemoration of Mícheál Ó Cléirigh in 1944. There was a commemorative stamp, many public lectures, lunches and dinners, the unveiling of busts and statues and two series of special ceremonies in Rome, one at St Isidore's on St Patrick's Day, which was attended by the President of Ireland, and further celebrations in October when most of the Irish bishops and members of the government were present. The city of Waterford conferred the freedom of the city on the Minister General of the order, Fr Augustine Stepinski. During the week of 17 March, Dublin's Theatre Royal staged 'A Pageant in Green', a series of living tableaux of events in the life of Luke Wadding. Fr Felix Butler, definitor and rector of Gormanston College was invited to throw in the ball at the Railway Cup match in Croke Park on St Patrick's Day in honour of Luke Wadding. A special concert in the Gaiety in October saw the premiere of a specially-composed *Salve Maria* in honour of Luke Wadding by Seoirse Bodley. Radio Éireann broadcast a play about Luke Wadding written by Teresa Deevy, which was subsequently staged in St Anthony's Hall at Merchants' Quay. Canice Mooney described the play as 'a good dramatization of a difficult subject', though he also noted that there were a lot of errors in the story. March 1958 saw the release of a documentary film 'Luke Wadding – the man who invented St Patrick', narrated by Eamonn Andrews, then one of the leading personalities on BBC television. Canice Mooney noted that it was 'titled (rather unhappily), with an eye to the American and English audiences, especially around St Patrick's Day'. It would be shown in most cinemas along with the film *Rooney*, the story of a Dublin dustman who was a champion hurler.[60]

The early 1960s brought renewed interest and concern with regard to the Irish language, concerns prompted by the succession of Sean Lemass as Taoiseach in place of Eamon de Valera. Lemass had little knowledge of Irish and little evident interest. His focus on economic growth was also seen as a threat to the Irish language and culture. The long-awaited report of the Commission on the restoration of the Irish language, which appeared in 1964, also added to the tensions. The Irish Franciscans were widely seen as playing a major role in the

community. **58** *Chronicle II*, 12 September 1958, p. 205. **59** Ibid., 19 July 1958, p. 202. **60** Ibid., 13 March 1958, p. 197. Additional details about *Rooney* courtesy of P.J. Daly.

renewal of the Irish language. The President of Conradh na Gaeilge commended the order for its role in introducing modern language teaching methods for Irish, a reference to the work of Fr Colmán Ó hUallacháin. Some months later Fr Ó hUallacháin was commissioned by the Minister for Education, Patrick Hillery to produce a new Irish language textbook that would drive the revival of the language using modern teaching methods.[61] A blunter, but perhaps a more significant, compliment to the order's role with respect to Irish language and culture came from the Irish writer Máirtín Ó Cadhain in an article published in *Feasta* in June 1962 when he stated that 'only for the Friars Minor there would hardly be any Ireland today!' He expressed hopes that 'the Holy Ghost would inspire the bishops to hand over the sad remnants of today's Gaeltacht to the care of the Franciscans'.[62]

The ultimate tribute to the order's centrality in the history and culture of the new state came in September 1962 when President Eamon de Valera decided to transfer his private papers to Dún Mhuire. The legal document was executed in October 1962, and the first batch of papers was brought to Dún Mhuire by Benignus Millett and Canice Mooney.

CONCLUSION

During the second half of the nineteenth century the Catholic church and the Catholic religious orders re-established a public presence throughout Ireland, but one that co-existed with a state that continued to be dominated by a protestant culture. The position was transformed in 1922 with the founding of the Irish Free State. In the decades that followed, the Catholic church, the Irish state and the overwhelming majority of the Irish people shared a common religious and cultural heritage, and this shared tradition is very evident in the story of the Irish Franciscans. The order made a significant contribution to re-establishing scholarship and learning relating to Ireland's Gaelic, Catholic heritage through the work carried out in Dún Mhuire, and the involvement of the order in the Dublin Institute for Advance Studies, UCG and other academic institutions. At the same time the Irish OFM houses in Rome and Louvain and OFM missions in China, Africa and the US maintained the order's traditional international outlook at a time when the new Irish state had not yet fully established its presence in the wider world.

61 *Chronicle II*, 12 February 1962, p. 252.   **62** Ibid., 6 October 1962, pp 259–60.

Recovering the charism, 1963–90

JOSEPH MAC MAHON OFM

The Second Vatican Council, which ended on 8 December 1965, left in its wake rather hazy hopes and dreams of new beginnings in the church. The Council had given its blessing to a shift from an understanding of the church and its ministry centred on institution and hierarchy to a renewed understanding based on mystery and service in the context of an increasingly pluralist world.[1] It invited religious institutes to a renewal of its members by rediscovering the gospel and the original inspiration of their founders.[2] For Franciscans this entailed the task of re-examining how St Francis of Assisi understood and lived the gospel in order to discover their own special character and purpose. Consequently, while continuing to respond to pastoral needs in a rapidly changing society, the history of the next three decades of the Irish Franciscans was a search for a renewed identity and vision, an understanding of who they are and what they ought to be doing in the light of their founding inspiration.[3] This search was not easy and there were many different and indeed conflicting views. It was far easier to respond to the new needs as they arose and in a sense these responses reflected how the friars saw themselves and their role in church and society at the time.

1960s: LITURGY, COMMUNICATION AND INSTITUTIONAL REFORM

Most of the changes initiated by the friars in response to Vatican II during the 1960s were of a practical nature touching on the liturgy (such as the setting up of temporary altars in the churches, the introduction of evening masses, the use of the vernacular and the relaxation of the laws governing the recitation of the divine office and other prayer practices), the gradual adjustments of their practices and customs to the changed conditions of the times (such as the wearing of clerical dress and the use of money), and an effort at improved communication and consultation among the friars. Two far more significant reforms, however, because they touched on the life and self-understanding of the friars, were the

---

1 Vatican II, *Dogmatic constitution on the church (Lumen gentium).* 2 Vatican II, *Decree on the appropriate renewal of the religious life (Perfectae caritatis),* n.2. 3 The following internal Irish Franciscan sources were consulted: *Chronicle of the Province of Ireland of the Friars Minor, 24 November 1963–8 July 1985; Proceedings of the Provincial Chapters of 1969–1990 with accompanying documentation; Acta Definitorii Provinciae Hiberniae, 1963–1990; Seanchas na mBráithre, 1961–1990; Definitory News, 1981–1990; Communications, 1967–1990; Franciscan News, 1988–1990;* various documents from the Provincial Office, La Verna, Gormanston.

establishment of community chapters in each house which, it was hoped, would help build fraternity and promote common projects, and changing the status of the lay friars.[4] Francis had welcomed into his fraternity men of every social and ecclesial status and all had shared the same rights and responsibilities as 'lesser brothers', but not long after his death it had been transformed into a clerical order so that the lay friars became a separate 'class' and were regarded as being at the service of the priest friars. Accordingly these reforms were intended as the first steps in moulding the order into a more fraternal fellowship, offering humble service to each other and to the wider world. The province changed its legislation to grant all friars the same rights, except those arising from holy orders, in local and provincial chapters. It was an easy matter to change the laws but it would take much longer before mindsets were altered and it would take years before a joint formation programme for both cleric and lay friars was established. Special attention was given to improving internal communication within the province and in 1961 an in-house newsletter, *Seanchas na mBráithre*, was established with the intention of disseminating news of what was happening in the province. A supplement to *Seanchas*, called *Communications*, was added in 1967 to carry the many official documents that were coming from the general curia and the provincial office dealing with renewal.

It was only in 1967 that the first major step in forging a new self-under-standing was taken when the general chapter in May of that year focused on the topic of Franciscan life and agreed a draft of new general constitutions which provided guidelines and directions for the renewal and adaptation of the order. The fruit of this examination was communicated to the Irish friars later in the year but absorbing this and translating it into reality would take time. Meanwhile a consultation process was initiated to seek the views of the friars in preparation for an extraordinary provincial chapter to be held in August 1968. At the chapter particular emphasis was placed on the formation of candidates 'in the context of the Franciscan ideal' but most attention was devoted to the apostolate and a plea was made for the friars to be trained in catechetics, youth work, counselling and the media; for specialized groups to update them in theology, liturgy and pastoral ministry; for friars to work with engaged couples, the unemployed and the badly housed. This was a long 'wish list' and some friars were sent for training in the above mentioned areas, but there was also frequent mention of lack of manpower even though there were eighty-six priests involved in friary ministry and another fifty-six in education in Ireland.[5] Large numbers of candidates had been entering the province up to the mid-1960s and with a steady stream of young men being

---

4 See *Seanchas na mBráithre*, 5:1 (1966), pp 1–2 for instructions on the formation of the lay friars issued by the general curia.   **5** *Acts of the Extraordinary Provincial Chapter 1968*.

added to the manpower pool there was a lot of vigour and enthusiasm about. Significant numbers had been allocated to pastoral ministry in the local friary churches, to the missions in South Africa and the then Southern Rhodesia and to education, particularly to the staffing of Gormanston College. A few had been sent to pursue post-graduate studies. New avenues of activity began to open. A strong missionary zeal had been characteristic of the province and new missions were accepted in Chile and El Salvador (1968); the first Simon Community shelter was established in the friary grounds at Merchants' Quay as were tea rooms for the poor in 1969; friars became chaplains to Irish emigrants in Britain, including Irish-speaking ones in the London area, and others were supplied as religion teachers to vocational schools in Dublin and Drogheda; a language institute was built at Gormanston in 1965 and two years later it was granted the status of the National Language Institute by the government; and a centre for former students of Gormanston attending University College Dublin was built in Donnybrook. Friars continued to contribute to scholarship in Celtic studies, Irish history, classics, philosophy, biblical studies, theology, sociology and theoretical physics.

Numerically the province reached its high water mark in 1965 with a total membership of 428 but already in 1964 the first signs of a change were showing when only seven candidates for the clerical state entered the novitiate, a considerable drop in numbers. From this time forward not only would the numbers entering be lower, though they were still adequate to meet existing needs, but fewer would stay the course. In 1965 fourteen novices were accepted for the clerical state and only two of these were eventually ordained. The problem at the time was not so much in attracting candidates but in keeping them. The fall out reflected both the upheaval taking place in society in general and the inadequate formation system in the province which caused unrest among younger friars who felt that the pace of reform was far too slow. For all that, at the end of the decade the minister general pronounced the province to be in a healthy state but encouraged communities to be more diligent in holding community chapters 'so that renewal appropriate to our time ... may be advanced prudently and firmly in accordance with Vatican II.'[6]

1970S: REFORMS, NEW PARISHES AND MISSIONARY ACTIVITY

The momentum of reform continued during the 1970s. Work on the adaptation and renovation of church sanctuaries went on.[7] Fact-finding commissions were

6 *Seanchas na mBráithre*, 8:2–3 (1969), pp 1–2.   7 A good example of this can be seen in the friary church

set up to examine the home apostolate, formation, teaching and post-graduate studies, and the foreign missions and to report on how these might be improved. The province accepted its first parishes in recent times when the friary church in Galway was given the status of a parish church in February 1971, followed by Merchants' Quay and the new parish of Ballywaltrim, Bray, both in 1974. In the same year the Irish friars in Leuven became official chaplains to the English-speaking Catholics in Brussels. A new agricultural college was built at Multyfarnham. There was a wide variety of activity which, apart from the traditional friary ministry, included such diversity as chaplaincies to CIE employees, hotel workers in the Dublin area, Catholic Boy Scouts and hospitals as well as adult education, social work, counselling and lecturing in the Dublin School of Speech Therapy. Overseas, the province withdrew from its mission in Chile in 1977 and a handful of friars went to Bolivia and California. The struggle for independence in Southern Rhodesia seriously disrupted missionary life and some friars were forced to leave the country. In early 1971 the Province accepted the de Valera papers which were housed in Killiney.[8] Two friars moved out of Merchants' Quay friary and into a flat in Benburb St in Dublin with the intention of getting closer to the people.

Apart from the activity, and there was much of it, the focus of debate began to shift from the external changes to the internal conversion of mind and heart requested by Vatican II. On the occasion of its general chapter in 1973, Pope Paul VI challenged the order to define its specific vocation in the contemporary world and its role in the church.[9] The questions being asked in the 1960s – 'what are we doing and how can we do it better' – changed in the 1970s to 'who are we and what are we supposed to be doing in the light of our Franciscan identity?'[10] This resulted in a lot more, and sometimes heated, debate during the decade and into the 1980s which would lead to a degree of polarization between those who were accused of wanting to jettison many of the distinguishing external marks of the Franciscans so as to be more 'relevant' and those who were regarded by their opponents as trying to resist the adaptation called for by the Council. Much of the debate was driven by the new ideas current at the time. Franciscan scholars had begun to produce critical editions of the writings of St Francis and the early Franciscans which showed how the order had become clericalist and to a degree had moved away from the saint's ideal of his followers being a community of simple and humble brothers 'intent on serving God and doing good works'.[11]

at Multyfarnham.   **8** For a list of the published writings of the Killiney friars see Millett & Lynch (eds), *Dún Mhuire Killiney* (1995).   **9** *General Chapter documents Madrid 1973* (1974), p. 2.   **10** See for example, *Seanchas na mBráithre* 13 (1974). Beginning in 1973 the enumeration sequence of *Seanchas na mBráithre* changed from volume to numbers.   **11** *Regula non Bullata*, vii; also W.J. Short, *The Franciscans* (1989), pp

Running alongside this seismic change in Franciscan self-understanding were new and sometimes bewildering ideas on theological topics, especially on ecclesiology as promoted by liberation theology, leading to a debate on the notion of ministry: was it to be limited mainly to that exercised in friary churches, principally sacramental, or should there be greater diversity?[12] In particular the priest-friars were faced with a changing model of priesthood. No longer was the well-defined pre-Vatican II model of priesthood fully acceptable, but now they had to work out how ministerial activity was to be conducted in a different world and in a way that would be consistent with their Franciscan identity. The friars responded to these changes and to events and ideas coming from the secular sphere (the struggle for justice and human rights, for example) with varying degrees of enthusiasm or revulsion, depending on the individual's stance. During the decade the call at provincial chapters was for a greater sense and practice of brotherhood, a deepening of community living and the use of the community chapter as a vital tool in improving pastoral ministry.[13] The last provincial chapter of the decade set out the priorities for the following three years: a deeper awareness of the Franciscan vocation, a clearer sense of direction and an increased capacity for effective service.[14] The visitator general challenged the friars to listen to the contemporary voices and trends in a changing Ireland, to articulate their mission and set measurable goals, to regard vocations and formation as the highest priority (numbers continued to drop) and to train guardians how to conduct community chapters. As a result of such demands serious efforts at planning followed during the 1980s and beyond.

1980s: NEW INITIATIVES AND RECOVERING THE CHARISM

Beginning in autumn 1980, a series of regional meetings were held to consider specific areas of concern in preparation for the chapter of 1981. Twelve areas were identified and corresponding long-term goals were agreed which would set the desired direction. The number of goals was later reduced to eight and included community life, justice and peace, missionary apostolate, ongoing formation, pastoral planning, prayer, preaching (missions and retreats) and youth and married couples. There was a high level of agreement with the plan but a low level of implementation. The response to it was met by personal and community inertia and a reluctance to make the choices it demanded and the risks associated with it. There was also a creeping feeling that the church in Ireland was becoming

133–4. **12** For example, see issues of *Seanchas na mBráithre* (1984). **13** *Proceedings of the Provincial Chapter 1972*, N. 22: Closing address. **14** *Proceedings of the Provincial Chapter 1978*, Report no. 7.

less relevant to the needs of the people and that the certainties of the past were beginning to crumble. Many friars felt themselves unqualified to address social issues in their preaching. It is little wonder that morale was beginning to wane somewhat because of these factors, as well as falling numbers in the province due to death, departures from the order and the decline in vocations. The last mentioned cause was graphically illustrated by the withdrawal during the decade from the colleges in Galway and Louvain which had been important centres of formation over the previous decades.

New initiatives were still being undertaken: two new parishes, Mell (Drogheda) and Ballinfoyle (Galway) were entrusted to the friars; the province acquired new bases in Belfast and Bray; Drogheda and Wexford friaries were extensively refurbished and the Galway Ministry Centre was set up in 1985 as a response to young people's need to do something for themselves. The friars at Merchants' Quay became aware of the drug problem and related issues and this eventually led to the creation of a project for people affected by drug use and HIV. But despite this evidence of vigour there was no hiding the fact that more radical measures were needed in order to respond to the three elements highlighted by the general chapter of the order of 1985 as essential to the recovery of the charism: the contemplative dimension, the 'option for the poor' through justice and peace activities and the formation of a missionary spirit. A major programme of ongoing formation, both in relation to personal human development and pastoral ministry and a more appropriate ecclesiology were needed. The quality of community life had no chance of improving until the human and spiritual growth of the individual friar was promoted. The topics of personal and community life-styles, poverty and the option for the poor clamoured for attention, and there was even a desire on the part of some to live a more radical and simple Franciscan way of life, 'a witness for genuine communities of poor and prayerful men of faith.'[15] Adding to the sense of urgency was an increasing reluctance among some younger friars to be part of the traditional friary ministry because it appeared to them to be out of touch with reality and instead they wanted to work in more challenging and relevant ministries.[16] The formation system in their view was merely training young friars to fit into already existing structures and ministries rather than preparing them to meet the challenges of the 'new' Ireland. It was even claimed that some candidates were leaving the formation programme because service of the poor was no longer a priority in the life of the province.[17]

It was clear from the debate that while the friars had a clearer notion of their identity they had not as yet charted a new direction for themselves. Brave efforts

---

15 *Seanchas na mBráithre* 98 (1982).   **16** See *Seanchas na mBráithre* 143 (1988).   **17** *Seanchas na mBráithre*

had been made to define their role in a rapidly changing Ireland but there was no common ground on what should be done to match the new reality. Learning from past attempts a new effort was launched at the 1987 provincial chapter which included the essential ingredient of implementation at individual, community and provincial levels.[18] A major exercise in consultation of the friars took place and in 1989 concrete decisions covering ten topics emerged from the process: ongoing formation, prayer, individual and community development, justice and peace, the marginalized, lay involvement and the Secular Franciscan Order, lifestyles, buildings, structures, visitation, communication, education, youth and sacramental and non-sacramental ministry.[19] These decisions, which would determine the agenda of the province for the next decade, were to be implemented by fixed dates and were intended to move the friars towards renewal.

CONCLUSION

Over the course of the three decades the friars had set out to forge a new identity and direction for themselves based on a renewed understanding of the Franciscan charism while at the same time attempting to respond to the new pastoral needs. Creating a new self-understanding is always a difficult undertaking and the task for the friars was not made easier in that it had to be done in a context in which so much self-questioning was taking place and when so much social change was happening. But the friars held steady. In its observations on the state of the province at the end of the 1980s the general definitory or council identified positive elements: a satisfactory level of religious observance, a good fraternal atmosphere, proper care for the elderly friars and service in many ministries.[20] However, manpower continued to decline and by 1990 the membership stood at 244, a decrease of nearly 200 in less than thirty years, though some of the decrease can be accounted for by the transfer of Irish friars to the newly independent entities in South Africa and Central America. But after three decades they possessed a clearer idea of the essential elements of the Franciscan life: life with God, life in fraternity and a life of service of others, especially of the poor, and doing all this after the manner of their founder who had instructed them in his rule: 'let them be meek, peaceful and unassuming, gentle and humble, speaking courteously to everyone, as is becoming.'[21] The challenge as they faced into the new millennium was how to make this a reality.

142–4 (1988).   **18** *Planning and renewal process* (1988).   **19** *Decisions which emerged from the meetings in Multyfarnham, June 1989, on ten topics.*   **20** *Seanchas na mBráithre* 140 (1988).   **21** *Regula Bullata*, iii.

The Poor Clare Order in Ireland

BERNADETTE CUNNINGHAM

The first Irish convent of Franciscan nuns of the Second Order, better known as the Poor Clares, is believed to have been established in Dublin about the feast of St Anthony of Padua in summer 1629.[1] While there are some tantalizing references to convents of Franciscan nuns in Ireland in the pre-Reformation period there is no clear evidence of any Poor Clare foundations.[2] The earliest history of the Poor Clare Order in Ireland, which consists of the memoir written in the 1670s by Mother Mary Bonaventure Browne, opens with an account of the Poor Clare convent established in Dublin in the 1620s.[3] While Mother Bonaventure's memoir dates the arrival in Dublin of the Irish Poor Clares to 'about the year 1625',[4] the accepted date for the arrival of the order in Dublin is 1629.[5]

FROM GRAVELINES TO DUBLIN, 1607–31

The six Irish women who comprised the first Poor Clare community in Dublin had joined the order in Gravelines in the diocese of Ypres in the Spanish Netherlands where an English convent had been founded by Mary Ward in 1607.[6] The community there lived under the Rule of St Clare, one of the strictest rules in the church. In the early years Jesuit confessors were appointed to the Gravelines community, and an Irish Jesuit, Henry Fitzsimon, was among those who played a role in encouraging Irish women to join convents overseas.[7]

---

1 Giblin, *Liber Lovaniensis*, p. 7. Various versions of the chronicle of the order, derived from the 1670s memoir of Mother Mary Bonaventure Browne, give 1625 as the date of the first Dublin foundation, but this date appears to be incorrect (Galway, Poor Clare Convent, Chronicle of Mother Mary Bonaventure Browne; Dublin, Poor Clare Convent, Harold's Cross, 'Register 3', consulted on NLI microfilm P3500). 2 D. Hall, *Women and the church in medieval Ireland* (2003), pp 90–1; on devotion to St Clare in medieval Ireland see Ó Clabaigh, 'The cult of St Francis' (2006), p. 153. 3 Galway, Poor Clare Convent, Chronicle of Mother Mary Bonaventure Browne, pp 1–15. C. O'Brien (ed.), *Recollections of an Irish Poor Clare* (1993), is a modernized version of pp 1–15 of this manuscript. I acknowledge the kind assistance of Sister M. Louis O'Donovan and of Dr Colmán Ó Clabaigh OSB in arranging access to the archive of the Poor Clares in Galway. 4 O'Brien, *Recollections of an Irish Poor Clare*, p. 1. Mother Bonaventure was generally imprecise about dates, and was writing in retrospect in the 1670s. She did not have first-hand knowledge of the earliest years of the order in Ireland. 5 Giblin, *Liber Lovaniensis*, p. 7; Thomas Strange to Luke Wadding, 4 Aug. 1629, in Jennings, *Wadding Papers*, p. 307. 6 P. Guilday, *The English Catholic refugees on the Continent* (1914), pp 28–9, 166; M.C.E. Chambers, *The life of Mary Ward* (1882–7). The link with the Gravelines convent was still remembered in the nineteenth century, and an account of its destruction by fire in May 1654 is preserved among the papers of the order in Ireland (NLI microfilm P3500). 7 J. Brady, 'Keeping the faith at Gormanston, 1569–1929' (1957), pp 408–10.

Following the foundation of a house of English Franciscan friars at Douai in 1618 the Poor Clares were placed under their jurisdiction.[8] According to the surviving register of the English Poor Clares at Gravelines, the first Irish woman to be professed there was Martha Cheevers on 25 December 1620, at the age of 21. Others followed in the next few years.[9] The high number of female religious attracted to the Gravelines convent necessitated expansion to other venues, and the Irish members of the community moved to Dunkirk in 1626 and on to Nieuport in 1627 where their confessor was the Irish Franciscan Fr Robert Rochford.[10] Two years later, encouraged perhaps by the revival of Franciscan activity in Ireland, the group decided that improved circumstances for Catholics in Ireland in the reign of King Charles I were such that a move to Ireland was a realistic option. The Dublin convent of the Poor Clares was accepted into the Irish Franciscan province on 15 August 1629 during the provincial chapter held at Limerick in that year. Fr Bonaventure Dillon, a Franciscan who was a relative of the abbess, was appointed their confessor.[11]

The Irish women who had joined the Poor Clares in Gravelines, and who subsequently returned to Ireland to establish a convent in Dublin, were all of Old English origin, but from a number of different parts of Ireland. The six were named in Mother Bonaventure Browne's memoir as 'Sister Mary Joseph and Sister Cecily Francis, daughters of Viscount Dillon of Costello, Sister Martha Mariana [Cheevers] of the highest stock in Wexford, Sister Magdalen Clare Nugent, daughter of an important gentleman, Sister Mary Peter [Dowdall], a native of Dublin, and Sister Brigid Anthony Eustace'.[12] The explicit reference to the high social status of Cheevers and Nugent was probably deemed unnecessary in the case of the Dillon sisters, whose family was well known. Their brother, Sir Lucas Dillon, was a member of the Irish privy council.[13] Their father, Theobald Dillon, originally from the barony of Kilkenny West, Co. Westmeath, had gained considerable prosperity as a political agent and land speculator in late sixteenth-century Connacht, and by the early seventeenth century owned vast tracts of land in Roscommon and Mayo.[14] By 1622 he was able to purchase the title Viscount Dillon of Costello Gallen, which helped confirm his enhanced status in Connacht society.[15] Theobald Dillon and his wife, Eleanor Tuite, had a large

8 Guilday, *English Catholic refugees on the Continent*, p. 287. 9 W.M. Hunnybun (ed.), 'Registers of the English Poor Clares at Gravelines' (1914), pp 34–5; Brady, 'Keeping the faith at Gormanston, 1569–1929', p. 410. 10 Mrs T. Concannon, *The Poor Clares in Ireland* (1929), pp 8–9. 11 Giblin, *Liber Lovaniensis*, p. 7; Concannon, *The Poor Clares in Ireland*, pp 10–12. Fr Bonaventure Dillon OFM, whose baptismal name was Christopher, was son of James Dillon (Jennings, *Louvain papers*, p. 57). 12 O'Brien, *Recollections of an Irish Poor Clare*, p. 1. 13 Concannon, *The Poor Clares in Ireland*, p. 15. 14 B. Cunningham, 'Theobald Dillon: a newcomer in sixteenth-century Mayo' (1986); Cunningham & Gillespie, *Stories from Gaelic Ireland*, pp 59–86; L. Cox, 'The Dillons, lords of Kilkenny West: part one' (2000), pp 71–87. 15 HMC, *Eighth report* (1881), appendix 2, p. 30.

family of eight sons and eleven daughters, who were reared as Catholics. Two of their sons, Edward and George, studied at Douai and became Franciscan priests,[16] and two daughters, Ellen and Cecilia joined the Poor Clares at Gravelines.[17] Their mother, Eleanor Tuite, who died on 8 April 1638 at Killinure, Co. Westmeath, was buried in the Franciscan monastery at Athlone.[18] The Dillons were also known for providing safe places in which Catholic clergy could reside in Meath and Westmeath.[19] Like the other Catholic Old English families whose daughters joined the Poor Clares, the Dillons enjoyed above average prosperity and would have encountered little difficulty in providing generous dowries for their daughters. The social status of others of the Poor Clare community was affirmed by the lord deputy who observed that when the mayor of Dublin went to arrest the occupants of the Dublin convent on 22 October 1630, he found 'sixteen of prime noblemen and gentlemen's daughters therein'.[20]

It is known that the initial Dublin foundation expanded rapidly with twelve postulants joining the community based at Merchants' Quay or nearby Cook Street. Their residence was located close to that of the Franciscan friars, 'in whose dangers and persecutions they shared'.[21] That proximity was symbolic of the close links between the Franciscan friars and the Poor Clares at a familial and a community level, links that were essential to the viability of the Poor Clares in Ireland. However, within two years the entire convent had relocated to a much more secluded rural location in the townland of Ballinacliffey, near Athlone, Co. Westmeath, on land owned by the Dillon family on the shores of Lough Ree. The place selected was given the name Bethlehem and a convent was built there, where the community resided for over ten years. The precise date of the establishment of a convent there is undocumented, but it is thought to have been in 1630 or 1631. The close links between the Poor Clares and the Franciscan community continued, the guardian of the Franciscan friary at Killinure, near Athlone, having a particular responsibility for the Poor Clare convent.[22] It is probably no coincidence that the guardian of the friary at Killinure in 1630 was yet another Dillon, Revd George Dillon.[23]

---

16 Jennings, *Louvain papers*, p. 72n.   17 J. Lodge, *Peerage of Ireland*, revised by M. Archdall (1789), iv, pp 182–9; Concannon, *The Poor Clares in Ireland*, p. 9.   18 Lodge, *Peerage of Ireland*, iv, pp 179–80.   19 R.J. Hunter, 'Catholicism in Meath, c.1622' (1971), p. 9.   20 A.B. Grosart (ed.), *The Lismore papers* (1886), iii, p. 106, cited in Concannon, *The Poor Clares in Ireland*, p. 18. The houses of all religious orders in Dublin, of which there were about ten, had been raided by the authorities on St Stephen's Day, 1629 (Brady, 'Keeping the faith', p. 412).   21 [Anon], 'History of the Franciscan Order in Ireland' (1896–7), p. 354. 22 Galway, Poor Clare Convent, MS A 1, profession of Sr Catherine of St Francis Browne was signed by Fr Patrick Plunkett, the guardian at Athlone. Killinure was the location of the temporary refuge of the Athlone friars.   23 In his capacity as guardian of the Athlone friary, he witnessed the completion of the Four Masters' work on the genealogies of saints and kings on 4 November 1630 (UCD-OFM, MS A16, f. xiii r). George Dillon was son of Theobald, and thus brother to Ellen and Cecilia Dillon (Jennings, *Louvain papers*, p. 57).

BETHLEHEM, ATHLONE TO GALWAY, 1631–52

Among the acquaintances of George Dillon who visited the Bethlehem convent during these years was the Franciscan scholar Mícheál Ó Cléirigh who made a transcript of an Irish version of the Rule of St Clare, in October 1636, for the use of the nuns.[24] The initial Irish translation had been made by two priests, Aodh Ó Raghallaigh and Séamus Ó Siaghail, and although the patronage of Toirdhealbhach Mac Cochláin is unacknowledged in this specific instance, the Ó Siaghail family were among those known to have enjoyed his patronage. Thus, it seems that the Poor Clares at Bethlehem had direct contact with the network of scholars and patrons cultivated by the Franciscans in that region.[25] That an Irish rather than an English version of the Rule of St Clare was in demand in the 1630s is an indication that at least some of these women from the Old English community in Ireland were more at home with that language.

The Bethlehem convent prospered for a number of years, and a daughter house was established in the town of Drogheda, Co. Louth, in 1641.[26] That proved to be a short-lived venture, however, because of the political instability of the mid-century.[27] The outbreak of rebellion in Ireland in 1641 had repercussions for the order and in 1642 the Poor Clares were forced to abandon not just their newly established convent in Drogheda but also the rural foundation at Bethlehem. The community was dispersed, some going to Wexford, Waterford, Sligo and Longford, while others from the Bethlehem convent remained with their local patron Toirdhealbhach Mac Cochláin, and yet others sought the protection of Sir Lucas Dillon, the politically influential brother of two of the nuns.[28] In January 1643 'in view of the disturbance of the times' permission was granted by the Franciscan provincial, Fr Anthony Geoghegan, to the Bethlehem community to found a convent at Galway.[29] Indeed, such a move had been considered even before the outbreak of rebellion in October 1641. A letter from Fr Valentine Browne to Hugh de Burgo dated 29 August 1641 observed that 'There are of the town and county of Galway religious Clares, and do intend to go from

---

24 Ó Cléirigh's manuscript, which was subsequently added to by Dubhaltach Mac Fhirbhisigh, survives as the opening part of RIA MS D i 2; for an edition, see E. Knott (ed.), 'An Irish seventeenth-century translation of the Rule of St Clare' (1948).   **25** On Franciscan patronage networks in the 1620s and 1630s, see B. Cunningham, 'The making of the Annals of the Four Masters' (2005), chap. 9.   **26** Lords Justice and Council to Secretary Vane, 30 June 1641, *Cal. S.P. Ire., 1633–47*, p. 307.   **27** Luke Netterville commented that 'were it not for some friars and nuns in that town [Drogheda] they would fire that town', 1641 Depositions, Co. Meath, TCD MS 816, f. 35.   **28** Galway, Poor Clare Convent, MS A3. Copy of a letter from a member of the Galway community, presumably Mother Cecily Dillon, dated 27 September 1642, the original of which was formerly in St Isidore's College, Rome; O'Brien, *Recollections of an Irish Poor Clare*, pp 10–18.   **29** Galway, Poor Clare Convent, MS A2, Licence to found in Galway. The document is signed by Fr Anthony Geoghegan, and since the date 30 Jan. 1642 is presumably old style,

Bethlehem to Galway. For many reasons they are deferred to go thither as yet'.[30] Browne also advocated the idea that one of the former Franciscan friary buildings in the west of Ireland be made available to the Poor Clare sisters, but this did not happen.[31] Valentine Browne had a direct interest in the matter as he was a relative of Mother Mary Bonaventure Browne one of the original members of the Galway convent. The initiative to establish a convent in Galway proved successful, and by July 1649 the Poor Clares had acquired permission from Galway Corporation to build a convent with garden and orchard on 'Islannaltenagh' a location that came to be better known as 'Nuns' Island'.[32] The corporation granted the request on condition that 'they make up a common and bridge to the other island'.[33] The sheriff, Martin Blake of Cummer, Co. Galway, ensured that the sisters were permitted to occupy the site, and on a pictorial map of the town dated 1651 the convent building of the Poor Clares, together with a low wooden bridge to the next island, is clearly marked.[34] Mother Bonaventure's chronicle described the first convent on the site as having been built of timber and other materials, and recorded that it was built at a cost of £200stg, paid for out of the dowries of members of the community.[35] The 1651 map listed a variety of other convents for religious women in the town, apart from the Poor Clares. Also recorded were the houses of Dominican, Augustinian and Carmelite sisters, the 'Rich Clares', the sisters of the Third Order of St Francis, as well as 'various residences of nuns (or pious ladies)'.[36]

Due to continuing growth in numbers, new Poor Clare convents were also established in the late 1640s in the town of Loughrea, Co. Galway,[37] and in Athlone, Co. Westmeath, an indication of the vibrancy of the community. Sr Cecily Dillon became abbess of Athlone, having previously been abbess in Dublin and in Bethlehem.[38] These particular locations at Loughrea and Athlone were probably chosen on the grounds of the presence of influential local Catholic patrons, notably the earl of Clanricard, the centre of whose lordship had traditionally been at Loughrea, and Sir Toirdhealbhach Mac Cochláin, the influential Catholic whose patronage the Athlone Franciscans enjoyed. However, given the

then the year in question was 1643.　**30** Cited in C. O'Brien, *Poor Clares, Galway, 1642–1992* (1992), p. 17.
31 Jennings, *Louvain papers*, no. 189, 12 March 1643.　**32** Galway, Poor Clare Convent, File A (large documents). The document is reproduced in O'Brien, *Poor Clares, Galway*, inside back cover.　**33** HMC, *Tenth report, Appendix. Part 5. The manuscripts of the Marquis of Ormond, the earl of Fingall, the Corporations of Waterford, Galway* (1885), p. 499.　**34** Galway, Poor Clare Convent, MS B7. The relevant section of the 1651 map is reproduced in O'Brien, *Poor Clares, Galway*, p. 18.　**35** Galway, Poor Clare Convent, Chronicle, pp 15–6.　**36** J. McErlean, 'Notes on the pictorial map of Galway' (1905–6), pp 140–1.
37 Galway, Poor Clare Convent, MS A6, [1647] agreement signed by nine Poor Clares concerning the establishment of the Loughrea convent. The agreement was overseen by two Franciscan priests, Fr George Dillon, then guardian of Galway, and Anthony de Burgo, confessor to the nuns; O'Brien, *Recollections of an Irish Poor Clare*, p. 11.　**38** O'Brien, *Recollections of an Irish Poor Clare*, p. 12.

reality of plague, which reached Galway in 1649, and the unsettled politics of the 1640s and 1650s, none of these towns proved to be a safe haven.[39] The Poor Clares were forced to leave Galway after the town surrendered to Sir Charles Coote, leader of Oliver Cromwell's forces in April 1652.[40] The convents at Loughrea and Athlone were also dispersed. Many of the community went to Spain, and only a few lived long enough to return to Ireland in the 1670s.

GALWAY AND SPAIN IN THE LATE SEVENTEENTH CENTURY

In the circumstances it is little wonder that a memoir written by one of the Galway community who was forced into exile in Spain, Mother Mary Bonaventure Browne, speaks of hardship and exile and the challenges posed 'in a country where the heretics had all jurisdiction and government'.[41] Mother Bonaventure, who was probably a native of Galway, had joined the Poor Clares at Bethlehem in 1632, a few years after the order had been established in Ireland. She was among the community of fourteen who subsequently moved from Bethlehem to Galway in 1642–3, and from 1647 to 1650 she was abbess of the Galway convent. She was forced to go into exile in Spain in 1652 or 1653 along with other members of the community.[42] It was not just the Poor Clare community that came under threat at this time, but also their social networks among the Catholic community of Galway and the surrounding area. With their support networks within the wider community in disarray, the nuns had little choice but to seek refuge abroad. Being part of an international religious order, coupled with the fact that some of their number had spent their youth in a convent in the Spanish Netherlands, meant that a move to Spain was a realistic option. The Irish Poor Clares who relocated to Spain in the 1650s went to a number of different locations there, Bilbao, Madrid, Malaga and Salamanca are among the places noted in Mother Bonaventure's chronicle as the destinations of nuns from Galway. Mother Bonaventure explained that they 'sought a haven in foreign countries where they might enjoy the sweet presence of their heavenly Spouse whom they longed for'.[43]

Among the key themes emphasized in Mother Bonaventure's narrative were the challenges posed for the fledgling Irish branch of the order by the hostility of the 'heretic'; the restrictions imposed on their activities; the sanctity of the nuns

39 Galway, Poor Clare Convent, MS A7, A letter from the Franciscan Provincial, Fr Thomas MacKiernan, granting permission to the Poor Clares to leave the convent when danger, disease or enemy approached the city. Dated 27 June 1650; On the broader context of the circumstances of the Poor Clares in the 1650s, see Millett, *The Irish Franciscans*, pp 224–34. 40 O'Brien, *Recollections of an Irish Poor Clare*, p. 11. 41 Ibid, p. 11. 42 Ibid., p. [v]. 43 Ibid., p. 12.

in the face of the trials brought about by the adversity of the times in which they lived; their perseverance in the face of adversity; and the support they received from unexpected quarters. Considerable space was devoted to accounts of the pious lives and holy deaths of individual members of the order, of special favours and miracles associated with them, and the high regard in which they were held on account of the sanctity of their lives.

Despite displaying the shortcomings of an eyewitness narrative of events written after quite a few years had elapsed, Mother Bonaventure's account of the early years of the Poor Clares in Ireland has provided the basis for all subsequent narratives of the history of the order in Ireland. Her original manuscript was reportedly destroyed in 1691 but a copy had already been made. The earliest surviving text does not merely contain Mother Bonaventure's chronicle, but has been systematically added to at intervals since the seventeenth century. Thus the Galway chronicle now documents events that occurred long after Mother Bonaventure's death, and records the succession of abbesses and the profession of new members of the community in the Galway convent down to the year 1915.[44] Even after a new register of professions was commenced in 1915, the old chronicle continued to be augmented by recording the deaths of members of the Poor Clare community. That practice had commenced in 1704 and the most recent entries date from 2003.[45] Nineteenth- and early twentieth-century adaptations and continuations of Mother Bonaventure's narrative are held in the convent in Harold's Cross, Dublin. These were prepared for the use of the Dublin convents that had been founded from 1712, and each elaborates on the foundation narrative in different ways.[46]

It was in the convent of El Cavallero de Garcia in Madrid that Mother Bonaventure wrote her memoir,[47] which has been dated to 1670–1, but the primary intended readership was those younger members of the order who would re-establish the community at Galway. Given the way it was subsequently copied and augmented, it clearly proved to be an inspirational text. Eventually, some of those who had moved to Spain were able to return to Galway, while it is believed that others, such as the first abbess, Mother Mary Gabriel Martin, had remained in the town throughout the Cromwellian period. She died in the town of Galway in 1672, and was buried in the Franciscan cemetery there.[48]

---

44 Galway, Poor Clare Convent, Chronicle, pp 15–32; for the ceremony of profession in the late eighteenth century see *The manner of receiving the poor Sisters of St Clare to clothing* (1795), FLK copy listed in H. Fenning, 'Dublin imprints of Catholic interest, 1790–1795' (2004–5), p. 138. 45 Galway, Poor Clare Convent, Chronicle, pp 32–7. Manuscript consulted by the present author in September 2006. 46 Microfilm copies of three variant versions of the narrative, prepared at various dates between 1826 and 1904, are available in NLI microfilm P3500. 47 Concannon, *The Poor Clares in Ireland*, pp xvff. 48 O'Brien, *Poor Clares, Galway*, p. 30.

The surviving documentation still preserved in the Galway convent indicates that the Poor Clares continued to have a presence in Galway city through the late seventeenth century, even though it was not always possible for them to live on the Nuns' Island site that had first been acquired from the corporation in 1649. In 1684, for instance, the standard letter of permission was issued by the Franciscan provincial to the abbess authorising the admission of new novices, but with the stipulation that it be done 'privately, however, and without any great solemnity'.[49] This is a clear indication of an awareness of the continuing need to maintain a low profile, but also a hint that such ceremonies may on occasion have been somewhat more elaborate than was strictly necessary. In 1690 the abbess was concerned to negotiate an agreement to have the full benefit of the fishing of the stream known as the 'Royal Stream' running alongside the convent which had been assigned them by James Reagh Darcy but later denied them.[50] But in the very same year the nuns were also forced to seek permission to live with relatives and friends, being 'reduced to such extremities that they cannot subsist together in cloister'.[51] It was also conceded in 1690 that 'in case of necessity they may eat meat'.[52] The dowries of the nuns, many of which were very substantial,[53] were generally linked to property in Galway and elsewhere and the losses incurred during the wars of the 1690s adversely affected the income available to the order.[54] The crisis of 1690–1 was severe, and during those years it was reported that most of the books and altar fittings and altar plate that had been in the Galway convent were lost. That this was indeed the case is confirmed by the fact that although one silver chalice dated 1661 and one ciborium dated 1644 survive, otherwise the altar plate that survives in the Poor Clare convent dates from the eighteenth century or later.[55] Some seventeenth-century printed copies of the Rule of St Clare are also preserved in the Galway convent, but at least some of these were acquired in later centuries. One important survival, however, from the earliest days of the Galway foundation, despite the turbulence of the times, is a wooden statue of the Virgin and Child. This statue, known as 'Our Lady of Bethlehem', is still in the Galway convent.

After the political crisis of the early 1690s new novices were again accepted in the Galway convent in 1696[56] but two years later the community was faced with a government instruction requiring all nuns to leave Ireland by 1 May 1698. The

49 Galway, Poor Clare Convent, MS A9.   50 Galway, Poor Clare Convent, MS A11.   51 Galway, Poor Clare Convent, MS A12.   52 Galway, Poor Clare Convent, MS A12.   53 On dowries, see Galway, Poor Clare Convent, MSS A4 (1643), B4 (1712), B14 (1779), and Chronicle, passim.   54 Galway, Poor Clare Convent, Chronicle, pp 16–19.   55 Galway, Poor Clare Convent, unpublished inventory of ecclesiastical silver plate, prepared by R.J. Lattimore (1997). Lavishly embroidered new vestments were also acquired, sponsored by local patrons, in the early eighteenth century, perhaps to replace ones that had been destroyed, see Plate 3.   56 Galway, Poor Clare Convent, MS A14.

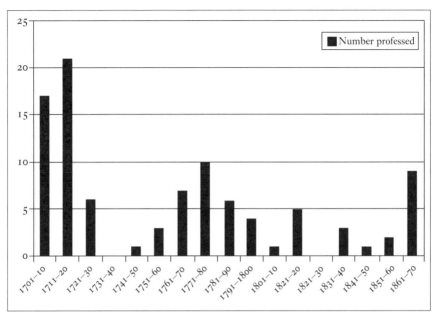

7 Statistical analysis of the number of Poor Clares professed, 1701–1870
(Bernadette Cunningham).

Poor Clares obtained permission in that year from the Franciscan provincial, Anthony O'Kelly, to go 'to some Catholic region, on the first available opportunity of travelling'. They were provided with a letter of commendation 'to all the faithful, whether lay folk or clergy, to whom you turn, as poor exiled daughters, lovingly in the Lord'.[57] However, it is clear that, as in earlier crises, at least some of the community remained in Galway, moving to live in private residences in the town. Thus, for example, another letter from Anthony O'Kelly, dated at Louvain on 12 July 1699, was addressed to the abbess, Mother Mary Gabriel as 'Mrs Mary Gabriel near Mr Ambrose Ruisse the Apothecary's house in Galway'.[58] Despite the disruptions caused by the turbulent politics of the time, by the year 1700 the Galway chronicle of the Poor Clares recorded that twenty-seven nuns had been professed and there had been four abbesses since the foundation of the convent in the early 1640s.

In May 1701, the abbess Mother Mary Gabriel Skerrett was exhorted by Fr Bonaventure Collin 'let not these troublesome times daunt your noble mind', and she was authorized to receive as many qualified postulants as she thought fit, 'to encourage the well-disposed minds to serve the lord'.[59] Professions continued

57 Galway, Poor Clare Convent, MS A15.   58 Galway, Poor Clare Convent, MS A18.   59 Galway, Poor Clare Convent, MS B1.

through the eighteenth century, though with a noticeable decline in the 1730s and 1740s. In 1779 there were twenty sisters apart from the abbess present at Galway and able to sign a document addressed to Thomas Blake.[60]

GALWAY AND DUBLIN IN THE EIGHTEENTH CENTURY

In the early eighteenth century, Galway was the only Poor Clare convent in the country, and the community generally resided in a house at Market Street in the town centre, rather than living on Nuns' Island. Then, in 1712, still under the leadership of Mother Mary Gabriel, who lived on until 1750,[61] the decision was taken to open a Dublin convent once more. At that stage there were more than forty nuns in the Galway convent, and six were sent to Dublin, with Mother Mary Augustine Lynch as abbess. The move to Dublin was done at the request of the archbishop of Dublin but essentially on the initiative of Revd Cornelius Nary. Dr Nary was also involved in encouraging Dominican and Carmelite nuns to establish convents in the same parish of St Paul in the northern part of the city – an expanding Catholic area.[62] The initiative was not without repercussions because it brought the order to the attention of the Dublin government once more. In consequence, the nuns were removed from their residence in Market Street, Galway, and the building was converted to a military barracks for some years. [63] Negotiations were conducted in London in the 1740s to reclaim the Nuns' Island residence, but these came to nothing, and it was only in June 1825 that the order was finally able to return to a newly constructed convent on that site. At that stage there were just sixteen in the Galway convent.[64]

The opening of a convent in Dublin in 1712 marked a new phase in the development of the Poor Clares in Ireland. With the assistance of Dr Nary they first established themselves in a former Benedictine convent building at Channel Row (now Brunswick Street), but this relatively high profile location had the disadvantage of attracting the attention of the government.[65] It was noted 'that an unlawful society of popish persons calling themselves nuns was lately transferred from the Towne of Galway to the City of Dublin, to be there settled and established by the pretended order of a person calling himself Brother John Burke of the Order of St Francis and Provincial of Ireland'.[66] The convent was raided

---

60 Galway, Poor Clare Convent, MS B14. 61 An inscription at Franciscan cemetery, Galway, recorded her death on 29 April 1750. 62 P. Fagan, *Dublin's turbulent priest: Cornelius Nary* (1991), pp 67–73.
63 Concannon, *The Poor Clares in Ireland*, p. 72. 64 Galway, Poor Clare Convent, Chronicle; Concannon, *The Poor Clares in Ireland*, pp 74–9. 65 Fagan, *Dublin's turbulent priest: Cornelius Nary*, pp 67–70. 66 Proclamation 'by the Lords Justice Generall and Generall governors of Ireland and Council' against Archbishop Edmond Byrne, Revd Cornelius Nary and Revd John Burke, 20 Sept. 1712, cited in

and two nuns arrested. However, the community survived and soon afterwards moved to a new location at North King Street, Dublin, where new postulants joined. In the initial stages of the Dublin foundation there was controversy over whether the convent was under the authority of the archbishop or the Franciscan provincial, and it was eventually agreed that their confessors should be appointed by the Franciscan provincial, subject to the approval of the archbishop.[67] As was also the case in Galway, the restrictions placed on them by the authorities meant that they could not normally wear the habit of the order and could not observe the strict Rule of St Clare. According to the evidence of a contemporary 'they wear no particular habit, only a black stuff gown and plain linen'.[68] The North King Street convent took lady boarders partly as a means of disguising the precise nature of their religious community.[69] They also obtained funding that allowed them to build a chapel, described in 1749 as a very good one with a 'handsome altar'.

> The altar-piece is a painting of the Crucifixion, having on the outside a picture of the Nativity and on the other of St Francis ... At the end of the chapel is the choir and stalls in it, over the choir a gallery for music, at the front of which is an organ, with an image of St Clare in her nun's habit holding the remonstrance in her hands, being the donation of the Countess of Fingal.[70]

In 1751 some members of the North King Street convent, including the abbess, Mother Jane Clare Joseph Geoghegan, moved to a new foundation first in temporary accommodation at Russell's Court and relocating shortly afterwards to the south side of Drumcondra Lane (now Dorset Street Lower), where they remained until 1803. As had happened on their first arrival in Dublin in 1712, a dispute arose over the competing jurisdictions of the Franciscan provincial and the archbishop of Dublin in respect of these convents.[71] The dispute being resolved the community in the Dorset Street convent ran a boarding school, there being a demand for such a service since there were few alternative venues where Catholic girls could receive instruction in the late eighteenth century.[72] A school

---

Concannon, *The Poor Clares in Ireland*, pp 87–8; R. Steele (ed.), *Tudor and Stuart Proclamations, 1485–1714* (1910), ii, Ireland, no. 1620. **67** Fagan, *Dublin's turbulent priest: Cornelius Nary*, p. 70. **68** Mrs Delany, cited in Concannon, *The Poor Clares in Ireland*, p. 96. **69** Dublin, Poor Clare Convent, Harold's Cross, Register '3', pp 39–42 (NLI microfilm P3500), summarized in Concannon, *The Poor Clares in Ireland*, pp 88–93. **70** N. Donnelly (ed.), *Roman Catholics: state and condition of R.C. chapels in Dublin* (1904), pp 19–20. **71** Concannon, *The Poor Clares in Ireland*, pp 95–101, 109. The Dorset Street convent was on a site adjoining Hardwick Street. **72** The Dublin Annals of the order, written in retrospect in 1826, record little or nothing for the years 1753–1803 in respect of either of these Dublin convents (Register '3', pp 43–4, on NLI microfilm P3500). On the role of female religious orders in Catholic Dublin in the late eighteenth

had also been established in the North King Street convent which continued to operate into the nineteenth century.

CONVENTS THROUGHOUT IRELAND IN THE NINETEENTH AND TWENTIETH CENTURIES

In 1812, following a request from the bishop of Limerick, three Poor Clare nuns from North King Street moved to Limerick to open a school for the poor in that city. The school functioned for almost twenty years until the Limerick convent was dissolved in 1831, the year in which a system of government-sponsored national primary education commenced in Ireland. The North King Street community moved to Kingstown (now Dún Laoghaire), Co. Dublin in 1826 but due to financial difficulties this house was dissolved in 1834.[73]

The Dorset Street convent, supported by lay benefactors including one Denis Thomas O'Brien and his daughter Maria, became involved in providing for the needs of orphans. As an extension of this work, a new convent was opened in Harold's Cross, Dublin, in 1804 to replace the Dorset Street convent. Charles Young, father of a Poor Clare sister, and Charles Lynch, brother of his business partner, together with Mary Teresa Mulally, were also significant benefactors.[74] A new building for an orphanage at the Harold's Cross site was ready for occupation by July 1806.[75] There was a brief involvement with another orphanage in North William Street in the late 1820s but this was handed over to the Carmelite order after a few years.[76] This commitment to providing orphanages and schools for the poor, and particularly for female children, set the pattern for the public role of the Poor Clares throughout the nineteenth century and well into the twentieth. That it was indeed a new departure is evidenced by a formal change to the observance of the rule at Harold's Cross from 1808. In that year, with Archbishop John Thomas Troy of Dublin acting as intermediary, a new form of profession was introduced incorporating a solemn vow of 'attending to the instruction of poor girls'. At the same time, a dispensation was given from the strict obervance of enclosure and from fasts and abstinences prescribed by the rule, probably in recognition of the demands of running an orphanage.[77] As a result, the Dublin-based sisters and those in convents subsequently founded

century, see Ronan, *An apostle of Catholic Dublin*, pp 41–7. **73** Concannon, *The Poor Clares in Ireland*, pp 102–7. **74** Ronan, *An apostle of Catholic Dublin*, pp 47, 80, 120–1. Mary Teresa Mulally had earlier been involved in establishing the Presentation convent at George's Hill, Dublin (1789). **75** Concannon, *The Poor Clares in Ireland*, **76** Poor Clare Convent, Harold's Cross, Register '3', pp 46–7 (NLI microfilm P3500); Concannon, *The Poor Clares in Ireland*, pp 130–1. **77** Extract from letter from Dr Concannon to Dr Troy, 25 Aug. 1808, Harold's Cross Convent, Document no. 11 (Photostat in NLI MS 8402).

directly or indirectly by them began to follow the Rule of St Clare in a form that combined a contemplative spirit with an active ministry, such as education and pastoral care.

More significant was the development of several convents in the archdiocese of Armagh, all of which took on an educational role. The convent of St Clare was established in Newry in 1830 by four sisters and one novice from North William Street and Harold's Cross. A school was started in the town in 1831 with a new school building ready for use in 1835. A work school for women was opened in 1840, teaching lace-making, embroidery and knitting. There were some sectarian tensions to contend with in Newry involving encounters with the Orange Order, but the convent prospered and expanded and in 1861 sisters from Newry founded new convents and schools in Cavan and in Kenmare, Co. Kerry.[78] The Cavan convent established a national school as well as St Joseph's Orphanage, the latter becoming an industrial school in 1869 as part of a system introduced by the state in 1868.[79] Further establishments in Keady, Co. Armagh (1871) and Ballyjamesduff, Co. Cavan (1872) also became involved in schools for the poor.[80] In addition to conducting national schools, the convent at Kenmare followed the example of Newry in establishing a lace school, and that at Keady also provided a night school for working women, in an attempt to use training and education as a means of alleviating the hardship experienced by impoverished women.[81] There was also an impact on devotional practice in the locality, with the introduction of a Christmas crib – a Franciscan devotion – at Newry in 1858, and the increased use of the ceremony of Benediction, formerly a very rare occurrence.[82] As an extension of their involvement with the education of adults, members of the Newry and Kenmare convents published explanatory booklets on the Christmas crib, on the *Portiuncula* indulgence, and on other topics such as the lives of the saints and Irish history. A lending library was also established for the use of the girls attending their schools.[83]

That such an active involvement in an educational role in the community was possible through the nineteenth century is a measure of the relaxation of

78 Sister Mary Francis Clare (Margaret Anna Cusack, 1829–1899), also known as 'The Nun of Kenmare' was one of the founding group of sisters. A woman of many parts: author of 35 books, critic of British misrule in Ireland, campaigner for the rights of the underprivileged and founder of the Sisters of St Joseph of Peace, she was a convert to Catholicism but returned to the Church of England later. See I.F. Eager, *The Nun of Kenmare* (1970). **79** A fire in the Cavan orphanage in 1943 resulted in the tragic deaths of 35 children. **80** Concannon, *The Poor Clares in Ireland*, pp 138–54, based on the Chronicle of the Newry convent. For a copy of archival material from the Newry convent, see Public Record Office of Northern Ireland, T1461. Material relating to Newry is also incorporated into the Harold's Cross 'Annals of the Poor Clares to 1901' (NLI microfilm P3500). **81** On the activities of the Kenmare convent see *In memoriam Mary O'Hagan* (1876). **82** Concannon, *The Poor Clares in Ireland*, pp 136–8. **83** Concannon, *The Poor Clares in Ireland*, pp 138–9; On the origin and Franciscan context of the *Portiuncula* indulgence see Ó

government restrictions on the activities of the Poor Clares. Even before the achievement of Catholic Emancipation in 1829, it had become possible for the sisters again to wear their habits from 1817, a consequence of the influence of the French emigré community in England whose attire made the habit of the Irish Poor Clares more acceptable to the authorities.[84] It was recorded in the Harold's Cross register for the year 1817 that 'We put on the religious habit the Sunday within the Octave of Saint Augustine – Feast of Our Lady of Consolation'.[85] Each convent following the modified form of the rule remained autonomous until 1944 when the northern houses amalgamated into a single congregation and were later joined by Harold's Cross and Kenmare. The congregation thus became an independent institute within the Franciscan movement and since its general chapter of 1984 is known as 'The Sisters of St Clare'. It continued to expand throughout the twentieth century with new houses in England, Wales, California and Florida. In the early 1970s it opened a house in Gotera, El Salvador where the Irish Franciscans had a mission and later it established more houses there and in Guatemala.[86]

Significant developments were also taking place in the contemplative wing of the Poor Clares. Towards the end of the nineteenth century, the Galway convent found it possible once more to return to the full observance of the strict Rule of St Clare, and this was implemented from 1892.[87] The arrival in Ireland in the following year of a group of Poor Clare Colettines, who observed this same strict rule, marked another new phase in the history of the order. This group had strong Belgian links, having evolved under the influence of Mère Dominique Berlamont. They established a convent at Graigue on the outskirts of Carlow. Both Carlow and Galway were instrumental in spreading the full Colettine observance of the rule to other parts of Ireland, Britain and elsewhere. Carlow founded St Damian's, Donnybrook (1906), Cork (1914), and Neath in South Wales (1950). In turn sisters from Dublin founded Belfast (1924) while Cork founded Bothwell in Scotland (1952) and Ennis (1958). From Galway came the foundations in Southampton (1934) and Sydney (1951). The latter joined with Ennis in co-founding a monastery in Papua New Guinea in 1971. From the late nineteenth century, therefore, there was a clear move towards a return to the strict observance of the Rule of St Clare, a rule that of necessity had been relaxed for centuries in Ireland because of government opposition to the activities of religious orders.

Clabaigh, 'The cult of St Francis', pp 148–9.   **84** Concannon, *The Poor Clares in Ireland*, pp 128–9. **85** Poor Clare Convent, Harold's Cross, Register '3', p. 49 (NLI microfilm P3500).   **86** See Sisters of St Clare, *Sisters of St Clare: a brief history* (1985) for an account of the evolution of this branch of the Poor Clares. I am grateful to Joseph MacMahon OFM, for researching material on the Poor Clares in the twentieth century for inclusion here.   **87** A Golden Jubilarian, 'Looking back fifty years' in S. O'Brien,

Responding to a recommendation made by Pope Pius XII preliminary steps were taken in 1958 towards forming a federation of the monasteries and following a lengthy process the federation of the six Irish monasteries and the three British ones founded from them was established in 1973.[88] The enclosed Franciscan Third Order convent at Drumshanbo, established in 1869, transferred to the Poor Clares in August 1973 and joined the federation. Each monastery retains its autonomy and distinctive identity while collaborating in promoting the spirit of the order, providing mutual assistance and engaging in common ventures, such as formation.

CONCLUSION

Given the generally unobtrusive nature of the work of the order and the imperative to avoid having a high public profile prior to Catholic Emancipation in 1829, the extant source documentation tends to emanate from within the order. The bicentenary of the Irish branch of the Poor Clares in 1829 seems to have prompted a revision of the original Galway chronicle, but it was only in 1929 that a commemorative volume was actually published.[89] The booklet issued for the tercentenary was edited by Sylvester O'Brien, a Franciscan priest based in the Abbey, Galway. In that same year, the contribution of the Poor Clares to Irish life was further recognized with the publication of Helena Concannon's *The Poor Clares in Ireland, 1629–1929*. That pioneering study was closely based on the archives of the order, particularly those still preserved in the convents at Galway, Harold's Cross and Newry. Although specific manuscripts are not referenced, Concannon's book closely reflects the contents of the extant documents in these convents. Among the archival sources preserved, the most substantial sources of information take the form of chronicles maintained over time within the various convents, as continuations of the chronicle commenced by Mother Bonaventure Browne of the Galway convent in the 1670s. The principal continuation taking the story into the nineteenth century was the work of Mother Mary Baptist Clancy, who was professed in 1771 and died in 1829, having spent much of her life in the Limerick convent.[90] This revision was partly derivative of printed secondary sources. A member of the Harold's Cross convent, Sr Mary Joseph Jane White, compiled a further chronicle of developments in Dublin, while the Newry convent likewise compiled its own annals. Each of these variants of the chronicle of the order concentrates on key events such as the dates of new foundations, the

Poor Clare tercentenary record, pp 45–6 for the events leading up to this. **88** The archives of the federation are held by its President during her term of office. **89** O'Brien, *Poor Clare tercentenary record*. **90** Galway, Poor Clare Convent, Chronicle; Concannon, *The Poor Clares in Ireland*, pp 69, 79.

appointment of abbesses and the profession and death of individual sisters. They are essentially self-contained narratives, external events being recorded only where there was a serious impact on the life of the community. Yet, in each generation it was important to the order that its achievements should be documented, as evidence of their commitment to continuing a tradition of piety and devotion established by St Clare, and as an example to those who would follow the same path. By force of circumstances that tradition had evolved into two strands, one active, which sought to bring the spirit of St Clare into contemporary society through its ministry, and the other enclosed, which brought the world into the heart of its prayer.

PART II

The Legacy of the Irish Franciscans

The Louvain achievement I: the Annals of the Four Masters

BERNADETTE CUNNINGHAM

The lively interest in historical writing in early seventeenth-century Ireland, exemplified in works such as the Annals of the Four Masters, was not something uniquely Irish. The study and interpretation of history had formed an important element of debate in Reformation and Counter-Reformation Europe in the sixteenth and early seventeenth centuries. The availability of print technology facilitated this development, which came on top of the earlier cultural renaissance, which had itself prompted a renewed interest in the primary sources for the past. It was an era of lively confessional debate about the origins of the early Christian church and an era of growing interest in the histories of individual nations. These European trends helped shape the environment from which the Annals of the Four Masters emerged, and the Franciscan network was important in facilitating movement of ideas between Europe and Ireland.[1]

HUGH WARD AND PATRICK FLEMING: INITIATING THE TASK

The need for a comprehensive history of Ireland had become apparent to those Catholic Irish who found themselves in the university towns of continental Europe in the early seventeenth century. The continental colleges were founded in university towns throughout western and central Europe, to support the education of Irish Catholics, many of whom were students for the priesthood. By the 1620s in St Anthony's College, Louvain at least two of the Irish Franciscan community there, Hugh Ward and Patrick Fleming, were actively researching the lives of Irish saints.[2] They travelled to various European towns in search of relevant manuscript materials and kept in contact with one another by letter. It is clear from their correspondence that a primary objective of their research was to enhance the image of Ireland by reference to the country's illustrious past.

With their plans for research into the lives of saints taking shape, Fleming commented to Ward in a letter dated 24 August 1624, 'What else remains except to make a history of the kings of Ireland with their reigns such as other nations

---

1 See Lyons, 'The role of St Anthony's College, Louvain' in this volume.   2 Cunningham, 'The culture and ideology of the Irish Franciscan historians' (1991), pp 11–30, 223–7. See Ó Riain, 'The Louvain achievement II: hagiography' in this volume.

have'.[3] A seminal moment, perhaps, because it may have been then the seed was sown for the scheme of historical research that culminated in the Annals of the Four Masters. The work could not have proceeded, however, without the availability of scholars trained in the interpretation of Irish historical sources. Ward soon identified one such scholar in the person of Mícheál Ó Cléirigh.

Mícheál Ó Cléirigh joined the Irish Franciscans at Louvain probably in the early 1620s, when aged about 30. A member of the Donegal family who had traditionally been hereditary historians to the O'Donnells, he had trained as an historian before leaving Ireland. He may have served for a time in the army in the Spanish Netherlands, a not-untypical move for younger sons in early seventeenth-century Ireland.[4] His older brother, Maolmhuire, had joined the Franciscans some years earlier, taking the name Bernardine, and pursued his seminary education at Salamanca and subsequently at St Anthony's College, Louvain.[5] He was ordained a priest at Brussels in 1619.[6] This family connection was one obvious link that would have drawn Mícheál Ó Cléirigh to Louvain, but the presence of others from learned families in Donegal and elsewhere who had also joined the Franciscan community at Louvain would have been an added attraction. Ó Cléirigh did not become ordained a priest, choosing to remain a lay brother, a fact that helped determine the course of his subsequent career in Ireland. Rather than provide pastoral ministry to the catholic community in Ireland, Ó Cléirigh was permitted to devote much of his time to scholarship. His expertise as a scribe and scholar had been recognized by fellow Donegal man, Hugh Ward. Almost immediately on becoming superior of St Anthony's College in 1626, Ward instructed Ó Cléirigh to return to Ireland to undertake the task of locating and transcribing manuscripts still preserved there that contained the lives of Irish saints.[7]

COMPILING THE ANNALS OF THE FOUR MASTERS, 1626–36

The Irish Franciscan community to which Mícheál Ó Cléirigh returned in Donegal in 1626 was no intellectual backwater compared to the world of the continental seminaries. Although forced to reside in temporary accommodation in the extreme south of Co. Donegal in the 1620s and 1630s, following the destruction of the original friary buildings at Donegal in 1601 at the height of the

---

3 Printed in Latin in B. Jennings, 'Documents from the archives of St Isidore's College' (1934), p. 216. 4 Jennings, *Michael O Cleirigh*, pp 11–18. 5 Listed as Moylerus Clery in D.J. O'Doherty, 'Students of the Irish College, Salamanca' (1913), p. 28; listed as 'Fr Milerus Cleri, nunc dictus Fr Bernardinus a Sancta Maria, dioecesis Rapotensis' in Jennings, *Louvain Papers*, p. 55. 6 Jennings, *Michael O Cleirigh*, p. 17. 7 Ibid., pp 26–40.

Nine Years War, the Donegal Franciscan community was still a vibrant one. Its members included Fr Bernardine Ó Cléirigh, Mícheál's brother, who had been educated alongside Hugh Ward at Salamanca;[8] Fr Muiris Ulltach, son of Seaán, a former provincial of the Franciscan order in Ireland and a man who was able to supply Ó Cléirigh with Irish translations of Latin texts;[9] and another Fr Muiris Ulltach, son of Donnchadh, who, along with Flaithrí Ó Maoil Chonaire, had been at the deathbed of Red Hugh O'Donnell in Simancas in 1602.[10] In 1624, some two years prior to Mícheál Ó Cléirigh's return from Louvain to Donegal, one Muiris Ulltach was already employing the services of Cú Choigcríche Ó Cléirigh to conduct hagiographical research for the Donegal community.[11] This initiative is interesting because it shows that the Donegal Franciscan community was fully in sympathy with the objectives of the Louvain hagiographical research project. The principle of collaboration with lay professional historians was already established, and the need for scholarly use of the most authoritative manuscript sources was clearly recognized. Part of the inspiration for the researches of Mícheál Ó Cléirigh may have come from Louvain, but the Franciscan community in Ireland were fully supportive of its objectives. The project also involved lay scholars who as far as we know had no direct continental experience.

Ó Cléirigh spent much of his time in the years from 1626 to 1630 transcribing saints' lives from manuscript copies preserved in various parts of Ireland, a task in which he made full use of the Franciscan network within the country. His travels, and his sojourns at a range of Franciscan houses mainly in the south and west have been eloquently described by Brendan Jennings.[12] With the hagiographical work nearing completion, Ó Cléirigh then embarked on a series of collaborative historical projects with a group of other chroniclers. However, it seems clear that he had planned such an undertaking for some time. In fact, he was actively assembling secular historical as well as hagiographical source material from the beginning of his researches in Ireland. In 1627, for example, after Ó Cléirigh had copied the Martyrology of Tallaght from the Book of Leinster he then proceeded to extract secular historical source material from the same source.[13]

Ó Cléirigh's first collaboration with another member of the Four Masters team appears to have been when he and Cú Choigcríche Ó Cléirigh worked on the first of two versions of the Martyrology of Donegal completed in 1628.[14] A

8 O'Doherty, 'Students of the Irish College, Salamanca', pp 28–9. **9** 'Brussels MS. 3410', p. 192. **10** *AFM*, vi, p. 2297; J.J. Silke, 'The last will of Red Hugh O'Donnell' (1984–8). **11** Preface by Mícheál Ó Cléirigh to the 1628 recension of the Martyrology of Donegal, BR MS 4639, ff 2–2v. **12** Jennings, *Michael O Cléirigh*, pp 51–98; some revisions of the dates cited in Jennings's book were published with explanations in P. Walsh, 'Travels of an Irish scholar' (1937). **13** Ó Cléirigh's transcripts of secular historical poems are preserved in RIA MS B iv 2, which has scribal colophons dated to 1627 and 1628. For a summary list of contents of MS B iv 2 see *Cat. Ir. Mss RIA*, pp 3021–9; see also Jennings, *Michael O Cleirigh*, pp 57–8. **14** Brussels, BR MS 4639.

second recension was completed by April 1630.[15] Then, in December 1630, the four scholars who came to be known as the Four Masters spent some time collaborating on the genealogies of the saints and kings of Ireland, a work sponsored by Toirdhealbhach Mac Cochláin of Co. Westmeath.[16] Aside from Mícheál Ó Cléirigh, the other three 'masters' were Cú Choigcríche Ó Cléirigh (probably Mícheál's third cousin), Cú Choigcríche Ó Duibhgeannáin and Fearfeasa Ó Maoil Chonaire. Ó Cléirigh was explicit about the purpose of this work.

> The four agreed that they should insert a list of the kings of Ireland in the beginning of the book they had commenced, for two reasons: the first, because it was impossible to trace the descent of the saints directly to their origins without first setting down the descent of the kings, for it is from these that the saints sprung; the second, that the reverence and devotion of the nobility for their saints, comharbs and churches might be increased by knowledge of their connexion and kinship with their holy patrons and with the tribal saints of the stock to which each family belonged, and by knowledge of the number of saints connected with each family.[17]

In the following year, 1631, the same four scholars prepared a new recension of the *Leabhar Gabhála* (Book of Invasions), sponsored by Brian Maguire in Co. Fermanagh.[18] This source, found in many medieval manuscript compilations, not least *Leabhar na hUidhre*, the Book of Leinster, the Book of Lecan and the Book of Ballymote, was deemed by seventeenth-century historians to form the essential framework of any account of the earliest phase of Irish history. Indeed, the opening section of the Annals of the Four Masters relied heavily on the version of the *Leabhar Gabhála* that the Four Masters had produced, while the framework of the succession of kings that they had outlined in the *Genealogiae regum et sanctorum Hiberniae* underpinned the entire structure of the early medieval portion of the annals.[19]

The Annals of the Kingdom of Ireland, sponsored by Fearghal Ó Gadhra, MP for Sligo in the 1634–5 Parliament, was the final major historical project on which

15 Brussels, BR MS 5095–6, f. 100v. Ó Cléirigh evidently intended to have a version of this martyrology published at Louvain, and it may have been to that end he collected approbations for it from a selection of scholars and bishops. Ó Cléirigh must have retained a copy of the 1630 recension of the martyrology in Ireland until he himself travelled to Louvain in 1637, because he obtained some approbations for it in late 1636 and early 1637 at the same time as the Annals of the Four Masters. See *MartD*, pp l–lv; *AFM*, i, pp lxviii–lxxi. **16** UCD-OFM MS A16. **17** *GSRH*, translation, pp 143–4. **18** RIA MS 23 M 70 is the fragmentary survival of Ó Cléirigh's autograph copy of the Four Masters' recension of the *Leabhar Gabhála*. For an edition of part of the text, based on other extant transcripts, see R.A.S. Macalister and J. MacNeill (eds), *Leabhar gabhála, part 1* (1916). **19** Cunningham, 'The making of the Annals of the Four Masters' (2005), pp 75–103.

the Four Masters team collaborated.[20] The patron of the annals, Fearghal Ó Gadhra, had a particularly close connection with the Irish Franciscan community. His father had died at an early age and the young Fearghal was made ward of court, and was educated under the care of Theobald Dillon, an Old Englishman from Westmeath. Dillon was a man who had made an enormous personal profit from the changes in landholding in late sixteenth-century Roscommon.[21] Two of his sons became Franciscan priests while two daughters were among the founders of the Poor Clare Order in Ireland in the 1620s.[22] Fearghal Ó Gadhra grew up in that same household, so as an adult he had close personal links to his foster family who included prominent Irish Franciscans. In addition, the Dillons were connected by marriage to the Mac Cochláins, an association that created an important link with another patron of the work of the Four Masters. This network of scholars and patrons transcended traditional ethnic and political boundaries in the cause of promoting research into the Irish past. Thus, it was under the influence of a centuries-old tradition of *seanchas*, combined with a new sense of the need for a comprehensive history of Ireland, that the Four Masters began to compile their new annals in January 1632. They had as their exemplars the Annals of Ulster and a range of other annals, together with other historical texts in prose and verse. They worked through into 1633, after which they appear to have taken a break. They resumed in 1635, completing the final section of the annals by August 1636.

Work had been in progress for some months before Mícheál Ó Cléirigh obtained official permission from Valentine Browne, the superior of the Franciscans in Ireland, to proceed with the annals project. In a letter dated 15 May 1632 Browne wrote as follows:

> Whereas … you have purposed to compile from the ancient and almost obliterated Irish records whatever concerns the annals of our kings, and relates to the state, both ecclesiastical and civil, of this kingdom; lest we might not appear to second your work, which is so virtuous, and fills such a long-felt want, we command you by the merit of holy obedience to persevere until the end, if God shall give you life, in this laborious work of the Annals which you have already begun, and to submit all that you shall compile to the judgment of men skilful in the Irish tongue, as you have done in the case of the smaller works.[23]

---

20 RIA MS C iii 3, p. iii.   **21** B. Cunningham & R. Gillespie, *Stories from Gaelic Ireland* (2003), pp 59–87. **22** For the Dillon members of the Franciscans and Poor Clares see Cunningham, 'The Poor Clare Order in Ireland', in this volume.   **23** Printed in Latin in Walsh, *Gleanings from Irish manuscripts*, p. 71. The English translation used here is printed in Jennings, *Michael O Cleirigh*, pp 134–5.

Browne, like other Franciscans, was clear that a new set of annals would 'fill a long-felt want'. The extensive use made of the annals by John Colgan in the notes to his published compilations of lives of the Irish saints shows that they were indeed useful to the Louvain hagiographical project.[24] Colgan generally cited them as the 'Annals of Donegal', which was a fair description, and would have appealed to him, being himself from Inishowen, in that county. It was Colgan, too, in the preface to his *Acta Sanctorum Hiberniae*, who applied the term 'Four Masters' to Ó Cléirigh and his collaborators, a name that has been in common use ever since.[25]

THE ANNALS OF THE FOUR MASTERS: FORM AND CONTENT

Two sets of autograph manuscripts of the Annals of the Four Masters survive. They are currently divided into five volumes and are housed in three different archives in Dublin. Franciscan MS A 13, recently transferred to University College Dublin from Dún Mhuire, the Franciscan House of Studies at Killiney, along with Royal Irish Academy MSS 23 P 6–23 P 7 are generally regarded as constituting the set that Mícheál Ó Cléirigh took to Louvain in 1637 with plans for publication. Royal Irish Academy MS C iii 3 and Trinity College Dublin MS 1301 together are usually regarded as being the set given to the patron, Fearghal Ó Gadhra.[26] The sources used included earlier annals compiled by members the Ó Maoil Chonaire, Ó Duibhgeannáin and Ó Cléirigh families,[27] and this in itself goes a long way towards explaining the composition of the Four Masters team. There were two scribal assistants, Muiris Ó Maoil Chonaire and Conaire Ó Cléirigh, the latter being an older brother of Mícheál. Contemporaries such as John Colgan and Fearfeasa Ó Maoil Chonaire were in no doubt, however, that there were just four masters, and we should accept their testimony: Mícheál Ó Cléirigh, Cú Choigcríche Ó Cléirigh, Cú Choigcríche Ó Duibhgeannáin, and Fearfeasa Ó Maoil Chonaire.[28]

The history of Ireland planned and executed by this team of scholars retained the traditional annalistic form – the simplest kind of history writing – but their chronological scope and interpretative framework was impressive. They were designed to document, by means of a systematic chronological outline, the full sweep of recorded time, from earliest times (AM 2242) to the present. They terminated with the death of Hugh O'Neill, earl of Tyrone in 1616.

---

24 Cunningham, 'The making of the Annals of the Four Masters', p. 34; B. Cunningham, 'John Colgan as historian' (forthcoming).   **25** Colgan, *AS*, sig b2v–b3v.   **26** N. Ó Muraíle, 'The autograph manuscripts of the Annals of the Four Masters' (1987).   **27** *AFM*, i, pp lxiii–lxvii.   **28** Colgan, *AS*, sig B 3v; Mhág Craith, *Dán na nBráthar Mionúr*, poem 39.

The Four Masters placed particular emphasis on the reigns of kings, beginning with Sláinghe, first king of the Fir Bolg in the year of the world 3266. From that year forward down to 5199 (or I BC), and then commencing again at AD I, they itemized every year of the reign of every king, even where no information other than the regnal year was available. This simple chronological approach was an effective means of projecting the idea of an Irish kingdom back into prehistory. The essential objective was to demonstrate the antiquity of the kingdom of Ireland. To this end, every year in which it could be stated that a king had ruled Ireland was a year worth recording.[29] The annalistic format helped reinforce that point.

As was also the case in their source texts, a new era was deemed to begin with the coming of St Patrick. The regnal lists began anew, itemising the reigns of kings after the coming of Christianity. Yet, the Four Masters devoted rather less space to saints than to kings. Essentially the Martyrology of Donegal had already chronicled the saints of Ireland, and the annals were designed to complement that work by focussing on secular history. Although many of the saints documented in the Martyrology of Donegal were mentioned in the annals, only the basic chronology was recorded. Inserting implausible stories or exaggerated claims about miracle-working saints was not part of the plan.[30]

The early Christian section of the annals contains a significant proportion of ecclesiastical entries, but that proportion decreased steadily over time. By the late medieval period, the lessened ecclesiastical focus was not so much on saints as on abbots and bishops. Significantly, in contrast to earlier annals such as the Annals of Ulster, the Four Masters paid attention to the sequence in which entries were arranged within any given year. In arranging obituaries, they almost invariably gave priority to ecclesiastical over lay people. Thus, for example, in the fourteenth-century section, although only about 10 per cent of the entries in the Four Masters were ecclesiastical, 57 per cent of years opened with an ecclesiastical item, as compared with 8 per cent in the Annals of Ulster and 8 per cent in the Annals of Loch Cé. This editorial policy created the impression of Ireland as a country in which particular respect had been shown to churchmen in the past.

Much of the text of the annals is comprised of obituaries of individuals, and in these the place of burial was frequently mentioned. Reference to burial in Franciscan friaries was not uncommon, and the recording of such details subtly enhanced the Franciscan dimension of the history. The Four Masters also added new Franciscan material not found in any earlier annals. At a late point in their work, the annalists inserted entries recording the foundation dates of Franciscan

---

29 The early part of O'Donovan's published text of the annals is heavily abridged, omitting many entries for regnal years recorded in the autograph manuscripts. For details see Cunningham, 'The making of the Annals of the Four Masters', p. 76.   **30** Cunningham, 'The making of the Annals of the Four Masters', pp 248–65.

friaries. This information was drawn from the early seventeenth-century list compiled by Francis O'Mahony (Matthews), *Brevis synopsis Provinciae Hyberniae fratrum minorum*.[31] O'Mahony had written his work in Latin, but the Four Masters used an Irish version of the *Brevis synopsis* translated by Muiris Ulltach mac Seáin, Franciscan guardian of Donegal.[32] The entries on the Franciscan friaries were inserted in the autograph manuscripts after most other entries had been written. It may have been an afterthought, but was still a deliberate and systematic addition. The principal scribe involved in this editorial phase was Cú Choigcríche Ó Cléirigh,[33] although Mícheál Ó Cléirigh added the entries on the friaries at Killeigh (1393) and Quin (1402).[34]

Obituaries of lay men and women, along with short narratives of military exploits, made up the bulk of the late medieval section of the annals. That there was a particular emphasis on the achievements of leading members of the O'Donnells of Tír Conaill is to be expected given that the Ó Cléirigh family were hereditary historians to the O'Donnells.[35] The closing section of the annals – from 1585 to 1602 – is dominated by an account of the exploits of Red Hugh O'Donnell during the Nine Years War. This section is derived from a biographical narrative of Red Hugh of O'Donnell – *Beatha Aodha Ruaidh Uí Dhomhnaill* – compiled by Lughaidh Ó Cléirigh.[36]

The annalists sought to put their own stamp on this material by adding some details of their own. It is no surprise, given their personal acquaintance with some of those present in Simancas at the time of Red Hugh's death, that they inserted the names of two Franciscan priests, Flaithrí Ó Maoil Chonaire and Muiris Ulltach son of Donnchadh who had been there.[37] They also added a sentence about those Irish who died abroad and were 'buried in strange places and unhereditary churches'.[38] This has the effect of giving greater meaning to the repeated recording of places of burial in earlier obituaries. These were not merely

31 Jennings, 'Brevis synopsis', edited from a manuscript in St Isidore's College, Rome. The author's name is variously translated as O'Mahony and Matthews. (Note that in this quotation Mícheál Ó Cléirigh gives the author's name in Irish as '*an tAthair Proinsías ua Mathghamhna*'.)   **32** Muiris Ulltach was guardian of Donegal between 1632 and 1635, 'Brevis synopsis', p. 142.   **33** For example, the entries in RIA MS 23 P 6 on Youghal (AFM 1224.16), Cork (AFM 1229.1), Waterford (AFM 1240.1), Timoleague (AFM 1240.7), Galway (AFM 1247.13), Ennis (AFM 1247.14), Buttevant [Kilnamullagh] (AFM 1251.3), etc. The entry numbers cited here are those assigned in the electronic edition of AFM published on the CELT (Corpus of Electronic Texts) website www.ucc.ie/celt.   **34** RIA MS 23 P 6, ff. 135r, 140v.   **35** For the O'Donnell context, see B. Cunningham, *O'Donnell histories: Donegal and the Annals of the Four Masters* (2007).   **36** P. Walsh (ed.), *Beatha Aodha Ruaidh Uí Dhomhnaill* (1948–67).   **37** *AFM*, vi, pp 2296–97 (AFM 1602.4). It is possible that both Muiris Ultachs were in Simancas at the time of Red Hugh O'Donnell's death in 1602 (see J.J. Silke, 'The last will of Red Hugh O'Donnell' (1984–8), p. 53). Both were present in the Donegal Franciscan convent in the mid-1630s when AFM was being compiled. They would have been able to supply their own personal memories of the death of Red Hugh. Personal recollections were also used in the compilation of Irish Franciscan history ('Brevis synopsis').   **38** *AFM*, vi, pp 2298–9.

formulaic but were, rather, a reiteration of connection to a traditional family burial place, in later times often a Franciscan one, regarded as a fitting conclusion to a Christian life.[39]

Perversely, given that Franciscan support had been vital to the work of the Four Masters, a dispute within the Franciscan chapter led to a deferral of plans to have the annals published. As stipulated by the Franciscan provincial, the completed annals were submitted to the judgment of two Irish scholars, Flann Mac Aodhagáin and Conchobhar Mac Bruaideadha, who provided formal approbations or letters of approval as to the worthiness of the finished work. Shortly thereafter the annals were criticized by Tuileagna Ó Maoil Chonaire, a Franciscan, who complained about perceived slights on Connacht history. Tuileagna publicized his case at successive Franciscan provincial chapters, drawing attention to five errors that he claimed required amendment before the work could be published. He even persuaded Mac Aodhagáin and Mac Bruaideadha to withdraw their appro-bations.[40] The ensuing debate dragged on for years, and Mícheál Ó Cléirigh himself had died – in 1643 – before the matter was resolved. Fearfeasa Ó Maoil Chonaire continued to defend the annals, but once the only Franciscan member of the team had died, the likelihood of publication had greatly diminished. The Louvain Franciscans devoted their energies instead to publishing the lives of Irish saints in two large folio volumes edited by John Colgan.[41] As already noted, the work of the Four Masters was cited extensively in Colgan's notes, but just as Colgan's own work remained unfinished, so two did the annals remain unpub-lished. Over the following centuries, the Louvain copy of the annals lay largely unread. One part of those annals was evidently brought back to Ireland in the late eighteenth century and was purchased by Sir George Petrie for the Royal Irish Academy in 1831.[42] The other part of the Louvain set, now UCD-OFM MS A 13, remained in Franciscan hands, and was taken back to Ireland in 1872.

Having acquired the only complete extant autograph copy of the post 1171 annals, George Petrie became the driving force behind plans to publish the work in a

---

39 Late fifteenth-century examples of such references to burials in Franciscan friaries are AFM 1470.13, 1475.7, 1480.1, 1481.2, 1487.9 and 1496.8. **40** Some of the documentation is printed, with translation, in *GRSH*, pp 131–8, 147–53. **41** Colgan, *AS*; John Colgan, *TT*. **42** W. O'Sullivan, 'The Slane manuscript

prestige dual language edition. The annals were eventually published in John O'Donovan's classic edition, in the years 1848–51, with the financial support of George Smith of Hodges and Smith.[43] The publication was viewed by contemporaries as an important cultural milestone. As Eugene O'Curry explained in his *Lectures on the manuscript materials of ancient Irish history*, the Annals of the Four Masters were 'the most important of all [annals] in point of interest and historic value'. He continued:

> In whatever point of view we regard these annals, they must awaken feelings of deep interest and respect; not only as the largest collection of national, civil, military, and family history ever brought together in this or perhaps any other country, but also as the final winding up of the affairs of a people who had preserved their nationality and independence for a space of over two thousand years, till their complete overthrow about the time at which this work was compiled. It is no easy matter for an Irishman to suppress feelings of deep emotion when speaking of the compilers of this great work and especially when he considers the circumstances under which, and the objects for which, it was undertaken.[44]

The reputation of Ó Cléirigh and his associates as the saviours of the Irish past was enhanced rather than diminished over the course of the following century, assisted in no small way by the existence of O'Donovan's edition, which was exemplary for its time. By 1919, the Franciscan community at Athlone found it beneficial to use the appeal of the Four Masters to enhance their fundraising activities for a new church in the town.[45] What might be termed the cult of the Louvain school and of Ó Cléirigh in particular received further boosts through the publication of Brendan Jennings's pamphlet on St Anthony's College in 1925, Tomás Ó Cléirigh's study of Aodh Mac Aingil in 1936, and by Jennings's engaging book on Ó Cléirigh's life and labours also published in 1936.[46] Less than a decade later, in the midst of the Second World War, on Sunday 25 June 1944, a gala concert was held in the Gaiety Theatre in Dublin, to mark the 300th anniversary of the death of Ó Cléirigh. The event honoured the memory of the Franciscan lay brother 'whose labours in the cause of Irish history, literature, and

of the *Annals of the Four Masters*' (1999). Petrie purchased the manuscript for £53, at an auction of the books of Austin Cooper, and arranged for it to be repaired and rebound in two volumes, now RIA MSS 23 P 6, 23 P 7. **43** B. Cunningham, 'An honour to the nation', (2006). **44** E. O'Curry, *Lectures on the manuscript materials* (1861), p. 140. **45** A copy of the souvenir brochure for the fundraising bazaar held in Athlone from 10–17 August 1919 is preserved in the FLK. **46** B. Jennings, *The Irish Franciscan college of St Anthony at Louvain* (1925); T. Ó Cléirigh, *Aodh Mac Aingil* (1936, repr. 1985); Jennings, *Michael O Cleirigh*.

language, saved our country's records from obliteration and our native tongue from extinction'.[47] The commemorative programme produced on the occasion included a special apostolic blessing from Pope Pius XII. The blessing was addressed to:

> His eminence Cardinal MacRory, primate of all Ireland, an Taoiseach Eamon de Valera, and other leaders of Church and State, together with many persons prominent in the religious, civil, educational, and cultural life of the Irish nation, assembling in Dublin to commemorate the tercentenary of the death of Ireland's great annalist, and historian, the Franciscan lay-brother, Michael Ó Cléirigh, known as 'The Chief of the Four Masters.[48]

A commemorative postage stamp, commissioned in 1944 as part of the same celebration, with its image of a scholar at work, was adopted as part of the definitive series of Irish stamps.[49] The stamps remained in current use until 1969, in denominations of ½*d.* and 1*s.* and helped enshrine Ó Cléirigh as a symbol of Irishness in the consciousness of a generation. Again in that same tercentenary year, 1944, a substantial collection of academic essays in memory of Mícheál Ó Cléirigh was published in Dublin under the editorship of Sylvester O'Brien OFM.[50]

The process that saw the emergence of something akin to a cult of Ó Cléirigh also permitted the dissemination of some misconceptions about the nature of the historical project on which the annalists had been engaged. A romantic view emerged of these annals as a last defiant rescue mission undertaken in the face of the passing of the old Gaelic order. That view was constructed by the nineteenth-century romantics, peripherally involved in the publication of the Annals of the Four Masters, and later popularized by Douglas Hyde, but it misrepresents the essence of the work of the Four Masters.[51] Writing in the early 1630s, theirs was not a salvage exercise, but the construction of a new history of the kingdom of Ireland appropriate to the changed political and cultural circumstances of the early seventeenth century.[52] A second mistaken idea – that all four 'masters' were Franciscans – has gained currency in the twentieth century. Perhaps the emphasis placed by twentieth-century historians on the influence of the Louvain Franciscans and on the scholarship of the 'poor friar', Mícheál Ó Cléirigh, inadvertently created the impression that it was an exclusively Franciscan project. In reality, the

---

47 *Comóradh i n-onóir Mhichíl Uí Chléirigh* (1944), p. [16].   **48** Ibid., p. [3].   **49** Don M. Buchalter, *Hibernian specialized catalogue of the postage stamps of Ireland* (1972), pp 50–1.   **50** O'Brien, *Measgra*. **51** D. Hyde, *A literary history of Ireland* (1899, rev. ed., 1967), pp 574–80; Cunningham, 'An honour to the nation'.   **52** B. Ó Buachalla, '*Annála Ríoghachta Éireann* agus *Foras feasa ar Éirinn*' (1982–3).

only Franciscan among the annalists and their scribal assistants was Mícheál Ó Cléirigh himself. Nevetheless it is true that the Franciscan dimension to the undertaking, which facilitated the work and moulded the contents, was crucial to this great historical enterprise from inception to completion. The annals evolved out of the Louvain hagiographical research project, but took on a life of their own. While their impact among contemporaries was muted, over the longer term their influence on Irish perceptions of the past was very considerable. Following publication of the Annals of the Four Masters in a dual-language edition in the mid-nineteenth century the scene was set for Mícheál Ó Cléirigh's version of Irish history to become an iconic text for modern Ireland in the late nineteenth and twentieth centuries.

The Louvain achievement II: hagiography

PÁDRAIG Ó RIAIN

The year 1607 saw the foundation of St Anthony's College, Louvain. Almost twenty years later the Louvain friars devised a scheme for the publication of a history of early and medieval Ireland, civil and religious.[1] Three other events dating from 1607 merit commemoration in connection with this foundation and its subsequent history, one of them well-known in Ireland, the others less so. The well-known event is, of course, the Flight of the Earls. Louvain figured prominently in the itinerary of the earls, who spent the winter of 1607 there, in a hostel called 'the Emperor's House'.[2] During their stay, they would almost certainly have visited the embryo community of St Anthony's College, which had been founded the previous spring. However, Tadhg Ó Cianáin made no reference to it in the part of his narrative describing the earls' stay in Louvain, which named one Irish Franciscan only, Diarmaid Ó Conchobhair from Dungiven, Co. Derry.[3] The name of the founder of the college, Flaithrí Ó Maoil Chonaire, gained mention earlier in Ó Cianáin's narrative. Following the arrival of the earls at Douai in Flanders, Ó Maoil Chonaire went there to meet them, and subsequently became part of their escort, first on the way to Louvain, then on the long journey to Rome.[4]

CONFESSIONAL HISTORIES AND HAGIOGRAPHY IN EUROPE

A third reason to remember 1607, although devoid of any immediate Irish involvement, was to be of great relevance to the form and progress of the Louvain scheme. A pamphlet entitled *Fasti sanctorum quorum vitae in belgicis bibliothecis manuscriptae*, which was published in that year by Heribert Rosweyde of the Society of Jesus, was destined to influence all subsequent hagiographical studies.[5] Rosweyde's plan, soon after much expanded from its original focus on the manuscripts of saints' lives in the libraries of Spanish Flanders, underlies the

1 For previous publications of mine touching on the Louvain project, see P. Ó Riain, 'John Colgan's *Trias thaumaturga*', in the 1997 reprint of Colgan, *TT*; P. Ó Riain, 'Irish hagiography of the late sixteenth and early seventeenth centuries' (2002). See Lyons, 'The role of St Anthony's College, Louvain in establishing the Irish Franciscan college network, 1607–60' and Cunningham, 'The Louvain achievement I: the Annals of the Four Masters' both in this volume. Thanks are due to my colleagues, Diarmuid Ó Murchadha and Kevin Murray, for having read and commented on this paper. I also wish to thank John Barry of the Department of Ancient Classics at UCC for helpful comments. **2** P. Walsh (ed.), *Flight of the earls* (1916), p. 56. **3** Walsh, *Flight of the earls*, p. 56. **4** Ibid., p. 36, 56n. **5** See H. Delehaye, *L'oeuvre des Bollandistes* (1920), pp 7–22.

great, and still ongoing, Bollandist series of *Acta Sanctorum*, which took its name
from one of Rosweyde's first disciples, Iohannes Bollandus (John van Bolland).[6]
Rosweyde's ideas also formed the basis of the more modest proposal devised by
the Irish Franciscans of Louvain almost twenty years later, in 1623. Furthermore,
some years before this latter plan was put in place, the appeal made in the *Fasti
sanctorum* for information on the whereabouts of hagiographical manuscripts
appears to have led to the transfer of the *Salmanticensis* collection of saints' lives
from the Irish College in Salamanca to Flanders, where it was placed in
Rosweyde's care.[7] As Paul Grosjean has shown, once their scheme was in place,
the Louvain Franciscans were to be among the earliest users of this hugely
important primary source.[8] And as we shall see, the germ of the idea that led to
Rosweyde's plan may itself have been the subject of some Irish influence.

A fourth event dating to 1607 that deserves to be recalled is the publication of
the twelfth and final volume of the celebrated 'Ecclesiastical Annals' (*Annales
ecclesiastici a Christo nato ad annum 1198*), compiled by the Oratorian historian,
Cardinal Cesare Baronius, in reply to the equally renowned 'Centuries'
(*Centuriae Magdeburgicae*), prepared at Magdeburg by the so-called Centuriators
under the direction of the Lutheran historian Matthias Flacius. The Magdeburg
work was a protestant history of the church, constituting what has been described
as a 'frontal attack' on catholicism, and the reply to it was a measure of the extent
to which ecclesiastical historians of the period were preoccupied with topical confessional issues.[9] In medieval times, the need to protect the interests of individual
churches, or groups of churches, and perhaps also the desire to edify by reference
to saintly example, might lie behind the compilation or collection of saints' lives.
By the early seventeenth century, the inspiration behind hagiographical schemes
lay far more in the desire to promote one branch of Christianity in the face of the
challenge posed by another. The confessional clash between rival Christian creeds,
reformers and counter-reformers, Protestants and Catholics, had, of course,
begun much earlier, but it attained particular vigour during the period that
followed the third, and most influential, session of the Council of Trent, held in
1562–3.[10] Among other developments, this session of the council saw the Jesuit
order, whose founder, Ignatius of Loyola, had died shortly before, in 1556, emerge
as one of the chief instruments of the papacy in its efforts to carry through a
reappraisal of the basic theological and doctrinal position of Catholicism, forced

---

6 For accounts of this scheme, see Delehaye, *L'oeuvre des Bollandistes*; M.D. Knowles, *Great historical
enterprises* (1962), pp 1–32.   **7** Heist, *Vitae SS Hib. Salmanticensi*, pp xxxi–viii; R. Sharpe, *Medieval Irish
saints' lives* (1991), pp 228–30.   **8** Unfortunately, this resulted in the loss of some folios: Heist, *Vitae SS
Hib. Salmanticensi*, p. xxxv (n); Sharpe, *Medieval Irish saints' lives*, p. 228n.   **9** C. Mooney, 'Father John
Colgan, O.F.M.' (1959), p. 14.   **10** For a brief account of the confessional background to the Louvain
scheme, see Mooney, 'Father John Colgan, O.F.M.', pp 13–15.

on it by the rise and spread of Protestantism. In effect, the two main branches of western Christianity were now required to justify their competing claims to be rightful heirs to the early church by re-examining and, if necessary, re-interpreting the ancient records, including those of the saints in all their forms. Thus, some years after the council had concluded its deliberations, a commission of ten scholars, established by Pope Gregory XIII, and including the author of the *Annales*, Cesare Baronius, set about preparing a new, and more authoritative, martyrology of the saints, the so-called *Martyrologium Romanum*, which is still in use today. The confessional background to this undertaking is shown by the title of the tenth and final chapter of Baronius's intoductory *Tractatio* on the subject, which reads: *De falsis haereticorum martyribus eorundemque pseudomartyrologiis*. A measure of its importance in the eyes of the papacy is the fact that the first part of the new martyrology was published on 15 October 1582, the same day as saw the introduction of Gregory's reform of the Julian calendar.[11] And in the half century that followed, the new Roman martyrology ran through several editions, including one prepared at Antwerp in 1617 by Heribert Rosweyde.[12]

RE-DISCOVERING IRISH SAINTS' LIVES: STANIHURST, FITZSIMON AND WHITE

Since the new-found interest in the records of the saints can be traced to a dispute between rival versions of Christianity, it is perhaps appropriate that its initial Irish manifestation involved a convert from Protestantism to Catholicism, Richard Stanihurst of Dublin.[13] While studying at the University of Oxford in 1563, Stanihurst, the son of a speaker of the Irish Parliament, came under the influence of Edmund Campion, converted to Catholicism, and, on returning to Ireland, became tutor to the children of the Earl of Kildare. Subsequently, having fallen foul of the authorities, he was forced into exile in the Netherlands. The publication in Antwerp in 1587, by the famous Plantin printing house, of Stanihurst's Life of St Patrick, pieced together from several sources, none of them biographical, was the first sign of the re-discovery of Ireland's early ecclesiastical history.[14]

---

11 H. Delehaye et al. (eds), *Propylaeum ad AASS Decembris* (1940); R. Aigrain, *L'hagiographie, ses sources, ses méthodes, son histoire* (1953), repr. with bibliographical supplement by R. Godding (2000), pp 91–9. Baronius's *Tractatio* is cited here from p. xlix of the 1902 edition, revised under Leo XIII.   12 H. Rosweyde, *Martyrologium Romanum* (1613).   13 For Stanihurst, see C. Lennon, *Richard Stanihurst* (1981). For criticism by his contemporaries of his views on Ireland, see B. Cunningham, *The world of Geoffrey Keating* (2000), pp 97–8.   14 R. Stanihurst, *De vita S. Patricii Hiberniae apostoli libri II* (1587).

The new phase of Irish hagiography, begun by Stanihurst, was distinctive in at least four ways. Firstly, by far the greater part of its achievement lay on the Continent, in one or other of the many colleges founded to train priests for missionary work, at such centres as Rome, Paris, Salamanca, Douai and Louvain.[15] Secondly, setting aside the vernacular hymns in praise of Patrick and Brigit, with which John Colgan prefaced his acts of the two saints, these publications were almost entirely in Latin.[16] Thirdly, as might be expected of scholarly activity carried out mainly on the Continent, the editors of these publications adopted, to the best of their ability, the standards of editorial practice and criticism that had evolved over the previous hundred years. Fourthly, the new, critical hagiography initially lay, almost exclusively, in the hands of Jesuits. Indeed, even if his own entry to the order is unlikely, Stanihurst appears nonetheless to have had strong Jesuit connections. His Life of St Patrick, for instance, was dedicated to Alessandro Farnese, a strong supporter of the Jesuits, and two of Stanihurst's sons later became well-known members of the order.[17]

In an address to Patrick Plunket, Lord Baron of Dunsany, at the beginning of the first book of his *De rebus in Hibernia gestis*, a history of Ireland written from an Old-English viewpoint and published in Antwerp in 1584, Stanihurst lamented the fact that Ireland alone of the countries of the world remained 'hidden in dense obscurity'.[18] His own failure to rectify this situation may be gleaned from the generally unfavourable reaction of contemporary Irish writers to his book.[19] His work on St Patrick was to prove less controversial, not least because it failed to excite much interest. Thus, while John Colgan noticed the book in his table of 'writers of the acts of St Patrick', he scarcely ever adverted to it in his extensive notes.[20]

By contrast, Colgan cited regularly the 'Catalogue of the principal Irish saints' (*Catalogus praecipuorum sanctorum Hiberniae*), compiled by Stanihurst's cousin, Henry Fitzsimon, who was likewise a convert to Catholicism.[21] Following his conversion, Fitzsimon had gone to the Continent in order to prepare for his reception into the Jesuit order. He studied first at Pont-à-Mousson, then at Douai, where he joined the novitiate, and finally at Louvain, which he entered in 1593 to pursue his theological studies.[22] In the confrontational atmosphere of the

---

15 For a general account of these Irish Colleges, see T.J. Walsh, *The Irish continental college movement* (1974). **16** Colgan, *TT*, pp 1–3, 515–18. **17** One of his sons, William, published several pious books, none of them, according to B. Millett ('Irish literature in Latin, 1550–1700', p. 575), showing originality of thought. Cf. T. Sweeney, *Ireland and the printed word* (1997), p. 755. **18** R. Stanihurst, *De rebus in Hibernia gestis* (1584). Cf. J. Barry, 'Richard Stanihurst's *De rebus in Hibernia gestis*' (2004). **19** Millett, 'Irish literature in Latin', p. 567. Cf. S.J. Connolly (ed.), *The Oxford companion to Irish history* (1998), p. 524. **20** J. Colgan, *AS*, 321ab; idem, *TT*, 219b, 257a. **21** For example, Colgan, *AS*, pp 153 (8), 165 (1), 230 (1, 5), 238 (7), 240 (1), 255 (13), 257 (15), 275 (1). **22** E. Hogan, *Distinguished Irishmen* (1894), pp 204–5.

time, it was perhaps natural that, by Fitzsimon's own account, the reputation of its members as 'janizaries of the Pope, who most impugn the impiety of heretics', should have been among the attractions of the Jesuits.[23] And it was perhaps at Louvain, where he formed a friendship with his fellow student, the previously mentioned Heribert Rosweyde, that Fitzsimon fully realized the potential value of recourse to the records of the saints as a means of overcoming the impiety of heretics. At this stage, he had already become, as he put it himself, an ardent 'ransacker of libraries in his way for his country's antiquities'.[24] While still a student in Pont-à-Mousson, Fitzsimon had been presented with a collection of ninty-four names by Richard Fleming, likewise an Irish Jesuit, who had begun to collect references to Irish saints in continental sources, and while in Louvain, he added to his collection over forty entries from the now lost Jesuit house martyrology known as *Florarium*.[25] Since one surviving copy of the *Catalogus* is mainly in Rosweyde's hand, contact between the two Jesuits clearly continued years after their meeting in Louvain.[26]

Once back in Ireland in 1596, Fitzsimon met the challenge of the reformers on two fronts, through polemics and historical exposition. First, he embarked on a preaching mission that led, according to contemporary reports, to the conversion of hundreds, among them 'many leading men'.[27] Then, emboldened by his initial success, he used what he himself termed his 'stentorian voice' to issue challenges to such noted proponents of reform as Luke Challenor and Meredith Hanmer, before being himself challenged, it would appear, by his kinsman, James Ussher, then not yet twenty years old.[28] Imprisonment followed, but he used his incarceration to good advantage by adding names of saints to his *Catalogus* from no less a source than the *Kilkenniensis* collection of saints' lives, now Marsh's Library MS Z 3.1.5. The longer version of Fitzsimon's *Catalogus*, which contains extracts from the Marsh's Library manuscript, originated, then, as a kind of prison manifesto. Moreover, although designed, as we shall see, to underpin the legitimacy of Catholicism, the composition of the *Catalogus* had been greatly facilitated by Fitzsimon's Protestant protagonist, Meredith Hanmer, who, as far as one can judge, was the source of the manuscript of saints' lives used by the Jesuit.[29] Similarly, one of the first copies to be made of the text, and arguably the earliest to have survived, appears to have been commissioned by the Jesuit's other

23 Hogan, *Distinguished Irishmen*, p. 204. **24** H. Fitzsimon, *A catholic confutation of M. Iohn Rider's clayme of antiquitie* (1608); the quotation is from the 'epistle dedicatorie'. **25** P. Grosjean, 'Édition du *Catalogus*' (1940), pp 340–1. **26** Ibid., p. 337. Even though one can only speculate, an exchange of ideas between the two men while still students, and long before Rosweyde's *Fasti sanctorum* was published, concerning the usefulness of hagiographical sources must seem extremely likely. **27** Hogan, *Distinguished Irishmen*, pp 208, 211. **28** Ibid., pp 224–31. **29** P. Ó Riain, '*Catalogus*' (1999), pp 396–430; at 401; P. Ó Riain (ed.), *Beatha Bharra: Saint Finbarr of Cork* (1994), pp 103–4.

protagonist, James Ussher.[30] These coincidences exemplify how doctrinal differences tended to give way to good working relations when it came to the use of scarce historical sources.

On his release from prison, Fitzsimon returned to the Continent, and there laid the foundation for his reputation as a founding father of modern Irish hagiography by arranging to have the *Catalogus* published at least four times between 1611 and 1621.[31] Never a mere antiquarian list of saints, its unambiguous purpose, especially in later editions, was to show how the Irish had remained in faithful communion with their early Christian past. To demonstrate this unbroken line of succession, Fitzsimon drew entries not only from the record of early Irish Christianity, but also from the ranks of more recent *notabiles*, including some martyrs. In this way, we find among the saints of Ireland Richard Fitz Ralph (†1360), primate of Armagh, whose opposition to the mendicant orders had in fact led to the foundering of the cause for his canonisation.[32] Only in his native Dundalk did Fitz Ralph attract veneration, which may explain why the name of the town accompanies his own in the *Catalogus*. The name of Richard Creagh (†1587), who died as a prisoner in the Tower of London, followed that of Fitz Ralph, and among other recent obits were those of two new martyrs, the Jesuit Brother Dominic Collins (†1602), and the Franciscan friar Cornelius O'Devany (†1612).[33]

Like most other Irish Catholic apologists of this period, Fitzsimon had also a non-confessional concern, the need to remedy the violence Scottish historians had been doing to the medieval records of the Irish saints. By taking *Scotia/Scotus*, which had usually denoted Ireland/Irish, to mean Scotland/Scot, historians such as Hector Boece and Thomas Dempster sought to deprive Ireland of many of her most famous sons and daughters. The outrage felt by Irish writers of the period can be gauged from the fact that almost all of them felt obliged to take part in the ensuing debate.[34] In retrospect, Ireland owes a debt of gratitude to the wayward Scottish historians because the indignation they caused gave an extraordinary impetus to the search for materials needed to rebut their audacious claims.

On the Continent, there was also a practical side to the dispute, brought about by the unsettled conditions that followed the Reformation. The linguistic equivalence between *Scotus* and Scot, *Scotia* and Scotland, exclusive of Ireland, had been used as evidence to support the claim of Catholic Scottish clergy, now forced to leave their homeland in great numbers, to churches on the Continent

---

30 Ó Riain, '*Catalogus*', pp 405–6.   31 Ibid., pp 402–5.   32 Grosjean, 'Édition du *Catalogus*', p. 386 (§600); K. Walsh, *A fourteenth-century scholar* (1981).   33 Grosjean, 'Édition du *Catalogus*', pp 355 (§149), 358 (§ 226). For Collins, see also Hogan, *Distinguished Irishmen*, pp 79–113.   34 Mooney, 'Father John Colgan O.F.M.', pp 13–21.

historically associated with the Irish. In this way, the *monasteria Scotorum* founded by Irishmen in the eleventh and following centuries, and still known in Germany and Austria as *Schottenklöster*, became targets of Scottish take-overs, with some success, as in Regensburg, Würzburg, and Vienna. But this development, too, had a positive side to it. The dispossessed in this case were German monks, who had earlier replaced the Irish monks of the *Schottenklöster*. Now, however, because of the Scottish influx, some of the manuscript remains of the earlier Irish tenure of these churches, such as necrologies and martyrologies, were held to be still useful, thus leading to their survival.[35]

Other Irish Jesuits of the period similarly became involved in the cultivation of hagiography for confessional purposes. Among these, Richard Conway, rector of the Irish College in Salamanca, assembled a calendrical list of Irish saints, drawn mainly from printed books.[36] The Clonmel Jesuit, Stephen White, Fitzsimon's colleague and friend, whom James Ussher described as a man 'of exquisite knowledge in the antiquities, not only of Ireland but also of other nations', became deeply involved in the so-called Scotic debate.[37] White also came under the influence of Heribert Rosweyde, and following the publication of *Fasti sanctorum* in 1607, engaged in a prolonged correspondence with his fellow Jesuit.[38] Like Fitzsimon, White ransacked libraries in search of relevant materials, especially in Germany, and was rewarded by the discovery in Reichenau of the earliest surviving Irish manuscript containing a saint's life, the copy of Adamnán's *Vita Columbae*, which Dorbéne had written on Iona shortly after 700.[39]

THE IRISH FRANCISCAN HAGIOGRAPHICAL SCHEME

Hugh Ward and Patrick Fleming

Despite the friendship formed by both Fitzsimon and White with Rosweyde, the Irish Jesuits never formalized their studies of the records of the Irish saints. This was left to the Irish Franciscans who, in 1623, as already stated, put in place a semi-formal scheme for the production of a *Thesaurus antiquitatum Hibernicarum*, a civil and religious history of Ireland. The scheme was launched not in Louvain but in Paris, at a meeting attended by three Franciscans, Aodh Mac Aingil, on his

---

35 D. Ó Riain-Raedel, 'Das Nekrolog der irischen Schottenklöster' (1992); P. Ó Riain, *Feastdays of the saints* (2006), p. 231. 36 M. Kelly (ed.), *Historiae Catholicae Iberniae* (1850), pp 47–51. 37 Only one of his many works has been published: M. Kelly (ed.), *Apologia pro Hibernia* (1849). For White see E. Hogan, 'Life of Father Stephen White, S.J.' (1897). 38 V. De Buck, 'L'archéologie irlandaise au couvent de saint Antoine de Padoue à Louvain', (1869), p. 590. Cf. Sharpe, *Medieval Irish saints' lives*, p. 44. 39 This is now Generalia 1 in the Stadtbibliothek, Schaffhausen, Switzerland. See A.O. & M.O. Anderson, *Adomnan's life of Columba* (1961; rev. ed. 1991), p. 3.

way to Rome, Patrick Fleming, who was accompanying Mac Aingil, and Hugh
Ward (Aodh Mac an Bhaird), and one secular priest, Thomas Messingham, rector
of the Irish College in Paris.[40] Moreover, the first publication to follow the
inauguration of the scheme, a florilegium or collection of lives of Irish saints, was
published a year later in Paris by Messingham.[41] Dissension with regard to where
transcripts of relevant materials were to be sent, however, soon led to the
exclusion of the Irish College in Paris, and preparations for the scheme were
concentrated in St Anthony's, Louvain. Here, with the approval and, where
possible, the financial assistance of the Irish Franciscan province, Hugh Ward
took all the necessary steps to put in place the collection of manuscript and
printed sources on which the success of the project ultimately depended.

Rosweyde's model had envisaged the publication of eighteen volumes *in folio*,
comprising three preliminary volumes, twelve devoted to the lives of the saints
preserved in manuscripts in local libraries, one containing martyrologies, and two
final volumes of notes, tables and indexes. The scheme worked out at the Paris
meeting would obviously have been more modest, and, when properly in place,
the proposal, as we know from an account given later by John Colgan, was to
publish two or three volumes on the Irish saints who had flourished 'within and
without the country', together with two others, one a prolegomenon devoted to
such matters as the meaning of *Scotia*, still clearly an issue of great concern, the
other containing a treatise on the kings of Ireland.[42] However, among additional
volumes also planned, but never published, was one, or perhaps more, devoted to
martyrologies. And although one cannot be sure of its accuracy, the fresco of
Colgan at work in his cell, now in St Isidore's, Rome, which was prepared some
twelve years after his death in 1658, reveals several bound volumes of lives of
saints, arranged according to the months of the year, together with miscellaneous
volumes, devoted to such subjects as genealogies and kings.

Once the Louvain scheme was in place, the transcription of hagiographical
materials relating to Ireland in the principal libraries of Italy, France, Belgium and
Germany, to be brought together in St Anthony's College, began in earnest. A
number of excerptors appear to have been available from the beginning,
including Patrick Fleming, who sent copies of many documents, collected mainly
in Rome, accompanying them with letters enthusiastically supportive of the
scheme.[43] Under Ward's direction, the bulk of the collecting activity was
completed, not least, as we shall see, because of his decision to dispatch Mícheál

---

40 For an account of the scheme, see Mooney, 'Father John Colgan O.F.M.', pp 13–21; Sharpe, *Medieval Irish saints' lives*, pp 46–74.   41 T. Messingham, *Patricii, Columbae, Brigidae* (1620).   42 C. McNeill, 'Rawlinson manuscripts class B' (1930), pp 143–4.   43 Jennings, 'Documents from the archives of St Isidore's', pp 203–17.

Ó Cléirigh to Ireland in 1626. And after Ward's death in 1635, reponsibility for
the preparatory work was taken over by John Colgan (Seán Mac Colgáin).

Unlike their Jesuit brethren, whose members were largely recruited from the
Catholic gentry of the area around Dublin, many of the Irish Franciscans in the
early years in Louvain were drawn mainly from the northwest and west of
Ireland. Moreover, those directing the Louvain scheme, although thoroughly
schooled in the new sciences John Colgan, for instance, had studied at Glasgow
University and had taught theology at several centres in Germany – belonged to
the native Irish professional classes.[44] Colgan was a member of a hereditary
ecclesiastical family, while his predecessor, Hugh Ward, belonged to a hereditary
bardic or poetic family.[45] Unlike their Jesuit counterparts, who depended in the
main on printed or manuscript works in Latin, the Franciscans could draw not
only on these but also on a wide range of native, vernacular sources. Moreover,
they remained in a position to profit from Jesuit resourcefulness, both previous
and current. Colgan's printed work benefited both from Fitzsimon's *Catalogus*
and from copies of texts that Stephen White continued to provide, including a
transcript of Adamnán's Life of Columba.[46] By way of acknowledgement, Colgan
gratefully and memorably praised White as 'a man thirsting for his country's
antiquities and most knowledgeable in them'.[47]

The work undertaken by the Louvain Franciscans attracted widespread
attention, and not only in Ireland, where most, if not all, bishops received appeals
for information on the saints of their dioceses.[48] Crediting the *patres* of the
convent in Louvain with *magna notitia sanctorum Hiberniae*, the Cologne Jesuit
Philipus Boebius made an enquiry in 1633 concerning the reputedly Irish St
Ursula.[49] In the process, Boebius showed himself to be thoroughly familiar with
the dispute concerning the meaning of *Scotia* 'because the English and Scottish
claim for themselves everything said by the ancients concerning *Britannia aut
Scotia*'.[50] And from the outset, as Robert Godding has shown, the Franciscans
maintained close contact with the Jesuits of Antwerp who, as previously stated,
were not only engaged in a similar, much more ambitious, project, but had also
custody of the *Codex Salmanticensis*.[51]

In Ireland, some of the material transcribed for the use of the Louvain scheme
became available through the good offices of Protestant scholars, including James
Ussher and James Ware, who now held the two major medieval collections of
saints' lives remaining in the country, the so-called *Kilkenniensis* and *Insulensis*.[52]

44 Ó Riain, 'John Colgan's *Trias thaumaturga*', §§ 2, 5.   **45** P.A. Breatnach, 'An Irish Bollandus: Fr Hugh
Ward' (1999).   **46** Colgan, *TT*, p. 372.   **47** Colgan, *AS* (*praefatio ad lectorem*).   **48** Ó Riain, 'John
Colgan's *Trias thaumaturga*', §5; C. Mooney, 'Colgan's inquiries about Irish placenames' (1950).
49 Jennings, 'Documents from the archives of St Isidore's', pp 221–3.   **50** Ibid., p. 224.   **51** R. Godding,
'Irish hagiography in the Acta sanctorum' (2001).

But all of these contacts and activities, external and internal, counted for little when compared to the benefits that accrued to the Louvain scheme from the Franciscans' intimate knowledge of Gaelic Ireland. Here, through years of war and consequent neglect, the manuscript materials were in greatest danger of perishing without trace, but the man entrusted with the duty of salvaging as much as could still be discovered of the early remains was equal to the task.

Mícheál Ó Cléirigh and John Colgan

The 'poor friar', Mícheál Ó Cléirigh, who belonged to a family skilled in vernacular history, arguably made the greatest contribution to the success of the Louvain scheme, after Hugh Ward and John Colgan. Sent from Louvain by Ward with instructions to copy faithfully whatever he deemed to be relevant, Ó Cléirigh travelled the length and breadth of Ireland in search of materials.[53] Although reputed to have copied hundreds of lives of saints, the extant texts of this kind in Ó Cléirigh's hand actually run to about fifty.[54] However, a measure of the enormity of his achievement is the fact that almost half of the corpus of extant vernacular lives of Irish saints was written by him. Moreover, besides compiling a martyrology of Irish saints in collaboration with his cousin Cú Choigcríche Ó Cléirigh, Mícheál also transcribed considerable sections of the Martyrology of Tallaght, since lost from the source manuscript, as well as the only surviving copy of the late twelfth-century Martyrology of Gorman.[55]

While the debt owed by posterity to Mícheál Ó Cléirigh is clearly huge, John Colgan also showed himself to have been fully aware of his colleague's truly remarkable achievement. In composing the *praefatio ad lectorem* of his *Acta sanctorum Hiberniae* a few months after Ó Cléirigh's death in 1643, Colgan paid a handsome tribute to his *confrater*. Moreover, although placing him third after Ward and Fleming, he devoted more space to Ó Cléirigh's contribution than to any other, describing him as 'a man exceedingly well versed in the antiquities of his country, to whose pious labours over many years, this, and the other works we are printing, owe most of all'.[56] Unfortunately, Colgan's *Acta* was the only published volume of what was intended to be four, covering the saints of the whole year. His other published work, *Triadis thaumaturgae*, was concerned with Ireland's three principal saints, Patrick, Brigit, and Colum Cille. Despite the semi-formal nature of their scheme, the Irish Franciscans of Louvain did not allow for the need to put their arrangements on a permanent footing, designed to

---

52 Sharpe, *Medieval Irish saints' lives*, pp 61–8.   **53** For Ó Cléirigh's travels, Jennings, *Michael O Cleirigh*; P. Walsh (N. Ó Muraíle (ed.)), *Irish leaders and learning* (2003), pp 350–70.   **54** C. Plummer (ed.), *Miscellanea hagiographica Hibernica* (1925), pp 179–97.   **55** Plummer, *Miscellanea hagiographica Hibernica*, p. 225; *MartO*, pp viii–ix; *MartT*, pp xv–xix.   **56** Colgan, *AS* (*praefatio ad lectorem*).

last well beyond the lifetimes of its originators. However, what remained after the collapse of the scheme was a large collection of mainly hagiographical manuscripts, many of them written by Mícheál Ó Cléirigh, and dozens of printed works, which, perhaps because of the dispersal of the library in the wake of the French Revolution, are but only now receiving due attention. Fortunately, the greater part of the manuscript collection has survived, and is now divided between the Bibliothèque Royale in Brussels and the Franciscan collection in the archives of University College Dublin.[57]

The hagiographers of the late sixteenth and early seventeenth centuries, both Jesuit and Franciscan, were the first to apply to the records of the Irish saints the editorial methods that had been developed by Renaissance scholars. Colgan has been justly accused of adopting a largely uncritical approach to the contents and provenance of his materials, often accepting hopelessly exaggerated claims concerning their antiquity.[58] Whether, as Canice Mooney suggested, he was disarmed by the consciousness that he was dealing with the lives of holy men written by other holy men, or whether, as Bieler pointed out, it was then too early to have expected the kind of textual criticism that we have become accustomed to, is beside the point.[59] Viewed from a modern perspective, Colgan's naivity was a blessing in disguise, because it encouraged him not only to use sources since lost, but also to write expansive notes, which in many cases constitute primary sources in their own right. Notable cases in point are his Latin translation of a version of the Tripartite Life that has since disappeared, and his citations from the Martyrology of Cashel, which are all that remain of this important source.[60]

A full study of Colgan's manuscript sources has not yet been made; nor has there been any systematic attempt to identify the library of printed works at his disposal. Studies such as these will no doubt eventually place the Louvain Franciscans in their proper historical context, together with the many other ecclesiastical historians of the period who felt the need to participate in an essentially confessional dispute concerning the legitimacy of Catholic claims to the Christian legacy. As already stated, Colgan's career included a period spent teaching in Germany, at a time when parts of central Europe were being laid waste by armies involved in the Thirty Years War (1618–48), which began as a religious conflict. Indeed, some of those participating in the Louvain scheme paid with their lives for their support of the Catholic cause, including one of its co-founders, Patrick Fleming.[61] Shortly after the scheme was inaugurated, Fleming,

---

57 For the Franciscan collection in UCD, formerly in FLK, see *Cat. Ir. MSS FLK*. A catalogue of the Brussels manuscripts has yet to be published. 58 Ó Riain, 'John Colgan's *Trias thaumaturga*', §8. 59 L. Bieler, '*Trias thaumaturga*, 1647' (1959), p. 48; Mooney, 'Father John Colgan O.F.M.', p. 31. 60 W. Stokes (ed.), *The tripartite life of St Patrick* (1887), i, pp i, x–xiv; P. Ó Riain (ed.), *Four Irish martyrologies* (2003), pp 162–84. 61 E. Hogan, 'Patrick Fleming OSF' (1870–1).

writing from Rome, exhorted Hugh Ward to persevere in the good work then just begun. Since Fleming's sentiments reflect a spirit typical of the time, they may serve here as a tribute to the magnificient service rendered by the Louvain Franciscans to their *religio et patria*.[62]

> *Vive in spe, Hugo magnanime; faciemus, faciemus, permittente glorificatore Sanctorum, ut aliquid nostra diligentia splendoris Hyberniae sanctis accedat.*

> Live in hope, generous Hugh; let us do it; let us do it, the glorifier of the saints permitting, so that by our hard work something of splendour may come to the saints of Ireland.

---

62 Jennings, 'Documents from the archives of St Isidore's College', p. 211.

The theological and philosophical accomplishments of the Irish Franciscans: from Flaithrí Ó Maoil Chonaire to Bonaventure Baron

M.W.F. STONE

> O gentle company far off on Ireland's plain
> Let us speak of learning and put grief away;
> Let us get down to business as all men must:
> On behalf of Ireland let us drink a toast.

Pádraigín Haicéad, *In Louvain 1630*[1]

While the speculative achievements of the Irish Observant Franciscans have been duly honoured by the historians of their own order,[2] there is a sense in which their notable contribution to early modern philosophical and theological discourse is still largely unknown. When the friars are remembered in Ireland, they are consigned to the custody of scholars of the Irish language and history, the assumption being that their accomplishments belong among the subjects of those disciplines, rather than to any reliable chronicle of the Irish legacy to early modern philosophy and theology.

The omission of the friars from most surveys of the intellectual history of Ireland needs to be redressed.[3] Their exclusion obscures the reputation that several Franciscans enjoyed as philosophers, theologians, and scholars in their own day,[4] and also fails to register the lasting and quite remarkable contribution which the friars, along with other members of the exiled Irish clergy, secular and regular, made to European learning in the seventeenth and eighteenth centuries.[5]

---

1 Pádraigín Haicéad (*c*.1600–54), a Dominican friar of the Cashel, Co. Tipperary, who visited Louvain in 1630 and 1652. Translation by M. Hartnett, *Haicéad* (1993), p. 20. **2** The subject has been treated in the works of Brendan Jennings, Canice Mooney, Cathaldus Giblin, Benignus Millett, and Ignatius Fennessy. It has also been discussed by European friars such as Lucien Ceyssens, and Charles (Carlo) Balič. **3** For a detailed discussion of the Irish friars and why they have been overlooked in many of the standard histories of Irish thought, see M.W.F. Stone, 'Punch's riposte' (2009). The present article reproduces some of this material, albeit in a very different form. **4** On Ó Maoil Chonaire see C. Heaney, *The theology of Florence Conry* (1935). Wadding's immense reputation is documented in *Father Luke Wadding: commemorative volume* (1957). On the fame of Mac Aingil, Punch, and Baron see C. Giblin, 'Hugh McCaghwell, O.F.M., archbishop of Armagh (†1626)' (1983–5) reprinted in Millett & Lynch, *Dún Mhuire*; M. Grajewski, 'John Ponce, Franciscan Scotist of the seventeenth century' (1946); and J.J. Silke, 'Irish scholarship in the Renaissance' (1973). **5** For a recent discussion of this topic see the excellent study by L. Chambers, *Michael Moore, c.1639–1726* (2005), which considers the contribution of Moore and other Irish exiles to the

Billeted in their colleges in the Iberian peninsula, the Low Countries, central and eastern Europe, Rome and other parts of Italy,[6] several Irish Franciscans broached the core issues of philosophy and theology as they were understood by the cognoscenti of post-Tridentine Catholicism.[7] In philosophy, these individuals made telling contributions to logic,[8] metaphysics,[9] and significantly aided the development of the modern school of 'Scotism', an enterprise which reached its zenith with the publication at Lyons in 1639 by Luke Wadding (1588–1657) of the first modern critical edition of the *Opera omnia* of John Duns Scotus (1265/6–1308), the highly influential Franciscan thinker of the Middle Ages.[10] Both before and after the printing of this monumental work, the friars published tomes of commentary, polemic, and novel works of analysis and synthesis, all of which purported to defend or to clarify Scotist teaching so as to make it one of the most dynamic schools of the period.[11]

In theology, Irish Franciscans considered and then rejected the controversial moral doctrine of probablism; hounded the minutiae of vexed issues concerning grace and human nature as they had been left open following the reluctance of successive popes to decide the *De auxiliis* controversy (1602–5) in favour of either the Jesuits or the Domincans; flirted with and then cooled in their attitudes toward Jansenism; and most importantly of all, defended with great alacrity and acumen the cause of the doctrine of the Immaculate Conception of Mary.[12] In all these areas, subjects that dominated the theological agenda of Catholic Europe

intellectual life of the University of Paris. For other publications see T. O'Connor (ed.), *The Irish in Europe, 1580–1815* (2001); O'Connor & Lyons, *Irish migrants in Europe after Kinsale* (2003). **6** For the best general discussion see Millett, *The Irish Franciscans*, pp 105–223. See also C. Giblin, 'The contribution of Irish Franciscans on the Continent' (1981). On the colleges see J. O'Boyle, *The Irish colleges on the Continent* (1935). **7** In 1661, John Punch, then based in Paris, could record that since the beginning of the seventeenth century there had been at least seventy-three Franciscan theologians, philosophers and canonists of high distinction that had held professiorial chairs and lectureships in the major universities of Catholic Europe; see *Scotus Hiberniae restitutus*, pp 23–4, prefixed to *Commentarii theologici*, I, pars prima (1661); and Stone, 'Punch's riposte', pp 185–91. **8** See especially John Punch's *Logica*, the first volume of his *Integer cursus ad mentem Scoti* (1643). This work was later republished as the *Integer philosophiae cursus ad mentem Scoti* (1649). **9** For evidence of the sophisticated metaphysics of the seventeenth-century friars note Aodh Mac Aingil [Cavellus]'s work, *In quatuor libros Sententiarum* (1620); and the courses on metaphysics offered by Bonaventure Baron, *Fr. Joannes Duns Scotus Ordinis Minorum Doctor Subtilis* (1664); and by John Punch, *Libri de generatione et corruptione, meteoris, anima, parvis naturalibus, et metaphysica*, this being the third volume of *Interger philosophiae cursus ad mentem Scoti* (1643). **10** The circumstances and publication of this edition are described by C. M. Balič, 'Wadding, the Scotist' (1957); and D. Scaramuzzi, 'La prima edizione dell'*Opera Omnia* di D. Duns Scoto (1639)' (1930). **11** On early modern Scotism see D. de Caylus, 'Merveilleux épanouissement de l'école scotiste au XVIIe siècle' (1910–11); an article that needs to be supplemented by P. Uriël Smeets, *Lineamenta bibliograhiae Scotisticae* (1942). For a general synthesis see B. Jansen, 'Zur Philosophie der Skotisten im 17. Jahrhunderts' (1936). For a more recent consideration see J. Schmutz, 'L'héritage des subtils' (2002). **12** On the Irish Franciscan contribution to all these debates see Stone, 'Punch's riposte'.

from the close of the Council of Trent in 1563 to the outbreak of the French Revolution in 1789,[13] the friars made a series of able and distinctive contributions that are worthy of comment.

This chapter will deal with the extent to which Irish Franciscans were embroiled in the major debates of their time. It will involve an examination of the salient components of the philosophical and theological thought of key figures whose writings and teaching helped to recast, and in some cases ameliorate, long standing debates that had either reached an impasse or were in need of renewal. Those whose works are considered include Flaithrí Ó Maoil Chonaire (Latinized to 'Conrius') (c.1560–1629),[14] Aodh Mac Aingil (Latinized to 'Cavellus') (1571–1626),[15] Anthony Hickey (Latinized to 'Hiquaeus') (1586–1641),[16] Luke Wadding,[17] John Punch (Latinized to 'Poncius') (1599 or 1603–1661 or 1672/3);[18] and Bonaventure Baron (1610–80).[19] All of them had important connections to Franciscan colleges in Salamanca, Louvain, Rome, and Prague.[20] While it is probably invidious to single out these individuals at the expense of others who are just as deserving of commentary and analysis,[21] or to leave the period after the death of Baron without substantial comment,[22] there is a sense in which the efforts of these six

13 For a general survey of Catholic dogmatic and moral theology in this period see M.W.F. Stone, 'Early modern Catholic theology' (forthcoming).   **14** The most recent biographical sketches of Ó Maoil Chonaire are by T. Clavin, 'Conry, Florence', *ODNB*, vol. 12 (2004), pp 996–8; D. Downey, 'Archbishop Florence Conry of Tuam' (2004), pp 86–90; A. McKenna et al., 'Florent Conry' (2004), p. 293. See Luke Wadding, *Scriptores*; M.R. Pazas, 'Religiosos irelandeses de la Provincia de Santiago' (1945).   **15** See T. Clavin, 'MacCaughwell, Hugh', *ODNB*, vol. 35 (2004), pp 82–3. See also Wadding, *Scriptores*, col. 120; and Nicholas Vernulaeus, *Rhetoricum Collegi Porcensis inclitae academiae Lovaniensis Orationum* (1657); A. Goyena Pérez, 'D. Fr. Hugo Cavello Francisco, Arzobispo de Armagh (1571–1626)' (1927); M. Mac Conmara, 'Mac Aingil agus an Scotachas Éireannach' (1988); and M. Dunne, 'Nicholas Vernulaeus, Aodh MacAingil and the anonymous author from the *Collegium Pastorale*' (2008).   **16** For Hickey's life and writings see P. É. d'Alençon, 'Hickey, Anthony', *Dictionnaire de théologie catholique*, vol. 6 (1920), cols 2358–9; Cleary, *Father Luke Wadding and St Isidore's College Rome* (1925), pp 73–8.   **17** I. Fennessy, 'Wadding, Luke', *ODNB*, vol. 56 (2004), 643–9 which includes an extensive bibliography.   **18** See T. Clavin, 'Punch, John (1599–1672/3)', *ODNB*, vol. 45 (2004), 561–2; A. Teetaert, 'Ponce, Jean', *Dictionnaire théologie catholique*, vol. 12 (1935), cols 2546–8. There seems to be some confusion about the year of Punch's death. Most scholars give 1673/3, but there is some evidence that he may have died as early as 1661, and that he was buried in the convent of the Parisian Conventuals. This can be established in the necrology, based on the Archives Nationales (series LL 1598–LL 1527A) published by J. Poulenc, 'Deux registers de religieux décédes au grand couvent de Paris' (1966), p. 344.   **19** See T. Clavin, 'Baron, Bartholomew', *ODNB*, vol. 4 (2004), pp 13–14; Cleary, *Father Luke Wadding and the College of St Isidore*, pp 85–100; B. Millett, 'Bonaventure Baron, O.F.M. *Hibernus Clonmeliensis*' (1950), reprinted in Millett, *The Irish Franciscans*, pp 469–73.   **20** See Millett, *The Irish Franciscans*, pp 105–223.   **21** For a useful list of individuals who need to be studied see B. Millett, 'Irish Scotists at St Isidore's College, Rome' (1968), iv, pp 412–9.   **22** The period from Ó Maoil Chonaire to Punch has been represented as a 'Golden Age' for the Irish Franciscans (see C. Mooney, 'The golden age of the Irish Franciscans'). The remaining years down to the outbreak of the French Revolution have not been examined. A close study of the FLK and UCD-OFM 'B' and 'C' manuscripts, which contain a great deal of theological and philosophical content, ought to provide a glimpse into these lost centuries. For a useful description of the B manuscripts see I. Fennessy, 'The B manuscripts in the Franciscan Library at Killiney' (1995).

highly talented friars encompass a diversity of interests that characterize the
unique legacy of the Irish Franciscans to early modern philosophy and theology.
Before examining their work, however, it is necessary to comment on the
scholastic schools of seventeenth-century Catholic Europe, and to describe the
leading school to which the Irish friars pledged their allegiance, Scotism.

SCHOLASTIC PHILOSOPHY AND SCOTISM IN EUROPE

For the past two centuries, early modern scholastic philosophy and theology, to
which the Irish Franciscans made a redoubtable contribution have been traditionally neglected by historians of European thought.[23] Recent studies, however,
have done much to dispel the unfair caricatures and negative assessments that
blighted its earlier analysis, and have begun to recapture a sense of the vibrancy
and innovation that were identifiable features of seventeenth-century scholastic
discourse. Collectively, these writings demonstrate that the scholastic schools of
the early modern period were not recalcitrant relics from the Middle Ages, but
were intellectually contiguous with the practices and concerns of early modernity.[24]
This fact is reflected in the Scotist school to which the Irish Observants belonged,
for it is important to emphasize that this community of ideas was neither a
monolithic nor a closed intellectual system. Even though there were effusive
admirers of Scotus among the ranks of Irish friars and elsewhere, there was no
overbearing official dogma in the school itself. Considerable disagreement on
issues in metaphysics, ethics, and philosophical theology was permitted and even
encouraged.[25]

   The 'school of Scotus' became an identifiable presence in European thought at
the beginning of the sixteenth century when the works of Scotus were collected,
published in several editions, and systematically analyzed. Though indebted to
earlier traditions of commentary in the fourteenth and fifteenth centuries,[26] early
modern Scotism, both intellectually and geographically, was much more expansive than earlier incarnations, providing a wider dissemination of its founder's
ideas and methods. Its progress in Catholic Europe and in the new colonies was
assisted from 1501 onwards, when regulations of general chapters of the

---

23 Negative assessments of early modern scholasticism have always been a feature of accounts of the
development of medieval philosophy and scholasticism going back at least as far as K. Werner, *Die
Scholastik des späteren Mittelalters* (1881–7). See also M. De Wulf, *Histoire de la philosophie médiévale* (1925),
ii, pp 243–94.   24 S. Knebel, *Wille, Würfel und Wahrscheinlichkeit* (2000); J. Schmutz, 'Bulletin de
scolastique moderne (I)' (2000); M. Forlivesi, *Scotistarum princeps: Bartolomeo Mastri* (2002); M.W.F.
Stone, 'Scholastic schools and early modern philosophy' (2006).   25 Schmutz, 'L'héritage des subtils', pp
60–80.   26 On the early school see C. Bérubé, 'La première école scotiste' (1984); L. Honnefelder, 'Scotus
und der Scotismus' (1995).

Franciscans recommended or directly prescribed the *doctrina Scotistae* as the teaching to be followed by the Observants and Conventuals.[27] Furthermore, in the late fifteenth and early sixteenth centuries, chairs of Scotist theology were established at the universities of Paris, Rome, Coimbra, Salamanca, Alcalá, Padua, and Pavia, thereby providing the school with a strong institutional foundation.

Scotism can be said to have approached its peak in the first half of the seventeenth century, when one observer, the Cistercian polymath Juan Caramuel y Lebkowitz (1606–82) was moved to remark: 'the school of Scotus is more numerous than all the other schools taken together'.[28] In the eighteenth century the movement still had an important following, especially in Germany, parts of southern Europe, and Latin America,[29] but subsequently fell into decline, a state of affairs explicable by the repeated suppressions endured by Franciscan communities in many countries,[30] and by the increasing tendency of several popes towards the end of that century to recommend the thought of the Dominican Thomas Aquinas (1224–74) as normative for Catholic theologians and philosophers.[31]

The Irish friars did not merely gravitate toward the teachings of Scotus on account of their shared Franciscan heritage. There were much stronger connections that bound them to his thought. First and foremost, there was the long-standing belief that Scotus himself was Irish, and that he had been born at Downpatrick in Ulster.[32] The very idea that Scotus was Irish provided the friars with sufficient cause to defend his honour against any attack on his reputation. A good example of such dedication to the cause is to be found in 1617, when a Polish Dominican Abraham Bzowski ('Bzovius') (1567–1637) penned a trenchant refutation of Scotus that so appalled a whole generation of Irish friars,[33] that they were moved to answer the Bzowski's charges in ever greater detail. Leading the counter-attack against the perceived calumnies was Aodh Mac Aingil who penned a *Vita Scoti* and an *Apologia*, in order to counter Bzowski's criticisms.[34] Tellingly,

---

27 See M.J.F.M. Hoenen, 'Scotus and the Scotist school' (1998). **28** Juan Caramuel y Lebokowitz, *Theologia moralis fundamentalis* (1657), Lib. II, disp. 10: '*Scoti schola numerosior est omnibus aliis simul sumptis*'. On the quotation see F. Bak, '"Scoti schola numerosior est omnibus aliis simul sumptis"' (1956). See also the remarks made by Wadding, *Annales*, ad an 1308, nn. 52 and 54. **29** On the Franciscans in the New World see M. Beuchot, *Historia de la filosofía en el México colonial* (1996), pp 15–43. **30** On the fortunes of the three orders of Franciscans, the Observants, Conventuals and Capuchins, see O. Chadwick, *The popes and European revolution* (1981), pp 13–14, 26, 35, 43–6, 60–5, 162–9, 214–18, 526–7, and 593–5. For an interesting account as to how the debates of the Enlightenment impacted upon one Franciscan community see T. Kogler, *Das philosophisch-theologische Studium der Bayrischen Franziskaner* (1925). **31** Schmutz, 'L'héritage des subtils', pp 60–80; Stone, 'Scholastic schools and early modern philosophy', pp 310–13. **32** It has now been firmly established that Scotus was born in Scotland. The evidence is presented and reviewed by C. Balič, 'The life and work of John Duns Scotus' (1965), pp 2–14. **33** A. Bzovius, *Annales ecclesiastici, XIII* (1617), pp 831–2. The gist of Bzowski's complaint was that the writings of Scotus were obscure and unintelligible, and lost in utter darkness. He even joked that the name 'Scotus' was derived from the Greek 'skotino' meaning 'dark'. **34** Both these works were included in his *In quatuor*

Mac Aingil's students Bonaventure Magennis (*fl.* 1623) followed in his footsteps
with the publication of the *Apologia apologiae pro Ioanne Duns Scoto*, which was
published at Paris in 1623, as did Anthony Hickey with his *Nitela Franciscanae
Religionis et abseterio sordium quibus eam conspurcare frustra tentavit Abrahamus
Bzovius*, which appeared in Lyons in 1627. After these others played their part,
with William Casey (*fl.* 1638),[35] the acclaimed hagiographer John Colgan,[36] and
John Punch,[37] all writing tomes of polemic to defend Scotus. Added to this list
was the earlier *Vita R.P. Joannis Duns Scoti* of Luke Wadding,[38] a work more
circumspect about Scotus's origin,[39] but one just as resolute in its defence of his
thought and piety.

SCOTISM AND THE IRISH FRIARS IN THE LATE MEDIEVAL PERIOD

By the seventeenth century Scotism constituted the very centre of the Irish friars'
theological outlook, but it was not always thus. At the end of the Middle Ages
there is hardly any evidence to suggest that Franciscans in Ireland were reading
the works of Scotus with the same frequency, expertise, and enthusiasm as their
early modern successors. Recent research on the late medieval friars paints a vivid
picture of their religious, liturgical, and disciplinary concerns, revealing them to
be much more exercised by the vicissitudes of preaching and other pastoral
responsibilities than with the demands of speculative theology and philosophy.[40]

The first ostensible connection between the Irish Franciscans and Scotism,
however, seems to appear in the person of the English Conventual, and former
Observant, John Foxall (*c.*1415–75).[41] A well-known exponent of Scotist theology,
Foxall enjoyed a considerable reputation in late fifteenth-century Rome and
Bologna due to his prowess in the debate *De arcanis Dei* on the role of future
contingents in divine foreknowedge.[42] For this and other reasons, he was raised to

libros Sententiarum (1620).   **35** William Casey, *Vindicationes apologeticae Doctoris Subtilis* (1638). This work
is listed by Ioannes a S. Antonio, *Bibliotheca universa franciscana* (1732), i, col. 45.   **36** John Colgan,
Tractatus de Ioannis Scoti, Doctoris Subtilis (1655). This work was written to refute the claims of an English
Franciscan Richard Angelus a S. Francisco Mason (1599–1678) that Scotus was an Englishman. Mason
wrote a reply to the *Tractatus*, with his *Apologia pro Scoto Anglo* (1656), Colgan was too ill to continue the
fight, dying on 15 January 1658. Punch then entered the fray with the work listed below in fn. 37.   **37** John
Punch, *Scotus Hiberniae restitutus*, in his *Commentarii theologici quibus Ioannis Duns Scoti quaestiones* (1661),
cols 1–39.   **38** This is added to the first volume of *Ioannis Duns Scoti, Opera omnia* (1639), i, cols 1–34. The
text was later published as self-standing tome, *Vita R.P.F. Ioannis Duns Scoti* (1644). For further discussion
see Balič, 'Wadding the Scotist', pp 463–74.   **39** Wadding, *Vita R.P.F. Ioannis Duns Scoti*, c. 1, p. 3: 'patria,
aetas, mors, haec plus ceteris incerta'.   **40** Ó Clabaigh, *Franciscans in Ireland*, pp 42–80, 106–57; B. Roest,
A history of Franciscan education (2000), pp 272–324.   **41** G.J. Etzkorn, 'John Foxal, OFM. His life and
writings' (1989); L. Di Fonzo, 'Il minorita inglese Giovanni Foxholes' (1999).   **42** C. Schabel, *Theology at
Paris, 1316–1345* (2000), pp 151, 163, 314, 325–6, 328.

the position of archbishop of Armagh on 16 December 1471 by his old friend and fellow friar Franciscus della Rovere OFM (1441–84), who later became Pope Sixtus IV.[43] Due to unpaid debts owed to the Roman Curia by his predecessor in Armagh, Foxall was never able to enter his diocese, and finished his days languishing in the London convent of the Conventuals.

The exploits of another Conventual friar, a native Irishman, Maurice O'Fihely (Ó Ficheallaigh) (*c*.1460–1513), seem to offer a more tangible link between the emerging Scotist school and the Irish friars. The facts of his early career are obscure and accounts of the period of his life before 1488 are a matter for conjecture.[44] Known as *Mauritius Hibernicus de Portu*,[45] and *Flos mundi* ('Flower of the World') for his erudition,[46] O'Fihely was appointed archbishop of Tuam in 1506, but remained in Italy for six more years. He died in Galway en route to take up his see. His fame rested on a long and celebrated academic career as an exponent of Scotist thought.[47] As with Foxall, O'Fihely's direct influence on the future direction of the Irish friars is difficult to determine, not least for the reason that the last twenty-three years of his life were spent teaching in Padua, a university which by the end of the fifteenth century had an established chair of Scotist theology.[48] An obvious consequence of his foreign residency was that O'Fihely had little or no contact with his native brethren (except those who may have studied at Padua), and this makes it difficult to gauge the extent of his influence on a later generation of Irish friars. In any case, the protracted squabbles and unseemly rivalry between the Conventuals and Observants in late medieval Ireland, may well have mitigated the extent of his influence had he returned to the land of his birth in the years before his episcopal election.[49] That said, his commentary on Scotus was used and consulted by sundry Scotists at Padua,[50] and

---

43 On Sixtus see E. Lee, *Sixtus IV and Men of Letters* (1978); L. Di Fonzo, 'Sisto IV. Carriera scolastica e integrazioni biografiche' (1986).   **44** C. Ó Clabaigh, 'O'Fihily, Maurice', in *Dictionary of Irish philosophers*, pp 263–4 and *DIB*, forthcoming.   **45** Luke Wadding interpreted the toponym *de Portu* as referring to the port town of Baltimore, Co. Cork. Other writers see it as deriving from the Augustinian monastery *St Maria de portu puro* in the diocese of Clonfert.   **46** J. Neary, 'Maurice O'Fihily, Flos Mundi and his times' (1925); P. Scapin, 'Maurizio O'Fihely editore e commentatore di Duns Scoto' (1976); idem, 'Il contributo dei formalisti padovani al problema delle distinzioni' (1966), pp 624–6; Conlan, *St Isidore's College Rome*, pp 61–102.   **47** G. Franchini, *Bibliosofia e memorie letterarie di scrittori francescani Conventuali* (1693), p. 454; Wadding, *Scriptores*, cols 172–3; M.K. Walsh, 'Irish books printed abroad' (1963), pp 23–4. O'Fihely's main work is Mauritius Hibernicus de Portu, *Epitomata castigationum, conformitatum atque elucidationum in questiones metaphysice, de primo principio tractatum, atque theoremata doctoris subtilis fratris Ioannis Duns Scoti*. This work was published for the first time as an appendix to *Ioannes Duns Scotus Questiones subtilissime in Metaphysicam* (1497). The most recent reprint of his work is Wadding's edition of the *Opera omnia* (1639) see vol. IV.   **48** On Scotism at fifteenth-century Padua see E.P. Mahoney, 'Duns Scotus and the school of Padua' (1979); A. Poppi, *Ricerche sulla teologia e la scienza nella Scuola padovana del Cinque e Seicento* (2001).   **49** On the tensions between the Observants and Conventuals in late medieval Ireland see Ó Clabaigh, *Franciscans in Ireland*, pp 19–42, 58–79.   **50** Mahoney, 'Duns Scotus and the school of Padua', pp 217–18.

later editors such as Mac Aingil, Wadding, and even the modern editors of Scotus's *Opera philosophica*, have incorporated his suggestions in their own versions of the relevant texts.[51] A learned commentator of Scotus, whose work has yet to be studied in the detail it deserves, O'Fihely is most undeserving of the ungracious comment by a celebrated historian of the Franciscan order that 'he added nothing new to human thought'.[52]

IRISH FRANCISCAN THEOLOGIANS IN THE SEVENTEENTH CENTURY

Although it might appear unlikely, the seeds of the long attachment of the Irish friars to Scotism were sown in Salamanca. Due to the political conflicts of late sixteenth- and early seventeenth-century Ireland, many students and clerics made their way to Spain in order to begin or resume an education denied to them at home due to the bleak realities of civil strife and displacement. Those inclining to a career with religious orders like the Observant Franciscans gravitated to their house of studies in university towns like Salamanca. By the time the Irish arrived, the Franciscan convent there already enjoyed a great reputation for learning, with theologians such as Andréas de Vega (*c.*1498–1549) and Alfonso de Castro (1495–1588) having made a significant contribution to the theological debates at the Council of Trent.[53] This tradition was upheld and improved upon in the early years of the seventeenth century, when Francisco de Ovando (*fl.* 1577),[54] Juan de Rada (*c.*1545–1608),[55] Mateus de Sosa (*fl.* 1629),[56] Francisco de Herrera (1551– 1609),[57]

---

51 See for instance the remarks of the editors of the *Quaestiones super libros Metaphysicorum Aristotelis,* libri I–V, pp xxxi–xxxii. **52** J.R.H. Moorman, *History of the Franciscan Order* (1968), p. 539. **53** B. Oromi, *Los Franciscanos españoles en el Concilio de Trento* (1947); R. Varesco, 'I Frati Minori al Concilio di Trento' (1948). On Vega see also H.A. Oberman, *The dawn of the Reformation* (1992), pp 204–33. **54** A Spainard who later spent many years in Peru, becoming bishop of Trujillo. Ovando's influential *Breviloquium scholasticae theologiae in quatuor libros Magistri Sententiarum,* was published Salamanca at 1584, and again at Madrid in 1587. See 'Ovando, François', *Dictionnaire de théologie Catholique,* vol. 11 (1932), col. 1674. **55** An eirenic thinker who sought to contrive a conciliation between the rival schools of early modern scholasticism, Rada is possibly less of a pure Scotist than his Salamancan contemporaries. His *Controversiae theologicae inter S. Thomam et Scotam super quatuor libros Sententiarum,* was published at Salamanca in 1586, with later prinitings at Venice, 1601, 1604, and 1617, and at Cologne, 1620. See I. Vázquez Janeiro, 'El arzobispo Juan de Rada y el molinismo' (1962). **56** A Portugese Scotist resident in Spain who was celebrated as an editor. His main work was *Optata diu articulatio et illustratio libri primi Sententiarum Doctoris Subtilissimi I.D. Scoti* (1629). **57** A major commentator on Scotus ever present in the *Covento de San Francisco* in Salamanca. His important works are *Disputationes thelogicae et commentaria in primum librum Sententiarum doct. Subtilis a 28 usque ad 48* (1589); *In Secundum* (1600); *Manuale theologicum et resolutissima dilucidatio principalium quaestionum quae communiter in quatuor libris Sententiarum disputantur* (1607), with later editions at Paris, 1616, and Venice, 1644. For further discussion see D. Savall, 'La interpretacíon escotista en la provincia de Santiago' (1939); and I. Vázquez Janeiro, 'Fr Francisco de Herrera, OFM' (1965).

and Juan Ovando de Paredes (d. 1610),[58] all wrote works of speculative theology that added to the depth and sophistication of Scotist school. Since three of the leading theologians of the Irish Franciscans, Flaithrí Ó Maoil Chonaire, Aodh Mac Aingil, and Luke Wadding, had direct connections with Salamanca, either as students or else as teachers,[59] it is reasonable to conclude that the enduring Scotist proclivities of the Irish friars owed as much to the intellectual tradition of the Franciscan house of studies at Salamanca, as it did to any other discernible influence. In this respect the theological and philosophical expertise of the friars might be said to have developed as a direct result of their condition as exiles.

Flaithrí Ó Maoil Chonaire

The first substantial theologian of the Irish Franciscans at this time was Flaithrí Ó Maoil Chonaire, an individual whose intellectual interests, political passions, quizzical personality, and general approach to theology, set him apart from many of his colleagues.[60] Although he maintained a resolute interest in the propagation of traditional Franciscan and Scotist doctrines such as the Immaculate Conception, thereby affirming an impeccable Salamancan provenance,[61] there is a sense in which Ó Maoil Chonaire was not a 'scholastic', at least in the sense in which that term might be used to characterize the methods and arguments employed by Mac Aingil, Hickey, and Punch. For unlike them, he drew his inspiration not from the medieval schoolmen but from the Fathers, specifically the writings of Augustine. Though his distinctive theological outlook never caused him to quarrel with Scotism as such,[62] it did move him to query the validity of the pronouncements of many contemporary scholastic theologians, especially members of the Jesuit order whom he particularly disliked, on topics such as grace, nature, limbo, and infant baptism. Ó Maoil Chonaire could not help himself from pointing out that elements of their teaching were contradicted by the teachings of the ancient church as upheld by Augustine.

---

58 Another influential Observant theologian in Spain, whose reputation was based on his work *Commentarii in tertium librum Sententiarum Ioannis* (1597); see I. Vázquez Janeiro, 'Los Juan de Ovando' (1978). **59** For an invaluable assessment of the relationship between the Irish friars and Spain, albeit one specified to consider the activities of Luke Wadding, see Manuel de Castro, 'Wadding and the Iberian Peninsula' (1957). **60** Something of the man is captured in the following studies: F. O'Byrne, 'Florence Conry, archbishop of Tuam' (1927); (1928); Heaney, *The theology of Florence Conroy*; Ceyssens, 'Conry, de Burgo, Wadding and Jansenism', pp 267–95; O'Connor, *Irish Jansenists*. **61** Ó Maoil Chonaire's debt to Salamanca is clear in his first published work *De Augustini sensu circa B. Mariae Virginis Conceptionem* (1619). The enthusiasm for the doctrine among the Salamancan Franciscans is documented by de Castro, 'Wadding and the Iberian Peninsula', pp 134–57; and Balič, 'Wadding the Scotist', pp 474–9. **62** This is probably due to the fact that Scotus's own theology is heavily reliant on so many facets of Augustine's thought. The Augustinian residue in Scotism is famously chronicled in the useful, if fundamentaly flawed, work by E. Gilson, *Jean Duns Scot* (1952), pp 111–15.

Even though he enjoyed the honour of being the first head of St Anthony's College, Louvain,[63] Ó Maoil Chonaire's posthumous reputation has undoubtedly suffered as a result of his less than cordial association with Cornelius Jansen (1585–1638), and the fact that many of his writings were circulated after his death by Antoine Arnauld (1612–94) and other supporters of the Jansenist cause of Port-Royal.[64] While it is true that he shared several points in common with these individuals, it would be unfair to view him as an influential figure in the development of the theological movement that bore Jansen's name, so-called 'Jansenism'.[65] When his work is liberated from the false perspective that he was a proto-Jansenist, Ó Maoil Chonaire can be appreciated as a historically engaged theologian whose position on the topical questions of his day was constructed on the basis of a detailed reflection upon Augustine. Moved to read Augustine's treatises with an eye to discerning the details of their author's development, and thus to locating their salience and truth,[66] Ó Maoil Chonaire's entire corpus is devoted to the advancement and defence of an Augustinian theology.

The first fruits of his rich conversation with Augustine can be seen in his translation into Irish of a Catalan work, known in Castilian as *Tratado llamado el Desseoso, y por otro nombre, espejo de religiosos*,[67] which Ó Maoil Chonaire called *Sgáthán an chrábhaidh* ('Mirror of piety') or *Desiderius*.[68] *Desiderius'* content is indicative not only of his general catechetical concerns for the Irish mission but also of his more specific aspiration to form the Irish in an orthodox Augustinian faith, that avoided the sort of compromising attitude towards the Protestant state he had so roundly condemned in his 1615 letter to Irish Catholic Members of Parliament.[69]

Further testimony of his commitment to an uncompromising Augustinian anthropology can be found in *De statu parvulorum*, perhaps his best known

---

63 Jennings, *Irish Franciscan College of St Anthony at Louvain*; Conlan, *St Anthony's College of the Irish Franciscans, Louvain*; Mooney, 'St Anthony's College, Louvain'; I. Fennessy, 'Guardians and staff of St Anthony's College, Louvain' (2000).   64 Ceyssens, 'Conry, de Burgo, Wadding and Jansenism', pp 303–31; O'Connor, *Irish Jansenists*.   65 R. Clark, *Sojourners and strangers at Port-Royal* (1930), pp 3–7.   66 J.-L. Quantin, *Le Catholicisme classique et les pères de l'église* (1999), pp 128–30, 137; M.W.F. Stone, 'Florence Conry on the *limbus infantium*' (forthcoming).   67 The Catalan original had probably circulated in manuscript before being published, anonymously, in 1515. On the dispute concerning the authorship of the work see S. Ua Súilleabháin, 'Údar sgáthán an chrábhaidh' (1989).   68 T.F. O'Rahilly (ed.), *Desiderius* (1955). See also B. Ó Cuív, 'Flaithrí Ó Maolchonaire's catechism of Christian doctrine' (1950).   69 'Remonstrance by Florence Conry to the Catholic members of the Parliament held in Dublin, 1613' [Valladolid, 1614] cited in C.P. Meehan, *The fate and fortunes of Hugh O'Neill, earl of Tyrone and Rory O'Donel, earl of Tyrconnell* (1868), pp 395–7. On Ó Maoil Chonaire's extensive political activities see Jennings, *Wild Geese*, pp 155, 209, 212–15, 217–19; M.K. Walsh, 'The last years of Hugh O'Neill' (1965–6); J.J. Silke, *Kinsale. The Spanish intervention in Ireland* (1970; repr. Dublin, 2000), pp 148, 161, 166–7; Henry, *The Irish military community*, pp 136, 142–3; M. Mac Craith, 'The political thought of Florence Conry and Hugh MacCaughwell' (2005).

theological work, where he treats the thorny issue of unbaptized infants. The immediate stimulus for the tract, Ó Maoil Chonaire revealed in the preface, was his own teaching experience, particularly his attempts to make sense of the sufferings of the just.[70] Some theologians, he claimed, had been tempted, perhaps in the interests of pastoral sensitivity, to adopt a benign line on the issue, by offering the hope of some version of eternal felicity to infants who died unbaptized. Ó Maoil Chonaire would allow nothing of the sort since Augustine and sacred scripture, he argued, denied any middle place between the eternal life of the kingdom and the perpetual punishment of hell.[71] As there was no limbo, the infants would suffer the pains of hell, albeit in a manner less horrific than that endured by the damned. Here was an issue, Ó Maoil Chonaire asserted, that revealed scripture and Augustine to have greater authority than the conjectures of modern scholastics.[72]

Following on from *De statu parvulorum* Ó Maoil Chonaire pursued another project which dealt more explicitly with the question of grace. This manuscript was entitled *Peregrinus*, and though completed by 1625, it remained unpublished for sixteen years. The work provides the most complete account of Ó Maoil Chonaire's engagement with the anti-Pelagian writings of Augustine, and his attempt to translate them into a practical pastoral programme. As such, the book amounts to nothing more than a strong defence of an Augustinian theory of grace and predestination. Significantly, the dominant conclusion of the work proved exceptionally popular with some of the students at St Anthony's College. John Barnewall OFM (*fl.* 1627),[73] for instance, in his lectures reiterated Ó Maoil Chonaire's grim doctrine,[74] and in 1627 he presided over a thesis entitled *Sententia S. Augustini* [...] *de gratia, libero arbitrio, praedestinatione et reprobatione ac simul proponitur disputatio de justificatione ac merito bonorum operum* defended by one Francis O'Farrell OFM (*fl.* 1627).[75] The presentation of Barnewall's

---

70 This was probably a reference to his tract *De flagellis justorum juxta mentem Sancti Augustini*, which dealt with the sensible punishment of original sin; see Heaney, *The theology of Florence Conry*, pp 41–2. No copy of this tract is known to exist. It appears to have been a substantial piece as Ó Maoil Chonaire writes, in *De Statu parvulorum*, 'late alibi tractavimus', p. 5, and 'alibi operose poenas originalis in hac vita deduximus', see p. 33.   71 *Tractatus de statu parvulorum* (1623). For a full discussion of Ó Maoil Chonaire's complicated views on this subject see Stone, 'Florence Conry on the *limbus infantium*'.   72 For further discussion of this aspect of Ó Maoil Chonaire's thought see D. Downey, 'Augustinians and Scotists' (2002).   73 Barnewall, who later became Provincial of the Irish Observants also defended a thesis on Scotus, *Universa theologia iuxta mentem Doctoris Subtilis* (1620). What little information on him that exists is recorded by Ceyssens, 'Conry, de Burgo, Wadding and Jansenism', pp 308, 310, 312, 324–5, 326, 344–5.   74 Peter Walsh, *History and vindication of the Loyal Formulary or Irish Remonstrance* (1674), Fourth treatise, p. 75. Peter Walsh (Petrus Valesius) (1610/8–1688) was an Irish Franciscan who had been educated at Louvain and was initially well disposed to Jansenism; see Clark, *Strangers and sojouners at Port-Royal*, pp 206–7; and Millett, *The Irish Franciscans*, pp 418–63. On O'Farrell see Ceyssens, 'Conry, de Burgo, Wadding and Jansenism', p. 325.   75 *Sententia D. Augustini eximii ecclesiae doctoris de gratia, lib. Arbit,*

lectures and O'Farrell's thesis indicates that Ó Maoil Chonaire's views on grace and predestination had set down roots among the early Franciscans at Louvain. Indeed, some years later, when, following the publication of Jansen's *Augustinus* in 1640, an ensuing controversy had polarized theological opinion both in Louvain and elsewhere, the Franciscan propositions were reprinted.[76] In this different and slightly hysterical episode, Hugh Bourke OFM (*c.*1592–1654), Patrick Brenan OFM (*fl.* 1627), and other Irish Franciscans came under pressure from anti-Jansenist quarters, to disown the 1627 propositions. They refused to do so, and with some justice denied that their position issued from Jansen, but pointed out that it was nothing more than the teaching of Augustine as interpreted by Flaithrí Ó Maoil Chonaire.[77]

In retrospect Ó Maoil Chonaire might be regarded as semi-detached from the theological views that are more readily associated with the so-called 'Golden Age' of the Irish Franciscans, not least for the reason that he promoted a neo-Augustinian theology that rejected a good deal of the apparel of early modern scholasticism. His stalwart enthusiasm for the doctrine of the Immaculate Conception, however, helped to keep him within the theological mainstream of his order, rather than that of his adopted home of Louvain, where theologians viewed the doctrine with some suspicion.[78] For all that, Ó Maoil Chonaire still cuts quite a dash in the intellectual landscape of his age, not least for his articulate advocacy of the view that Catholic theology should always be firmly grounded in the authority of scripture and the Fathers, so that it might avoid heresy and uphold the verities of the ancient church.

Aodh Mac Aingil

The learned Aodh Mac Aingil arrived in Louvain sometime in the summer of 1607 having received a thorough education in Scotist thought at Salamanca.[79] Notwithstanding the earlier efforts of Maurice O'Fihely, the venerable tradition

---

praedestinatione et Reprobatione publice defense, Lovanii in Collegio S. Antonii de Padua FF. Minorum Hibernorum strictioris observantiae, praeside V.F.P. Ioanne Barnewallo Sacrae Theologiae Lectore. Respondente F. Patricio Brinan, die 9. Septembris 1627, hora 9. Ante et 3 post meridiem. Facta omnibus oppugnandi Copia. Secunda editio. Lovanie, apud Iacobum Zegers anno 1641. See Dom Gabriel Gerberon, *Histoire générale du jansénisme* (1700), i, pp 21–3. On the theses published by the Irish friars see I. Fennessy, 'Canon E. Reussen's list of Irish Franciscan theses in Louvain' (2006). **76** Ceyssens, 'Conry, de Burgo, Wadding and Jansenism', p. 324. The propositions were originally published by Jacob Zegers in Louvain and were later republished in Paris, in 1641. **77** Ceyssens, 'Conry, de Burgo, Wadding and Jansenism'. **78** The doctrine of the Immaculate Conception did not find favour among the *Lovanienses*, even from the foundation of their Theology Faculty in 1432. Their reluctance to embrace the idea was further strengthened by their allegiance in the early modern period to several neo-Augustinian doctrines rightly or wrongly associated with 'Jansenism'. **79** On Mac Aingil's life and work see C. Giblin, 'Hugh MacCaghwell O.F.M. and Scotism' (1968); idem, 'Hugh McCaghwell, O.F.M., archbishop of Armagh (†1626)' (1995); J. McEvoy, 'Aodh MacCawell OFM and the Scotist theology of the Immaculate Conception of Mary' (forthcoming).

of Irish exegesis and reflection on Scotus might be said to have begun with Mac Aingil, not least by dint of his influence on a whole generation of friars, and by virtue of his creativity as a commentator and editor of Scotus's works. In 1620 while still at Louvain, Mac Aingil published at Antwerp his two volumes of commentaries of the four books of *Sentences* according to Scotus. This indefatigable work of nearly one thousand pages of large folio contains an edition of the *Opus Oxoniense* (this being the *Sentences* commentary which Scotus composed at Oxford), a life of Scotus which includes a charming and picturesque description of the environs around Downpatrick which Mac Aingil took to be the birthplace of Scotus,[80] the aforementioned defence of Scotus against Bzowski, and a small work entitled *Rosarium Beatae Mariae Virginis*, in which Mac Aingil argued that Scotus was not the progenitor of the doctrine of the Immaculate Conception, but its most formidable advocate.

Sometime in the summer of 1623, Mac Aingil left Louvain and went to Rome where he was appointed professor of theology at the Franciscan convent of Aracoeli. Combined with his teaching responsibilities, he continued to work with skill and energy on further editions of Scotus he had begun while in Louvain, and by 1625 no less than six further tomes had appeared in Venice and Cologne.[81] Two further volumes, editions of Scotus's *Reportata Parisiensia* and *Quaestiones quodlibetales*, were published some nine years after his death in 1635. Any cursory examination of Wadding's later edition will reveal that he drew lavishly from Mac Aingil's earlier attempts to make Scotus's writings available to the modern age, and for this reason it is important that Mac Aingil be apportioned sufficient credit for the extent of his contribution to the whole enterprise.[82]

Given the size of Mac Aingil's theological corpus, it is perhaps unsurprising that few scholars have attempted to present a synoptic analysis of its content and quality. This is to be regretted, since much is to be learned about early modern Catholic theology in the early seventeenth century from a study of its teaching on grace, divine providence, and the sacraments. Like his fellow Irish commentators, save with the possible exception of Baron, Mac Aingil is rarely content to restate the views of Scotus, but rather uses the text of Scotus as a canvas on which he paints his own views on a diversity of topical subjects. Though committed to

A list of his Latin works is provided by Giblin, 'Hugh MacCaughwell O.F.M. and Scotism', pp 391–3, and A. Mac Giolla Comhaill, *Bráithrín Bocht ó Dhún* (1985). Mac Aingil's learning was quite remarkable, as can be displayed by an examination of his writings in the Irish language, see Ó Cléirigh, *Aodh Mac Aingil.* Of further interest are his pastoral writings such as the *Sgáthán Shacramuinte na hAithridhe* of 1618, see S. Ryan, 'Steadfast saints or malleable models?' (2005). **80** Mac Aingil's description of these places is enhanced by virtue of his own acquaintance with Downpatrick and its historical sites. See Giblin, 'Hugh McCaghwell O.F.M., archbishop of Armagh (†1626)', pp 89–94; McEvoy, 'Aodh MacCawell OFM and the Immaculate Conception of Mary'. **81** Giblin, 'Hugh MacCaughwell O.F.M. and Scotism', pp 391–3. **82** Wadding was generous in his acknowledgement of Mac Aingil's achievements, *Annales*, vi. cols 50–1.

depicting Scotus's thought in the best possible light, Mac Aingil is not above going beyond the letter of the Scotist position, and proves himself most able in teasing out the many ambiguities and obscurities that attend the text.

If we lack a solid treatment of his theological ideas, then the very same thing could be said of Mac Aingil's philosophy. His interesting account of the epistemology of decision-making in *De evidentia*, which features a novel analysis of concepts such as doubt (*dubia*) and probable certainty (*certitudo probabilis*), as well as his more general account of human psychology in the *De anima*, are two topics which could be usefully studied by historians of early modern philosophy.[83] Likewise a full and impartial treatment of his work as a textual scholar of Scotus is warranted. On any general assessment, Mac Aingil was an interventionist editor prepared to gloss, embellish, omit, and restore anything he believed to be either superfluous or else necessary to the understanding Scotu's texts.[84] While his particular editorial traits have been rejected by modern scholars of the *Subtle Doctor*,[85] it would still be of great interest to learn just how his methods of preparing a critical edition helped to fashion Scotism in the early modern period, and the degree to which this school was or was not faithful to the claims of the putative 'historical Scotus' that is studied by students of medieval philosophy today. Mac Aingil left an impressive corpus in the fields of theology, philosophy, and textual editions; his work is surely deserving of greater attention.

Anthony Hickey

Anthony Hickey plays something of a lesser part in this story, not least for the fact that his figure is so often obscured by the long shadows cast by his teacher Mac Aingil and his pupil Punch.[86] Nevertheless, he can be considered an important conduit through which Scotist thought was filtered onto the stage of European letters, and his writings (though for the most part unstudied) are of some consequence. Hickey received the habit in Louvain on 1 November 1607,

---

83 M. Dunne, 'Hugo Cavellus (Aodh Mac Aingil, 1571–1626) on certitude' (forthcoming). Giblin, 'Hugh McCaghwell, O.F.M., archbishop of Armagh (†1626)', pp 91–2 cites evidence that Mac Aingil influenced Descartes. In my view such a link is tenuous since on the basis of the available evidence, it appears that Descartes was never really cognisant of the central debates of seventeenth-century scholasticism, let alone Irish Scotism, and that his interest in the schools was selective and driven by his own research. Other scholars have attempted to place some of Descartes' views in the context of Parisian scholasticism (which was heavily influenced by Scotism), and have argued that links are by no means spurious. See R. Ariew, *Descartes and the last scholastics* (1999).   **84** Mac Aingil tells us, for example, that in the first book of the *Sentences*, he alone made 400 changes; see *In quatuor libros Sententiarum*, i (ad lectorem).   **85** See, for instance, the comments made by the various modern editors to the *B. Ioannis Duns Scoti Opera Philosophica* (1997–2005), iii pp i–l; v, pp 1–144, of texts edited by Mac Aingil. For a reasoned defence of Mac Aingil's editorial practices see Mac Conmara, 'Mac Aingil agus an Scotachas Éireannach' (1988), p. 80; Dunne, 'Hugo Cavellus (Aodh Mac Aingil, 1571–1626) on certitude' (forthcoming).   **86** On Hickey's writings see Wadding, *Scriptores*, pp 26–7; Francis Harold, *Vita fratris Lucae Waddingi*, pp 24, 32.

and later joined Mac Aingil on his journey to Rome to attend the general chapter of the order in 1612. There, he distinguished himself in the midst of his brethren by defending theological theses, and by 1619 his reputation was such that he was teaching theology back in Louvain and then in Cologne. His Rhienland sojourn was cut short when he was summoned to Rome to assist Luke Wadding in his multiple scholarly endeavours. There Hickey remained until his death in 1641, becoming the first professor of theology at the newly instituted St Isidore's College in June 1625.[87]

Ever faithful to the intellectual legacy of Mac Aingil, Hickey through his research and teaching helped to make St Isidore's one of the most renowned centres of Scotistic studies in the seventeenth century.[88] Originally intending to write commentaries on all the four books of *Sentences* '*iuxta mentem Scoti*', a project which remained incomplete at the time of his death, Hickey did succeed in compiling the commentaries of the fourth book and these were later published by Wadding as volumes eight, eleven, and ten of the *Opera omnia* of 1639. Hickey used the text of the fourth book which had been corrected and emended by Mac Aingil in 1620, and followed verbatim the *scholia* adopted by his former teacher. Apart from his polemical *Nitela Franciscanae Religionis* which he published under the pseudonym Dermitius Thaddaeus, which as we noted earlier sought to defend the honour of his order, Scotus, and former teacher Mac Aingil, Hickey also published a work on the Immaculate Conception.[89] Though his fame at the time of his death was such that his pupil, John Punch, intended to publish his work, the volumes were never printed.[90] Hence Hickey remains an enigmatic figure known to few and read by fewer.

Luke Wadding

It should never be forgotten that the great historian of the Franciscan order, Luke Wadding, was also a theologian of some substance.[91] His formative years as a Franciscan were spent in the Iberian peninsular, first in Portugal and then in Spain, especially at Salamanca, where he was taught by such luminaries of early modern scholaticism as the Jesuit Francisco Suárez (1548–1617) and the Augustinian friar Gil da Presentaço (1593–1629), both of whom can be said to have exerted some influence on his mariology.[92] Since the literary output of Wadding is enormous,[93] it is important to discriminate among his published

87 Cleary, *Father Luke Wadding and St Isidore's College*, pp 74–8. **88** Millett, *The Irish Franciscans*, pp 465–87. **89** Cited in H. Maracci, *Biblioteca Mariana* (1648), p. 125. **90** John Punch, *Commentarii theologici*, iii, 109. **91** Balič, 'Wadding the Scotist'. **92** De Castro, 'Wadding in the Iberian Peninsula', pp 120–62. On Suarez's mariology see R. Fastiggi, 'Mary's Coredemption according to Francisco Suarez, S.J.' (2004); for Fray Gil see E.D. Carretero, 'Tradicion Immaculista agustiniana' (1954). **93** C. Mooney, 'The writings of Father Luke Wadding' (1958); B. Millett, 'Guide to material for a biography of Father Luke

works in order to highlight works of greater theological moment. Beside the publication in 1639 of Scotus's *Opera omnia,* which is surely his greatest service to the cause of Scotism, four learned tracts defending Scotist mariology must surely rank among his more considerable theological accomplishments.

His first major theological work *Legatio Philippi III et IV catholicorum regnum Hispaniarum ad SS.DD.NN. Paulum PP. V et Gregorium XVnde definienda controversia Immaculatae Conceptionis B. Virginis Mariae per Ill. Mum ed. Rev. mum Dom. D. F. Antonium a Trejo,* was published at Louvain in 1624 and in a second edition at Antwerp in 1641. For a work that contains many sober documents relating to the official Spanish mission to the Holy See to plead the cause for the Immaculate Conception, of which Wadding was a member,[94] it is surprisingly fresh and full of novel insights, and significantly, reveals Wadding's own commentary on the long and sophisticated debate on the Immaculate Conception that had been a feature of late medieval theology, and of the University of Salamanca during his time there as a student and teacher.

Three other short works on the death,[95] the redemption,[96] and the baptism of the Virgin Mary,[97] were published in Rome between 1655–6, and yet again, were the by-product of Wadding's membership of the Spanish mission. The first and second of these tracts purport to be a commentary on Scotus's own teaching concerning the preservative redemption of the Virgin Mary, but as scholars such as Balič have pointed out,[98] Wadding's extensive theological learning and use of clear scholastic reasoning were such that they helped to ground and justify the dogmatic definition of the doctrine for a new generation of Catholic theologians. In this respect, the Waterford friar's mariological writings rank among the more significant of the early modern period, and serve to illustrate the manner in which Wadding's hard-won erudition, gained from long hours of study of original documents and ancient texts, was applied to one of the contentious theological debates of the period.

John Punch

A remarkable philosophical talent among the Irish friars was John Punch of Cork,who proved to be one of the more creative yet controversial scholastic metaphysicians of the mid-seventeenth century. As with Mac Aingil, Punch's corpus of published work is imposing, presenting itself as a mixture of original philosophical and theological reflection accompanied by exacting commentary on

Wadding' (1957), pp 235–42; idem, *The Irish Franciscans,* pp 464–7.   **94** On the work's content and the circumstances in which it was composed, see Balič, 'Wadding the Scotist', pp 474–80.   **95** *Immaculatae Conceptioni B. Mariae Virginis non adversari eius mortem corporalem* (1655).   **96** *De redemptione B. Mariae Virginis* (1656).   **97** *De baptismo B. Mariae Virginis* (1656).   **98** Balič, 'Wadding the Scotist', pp 474–5.

the texts of Scotus.[99] Though heartily committed to Scotism, an allegiance which expressed itself with great force in his *Scotus Hiberniae restitutus*, a treatise written to defend Scotus's reputation and Irish nationality, Punch's mind was blessed with a cultivated critical acumen that is indispensable to the successful prosecution of abstract argument.[1] Tellingly, his achievements are spread over the central areas of scholastic philosophy: logic and metaphysics, coupled with intelligent excursions into areas of natural philosophy, psychology, and ethics.[2]

Initially educated at Louvain, before being groomed by Hickey at St Isidore's, Punch left Rome in 1648 bound for France, and the Franciscan convent in Paris. There, he taught with a sense of autonomy and originality which led him away from many positions associated with the heritage of Scotus, toward ideas more readily associated with other scholastic schools, most notably those of the Jesuits.[3] For this and other reasons, Punch's philosophical labours began to attract the censure of some of his fellow Franciscans, and he met his match in the form of two highly capable Italian Conventuals, Bartolomeo Mastri da Meldola or 'Mastrius' (1602–73),[4] and Bonaventura Belluto (1600–76),[5] authors of one of the most influential Scotist textbooks of the seventeenth century, the *Cursus integer philosophiae ad mentem Scoti*.

For Belluto, and especially Mastri, Punch was a renegade Scotist whose ideas had strayed too far from the original and authoritative texts of the school's founder. If strict fidelity is a hallmark of intellectual excellence, then the case of the Italian Conventuals could be conceded, especially since it is clear that in important areas of metaphysics Punch is very much his own man, being led by the force and direction of an argument rather than by an appeal to prior authority. This is not to say, however, that Mastri and Belluto were servile Scotists concerned to criticize Punch for doctrinal impurity,[6] but that, unlike them, the Irish Observant took the view that, in specific instances, Scotus was not always

---

99 M. Grajewski, 'John Ponce, Franciscan Scotist of the seventeenth century' (1946), pp 71–92; M. Forlivesi, '"*Ut ex etymologia nominis patet*"' (forthcoming).   **1** J. Coombs, 'The possibility of created entities in seventeenth-century Scotism' (1993); S. Sousedik, 'Der Streit um den wahren Sinn der scotischen Possibilienlehre' (1996); T. Hoffmann, '"*Creatura intellecta*". *Die Ideen und Possibilien bei Duns Scotus* (2002).   **2** A synoptic portrayal of his philosophical achievements is furnished by Grajewski, 'John Ponce, Franciscan Scotist of the seventeenth century', pp 71–92; although some points of his analysis have been surpassed by the more recent scholarship listed above, fn. 99.   **3** For an excellent discussion of this issue, which takes place in the course of an analysis of Mastrius, see J.P. Doyle, 'Mastri and some Jesuits on possible and impossible objects of God's knowledge and power' (2006), pp 443, 452–3.   **4** On Mastrius see Forlivesi, *Scotistarum princeps: Bartolomeo Mastri (1602–1673) e il suo tempo* (2002); and his more recent edited collection, *Rem in Seipsa Cernere* (2006).   **5** On Belluto see D. Scaramuzzi, *Il pensiero di Scoto nel Mezzogiorno d'Italia* (1927); V. Di Giovanni, *Storia della filosofia in Sicilia dai tempi antichi al secolo XIX* (1872), i, p. 144.   **6** For a useful discussion of Mastrius's general approach to Scotus see F. Bottin, 'Bartolomeo Mastri' (2006).

the best guide for resolving questions that had arisen since his death in the fourteenth century as a result of important changes in scholastic philosophy.[7]

The disagreements between Punch and his Franciscan critics are instructive because they demonstrate the extent of principled dissension that existed within the Scotist school, especially on some of the more profound aspects of metaphysics and ontology. On this last topic, which concerns the study of being and other cognate concepts, Punch advanced a radically essentialist position, whose merits and drawbacks would be debated by successive generations of Observant theologians. Even as late as the eighteenth century, an Irish Franciscan based at Valladolid in Spain, Anthony Rourke or Ruerk (*fl.* 1746) published a *Cursus theologiae scholasticae*, which advanced several trenchant criticisms of Punch's theory of 'autonomous possibles'.[8]

The thorough scrutiny and protracted discussion of Punch's work stands testimony to the fact that his philosophical writings were widely debated within scholastic circles, and that he enjoyed a reputation for innovation and rigour, even if his views were not always greeted with universal approval. A technically proficient philosopher who wrote at the highest level of abstraction, and whose use of dense argument and incremental analysis is reminiscent of the methods used in contemporary English-speaking philosophy, Punch's ideas are not readily accessible to those uninitiated in the scholasticism of his time. And yet, his extant corpus reveal a metaphysican of the uppermost calibre who commanded the respect and attention of a whole generation of European schoolmen.

Bonaventure Baron

The last of the friars discussed in this survey is the gifted humanist and theologian Bonaventure Baron.[9] Nephew of Luke Wadding, he quickly acquired expertise as a theologian, and became a respected Latin stylist, composing some of the most accomplished Latin verses of his generation of Irish scholars. He enjoyed the favour and friendship of Popes Urban IV and Alexander VII, as well as Cardinal Barberini. Baron taught at St Isidore's, and then spent some time in Hungary engaged in duties for his order. Later, he was appointed provincial commissary for the Franciscan order, and in 1676 Cosimo de Medici, the Grand Duke of Tuscany, honoured him with the office of historiographer in recognition of his

---

7 For informative discussions of the Punch-Mastrius dispute see the very different interpretations advanced by Hoffmann, *Creatura Intellecta, Die Ideen und Possibilien bei Duns Scotus* (2002); L. Novak, 'Scoti de conceptu entis doctrina a Mastrio retractata et contra Poncium propugnata' (2006); M. Forlivesi, 'The nature of transcendental being and its contraction to its inferiors in the thought of Mastri and Belluto' (2006). **8** *Cursus theologiae scholasticae in via venerab. P. Subt. que doct. Joannis Duns Scoti, decursus per quatuor eiusdem sententiarum libros* (1746–64), i, §§ 387–98. For further discussion of this debate in the seventeenth century see Coombs, 'The possibility of created entities'; S. Sousedik, 'Der Streit um den wahren Sinn der scotischen Possibilienlehre'. **9** Millett, *Irish Franciscans*, pp 469–73.

eminence as a scholar and Latinist.[10] After a period of residence in Florence, his last years were spent at St Isidore's in Rome. A seemingly humble man, who was moved nevertheless to quarrel with several of his *confrères*, he is said to have declined several bishoprics and even the guardianship of the college.

Baron's elegant and learned publications were extensive, ranging from occasional verse to philosophical and theological treatises with a pronounced Scotist flavour.[11] Of special interest are his tract *De Deo uno*,[12] which presents a nuanced discussion of some of the central conundrums of philosophical theology, and a small work on angels which aimed to situate Scotus's own views on the heavenly host in the on-going modern debate about the nature and role of these spiritual creatures.[13] These works were the fruit and development of Baron's lectures in the classrooms of St Isidore's, as indeed were his earlier volumes of Scotist philosophy. Together they represent a solid addition to the school of Scotus, which by the time Baron's writings had been disseminated was firmly entrenched in the intellectual life of Catholic Europe and the New World.

While it would be unfair to compare Baron's philosophical and theological works with the acute and penetrating analysis of Punch, or the magisterial understanding of Scotus to be found in Mac Aingil, the careful exegesis of Hickey, the impressive historical learning of Wadding, or even the sheer theological boldness of Ó Maoil Chonaire, his reasoned and balanced approach reveals something of his own considerable talent. For Baron provides clear and earnest instruction in the doctrines of Scotus by means of crisp, lucid, and economical Latin prose, a style that more often than not, helps to render the salient features of Scotus's thought less obtuse and more amenable to philosophical reflection. An acknowledged master of Latinity, Baron managed to communicate the meaning of Scotus's often taxing concepts in simple terms without contrivance and embellishment. Though not as original in his interpretations of the texts as many of his peers, Baron ought to be acknowledged for helping to make one of the difficult thinkers of the Middle Ages tractable and interesting.

---

10 On Baron the humanist see, T. Wall, 'A distinguished Irish humanist' (1946), pp 92–102; 'Parnassus in Waterford' (1947); Silke, 'Irish scholarship and the Renaissance'. **11** The principal philosophical and theological works of Baron are: *Panegyrici sacro-prophani* (1643) and (1656); *Prolusiones philosophicae, logicis et physicis materiis bipartitae* (1651); *Divus Anitius Manlius Boctius absolutus: sive De consolatione theologiae, libri quatuor* (1653); *Fr. Ioannes Duns Scoti per universam philosophiam, logicam, physicam, metaphysicam, ethicam contra adversantes defensus, quaestionum novitate amplificatus*, 3 vols (Cologne, 1664); and *Opuscula* (1669). A full list of his works can be found in Sbaralea, *Supplementum*, pp 185–6. **12** *Ioannes Duns Scotus … de Deo trino, contra adversantes quosque defensus* (1668). **13** *Ioannes Duns Scotus defensus et amplificatus de Angelis* (1676). On Scotus's views on angels see Gilson, *Jean Duns Scot*, pp 391–431; and on the early modern debate see P. Marshall & A. Walsham (eds), *Angels in the early modern world* (2006).

CONCLUSION

The six thinkers surveyed above by no means exhaust the philosophical and theological achievements of the Irish friars of the early modern period, since there is no overwhelming evidence to suggest that a protracted intellectual decline in the quality Irish Franciscans ensued from the time of Baron's death in 1680. The truth of the matter, however, is that until such times as the published writings and multiple manuscripts of friars resident at colleges in Louvain, Rome, Bolzano, Salamanca, Paris, and Prague, are collated, catalogued, and then fully studied, we will remain in a position of ignorance concerning the philosophical and theological work of the Irish Franciscans in the years down to the outbreak of the French Revolution. In the light of this, we cannot rule out in advance that other figures of substance will emerge and reclaim their place in the annals of Irish Franciscan thought, or continue to presume that Baron's death represents the terminus of a 'Golden age'.

The Irish Franciscans made a significant contribution to European philosophy and theology and their efforts were judged by their peers to be genuine bequests to some of the central debates of seventeenth-century scholasticism. Because scholasticism at this time can be shown to have been a cosmopolitan, rigorous, pluralistic, as well as intellectually compelling phenomenon, the writings of the Irish friars can be viewed as contributions to a truly international set of debates that were conducted throughout Catholic Europe and the New World. The formal study of the philosophical and theological labours of the Irish friars of the Franciscan Observance is in its infancy; it has not even reached its adolescence let alone attained maturity. There is a great deal left to do.

A wooden key to open Heaven's door: lessons in practical Catholicism from St Anthony's College, Louvain

SALVADOR RYAN

In the preface to *Desiderius*, otherwise known as *Sgáthán an Chrábhaidh*, published at Louvain in 1616, Flaithrí Ó Maoil Chonaire advises his readers why he does not consider the pursuit of a polished and fluent style of Irish as a priority. In doing so, he chooses the words of St Augustine as expressed in his *De Doctrina Christiana* to convey his point:

> What is the benefit of a golden key if it does not open the thing that we wish to open, when we have no other use for it than that? Or why should we consider a wooden key inferior if it opens the thing for us?[1]

He explains the rationale behind the production of what was essentially an Irish translation of a popular Catalan devotional work published in 1515, which had been previously translated into Spanish, Italian, French, German and Latin:

> We believed, as did others (who are concerned to help their friends and neighbours to depart from this pilgrimage to the land of truth – heaven) that it would be worth translating into Irish, to enlighten those of our land, who do not understand other tongues, regarding the sacred things that it teaches.[2]

Furthermore, Ó Maoil Chonaire states that by writing in a manner that is 'clear and easily understandable', judicious and discerning readers will more likely commend the work than criticize it for its simplicity of style, which was used 'particularly for the sake of the simple people who are not expert in the intricacies of the language'.[3]

Similar statements appear in some of the other notable religious works that were published by the friars of St Anthony's College, Louvain in the first half of the seventeenth century. Aodh Mac Aingil, in the preface to his work on the Sacrament of Penance, *Sgáthán Shacramuinte na hAithridhe*, published in 1618,

---

1 Flaithrí Ó Maoil Chonaire, *Desiderius*. ed. T.F. O'Rahilly (1955), p. 2.   2 Ibid., p. 1.   3 Ibid., p. 2.

admitted that his text was written in 'simple, imprecise Irish in order to teach and draw all to devotion and faith through the Sacrament of Penance'.[4] He implored his readers not to allow the simplicity and poor expression of the language obscure the value of its teaching on the cure of the soul. Indeed, he states unequivocally: 'Learn it well and it will bring you to the gate of heaven'.[5]

For Ó Maoil Chonaire and Mac Aingil to maintain that their texts were written rather badly and in an imprecise style of Irish, constituted a surrender to a trope of humility on their part. Ó Maoil Chonaire belonged to a famous learned family that for centuries provided *ollamhain* ('chief poets') to the O'Conors and Mac Dermots of Connacht.[6] Mac Aingil had a similar scholarly background and had once been employed as tutor to the two sons of Hugh O'Neill.[7] Downplaying their literary achievements was not just a rhetorical device, but an acknowledgment that there was a more pressing matter at stake, namely, the salvation of their readers' souls. The publication of catechisms and devotional works in Irish at Louvain was clearly aimed at counteracting the influence of the 'heretical' works of the reformers and instructing Irish Catholics in the fundamentals of their faith. The declaration of permission to publish Bonaventure Ó hEodhasa's *An Teagasg Críosdaidhe* given by Archduke Albert, ruler of Spanish Flanders, on 20 June 1611 noted that the work would be used 'against the false doctrine of other religions contrary to our holy faith'.[8] This was also the rationale cited by Ó hEodhasa when applying to the archduke for permission to print a second edition three years later.[9] Aodh Mac Aingil admitted that his work on penance was partially a response to the publications of 'heretics' who produced a version of the Book of Common Prayer in Irish in addition 'to much of the Bible'.[10] For these reasons, therefore, the Irish language publications that were produced at St Anthony's College, Louvain tended to favour expedience over elegance. These works had a practical purpose, to instruct Catholics in the fundamentals of Christian doctrine and to provide counsel on how Christians were expected to behave and, not least, how they should pray. It is to the second and third of these categories that attention is drawn in this study. They encompass what might be called the practical elements of early modern Catholicism. The audience addressed in the first of these works, *Desiderius*, is clearly not simply the Irish migrant population in the Low Countries, for certain passages, which discuss contemporary political and religious realities, relate to situations arising in Ireland itself. Similarly, the second work, *Parrthas an Anma*, written by Antoin Gearnon and published in 1645, shortly after Gearnon

4 Aodh Mac Aingil, *Sgáthán*: ed. C. Ó Maonaigh (1952), p. 5. 5 Ibid. 6 O'Rahilly, *Desiderius*, p. viii. 7 Ó Cléirigh, *Aodh Mac Aingil*, p. 46. 8 Jennings, *Louvain Papers*, pp 32–3. 9 S. Ryan, 'Bonaventura Ó hEoghusa's *An Teagasg Críosdaidhe*' (2004), p. 263. 10 Ó Maonaigh, *Sgáthán*, p. 5.

returned from a five-year period of mission in Ireland, convinced him of the urgent need for catechesis. He was to return to Ireland again two years later when he was appointed as guardian of the Franciscan convent in Dundalk.[11] Although arguments have been made in favour of the members of the Irish miltary in Flanders and their families being the primary target audience for Ó hEodhasa's catechism of 1611 and 1614, there are many reasons why it might be argued that the Irish Franciscans at Louvain took a broader and more far-sighted approach to the question of catechesis.[12]

PREVENTION BETTER THAN CURE

In one notable section of his devotional work, *Desiderius*, Flaithrí Ó Maoil Chonaire concerns himself at length with providing advice to Irish Catholics who might be influenced by reformist doctrine.[13] The section comprises a dialogue between the main character (the pilgrim Desiderius) and a spiritual guide, Simplicity (*An tSimplidheachd*). Ó Maoil Chonaire, through his character Simplicity, stresses the importance of consultation with clergy for spiritual guidance and expresses disappointment that Desiderius believes he can avoid sin without their help.[14] Citing one of Aesop's fables, Ó Maoil Chonaire relates how wolves tricked a flock of sheep into surrendering the protection of their hounds in exchange for a peace pact which, of course, the wolves reneged on as soon as the hounds departed. In the same way, compliance with the heretical powers of government at the expense of the protection of Catholic clergy, could only lead to ruin.[15] In another scene, Desiderius is asked by Protestant prelates to pass judgment on some priests and friars who are imprisoned. He is about to capitulate out of fear when Simplicity advises him that by law a layperson has no right to judge clerics and that what he terms the 'pseudo-bishops' have no authority to do so either.[16] Desiderius then asks whether he has a right to forward the names of Catholics who do not attend Protestant services, as required by law, to the Protestant bishops.[17] In response, Simplicity explains that such an action would be an offence against the Mystical Body of Christ, which is the church. Since Catholics are the church and the church is the Body of Christ, who is its head, whatever is done against that body is done against Christ.[18]

These questions were significant in early seventeenth-century Ireland. From the summer of 1614, government activity against the Catholic laity had increased.

11 Antoin Gearnon, *Parrthas an Anma*: ed. A. Ó Fachtna (1953), pp ix–x. **12** See Ryan, 'Bonaventura Ó hEoghusa'. **13** O'Rahilly, *Desiderius*, pp 113–64 (lines 3411–5050). **14** Ibid., p. 115. **15** Ibid., p. 116. **16** Ibid., pp 122–4. **17** Ibid., p. 129. **18** Ibid.

It was not unknown for civil proceedings to be brought against jurors who were not prepared to present the names of Catholics who breached the law.[19] Yet, many Catholics continued to function in official capacities while simultaneously flouting the law. In Kilkenny, for example, David Edwards notes how twelve justices of the peace, three coroners and four constables of baronies harboured twenty-two Catholic clerics in their homes.[20] Early on in this section, Desiderius appears unequal to the same level of commitment to the protection of Catholic clerics. He admits that while he has promised out of fear never to allow clergy into the same house as himself, he nevertheless expects to see them in hiding in his friends' houses.[21] Admitting that he is sometimes confounded when confronted with the arguments that reformers draw from scripture, Desiderius is advised by Simplicity to ensure that he is not disarmed of the sword of faith and, furthermore, that if an angel came from heaven to preach against the articles of faith, his sermon should be dismissed.[22]

Entering into disputation with the reformers on these issues is also discouraged, for these things should properly be left to prelates and learned men.[23] The fear of laypeople misinterpreting passages of scripture without the guidance of the teaching office of the church caused the Franciscan, Antoin Gearnon, to conclude that reading the Bible in the vernacular was forbidden to Catholics. He outlined this belief in his devotional and catechetical work, *Parrthas an Anma*, published at St Anthony's College, Louvain in 1645.[24] Paradoxically, the low standard of literacy and catechetical knowledge among the population at large often worked in favour of the continentally-trained clergy's efforts to implement tridentine reform in Ireland. It may even have inadvertently shielded many from the arguments of the reformers. Indeed the Catholic laity was urged primarily to profess belief in the fundamental teachings of their church before attempting to grapple with the finer points of its doctrine.[25]

DAILY LIVING IN 'PARRTHAS AN AMNA'

While the concerns of Ó Maoil Chonaire regarding the dealings of Catholics with the state and the established church were relevant to many in early seventeenth-century Ireland, the catechetical publications of the friars at Louvain in general focused on what might be considered the mundane matters of daily life. In

---

19 A. Clarke with R. Dudley Edwards, 'Pacification, plantation and the Catholic question, 1603–23', *NHI* iii, p. 217.   **20** D. Edwards, *The Ormond Lordship in County Kilkenny* (2003), pp 267–8; cited in T. Ó hAnnracháin, 'Catholicism in early modern Ireland and Britain' (2005), p. 10.   **21** O'Rahilly, *Desiderius*, p. 114.   **22** Ibid., p. 155.   **23** Ibid., p. 158.   **24** Ó Fachtna, *Parrthas an Anma*, p. 39.   **25** S. Ryan, '"New wine in old bottles"' (2007).

Desiderius, Ó Maoil Chonaire advises his audience to practise daily contemplation of their own death:

> When we rise in the morning let us fear that we will not reach the night and when we lie in our beds let us have the same fear that we will not survive until the morning; and if we do this, we will easily conquer the desires and weaknesses of the body and the fear of the world will not compel us to abandon God.[26]

The effective sanctification of time was a favourite topic of Antoin Gearnon, who provides an elaborate routine of prayer and practice for his readers in *Parrthas an Anma*. Gearnon studied on the Continent and was ordained priest in 1635. He spent some years working in Ireland before being appointed as superior of St Anthony's College, Louvain in 1644. Three years later, he returned to Ireland and was appointed guardian of the Franciscan convent in Dundalk.[27] The compilation of *Parrthas an Anma* most likely grew out of his pastoral experience in Ireland and recognition of the needs of those to whom he ministered.

Gearnon's work is divided into twelve sections: Daily Prayer and Practice, Faith, Hope, Charity (Love), Sacraments, Virtues and Vices, Prayer, Mass, Sacramental Practice, The Tree and Clock of the Passion, the Last Things and the Spiritual Alphabet. These are depicted as twelve trees in the garden of paradise from which the reader is encouraged to pick nourishing fruit. In the preface to *Parrthas an Anma*, Gearnon emphasizes the importance of daily spiritual practices, citing the Pauline exhortation 'whether you eat or drink or whatever you may do, it all for the glory of God' (1 Corinthians 10:31–3).[28] Gearnon's observation that 'there is more value and perfection in the mundane works when they are done for the greater glory and honour of God than any other works that do not have this quality, no matter how great they are' succinctly captures the approach adopted throughout this devotional work.[29]

Daily prayer

The first section of Gearnon's work suggests various ways in which elements of daily routine can be sanctified. In each case, suitable prayers for recitation are provided and were presumably expected to be learnt by heart. However, a balance is struck between verbal prayer and the sort of silent meditation that is recommended as an accompaniment to simple tasks. When dressing each morning, individuals are advised to meditate on the Instruments of Christ's Passion, a medieval devotion that was particularly popular in Franciscan

---

26 O'Rahilly, *Desiderius*, p. 146.   **27** Ó Fachtna, *Parrthas*, pp ix–xvii.   **28** Ibid., p. 4.   **29** Ibid.

spirituality.[30] The spiritualization of the routine was quite detailed: when putting on shoes, the focus was to be on the nails in Christ's feet and the crown of thorns on his head; when closing the buttons on one's clothes, on the scourging of Christ and the purple robe in which he was dressed.[31] Once dressed, Gearnon advised kneeling in prayer, giving thanks to God for his gifts and how he had helped him up to that point, reciting, hands joined together, 'In the name of the Father and of the Son and of the Holy Spirit, Amen'.[32] These very precise guidelines suggest that he felt it necessary that there should be clear direction in these matters and he did not presume that his audience had prior knowledge of prayerful posture.

The Confiteor, the text of which is also provided in Gearnon's work, followed the Morning Offering.[33] Traditionally in the Middle Ages, a wide variety of saints could be invoked in this prayer. Religious orders, for instance, routinely included their founders in the list. Gearnon suggests that Patrick, Colum Cille and Francis among others be included.[34] An Examination of Conscience should be followed by a prayer of contrition. At one point in the prayer, addressing Christ, the person resolves 'in the presence of the Glorious Virgin Mary, your sweet mother, and in the presence of my Angel Guardian, and the heavenly court, not to sin against you again …'[35] Here, Gearnon inserts a note of further advice. He suggests that the person resolve never to commit any sin again, but 'to especially avoid that day the sins towards which he has a natural inclination'.[36] After some further short invocations, a translation of a traditional Latin prayer to one's guardian angel is provided. This is followed by the short prayer of blessing 'May the Lord bless us and keep us from all evil and bring us to everlasting life', which is found in the Roman breviary for the Office of Prime. Some thought was now expected to be given to routine daily tasks.[37]

Mass

Gearnon encourages readers to proceed without delay to church to pray to God, hear Mass and listen to the sermon.[38] If it be an occasion for receiving indulgences or a period of special devotion, the person should confess their sins and receive Holy Communion. One should travel to Mass with the same mindset as if one was going to Mount Calvary, Gearnon continues that, on arrival, one should imagine being under the cross with Mary, John and Mary Magdalene. Those who

---

30 For a more detailed discussion of this devotion, see S. Ryan, 'Weapons of redemption: piety' (2007). **31** Ó Fachtna, *Parrthas*, pp 17–18. **32** Ibid. **33** The text, following its well known traditional formula begins 'I confess to Almighty God, to Blessed Mary, Ever Virgin, to Michael the Archangel, to John the Baptist, to the holy apostles Peter and Paul, and to all the saints, that I have sinned greatly …' **34** Ó Fachtna, *Parrthas*, p. 19. **35** Ibid. **36** Ibid. **37** Ibid., p. 20. **38** Instructions on how to most profitably hear a sermon are given later in the text (p. 141).

attend Mass offer the Sacrifice of Christ's Body and Blood to the Heavenly Father through the hands of the priest. Participants should, therefore, contemplate the mysteries of the Passion and Death of Christ. They should also make a spiritual communion in every Mass they attend, at least at the same time as the priest receives the Eucharist. This should be done with humility, fervor and appropriate devotion.[39] This section of Gearnon's work, which focuses on recommended activity for morning time, concludes with the text of the Angelus prayer, which was to be recited three times a day – in the morning, at midday and in the evening.[40] A later section examines the Mass in more detail, explaining the symbolism of the priest's vestments and each part of the liturgy. The actions of the priest are explained in terms of the various episodes of the Passion story; for example, when the priest stretches his hands out over the chalice and then takes the host in his hand, this symbolized the arrest of Christ, his being bound and scourged and the placing of a crown of thorns on his head.[41] The priest dressed in his vestments before the beginning of Mass should call to mind Christ carrying the cross on his shoulders to Calvary.[42] Participants were thus encouraged to participate in the story of the Passion through the liturgy. In this section, Gearnon also deals with the more practical matter of how to behave during Mass. One should remain on one's knees except at the time when the Gospel is read, not distract the priest or the others attending Mass, not cough loudly, not speak with anyone else during Mass, nor continually look at who is coming in or going out but, instead, fix one's attention on the mystery of the Eucharist with reverence .[43] Gearnon supplies the reader with prayers to be recited during Mass.[44] Various benefits of the Mass, outlined by Gearnon, bear much resemblance to standard late medieval lists. The three principal benefits are that it restrains God's anger, bestows many gifts on us in this life and also on the souls in Purgatory.[45]

Daily tasks and prayers

One of the most notable features of *Parrthas an Anma* is its instruction on how to punctuate each day with moments of prayer and self-offering. However, these were not limited to occasions in church or encounters with religious iconography. While Gearnon includes a prayer to be recited when passing a crucifix (which might have been employed when travelling by a wayside cross, for instance), he accompanies this with a prayer to be used when meeting a neighbour. When passing a cross, one should bow one's head and say 'I venerate your cross, O Lord, in honour of your glorious Passion, through which you freed and saved us.

---

39 Ibid., pp 21–2.   **40** Ibid., p. 22.   **41** Ibid., p. 135.   **42** Ibid., p. 137.   **43** Ibid.   **44** Ibid., pp 138–40.
45 Ibid., p. 133. On the effects of Mass on God's anger, see S. Ryan, 'Reign of blood: aspects' (2002).

Through the sign of the holy cross (bless oneself at this point), free us (bless oneself a second time), O God (and a third time) from our enemies'.[46] When meeting a neighbour, Gearnon suggests that the following blessing should be employed: 'Praise be Jesus Christ'. He notes that this prayer of blessing has fifty days' indulgence attached to it by Pope Sixtus V (1585–90).[47]

The regulation of neighbourly relations is the subject of a later passage in *Parrthas an Anma*. A person should do his best not to cause his neighbour spiritual or temporal harm. Readers are encouraged to look with love on their neighbours and to imagine that they are in the image of Christ or the Virgin Mary. Gearnon states that as God is everywhere, he should be thought of as dwelling in the soul of each person to whom the reader is speaking and, therefore, should be approached with humility and love.[48] All dangerous conversation should be avoided and nothing should lead to later scruples in confession. Topics that might cause disgust or displeasure should be shunned and, concomitantly, every good thing that might benefit both soul and body should be encouraged.[49]

Every daily task had the potential to be transformed into a prayer. Readers are instructed to begin their tasks by reciting the words 'I begin this work for the glory and honour of God and for the salvation of my soul'.[50] They should, at times, imagine Christ and Mary at their side, assisting them in their chores.[51] Gearnon suggests that readers take the opportunity to adopt wholesome and beneficial thoughts according to the manner of work in which they are engaged: for example, when working near a fire, contemplate the fires of hell or if, performing an enjoyable work, imagine the glory of heaven. When work is difficult, one should pray the words 'Glory be to the Father and to the Son and to the Holy Spirit, as it was in the beginning, is now and ever shall be, Amen'. By this action, Gearnon continues, the person shows that he is not vanquished in his difficulty.[52] Gearnon advises his readers that they should place themselves in the company of Christ on the cross, uniting their suffering with his.[53] At other times, one might contemplate that no suffering can compare with the pains of hell. Gearnon stresses that this will render every kind of work light and easy to bear.[54]

Mental association with Christ's Passion at various stages of the day is strongly recommended throughout *Parrthas an Anma*. Gearnon calls this kind of prayer 'the most beneficial prayer' and suggests that readers contemplate from within, and on their knees, for an hour or longer, everything that Christ suffered.[55] Devices such as the Clock of the Passion, lists of the people who crucified Christ

---

46 Ó Fachtna, *Parrthas*, p. 23. The power of the Sign of the Cross was widely acknowledged in medieval spirituality. In prayers of blessing and exorcism, in particular, repeated 'crossings' were routinely prescribed at various points.   **47** Ibid. This form of greeting was quite common in continental Europe at the time and is still used in some regions today.   **48** Ibid., p. 27.   **49** Ibid., pp 27–8.   **50** Ibid., p. 24.   **51** Ibid.   **52** Ibid.   **53** Ó Fachtna, *Parrthas*, p. 24. See also 2 Cor 4:10–12.   **54** Ibid., p. 25.   **55** Ibid., p. 161.

and the places he walked along the way, the twelve pains of Christ and the seven occasions he spilled blood, the seven last words of Christ and the seven sorrows of Mary, all facilitated recollection of the principal events of Christ's suffering and death. However, one did not have to kneel to recall Christ's Passion. The audience or readers of *Parrthas an Anma* were encouraged to keep the events of Christ's life and death in mind at all times.[56]

In addition to these thoughts, Gearnon encouraged the frequent use of the short aspirations, 'Jesus' and 'Mary', noting in this case that twenty-five days' indulgence was granted by Pope Sixtus V to all who uttered these names prayerfully. Furthermore, a plenary indulgence from all sin at the hour of death was accorded persons who were in the habit of reciting these names, or either one of them, frequently. A similar indulgence was granted to preachers who spread the devotion.[57] At times, however, the practice of transforming some daily tasks into 'prayers' and indulgences had to be regulated. In his tract on penance, *Sgáthán Shacramuinte na hAithridhe*, Aodh Mac Aingil felt it necessary to caution against a belief in the Low Countries, which affected the Irish living there, that an indulgence from the Pope was obtained every time a person drank from his cup after saying grace after meals: 'I would consider as sinful the people who, after grace, knock back drinks together for fun in order to obtain an indulgence, for spiritual things are not suitable for entertainment'.[58]

Mealtime prayers of blessing and thanksgiving (translations of traditional Latin versions) are also included in *Parrthas an Anma*. These reinforce the Pauline idea that every action that one performs should be directed to the glory of God. After eating, readers are invited to retire to a quiet place and recite five Our Fathers and Hail Marys in honour of the five wounds of Christ and to thank him for having satisfied them through his great goodness.[59] At this point, they are encouraged to make a further examination of conscience and to ask themselves whether they have fulfilled every good intention they made that morning and, in particular, whether they subsequently fell into mortal sin.[60] Before retiring to bed, another and more detailed examination of conscience is recommended, in the middle of the Confiteor. This was to entail an examination of all works, words and thoughts from the moment of rising, how every hour was spent, and whether there were lapses into venial or mortal sin.[61] Readers were to adopt the attitude that they might not be alive the following day and were, therefore, not to allow themselves to fall asleep before making an act of contrition. Every intention that was made that morning was to be called to mind and, if not fulfilled, the intention was to be renewed for the following day. When this was completed, readers were advised to finish reciting the Confiteor and then pray the following: 'Save us Lord while we are awake, protect us while we sleep, that we may keep watch with Christ and rest with him in peace'.[62] Once again, this prayer derives from compline in the Roman breviary. Considerable time was to be spent contemplating death and judgment.[63] Then, when undressing before bed, Gearnon advised his readers to remember how the Jews stripped Christ for crucifixion and beseech him, for the sake of the pain which he endured at that time, to strip away all inordinate desires and passions from their hearts.[64] Finally, when lying in bed, readers were to imagine how they would be stretched out in a grave at the end of their lives. They were, therefore, to stretch themselves out while imagining themselves lying with Christ in the tomb. God, in turn, would then preserve them from a difficult sleep.[65]

This contemplation was not the end of one's spiritual duties. At midnight one was expected to rise to recite a choice of prayers according to one's station. Suggestions include the canonical hours (for clergy and religious), the hours of Mary (a popular lay alternative), the Chaplet of Jesus,[66] the Rosary,[67] the Litany of Jesus, Mary or the saints,[68] 'or whatever prayers God reveals to him according to his capability …'[69] Prayers at this hour were to be directed towards the souls in Purgatory, contemplation of the Passion of Christ and the last things. Gearnon assures his readers that there is no better time to pray 'for the mind is tranquil and at rest'.[70] He continues by noting another reason for the tradition of midnight prayer: it is about this time that Christ was born and also, according to some holy fathers, would return in judgment.[71] Noting the tradition of praying at midnight among religious orders, Gearnon adds an interesting comment, which demonstrates that he is primarily addressing a lay audience: 'It was not long ago that this blessed custom was common across Ireland among all sorts of people who loved God and cared for the salvation of their souls'.[72] He asks that this custom not be wholly abandoned through laziness or desire for comfort.[73]

62 Ibid.   63 For the wider context see Salvador Ryan, 'Fixing the eschatological scales: judgment of the soul in late medieval and early modern Irish tradition' (2009).   64 Ibid., p. 30.   65 Ibid.   66 This prayer consisted of thirty-three Our Fathers and Hail Marys in honour of the thirty-three years of Christ's life. Devotees were expected to meditate on various scenes of Christ's passion throughout the three decades and on the Resurrection, Ascension and Last Judgment for the final three prayers. Instruction on how to recite this chaplet is included later in *Parrthas* (p. 116).   67 The form of the Rosary, as outlined in *Parrthas*, consisted of seven decades of Hail Marys in addition to two Hail Marys at the end, in honour of the number of years Mary spent on earth – seventy-two. This was a Franciscan creation known as the *Seven Joys of Mary*. Instruction on how to recite this prayer properly is included in *Parrthas* (pp 117–19).   68 These litanies are also included in the section on prayer in *Parrthas* (pp 120–31).   69 Ibid., p. 31. Here, Gearnon, while providing the texts of suggested prayers, allows for a degree of spontaneity in prayer, a fact that was of some importance in the Tridentine effort to move away from prayers performed exclusively by rote. For wider discussion on this see S. Ryan, 'From late medieval piety to Tridentine pietism?' (2006).   70 Ó Fachtna, *Parrthas*, p. 31.   71 Ibid. 72 Ibid., p. 32.   73 Ibid.

The Spiritual Alphabet

The Spiritual Alphabet, the final section of *Parrthas an Anma*, functions as an *aide-memoire* for many of the daily practices that Gearnon wishes to encourage in his readers. He intends the alphabet to be committed to memory and that it, or at least its principle points, might be recalled at the time of Morning Prayer in order that some of it might be put into practice that day 'for the glory of God … and on account of the love that is his due'.[74] This should also be repeated at night time in order that one might make an assessment of how well this was achieved. Among the most important points included in the *Spiritual Alphabet* were daily prayer (morning, midday and night time), the frequent use of the sign of the cross to begin and end both spiritual and temporal duties, the disciplining of one's desires through observance of the Ten Commandments and precepts of the church, the hearing of Mass and daily spiritual communion, weekly or monthly confession and Holy Communion, almsgiving (to the materially poor by means of a daily contribution from one's possessions and to the spiritually poor through daily remembrance of the souls in Purgatory), daily prayer for the adoption of virtue and the grace to free oneself from sin, devotion and recourse to the merits of Christ's Passion, contemplation each night of one's death and the last things, awareness that every day may be one's last and that contrition for sin must, therefore, be part of it; daily offering of oneself to the Creator and acceptance of one's lot, both good and bad; the practice of examining one's conscience three times a day – in the morning, at midday and at night, the instruction of the ignorant in Christian doctrine and the avoidance of both sinful occasions and company; in times of distress to remember the feast days of Mary and the saints and all they suffered in life for the sake of Christ and the crown of glory they received as a result. The *Spiritual Alphabet* concludes, as does the work as a whole, in the manner of many medieval sermons, with the aspiration that Christ, in his great mercy, will bestow that crown on its readers.

CONCLUSION

Works such as Ó Maoil Chonaire's *Desiderius*, Aodh Mac Aingil's *Sgáthán Shacramuinte na hAithridhe* and Antoin Gearnon's *Parrthas an Anma* should not be simply regarded as some of the earliest examples of Catholic printed publications in the Irish language. More generally, they form part of a much larger tridentine project that spanned Europe and indeed the New World. The production of catechisms in the catholic world was followed closely by a huge

---

74 Ibid., p. 193.

output of devotional literature. The latter was not replicated in Protestantism to the same extent as is evidenced by the demand, even among many Puritans, for sanitized versions (usually excising references to Purgatory, the Virgin Mary, etc.) of Catholic devotional tracts to fill this need.[75] While the Jesuit order was at the forefront of the development of Catholic catechisms in sixteenth-century Europe, by the succeeding century many secular clergy were also involved in producing their own versions. In the period in which *Parrthas an Anma* was produced, it was becoming more common to include devotional material as appendages to catechisms, as is evidenced, for instance in a later example, the 1672 *Abstract of a Douay catechism.*[76]

Antoin Gearnon's *Parrthas an Anma* was not simply designed as a catechism. While it contains much catechetical material, it presumably functioned best as a prayer book. Here, outlined in a simple and accessible form, were a host of devotional exercises that could be performed by all. While the longer prayers might require some time to learn, many of the devotions required nothing more than an active religious imagination and a willingness to spend time in quiet meditation. This is an important point, which is exemplified in copies of sections of Gearnon's work found in the manuscript tradition. It is through this tradition that the reception and use of Gearnon's work can best be appreciated.[77] Invariably, the sections which are copied into manuscript collections are those dealing with everyday prayers and rituals: morning prayers, evening prayers, grace before and after meals, prayers before and after Communion, litanies and instructions on how one should behave during Mass and when listening to a sermon – essentially the practical elements of one's religious life.

Gearnon allowed for the potentially busy lives of his audience by incorporating into his work recommendations on how to transform every task into a prayer. While acknowledging the central role of the sacraments, many of the devotions that Gearnon presents to his audience do not require the presence of a priest or even proximity to a church to be performed. Here, then, is an important text centered on the spiritual requirements of the laity in early modern Ireland – a text which advocates the use of what might be termed the 'wooden key' of daily practice to achieve personal holiness and the unlocking of that heavenly door.

75 D. MacCulloch, *Reformation: Europe's house divided* (2004), p. 588.   **76** G. Scott, 'The education of James III' (2004), p. 274.   **77** See R. Flower, *BL Cat. Ir. MSS.* The following manuscripts held at the British Library all contain material from *Parrthas an Anma*: Sloane 3567 (1664–5), Egerton 196 (1688), Egerton 198 (1717), Egerton 193 (late eighteenth century), Additional 33196 (1797).

'Collegium S. Antonii Lovanii, quod Collegium est unicum remedium ad conservandam Provinciam' (Donnchadh Ó Maonaigh, 1617–18)

MÍCHEÁL MAC CRAITH OFM

Ceapadh an t-iarollamh file Flaithrí Ó Maoil Chonaire mar mhinistir proibhinsil ar Phroinsiasaigh na hÉireann ag caibidil ghinearálta an oird i Toledo sa bhliain 1606. Go luath ina dhiaidh sin scríobh sé chuig Pilb III na Spáinne ag iarraidh ceada chun coláiste a oscailt i Lobháin san Ísiltir Spáinneach chun Pronsiasaigh óga na hÉireann a oiliúint don tsagartóireacht. Tugadh an cead, fritheadh bulla toilithe ón bPápa 3 Aibreán 1607 agus chuir an chéad chomhluadar de na bráithre fúthu i Lobháin i mí na Bealtaine.

B'fhéidir go dtugann na fíricí loma sin le fios gur cinneadh an-tobann ba chúis le bunú Choláiste San Antoine i Lobháin. Is cosúil gur a mhalairt ghlan a bhí i gceist. Ní anuas ón spéir a tháinig an Lobháin ach ba thoradh é ar pholaitiú reiligiúnda na bProinsiasach a bhí ar siúl le seachtó bliain roimhe sin.

AN LEASÚCHÁN OBSARVAINTEACH

Chun léargas níos soiléire a fháil ar an bpróiséas seo ní mór dul siar go dtí an ceathrú haois déag san Iodáil nuair a tháinig gluaiseacht leasúcháin chun cinn san ord a bhí ag iarraidh filleadh ar úire agus ar dhíogras na laethanta tosaigh nuair ba bheo do Phroinsias féin. Chuaigh an ghluaiseacht i dtreis go háirithe sa chéad leath den chúigiú haois déag nuair a tháinig ceathrar ceannairí iomráiteacha chun cinn a dtugtar ceithre cholún na hObsarvainteachta orthu, agus díol spéise gur naomhaíodh iad go léir ach amháin an chéad duine: Alberto da Sarteano (1385–1450), Bernardino da Siena (1380–1444), Giovanni da Capestrano (1386–1456) Giacomo della Marca (1394–1476). Cé gurbh é cuspóir na gceannairí go leasófaí an t-ord ar fad, ní mar sin a tharla agus bhí sé á scoilt ina dhá champa, lucht tacaíochta an leasúcháin ara dtugtar na hObsarvaintigh, agus lucht diúltaithe an leasúcháin ara dtugtar na Coinbhintigh. Sa bhliain 1446 bhunaigh an Pápa Eugene IV córas viocáireachtaí do na hObsarvaintigh. Go teoiriciúil bhí siad le bheith faoi cheannas an mhinistir ghinearálta, ach go praiticiúil bhí siad neamhspleách air. Ní raibh ann ach ceist ama go ndaingneofaí an scoilt go foirmeálta, áfach, rud a tharla sa Róimh 29 Bealtaine 1517 nuair a d'aithin an Pápa

Leo X na hObsarvaintigh mar chomharbaí dlisteanacha San Proinsias, agus d'ordaigh sé gur orthu sin feasta a thabharfaí an teideal Ord na mBráthar Mionúr. Dhiúltaigh na Coinbhintigh glacadh le dlínse na nObsarvainteach agus thogh siad ministrí ginearálta dá gcuid féin. Cé nár ghlac an Pápa i dtus báire leis an socrú seo, ghéill sé sa deireadh agus 12 Meitheamh 1517 d'athbhunaigh sé na Coinbhintigh mar ord ar leith[1].

AN LEASUCHÁN OBSARVAINTEACH SNA hOILEÁIN SEO

Éire

Maidir leis na hoileáin seo tá fianaise ann go raibh Proinsiasaigh áirithe in Éirinn báúil leis an leasuchán faoi bhlianta tosaigh an chúigiú haois déag. Faoin mbliain 1417 bhí dóthain misnigh acu chun Riail San Proinsias a chleachtadh go follasach faoina híondéine, ach iad fós faoi dhlínse na ministrí proibhinsil. Sa bhliain 1458 chuaigh Nehemias Ó Donnchadha chuig caibidil ghinearálta an oird sa Róimh. Chuir sé cás na leasaitheoirí in Éirinn chun cinn go tréan agus d'éirigh chomh maith leis gur údaraigh an chaibidil viocáireacht Obsarvainteach a bhunú in Éirinn le Nehemias mar viocáire. Toisc nár éirigh leis filleadh abhaile go dtí an bhliain 1460, sin í an bhliain is gnách a lua le bunú na viocáireachta Obsarvaintí in Éirinn. Ón am sin i leith tháinig borradh éachtach faoi na hObsarvaintigh abhus. Idir 1460 agus 1536 bhunaigh siad deich dteach nua, a bhformhór acu i gceantar na nGael, agus ghlac ocht dteach is fiche as an ocht dteach is daichead a bhí ag na Coinbhintigh leis an leasúchán[2].

Ar na tithe nua Obsarvainteacha ab iomráití, ní mór aird ar leith a dhíriú ar mhainistir Dhún na nGall. Aodh Ruadh Ó Domhnaill, taoiseach Thír Chonaill agus a bhean chéile, Nuala Ní Bhriain, a bhunaigh í sa bhliain 1473 nó 1474.[3] Is iad tuismitheoirí Aodha Ruaidh, Niall Garbh Ó Domhnaill agus Nuala Ní Chonchobhair a thóg an Treas Ord Rialta go Machaire Beag i dTír Chonaill roinnt blianta roimhe sin. Nuair a fágadh ina baintreach í don dara huair sa bhliain 1444, chuaigh Nuala abhaile go hUíbh Fháilí agus chaith sí an chuid eile dá saol i mbun guí agus aithrí láimh le teach na bProinsiasach i gCill Shléibhe.[4] Níorbh iontas ar bith é dá dtabharfadh sí lántacaíocht dá mac agus dá hiníon chéile nuair a bheartaigh siad teach a bhunú do na hObsarvaintigh i nDún na nGall.[5] Thug taoisigh Thír Chonaill an-tacaíocht do na bráithre bochta. Is sa mhainistir sin a adhlacadh Aodh Ruadh nuair a bhásaigh sé sa bhliain 1505 agus a

---

1 Moorman, *History of the Franciscan order* (1968), ll 441–585; Robson, *Franciscans in the Middle Ages* (2006), ll 181–223. 2 Ó Clabaigh, *Franciscans in Ireland*, l. 53. 3 C. Mooney, 'The founding of the friary of Donegal' (1954–5), l. 20. 4 Ibid., ll 16–7. 5 Ibid., l. 20.

bhean chéile Nuala sa bhliain 1528. Is ann leis a adhlacadh Mánas Ó Domhnaill nuair a bhásaigh sé sa bhliain 1563.[6] Ní hamháin go n-adhlactaí na Dálaigh mhóra ar fad ansin, ach go leor eile d'uaisle iarthuaisceart Uladh chomh maith.

Albain

Fuair na hObsarvaintigh cuireadh teacht go hAlbain sa bhliain 1436 agus bhunaigh siad a gcéad teach i nDún Éideann sa bhliain 1447.[7] Sa bhliain 1463 scríobh an Pápa Pius II chuig an vicáire ginearálta ciosalpach á údarú chun trí nó ceithre theach a bhunú do na hObsarvaintigh in Albain agus glacadh le dhá theach nó trí cinn de chuid na gCoinbhinteach ar son an leasúcháin. Mhol an Pápa díograis na banríona, Máire de Gueldres, baintreach Shéamais IV (1471–1513), agus díograis an phobail araon as na hObsarvaintigh a lorg.[8] Ocht dteach ar fad a bhí ag na hObsarvaintigh in Albain i ndeireadh na dála, Dún Éideann, Saint Andrews, Obair Dheáin, Peart, Glaschú, Elgin, Ayr agus Stirling. Séamus IV a bhunaigh an teach i Stirling agus ba bhreá leis an tSeachtain Mhór a chaitheamh ann, duine nár dheacair leis an diantréanas agus an drabhlás a chleachtadh in uainíocht ar a chéile.

Sasana

Bhí Éire agus Albain chun tosaigh ar Shasana maidir le teacht na nObsarvainteach. Is cosúil gur thug Annraoi VI cuireadh do Giovanni da Capestrano sa bhliain 1454 teacht go Sasana chun na hObsarvaintigh a bhunú ann, ach bhí Capestrano róghafa le hiarrachtaí chun Constantinople le fáil ar ais ó na Turcaigh chun rud a dhéanamh air.[9] Níor tharla dada go ceann breis agus tríocha bliain ina dhiaidh sin. Phós deirfiúr an rí Eadbhard IV, Mairéad Eabhrac, Cathal Dána, Diúca na Burgainne sa bhliain 1468. Tháinig cúirt ríoga Shasana go mór faoi anáil na Burgainne de bharr an chleamhnais seo agus bhí athair céile Mhairéad an-tógtha ar fad leis na hObsarvaintigh. I samhradh na bliana 1480 d'fhill sí ar Shasana chun tacaíocht an rí a lorg ar son na Burgainne in aghaidh na Fraince. Is cosúil gur thapaigh sí an deis le linn na cuairte chun bolscaireacht a dhéanamh ar son na nObsarvainteach. D'eisigh an Pápa bulla 24 Meán Fómhair 1480 a cheadaigh trí theach a bhunú sa ríocht. Tháinig na hObsarvaintigh go Sasana don chéad uair 2 Iúil 1482 agus tugadh láithreán dóibh i Greenwich in aice leis an bpálás ríoga.[10]

D'ainneoin an chuiridh ríoga, áfach, ní raibh cúrsaí go maith ag na bráithre go dtí gur tháinig Annraoi VII i gcoróin sa bhliain 1485. Sa bhliain 1498 fuair an rí cead ón bPápa chun trí theach Choinbhinteacha a ghlacadh chun an leasuchán a

6 Mooney, 'Friars and friary of Donegal', ll 46–9.   7 Mooorman, *History of the Franciscan order*, l. 491.
8 Robson, *Franciscans in the Middle Ages*, ll 216–17.   9 K.D. Brown, *The Franciscan Observants in England* (1986), ll 19–20.   10 Ibid., ll 24–32.

chur cinn iontu, Canterbury, Newcastle agus Southampton. Dealraíonn sé nach cúrsaí cráifeachta amháin ba bhun leis an gcinneadh seo, ach leas an stáit. Bhí an rí tar éis conradh cleamhnais a dhéanamh leis an Spáinn sa bhliain 1496, cleamhnas a chuirfeadh le gradam na dTudorach. De réir an chonartha phósfadh Artúr, mac an rí, Caitríona Aragon, iníon Ferdinand agus Isabella na Spáinne, nuair a thiocfadh an bheirt óg in inmhe. Is maith a thuig Annraoi an borradh reiligiúnda a bhí ar siúl sa Spáinn ag an am. Bhí Fray Francisco Ximines de Cisneros, bráthair Obsarvainteach agus Ardeaspag Toledo, mar oide faoistine ag an mbanríon. Agus lántacaíocht na monarc aige, bhí clár leathan leasucháin ar bun ag Cisneros sa Chaistíl ach go háirithe. De bharr léasuchán Ximines bhí an ruaig á cur ar na Coinbhintigh as a gcuid tithe agus Obsarvaintigh á gcur ina n-áit. Bhí Caitríona féin chomh tógtha leis na hObsarvaintigh is a bhí a máthair, rud nach ndeachaigh amú ar Annraoi. Má bhí uaidh dea-mhéin na Spáinne a thabhú do féin, ní fearr rud a dhéanfadh sé ná an tacaíocht chéanna a thabhairt do na hObsarvaintigh is a bhí á tabhairt ag tuismitheoirí bhean a mhic.[11]

Thóg Annraoi pálás taibhsiúil ag Richmond idir 1498 agus 1501 in ómós don chleamhnas idir Artúr agus Caitríona. Thóg sé teach do na hObsarvaintigh ag Richmond freisin, teach a bhí ar aon dul le galántacht an pháláis, teach a raibh na bráithre féin thar a bheith míshuaimheach leis agus iad tiomnaithe chomh mór sin do chleachtadh an dianbhochtanais. Pósadh Artúr agus Caitríona 14 Samhain 1501 ach thit an lug ar an lug ar Annraoi nuair a bhásaigh Artur go tobann den tinneas allasach 2 Aibreán 1502. Bhásaigh Annraoi féin sa bhliain 1509, teach Obsarvainteach nua bunaithe aige an bhliain roimhe sin i Newark i Nottinghamshire, ach leas a anama agus ní leas na ríochta a bhí ag déanamh buartha dó an babhta seo. Sé seachtaine i ndiaidh adhlacadh a athar, 11 Meitheamh 1509, phós an rí nua, Annraoi VIII, Caitríona Aragon i searmanas ciúin in aireagal na mbráithre i Greenwich.[12] Bhí seisean nach mór ocht mbliana déag d'aois, bhí sise fiche trí. Toisc go raibh Annraoi ag pósadh bhaintreach a dhearthár, b'éigean dispeansáid speisialta a fháil ón bPápa le go bhféadfadh an pósadh dul ar aghaidh. Bhí na hObsarvaintigh mar shéiplínigh chúirte faoin ritheaghlach nua. Is i séipéal na mbráithre i Richmond a baisteadh an prionsa Annraoi 5 Eanáir 1511, leanbh nár mhair ach seacht seachtaine go leith. Rugadh marbhghin fhireannach do Chaitríona i mí na Nollag 1514 agus nuair a saolaíodh an banphrionsa Máire, 8 Feabhra 1516, níor léir go raibh an rí díomúch.[13] Baisteadh an naí nua i séipéal na mbráithre i Greenwich.

---

11 Ibid., ll 32–40.   **12** G. Mattingly, *Catherine of Aragon* (1942), l. 106.   **13** Ibid., l. 144.

'Ábhar Mór an Rí'

Nuair nár éirigh le Caitríona oidhre fir a sholáthar chun rítheaghlach na dTudorach a chur ar lámh shábhála, áfach, tháinig an pósadh faoi bhrú. Rugadh marbhghin do Chaitríona 18 Samhain 1518, leanbh mná. Níorbh fhada torrach í gur thosaigh an rí ag caitheamh a shúil thar a chuid. Meitheamh 1519 rugadh leanbh sláintiúil fir dá leannán, Bessie Blount. Annraoi FitzRoy a tugadh air. Thóg bean óg darbh ainm Mary Boleyn áit Bessie Blount mar *maîtresse-en-titre* go dtí gur phós sí sa bhliain 1521. Chun todhchaí an rítheaghlaigh a dhaingniú, thosaigh na húdaráis ag faire amach chun cleamhnas straitéiseach a dhéanamh don bhanphrionsa Máire. Luadh an Dauphin, an tImpire Séarlas – nia Chaitríona, Séamas V na hAlban, ach níor tháing dada as na comhráite go léir. D'ídigh Annraoi a racht ar Chaitríona nuair a phós an tImpire Isabella na Portaingéile i ndeireadh na dála sa bhliain 1526. An bhliain chéanna thit an rí i ngrá le hAnne Boleyn, duine de mhná coimhdeachta na banríona, an dara hiníon leis an ambasadóir cumasach, Sir Thomas Boleyn, deirfiur Mháire a luadh thuas.[14] Ansin sa bhliain 1527, d'fhógair an rí go raibh a choinsias á chrá – 'ábhár mór an rí', mar a tugadh air – nach raibh sé pósta go bailí le Caitríona chor ar bith. Nach raibh sé de cheart ag an bPápa dispeansáid a thabhairt dó chun baintreach a dhearthár a phósadh. Ar an láimh eile bhí Caitríona chomh diongbháilte céanna gur pósadh bailí a bhí ann toisc nár cuireadh an chéad phósadh le hArtúr riamh i gcrích. Chun an scéal a dhéanamh níos casta fós bhí an Pápa, Clemens VII, agus nia Chaitríona, an tImpire Séarlas V, in adharca a chéile ag an am, an Pápa mar phríosúnach ag an Impire ó chreach fórsaí Shéarlais an Róimh sa bhliain 1525. Sheol an Pápa an Cairdinéal Campeggio go Sasana chun bailíocht an phósta ríoga a fhiosrú i dteannta an Chairdinéil Wolsey. B'fhearr go mór fada le Caitríona go ndéanfaí an cás a phlé sa Róimh ná i Sasana agus chuir sí iarratas dá réir sin chuig an bPápa.[15]

Domhnach Cásca 1532 thug William Peto, ministir proibhinsil na nObsarvainteach i Sasana, seanmóir os comhair an rí i séipéal na mbráithre i Greenwich, inar thug sé le fios go lífeadh madraí fuil an rí faoi mar a tharla don drochrí Achab sa Sean Tiomna (1 Ríthe 21:19), dá bpósfadh sé Anne Boleyn. Ar éigean a d'fhéadfaí seanmóir ba lú íogaireacht a roghnú gusan tagairt fholaithe d'Ízeibil, ní áirím téacs nach raibh baint dá laghad aige leis an Aiséirí. Tá gach cuma ar an scéal nach as a sheasamh a thug Peto an tseanmóir seo, ach gur beart tomhaiste a bhí ann ar an Domhnach ba shollúnta sa bhliain nuair a bhí a fhios aige go maith go mbeadh Annraoi i láthair. B'shin fianaise ghlé ar an bhfreasúra poiblí in aghaidh chealú an phósta. Ba léir freisin go raibh William Peto agus

14 A. Fraser, *Six wives of Henry VIII* (1992), ll 113–62. **15** Mattingly, *Catherine of Aragon*, ll 191–271; Fraser, *Six wives of Henry VIII*, ll 163–91.

Henry Elston, bardach na nObsarvainteach i Greenwich, i ndlúthpháirt le tacadóirí Chaitríona. Ar na tacadóirí seo bhí John Fisher, easpag Rochester, Sir Thomas More, an Seansailéir, agus ambasadóir an Impire, Eustace Chapuys, a tháinig go Sasana mar thaidhleoir sa bhliain 1529.

Labhair Annraoi le Peto tar éis na seanmóra agus chuir an Proinsiasach in iúl go neamhbhalbh don rí go raibh an choróin i mbaol dá rachadh sé ar aghaidh leis an gcolscaradh. Ní fhéadfadh an rí bean eile a phósadh fad ba bheo do Chaitríona, ach amháin sa chás go bhféadfaí a chruthú nach raibh cuid aici d'Artúr. Agus bhí an leabhar tugtha aici féin go sollúnta gurbh shin go díreach a bhí fíor. Bhí Caitríona chomh hionraic sin nach bhféadfaí gan í a chreidiúint. Luaigh Peto chomh maith na luaidreáin a bhí sa timpeall faoi iompar an rí, ní hamháin le hAnne Boleyn ach lena deirfiúr agus lena máthair chomh maith.[16]

D'ainneoin fhreasúra poiblí Peto, thug an rí cead dó freastal ar chaibidil ghinearálta an oird um Chincís i Toulouse. Ar éigean a thuig an rí go raibh leabhar á réiteach ag Peto chun cás Chaitríona a chur chun cinn agus go dtapódh sé an deis agus é thar lear leis an leabhar a phriondáil. An Domhnach dar gcionn, bhí Peto as láthair ag caibidil an phróibhinse i Canterbury. D'ordaigh Annraoi do dhuine dá shéiplínigh féin, an Dr Richard Curwen, seanmóir a thabhairt i Greenwich ar neamhchead do thoil an bhardaigh, Henry Elston, agus rud a bhí go huile is go hiomlán in aghaidh gnáis. Bhréagnaigh Elston go poiblí maoímh Curwen go raibh na hollscoileanna ar fad ar son an cholscartha. Bhí an rí le ceangal agus nuair a dhiúltaigh Peto Elston a bhriseadh mar bhardach cuireadh an bheirt acu i bpríosún. Nuair a díbríodh thar lear iad chuaigh siad chuig teach na nObsarvainteach in Antwerp, áit ar lean siad ar aghaidh ag stocaireacht i gcoinne an rí i dteannta bráithre eile ó Greenwich, Richmond agus Canterbury. Bhí tráchtas Laidine á réiteach acu in aghaidh argóintí an rí agus seoladh ochtó cóip ar ais go Sasana trí bhithín na mbráithre. Is cosúil freisin gur fhan Peto i ndlúth-theagmháil le Caitríona agus go mbíodh Obsarvaintigh ón iasacht ag taisteal os íseal chun cuairt a thabhairt ar an mbanríon thar a cheann.[17]

Phós Annraoi Anne Boleyn go rúnda ag deireadh Eanáir 1533. 23 Bealtaine thug Cranmer, Archeaspag Canterbury, a bhreithiúntas go raibh pósadh Annraoi agus Caitríona neamhbhailí ach chuir an Pápa breithiúntas Cranmer ar ceal i mbulla a d'eisigh sé 11 Iúil. Rinneadh Anne a choróiníú go foirmeálta 1 Meitheamh 1533. Saolaíodh an banphrionsa Eilís dóibh 7 Meán Fómhair agus baisteadh í i séipéal na nObsarvainteach i Greenwich. Seacht mí ina dhiaidh sin, Márta 1534 d'fhógair an Pápa in antráth go raibh pósadh Annraoi agus Cháitríona bailí ón tús.

16 Brown, *Franciscan Observants in England*, II 138–40; Fraser, *Six wives of Henry VIII*, l. 212; G.W. Bernard, *The king's reformation* (2005), l. 152.   17 Brown, *Franciscan Observants in England*, ll 140–7.

Cé go raibh William Peto agus Henry Elston ar thús cadhnaíochta maidir leis an bhfreasúra in aghaidh an rí, bhí Proinsiasaigh Obsarvaintecha eile a thug seanmóintí ina choinne. Bhí roinnt de na hObsarvaintigh thar a bheith báiúil le Elizabeth Barton, 'cailleach Kent'. Ní hámháin go raibh cáil na cráifeachta uirthi, ach b'fhísí í a raibh físeanna aici, más fíor, a chaith anuas ar pholasaí an rí i leith an cholscartha. Beirt d'Obsarvaintigh Canterbury, Hugh Rich agus Richard Risby, bhí siad gnóthach go maith ag scaipeadh foilseacháin na caillí. Crochadh agus dícheannaíodh iad ina teannta maraon le roinnt eile dá tacadóirí 15 Aibreán 1534.[18]

Ritheadh Acht an Cheannais agus Acht na Comharbachta Márta na bliana 1534, an chéad acht a d'fhógair gurbh é an rí féin ceannaire na hEaglaise sa ríocht, an dara ceann a d'fhógair bailíocht an phósta idir Annraoi agus Anne Boleyn. B'éigean do gach duine fásta sa ríocht an dá mhóid seo a ghlacadh ach ceapadh leagan ar leith díobh do na hObsarvaintigh, d'aon ughaim chun tuilleadh brú a chur orthu. Dhiúltaigh formhór na mbráithre an mhóid a thógáil, ach amháin i Canterbury, mar ar thug gach duine ach beirt í. I mí an Mheithimh 1534 tógadh dhá thrucail lán le hObsarvaintigh chuig Túr Londan. Scríobh Eustace Chapuys, ambasadóir an Impire, chuig Séarlas V i ndeireadh Lúnasa gur díbríodh na hObsarvaintigh as a gcuid tithe go léir. Luann cáipéis amháin 32 bráthair a fuair bás, 36 'exemptorum' toisc gur ghlac siad an mhóid, de réir dealraimh, 30 a chuaigh ar deoraíocht (19 acu go hAlbain) agus 45 scaipeadh ar fud na tíre, i dtithe na gCoibhinteach don chuid is mó.[19] Fuair Caitríona Aragon bás in Eanáir 1536. Theastaigh uaithi go ndéanfaí í a adhlacadh i séipéal Obsarvainteach ach faoin am sin ní raibh teach ar bith fágtha acu i Sasana. Aistríodh an teach i Greenwich chuig na Coinbhintigh 1536–7; tugadh Newark, Richmond agus Southampton do na hAgaistínigh; is cosúil gur ligeadh d'Obsarvaintigh dhílse Canterbury fanacht sa teach. Rinne roinnt de na bráithre a chuaigh go hAlbain seanmóireacht in aghaidh an rí agus bhí baint ag dornán de na bráithre a d'fhan i Sasana le hOilithreacht an Ghrásta sa bhliain 1536. Ní cóir dearmad a dhéanamh ach an oiread den bhráthair bocht John Forest a dódh go poiblí ina bheatha sa bhliain 1538, cé gurb eagal le Keith Brown nach bhfuil cuntas an mháirtreolaí cháiliúil Thomas Bourchier (Páras, 1582) saor ó locht, agus gur nós leis dul i muinín na samhlaíochta ar mhaithe le bolscaireacht reiligiúnda.[20] Dá uaisle é freasúra na nObsarvainteach in aghaidh pholasaí an rí, áfach, measann G.W. Bernard nach raibh an freasúra seo sách eagraithe. Is aisteach leis nach ndeachaigh siad i bpáirt le hoird eile agus nár fhéach siad le tacaíocht a fháil ó na heaspaig agus ó na huaisle. Is trua le Bernard nár eagraigh siad feachtas seanmóireachta nó

18 Ibid., ll 169–79. 19 Ibid., l. 200; Bernard, *The king's reformation*, l. 159. 20 Brown, *Franciscan Observants in England*, ll 211–17.

foilsitheoireachta, go háirithe i mBéarla. Ach i ndeireadh na dála is beag a d'fheadfadh siad a chur i gcrích, tharla cumhacht an rí a bheith chomh láidir sin.[21] Ba mhór idir freasúra na nObsarvainteach i Sasana agus in Éirinn, áfach, cé go raibh nasc thábhachtach idir an dá chineál agóidíochta.

OBSARVAINTIGH NA hÉIREANN AGUS 'ÁBHAR MÓR AN RÍ'

Níor atoghadh William Peto i gcaibidil na nObsarvainteach i Sasana i bhfómhar na bliana 1532 ach níor toghadh comharba air ach an oiread. I ndeireadh na dála, sheol an ministir ginearálta ball de phroibhinse Pháras, Francis Faber, go Sasana agus toghadh mar mhinistir probhinsil é go luath in Aibreán na bliana 1533. Ní raibh cur amach ceart ag Faber ar chúrsaí i Sasana agus is í an aidhm is mó a bhí aige sna míonna tosaigh an rí a shásamh. Díbríodh John Forest, duine de na bráithre ba ghlóraí in aghaidh Annraoi chuig ceann de na coinbhintí ó thuaidh agus rinne Faber iarracht srian a chur le beartas Peto chun leabhair threascracha a sheoladh ó Antwerp go Sasana. Ach de réir a chéile thuig sé nárbh fhada go mbeadh air rogha a dhéanamh idir a dhualgas don rí agus a dhualgas do riail na mbráithre, agus thuig údaráis na corónach nach bhféadfaí brath air a thuilleadh. Tugadh cead dó fiosrú oifigiúil a thabhairt ar thithe an oird in Éirinn Aibreán 1534. Roimh imeacht dó gheall sé do Chapuys 'that he would brew up there all he could for the preservation of the authority of the Holy See …'[22] Ba léir go raibh cur amach aige ar cháil na mbráithre in Éirinn, agus an tionchar a bhí acu i gceantair na nGael ach go háirithe:

> … in which he (Faber) may do wonderful service, especially among the wild Irish, by whom these Cordeliers [*Obsarvaintigh*] are feared, obeyed and almost revered not only by the peasants but by the lords who hold them in such reverence as to endure from them blows from a stick [23]

Ar an drochuair níl a fhios againn cad a rinne Francis Faber in Éirinn. Imíonn sé ar fad as an stair, agus tá an chuma ar an scéal nár fhill sé ar Shasana ar aon nós. Díol spéise freisin an nóta seo i gcáipéisí an tSeansailéara Cromwell, 7 Iúil 1534 'the ffreers of Greenwiche to have licence to go into Irelonde'.[24] Cheap Annraoi VIII George Browne mar Ardeaspag ar Bhaile Átha Cliath sa bhliain 1536. Bhí sé mar phroibinsial ar na hAgaistínigh i Sasana tráth, agus is air a thit an cúram na hObsarvaintigh thall a mhionnú faoin leagan ar leith d'Acht an Cheannais a

21 Bernard, *The king's reformation*, l. 160. **22** J. Gairdner, *Letters and papers, foreign and domestic, of the reign of Henry VIII* (1892 repr. 1965), vii, ll 366, 957 (1534). **23** Ibid. **24** *Cal. S.P. Spanish*, 1534–5, n. 70 (Gairdner, vii. l. 957).

ceapadh dóibh. Theip go tubaisteach air é sin a dhéanamh agus is cosúil gur leathnaigh a cháil roimhe go hÉirinn. Bhí sé níos déine ar na hObsarvaintigh abhus ná ar aon ord eile, ach d'admhaigh sé go poiblí gur theip go hiomlán air Obsarvaintigh Bhaile Átha Cliath a mhionnú.[25] Sa bhliain 1538 luann Thomas Aagarde, oifigeach de chuid na corónach i mBaile Átha Cliath, diongbháilteacht na mbráithre:

> Here as yett the blude of Criste is cleane blottyed owte of al mens herttes, what with that monsttyr, the Byschope of Roome, and his adherenttes, in espeschially the false and crafty bludsukkers, the Observauntes, as they wilbe callid most hollyeste, soo that ther remaynz more vertu in on of ther cootes and knottyd gyrdylles, than ever was in Criste, and his Paschion.[26]

In alt tuisceanach a fhiosraíonn na torthaí difiriúla a bhí ar an Reifirméisean i Sasana, in Éirinn agus sa Bhreatain Bheag, leag Brendan Bradshaw béim láidir ar thionchar na nObsarvainteach in Éirinn chun an tír seo a ghnóthú don Leasuchán Creidimh Caitliceach,[27] Cé nach dtógann Bradshaw ceann a dhóthain de fhreasúra na nObsarvainteach i Sasana in aghaidh pholasaí Annraoi VIII, agus den tionchar a bhí acu ar a gcomhbhráithre in Éirinn, fós féin, díol spéise a chuid conclúidí:

> Unlike Wales or indeed England, Ireland uniquely possessed in the orders of friars a spiritual élite – the fruits of the Observant reform movement – numerous, widely dispersed, pastorally dynamic, respected by the laity of all social degrees, and well attuned to the vernacular as a mode of evangelisation.[28]

Maidir le díscaoileadh na dtithe rialta in Éirinn bhí an scéal i bhfad ní ba chasta agus an próiseas i bhfad ní b'fhaide ná i Sasana.[29] Nuair a baineadh triail as na mainistreacha a chur faoi chois don chéad uair sa bhliain 1540, meastar gur éirigh le seasca faoin gcéad díobh teacht slán. Buntáiste mór amháin a bhí ag na hObsarvaintigh thar na hoird eile gur thaitin siad leis an bpobal áitiúil agus leis na tiarnaí chomh maith. Is minic a d'fhág na bráithre an teach sular tháinig na coimisinéirí chun an díscaoileadh a chur i bhfeidhm, rud a rinne na Proinsiasaigh i Muilte Fearnáin agus i Luimneach. D'fhéadfaí earraí luachmhara agus soithigh altóra a thabhairt do chairde iontaobhacha le coimeád slán dóibh fad a bhí siad imithe.[30] Chabhraigh deighilt na tíre idir na ceantair faoi smacht na corónach

25 C. Mooney, *First impact of the Reformation* (1967), l. 26. 26 Ibid., l. 26. 27 B. Bradshaw, 'The English Reformation and identity formation in Ireland and Wales' (1998), l. 99. 28 Ibid., l. 90. 29 Féach Lennon, 'The dissolution to the foundation of St Anthony's College, Louvain' san imleabhar seo. 30 Féach Krasnodębska-D'Aughton, 'Franciscan chalices, 1600–50' san imleabhar seo.

agus na ceantair faoi smacht na nGael go mór leis na Proinsiasaigh ach go háirithe. Nuair a chuaigh an crú ar an tairne i dtailte na corónach, d'fhéadfaí éalú go héasca go ceantar a bhí saor ar údarás an rí.[31] I ngeall ar chomh dáiríre a thóg na hObsarvaintigh cleachtadh na bochtaineachta, ní raibh mórán tailte acu, rud a d'fhág nach raibh siad chomh tarraingteach sin do lucht na sainte. Choinnigh na teagmhálacha a bhí acu lena gcomhbhráithre i Sasana ar an eolas iad faoi leasúchán Annraoi VIII, agus ba mhaith an deis iad caibidlí idirnáisiúnta an oird chun na 'friars obstinates' a choinneáil i dteagmháil le himeachtaí ar an mór-roinn.[32] Ní háibhéil ar bith a rá, déanta na fírinne, go raibh na hObsarvaintigh ar thús cadhnaíochta maidir le nasc a bhúnú idir an freasúra in aghaidh pholasaí reiligiúnda na corónach in Éirinn agus gluaiseacht an Leasúcháin Chreidimh Chaitlicigh a bhí ag bailiú nirt ar an mór-roinn.[33]

POLAITIÚ NA nOBSARVAINTEACH

Nuair a cuireadh éirí amach na nGearaltach faoi chois sa bhliain 1537 tháinig roinnt taoiseach Gaelach agus roinnt tiarnaí de chuid na Sean-Ghall le chéile chun oidhre óg na nGearaltach a chosaint. Mar chuid den straitéis seo phós Mánas Ó Domhnaill Eileanóir Nic Gearailt, aintín an bhuachalla. Díol suntais an chomhghuaillíocht seo ar go leor cúiseanna. Ba í an chéad chomhghuaillíocht mhór idir na Gaeil agus na Sean-Ghaill í in aghaidh chumhacht na corónach in Éirinn. Ina theannta sin bhí gné láidir den taidhleoireacht idirnáisiúnta i gceist agus rinneadh teagmhálacha leis an Impire, Séarlas V, le Proinsias I na Fraince agus le Séamas V na hAlban. Bhí toise reiligiúnda ag baint leis an bhfeachtas chomh maith. Dúirt ceannaí ó Ghaillimh a bhí i nDún na nGall ar chúraimí gnó sa bhliain 1539 go raibh na Proinsiasaigh ag tacú le Mánas san ionradh á bhí á bheartú ar an bPáile aige agus go raibh siad ag seanmóireacht sna téarmaí seo a leanas:

> Every man ought, for the salvacion of his sowle, fight and make warr ayenste Our Soverayne Lord the Kinges Majestie, and his trewe subjectes; and if any of theym, which soo shall fight ayentste His said Majestie, or his subjectes, dy in the quarrell, his sowle, that so shallbe dedd, shall goo to Heven, as the sowle of Saynt Peter, Pawle, and others, which soffered death and merterdom of Godes sake.[34]

31 Mooney, *First impact of Reformation*, ll 24–8. **32** Ó Clabaigh, *Franciscans in Ireland*, ll. 78–9. **33** Bradshaw, 'The English Reformation and identity formation in Ireland and Wales', l. 100. **34** *Cal. S.P. Ire.* 3 Henry VIII, no. cclxxii, l. 141.

23 Meitheamh 1539 rinneadh conradh idir Mánas Ó Domhnaill agus Tadhg Ó Conchobhair Shligigh inar tugadh caisleán Shligigh do Thadhg ar choinníollacha ar leith, mar atá go bhfanfadh sé dílis do Mhánas in aghaidh Gael agus Gall faoi seach agus go dtabharfadh sé úsáid an chaisleáin do Mhánais le linn éigeandála. Bhí go leor easpag agus filí i láthair. Bhagair na heaspaig pionós an choinnealbhá ar cheachtar den dá pháirtí dá mbrisfidís an conradh agus bhagair na filí pionós na haoire. Dá spéisiúla an ní é smachtbhannaí na n-easpag agus na bhfilí araon a bheith ar chomhchéim, is spéisiúla fós gur síníodh an conradh seo i mainistir na bProinsiasach i nDún na nGall, go raibh an comhluadar ar fad mar fhinnéithe ar an gconradh, agus gur shínigh triúr de na baill ba shinsearaí an cháipéis, an proibhinsial, Toirrdhealbhach Ó Conchobhair, ina measc.[35] Gné lárnach den chomhghuaillíocht ab ea an conradh seo agus seo é an chéad sampla follasach de pholaitiú na bProinsiasach sa séú haois déag. An bhliain dar gcionn chuaigh viocáire proibhinsil na nObsarvainteach go dtí an Pápa ag lorg cabhrach chun Éire a choiméad slán sa chreideamh caitliceach.[36] Nuair a bhuaigh fear ionaid an rí ar fhórsaí na comhghuaillíochta i Lúnasa 1539, níorbh fhada gur éirigh Mánas as léig na nGearaltach agus gur ghéill sé do na húdaráis. D'imigh Eileanóir ar ais go Má Nuad agus sheol sí a nia óg thar lear. Sa bhliain 1542 sheol Iognáid Loyola beirt Íosánach go hÉirinn, Paschasius Brouet agus Alphonsus Salmeron. Bíodh is go raibh litreacha molta ón bPápa acu, dhiúltaigh Mánas agus Conn Ó Néill teagmháil leo, cé gur thairg Mánas bualadh leo ós íseal. D'fhan na hÍosánaigh ceithre lá is tríocha i gCúige Uladh ach chaill siad dóchas go tapaidh agus d'fhill siad abhaile. Nuair a chuala Iognáid a dtuarascáil b'eagal leis go raibh Éire caillte agus gur mheasa an scéal abhus ná sa Ghearmáin féin.[37]

Níl mórán eolais againn faoi ról na bProinsiasach sna caogaidí agus na seascaidí ach sa bhliain 1572 scríobhadh tuairisc ó Ghaillimh go raibh suas le fiche bráthair tar éis teacht le chéile sa chathair, roinnt acu as cúige Uladh, gur thug bráthair Ultach seanmóir sa mhainistir, a bhí fós slán, de réir dealraimh, agus go raibh sé ag gríosú na ndaoine chun ceannairce.[38]

Seon Carsuel, 1567

Ní miste súil a chaitheamh ar cad a bhí ag tarlú in Albain sna blianta céanna. Tháinig Giolla Easpaig Cambeul, cúigú hIarla Earra Gael i seilbh na hiarlachta sa bhliain 1558, agus é fiche bliain d'aois. Ceithre bliana roimhe sin phós sé Jane Stewart, iníon neamhdhlistineach leis an rí Séamas V. Nuair a d'fhill Máire

35 M. Carney, 'Agreement between Ó Domhnaill and Tadhg Ó Conchubhair concerning Sligo castle' (1942–3); Mooney, 'Friars and friary of Donegal', l. 7.   **36** J.J. Silke, 'Raphoe and the Reformation' (1995), l. 277.   **37** Mooney, *First impact of Reformation*, l. 30; Silke, 'Raphoe and the Reformation', l. 277.   **38** P. Corish, *The Irish Catholic experience* (repr. 1985), l. 75.

banríon na nAlbanach ar Albain ón bhFrainc sa bhliain 1561 d'éirigh sí an-mhór le
Jane, cheap mar dhuine dá mhná coimhdeachta í agus is minic a ligeadh sí a rún léi.
D'fhág an pósadh seo go leor dlúthnascanna ag an iarla le saol na cúirte.[39]

Sa bhliain 1555 bhí Calbhach Ó Domhnaill in achrann lena athair faoi
cheannas thiarnas Thír Chonaill. Theastaigh cabhair mhíleata uaidh chun
cumhacht a athar a bhriseadh agus thaistil sé go hAlbain ar an 13 Iúil 1555 chun
conradh a dhéanamh leis an gceathrú hiarla, athair Ghiolla Easpaig. De bharr an
chonartha seo chuaigh Giolla Easpuig ar fheachtas míleata go hÉirinn, fórsa láidir
gallóglach aige, gunnaí móra agus tacaíocht ó Dhomhnailligh Aontroma, a raibh
aintín leis pósta aige orthu. Tháinig an t-arm Albanach i dtír lá Samhna 1555, agus
bhí sé i bhfad róláidir do thrúpaí Mhánais. Rinneadh príosúnach go luath de agus
chaith sé an chuid eile dá shaol i mbraighdeanas ag a mhac. Bhí tionchar mór ag
na gunnaí móra ar thoradh an fheachtais, thug na hannálaithe dúchais suntas don
'ghunna cam' agus b'údar imní do na húdaráis i mBaile Átha Cliath airm chomh
nua-aimseartha sin a bheith ar fáil ag tiarna aonair.[40] Tógadh Giolla Easpaig mar
Phrotastúnach agus bhí sé an-tógtha le John Knox nuair a thug sé cuairt rúnda
seanmóireachta ar Albain i bhfómhar na bliana 1555. Theastaigh ó Ghiolla Easpaig
go rachadh sé i mbun soiscéalaíochta go poiblí agus gheall coimirce na
gCambeulach dó. B'éigean do Knox filleadh ar Geneva ach gheall sé go bhfilleadh
sé dá n'iarrfaí a leithéid air. Chuir Giolla Easpaig ainm le litir ag iarraidh air
filleadh sa bhliain 1557. D'fhógair roinnt de na huaisle ba ghradamúla in Albain
go raibh siad ag tacú go poiblí le cúis an Phrotastúnachais, ceathrú hIarla Earra
Gael ar thús cadhnaíochta. Nuair a fuair a athair bás an bhliain i 1558, bhí Giolla
Easpuig réidh leis an gcreideamh nua a chur chun cinn.[41] Thug sé geallúint
shollúnta dá athair agus é ar leaba a bháis go ndéanfadh sé a sheacht ndícheall fáil
réidh leis an aifreann ar fud an hAlban agus foirm Phrotastúnach adhartha a
thabhairt isteach.[42]

D'éirigh na tiarnaí Protastúnacha, Tiarnaí an Chomhthionóil mar a thug siad
orthu féin, amach sa bhliain 1559. Greamaíodh Toghairm na mBacach do dhoirse na
mainistreacha Lá Coille. Mura leasódh na bráithre a saol go huile is go hiomlán
dhíbreofaí iad ar 12 Bealtaine, 'flitting Friday' an lá bliantúil chun tionóntaí a
ruaigeadh. D'fhill John Knox ó Geneva agus thug seanmóir cháiliúil i Perth 11
Bealtaine. Bhí Iarla Earra Gael i láthair. Nuair a d'fhéach sagart le haifreann a
léamh ag deireadh na seanmóra bhris círéib amach, briseadh íomhánna agus
dealbha agus réabadh mainistreacha agus clochair Perth. Bhí Iarla Earra Gael go
mór ar son an íonghlanta seo. Ar 10 Meitheamh chuaigh sé féin agus an Tiarna
James Stewart chuig St Andrews, príomhchathair eaglasta na hAlban. An lá dar

39 J.E.A. Dawson, *The politics of religion in the age of Mary, Queen of Scots* (2002), ll 19–20.   40 Ibid., ll
20–6.   41 Ibid., ll 23–5.   42 Ibid., l. 87.

gcionn thug Knox seanmóir i séipéal an pharóiste faoi choimirce an Iarla arae bhagair an t-ardeaspag go scaoilfi é. Tar éis na seanmóra tarraingíodh na híomhánna anuas den séipéal, den ardeaglais agus de shéipéil na hollscoile, tógadh go lár an bhaile iad agus dódh go deasghnáthach iad. Tharraing an t-ardeaspag siar ón gcathair gona thrúpaí Francacha. Gan freasúra ar bith fágtha ina choinne, d'eagraigh an t-iarla scriosadh na ndealbh ar bhealach sistéimeach córasach. Dhírigh sé go speisialta ar na Doiminicigh agus ar na hObsarvaintigh Phroinsiasacha, an bhagairt is mó ar an bProtastúnachas, dar leis na leasaitheoirí, agus scriosadh an dá theach go huile is go hiomlán.[43] D'ainneoin a ghafa a bhí Iarla Earra Gael leis an leasúchán creidimh, áfach, ní dhearna sé faillí ina chuid comhghuaillíochtaí abhus, agus i dtús na bliana 1560 phós a leasmháthair, Katherine MacLean, Calbhach Ó Domhnaill. Nuair a fuair Calbhach suas le dhá mhíle gallóglach mar spré, bhí sé lánsásta a chearta chun tailte a mhná céile in Albain a scaoileadh uaidh.[44]

Sa bhliain 1561 ceapadh Seon Carsuel mar dhuine den chúigear stiúrthóirí le bheith i gceannas ar an eaglais leasaithe, an Kirk, sna Gairbhchríocha, ceantar Earra Gael agus na n-oileán faoina chúram. Sa bhliain 1567 d'aistrigh Carsuel saothar John Knox, *Book of Common Order*, go Gaeilge agus d'fhoilsigh Roibeard Lekprevik, clódóir na heaglaise leasaithe, i nDún Éideann é. Díol suntais an leabhar seo, *Foirm na nUrrnuidheadh* ar go leor cúiseanna.[45] Mar aon ní amháin is é an chéad leabhar Gaeilge a cuireadh i gcló riamh é. Baineadh leas as an gcló rómhánach ar chúiseanna praiticiúla toisc gurbh é ab fhearr a d'fheil don chlódóir Roibeard Lekprevik, clódóir na gCailvíneach i nDún Éideann. Scríobhadh sa Ghaeilge chlasaiceach é, rud a chiallaigh go dtuigfí ar an dá thaobh de Shruth na Maoile é agus díríodh go sainiúil ar fhir Alban agus Éireann in éineacht é. Déanta na fírinne déantar tagairt d'Albain agus d'Éirinn mar aonad cultúrtha sé huaire ar fad san aitheasc don léitheoir agus sa dán seolta a ghabhann leis an leabhar. Tiomnaíodh an saothar d'Iarla Earra Gael agus is é dóichí ná a mhalairt gurbh iad a aidhmeanna agus a fhadcheannacht siúd ba chúis le díriú ar Éirinn chomh maith le hAlbain. Sa réamhrá tiomnaithe tugtar an-mholadh go deo don iarla mar Phrotastúnach Leasaitheach. Mar ba dhual do thraidisiún na Gaeilge, déantar comórtas idir an t-iarla agus laochra na sean, ach an t-am seo timpeall ní ar laochra na scéalaíochta dúchais a bhunaítear an comórtas ach ar laochra an tSean Tiomna, eisiomláirí scrioptúrtha fearacht Mhaois, Gideón, Hiziciá agus Dáibhí. Ní hamháin sin ach cuirtear béim ar leith ar Earra Gael mar loiscneoir dealbh agus íol agus díríonn Carsuel aird an iarla ar eachtraí dealbhloisceacha Mhaois agus Hiziciá. Is mar phrionsa diaga de chuid an Leasúcháin Chreidimh a mhórann agus a láithríonn Carsuel an t-iarla.[46]

43 Ibid., ll 87–96. **44** Ibid., ll 105–6. **45** R.L. Thomson (ed.), *Foirm na n-Urrnuidheadh* (1970). **46** D.E. Meek, 'The Reformation and Gaelic culture' (1998), ll 42–7.

Leanann dán beag cúig rann an t-aitheasc don léitheoir, dán a chum Carsuel féin. Baineann an chéad rann leis an iarla féin agus críocha Earra Gael. Sa dara rann seoltar an leabhar ar fud na hAlban, gan bacadh le Sasana. Sa tríú rann seoltar an leabhar go hÉirinn:[47]

> Dá éis sin taisdil gach tond
> go crích Eireand na bfond fial;
> gé beag ar na bráithribh thú,
> gluais ar amharc a súl siar.

Ní hamháin go bhfuil Carsuel agus a phátrún ag iarraidh an Leasúchán Creidimh a chraobhscaoileadh in Éirinn, ach tá an bac is mó agus an namhaid is mó spriocroghnaithe acu ón tús, na bráithre, na Proinsiasaigh Obsarvainteacha ach go háirithe. Seo téacs Gaeilge, an t-aon téacs Gaeilge amháin, b'fhéidir, a shainíonn na bráithre mar an dream nach mór a chur faoi chois más áil leis na húdaráis an Leasúchán Creidimh a chur chun cinn. Meabhraímis, áfach, gurb é an leasuchán creidimh Albanach Cailvíneach atá i gceist anseo, nach ionann é agus an leagan a bhí á chraobhscaoileadh i mBáile Átha Cliath. Ciallaíonn leabhar Carsuel go raibh dhá chraobh den Phrotastúnachas in iomaíocht le chéile in Éirinn, leas á bhaint ag craobh amháin acu as an nGaeilge mar mheán soiscéalaíochta. Is í an imní a ghin an tuiscint seo i mBaile Átha Cliath, a mhúscail na húdaráis as a suan agus a spreag iad, más go mall féin é, chun ábhar reiligiúnda a sholáthar i nGaeilge a mhíneodh Protastúnachas na heaglaise státbhunaithe. I ngeall ar comhghuaillíochtaí Iarla Earra Gael i dTír Chonaill agus in Aontroim, ba dhóigh liom gurbh é Cúige Uladh i gcéaduair agus go príomha a bhí i gceist aige le hÉirinn. Agus i ngeall ar thaithí phearsanta an iarla i St Andrews, níl aon amhras ach gurbh iad na hObsarvaintigh Phroinsiasacha ach go háirithe a bhí i gceist aige mar namhaid, Proinsiasaigh Dhún na nGall thar aon dream eile.

Bhí Sir James MacDonald, taoiseach Ghleannta Aontroma pósta ar Lady Agnes Campbell, aintín le hIarla Earra Gael, agus nuair a fuair Sir James bás ó na créachtaí a d'fhulaing sé i gcath Ghleann Seisce sa bhliain 1565, rinne an t-iarla cleamhnas dúbalta chun a chuid cumhachta i gCúige Uladh a neartú tuilleadh. Phós Lady Agnes Toirdhealbhach Luineach Ó Néill agus phós a hiníon Fionnuala, Aodh Ó Domhnaill, a tháinig i gcomharbacht ar a dheartháir Calbhach nuair a bhásaigh seisean sa bhliain 1566. Níor adhlacadh Calbhach i mainistir na nObsarvainteach i nDún na nGall, an chríoch ba dhual do thaoisigh Thír Chonaill. Tharlódh go raibh baint aige seo leis an dlúthchaidreamh a nasc Calbhach agus príomhcheannaire an Chailvíneachais in Albain le chéile. Ar an

---

47 Thomson, *Foirm na n-Urrnuidheadh*, l. 13.

chaoi ceiliúradh an dá phósadh ar oileán Reachlainn an lá céanna i dtús Lúnasa sa bhliain 1569.[48] Bhí Iarla Earra Gael féin i láthair don ócáid le ceithre mhíle fear as Albain. Ioróineach go maith is iad an dá bhainis seo a chuir deireadh leis an naimhdeas traidisiúnta idir Ó Néill agus Ó Domhnaill agus a ghin an chomhghuaillíocht cháiliúil idir Aodh Mór Ó Néill agus Aodh Ruadh Ó Domhnaill ba bhun le Cogadh na Naoi mBliana. D'ainneoin chomh tréan is a d'oibrigh Earra Gael chun na hObsarvaintigh a chur faoi chois mar chuid dá fheachtas chun an Leasuchán Creidimh a chur chun cinn in Albain, a mhalairt ghlan a bhí mar thoradh ar a chuid iarrachtaí in Éirinn, agus bhí baint mhór ag na hObsarvaintigh le lorg tréan Caitliceach a chur le feachtas na dtiarnaí Ultacha ag deireadh an séú haois déag.[49]

EOGHAN Ó DUBHTHAIGH (+1591)

Bhí clú agus cáil ar Eoghan Ó Dubhthaigh mar sheanmóirí sa dara leath den séú haois déag agus d'fhág Donnchadh Ó Maonaigh cuntas spéisiúil dúinn ar chur chuige Uí Dhubhthaigh agus é i mbun proiceapta. Gur nós leis achoimre fhileata a thabhairt ar gach seanmóir nuair a bhíodh deireadh déanta aige agus go raibh mianach na maitheasa sna véarsaí chomh torthúil sin gur dhóigh leat gur mó a spreag grásta an Spioraid Naoimh iad ná spiorad na filíochta féin.[50] Ar an drochuair níor tháinig ach dhá dhán leis an Dubhthach anuas chugainn. Ar éigean is féidir a rá gur achoimrí ar sheanmóirí iad na dánta seo ach, fós féin, tugann siad léargas iontach luachmhar dúinn ar pholaitiú na bProinsiasach agus léiríonn siad freisin gur maith a thuig na Proinsiasaigh nach iarmairtí reiligiúnda amháin a bheadh mar thoradh ar an Reifirméisean in Éirinn, ach iarmairtí polaitíochta agus cultúrtha chomh maith. Sa chéad dán acu seo, *A Bhanbha, is truagh do chor*, gan ach seacht rann ann, deir an Dubhthach gur díol trua í Éire agus sluaite Saxan agus fir Alban sa tóir uirthi agus impíonn an file ar Éirinn bheith dílis di féin agus dá dúchas creidimh. Mura ndéanann sí amhlaidh ní bheidh inti ach Saxa óg. Léiríonn sé an t-achrann creidimh in Éirinn mar choimhlint idir *Caiptín Lúitéir 's Caiptín Cailbhín* ar láimh amháin agus *Pádruig do ghénéral féin* ar an láimh eile. Is deas mar a nascann an file an creideamh a thóg Pádraig leis go hÉirinn fadó le feachtas an Leasúcháin Chreidimh Chaitlicigh. Ní cúrsaí cráifeachta agus ársaíochta amháin a bhí taobh thiar den spéis sa naomhsheanchas a bhí ar tí borradh ar fud na hEorpa, ach bhainfí leas as freisin

---

48 Tugann Mooney ('Friars and friary of Donegal', ll 46–9) liosta na dtaoiseach agus na n-uaisle a adhlacadh i mainistir na bProinsiasach i nDún na nGall idir 1474 agus 1600 agus díol suntais nach bhfuil Calbhach Ó Domhnaill ina measc.   **49** Dawson, *Politics of religion in age of Mary, Queen of Scots*, ll 162–5.   **50** Ó Clabaigh, *Franciscans in Ireland*, l. 144; 'Brussels MS. 3947'.

mar arm éifeachtach bolscaireachta i gcogaí na reiligiún. Chomh fada agus a bhaineann leis an Dubhthach de, ní féidir idirdhealú a dhéanamh idir an concas Eilíseach agus an Reifirméisean in Éirinn. Is dhá thaobh den bhonn céanna iad.[51]

Chum Ó Dubhthaigh an dara dán, *Léig dod chomórtas dúinn*, go mall sa bhliain 1578, dán fada a bhfuil naoi rann is ochtó ann.[52] Dán molta na Maighdine Muire an dán seo, chomh maith le hionsaí binbeach ar thriúr Gael atá tar éis iompó ón gcreideamh Caitliceach le bheith ina n-easpaig in Eaglais na hÉireann: Mathghamhain Seidhin, Easpag Chorcaí (1572–82/3), Uilliam Ó Cathasaigh, Easpag Luimnigh (1571–91), Maol Muire Mac Craith, Ardeaspag Chaisil (1571–1622). Nuair a chuirtear san áireamh go raibh Maol Muire ina Phroinsiasach tráth, ní hiontas ar bith é gur air siúd a ídíonn an Dubhthach an chuid is fraochmhaire dá fhíoch. Ní sparálann sé a bhean chéile, Áine Ní Mheadhra, ach an oiread, á mholadh go searúsach gur chóir ainm a iarbhráthar a athrú ó Mhaol Muire go Maol Áine. Déanta na fírinne, cuireann an Dubhthach béim láidir ar dheabhóid do Mhuire mar cheann de shaintréithe an Chaitliceachais Thriontaigh; má thréigeann tú an deabhóid sin, tréigfidh tú gnéithe riachtanacha eile den Chaitliceachas chomh maith:[53]

> A Mhaoil gan Mhuire, ataoi leamh,
> Dul ar neamh ní hé do thriall;
> Maol gan Aifrionn, Maol gan ord,
> Maol go hIfrionn is borb pian.

Ní leasc leis an bhfile dul i muinín na gáirsiúlachta ar uairibh chun barr maise a chur ar a bhinb:[54]

> Maol mór reamhar gránna dubh—
> Ní maith ar mhnaoi na gcruth chaomh:
> Do réir fhiadhnaise na bhfear,
> Ní maith bean ar a mbí Maol.

Ceann de na tréithe is suntasaí faoin dán seo, déanta na fírinne, is ea an bealach tobann a n-athraíonn sé ón bhfogha fíochmhar pearsanta go véarsaí a léiríonn an urraim agus an deabhóid is caoine don Mhaighdean. Agus fiú más ait leis an léitheoir nua-aimseartha an chodarsnacht seo, caithfidh gur oibrigh sé go han-éifeachtach ar fad mar láithriú poiblí, rud a raibh an-taithí ag an Dubthach air.

---

51 Mhág Craith, *Dán na mBráthar Mionúr*, ll 151–3; Caball, *Poets and politics* (1998), l. 79; M. Caball, 'Faith, culture and sovereignty' (1998), ll 134–5; M. Caball, 'Innovation and tradition' (1999), l. 77.
52 Mhág Craith, *Dán na mBráthar Mionúr*, ll 127–51.   53 Ibid., l. 135, rann 29.   54 Ibid., l. 136, rann 34.

Baineadh leas as roinnt de na véarsaí deabhóideacha seo don iomann cáiliúil *'S maith an bhean í Muire mhór*, cé gur beag duine de na fíréin a bheadh ar an eolas faoi bhunús polaimiciúil na véarsaí céanna.

Nascann an Dubhthach Naomh Pádraig arís leis gCaitliceachas Triontach nuair a deir sé nach raibh sa naomh ach 'duine leamh' má éiríonn leis an 'gcliar ghliogair' neamh a bhaint amach (rann 69a). Cuireann sé béim arís ar ghalldacht agus coimhthíos an Reifirméisin, is dream anall iad an chléir nua, cliar dhall ar a ndeachaigh ceo:[55]

> An chliar-sa anois tig anall,
> cliar dhall ar a ndeachadh ceo,
> ní mó leo Muire ná *dog*,
> dar *by God*, ní rachaidh leo.

> 'S a mháthair Airdrígh na ndúl,
> ríoghan ur darab oighre Dia –
> ní fhuighe ach dorn ar a dúid,
> istigh i gcúirt Átha Cliath.

Má nascann an file urraim do Mhuire leis an gCaitliceachas iarThriontach, nascann sé an easurraim chomh maith céanna leis an Reifirméisean. Is deas mar a éiríonn leis an Reifirméisean agus an concas a shnaidhmeadh le chéile nuair a luann sé an drochíde a thabharfaí do Mhuire dá dtabharfadh sí cuairt ar chaisleán Bhaile Átha Cliath, lárionad na cumhachta gallda in Éirinn chomh maith le lárionad an chreidimh ghallda. Díol suntais freisin an earraíocht a bhaintear as focail Bhéarla sa dán, ní hamháin toisc gur fianaise an-luath í seo ar úsáid an Bhéarla i bhfilíocht na Gaeilge, ach toisc go gceanglaíonn na focail seo úsáid an Bhéarla le teacht chun cinn an Reifirméisin agus an choncais. Cuid suntais freisin na bríonna diúltacha tarcaisneacha atá ag na focail a roghnaíonn an Dubhthach:[56]

> Dream do *sheduction* lán
> Do chuir *corruption* sa chóir;
> Biaid na préaláide gona gcléir
> I bhfad i bpéin-phioláid mhór.

Is léir go gcreideann an Dubhthach go daingean go bhfuil impleachtaí polaitiúla agus cultúrtha ag an Reifirméisean chomh maith le himpleachtaí reiligiúnda, agus

---

55 Ibid., ll 133–4, rannta 25–6.   56 Ibid., l. 138, rann 42.

go dteastaíonn uaidh foláireamh dá réir sin a thabhairt dá lucht éisteachta. Má chiallaíonn an Reifirméisean galldacht agus daoirse, ciallaíonn an Caitliceachas ar an gcuma chéanna Gaelachas agus saoirse. Ní fhéadfadh an teachtaireacht a bheith níos soiléire.

Cé nárbh fhile gairmiúil é an Dubhthach, b'fhiú leis an Sean-Ghall Stanihurst aird a dhíriú ar a bhuanna liteartha nuair a thagair sé dó sa nath seo a leanas: 'Owen Odewhee a preacher and maker in Irish'.[57] B'fhiú le Luke Wadding freisin cuntas a thabhairt air agus luann sé gur nós leis tairngreachtaí a dhéanamh ina chuid filíochta:[58]

> Eugenius O Dowhee Hibernus, Reg Ober. Insignis concionator. Composuit idiomate Hibernico Poemata multa sacra, in quibus vatis more multa praedicit. Passim memoriter ab Hibernis recitantur. Vixit sub anno 1600.

Mar bhall d'ord rialta a bhí ar thús cadhnaíochta maidir le cur i gcoinne pholasaí reilgiúnda an stáit, bhain Eoghan Ó Dubhthaigh leas as na buanna fileata agus seanmóireachta a bhí aige chun a theachtaireacht a chraobhscaoileadh go forleathan. Ní hamháin go ndeachaigh sé i gcionn ar an bpobal i gcoitinne, ach mar phroibhinsial ar bhráithre bochta na hÉireann sna blianta 1581–3, bhí deis aige bualadh le huasaicme na tíre idir Ghael agus Sean-Ghall, idir chléir agus tuath. Óna ndúirt Ó Maonaigh, Stanihurst, agus Wadding faoi, dealraíonn sé gur chum sé i bhfad níos mó dánta ná an dá cheann a tháinig anuas chugainn, ach sa mhéid sin féin ní féidir gan ceann don tuiscint ghlé a bhí aige ar an bhféiniúlacht Éireannach. Áitíonn Marc Caball go raibh machnamh ar cad ab Éireannachas ann á chothú i measc an aosa léinn de réir mar a bhí an concas Eilíseach ag dul i nirt. Luann sé an file gairmiúil Tadhg Dall Ó hUiginn, a dheartháir, Maol Muire, Ardeaspag Thuama (1586–*c.*1590), agus an file amaitéarach de shliocht na Sean-Ghall, Uilleam Nuinseann,[59] ach is dóigh liom gur tathagaí go mór fada an tuiscint ar Éireannachas a d'fhorbair Eoghan Ó Dubhthaigh. B'fhéidir nár chuir sé béim chomh follasach sin ar an ngá le comhaontú idir Gael agus Sean-Ghall, ach is mó a rinne sé talamh slán dó ná aon rud eile. Bhain sé earraíocht as acmhainní na saíochta dúchais chun an Leasúchán Creidimh Caitliceach a chur chun cinn agus chuir sé impleachtaí an choncais Thudoraigh in iúl dá thréad gan fiacail a chur ann, idir impleachtaí reiligiúnda, impleachtaí polaitiúla agus impleachtaí cultúrtha. Bhí práinn ag baint lena chúram agus ba mhóide an phráinn gur ghéill duine dá chomhbhráithre féin do thathaint na nGall. Mar a dúirt Marc Caball:[60]

---

57 Ó Cléirigh, *Aodh Mac Aingil*, l. 100. **58** Ibid., 101. **59** Caball, *Poets and politics*, ll 45–50, 66–7, 80; idem, 'Faith, culture and sovereignty', ll 125–8; 'Innovation and tradition', ll 72–5. **60** Caball, *Poets and politics*, l. 82.

Crucially, the work of the cleric Ó Dubhthaigh charts the emergence of a concept vital to the transformation of the Gaelic mindset and the formation of an early modern Irish identity. His portrayal of Protestantism as an alien and intrusive English imposition is in implicit contrast to the 'nativeness' of Catholicism. Such cultivation of popular perception of the reformation as the religious arm of hegemonic colonialism was to become a serious obstacle to the advancement of Protestant evangelisation in Ireland.

Is beag, déanta na fírinne, idir na tuairimí a nocht Ó Dubhthaigh ó bhéal i ndeireadh na 1570idí agus na tuairimí a chuir a gcomhbhráithre i gcló san Ísiltír Spáinneach tríocha bliain níos moille. An difríocht is mó a bhí eatarthu, seachas an bheachtaíocht friotail a forbraíodh thar lear, gur éirigh leis na Proinsiasaigh i Lobháin teacht i dtír ar acmhainní theicneolaíocht na clódóireachta, rud nach raibh fáil air do Chaitlicigh abhus. Cúrsaí caiticéise go príomha a bhí ag dó na geirbe ag an Dubhthach, leathnaigh tionscadal Lobháin amach go cúrsaí naomhsheanchais is staire chomh maith. An fhadhb a chráigh na bráithre thall faoi shimpliú na teanga ar mhaithe leis an teachtaireacht, ní dhearna sé scim dá laghad don Dubhthach, tharla gurbh í an tseanmóireacht ó bhéal ba chúram dó. Ní háibhéil a rá go raibh fadhb Lobháin réitithe aige tríocha bliain fiú sular aithníodh mar fhadhb í. Ar mhuintir na hÉireann amháin a bhí an Dubhthach dírithe, lucht éisteachta i bhfad ní ba leithne a bhí i gceist ag Proinsiasaigh Lobháin. Fearacht an Dubhthaigh, ba iad muintir na hÉireann a bpríomhchúram gan amhras, ach ba dhual dóibh freisin freastal ar dheoraithe Éireannacha ar an Mór-roinn. Ach má b'áil le bráithre Lobháin tacaíocht dá dtír dhúchais a mhealladh ó phrionsaí na hEorpa idir chléir is tuath, níor mhiste a léiríu dóibh nár shuarach an náisiún é ar shaoránaigh de iad. Móradh an náisiúin Éireannaigh os comhair mhuintir na hEorpa ab aidhm cuid mhaith le saothrú an naomhsheanchais agus an stairsheanchais a saothraíodh i Lobháin. Ach d'ainneoin na ndifríochtaí seo, soláthraíonn an méid de shaothar Uí Dhubhthaigh atá tagtha anuas chugainn fianaise ghlé shoiléir ar pholaitiú reiligiúnda na bProinsiasach in Éirinn, agus ar an dlúthnasc a bhí á chothú acu idir dúchas agus creideamh. Is ón meonteilgean nua seo a d'eascair Lobháin. Níor leor an aeráid cheart chultúrtha, áfach, dá bháúla féin í, chun a leithéid de thogra a cheapadh is a chur a gcrích. Níor mhór duine ar leith le fís ar leith san áit cheart agus san am cheart. Ba é Flaithrí Ó Maoil Chonaire an duine sin.

FLAITHRÍ Ó MAOIL CHONAIRE (1560–1629)

Níorbh ann do Lobháin, ar ndóigh, mura mbeadh Flaithrí Ó Maoil Chonaire, ollamh file, bráthair bocht, comhairleoir i gcúirt ríoga na Spáinne, ministir proibhinsil Phroinsiasaigh na hÉireann, Ardeaspag Thuama. Níl cur amach againn ar na cúinsí a thug air cúl a thabhairt don fhilíocht agus dul le sagartóireacht ar an Mór-roinn. I litir a scríobh an Infanta Isabella chuig Pilib IV na Spáinne, 22 Deireadh Fómhair 1626, deir sí go bhfuil Fr Florencio Conryo tar éis a mheabhrú di go bhfuil ceithre bliana is tríocha ann ó chéadcheap uaisle na hÉireann é chun cúrsaí tromchúiseacha na hÉireann a phlé lena hathair, Pilib III, agus go bhfuil sé ag gabháil don cheird sin ó shin i leith.[61] Ciallaíonn sé seo go raibh sé sa Spáinn ón mbliain 1592 i leith agus go raibh sé ar na chéad mhic léinn sa choláiste Éireannach i Salamanca a bhunaigh an tIosánach Thomas White an bhliain chéanna. Mura mbeadh gur éirigh idir Flaithrí agus White faoin bhfábhar a bhí á thaispeáint aige do mhic léinn de shliocht na Sean-Ghall as Cúige Laighean agus Cúige Mumhan le hais an bhealaigh ar chaith sé le mic léinn Ghaelacha as Cúige Chonnacht agus Cúige Uladh, cá bhfios cén treo a ngabhfadh saol Uí Mhaoil Chonaire? B'fhéidir go ndéanfaí sagart deoise de, b'fhéidir go rachadh sé isteach sna hIosánaigh féin. Ar chuma ar bith is cosúil go raibh baint aige le feachtas chun White a bhriseadh as a phost mar reachtaire agus d'fhág sé an coláiste, pé acu dá dheoin féin nó dá ainneoin ní fios, agus chuaigh sé isteach sna Proinsiasaigh a raibh coláiste gradamúil acu i Salamanca.[62] Ní fios ach an oiread an raibh sé ina shagart faoin am go ndeachaigh sé isteach sna Proinsiasaigh nó nach raibh. Maidir le dátaí beachta cláraíodh mar mhac léinn sa tríú bliain in Ollscoil Salamanca sna Dána agus san Fhealsúnacht é 19 Meán Fómhair 1594, agus luaitear mar mhac léinn chéad bhliana sa diagacht é don tréimhse 1595–6.[63] Sa bhliain 1593 d'aistrigh sé *El texto de la doctrina Cristiana* (1591), teagasc críostaí a chum an tIosánach Jerónimo de Ripalda, oide faoistine Threasa Avila, go Gaeilge.[64] Ba é an teagasc críostaí seo is mó a bhí in usáid i Meicsiceo chomh fada leis an gcéad leath den fhichiú haois[65] agus ní raibh aon deacracht agam teacht ar chóip a foilsíodh chomh mall leis an mbliain 1998. Saothar an-simplí is ea an buntéacs, léargas a thabhairt do pháistí ar bhuneolas an chreidimh i bhfoirm ceiste agus freagra, 'leanbh' a fhreagraíonn na ceisteanna a chuireann an 'máistir' air. Is cinnte nach mbeadh aon dúshláin aistriúcháin i gceist sa saothar seo, go háirithe ó dhuine a raibh oiliúint ghairmiúil ollaimh fhile air. Sheol Flaithrí an t-aistriúchán go hÉirinn sa bhliain 1598 ach ní fios cé chuige ná cad chuige. Ar éigean a bhí sé i gceist aige go bhfoilseofaí in Éirinn

61 Jennings, *Wild Geese*, l. 209. **62** T. O'Connor, '"Perfidious Machiavellian friar"' (2002), l. 92. **63** Ibid., l. 91. **64** B. Ó Cuív, 'Flaithrí Ó Maolchonaire's catechism of Christian doctrine' (1950). **65** B.L. Marthalet, *The catechism yesterday and today* (1995), l. 60.

é. Mar aon ní amháin bhí tionscal nuabhunaithe na clódóireachta abhus i seilbh na n–údarás nach bhfoilseodh ábhar reiligiúnda ar bith ach é siúd a bhainfeadh leis an eaglais bhunaithe.

Chuaigh sé go Ceann tSáile le feachtas Don Juan del Aguila sa bhliain 1600 agus deir Wadding linn gurbh é an Pápa Clemens VIII a sheol ann é chun comhairle a chur ar arm na Spáinne.[66] D'fhill sé ar an Spáinn i ndiaidh na tubaiste le hAodh Ruadh Ó Domhnaill agus bhí sé i láthair mar anamchara agus Aodh ag saothrú an bháis i Simancas 9 Meán Fómhair 1602. Cúpla mí roimhe sin chuir sé meamram thar ceann Aodha Ruaidh faoi bhráid an rí inar cháin sé Thomas White uair amháin eile gona shaobhchlaonadh in aghaidh mhic léinn Chonnachtacha agus Ultacha i gColáiste Éireannach Salamanca. Ní hamháin sin ach d'ídigh sé a racht chomh maith ar na Sean-Ghaill i gcoitinne agus ar na hÍosánaigh ach go háirithe siocair nár thacaigh siad le hAodh Ó Néill le linn Chogadh na Naoi mBliana.[67] De réir mar a bhí líon na ndeoraithe Éireannacha sa Spáinn ag dul i méid, agus fadhbhanna dá réir sin á gcruthú acu do státchóras na Spáinne, d'ainmnigh Pilib III an Conde de Puñonrostro mar choirmiceoir orthu agus cheap sé Flaithrí mar chomhairleoir ag an Conde, post a choinnigh sé go dtí an bhliain 1617. Ina theannta sin ba dhual do Fhlaithrí urraíocht a dhéanamh ar uaisle Éireannacha a bhí ag iarraidh ballraíocht a fháil in oird niachais na Spáinne. Anuas air sin ar fad chabhraigh sé le reismint Éireannach a bhunú in arm na Spáinne, an tsíocháin á coinneáil aige idir na Gaeil agus Sean-Ghaeil, ach ag féachaint chuige ag an am céanna go gceapfaí Annraoi Ó Néill, an mac ba shine ag Aodh Mór Ó Néill, mar choirnéal ar an reismint sa bhliain 1604.[68]

Ní raibh Proinsiasaigh na hÉireann in ann caibidil phroibhinse a thionól sa bhliain 1605 i ngeall ar chúinsí corraithe na tíre. An bhliain dar gcionn tionóladh caibidil ghinearálta den ord i Toledo na Spáinne i mí na Bealtaine. Siúd is gur faoi chaibidil an phroibhinse ba ghnáth – agus is gnáth fós – ministir proibhinsil a thoghadh, thóg an chaibidil ghinearálta ceann de thoscaí urghnácha na hÉireann ag an am, agus d'ainneoin agóidí na mbráithre Éireannacha eile a bhí i láthair faoin sárú gnáis agus cirt, ceapadh Flaithrí Ó Maoil Chonaire mar phroibhinseal. Toisc go raibh toirmeasc curtha ag na Sasanaigh air filleadh abhaile, d'ainmnigh sé Muiris Ó Duinnshléibhe (Muiris Ultach) mar ionadaí thar a cheann agus sheol ar ais go hÉirinn é. Níorbh fhada i mbun a chúraim nua dó gur chuir Flaithrí iarratas faoi bhráid rí na Spáinne agus cead á lorg aige chun coláiste a bhunú i Lobháin chun Proinsiasaigh óga na hÉireann a oiliúint don tsagartóireacht. Tugadh an cead agus scríobh an rí ina thaobh chuig Albert, Ard-Diúca na hÍsiltíre

66 Carpenter & Harrison, 'Luke Wadding (1558–1657)', l. 262. 67 O'Connor, '"Perfidious Machiavellian friar"', ll 94–5. 68 Ibid., ll 95–6.

Spáinní, 21 Meán Fómhair 1606. D'eisigh an Pápa Pól V bulla bunaithe 3 Aibreán 1607 agus bhog an chéad chomhluadar isteach an mhí dar gcionn.[69]

Tá roinnt ceisteanna fós gan fhreagairt maidir leis an gcinneadh seo a raibh iarmairtí chomh tábhachtach aige do shaíocht na Gaeilge. Cén fáth Lobháin? Nárbh fheiliúnaí go mór fada Salamanca, coláiste mór le rá ag na Proinsiasaigh ann cheana féin, dochtúireachtaí ó Salamanca gnóthaithe ag na chéad léachtóirí a chuaigh go Lobháin, Donnchadh Ó Maonaigh, Aodh Mac Aingil, Roibéard Mac Artúir.[70] Dealraíonn sé, áfach, gurbh ábhar buartha do Fhlaithrí an fhaillí a bhí á déanamh ag na hÍosánaigh sa Ghaeilge sna cliarscoileanna Éireannacha a bhí faoina stiúir i Salamanca agus in áiteanna eile sa Spáinn. Straitéis thréadach agus ní cúrsaí cultúrtha ba chúis leis an imní seo. Cad ab fhiú sagairt de shliocht na Sean-Ghall ar bheagán nó ar easpa iomlán Gaeilge a chur ag seanmóireacht i measc na nGael? I litir a scríobh sé chuig Francisco de Valdivieso, prócadóir ginearálta na nÍosánach, sa bhliain 1604, rinne Ó Maoil Chonaire comórtas idir suíomh teanga na hÉireann agus suíomh teanga na Spáinn. Faoi mar a bhí an dá theanga *castillano* agus *gallego* sa Spáinn, iad á labhairt i gceantair dhifriúla faoi seach, ar an gcuma chéanna bhí dhá theanga in Éirinn, Gaeilge agus Béarla. Bhain an Béarla leis na bailte agus an Ghaeilge leis an tuath. Fiú dá bhféadfaí Gaeilge a chloisint sna bailte, ar éigean beo a chloisfí Béarla faoin tuath. Dá gcuirfí sagart ó na bailte ag seanmóireacht faoin tuath, ní thuigfeadh an pobal é, bheadh sé chomh doiléir le tairngreacht, *tan obscuro como prophesia*. Bhí na hÍosánaigh ag áiteamh ar an láimh eile go raibh an Ghaeilge ar cheann de na teangacha ba dheacra ar domhan, agus go fiú i measc na gcainteoirí ba líofa, nach raibh ach triúr as tríocha míle a raibh léamh agus scríobh na teanga acu. Mhaígh siad chomh maith gurbh é an Béarla teanga na Cúirte, teanga an dlí, teanga na bhforógraí, teanga an dioscúrsa phoiblí i gcoitinne, gur i mBéarla amháin a dhéanfaí rud ar bith a raibh tábhacht ag baint leis, *apenas se haze o se deshaze cosa de momento o de concierto sino es en la lengua inglesa*.[71] Is deacair drogall na hÍosánach an Ghaeilge a úsáid a thuiscint nuair a chuirtear san áireamh go raibh foghlaim teangacha agus soláthar áiseanna foghlamtha teangacha mar ghné riachtanach dá stráitéis mhisinéireachta ina liacht sin tíortha sa domhan nua. B'fhéidir gur ghabh an col eitneach lastuas den díograis chreidimh i gcás roinnt Íosánach de chuid na Sean-Ghall. Níorbh iontas ar bith é ar an ábhar sin, dá gceapfadh Ó Maoil Chonaire gur mhithid coláiste a bhunú ina mbeadh ionad lárnach ag an nGaeilge mar ghné riachtanach d'oiliúint thréadach na n-ábhar sagart.

---

69 Féach Lyons, 'The role of St Anthony's College Louvain is establishing the Irish Franciscan college network, 1607–60' san imleabhar seo.   **70** O'Connor, '"Perfidious Machiavellian friar"', ll 99–100.   **71** O. Recio Morales, 'Irish émigré group strategies of survival, adaptation and integration' (2006), ll 254–5.

Gné eile nach mór a chur san áireamh, áfach, gur mó a bhí údaráis na Spáinne ag breathnú ar inimircigh as Éirinn faoin tráth seo mar ualach agus crá croí seachas a mhalairt, agus b'fhéidir gur bhraith Ó Maoil Chonaire nár chóir brú ar an doicheall agus cead a lorg chun coláiste a bhunú sa Spáinn féin.[72] Ar an láimh eile níor mhór a admháil go raibh clú agus cáil ar ollscoil Lobháin mar lárionad intleachtúil an Leasucháin Chreidimh Chaitlicigh i dTuaisceart na hEorpa. Buntáiste eile a bhain le Lobháin is ea go raibh ceanncheathrú reismint nuabhunaithe an Choirnéil Annraoi Ó Néill (1605) lonnaithe in aice láimhe sa Bhruiséil, agus pobal Éireannach bunaithe sa chathair.[73] Ach cuma cé na cúiseanna ba bhun le roghnú Lobháin, sna blianta tosaigh ní raibh trácht ar bith ar fheachtas foilsitheoireachta, ná lua ar ábhar cráifeach, naomhsheanchas nó stair. Fir óga a thraenáil mar shagairt Phroinsiasacha do mhisean na hÉireann an t-aon chloch amháin a bhí ar a bpaidrín acu.

Ar an 21 Deireadh Fómhair 1607 chuaigh Flaithrí Ó Maoil Chonaire agus an sagart deoise Roibéard Mac Artúir (Chamberlain), oide faoistine Aodha Uí Néill, go Douai chun fáilte a chur roimh na hIarlaí. Chaith siad an geimhreadh i Lobháin agus chuir siad chun bealaigh chun na Róime 28 Feabhra 1608, Ó Maoil Chonaire agus Mac Artúir á dtionlacan. Táimid go léir faoi chomaoin ag an gcuntas atá fágtha ag Tadhg Ó Cianáin againn ar an turas seo.[74] Ach más é an Cianánach a chum is a cheap an téacs, ta barúil an-láidir agam go raibh tionchar an-láidir ag Ó Maoil Chonaire, ní hamháin ar leagan amach an turais ach ar mhúnlú na smaointe féin[75]. Mar aon ní amháin is téacs iontach Proinsiasach é. 25 Aibreán 1608 tugann na taistealaithe cuairt ar Assisi, baile dúchais San Proinsias agus cliabhán an oird a bhunaigh sé.[76] Ach toisc gurbh éigean dóibh casadh siar ag Foligno ó phríomhthreo an turais chun an chuairt seo a dhéanamh, is léir gur cinneadh tomhaiste é seo a tógadh d'aon ghnó. Is cinnte nach ligfeadh Flaithrí a leas ar cairde gan an deis seo a thapú chun cuairt a thabhairt ar an gcathair iomráiteach sin. Luann an téacs chomh maith go raibh ginearál an oird i láthair sa chathair ag an am. B'shin Arcangelo Gualterio da Messina, an fear a toghadh ag caibidil ghinearálta an oird i Toledo beagnach dhá bhliain roimhe sin, an chaibidil chéanna a cheap Flaithrí mar mhinistir proibhinsil ar bhráithre na hÉireann. Is maith a chuimhneodh an bheirt acu araon na cúinsí eisceachtúla ba shiocair le ceapachán Fhlaithrí. Bheadh aidhmeanna praiticiúla chomh maith le

72 E. García Hernán, 'Irish clerics in Madrid' (2006), ll 280–5.   73 Henry, *Irish military community*, ll 62–3, 81–5.   74 Walsh, *Flight of the earls* (1916); Ó Muraíle, *Turas na dTaoiseach nUltach* (2007).   75 Díol spéise an ráiteas seo a leanas ó James Loach, cócaire Annraoi Uí Néill, Nollaig na bliana 1607: 'Saith that, upon his coming from thence, the Earl of Tyrone was instantly bound to Rome, accompanied by Father Flarie O' Molconery as his principal guide … '. C.W. Russell & J.P. Prensergast (eds), *Cal. S.P. Ire.*, James I, 1606–1608 (1874, repr. 1944), nos. 493, 359.   76 Walsh, *Flight of the earls*, ll 162–5; Ó Muraíle, *Turas na dTaoiseach nUltach*, ll 260–1.

haidhmeanna cráifeacha ag an mbráthair bocht Éireannach le cuairt a thabhairt ar cheanncheathrú an oird. Cé go dtugann an tagairt do 'Gheinearál an Uird Mhionúir' ar fud na Críostaíochta le fios gurbh é ceannaire na nObsarvainteaich a bhí i gceist ag an gCianánach, d'fhéadfaí a áiteamh freisin gur ar Ghinearál na gCoinbhinteach a bhí sé ag trácht. Is faoi stiúir na gCoinbhinteach a bhí Baisleac San Proinsias, ionad adhlactha an naoimh. Daingníodh an tuama chomh tréan sin ar eagla go ngoidfí an corp nárbh fhios go beacht cá raibh sé go dtí gur fritheadh an tuama sa bhliain 1818. D'eascair go leor finscéalta mar gheall ar an aineolas seo, finnscéalta ar tugadh aitheantas dóibh dá n-áiféisí féin iad. Is ar na an finnscéalta sin a bunaíodh cuntas Uí Chianáin.

Nuair a bhaineann na taistealaithe an Róimh amach is ar chomhluadar na bProinsiasach Spáinneach i San Pietro in Montorio is mó a dhíríonn an cuntas. Is é an fócas beacht seo, béim ar an toise Proinsiasach agus ar an toise Spáinneach in éineacht, saintréith théacs Uí Chianáin, saintréith atá go mór faoi chomaoin ag Flaithrí Ó Maoil Chonaire. Is do Ferdinand agus Isabella na Spáinne, tuismitheoirí Chaitríona Aragon, a tógadh an séipéal seo idir 1481 agus 1500. Is mar ghníomh bolscaireachta do stádas na Spáinne a bhunaigh Ferdinand agus Isabella an séipéal seo. Is mar ghníomh bolscaireachta freisin a rinne siad pátrúnacht ar Bramante, a thóg an *Tempietto* i gclabhstra San Pietro os ceann na háite in ar céasadh Naomh Peadar de réir an tseanchais.[77] Is ceann de sheoda móra ealaíne an *Renaissance* é an *Tempietto*, seoid a ndéanann Ó Cianáin saintagairt di.[78] Is fiú a lua freisin gur lean comharbaí Ferdinand agus Isabella, Séarlas V, Pilib II, Pilib III agus Pilib IV don phátrúnacht fhial ar an séipéal seo.[79]

Maidir le séipéil na bProinsiasach Iodálach sa Róimh, cuirtear béim ar San Francesco a Ripa, ar thug na hIarlaí cuairt air 4 Deireadh Fómhair 1608, lá fhéile an naoimh féin, ní a luaitear go sainiúil sa téacs.[80] Ach toisc gur suíomh é seo a gcaitheadh San Proinsias seal ann agus cuairt á tabhairt ar an Róimh aige, agus go raibh an ceall ina nguíodh sé fós ar marthain, is geall le hathAssisi é. Tá toise an *pietas* go mór i gceist anseo agus i ngeall air sin braithim lorg Uí Mhaoil Chonaire go tréan ar an insint. Maidir le Santa Maria d'Aracoeli, ceanncheathrú na bProinsiasach Iodálach sa Róimh, siúd is gur foirgneamh taibhseach ar an gCampidoglio é, a tógadh d'aon ughaim mar aithris ar bhaisleac San Proinsias in Assisi, ní dhéanann Ó Cianáin ach seachthagairt dó. Is léir nach raibh sé ar thús cadhnaíochta a chuid tosaíochtaí aige féin ná ag Ó Maoil Chonaire ach go háirithe.

---

77 T.J. Dandalet, *Spanish in Rome* (2001), ll 1–3, 9. **78** Walsh, *Flight of the earls*, l. 214; Ó Muraíle, *Turas na dTaoiseach nUltach*, ll 332–3. **79** Dandalet, *Spanish in Rome*, l. 222, nóta 6. **80** Walsh, *Flight of the earls*, ll 248–51; Ó Muraíle, *Turas na dTaoiseach nUltach*, ll 384–5.

Má tá lorg an Phroinsiasaigh chomh tréan sin ar an turas féin, cad faoin
smaointeoireacht a eascraíonn amach ón téacs? Seo saothar próis a bhaineann leas
as an bhfocal *Éireannach* dosaen uair ar fad, seo é an chéad téacs go bhfios dúinn
a bhaineann leas as an bhfocal *náisiún* sa Ghaeilge, ocht n-uaire ar fad. Bhí neart
taithí ag Flaithrí ar na teannais eitneacha idir Gael agus Sean-Ghall sa choláiste
sagartóireachta i Salamanca. Is géar a cháin sé na teannais chéanna agus an chaoi
ar chriog siad feachtas Aodha Uí Néill agus Cogadh na Naoi mBliana, agus is
maith a thuig sé an dochar a dhéanfadh na teannais chéanna d'aontacht reismint
Annraoi Uí Néill. Má bhí faoi na hinimircigh dul i bhfeidhm ar phrionsaí
Chaitliceacha agus ardeaglaisigh na hEorpa, níor mhór tús áite a thabhairt don
aontacht thar gach ní eile, agus chuige sin b'áisiúil ar fad é an téarma neodrach
Éireannach chun na deighiltí a chlúdach agus béim a chur ar na snáthanna
aontachta, aontacht bunúis, creidimh agus cultúir. Tá againn anseo trí cinn de na
hairíonna riachtanacha a chuimsíonn coincheap an náisiúin. Gan in easnamh
orthu ach aontacht polaitíochta, ach nach raibh na deoraithe seo faoi choimirce rí
na Spáinne ar aon nós agus iad mar dhílseánaigh aige? Seo iad saintréithe an
náisiúin Éireannaigh mar ba léir do Fhlaithrí Ó Maoil Chonaire iad, siúd is go
bhfuil siad claonta níos mó ar son na nGael ná ar son na Sean-Ghall. Díol
suntais, dá bhrí sin, go mbaineann Ó Cianáin earraíocht as *Éireannach* agus
náisiún i dteannta a chéile mar is léir ón sampla seo a leanas i bhfómhar na bliana
1607 nuair a bhuaileann an Coirnéal Annraoi Ó Néill lena athair don chéad uair
le seacht mbliana ag Notre Dame de Halle in aice le Waterloo:[81]

> Ar n-a mhárach trá 31 Octobris tig mac Uí Néill, coirnéal na nÉireannach,
> chuca go mbuidhin ndearmháir ndeighinnill do chaiptínibh, do dhaoinibh
> uaisle do Spáinneachaibh agus d'Éireannchaibh agus do gach naisión
> archena dia mbádar.

Ní hamháin gur náisiún Caitliceach í Éire ach tá na hÉireannaigh agus na
Spáinnigh ar thús cadhnaíochta i measc náisiún Chaitliceacha na hEorpa. Nuair
a thugann na hIarlaí cuairt ar chaisleán Antwerp, 19 Feabhra 1608, deireann Ó
Cianáin go bhfuil sé ar cheann de na dúnfoirt is mó sa Chríostaíocht idir mhéid,
ghunnaí móra agus ordanáis. Ansin scríobhann sé an t-aguisín seo a leanas le
teann bróid agus mórtais chine: 'Ní leígid naisión ar bith oile d'fhéachain nó do
bhreathnughadh na hoibre acht Spáinneach nó Éireannach amháin'.[82] Nuair a
shroicheann na hIarlaí Milano, 23 Márta 1608, caitheann siad trí seachtaine sa
chathair sin agus is fiú leis an gCianánach trácht a dhéanamh arís ar chaisléan na
cathrach gona chuid daingnithe, agus uair amháin eile cuireann sé na hÉireannaigh

---

81 Ó Muráile, *Turas na dTaoiseach nUltach*, l. 92.   **82** Ibid., l. 124.

agus na Spáinnigh ar chomhchéim: 'Ní líonmhar a léigthear ann acht Spáinnigh agus Éireannaigh amháin'.[83] Is iad an toise Proinsiasach Spáinneach agus múnlú choincheap an náisiúin Éireannaigh Chaitlicigh an dá thréith is mó a shainíonn téacs Thaidhg Uí Chianáin, ach ní mar thoradh ar a chumas braistinte siúd is fearr liom breathnú ar an gcomaoin seo, ach mar idé-eolaíocht a gaibhníodh as taithí na gcúig bliana is fiche a bhí caite ag Ó Maoil Chonaire i dtimpeallacht chúirt ríoga na Spáinne agus prionsaí na heaglaise Caitlicí.

Bhí ard-deoise Thuama folamh ón mbliain 1595 agus d'ainmnigh an Pápa Pól V Flaithrí Ó Maoil Chonaire leis an bhfolúntas a líonadh 20 Márta 1609, agus cé nach raibh seans ar bith ann go bhféadfadh sé filleadh ar Éirinn chun cúraimí an phoist a chomhlíonadh, chuaigh tacaíocht Iarla Thír Eoghain do Fhlaithrí i bhfeidhm go mór ar údaráis na Vatacáine. Choisric an Cairdinéal Maffeo Barberini (an Pápa Urbanus VIII 1623–44) mar ardeaspag é cúig seachtaine níos déanaí agus go luath ina dhiaidh sin d'fhill Ó Maoil Chonaire ar an Spáinn chun cás Uí Néill a chur chun cinn. Thart ar an am céanna d'fhill Roibéard Mac Artúir ar an Ísiltír Spáinneach agus chuaigh isteach sna Proinsiasaigh i Lobháin 7 Feabhrú 1610. Níorbh ait liom dá mba rud é go raibh tionchar nár bheag ag na cuairteanna a thug Mac Artúir ar Assisi, San Francesco a Ripa agus San Pietro a Montorio ar an gcasadh is deireanaí i bhforbairt a ghairme, ní áirím an cairdeas speisialta le hArdeaspag Thuama. Bliain bheacht ina dhiaidh sin, 7 Feabhra 1611, rinne sé a uacht sular ghlac sé a chuid móideanna rialta, thug uaidh a raibh aige agus dhiúltaigh do dhílseacht, do sheilbh agus do thiarnas nithe ar bith as sin amach. Díol spéise go háirithe a ndearna sé leis an bpinsean a bhí ag dul dó ó rí na Spáinne:[84]

> Fágaim an mhéid atá agam ar an rígh re h-aghaidh an clodh-Gaoidhilge agus neithe do chur a ccló do rachas an onóir do Dhia, a cclu dár násion agus d'Órd San Froinsias.

Seo é an chéad uair a chloistear trácht ar thionscadal clódóireachta na mbráithre i Lobháin. Údar suntais freisin nach bhfuil anseo ach an dara téacs sa Ghaeilge a bhaineann earraíocht as an bhfocal *náisiún*, agus de bhrí go raibh Mac Artúir in éineacht le Flaithrí Ó Maoil Chonaire agus Tadhg Ó Cianáin ar thuras na nIarlaí chun na Róimhe, tá gach cuma ar an scéal go raibh sé páirteach sa bhreogadán intleachtúil céanna a ghaibhnigh coincheap an náisiúin Éireannaigh Chaitlicigh agus a cheap friotal dó dá réir. An iontas ar bith é gur tháinig ann don téarma *náisiún Éireannach* díreach ag an am céanna agus san áit chéanna a raibh an

---

83 Ibid., l. 160.   84 C. Ó Lochlainn, *Tobar fíonghan Gaedhilge* (1939), l. 97.

Spáinn ag baint earraíochta as an téarma *nación española* chun aontacht a chothú i measc na náisiún Ibéireach go léir sa Róimh?[85]

Corradh beag le ceithre mhí ina dhiaidh sin, 17 Meitheamh 1611, thug Ardeaspag Malines cead foilsithe do leabhar a bhí scríofa ag ball den chomhluadar i Lobháin, Bonabhentura Ó hEodhasa 'ut conatibus haereticorcum ad pervertendam gentem Hybernicam iam libros hoc idiomate conscriptos evulgantium contraeatur'.[86] Ar 20 Meitheamh thug rialtóirí na hÍsiltíre Spáinní, Albert agus Isabella, an cead céanna tar éis dóibh deimhniú an chairdinéil a fheiceáil, an stát agus an eaglais ag obair as lámha a chéile:[87]

> Ung livre intitulé Catechismus … en la langue hybernique pour servir à la jeunesse et aultres braves gens dicelluy pays contre la faulse doctrine des autres religions contraires à nostre saincte foy et nostre mère la Saincte Eglise Catholique de Rome …

Ba iad Aodh Mac Aingil agus Roibéard Mac Artúir a dhearbhaigh don easpag go raibh an teagasc críostaí saor ó earráidí foirceadail. Pé acu a spreag uacht Mhic Artúir síolta na clódóireachta a chéaduair in intinn Uí Eodhasa nó nach ndearna an uacht ach bonn airgeadaithe a chur faoi phlean a beartaíodh cheana, is deacair a rá agus dáiríre is cuma. B'fhéidir nár mhiste a mheabhrú, áfach, nach raibh i bproifisiún Mhic Artúir ach réaladh foirmeálta, dá sollúnta féin é, ar cinneadh a tógadh bliain roimhe sin, agus nach gá mar sin gur aireag meanman gan choinne é coincheap an teagaisc chríostaí. Níor mhiste a mheabhrú ach chomh beag, d'ainneoin na mbuntáistí follasacha a bhí ag Ó hEodhasa mar dhuine a raibh oiliúint ghairmiúil sa Ghaeilge agus sa diagacht aige faoi seach, go raibh dochtúireachtaí sa diagacht ó Salamanca ag Mac Artúir agus ag Mac Aingil araon agus taithí níos fairsinge acu ar shaol na hEorpa. Ar éigean a bheidh fhios againn go deo cé acu mar thogra aonair nó mar thogra foirne is fearr breathnú ar theagasc críostaí Uí Eodhasa. Rud amháin atá cinnte, áfach. Faoi dheireadh an Mheithimh 1611 bhí tionscadal foilsithe bhráithre bochta Lobháin faoi lánseol.

85 Dandalet, *Spanish in Rome*, ll 113–21.   **86** F. Mac Raghnaill (eag.), *Bonabhentura Ó hEodhasa, An teagasg Críosduidhe* (1976), l. 95.   **87** Jennings, *Louvain papers*, ll 32–3.

The secular Franciscans

PATRICK CONLAN OFM

The twelfth and thirteenth centuries in Europe saw the emergence of a religious movement known as the 'order of penitents', whose origins lay in the ritual of public penance practised from the earliest period of Christianity. This involved the performance of public ascetic acts such as undertaking pilgrimages, fasting and abstinence, wearing penitential garb like sackcloth or ashes during Lent. Almsgiving was also a common practice of medieval public penitents. During his early period of conversion St Francis was influenced by the lifestyle of the 'order of penitents' and, attracted by his charismatic personality, lay people sought his guidance for renewal of their lives. Thus, as the friars began to preach throughout continental Europe, their message encouraged lay religious movements such as the 'order of penitents'.[1] Between 1209 and 1215 St Francis compiled his *Letter to all the Faithful* and a rule for the Third Order of St Francis was approved verbally by Pope Honorius III in 1221. This gathered the members, or tertiaries as they were called, into an order called the Brothers and Sisters of Penance. Observing abstinence and regular fasts, they dressed simply and avoided public spectacles such as festivals and plays. Their daily lives were regulated by prayer. Regular confession and communion were encouraged. As people of peace, they did not carry weapons. They met monthly for mass and discussion on spiritual matters. Pope Nicholas IV promulgated a formal rule for the Third Order in 1289. Gradually a small scapular and cord worn under lay clothes replaced the wearing of a formal habit. Some tertiaries took the rule as a basis for a full religious life known as the Third Order Regular, while the lay movement was the Third Order Secular.

Emergence and consolidation in Ireland, 1425–1800
The earliest references to the existence of the two branches of the Franciscan Third Order in Ireland appear in the 1420s and are most particularly associated with the diocese of Clonfert where the first contemporary reference to a Third

---

1 The question of the Order of Penitents and its relationship with the Franciscan and Dominican movements has generated much academic controversy. Useful modern surveys include G.G. Meerssemann, *Dossier de l'Ordre de la Pénitence au xiii siècle* (1961); M. D'Alatri, *Aetas Poenitentialis: l'antico Ordine Francescano della Penitenza* (1993); R. Pazzelli, *St Francis and the Third Order* (1991); R.M. Stewart, *De illis qui faciunt penitentiam: The rule of the secular Franciscan Order* (1991). For the early development of the tertiaries in Ireland see P. Conlan, *Secular Franciscans down the ages* (1996) pp 6–9; Ó Clabaigh, *Franciscans*

Order friary occurs in 1426. The history of the Third Order in Ireland is mainly associated with the spread of the Observant reform movement in the latter half of the fifteenth century. Many communities flourished in the shadows of newly founded friaries and the patrons of such foundations, members of noble families such as the O'Kellys who were linked ot the friary of Kilconnell, Co. Galway, were secular tertiaries.[2] When the friars were forced to hide or go into exile from the end of the sixteenth century, tertiaries continued to follow the Third Order rule and to support the friars. Notable members included the parents of Luke Wadding who belonged to the merchant class of Clonmel and Waterford. A number of priests and bishops in seventeenth-century Ireland were tertiaries. They included the martyr Patrick O'Loughran (d. 1612), Bishop Redmond Gallagher of Derry (d. 1601), Bishop Edmund Dungan of Down and Connor, (d. 1628), and Thomas Morrissey, vicar choral of Cashel (d. 1647).[3] The Third Order was regarded as an ideal instrument of the Counter-Reformation. Pope Sixtus V founded the Cordbearers of St Francis in 1585 as a less complex form of the Third Order. Members met regularly to pray and spread devotion to Francis. The Irish Franciscan provincial chapter of 1612 ordered that confraternities be introduced and the wording of the decision suggests that Cordbearers were intended rather than established tertiaries.[4] Cordbearers were active in Drogheda in 1619. The Franciscan general chapter at Toledo in 1633 encouraged the restoration of the Third Order by renewing its practices and bringing it into new areas. The guardian of St Anthony's College, Louvain, Brian Mac Giolla Coinnigh translated the Rule of the Third Order into Irish and printed it as part of a handbook at Louvain in 1641.[5] This contained an historical background, the rule of Nicholas IV translated from the Wadding edition, an exhortation, a list of Franciscan saints, famous members of the Third Order, and the formulae for reception and profession in the order.

When religious were forced into hiding or exile during the Cromwellian period and later following the Banishment of Religious Act of 1697, the members of the Third Order continued to live a Franciscan lifestyle. This proved difficult in the circumstances and their numbers declined due to lack of regular meetings. The friars emerged in public again after 1735 and Francis Fleming OFM is reputed to have re-introduced the Third Order into Ireland. He got permission from the provincial definitory on 20 February 1759 to re-establish a fraternity of the Third Order for ladies at Adam and Eves, Merchants' Quay in Dublin. The fact that he had already got a ciborium for the use of the Third Order in Dublin the previous year implies that an existing group needed formal re-organisation. A

in Ireland, p. 82. **2** Ó Clabaigh, *Franciscans in Ireland*, pp 80–105. **3** 'Brevis synopsis', p. 178.
4 'Brussels MS. 3947', p. 122. **5** P. Ó Súilleabháin (eag.), *Rialachas San Froinsias* (1952), pp 1–57.

register of male and female members at Merchants' Quay exists for 1760–85. Fleming prepared a handbook in 1762 under the title of *The Rule of the Third Order of Penance instituted by the Seraphical Patriarch Saint Francis for Secular Persons of both sexes who desire to live Religiously in the World.*[6] The handbook was still in use many years later. It opens with an exhortation related to that issued at the Franciscan general chapter at Toledo in 1606 and lists the Franciscan calendar with the favours and spiritual advantages of joining as set out by the relevant Roman congregation in 1693. The differences between the Third Order and the Cordbearers are listed. The rule of Nicholas IV is accompanied by a commentary based on the constitutions of Pope Innocent XI. There are hymns and prayers for use at the monthly meetings and during the daily office. Finally texts are given for reception and profession. Among the stranger items is a note that those whose blood had been let were allowed to eat three meals during times of fast and that, where fraternities of men and women existed, they could not communicate with each other. Despite the mention of ladies only, the evidence is that there were different fraternities for ladies and gentlemen in Dublin at that time.

Expansion of the Third Order in Ireland, 1800–1963

There is evidence that the Third Order flourished in Ulster early in the nineteenth century. Nathaniel Greacen of Monaghan printed several booklets on St Francis and the Franciscan spirit. He wrote to Rome in 1819 for permission to establish the Third Order since the friars had recently left the area, but this request was refused. Only First Order priests could direct the Third Order.[7] He was encouraged to introduce the Cordbearers instead and this proved to be popular. Several handbooks were printed explaining that 'the object of this confraternity is to promote acts of reparation to the Most Holy Heart of Jesus, the veneration of the Blessed Virgin Mary, of Saint Francis of Assisi, and the relief of the suffering souls in purgatory'.[8] Members met regularly but were not associated with a particular friary. The Third Order was a way of life that needed continual nourishment by Franciscan religious if it was to flourish.

Some tertiaries in the nineteenth century imitated those of the medieval period and took the Third Order rule as a basis for a religious form of life. Laymen assisted priests in friaries as perpetual or quasi-religious tertiaries. When Fr Henry Young, who was a curate in the parish of St Nicholas in Francis Street, Dublin, which extended out as far as the village of Milltown, requested the help

---

6 Details of Fleming's life in *Liber Dubliniensis*: the permission is on pp 336–7. The ciborium is in a Dublin friary. The registers are in FLK MSS C85–6. The three versions of the handbook are UCD-OFM MSS B110–1 and B116. B110 is the most complete while B116 has a Cork provenance.   **7** P. Conlan, 'A short calendar of material of Irish interest' (1978), p. 108; APF, *SC Irlanda*, xxii 264–7.   **8** *Life of Saint Francis and Rule of the Confraternity of the Cord* (1820).

of the Franciscans in establishing a school in Milltown in 1820, John (Francis) Dunne OFM, who was Director of the Third Order at Merchants' Quay, approached the tertiaries. Some of them decided to dedicate their lives as religious to teaching the poor children and illiterate adults of the locality. They opened a residence and school named Mount Alverna at Milltown in May 1820.[9] The superior of the community of ten was Owen Smyth while John Dillon was the local director. They ran a day school, an evening school and a Sunday free school. A second foundation, also called Mount Alverna, was established at Dalkey, Co. Dublin in November 1820. Patrick Smyth was superior of that small community. They looked after two schools and one hundred children.

Dublin tertiaries were also involved in three other institutions. St Francis of Assisi Orphan Society was founded on 7 January 1817 with the aim of providing accommodation for orphans until they were apprenticed. The president, vice-president and twelve guardians met monthly and supported the education of twenty-four orphans at Tullow, Co. Carlow. An appeal in 1837, when Henry Hughes OFM was president, claimed that they had helped 156 helpless innocents, seventy of whom were dependent on charity.[10] The Patrician Orphan Society, with an even earlier origin, cared for well over a hundred boys and girls at Ballybrack, Co. Dublin until they moved to near Clane, Co. Kildare around 1815. It was still active in the early 1830s, when it was looking after forty children, but had closed before 1840.[11] St Bonaventure's Charitable Institution was founded on 14 November 1820 to provide an asylum for poor catholic children rescued from schools 'dangerous to faith and morals'. Again the inspiration came from the efforts of Fr Young to oppose the activities of a Protestant school at Harold's Cross in Dublin. The president in 1837 was John Murphy OFM.[12]

The tertiaries in Milltown and Dalkey were under the direction of the Franciscans at Merchants' Quay. A similar movement began in the west of Ireland when Christopher Dillon Bellew of Mount Bellew estate, Co. Galway, with the consent of Archbishop Oliver Kelly of Tuam, invited some of the brothers from Dublin to come to Mount Bellew in 1818.[13] The foundation stone of a permanent monastery was laid in 1823. Bonaventure Lee and Michael Dillon opened a free school that attracted pupils from a large area. The boys lodged in local cottages and repaid their board by teaching the families with whom they lived, particularly

9 Ronan, *An apostle of Catholic Dublin,* pp 95, 99; Fr Henry Young, 'The Catholic Directory for 1821' (1959), pp 338, 357. Fr Young may have lived with the friars in Merchants' Quay for a while before moving out to Harold's Cross.   **10** Young, 'The Catholic Directory for 1821', p. 341; Ronan, *An apostle of Catholic Dublin,* p. 301; *The Catholic Directory for 1838,* p. 322.   **11** Ronan, *An apostle of Catholic Dublin,* pp 54, 229; *The Catholic Directory for 1838,* p. 322.   **12** Young, 'The Catholic Directory for 1821', p. 341; Ronan, *An apostle for Catholic Dublin,* pp 100–1; *The Catholic Directory for 1838,* p. 322.   **13** *The Franciscan brothers of the west of Ireland* (1934).

in Christian doctrine. The pupils also learned farming and some trades. Mount Bellew became a full agricultural college in 1904. A small landowner and tertiary near Clara in Co. Offaly, Matthew Delahunty, and some companions adopted the religious life of the Third Order Regular in 1821. They followed the constitutions of the brothers in Mount Bellew but under the jurisdiction of Bishop Patrick Joseph Plunkett of Meath. Both branches eventually amalgamated to form a single congregation.

When it appeared that the Catholic Emancipation Act could result in the extinction of the older religious orders, including the Franciscans, the brothers in Mount Bellew requested Archbishop Kelly to take them under his protection.[14] The archbishop's request to Propaganda Fide to remove them from the control of the First Order and make them a diocesan congregation was granted on 13 September 1830. Similarly, Clara came under the jurisdiction of the bishop of Meath. The order expanded rapidly in the west of the country, in Galway, Mayo and Roscommon and established a foundation in Brooklyn in 1858.[15] The Brothers now have missions in Kenya and the US. They became a full pontifical brotherhood in 1938.

The Third Order suffered from the decline of the Friars Minor and Capuchins between 1820 and 1860 but the records show that during the second half of the century it went through a process of re-organization in Drogheda (1858), Killarney (1860), Wexford (1862), Waterford (1864), Cork-St Francis (1867), Cork-Holy Trinity (1870), Carrick-on-Suir (1880), Athlone (1882) and Clonmel (1883).[16] Many of those who rejoined had been tertiaries in their youth. Pope Leo XIII issued an encyclical in 1882 for the seventh centenary of the birth of St Francis. He promoted the Third Order as the most appropriate way of life for contemporary Catholics. Leo hoped to cure the ills of humanity by restoring Christian values and culture. The following year he issued a revised version of the 1289 rule promulgated by Nicholas IV and by doing so sought to make the rule so simple that anyone striving for Christian perfection could follow it. Tertiaries would wear the small scapular and cord, observe the commandments, avoid extremes in their lifestyles, go to confession and communion monthly, attend mass daily if possible, attend their monthly meetings and recite a daily office of twelve Our Fathers, Hail Marys and Glorias.[17] Bishops followed Leo XIII's advocacy of the Third Order and as a result the order expanded rapidly. From about a million and three-quarter tertiaries in nearly 10,000 fraternities worldwide in 1900, it grew to nearly four million in 24,000 fraternities by 1934.

14 Ibid.   **15** The texts of the papal documents have been published in *Rule and general constitutions of the Franciscan brothers* (1910), pp 1–15.   **16** Minute books of the various fraternities and friary house books. **17** Iriarte, *Franciscan history* (1983), pp 504–5; statistics pp 508–10.

Following a particular interpretation of papal support for the Third Order, tertiaries became involved in catholic action until a decree issued by Pius X in 1912 stated that individual sanctification was the primary purpose of the Third Order. It was not a group dedicated to acts of charity.

During this period and in line with European trends, Third Order publications appeared in Ireland. National Third Order directories containing details of meetings were issued from as early as 1881.[18] *The Franciscan Tertiary* appeared in 1890–9 and again in 1911–14 while the *Father Matthew Record* started in 1908. The Friars Minor produced *Assisi* (1929–66) and *The Franciscan* (1975–2003). *The Franciscan Almanac* appeared in the period 1926–31 and *The Capuchin Annual* from 1929. Augustine O'Neill OFM published the first edition of a Franciscan Manual for tertiaries in 1924. The Third Order in Ireland followed the wish of various popes by promoting christian literature. Tertiaries in Dublin staffed a street bookstall during the 1930s and catholic lending libraries were established in Athlone, Cork and Dublin. Others developed special works such as promoting the Franciscan Missionary Union to help finance foreign missionary activity. Tertiaries in Limerick helped organize the Franciscan Pilgrimage to Lourdes. The Athlone fraternity leased vegetable plots on which needy families could grow food.

The contemporary hierarchical structure of the church is quite clearly evident in the management and activity of the Third Order. In 1909 the provincial reminded tertiary councils that they were acting invalidly if they made decisions without a spiritual director. Brothers and sisters sat in different sections within the same fraternities. They attended a morning mass and an evening meeting each month. A wife needed her husband's permission before joining. The order in Dublin and Cork was split into separate fraternities for men and women in 1918. Athlone followed in 1921 with Ennis, Galway, Killarney, Limerick and Wexford following suit in 1922. The last fraternity divided about 1937.

The Third Order became involved in external acts of piety. Tertiaries encouraged people to erect blue IHS plaques over the front doors of their houses to signify the protection given by the Holy Name of Jesus. They marched as a body under their own banners in religious processions with the brothers wearing the habit. This was also worn during meetings and both brothers and sisters could be buried in the habit if they wished. Third Order pilgrimages became common. Initially local groups went to nearby friary ruins such as those at Askeaton or Claregalway. A national pilgrimage to Cashel was organized for the centenary of Catholic Emancipation in 1929. Tertiaries were among the early pilgrims to Knock. Five thousand travelled from Limerick in 1937 on what may have been

18 There is a comprehensive collection of Third Order directories in FLK; Mooney, *Devotional writings*, (1952), pp 40–8.

the first organized pilgrimage to the shrine. The annual Franciscan Day in Knock on the last Sunday in June became a major event. The first National Franciscan Pilgrimage to Lough Derg took place in 1935. Many tertiaries travelled on the Franciscan Pilgrimage to Lourdes, which began in 1929.[19]

The number of tertiaries attached to Franciscan houses in Ireland increased from 5,000 in 1905 to over 10,000 by 1920, 20,000 by 1930 and 30,000 between 1940 and 1970. The Third Order also appeared in places away from friaries where growth or decline depended on the interest of the local clergy. The first such fraternity started around 1910 in Derry's Waterside. Old members recall crowds crossing the bridge from the Cityside to attend meetings. Cordbearers at the Cathedral in Belfast changed to the Third Order in 1917. Other groups started in Newry (1927), Athenry (1930), Portlaoise (1931), Lurgan (1933), Cloone (1936), Ballaghdereen (1938), Dundalk (1940), Castleblaney (1942 and revived in 1979), Kiltimagh (c.1951–80), Ballyjamesduff (1954) and Monaghan (1954).[20]

The seventh centenary of the Third Order was marked by three days of events in Killarney in 1921.[21] Tertiaries commemorated the seventh centenary of the Stigmata of St Francis at the Abbey graveyard in Athlone on 6 July 1924, where they were addressed by the minister general, Bernadine Klumper OFM.[22] Trains from many locations brought pilgrims, including the Dublin Transport Band, to Athlone to celebrate the seventh centenary of the death of St Francis on 1926.[23] Meetings of local directors were held in 1927–30 and a national conference on the theme of the Third Order and Catholic Action took place in Dublin in 1931.[24] Another conference followed four years later with both Friars Minor and Capuchins involved.[25] These meetings were inspired by similar events in the US. Local directors met again in 1949 and were wrongly informed that Pius X had forbidden the order to become involved in social action.[26] The Third Order in Ireland seemed to be in good condition when John XXIII became pope in 1958. This was confirmed at a congress of spiritual directors in Cork in 1961. Devout tertiaries attended their morning and evening monthly meetings in good numbers.

19 Details of such events may be found in the contemporary issues of *The Franciscan Almanac* and *Assisi* – the 'Chronicle' in the former and 'Franciscan Echos' in the latter give an excellent account of Third Order activities from 1925 on; the Cashel pilgrimage is described in *The Franciscan Almanac* (1930), pp 94–5 and in *Assisi*, I (1929), pp 94–5, 230–1, 256. FLK has a brochure on it (XB530) and on Buttevant in 1927 (XB58). 20 Details in *Assisi*.   21 Copy of the souvenir brochure in Killarney Friary Archives.   22 *The Westmeath Independent*, 10 July 1924.   23 FLK old file L16.   24 Minutes of some of the meetings of directors in FLK box Provincial varia; report on the congress in *Assisi* 3 (1931), pp 235–7.   25 'The Letter of Most Rev. Fr Leonard Bello, O.F.M., minister general, to the National Congress of the Franciscan Tertiaries', *Assisi* 10 (1938), pp 484–5; 'The Pope and the Congress' *Assisi* 10 (1938), pp 595–623. There is a copy of the souvenir brochure in FLK (XB360).   26 See the letters of Fr Adrian Lyons OFM national director, in the Franciscan Third Order files, Franciscan Friary, Cork.

Many tertiaries were deeply spiritual people. The most renowned Irish tertiary was the Venerable Matt Talbot.[27] Born in Dublin in 1856, he went to work at the age of twelve. His life was marred by alcohol and it is related that one night in 1884 he had no money and no one among his workmates was willing to assist him. He saw the futility of his situation and took the pledge to refrain from alcohol. He turned to God as a penitent and sought to make reparation for his past by following an ascetical lifestyle. Matt was received into the Third Order at Adam and Eve's in 1890 and missed only two meetings in his first twenty years as a tertiary. He developed a dedication to the Eucharist, respected all people and promoted peace. He died in 1925 and was buried in the Franciscan habit in Glasnevin. Other examples include John McGuinness, a civil servant who joined the Third Order at Merchants' Quay in 1935 and dedicated his energies to improving the lot of the poor in Dublin.[28] Frank Duff, founder of the Legion of Mary, joined the Third Order at Church Street in 1927. The famous Legion envoy in Africa, Edel Quin, was also a tertiary.

The impact of Vatican II, 1963–90

New constitutions were approved by Pope Pius XII in 1957 in part response to a feeling that the Rule of Leo XIII was inadequate for the mid-twentieth century. This initiative was overtaken by the Second Vatican Council which challenged all Catholics to undertake genuine renewal. The Sacred Congregation for Religious gave permission to update Third Order legislation in 1966 and the four commissaries general (Franciscans, Capuchins, Conventuals and Third Order Regular) proposed a revision of the rule, constitutions and rituals, the proposal in turn being passed on to the national commissaries. An international gathering of friars discussed the results at a meeting in Assisi in January 1968 but without involving the tertiaries themselves. The First International Interobediential Congress of the Third Order met in Assisi in the summer of 1969 and drafted guidelines for the future. The order was defined as a community of brothers and sisters journeying towards the Father, by living the gospel as secular people following the spirit of Francis in communion with all Franciscans. The way of life was clarified in terms of seventeen essential elements. The congress stressed that there was just one order of tertiaries, which must tend towards a unity of structures while reflecting different local traditions. The drafting of a new rule was begun and Pope Paul VI promulgated the finished version for the renamed Secular Franciscan Order (SFO) on 24 June 1978. And following discussions at a series of international congresses new constitutions were finally approved in 1991.[29]

27 J.A. Glynn, *Life of Matt Talbot* (1932); S. O'Byrne, *Venerable Matt Talbot* (1999); Membership records in the SFO Archives, Merchants' Quay, Dublin.   **28** S. O'Brien, *John McGuinness* (1948).   **29** Stewart, 'De

Considerable renewal took place among the followers of St Francis in Ireland in the wake of the Vatican II. Initially tertiaries reacted to the council by making practical changes. The new law on the eucharistic fast and the introduction of evening masses resulted in the monthly morning mass and evening meeting being amalgamated to become an evening mass and meeting. The Irish Franciscan and Capuchin provincials with their Third Order commissaries meeting in Dublin in January 1971 agreed to foster unity and set up a national interobediential council. A meeting of spiritual directors was held in Dublin the following April. In October 600 tertiaries met in Dublin to celebrate the 750th anniversary of the founding of the Third Order. The archbishop of Dublin, John Charles McQuaid, presided at the mass. The keynote address was delivered by Agnellus Andrew OFM and replies came from politicians from both sides of the Dáil: the Taoiseach, Liam Cosgrave (Fine Gael), and Celia Lynch (Fianna Fáil).[30]

The inaugural meeting of the Irish National Interobediential Council was held in Dublin in October 1971. Agreement on a permanent national council proved difficult as it was felt that tertiaries from different fraternities did not know each other sufficiently. The text of a proposed new international rule was circulated to all national bodies in 1975 and an Irish National Congress met in Gormanston in July at which an interim rule for Ireland was adopted for three years.[31] A joint Friar Minor/Capuchin directory containing daily offices was published in 1976. Four regions were set up with a unit in Cork for 'isolated' tertiaries – those living too far from a fraternity to attend meetings. Statutes were agreed which proposed an annual general assembly. This assembly became a regular event for a weekend in August in Multyfarnham. Gradually tertiaries in Ireland got to know and appreciate each other and to share ideas. Fraternities of brothers and sisters amalgamated to promote renewal. The old passive style of quasi-anonymous monthly meetings faded as the influence of small group dynamics replaced the old system. Spiritual assistants who advised replaced spiritual directors who gave orders.

The first elective chapter of the Irish Secular Franciscans took place at Harold's Cross, Dublin, on 18 February 1979.[32] Provisional national statutes were adopted. Pat Cox from Dublin was elected president with William O'Brien from Waterford as vice-president. The new national council met for the first time in at Broc House in Dublin on 21 October where it discussed finances, communication with fraternities and filled vacancies on the council. The first annual general

illis qui faciunt Penitentia', pp 248–52.   **30** Details of the directors' meeting are in the Dublin friary chronicle; the celebrations are in *Seanchas na bBráithre* (internal Irish Franciscan newsletter) December 1971.   **31** *The Franciscan People* (June and August 1975).   **32** There are copies of most of the documents from 1979 on in the archives at National Headquarters in Dublin. The annual reports are particularly useful.

meeting took place in Tallaght in May 1980. After confirming the elections of 1979, the AGM discussed the setting up of the regions, formation, communications and plans for the celebration of Franciscan Year in 1982. The national council was recognized by the international council and got its own international delegate. The President and vice-president attended the international congress in Rome in 1982.

This renewal brought about a sense of revitalisation among the fraternities. The First Order established fraternities in their new houses: the Capuchins in Ards (1930), Raheny (1947), Priorswood (1975), Carlow (1977), Ballyfermot (1978), Gurranabraher (1983) and Blanchardstown (1988); the Friars Minor in Rossnowlagh (1947) and Bray (1987); the Conventuals in Fairview (1987). Religious sisters and lay people realized the spiritual value of the Secular Franciscans and set up new fraternities in places where the friars were not present: Ballinasloe (1982), Maynooth (1982), Finglas (1983), Tullamore (1984), Cookstown (1988), Ballincollig (1994), Ballycastle (1995), Ballymena (1995), Keady and Wicklow. Older groups were given fresh life in Belfast, Castleblaney, Gormanston and Derry.

CONCLUSION

During the twentieth century the Third Order in Ireland gave tertiaries the spiritual background that enabled them to engage in apostolic work through organisations like the Society of St Vincent de Paul. The fresh energy provided by the Pauline Rule has seen a growth in new activities by the fraternities themselves. These vary from prayer to study groups, care of young people and the aged, the provision of caravan holidays for the those in need and supporting refugees.

The celebration Franciscan Year of 1982 was an enriching experience for all orders of St Francis in Ireland. The SFO met in Multyfarnham to celebrate the year. Tom Purcell of the Bray fraternity, who was elected president in 1988, laid great stress on a proper programme of formation: the eastern region established the Franciscan School of Formation and Training while a formation handbook was produced by a tertiary from Belfast. A national headquarters was opened at San Damiano, Harold's Cross, Dublin on 11 July 1992 through the offices of the Sisters of St Clare. This made the publication of a national monthly newsletter much easier. Proper national statutes were adopted at the 1994 chapter, where Maura Noone of Galway was elected president. Tom Purcell took on the role of International Councillor, undertaking visitations in other countries. Celebrations were held on a local level to commemorate the 775th of the foundation of the order in 1996.

The Secular Franciscans in Ireland were in a robust state at the turn of the second millennium. Ita O'Neill of Dublin was elected president in 2000. There were over 8,000 tertiaries in forty-three fraternities. A group of committed tertiaries with experience of working at national level was able to give committed local leadership. Regular meetings prepared and helped the spiritual assistants and local presidents for their ministry. The six regions were functioning, some more successfully than others. International visitors were more than happy at the pace of renewal in Ireland. With the decline in numbers of the First Order, the Third Order has rediscovered its role of maintaining the Franciscan way of life in society in Ireland.

Missions and missionaries

PATRICK CONLAN OFM

Though Ireland was never a colonial power, membership of the British Empire and the pastoral needs of the Irish diaspora provided an outlet for Irish missionaries throughout the English-speaking world.[1] The vocations boom of the late nineteenth and twentieth centuries saw the emergence of numerous Irish missionary organizations and orders, while older orders, including the Franciscans, expanded their activities to the mission fields. For the friars this was the development of a well-established tradition as missionary activity had always been a feature of the province. In the fourteenth century Friar James of Ireland accompanied Blessed Odoric of Pordenone to China. In the late fifteenth century Irish Observant friars engaged in preaching tours in Scotland.

The devotion of St Francis to the Holy Land meant that it held a particular attraction for his followers. An account survives of the 1323 pilgrimage of two Irish friars, Hugh the Illuminator and Simon Semeonis to the Holy Land. The Franciscan Custody of the Holy Land was formally erected in 1342.[2] This survives as an international unit serving the needs of pilgrims and the local Christian population. In the modern period a number of Irish friars have served in the Holy Land: Fr Aloysius Stafford ministered in the Basilica of the Holy Sepulchre from 1861 to 1868. Fr Eugene Hoade, author of a celebrated pilgrims' guide, worked mainly at the shrine at the Garden of Gethsemane from 1929 to 1956. He was also chaplain to the Palestinian police, strongly supporting them in their struggle after 1948. Fr P.J. Giblin taught in Bethlehem in 1957–9. Br Conrad McEvoy was well known to Irish visitors while stationed at the Church of the Holy Sepulchre in Jerusalem and the Church of the Nativity in Nazareth in 1983–9.

SCOTLAND

The first Irish Franciscan mission for which a detailed account survives was the mission to the Highlands and Islands of Scotland in the early seventeenth century.[3] As with the change of religion elsewhere, the reformation in Scotland was complex, linked in particular to the politics of the Scottish monarchy and its relations with England and Europe. The period of reformation in Scotland was

1 P. Conlan, *The missionary work of the Irish Franciscans* (1996).   2 E. Hoade & C. Giblin, 'Ireland and the Holy Land' (1952), pp 69–77.   3 Giblin, *Irish Franciscan mission to Scotland*.

marked by great theological debates, by social upheaval and often by violence.[4] The Franciscans (Greyfriars) in Scotland, for example, found it difficult to maintain an active presence in the country and many went to the Continent, attracted to the same locations as Irish Franciscans.[5] By the early seventeenth century it would appear that society in parts of Scotland, especially in the Highlands and Islands, had virtually lost contact with formal religion because neither the Catholic Church nor the Calvinist Reformed Church could minister to these remoter regions. That the population was Gaelic-speaking has been cited as one of the reasons that the Scottish seminaries on the Continent did not send priests to the Highlands and Islands.[6] The initial stage of the Irish mission to Scotland came when John Ogilvie and John Stuart, both Scots, travelled from St Anthony's College, Louvain to Scotland in 1612–13 to assess the situation there. They were followed in 1619 by two Irish Franciscans, Patrick Brady and Edmund McCann, who went to work in the Highlands and the Hebrides. Rome, mainly through the Papal Nuncio in Brussels, had persuaded the Irish Franciscans in Louvain to embark on this mission and by 1623, eight Franciscans were approved as missionaries by Pope Urban VIII and were to receive an annual allowance from Propaganda Fide to whom they were to report on their mission. Four Irish friars worked in Scotland during periods from 1626 to 1637: Patrick Brady, Patrick Hegarty, Edmund McCann and Cornelius Ward. Their mission was difficult, hampered by constant danger of capture and by lack of assistance from Rome. At various times they withdrew from Scotland. In 1631 Patrick Hegarty took up residence in the abandoned Third Order friary at Bonamargy, Co. Antrim and ministered to Scots who sought him out there. Cornelius Ward travelled to the Continent on a number of occasions to seek assistance from Propaganda Fide. He spent two years in prison in London following his capture in 1630 when returning to Scotland from the Continent. The mission effectively ended in 1637 due to lack of funding. Efforts to re-open the mission in 1647 failed. Two young priests, Mark and Francis McDonnell, set out in 1667. Mark died in 1671 and ill health forced his brother to retire to Ireland in 1679. It was reported in 1703 that five Irish friars were ministering in Scotland and there were at least two Irish friars working in the Highlands and the Isles as late as 1743.[7]

Despite all its difficulties, the detailed accounts of the mission that survive, and particularly the reports written by Patrick Hegarty and Cornelius Ward, are testaments to the ceaseless activity of the Irish Franciscans in Scotland over almost twenty years. The documents are all the more important as they provide a

4 D. Roberts (ed.), *Essays on the Scottish Reformation* (1962). 5 A. Ross, 'Some notes on the religious orders in pre-Reformation Scotland' (1962), pp 228–30. 6 Giblin, *Irish Franciscan mission to Scotland*, p. viii. 7 C. Giblin, 'The Irish mission to Scotland in the seventeenth century' (1952), p. 24.

valuable insight into a society which maintained traditions of a religion that had been lost by continuing, for example, to venerate the cults of medieval saints such as Columba, Donnan and Ninnian. They also offer important evidence with regard to the process of conversion and the methods adopted by competing religions in influencing a society and in particular in persuading the nobility to their side.

NEWFOUNDLAND

The first five bishops in Newfoundland, where a third of the population in 1763 were Irish-speaking Catholics, were Irish Franciscans.[8] Neglected and suffering semi-official persecution, the Irish of Newfoundland frequently travelled back to Ireland to receive the sacraments. In 1784 three Waterfordmen applied successfully to the British government for a resident priest and later that year an Irish Franciscan, James Louis O'Donnell, arrived as prefect apostolic.[9] Born in Knocklofty, outside Clonmel, Co. Tipperary he studied in Rome and Prague before his ordination in 1770. He served as minister provincial from 1779 to 1782. Although it was not an official mission and depended on the willingness of volunteers, other friars joined him. The prefecture was elevated to a vicariate in 1796 and O'Donnell was consecrated bishop in Quebec on 2 September 1796. He reported that the population of Newfoundland in 1800 was 35,000 of whom 27,000 (75%) were Catholics. Serious difficulties faced the mission. The island was divided into four areas for pastoral purposes but there were only six priests and the authorities were slow in paying the promised allowance of £75 p.a. The Napoleonic wars compounded the difficulties in that supplies were occasionally seized by French warships and the missionaries had also to cater for the spiritual needs of French captives. O'Donnell resigned in 1807 and returned to Ireland where he died in 1811.

Patrick Lambert who had been minister provincial in 1803–4 and coadjutor bishop to O'Donnell since 1806, became the second bishop 1807.[10] He resigned in 1817 and was replaced by his nephew, Thomas Scallan.[11] The latter had arrived in Newfoundland in 1812, gone home in 1814 but agreed to return two years later as coadjutor bishop to his uncle. He died in 1830 and was succeeded by Michael Anthony Fleming who was to oversee a significant expansion of the mission. Fleming arrived in Newfoundland in 1823, was appointed coadjutor bishop in

---

8 M.F. Howley, *Ecclesiastical history of Newfoundland* ii, (1888); P.W. Browne, 'Talav an Eask' (1915); P. Conlan, 'The Irish Franciscans in Newfoundland' (1984). **9** P. O'Connell, 'Dr. James Louis O'Donnell' (1965); Byrne, *Gentlemen-bishops and faction fighters*, pp 33–232. **10** Ibid., pp 234–95. **11** Ibid., pp 296–352; J.D. Darcy, *Fire upon the earth Bishop M.A. Fleming* (St Johns, 2003).

1827 and was the first bishop consecrated in Newfoundland. He set out to persuade the authorities that the Catholic Emancipation Act applied in Newfoundland. He succeeded in recruiting more priests, both religious and secular, in Ireland. In 1837 he reported that seventeen priests served ten districts with ten good churches and twenty-two others. There were thirty-two Catholic schools. He also sent the first priest to minister in Labrador. Fleming laid the foundation stone of a cathedral in 1841 and became the first bishop of St John's when the vicariate was erected into a diocese in 1847. He was given a coadjutor in that year and later retired to a residence where he hoped to house a Franciscan community. The new cathedral was finished in time for him to celebrate the first mass there some months before his death in 1850.

He was succeeded by Thomas Mullock, who, while in Rome on Franciscan business, was nominated coadjutor bishop to Fleming in 1847.[12] A determined individual, he set about re-organizing church structures. By 1855 he could report that thirty priests were looking after 50,000 Catholics out of a population of 70,000.[13] In the same year Labrador, Greenland and all areas extending to the North Pole were detached from Newfoundland to become the Prefecture Apostolic of the North Pole and instead Mullock was given responsibility for a second diocese, Harbour Grace, in 1856. Mullock believed that the time was ripe for the withdrawal of the Irish Franciscans and he set up a minor seminary as a first step towards providing a local clergy. He died in 1869 and was succeeded by Canon Thomas Power, president of Clonliffe College in Dublin. The last Irish friar to serve in Newfoundland was Peter A. Slattery who retired as president of the local seminary and returned to Europe in 1877. He would later head the Irish Franciscan mission in Sydney. In eighty years the Irish friars had solidly rooted the church in Newfoundland but had failed to implant the order.

THE UNITED STATES

Individual friars ministered in the United States. Michael Egan (1761–1814) joined the friars in Louvain and was ordained in Prague.[14] He did tremendous work saving St Isidore's College from bankruptcy in the 1780s before returning to Ireland. Catholics in Lancaster, Pennsylvania, invited him to the United States but on his arrival in 1802, he moved to Philadelphia. He was granted permission in 1804 to erect an independent province of the order but nothing came of this.

12 R. Howley, 'The Right Rev. Dr. Mullock O.S.F.' (1889); Conlan, *St Isidore's College Rome*, p. 167. 13 Report of Mullock to Rome in APF, *Acta* 200, pp 177–8. 14 M.J. Griffin, *History of the Rt. Rev. Dr. Michael Egan* (1893).

8 Cathedral of St John the Baptist, St John's Newfoundland.

He was appointed first bishop of Philadelphia in 1808 and had a difficult time integrating the different emigrant groups there.

Charles Maguire (1768–1833) joined the friars in Louvain.[15] Later he lectured in philosophy and theology at St Isidore's College, Rome and fled to Graz when the French captured Rome. Having a substantial income, he joined the members of his family who had migrated to the US and ended up near Pittsburgh in 1817. He was given permission to introduce the Franciscans in the US and in 1822 built a two-storey log cabin and chapel for six friars at one end of a 113-acre property with a log cabin for Poor Clare Sisters at the other end. The project failed after two years due to lack of vocations.

John Daly from Athlone joined the friars in 1828 and moved to the US soon after his ordination.[16] Bishop Fenwick of Boston assigned him the southern half of the state of Vermont. Helped by the Irish working on railway construction, he was an active missionary and is regarded as the founding father of the diocese of Burlington. Following the appointment of the first bishop of Burlington in 1854 he retired to New York where he met the newly arrived Italian Franciscans, and

15 A. Faulkner, 'Letters of Charles Bonaventure Maguire, O.F.M.' (1979–81); Faulkner, 'Letters of Charles Bonaventure Maguire, O.F.M.' (1982–3).   **16** P. Conlan, 'John Benedict Daly, O.F.M.' (1978).

died in 1872. Other Irish friars to serve in the US in the nineteenth century include Patrick Lonergan who worked south of Pittsburgh and Henry Francis on Prince Edward Island. In the twentieth century Irish friars worked in the American Franciscan provinces, where they ran parishes, looked after migrant groups and specialized in missions and retreats or pursued special studies.

AUSTRALIA AND NEW ZEALAND

Individual friars responded to calls for priests in Australia and New Zealand. Hearing from his brother in Australia of the need for priests, Richard Hayes petitioned Rome for help in 1816, as a result of which the first clergy left for that mission.[17] Fr William Ullathorne OSB, vicar general of the diocese of Sydney, recruited two Irish friars while on a visit to Ireland. Patrick (Bonaventure) Geoghegan travelled back with Ullathorne in 1838.[18] He worked around Melbourne and is known as the 'Pioneer Priest' of Victoria. He celebrated the first mass there at Port Philip on 19 May 1839. Appointed the second bishop of Adelaide in 1859, he died of cancer in Dún Laoghaire in 1864. Ullathorne's other friar was Nicholas Coffey who went to Australia in 1842 and worked mainly around Sydney and Parramatta until his death in 1857. Lawrence (Bonaventure) Sheil, arrived in Melbourne in 1853, succeeded Geoghegan as bishop of Adelaide in 1864 and died in 1872. He was the only Irish Franciscan at the First Vatican Council.[19] His hope of establishing a Franciscan base in Australia came to nothing. Six other Irish friars worked in Australia around this time.[20]

Following his failure to reform the Irish province in the 1840s, Peter (Francis) O'Farrell went to Australia in 1854 and worked mainly in the diocese of Sydney.[21] He too hoped to establish the order in Australia and saved nearly £4,000 for that purpose. Archbishop Polding of Sydney and others knew of the fund and tried to force him to use it for diocesan purposes but the Franciscan's reply was simple: 'No friars, no money'. When O'Farrell died in 1875 Archbishop Vaughan OSB, coadjutor archbishop, tried and failed to overturn the friar's will and then opened negotiations with the Franciscans.[22] His offer of a Franciscan District in Sydney

---

17 P. Conlan, 'The Irish Franciscans in Australia in the nineteenth century' (1981); C. Giblin, 'James Dixon and Jeremiah O'Flynn, two prefects apostolic in Australia' (1983).   18 P. Conlan, 'The Irish Franciscans in Australia – Patrick Bonaventure Geoghegan' (1981–2); J. Fitzgerald, *Sowers of the seed – Irish Franciscans in Victoria during the 19th century* (1976).   19 P. Conlan, 'Lawrence Bonaventure Sheil' (1982).   20 P. Conlan, 'Daniel MacEvey, James Platt, Nicholas Coffey' (1982). MacEvey was a Discalced Carmelite and Platt was a member of the Turin Province; P. Conlan, 'William Cunningham, John Cronin, Thomas Barry, Joseph Clampett, Charles Hugh Horan, Patrick Keating, Patrick O'Keeffe' (1983).   21 P. Conlan, 'Fr Peter Francis O'Farrell, O.F.M.' (1984); M. Carmody, 'Peter Francis O'Farrell, O.F.M.' (1982).   22 P. Conlan, 'The Irish

was accepted by the Irish provincial definitory in 1876. The area just happened to include the two poor parishes that O'Farrell had refused to finance. A provisional contract was agreed in January 1879 and the first friars, Peter (James) Hanrahan, Martin (Augustine) Holohan and Br Paschal McGinley, set sail in March for Sydney. Br Paschal soon returned to Ireland but another three priests arrived.

One problem bedevilled the Australian mission for thirty years: how could five friars staff three parishes while forming one religious community? The obvious solution was to recruit more friars but none were available. The reform of the home province was consuming the manpower in Ireland. The superior in Waverly was guardian of the community as well as the religious superior of the mission. After experiments in 1889–93 the mission was erected into a commissariate under the Irish province in 1899. By 1908 there were only nine friars (including two on loan from the English province) although the first Australian students were approaching ordination. The population of the Franciscan District was increasing rapidly. The archbishop considered that more priests were needed and was in dispute with the friars about their contribution to diocesan funds. The friars did not object when two areas were taken from the Franciscan District in 1885 but resisted vehemently when the archbishop tried to remove other districts in 1906.[23] The case went to Rome in 1909. It seems that Propaganda Fide decided in favour of the friars but did not publish its decision. An inconclusive agreement was reached in 1915.

The friars were intent on establishing the order in Sydney and they got permission to do so in 1915. Attempts were made between 1916 and 1925 to erect a seraphic college at Rydal for boys interested in joining the Franciscans. By this time the reform was firmly established in Ireland and vocations were growing. Hubert Quinn was elected provincial in 1924. A man of vision and energy, he conducted the first visitation of the Australian mission in 1925 and decided that the time was ripe for expansion.[24] Fidelis Griffin was appointed commissary in 1927 and given the clear target of expanding the mission so that it could become an independent province.[25] The first house outside Sydney was established at Kedron near Brisbane in 1929. A seraphic college with twelve students started at Waverley in January 1928 and had thirty-five students the following year. A novitiate was also opened in Waverley in 1930. A student house in Waverley followed in 1932 which meant that Australian students no longer had to go to Ireland. The friars obtained a retreat house at Kew near Melbourne in 1931.

Franciscans in Sydney' (1986–7); J.E. Keane, *Striving for the stars* (1990), pp 16–43; C. Kelly, 'Calendar of source material … Franciscan community in Australia 1879–1905' (1953); P. Conlan, 'A short-title calendar of material of Irish interest (Australia)' (1978), pp 130–46. **23** Keane, *Striving for the stars*, pp 50–5. **24** Ibid., pp 65–7. **25** Ibid., pp 68–81.

Following extensive negotiations the friars received three canonical foundations in their original district in Sydney but surrendered their claim to the parts that the archbishop had reclaimed. They now had five foundations and formation was done locally. Eight foundations were needed for an independent province. This was the target when Sylvester O'Brien replaced Fidelis Griffin as commissary in 1933.[26] St Paschal College, a new student house at Box Hill near Melbourne, opened in 1934. That same year the novitiate was transferred to a proper foundation at Campbelltown also in Sydney.

Bishop Pompalier, bishop of Auckland, asked the Franciscan minister general for help in 1859.[27] Some Italian friars were sent and were given an area around Parnell. They intended opening schools but were prevented by Maori wars and financial problems. Two Irish friars arrived to help them in 1867. One became ill and died in Australia. When Bishop Croke, later archbishop of Cashel, succeeded Pompalier in 1871, seven of the sixteen priests in the diocese were Franciscans. Croke wanted them to become diocesan clergy and refused a foundation. As a result six friars withdrew from Auckland in 1874 and the remaining one, James (Anthony) O'Mahoney, became vicar general and died there in 1890.

Damian Nolan replaced Sylvester O'Brien as commissary in 1936 and looked towards New Zealand.[28] He accepted the bishop of Auckland's offer of a house for missions and retreats. The friary opened in 1939. The requisite number of eight houses was in place and the new Province of the Holy Spirit covering Australia and New Zealand was erected on 31 October 1939 consisting of 123 religious. An Irishman, Andrew Wogan, was appointed provincial. The Second World War delayed development and the first Australian-born provincial, Joseph Gleeson, was not elected until 1948. A very successful mission was started in New Guinea in 1949 and became the vice-province of Papua New Guinea in 1985. The last Irish friar to serve in Australia left in 1972.

CHINA

While attending the Eucharistic Congress in Dublin in 1932, the delegate general for China, Gerard Lunter OFM, met the Irish provincial, Flannan O'Neill, and discussed the possibility of an Irish mission in China.[29] Vocations were increasing, the mission in Australia was prospering and it was time for a new challenge. The

---

26 Ibid., pp 82–5.   **27** *Historia Missionum O.F.M., I Asia centro-orientale et Oceania* (1967), pp 321–3; P. Conlan, 'A short-title calendar of *Hibernia*' (1977), p. 168.   **28** Keane, *Striving for the stars*, pp 86–92. **29** A. Camps & P. McCloskey, *The Friars Minor in China, 1294–1955* (1995), pp 185–93. This section is based on a more detailed typescript: P. Conlan, *The Irish Franciscans in the prefecture of Suihsien* (1988, copy in FLK); E. Hoade, 'Chinese mission memories' (typescript, 1985, copy in FLK).

9 The first group of Irish Franciscan missionaries to China, 1934 (FLK).

provincial consulted Maurice Connaughton, an Irish friar who had been ministering in China since his ordination in Hankow in 1913, and on his recommendation an offer from Bishop Eugenio Massi OFM, vicar apostolic of Hankow, was accepted in 1935. The Irish would take over four administrative regions in the province of Hupeh. The capital was Suihsien and the nearest town to Hankow was Anlu.

Seven Irish friars arrived at Shanghai on 18 December 1935 and were joined by Connaughton as head of the mission. They headed for Anlu to learn Chinese and had their initial pastoral experience in the summer of 1936. In June 1937 Propaganda Fide erected the Prefecture Apostolic of Suihsien and Mgr Connaughton was installed as prefect on 4 October 1937. By then four Irish friars were studying Chinese in Peking, another acted as procurator in Hong Kong and six worked in the prefecture along with two Italian friars and two Chinese secular priests. A year later the missionaries were living at eight stations and serving thirty-five Christian communities. A minor seminary had opened in Anlu and work had begun on a residence for the prefect at Suihsien.

10 The church and residence built by Irish Franciscans in Suishen (FLK).

War broke out between the Japanese and Chinese in July 1937. The friars
opened camps for thousands of refugees as the Japanese army approached. Anlu
fell in October 1938 and Suihsien the following spring. The front stabilized with
one mission, Liaochiatsi, under Chinese control and the rest under the Japanese.
Missionaries in the Chinese area worked as normal and maintained contact with
Ireland. Those under the Japanese were treated well at first. The refugee camps
flew the tricolour. But the situation changed drastically after the attack on Pearl
Harbour in December 1941 and English speakers were treated with suspicion.
Bank accounts were frozen. All missionaries except those in Anlu were arrested in
April and placed under house arrest in a Franciscan College near Hankow.[30]
Three friars joined Mgr Connaughton and his companions in Anlu in February
1944 but these too were placed under house arrest. Missionaries could not return
to their stations until after the Pacific War ended in August 1945. The strain of the
war years took its toll. Several friars, no longer fit for ministry, returned home. By
1947 all missions were functioning, looked after by twelve priests, though not all
Irish. Five more priests and five Franciscan Missionaries of the Divine
Motherhood arrived in August of that year.

Conflict between the Communists and Nationalists was dormant during the
war but re-emerged in 1945. The Communists attacked the region and by
Christmas 1947 all areas except Anlu were under their control.[31] On the
instructions of the Franciscan delegate general, the Irish withdrew. It was

30 Hoade, 'Chinese mission memories', pp 15–22.   31 Ibid., pp 33–7.

anticipated that the Nationalists would retake the area with American help but this was discontinued and the Communists triumphed. Most of the Irish escaped and the four Chinese friars went underground. Mgr Connaughton and an Irish companion maintained a Catholic presence under house arrest in Anlu. Rome ordered Mgr Connaughton to resign. He left Hankow on Good Friday 1951 and went into exile in California. Dominic Ch'en OFM, took over and was probably martyred by Red Guards in Hankow in 1970. The last Irish friar left in December 1951. A few Irish friars worked in the international friaries in Hong Kong and Singapore. Immediately after the Second World War two Irish friars went to work in Ernakulam, Cochin, India but soon withdrew.

SOUTH AFRICA

An Irish friar, Daniel Burke, accompanied Bishop Raymund Griffith OP, to South Africa in 1837.[32] Another friar, Bonaventure Bradley, was a chaplain during the Boer War. The area around Kokstad, South Africa, under the control of the Bavarian Franciscans since 1932, was eventually raised to the status of a vicariate in 1939 with Sigebald Kurz OFM as bishop.[33] The bishop and most of the friars were interned as enemy aliens during the war and following their release were depleted in numbers and unable to get help from Germany. The apostolic delegate, Archbishop Martin Lucas, whose secretary was an Irish friar, invited the Irish Franciscans to help the Germans. The first four friars arrived in Kokstad on 27 December 1946. Three more followed in 1947. The minister provincial, Evangelist McBride, decided to join them and was consecrated bishop on 25 July 1949. Two years later there were about 4,500 Catholics out of a total population of 400,000 in the diocese (1%).[34] There were thirteen Irish priests, nine German and an Austrian, with two Irish brothers and four German. Seventy nuns, fifty catechists and eighty teachers helped in eleven mission stations and seventy-six outstations. Bishop McBride retired in 1978 and was replaced by Bishop Wilfrid Napier OFM. Born in the diocese, he had joined the Franciscans and studied in Ireland and Belgium before his ordination in 1970. He reported that Catholics numbered some 45,000 out of a total population of 925,000 (5%). They were served by 18 Franciscans, 47 nuns and 127 catechists. Bishop Napier moved to Durban in 1992 as archbishop and was made a cardinal in 2001. Another Irish friar, Liam Slattery, took over as bishop in Kokstad in 1994.

32 B. Doyle, *The Irish contribution to the church in South Africa 1820–1900* (1963, copy in FLK MS XV14).
33 M. Dischl, *Transkei for Christ – a history of the Catholic Church in the Transkeian territories* (1982), pp 163, 255–80.   **34** All statistics are based on copies of reports to Propaganda Fide in Kokstad Diocesan Archives.

A second mission in South Africa was established when Archbishop Lucas invited the friars to staff a major seminary for white clerics.[35] This was before the introduction of apartheid. Two Irish friars started a temporary seminary at Queenstown in 1948. A new seminary opened in Pretoria on 1 March 1951 with a staff of twelve Irish friars. It was decided to desegregate the seminary in 1977 even though it was in a designated white area. The faculty of philosophy moved to Hammanskraal in 1985 due to overcrowding in Pretoria. The friars have recently withdrawn from the seminary.

This mission was extended when the bishop of Johannesburg invited the Irish Franciscans to take over much of the Vaal Triangle south of the city. The first friars arrived in 1955. They ministered in two large white parishes and a retreat centre as well as a series of large black townships, including Sharpville where the massacre of 1960 was one of the factors that ultimately led to the overthrow of the apartheid regime. The friars worked closely with the black population in their struggle for social justice.[36] Further to the south, the friars ran a minor seminary and parish at Boksburg. They took over a new coloured township called Reiger Park in 1965 and developed a large complex with medical facilities, a day centre, language laboratories, computer services and small factories.

Irish, Bavarian and English Franciscans (the latter both working in the province of Kwazulu Natal) functioned independently of each other in the country and candidates for the order had to go to Europe for their formation. Re-organisation was necessary to implant the order and thus the Franciscan Federation of Southern Africa was formed in 1977. A novitiate was opened at Besters in 1980 followed by a student house near Pretoria in 1980 and a pre-novitiate in 1982. Initially friars remained members of their home provinces until the vice-province of Our Lady Queen of Peace in Southern Africa was set up on 12 April 1985 with eighty solemnly professed friars and ten in simple vows. About half were Irish. It became a full province in 1999. The province is flourishing and ministries have been re-arranged: for example, the seminary in Pretoria was handed back to the hierarchy, non-friar priests were brought into Kokstad and the friars have established a mission in Namibia. Seventeen Irish friars still work in South Africa.

The Irish friars extended their mission northwards into Southern Rhodesia when they signed a contract with the archbishop of Salisbury in 1958 to run the parish of Waterfalls.[37] The following year they agreed to take over the rural

35 J.B. Brain, *St John Vianney seminary* (2002).   36 St Anthony's Education Centre (Boksburg, 1982 & 1985) and other material in FLK, 'Other Mission Box'; P. Noonan, *They're burning the churches. The final dramatic events that scuttled apartheid* (2003).   37 *Rhodesia Franciscans 1958–1972* (Salisbury, 1972); *The Rhodesian Franciscans* (Salisbury, 1975).

districts of Charter and Buhera to the south of the capital. The friary at Waterfalls opened in April 1960 and the first friars moved into the rural area in November. The new mission expanded steadily despite the tensions caused by UDI in 1965. By 1975 the mission consisted of the friary in Waterfalls and eight rural missions staffed by twenty friars who also established schools and health clinics. The civil war of the late 1970s caused major problems. Three friars were expelled by the Smith government and several suffered severe stress. At one stage only four missionaries were active.

The war ended in 1980 and Rhodesia became Zimbabwe and Salisbury changed to Harare. The new government was favourable towards the friars who had been identified with the struggle of the black population during the troubles. The first local vocations went to Ireland for formation. The civil war had hindered efforts to develop a novitiate but it opened in Marondera in 1983 before moving to Gandachibvuvu. A postulancy started in Nharira in 1986. The professed initially joined their South African *confrères* in Pretoria until a Franciscan institute for philosophy and theology opened in Livingstone in Zambia in 1988 to serve the needs of the Franciscans, Conventuals and Capuchins in East Africa, Mozambique, Zambia and Zimbabwe. It now has a permanent campus in Lusaka. Recently the friars in conjunction with four other religious groups opened a theological institute at Tafara, Harare. Students begin their studies in Lusaka before finishing in Tafara.

In 1977 the mission in Rhodesia became an autonomous entity alongside Kokstad Mission and the Custody of South Africa, all of them dependent on the Irish province, within the Franciscan Federation of Southern Africa. When the vice-province of Our Lady Queen of Peace in Southern Africa was set up in 1985 Zimbabwe remained outside and became the Custody of the Good Shepherd on 9 October 1990. It enjoys some autonomy while still dependent on the Irish province.

The archbishop of Salisbury intended that Enkledorn would become a diocese and this remained the situation until 1990. The major achievement of the friars was a system of training catechists that was adopted throughout the country. At the initial custodial chapter held in 1992 the friars made inculturation their first priority, followed by work for justice and peace, youth ministry and healing. They handed back some of their missions, thus allowing them to move into other dioceses.[38] This would facilitate implanting both the order and the church. Two years later a third of the rural mission was handed back to the diocese. With the help of friars from other provinces, houses with viable communities have replaced

---

38 'Minutes of the Custodial Chapter' as reported in *Seanchas na mBráithre* (Winter, 1992).

the old mission stations. The total number of friars including those in formation is twenty-eight, with all but five of them Zimbabweans. There are hopes that Zimbabwe will eventually become a full province.

CENTRAL AND LATIN AMERICA

Irish missionary activity to Central and Latin America was a mid-twentieth century phenomenon. The region was regarded by many churches worldwide as having been evangelized in the sixteenth century and the Irish diaspora there was sparse. Indeed any Irish missionary activity in the region tended to concentrate on that diaspora, especially the Irish community in Argentina.[39] When Pope John XXIII appealed for priests to look after the neglected Catholics of Latin America an Irish friar went to Chile in 1964 after the local Franciscans sought help. By 1972 seven Irish priests were in the country helping in three friaries. They experienced difficult times under the oppressive Pinochet military regime. Some were placed under house arrest for a time and others were added to the regime's 'black list' and subject to surveillance. They helped to publicize abroad the repression taking place in the country and to aid its victims. Due to changing circumstances, it was decided to leave Chile in 1977. Some of the friars went to California to work with Hispanic migrants and one remained behind until the government expelled him in 1983. A handful of friars also worked in Bolivia from 1974 and the last of them left in 1988.

Also in the spirit of John XXIII, the Irish friars accepted an invitation to minister in El Salvador. The first four took over the rural parish of Gotera in the diocese of San Miguel in 1968. They helped form basic Christian communities as outlined in the Medellín documents. More friars were available to serve in El Salvador after the withdrawal from Chile and Bolivia and by 1984 there were nine Irish priests and two deacons there. In 1974 the minister general gathered the various Franciscan entities in Central America into a federation. This became the vicariate of Our Lady of Guadalupe on 12 December 1983 and a full province on 7 June 1987. The Irish played a major part in building up the new entity, continue to do so and have filled many posts of responsibility, particularly in formation. One was elected vicar provincial and later became the definitor general for Latin America between 1997 and 2003 while another ran the order's Justice and Peace desk at the General Curia in Rome. There are now seven Irishmen in the

---

39 The history of the Latin American missions is based on items from the *Irish Definitory News* and the minutes of the Irish Provincial Chapters. See also P. Kirby, 'Forging links: the Irish church in Latin America' (1992).

province, serving in Guatemala, El Salvador, Honduras, Costa Rica and Columbia.

The Irish friars living and working in Latin America were influenced not only by the wind of change blowing through the post-Vatican II Church but also to a greater or lesser extent by socio-political ideas then current and influenced by liberation theology. Missionary work in Latin America in the 1970s and 1980s had a marked political and social impact on Irish orders and on Irish foreign policy. The missionaries encountered a church in Latin America which espoused the spirit of Vatican II energetically. This involved greater pastoral work in a community-based church with the active involvement of lay people. As a result of the political and social upheaval so prevalent in Latin America during that period, the church was politicized and was central to social justice movements. Franciscans in El Salvador played a vital role in providing first-hand accounts of the civil war there during the 1980s and the impact the violence was having on their communities. This evidence, along with evidence from other sources, led to the formation of a vocal human rights lobby group in Ireland and on occasion, influenced Irish foreign policy positions adopted in the European Community and the United Nations.

CONCLUSION

Since the seventeenth century the Irish Franciscans have laboured as missionaries on all five Continents. The Scottish mission was a difficult and frustrating one and, in spite of heroic efforts by the friars, had little chance of succeeding given the hostile attitude of the authorities and the inadequate resources, both personnel and financial. The mission to Newfoundland offered a better chance of success since the friars had the resources to establish the necessary structures for the growth of a strong and flourishing community. Their aim was to build up the local church and when that was achieved they withdrew.

In contrast to the above, the missionaries to Australia evolved an intentional dual purpose, namely, to develop already existing church structures and to establish the order. They succeeded in doing both. The Chinese mission had a similar dual aim but its implementation was seriously disrupted by the war and the expulsion of the missionaries by the communist authorities. However, they did have the satisfaction of knowing that both the local church and the Franciscans survived the years of persecution. The mission to southern Africa set out initially to develop the local church through attending to its pastoral needs in a broad sense and the training of diocesan clergy. It was only after several decades and when they were also more clearly aware of their own Franciscan identity that they turned their attention to attempts to implant the order in the area, which they did very successfully.

The various missions to Latin America were somewhat different from the above, apart from China, in that the invitation to work there as missionaries came from Franciscan sources, either from Franciscan bishops or from a centuries-old province, as in the case of Chile. The Irish friars were invited to collaborate with their local *confrères*.

A large number of Irish friars have ministered on the missions. In the fifty years of the Zimbabwean mission alone forty-two friars, most of them Irish, have served for longer or shorter periods. All have given generous service characterized by a strong innate sympathy for the oppressed. But the friars have also been greatly enriched from their experiences. The image of the empty vessel may be used to describe the process: they came like empty vessels and were filled by the host peoples and their cultures. They learned new forms of relationships within the Christian community where service and a strong option for the poor shaped their self-understanding both as Christians and as Franciscans.

Franciscan chalices, 1600–50[1]

MAŁGORZATA KRASNODĘBSKA-D'AUGHTON

On 13 July 1654 in Brussels, the dispossessed landowner Bernard O'Flaherty handed over sacred objects belonging to the Franciscan friary of Kilconnell, Co. Galway to Fr Patrick O Aodh OFM. O'Flaherty appears to have brought the objects to the Continent for safekeeping at the request of the friars in Kilconnell. A few weeks later, on 10 August 1654, an inventory of the Kilconnell vestments and altar plate was endorsed by the sacristan of St Anthony's College, Louvain. That inventory listed over thirty vestments as well as three silver gilt chalices, one silver chalice and a ciborium.[2]

Subsequent lists of the Kilconnell material and inventories from other Irish Franciscan houses, scrupulously compiled by the friars in the latter half of the seventeenth century, along with other written sources provide us with an invaluable insight into the quantity of late medieval and early modern liturgical objects once owned by the Franciscan order in Ireland. When compared with the number of surviving objects, these documents present a distressing picture of the loss of objects dating to this period.

Existing evidence, both written and artistic discussed in this essay, shows that the majority of liturgical objects associated with the Franciscans were chalices produced between 1600 and 1650. It is possible, on the basis of such evidence, to document chalices made for friaries between 1600 and 1649:

Buttevant and Timoleague (1600)	Galway (1629)
Kilkenny (1606)	Adare (1630)
Cork (1610)	Carrick (1632)
Ardfert and Cork (1611)	Donegal, Galway, Kilconnell, Meelick,
Clonmel (1614)	Rosserrilly and Trim (1633)
Meelick (1616)	Cork, Elphin, Meelick and Monaghan (1634)
Limerick (1619)	Meelick (1635)
Galway and Kilconnell (1621)	Kilconnell (1636)
Kilkenny (1622)	Galway, Meelick and Kilconnell (1638)
Limerick (1626)	Cork (1639)

1 I wish to thank the following individuals for their generous assistance in the preparation of this paper: Edel Bhreathnach, Mark D'Aughton, Alison FitzGerald, John McCafferty, Rachel Moss, Elizabeth Mullins, Tessa Murdoch, †Conor O'Brien, Colmán Ó Clabaigh and Raghnall Ó Floinn as well as the members of the Irish Franciscan province for accommodating my work. The research on this paper was carried out in the UCD Mícheál Ó Cléirigh Institute as part of the IRCHSS-funded project on the material culture of the mendicant orders in Ireland. 2 FLK MS C426. F.J. Bigger, 'The Franciscan friary of Killconnell'

Kilconnell, Limerick and   Kilconnell, Meelick and Rosserrilly (1640)
   Cork (1627)   Clonmel (1645, 1648)
Kilconnell and Timoleague (1628)   Kilconnell (1649)

The number of silver objects made for the Irish Franciscans and the frequent donations to individual friaries indicate a period of intense silver production that goes beyond the simple provision of chalices for liturgical purposes. Why would the friars of Kilconnell need more than ten chalices and the friars of Meelick more than six at a given time? This is indicative of an increased number of friars in the Irish province, as a chalice was needed for each friar-priest in a community to celebrate private masses every day.[3] An increase in the production of altar plate for Franciscan friaries reflects a trend of Catholic silverware in general in the first half of the seventeenth century that exceeds the number of extant Protestant ecclesiastical silver objects produced during the reigns of James I and Charles I. Furthermore, the growth in silver objects probably corresponds to a new vitality among the friars' patrons.[4]

This chapter concentrates on the creation of early seventeenth-century Irish Franciscan chalices by analyzing evidence regarding iconography, makers, donors and beneficiaries.

THE MAKERS AND THE STYLE

In his seminal study on Irish altar plate, J.J. Buckley listed over one hundred and forty chalices made for different religious houses, including the Franciscan ones, during the period under discussion. Four of these chalices bear the names of their Irish makers. Thadeus Gahy inscribed his name on the 1630 chalice, Richard Roch on the 1632 chalice, John O Mullarkey on the 1633 chalice and William Gallant on the 1641 chalice.[5] Chalices engraved with the makers' names provide significant evidence for the production of early seventeenth-century altar plate and allow us to place other silver objects more firmly within an Irish context.

An example of such an object is the chalice made by John O Mullarkey, which was donated to the Franciscan friary in Donegal. This is the only surviving Franciscan chalice produced in the first half of the seventeenth century to have an identifiable maker and the only surviving chalice from that period to have an inscription written in Irish. This is important as John O Mullarkey describes himself on the inscription as silversmith to the O'Donnells, who were the founding patrons of Donegal friary. A certain Edmund Mullarkey, probably a

(1900–1), p. 156; Jennings, 'Chalices and books of Kilconnell abbey (1944–5)'.   **3** Ó Clabaigh, *Franciscans in Ireland*, p. 107.   **4** T. Sweeney, *Irish Stuart silver: a short descriptive catalogue* (1995), pp 7–8.   **5** J.J. Buckley, *Some Irish altar plate* (1943), pp 5, 52–4, 58, 85 (plates XVII, figs 1 and 2, plate XXXII, fig. 1).

relative of John the silversmith, was a member of the community at that time.[6] This possibility suggests that both the patrons and makers of chalices, occasionally had family associations with friaries.

When compared with continental and English chalices of the same period, Irish chalices can be distinguished by certain characteristics: they retain the medieval shape of their feet, which are either hexagonal or octagonal, their feet are tall, the knop tends to be globular, the chalices are simple and usually limit their engraved decoration to the foot. A chalice was primarily a liturgical vessel used to contain the Eucharistic wine that was a symbolic manifestation of the wine of the Last Supper and of Christ's blood shed on the Cross. The very form of the chalice, that is its shape and imagery, helped express visually its symbolic meanings. As the chalice was held by a large knop, it displayed the image of the Cross or the Crucifixion engraved on its elongated foot. Given the limited nature of visual expression in the Irish Catholic church at the time, which lacked Baroque frescoes and altarpieces common in Counter-Reformation continental churches, these chalices provided the faithful with important images and symbols of their faith.[7]

The sheer number of chalices, their form and the fact that Irish makers are named on some of these chalices, indicate that Catholic silver, including silver associated with the Irish Franciscans, was produced in Ireland. Although the newly established Company of Goldsmiths of Dublin introduced compulsory silver marking with a date-letter stamp starting with the year 1638–9, the law appears not to have been immediately implemented and marks are hardly ever found on surviving Catholic silver produced before 1650. It is of interest that a chalice stamped with Dublin marks for 1641 was made by William Gallant, unlikely to be a Catholic silversmith, while a Franciscan chalice given to Timoleague friary bears London hallmarks for 1633–4.[8]

Early seventeenth-century chalices donated to Franciscans friaries are marked by distinctive regional styles, which correspond to the styles of other Catholic chalices from the same period. Regional styles can be discerned for Cork, Limerick, Kilkenny and Galway. While no Franciscan chalice from that time survives which might be associated with Dublin, a Dublin style of chalice can be identified on the basis of non-Franciscan silver objects. Dublin chalices dated to the 1630s have a deep bowl, a globular knop chased with rosettes, and a hexagonal foot with slightly incurved base lines.[9]

6 Mooney, 'Friars and friary of Donegal', p. 12. **7** C. Hernmarck, *The art of the European silversmith* (1977); C. Oman, *English church plate* (1957), pp 39–153; idem, *English engraved silver* (1978), pp 33–70; A. M. Claessens-Peré, *Silver for Sir Anthony* (1999); P. Glanville, *Silver in Tudor and early Stuart England* (1990). **8** Buckley, *Some Irish altar plate*, p. 185. I am grateful to the late Conor O'Brien for these two references. **9** For example, the Russell-Taaffe chalice made by William Gallant (1641) (Buckley, *Some Irish*

Chalices produced in Cork have a deep bowl, often with an engraved calyx of six sepals, and a hexagonal stem (Plate 10). The knop is either globular with vertical flutings or decorated with openwork motifs. The hexagonal pyramidal foot with incurved base lines has facets, alternately plain and engraved: one with the Cross or the Crucifixion, and the others with an acanthus motif.[10] Chalices associated with Limerick are similar in their proportions to Cork chalices: their bowls are deep, their knops globular and feet hexagonal (Plate 11). However, the base lines of their feet are only slightly incurved. The knops of Limerick chalices are either fluted or retain late Gothic features of pointed leaf designs, openwork and circular bosses.[11] Franciscan chalices donated to the Kilkenny friary have a distinctive flattened knop engraved with deep relief patterns and low feet with straight base lines.[12] Early seventeenth-century Galway chalices have chased and pierced knops reminiscent of late Gothic and octagonal pyramidal feet with straight base lines (Plate 12). Galway chalices from the 1630s have globular knops chased with rosettes and hexagonal feet with slightly incurved base lines (Plate 13). It is possible that new styles of chalice, replicated by chalices associated with Galway, Cork and Dublin, were introduced into Ireland in the 1630s.[13]

Despite their regional differences many Franciscan chalices dated between 1600 and 1650, employ a mixture of pointed Gothic motifs, seen especially on knops and feet, and Renaissance motifs, such as foliate scrolls or egg-and-dart designs. This combination of Gothic and Renaissance elements suggests likely influences from the Low Countries or Germany, where these two styles featured together on silver produced in the early sixteenth century.[14]

A new Spanish style of chalice with a decorative baluster stem and a domed foot appeared in Ireland c.1625. The style rarely occurs on early seventeenth-century Irish chalices, but a less ornate format is adopted for the Timoleague chalice (1628). Another new shape of chalice was introduced to Ireland c.1640: the foot became either octafoil or hexafoil and a baluster knop with cherubs' heads replaced the earlier globular knop. These new designs first appeared on chalices

altar plate, p. 85, plate XXXII, fig. 1); the Kelly chalice made for the Augustinian priory in Dublin in the 1630s. **10** The Nicholas Sinan chalice (1600); the Dale-Browne chalice (1600); the William Ferris chalice (1610); the William Ferris chalice (1611); also the Elina Moirane chalice (1611) and the James Daniel chalice (1614). See Buckley, *Some Irish altar plate*, pp 30, 35, 36, plate IX fig. 1. **11** The John Farrell chalice (1619); the Anastasia Rice chalice (1626); the Robert Creagh chalice (1621); the Richard Arthur chalice (1626); the Creagh-White chalice (1627). See Buckley, *Some Irish altar plate*, pp 39, 42, 48, 50, plate XIII fig. 2, plate XVI figs 1 and 2, plate XV fig. 3. **12** The Walter Archer chalice (1606); the John Brenan chalice (1622); the O'Fogarty chalice (1598); the Robert Woolferston chalice (1612); the Barnaby Patrick chalice (1613). See Buckley, *Some Irish altar plate*, pp 33, 45, 27–28, 36, 37, plate XI fig. 1, plate XV fig. 1, plate VII fig. 1, plate X fig. 2, plate XII fig. 1. **13** The Font-Butler chalice (1621, Galway); the French-Darcy chalice (1638, Galway); the Maria Montij Jennings chalice (1633, Rosserrilly); the Paul Mulgeehy chalice (1640, Meelick). See Buckley, *Some Irish altar plate*, pp 44, 75, 55, 84, plate XVIII fig. 2. **14** J.J. Murray, *Flanders and England. A cultural bridge* (1985), p. 42. See also P. Fuhring, *Ornament prints in the Rijksmuseum II* (2004).

associated with prominent ecclesiastics who played an active role in Irish international politics such as Malachy O Queely, and they reflect an increased exposure of the Irish church to the art of Counter-Reformation Europe.[15]

Despite the fact that from the mid-1620s Irish silversmiths became familiar with the new opulent Baroque style they continued to employ older styles on their chalices well into the late seventeenth century. Moreover, the varying regional styles of Franciscan chalices employ different iconographic themes and types of script on their inscriptions. This suggests that they were produced in different workshops, which were subject to diverse influences. For example, Cork chalices tend to have inscriptions executed in upper case and employ the motif of the Cross as the Tree of Life, while Galway chalices have inscriptions in lower case and introduce the theme of the Mercy Seat.

ICONOGRAPHY: THE CROSS AND THE CRUCIFIXION

The most common iconographic themes encountered on Franciscan chalices produced between 1600 and 1650 are the Cross and the Crucifixion. Variants of these themes are numerous and traditional: they range from simple crosses, to the images of the Tree of Life, to elaborate Crucifixions with the Instruments of the Passion and accompanying figures set in the midst of architectural settings, and finally, to the complex imagery of the Mercy Seat.

When the Cross is depicted as the Tree of Life, plant scrolls are engraved sprouting from the top of the Cross and/or on either side at the foot of the Cross (Plate 14). The identification of the Cross as the Tree of Life which had its source in biblical, patristic, apocryphal and liturgical texts, received a new stimulus from *The Meditations on the Life of Christ*, a text that encouraged an emotive response to the life and death of Christ.[16] It enjoyed great popularity in late medieval Europe and was translated into Irish around 1443.[17] The text describes the Cross as a tree full of leaves and flowers, which bore fruit for Christians to eat. Many chalices depict the Cross as the life-giving tree, where a Crucifixion scene is flanked by designs of flowering and fruit-bearing plants.[18]

Crucifixion images on Franciscan chalices often include the Instruments of the Passion. For example, the John Farrell chalice (1619) has a Crucifixion scene flanked by the column to which Christ was tied, pincers with three nails, a spear,

15 The Richard Arthur chalice (1625), see Buckley, *Some Irish altar plate*, p. 46, plate XVIII fig. 1 and also J. Hunt, 'The Arthur cross' (1955). The Malachy O Queely chalice (1641), see Buckley, *Some Irish altar plate*, pp 86–7, plate XXXI fig. 1. **16** G. Schiller, *Iconography of Christian art* (1969), ii, p. 314. **17** Ó Clabaigh, *Franciscans in Ireland*, pp 102, 111, 176. **18** The Nicholas Sinan chalice (1600); the Dale-Browne chalice (1600); the William Ferris chalice (1610); the Elina Moirane chalice (1611); the James Daniel chalice (1614).

scourges and a ladder (Plate 15). On other chalices, the Instruments of the Passion not only appear as part of the Crucifixion on the foot, but are also grouped around the bowl or around the knop.[19] The recurrence of this motif on chalices reflects the popularity of the cult of the Instruments of the Passion, which developed during the Middle Ages. These are often depicted on Irish tombs, wayside and market crosses,[20] and their presence on chalices assumes a greater significance: the chalice becomes a symbol of Christ's sacrifice that is re-enacted during Mass.

The number of Instruments is frequently limited to a spear, which is shown as pointing at Christ's side.[21] Emphasis on the spear is a visual reminder of the origins of the Eucharist, as expressed by John the Evangelist who described how a soldier opened Christ's side with a spear, and 'immediately there came out blood and water' (Jn 19:34). It also reflects a special devotion to Christ's side wound and a belief that the wound allowed direct access to Christ's heart as the seat of love.[22] The blood drops issuing from the side wound, from the wounds in his hands and his feet are a common motif on Franciscan chalices of the period. The image forms a visual response to the devotion to the Five Wounds, which became popular in late medieval Europe. In Irish art the figure of Christ displaying the Five Wounds was carved on late medieval tombs, crosses and at least on one font,[23] which indicates that the image was not limited to a funerary context. The Franciscans, who had a special devotion to the Five Wounds due to their affinity with the stigmata of St Francis, may have been instrumental in spreading such cults in Ireland.[24]

The image of Five Wounds had many aspects to it: it reminded the faithful of Christ's suffering and death on the Cross; it carried an eschatological significance bringing to mind the Last Judgment, when Christ will be recognized by those who pierced him (Rev 1:7), and devotion to the Five Wounds was especially linked to indulgences and deliverance from Purgatory.[25] It also had an immediate Eucharistic application. The Eucharistic aspect of the Five Wounds is expressed in continental and English images of the chalice of life or the well of life. On such late medieval images the blood from the wounds of Christ is shown as being

See note 10 above.   **19** The William Ferris chalice (1634, drawing in FLK); the Everard-Naish chalice (1648). The Instruments of the Passion are engraved on the knop of the Font-Brown chalice (1621).   **20** C. Tait, 'Irish images of Jesus' (2001), pp 50–1.   **21** Examples include the William Ferris chalices (1610 and 1611); the James Daniel chalice (1627) has the spear and the lance with a sponge.   **22** E. Duffy, *The stripping of the altars* (1992), pp 238–48. Tait, 'Irish images of Jesus', p. 51.   **23** H.A. King, 'Late medieval crosses in County Meath' (1984), plate XVIII; M.M. Phelan, 'Irish sculpture portraying the Five Wounds of our Saviour' (1987).   **24** Tait, 'Irish images of Jesus', p. 51. Ó Clabaigh, 'The cult of St Francis'. **25** Duffy, *The stripping of the altars*, p. 246.

collected into a single chalice or several chalices usually held aloft by angels.[26] The image was known in Ireland in the late fifteenth century and it appears in a Franciscan context on a panel on the MacMahon tomb in Ennis friary dating to *c.*1470, and is preserved on at least two seventeenth-century carvings.[27] The Eucharistic aspect of Christ's wounds is also mentioned in late medieval religious poetry in Irish, where poets describe the powerful image of Christ 'lying in his wine-blood' or Christ washing away our sins by using his wine-blood.[28]

Some Crucifixion images on chalices include the motif of the skull and bones engraved at the foot of the Cross[29] (Plates 16, 19). The skull identifies the site of the Crucifixion as Golgotha or 'the place of the skull' (Jn 19:17). The skull also refers to the skull of Adam, and it visually expresses the typology of Christ as the second Adam, which was based on biblical and exegetical texts as well as on apocryphal stories that viewed the hill of Golgotha as the burial place of Adam's skull. In late medieval Ireland this image finds its expression in sculpture as well as in Gaelic poetry.[30] According to one poem, Christ found Adam's race, for which he had been searching, in his side wound. Other poems speak of Christ's blood falling on Adam's race and of Adam robbing the Tree of the Tithe through his sin and Christ's Cross undoing the harm.[31]

The image of the Mercy Seat, which combines the Holy Trinity with the Crucifixion, appears on chalices associated with the west of Ireland, as far as the surviving evidence allows us to discern[32] (Plates 16, 17, 18). A popular theme in late medieval art, it appeared in Irish art from the mid-fourteenth century onwards.[33] On Franciscan chalices, the figure of God the Father wearing a papal tiara, holds the crucified Christ aloft, and the dove of the Holy Spirit hovers above the scene. Mary and John the Evangelist engraved on either side of the Mercy Seat, do not occur in other Irish media, but they are found in contemporary and earlier continental art. This suggests that the iconography of the Mercy Seat as depicted on chalices may not draw from native examples, but rather looks to continental models as sources of inspiration.[34]

---

26 C.M. Kauffmann, *Biblical imagery in medieval England* (2003), pp 252–3. **27** P. Harbison, *The crucifixion in Irish art* (2000), plates 18, 22, 28, 29. **28** S. Ryan, 'Reign of blood', pp 147–8. **29** Examples include: the Font-Butler chalice (1621); the Anastasia Rice chalice (1626); the Elizabeth Forth chalice (1633); the William Ferris chalice (1634); the Boetius Egan chalice (1634); the Francis Guiffe chalice (1638); the French-Darcy chalice (1638). See Buckley, *Some Irish altar plate*, pp 44, 48, 58 (plate XX fig. 1), 60, 73, 75. **30** Schiller, *Iconography of Christian art*, ii, pp 130–3; Harbison, *The Crucifixion in Irish art*, plates 32, 34. **31** Ryan, 'Reign of blood', pp 140–2. L. McKenna (ed.), *Philip Bocht O Huiginn*, (1931), pp xv–xviii. **32** The Font-Butler chalice (1621, Galway); the Boetius Egan chalice (1634, Elphin); the Anastasia Rice chalice (1626, Limerick). **33** H.M. Roe, 'Illustrations of the Holy Trinity in Ireland' (1979) and idem, 'Illustrations of the Holy Trinity in Ireland: additamenta' (1980).

It is possible that the presence of John and Mary in the scenes of the Mercy Seat was inspired by prints brought to Ireland from the Continent. This potential influence can be detected in particular in the image of the Mercy Seat on the chalice donated to Galway friary (1621) where the deep cut and nearly coarse outlines of the figures are strikingly similar to continental woodcuts (Plate 16). On the 1626 Anastasia Rice chalice made for the Limerick friars, the Mercy Seat is engraved with great finesse and evokes the near impressionistic depictions of the Holy Trinity by Albrecht Dürer on his famous woodcut and painting of that theme, both of which he executed in 1511 (Plate 18).[35] Books with mass-produced woodcuts and engravings of devotional images, including those by Dürer, might have been known in sixteenth-century Ireland. Continental prints were definitely used as source for imagery on English recusant silver, as exemplified by a late seventeenth-century paten from Southwell Cathedral displaying the image of the Virgin and Child, copied after Dürer.[36] In the early seventeenth century single sheets with printed images arrived in Ireland as illustrated by the incident of a Spanish ship seized in Cork in 1617 that carried Catholic books and 'diverse printed pages with pictures'.[37] Printed sheets, brought from the Low Countries were also distributed by a Franciscan in 1632 in the diocese of Cashel. These included texts relating to the Franciscan order as well as printed images of St Francis.[38]

ICONOGRAPHY: ST FRANCIS AND OTHER FRANCISCAN SAINTS

The Passion of Christ, a devotion which played an important role in Franciscan spirituality, had a clear affinity with the stigmatisation of St Francis. The two events are engraved together on eight surviving Irish chalices from the seventeenth century[39] (Plate 19). The chalice donated to the Cork friars by John Colman and his wife Catherine Gould in 1639 depicts Christ crucified, with blood flowing from his wounds. On the panel immediate to the right of the Crucifixion, St Francis kneels with his arms outstretched to receive the stigmata. Drops of blood from the figure of Christ crucified are engraved directly above the figure of the seraphic Christ, whose wounds in turn are linked to those of Francis by five fine lines. An obvious visual link is thus established between the Cross and the stigmata.

34 Schiller, *Iconography of Christian art*, ii, plates 412, 774, 777–80.   35 P. Strieder, *Dürer* (1982), p. 314, plates 413–16.   36 B. Cunningham, 'Illustrations of the Passion of Christ in the *Seanchas Búrcach* manuscript' (2006), p. 20; Oman, *English engraved silver*, p. 65, plate 71.   37 Gillespie, *Reading Ireland*, p. 151.   38 For earlier prints of St Francis's stigmata see H. van Os (ed.), *The art of devotion in the late middle ages in Europe* (1994), plate 19 (Master Caspar, Regensburg, *c*.1470–80) and Strieder, *Dürer*, plate 168.   39 The Walter Archer chalice (1606) (Buckley, *Some Irish altar plate*, p. 33, plate X fig. 1); the Colman-Gould

The resemblance between Christ's wounds and Francis's stigmata was expressed in the life of St Francis, known as the *Legenda maior* composed by Bonaventure before 1263. The text compares Francis to an angel that bears on his own body the seal of the likeness of Christ crucified. It has been argued that the *topos* of Francis as the second Christ is present in late medieval Irish writing as well as being evoked visually.[40] The Irish friars were familiar with the *Legenda maior* as early as the fourteenth century, and references to the text of the *Legenda* are found in the poetry of the Franciscan bardic poet, Philip Bocht Ó hUiginn (d. 1487), who speaks of Francis being stamped by Jesus's Five Wounds.[41] The intercession through the wounds of Francis is evoked by Philip Bocht, who calls upon Francis bearing his wounded breast to plead for forgiveness for the sins that wounded Christ's breast.[42] The iconography of the seventeenth-century chalices reinforces such typology and is best exemplified by the Colman-Gould chalice, where Mary and St Francis, rather than a more usual John the Evangelist, witness the Crucifixion. Thus Mary and Francis intercede for humanity by sharing in the sufferings of Christ.

Other Franciscan saints were known in Ireland as evidenced by written sources, such as the lives of the saints or liturgical material as well as by visual representations.[43] However, Franciscan saints do not feature frequently on chalices. The rarity of such representations corresponds to the rarity of portrait figures on chalices in general, with figural scenes usually being limited to Christ and the Virgin Mary. The Colman-Gould chalice is quite exceptional in that it presents a family of the Franciscan saints: St Francis of Assisi, St Clare, St Elizabeth of Hungary and St Anthony of Padua accompanied by the images of Christ crucified and the Virgin Mary (Plate 20).

ICONOGRAPHY: MARY

Along with the Passion and St Francis, the next most popular iconographic theme on the Franciscan chalices is that of the Virgin Mary, who appears in three traditional guises: she is shown at the foot of the Cross, with the Child or as the Apocalyptic Woman. Interestingly, the majority of surviving chalices donated to

chalice (1639) (Buckley, *Some Irish altar plate*, p. 75, plate XXVII fig. 1); the Gerard Gould chalice (1641, made for the Dominicans); the Everard-Donoghue chalice/monstrance, (1667) (Buckley, *Some Irish altar plate*, p. 105); the Malachy ffalon chalice (1688); the Donnellan-Mostion chalice (1640); the 'Michael Davitt' chalice (mid-seventeenth century and 1874–5); undated chalice (Buckley, *Some Irish altar plate*, p. 186, plate LIX fig. 1). Also the early seventeenth-century crucifix reliquary, probably Spanish, now in the NMI, Turlough Park, Co. Mayo, J.M. Connaughton, 'Pendant reliquaries in Ireland: an overlooked tradition?' (2005), p. 104.   **40** Ó Clabaigh, 'The cult of St Francis', p. 156.   **41** McKenna, *Philip Bocht*, p. 129.   **42** Ibid., p. 130.   **43** Ó Clabaigh, 'The cult of St Francis', pp 152–3.

the Franciscans that bear the image of Mary include the names of women among their benefactors.[44]

When depicted at the foot of the Cross, Mary is shown not so much as a grief-stricken mother, but rather as an advocate who intercedes for humanity. She either kneels or stands at the Cross with her hands folded in prayer. The role of Mary as a mediator and advocate, expressed in the writings of the early church fathers, increased in popularity during the later Middle Ages, and found renewed expression in Irish poetry of the late medieval and early modern period as well as in Franciscan catechetical material composed in the first half of the seventeenth century (Plates 16, 17, 19).[45]

Portrayals of the Virgin and Child on Franciscan chalices present Mary as either seated or standing, holding the Infant. On the now missing Walter Archer chalice (1606), the Child's divinity was expressed as he pointed to 'the star' with his fingers in the act of blessing,[46] while on the later Everard-Donoghue chalice (1667), the Child holds a globe in his left hand. Such depictions present the mystery of the Incarnation, by alluding to the humanity and divinity of Christ, and they also stress Mary's status as the Mother of God. The choice of iconography on these chalices is fitting in a Franciscan context, since the Marian images appear alongside the Crucifixion and St Francis's stigmata.

The Everard-Donoghue chalice presents Mary not only as the mother, but also as the Apocalyptic Woman wearing a crown and star-covered garment, with the crescent moon under her feet (Rev 12:1, 5). The image of the Apocalyptic Woman holding the Child appears often in late medieval continental art and is particularly popular in sixteenth-century books of hours.[47] On the Anastasia Rice chalice (1626), Mary as the Apocalyptic Woman wears a crown, and her entire figure is enclosed within a sunburst, above her there are stars, beneath her feet, the crescent moon, and on either side is a cord with three Franciscan knots (Plate 21). She is without the Child. From the late sixteenth century, following the Council of Trent the image of the Apocalyptic Woman depicted as praying and without the Child, became the most frequent way of representing the Immaculate Conception of the Virgin. This image was subsequently made popular by Flemish printmakers. Devotion to the Immaculate Conception was a key doctrine promoted by Irish Franciscans based on the Continent. Luke Wadding, for instance, in one of his letters argued in relation to the images of the Immaculate Conception that they enabled the faithful to contemplate and admire the mystery

---

44 Mary at the Cross: the Font-Butler chalice (1621); the Colman-Gould chalice (1639); the Donellan-Mostion chalice (1640). Mary with the Child: the Walter Archer chalice (1606); the Everard-Donoghue chalice (1667). The Apocalyptic Woman: the Anastasia Rice chalice (1626).   45 S. Ryan, 'Popular religion in Gaelic Ireland, 1445–1645' (2002), pp 180–91. M. O'Reilly, 'Seventeenth-century Irish catechisms' (1996). 46 See n. 45.   47 S.L. Stratton, *The Immaculate Conception in Spanish art* (1994), p. 50.

of the Conception and that they were as important as words.[48] Several other Irish Franciscans wrote tracts on the doctrine of the Immaculate Conception.[49] The image and devotion were also known in Ireland. The feast was declared as a holy day in Ireland at synods in 1614 and 1631, and Mary was proclaimed patroness of Ireland as the Virgin of the Immaculate Conception in 1650.[50] Limerick and Waterford friars had an altar dedicated to the Immaculate Conception and it was to the altar of the Conception of the Blessed Virgin in Limerick friary that Anastasia Rice, a Franciscan tertiary, donated a chalice bearing the image of the Immaculate Conception in 1626.[51]

THE DONORS

Chalices donated to Franciscan friaries between 1600 and 1650 commemorate the names of the people who 'caused the chalices to be made' (*'me fieri fecit'* or *'me fieri fecerunt'*) and who in most cases were either members of the Franciscan order or lay benefactors.

One of the most exquisite Franciscan chalices is a silver gilt chalice commissioned by Boetius Egan, bishop of Elphin in 1634. Egan, who was a Franciscan, received his religious education in the Low Countries, where he would have encountered liturgical objects produced there. The iconography of the Egan chalice to a large extent calls to mind an earlier chalice made for the Galway friars in 1621. In contrast, however, it introduces a much richer variety of flora and fauna placed close to the Mercy Seat and which is reminiscent of decoration found in continental missals or books of hours[52] (Plates 17, 22, 23). When commissioning the chalice, Boetius Egan was probably familiar with different visual sources, but the choice of images may mirror the bishop's own reflections on biblical texts that describe certain images of nature. For example, the Prophet Isaiah paints a picture of a wasteland inhabited only by wild birds – a pelican, a bittern, an owl and a raven, and by wild plants – thorns, nettles and thistles, all of which are shown on the Egan chalice. According to Isaiah's prophecy, the wasteland in due time will flourish like a lily, a plant also engraved on the chalice, and the prophet encourages the fainthearted to take courage and not to fear, for God will bring their salvation (Isaiah 34–35, cf Ps 102). In a report sent to Rome in 1630 about the state of his diocese, Bishop Egan described the desolate

48 Ibid., pp 60–3, 86–7. **49** P. O'Dwyer, *Mary: a history of devotion in Ireland* (1988), p. 211. See M.W.F. Stone, 'The theological and philosophical accomplishments of the Irish Franciscans' in this volume. **50** O'Reilly, 'Seventeenth-century Irish catechisms', p. 106. **51** C. Tait, 'Art and cult of the Virgin Mary in Ireland, *c.*1500–1660' (2006), pp 178–9. **52** D. Bland, *A history of book illustration* (1969), plate 99.

condition of Catholics and the destruction of their churches. The Elphin friars, to whom the chalice was given by Bishop Egan, saw their friary demolished and its stones used to build a palace for a protestant bishop. Read against Egan's own letters and reports, the iconography of his chalice and the underlying biblical texts may allude to the contemporary political situation in Ireland and evoke a sense of hope, a notion further emphasized by the image of a peacock, an ancient symbol of resurrection (Plate 23).[53]

The choice of iconography on the Egan chalice as well as on other Franciscan chalices focuses on the spirituality of their donors. Franciscans such as Nicholas Sinan and John Farrell had the Cross depicted on their chalices as the Tree of Life flanked by the Instruments of the Passion. While the imagery of the chalices draws from standard iconography, the devotional nature of the images also reflected the spiritual training of the donor, who in the case of John Farrell was known as a preacher and Latin poet, who composed a poem on the stigmata of St Francis.[54] Members of the Third Order of St Francis, Anastasia Rice, Honora McCormockan[55] and Gerard Gould, are commemorated on three extant chalices, whose inscriptions mention the tertiary status of their donors.

Names of benefactors engraved on Franciscan chalices include Irish and Old English names. Chalices associated with the rural friaries of Adare, Donegal, Kilconnell, Meelick and Rosserilly usually carry Irish names, while the Old English names tend to feature on chalices donated to the friaries in the towns of Cork, Kilkenny, Galway and Limerick. Some Irish names, such as Mary O'Rourke Maguire who donated a chalice to the Donegal friars, represent families whose members had been for at least two centuries supporting the friars, thus showing a continuity of patronage into the seventeenth century.[56]

In the case of the Old English patrons, they represented prominent merchants and land owners of the period: the Flemings had considerable lands in Meath; Richard Barnewall was a landowner in Meath; William Sarsfield in Cork; Walter Coppinger was a leading Cork merchant and the Archers were a mercantile family in Kilkenny.[57] Members of these Old English families frequently belonged to the Franciscan First Order. The Barnewalls, Coppingers, Darcys, Everards,

---

53 C. Mooney, 'Bishop Boetius MacEgan of Elphin' (1952); J. Hagan, 'Miscellanea Vaticano-Hibernica, 1580–1631' (1914), pp 359–65. See also B. Cunningham, '"Zeal for God and souls": Counter-Reformation preaching' (2001), pp 124–5 on Geoffrey Keating's awareness of the current political and social situation as reflected in his theological writings.   54 On Nicholas Sinan see C. Mooney, 'The mirror of all Ireland' (1949), p. 13; on John Farrell see 'Franciscan altar plate' (1952), pp 53–4, also Giblin, *Liber Lovanensis*, pp 19, 134.   55 The Honora McCormockan chalice (1630) (Buckley, *Some Irish altar plate*, p. 53).   56 Mooney, 'Friars and friary of Donegal', pp 3–18.   57 A. Clarke, *The Old English in Ireland* (repr. 2000), pp 33, 51–2, 127, 135, 179; J.E. McKenna, *Diocese of Clogher: parochial records* (1920), i, p. 12; J. Robertson, 'Notes referring to the Archer chalice' (1899), pp 28–31.

Frenchs, Goulds and Sarsfields, whose names are inscribed on the early seventeenth-century chalices, held positions as provincials, guardians, confessors and definitors of the Franciscan order during that period.[58]

INVENTORIES

With the great exodus of Irish Catholics between 1650 and 1654, many friaries probably gave some of their portable objects to the exiles fleeing to the Continent, as the Kilconnell friary did.[59] Altar plate was rescued for its liturgical as well as its symbolic value. It is significant that during the Cromwellian wars only five pieces of altar plate were brought from Kilconnell to the Continent. They included two objects, now missing, which stood as landmarks in the history of the friary: the chalice dated 1409 given to the friary by its founder William O'Kelly and the ciborium given to the friary by William's son, Malachy O'Kelly, who introduced the Observant reform to Kilconnell.[60]

During the 1650s some church silver was also distributed locally among trusted lay people. Indeed there was an effort some years later by the religious to retrieve their plate from the laity. The provincial synod of Cashel in 1661 instructed parish priests 'to enquire diligently as to the whereabouts of chalices, vestments and other church furnishings deposited with the laity at the commencement of the Puritan persecution'.[61]

Inventories compiled towards the end of the century are important sources of information on early seventeenth-century chalices. In many cases these inventories contain detailed information on the date and material of a chalice, the name of a donor and even some brief description of its decoration. Some inventories also provide the names of people who received chalices into their custody. These inventories were compiled following a meeting held on 15 February 1698, when the definitory of the Irish Franciscan province took the decision to obey the Act of Banishment issued a few months earlier which exiled all Catholic clergy from the country.[62] It was decided at the meeting that

---

58 The Fleming-Barnewall chalice (1634); the Sarsfield-Coppinger chalice (1627); the French-Darcy chalice (1638); the Everard-Naish chalice (1648); the Colman-Gould chalice (1639); see Giblin, *Liber Lovanensis,* pp 21, 356 (John Barnewall); pp 26, 35, 356 (Richard Barnewall); pp 58, 65 (Francis Coppinger); pp 6, 17, 20, 24, 356 (Peter Darcy); pp 16, 23, 169 (John Everard); pp 5, 8, 16, 27, 36 (Joseph Everard); p. 30 (Francis French); p. 16 (John Gould); pp 58, 65 (Francis Gould); pp 17, 23 (John Sarsfield). See C. Lennon, 'The dissolution to the foundation of St Anthony's College, Louvain, 1530–1607' in this volume. **59** B. Millett, 'Survival and reorganization 1650–95' (1968), p. 5. **60** Bigger, 'The Franciscan friary of Killconnell' (1900–1), pp 145–67; 2 (1902), pp 3–20; 3 (1903–4), pp 11–5; Ó Clabaigh, *Franciscans in Ireland,* pp 44, 65. **61** Millett, 'Survival and reorganization', p. 14; Millett, 'Statues of the provincial synod of Cashel' (1966), pp 45–52. **62** See J. MacMahon, 'The silent century, 1698–1829', in this volume.

the furniture, utensils and other goods in the friaries were to be handed over for safekeeping to benefactors and patrons who were known for their attachment and loyalty to the friars, and every person receiving such items was to sign a document which stated what goods they had received. Besides, an inventory was to be made of the goods from each convent, which were given into the custody of others on this occasion, and these inventories were to be given to the syndics of the various convents. Neither the syndics nor the people to whom the goods were entrusted were to part with the inventories or the goods to any third person except with the express permission of the definitory or of the community of the convent to which the goods belonged.[63]

Late seventeenth-century inventories survive for the friaries of Kilconnell, Meelick, Killeigh and Donegal. Two documents dating to 1698 contain information on the silver plate from Kilconnell. The first document lists one ciborium, namely the Malachy O'Kelly ciborium, and twenty-seven chalices that range in date from the 1409 (the William O'Kelly chalice) to 1685 (the Hugo Kelly chalice), a fact that in itself is invaluable testimony to continuity of patronage enjoyed by the friary from the O'Kellys. A list of twenty-eight silver objects gives the dates of thirteen of them, of which all but one are earlier than 1650, and they include five items, which had been taken by Bernard O'Flaherty to Brussels in 1654. The second Kilconnell inventory gives the names of people and an itemized list of the objects they had received from the friars. One of the Catholics mentioned is Ulick Burke of Glinsk, who was a patron of Bishop Egan of Elphin. While the friars gave most of their altar plate away for safekeeping, they seem to have retained some chalices, including the chalice of their founder, William O'Kelly. Of thirty items of liturgical silverware listed in the two 1698 Kilconnell documents, only five can now be identified as being in known locations.[64]

An inventory of goods belonging to Meelick friary made in 1698 lists fourteen silver chalices, six of which date back to before 1651, one is dated to 1664, one to 1667 and the remaining ones are without dates. It also details the names of individuals into whose care the chalices were entrusted.[65] The first name on the list is that of Darcy Hamilton, a Catholic lawyer and benefactor of the Meelick friars.[66] Of the fourteen chalices listed in the inventory, only two can now be securely identified.[67]

63 Giblin, *Liber Lovanensis*, pp xxi, 225. 64 The Folain-Mac Sweeney chalice (1628); the Francis Guiffe chalice (1638); the Boetius Egan chalice (1634); the Maria Woodfall chalice (1640); the Simon Morris chalice (1683). 65 Millett, *Irish Franciscans*, 88; FLK MS M, notebook 1 of E.B. Fitzmaurice, pp 684–5. The Father Thadeus Kelly chalice, made in 1649 for the Kilconnell friary, is not listed in either document. 66 C. Giblin, 'Papers relating to Meelick friary' (1973), p. 69. The chalices were to be returned to the friars when requested 'att any tyme hereafter on demaund, casualtie of warr, robbery, fire or power by which the chalices may be lost or taken away'. 67 The Paul Mulgeehy chalice (1640); the Elizabeth Butler chalice

A 1698 document from Killeigh friary contains acknowledgements by eight individuals who confirm that they had received six silver chalices, one pewter chalice, two other chalices, two pyxes, a cup, an oil box, a ciborium and a bell as well as some vestments. Among the recipients were three lay people named Molloy, who were probably related to Hugh Molloy, guardian of Killeigh at the time and one of the signatories of the same document. William Shiell in turn, who received as many as three items might have been related to Michael Shiell, another signatory who became the guardian of Killeigh in 1693 and both probably were members of the Ó Siadhail family, who had long associations with the Franciscans in the midlands.[68]

An inventory of possessions from Donegal friary dated to 1699 lists four chalices as being lost through the deaths of the friars and twenty-one chalices as being given to various people, among them Laurence Colin, a parish priest and Thaddeus Coan, a merchant of Ballyshannon, who dealt with the financial affairs of the friars.[69] Donatus Mooney mentions that in 1600 Donegal friary had sixteen silver chalices and two ciboria. In 1602 the friary was raided and its valuables were taken: chalices were turned into drinking cups and vestments were torn. While some of these old chalices must have been rescued, it is quite possible that many of the twenty-five chalices recorded in 1699 were made in the early seventeenth century.[70]

The Killeigh and Donegal inventories only provide the names of people who had received silverware, but they do not identify items in any detail. Among surviving plate whose current locations are known, no item has a clear connection with Killeigh. As for the Donegal silver plate, only one chalice is identified as being made for the Donegal friars, the Mary O'Rourke Maguire chalice, made in 1633 and now in the diocese of Quebec. It is uncertain, however, if the chalice was among those given for safekeeping in 1698.

These inventories contain valuable information not only on the quantity of liturgical silver once kept in Franciscan friaries, but they also illustrate the existence of an unbroken patronage and of a close trustworthy network established between the friars and the local community, especially among family members.

CONCLUSION

Chalices donated to the Franciscan order in Ireland in the first half of the seventeenth century offer an insight into the manifold significance of these

(1667).   **68** FLK MSS C12; Giblin, *Liber Lovanensis*, p. 195.   **69** FLK MSS C12; Millett, *Irish Franciscans*, p. 88; K. MacGrath, 'Some Donegal Franciscan chalices' (1952), pp 73–8; B. Egan, 'Inventory of articles belonging to the friary of Donegal, 1698' (1952), pp 113–17.   **70** 'Brussels MS. 3947', p. 40; Mooney, 'Friars

objects as visual signs of religious ideas as well as into a variety of processes, which bring about the making and preservation of a liturgical object. The creation of a chalice involved craftsmen, beneficiaries, the friars, and donors, some of whom were Franciscans themselves. Each of these groups left an imprint on the appearance of an object. The craftsmen were certainly people of great skill who created distinctive regional styles and were open to ideas imported from abroad. The donors who had their names inscribed on their chalices were usually either Franciscans or lay benefactors, both Irish and Old English with close personal links to the order. The quantity of chalices and their sophisticated styles were also an expression of the wealth of patrons. The choice of iconography reflects the donors' devotional practices that in turn echo popular late medieval and early modern devotions, many of which were disseminated by the Franciscans.

The style and iconography of these chalices is shared by other Catholic chalices of the period and precludes one from speaking of a 'typical' Franciscan chalice. Their iconography, in particular, belongs to the international repertoire of well-established themes, which are reflected in the written word and other visual media, both earlier and contemporary. Some aspects of iconography, however, might have been introduced into Ireland for the first time at the start of the seventeenth century through popular woodcuts or engravings. These new images, some associated with the Counter-Reformation, are engraved on chalices that consciously retain late medieval styles.

For the friars who received these chalices, the objects acted as sacred vessels central to the celebration of the Eucharist. The significance of chalices and of other liturgical items was addressed by the founder of the order, St Francis, who in a letter to all clerics wrote about the proper celebration of the Eucharist: 'Those who are in charge of these sacred mysteries (…) should realize that the chalices, corporals and altar linens where the Body and Blood of our Lord Jesus Christ are offered in sacrifice should be completely suitable.'[71] The early seventeenth-century chalices donated to Irish friaries that so strongly focus on the image of the Cross, undoubtedly fulfill the aspiration regarding suitability of altar plate declared by St Francis.

and friary of Donegal', p. 15.   **71** 'Letter to all clerics' in M.A. Habig, *St Francis of Assisi* (1973), pp 100–1; Ó Clabaigh, 'The cult of St Francis', p. 145.

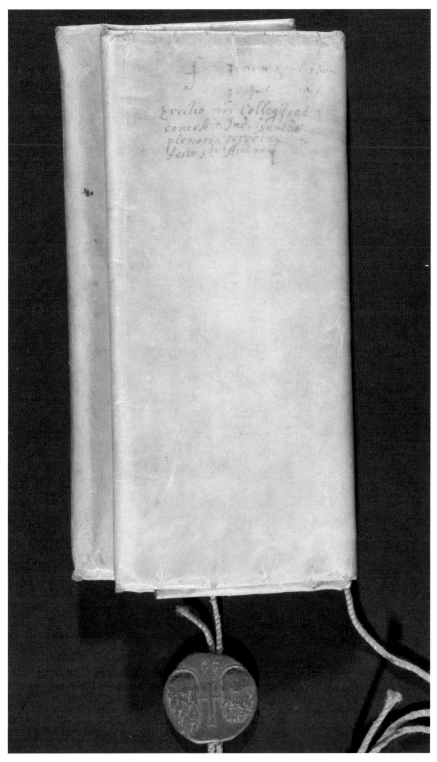

1 Papal bull of foundation for St Anthony's College, Louvain issued by Pope Paul V, 3 April 1607 (UCD-OFM Partnership/David Davison).

2 Document issued from St Anthony's College, Louvain incorporating the college's seal, November 1630 (UCD-OFM Partnership/J. McCafferty).

3 Antependium, Poor Clare convent, Galway, eighteenth century.

4 Signature page of the Four Masters (UCD-OFM Partnership/David Davison).

IESVS MARIA
FRANCISCVS.

ANNO DOMINI 1658. 15. Ianuarij Lovanij in Collegio
S. ANTONII DE PADVA Fratrum Hibernorum ſtri-
ctioris obſervantię, omnibus Eccleſię Sacramentis pręmu-
, migravit ad Dominum anno ſuę ætatis 66. Sacerdotij 40.
ͦonis 38. R. A. P. Fr. IOANNES COLGANVS S. Theo-
ͦr Iubilatus, & Collegiorum ſuę Provinciæ aliquamdiu
s. Vir erat ab eruditione, pietate , & animi candore
ͭendabilis,& pręclarè meritus de ſuo Inſtituto, Patriâ,
quorum actis in publicam notitiam proferendis,
& amplius annis pertinaci labore , in defeſſoque
ͭque ſedulus incubuit, Patrocinium prome-
ͦ humana fragilitate aliquid adhuc luen-
ͭ veſtris precibus enixè commendamus.

Requieſcat in pace.

5 Death notice of John Colgan OFM, 15 January 1658
(UCD-OFM Partnership).

6 Maurice O'Fihely (*c.*1460–1513), archbishop of Tuam and theologian: from a fresco in St Isidore's College, Rome painted by Fra Emanuele Da Como (Foto Gioberti Studio, Rome).

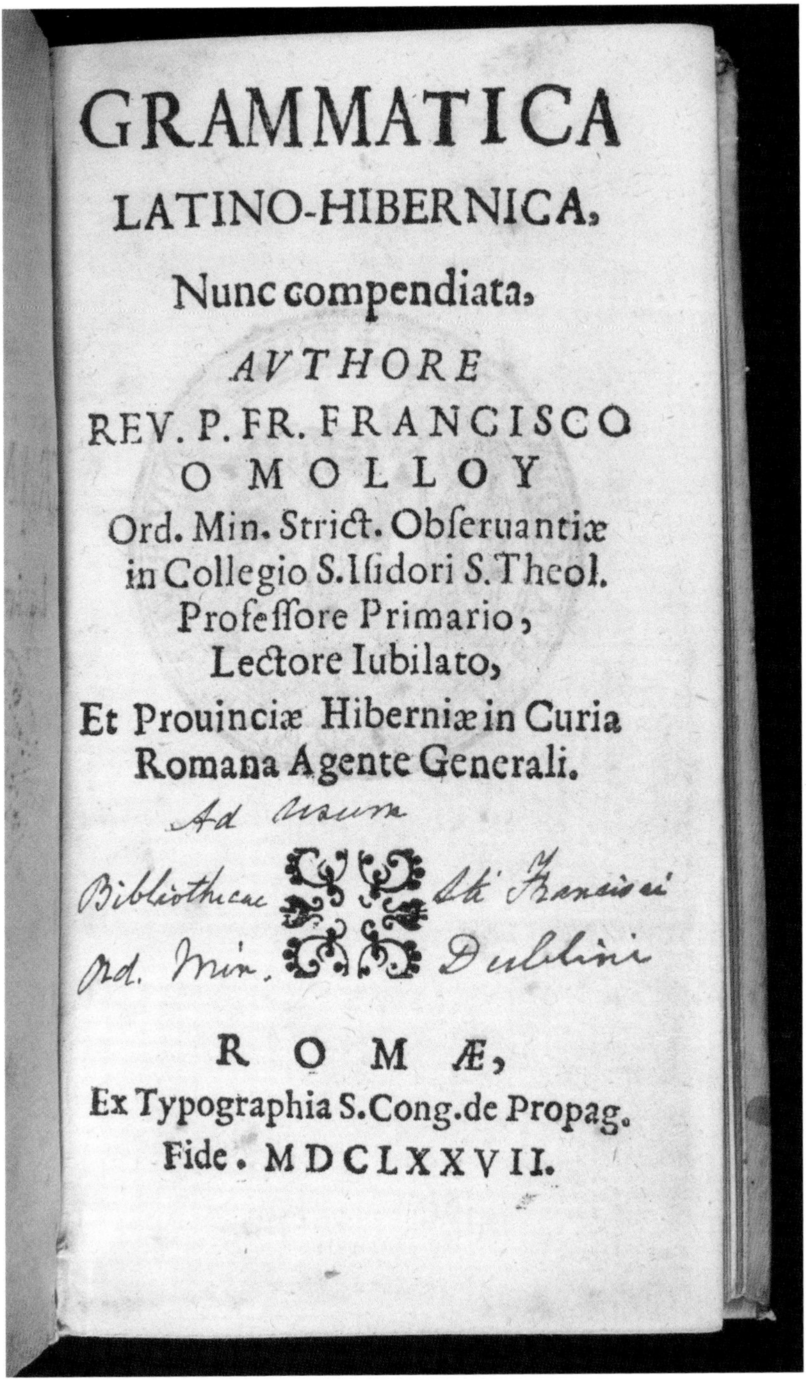

GRAMMATICA

LATINO-HIBERNICA,

Nunc compendiata,

AVTHORE

REV. P. FR. FRANCISCO
O MOLLOY
Ord. Min. Strict. Obseruantiæ
in Collegio S. Isidori S. Theol.
Professore Primario,
Lectore Iubilato,

Et Prouinciæ Hiberniæ in Curia
Romana Agente Generali.

Ad usum

Bibliothecae ❧❧ *St. Francisci*

Ord. Min. ❧❧ *Dublini*

ROMÆ,
Ex Typographia S.Cong.de Propag.
Fide. MDCLXXVII.

7 Francis O'Molloy, *Grammatica Latino-Hibernica*, Rome, 1677 (FLK/David Davison).

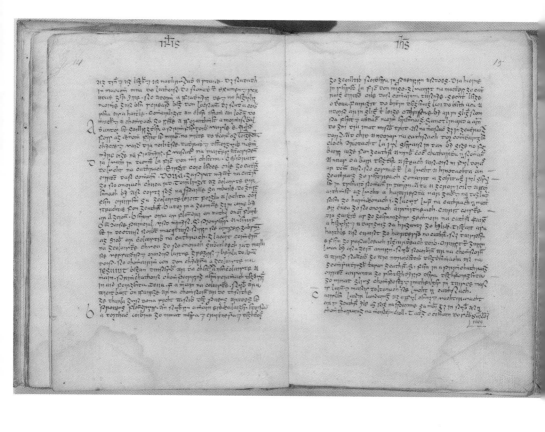

8 UCD-OFM MS A 21, the diary of Tadhg Ó Cianáin
(UCD-OFM Partnership/David Davison).

9 Everard-Donoghue chalice, Clonmel, 1667 depicting St Francis receiving the stigmata (National Museum of Ireland).

10 Dale-Browne chalice, Timoleague, 1600 (National Museum of Ireland).

11 Anastasia Rice chalice, Limerick, 1626 (National Museum of Ireland).

12 Font-Butler chalice, Galway, 1621 (National Museum of Ireland).

13 French-Darcy chalice, Galway, 1638 (UCD-OFM Partnership/M.K. D'Aughton).

14 *The Cross as the Tree of Life*, Dale-Browne chalice, Timoleague, 1600
(National Museum of Ireland).

15 *The Crucifixion*, John Farrell chalice, Limerick, 1619 (National Museum of Ireland).

16 *The Mercy Seat*, Font-Butler chalice, Galway, 1621 (National Museum of Ireland).
17 *The Mercy Seat,* Boetius Egan chalice, Elphin, 1634
(UCD-OFM Partnership/M.K. D'Aughton).

18 *The Mercy Seat*, Anastasia Rice chalice, Limerick, 1626 (National Museum of Ireland).
19 *The Crucifixion and St Francis*, Colman-Gould chalice, Cork, 1639
(National Museum of Ireland).

20 (above) *SS Francis, Clare, Elizabeth of Hungary*, Colman-Gould chalice, Cork, 1639 (UCD-OFM Partnership/ M.K. D'Aughton).
21 *The Apocalyptic Woman*, Anastasia Rice chalice, Limerick, 1626 (UCD-OFM Partnership/M.K. D'Aughton).

22 *Birds (including an owl) and plants*, Boetius Egan chalice, Elphin, 1634
(UCD-OFM Partnership/M.K. D'Aughton).
23 *Peacock*, Boetius Egan chalice, Elphin, 1634
(UCD-OFM Partnership/M.K. D'Aughton).

24 Rosserrilly aerial
photograph from SE
(Dúchas).

25 Claregalway crossing
tower. Tall slender
fifteenth-century tower
inserted into a
thirteenth-century
friary.

26 Adare refectory, tall stacks and jogged fireplace mantles.
Clear links to domestic architecture.
27 Ennis friary, south transept eastern chapels with a variety of tracery types.

28 Timoleague, junction of aisled transept and aisled nave. Example of crashing arcades.
29 Kilconnell. Cloister arcade with 'minimalist' dumb-bell piers and large well-cut voussoir blocks to the arches.

30 Quin, south transept. The ashlar quality of the walling is achieved by the use of hard-wearing carboniferous limestone. The slim tall crossing tower is also a prominent feature.

31 Quin, integrated cloister. The domestic ranges are carried out over the vaulted cloister
alley, giving more room to the upper floor but giving a castellated feel to the cloister garth.

32 Moyne, nave and crossing.

33 Buttevant, choir. Spectacularly sited on the banks of the river Awbeg. Some of the earlier
lancets have received later reticulated (net-like) tracery.

34 Kilkenny, fourteenth-century crossing tower.

35 Kilkenny, choir and east window.

36 Askeaton, dumb-bell piers of integrated cloister.

37 Adare, dumb-bell piers of lean-to cloister.
38 Ardfert, integrated cloister.

39 Muckross, vaulted cloister alley.

40 Rosserrilly, dumb-bell piers of integrated cloister. Here a trabeated system of Liscannor stone roof of cloister obtained.

41 Timoleague, cloister. Lean-to cloister with triple-sub arches to each opening.

42 Wall tomb composition: Adare, Ardfert, Askeaton and Ennis.

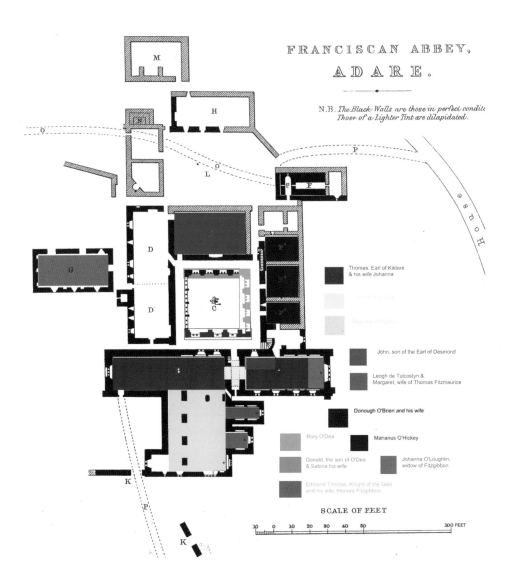

FRANCISCAN ABBEY,

ADARE.

Thomas, Earl of Kildare
& his wife Johanna

John, son of the Earl of Desmond

Leogh de Tulcostyn &
Margaret, wife of Thomas Fitzmaurice

Donough O'Brien and his wife

Rory O'Dea

Marianus O'Hickey

Donald, the son of O'Dea
& Sabina his wife

Johanna O'Loughlin,
widow of Fitzgibbon

Edmond Thomas, Knight of the Glen
and his wife, Honora Fitzgibbon

SCALE OF FEET

10   0   10   20   30   40   50   100 FEET

43 Adare. Plan showing patterns of patronage involved in building the friary.

44 Ennis, crossing tower. Figure
of St Francis.
45 Ennis, chancel. MacMahon
tomb. Panel of deposition.

46 Kilconnell, tomb in nave.

APPENDIX: CHALICES DONATED TO FRANCISCAN FRIARIES, 1600–50

The list is based on the evidence of surviving chalices and written sources, and includes the chalices donated to specific friaries by identified individuals. Names of the donors follow Buckley, *Some Irish altar plate* where possible.

Date of chalice	Name of friary to which the chalice was donated	Name(s) of Donor(s)	Location
1600	Buttevant, Co. Cork	Nicholas Sinan	Known
1600	Timoleague, Co. Cork	Carol Dale and Eliza Browne	Known
1606	Kilkenny, Co. Kilkenny	Walter Archer	Unknown
1610	Cork, Co. Cork	William Ferris	Known
1611	Cork, Co. Cork	William Ferris	Known
1611	Ardfert, Co. Kerry	Elina Moirane	Known
1614	Clonmel, Co. Tipperary	James Daniel	Known
1616	Meelick, Co. Galway	James Coughlon	Unknown
1619	Limerick, Co. Limerick	John Farrell	Known
1621	Galway, Co. Galway	Martin Font and Eliza Butler	Known
1621	Kilconnell, Co. Galway	Conn O Neill	Unknown
1622	Kilkenny, Co. Kilkenny	John Brenan	Unknown
1626	Limerick, Co. Limerick	Anastasia Rice	Known
1627	Cork, Co. Cork	Margaret Sarsfield and Walter Coppinger	Known
1627	Limerick, Co. Limerick	Leonard Creagh and Joanna White	Known
1627	Kilconnell, Co. Galway	Conn O Neill and Rosa McMorisey	Unknown
1628	Timoleague, Co. Cork	Dermot Hanin	Known
1628	Kilconnell, Co. Galway	Nehemias Folain and Catherine Mac Sweeney	Known
1628	Kilconnell, Co. Galway	John Cluan	Unknown
1629	Galway, Co. Galway	Nicholas Martin and Margaret Browne	Unknown
1630	Adare, Co. Limerick	Honora McCormockn	Unknown
1632	Carrick, Co. Tipperary	Paul O Neill	Uncertain

$\longrightarrow$

Date of	*Name of friary to which the chalice chalice*	*Name(s) of Donor(s) was donated*	*Location*
1633	Galway, Co. Galway	Elizabeth Forth	Known
1633	Donegal, Co. Donegal	Mary O'Rourke Maguire	Known
1633	Rosserrilly, Co. Galway	Maria Montij Jennings	Known
1633	Trim, Co. Meath	Alexander Plunkett	Known
1633	Kilconnell, Co. Galway	Thomas de Burgo	Unknown
1633	Meelick, Co. Galway	Thomas de Burgo	Unknown
1634	Elphin, Roscommon	Boetius Egan	Known
1634	Monaghan, Co. Monaghan	James Fleming and Brigida Barnewall	Known
1634	Meelick, Co. Galway	Michael Tully	Unknown
1634	Cork, Co. Cork	William Ferris	Unknown
1635	Meelick, Co. Galway	Louis Cormacone	Unknown
1636	Kilconnell, Co. Galway	John Guiffe	Unknown
1638	Kilconnell, Co. Galway	Francis Guiffe	Known
1638	Galway, Co. Galway	Edward French and Megina Darcy	Known
1638	Meelick, Co. Galway	Francis Madden	Unknown
1639	Cork, Co. Cork	John Colman and Catherine Gould	Known
1640	Kilconnell, Co. Galway	Maria Woodfall	Known
1640	Kilconnell (?), Co. Galway	John Donellan and Dorothy Mostion	Uncertain
1640	Rosserrilly, Co. Galway	Malachy O Queely	Known
1640	Meelick, Co. Galway	Paul Mulgeehy	Known
1645	Clonmel, Co. Tipperary	John English and Margaret Power	Known
1648	Clonmel, Co. Tipperary	Edmund Everard and Joanna Naish	Known
1649	Kilconnell, Co. Galway	Roger Jennings (?)	Unknown

Irish Franciscan friary architecture: late medieval and early modern

MICHAEL O'NEILL

Chronicling all aspects of Irish Franciscan history has been accomplished by the friars themselves over many centuries and the history of Irish friary architecture is no exception. Canice Mooncy pioneered the modern study of pre-Reformation friary architecture, particularly in a series of articles published in the *Journal of the Royal Society of Antiquaries of Ireland* between 1955 and 1957.[1] While Mooney had the model of A.R. Martin's *Franciscan architecture in England* to work with, the more intact state of Irish friaries allowed him and others to adopt a thematic approach to the subject. Published several years before Harold Leask's third volume on Irish church architecture, it is possible that Leask's less monographic approach in that volume was influenced by Mooney's study.[2] In an earlier period the friar-chronicler, Donatus Mooney's account of 1617–18 is uniquely important, not only for providing the foundation dates of friaries, but also for details relating to the architecture, furnishings and condition of friary buildings at the time. Unlike contemporary episcopal visitation reports, he also made aesthetic judgements regarding what he saw during his visitation.[3] This present chapter adopts a thematic approach to the subject and attempts to highlight the place of friary architecture in late medieval and early modern Ireland.

IRISH FRIARIES: AN INITIAL ASSESSMENT

Irish Franciscan friaries in the late medieval and early modern period formed an integral part of the great building boom which started in Ireland in the early fifteenth century. This expansion included the rebuilding and remodelling of parish churches as well as the development of that remarkable architectural phenomenon in the Irish landscape, the tower house. By the very nature of their daily and liturgical use, friary churches were often spatially more complex than most parish churches and many cathedrals. As regards areas used for accommodation and circulation, they remained faithful in plan to the centuries old cloister-centred model, while the vertical accommodation plan of coeval tower

---

1 C. Mooney, 'Franciscan architecture in pre-reformation Ireland' (1955–7).   2 H.G Leask, *Irish churches and monastic buildings,* iii (1960).   3 'Brussels MS. 3947'.

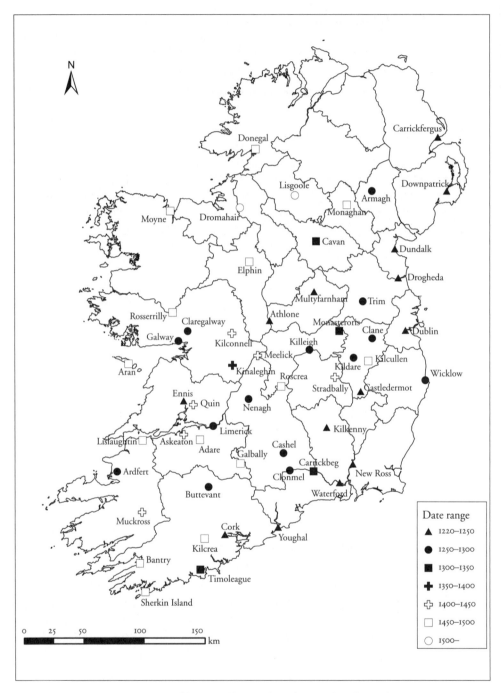

5 Location map of friaries – after Conlon, showing foundation dates.
Drawn by Anthony Corns.

houses was probably reflected in the friaries' sharply silhouetted belfry towers (Plates 24 and 25). Inserted at the crossing on east and west walls, pierced by tall arches supporting the upper stages they seem to reflect tower house construction techniques. In another example of the transmission of architectural forms from secular to ecclesiastical, it is evident that the multi-gabled domestic ranges with jogged fireplace lintels and prominent chimney stacks of friaries are linked to the fortified houses and strong houses of the seventeenth century, of native and planter alike (Plate 26). For example, the guardian's house at Ross and at Moyne have as much to do with secular architectural developments as with ecclesiastical architecture.

The late survival of many of the western friaries, the remarkable – albeit ruinous – condition of the buildings, and the often breath-taking isolated locations, make Irish friaries as iconic (though more complex) in Irish architecture as Maurice Craig's classic indigenous triumvirate of the round tower, ball alley and spirit grocery.[4] Many architectural features of the friaries, such as Perpendicular-style west doors and window forms, resonated in the Gothic revival architecture of the late eighteenth and early nineteenth century, until Puginian and ecclesiological sensibilities made these late gothic idioms unpopular.[5] At an earlier date, the window forms employed at the end of the seventeenth century by Sir William Robinson at Lismore Cathedral and in the first decade of the eighteenth century at St Mary's parish church in Mary Street Dublin, may arguably derive from Rosserrily friary.

Late medieval Irish architecture can be daunting. The standard classification of the Gothic style as flowing from Early English to Decorated to Perpendicular forms often provides little guidance to the architectural historian examining Irish friary architecture.[6] One is confronted with a bewildering array of forms – pointed windows juxtaposed with round-headed arcade arches, tracery bristling with cusps in close proximity to toothless and switch-line (intersecting) forms – all evidently employed within a close chronological sequence (Plate 27). Exquisitely wrought arcade piers die or merge into large unarticulated areas of wall; nave and transept arcades collide awkwardly (Plate 28); inserted towers of ashlar masonry partially obscure earlier windows and cloister arcade ranges are not uniform, the arcade piers sometimes verging towards a medieval 'Brutalist' style (Plate 29). Yet this jumbled architecture is more often than not executed in costly and crisply-dressed limestone, suggesting a deliberately created awkwardness and dissonance, perhaps reflecting the paradox of expensively executed buildings for a mendicant order (Plate 30). The ultimate manifestation of the dilemma of questing friars

---

4 M. Craig, *The architecture of Ireland* (1982), p. 17.   **5** The coincidence of late Gothic and early Gothic revival can be seen in the treatment of the pinnacles on the crossing tower of Ennis friary.   **6** Discussed by R. Stalley, 'Irish Gothic and English fashion' (1984).

living in exquisite buildings is best revealed in the location of the cloister range on the north side of the church – cold, dark, damp and penitential in the cooler northern climate. This aspect is further emphasized by the phenomenon of integrated cloisters, where not only is the cloister garth (garden) itself enclosed by cliff-like walls but the alleys and ground-floor chambers behind are narrow and seemingly claustrophobic (Plate 31).

The curious nature of the architecture of Irish friaries cannot be explained by workshops or schools of masons working in isolation and perpetrating architectural solecisms. The evidence, admittedly limited, from later friaries in the east of the country strongly suggests that the same masons worked, or at the very least employed the same styles, both east and west of the Shannon.[7] Two other factors must have contributed to this trend. One was the deliberate return to the earlier medieval forms of Romanesque and Transitional: round-headed arcade arches and, in particular, large well-cut voussoirs to rear-arches of windows and niches became very popular (Plate 32). The second factor was the constant reuse in windows of Decorated or Flamboyant tracery styles over the two centuries, fifteenth and early sixteenth, and the persistent use of switch-line (intersecting) forms. Both these styles were a clear rejection of the English Perpendicular parallel vertical tracery bars in the heads of windows.[8] While these forms are also found in the later parish churches in Ireland, the difference seems to be that the Decorated style continued to be incorporated into friary building construction well into the fourteenth century. Examples of this trend are evident in the friaries at Buttevant, Castledermot and Kilkenny (Figure 14 and Plate 33). When the building boom resumed in the fifteenth century, these idioms may have provided specific stylistic precedents for masons and craftsmen employed by the friars and their patrons.

A vital missing element in Ireland is the wooden architecture of the friaries – tomb canopies, crossing and altar screens, choir stalls, altar reredos, statue brackets and roof timbers. These highly portable pieces of architecture, some of them probably imported from Europe and England must have influenced the surviving stone tracery styles of tomb canopies, windows and west door surrounds. Recesses for wall hangings, set-backs below east windows for the altar reredos, evidence for wall paintings, ex-situ statuary and rood crosses, all help to present a more complete picture of friaries in late medieval and early modern Ireland.

---

7 Compare for instance the sketch by Austin Cooper of Kilcullen and Kildare friaries with Rosserrilly friary choir. For Cooper's sketch of 1782 see P. Harbison, *Cooper's Ireland* (2000), pp 94–5, 136–7. For Kildare friary see also Francis Grose, *The antiquities of Ireland* (1791), ii, pl. 25.   **8** J. Harvey, *The Perpendicular style* (1978), fig. 9 on p. 71. Perpendicular style tracery is occasionally found in the churches of the Pale, indicating that the style was not unknown.

THE LAYOUT OF EARLY FRIARIES

The basic plan

As the plan of the friary complex in Ireland developed over a three-hundred-year period from the thirteenth century onwards, late medieval and early modern convents were thus the inheritors of many centuries of experimentation and adaptation. The earliest foundations appear to have consisted of long rectangles with un-aisled choirs and naves as found at Ardfert, Armagh, Buttevant, Clane, Castledermot, Ennis, Kildare, Kilkenny, Multyfarnham, Nenagh and Waterford. Evidence for early cloisters is sparse, they having been destroyed for various reasons. Some examples can be detected in Armagh, Castledermot, Kilkenny, Kildare, Multyfarnham, Nenagh and Waterford. Other early cloisters were rebuilt in the late medieval period as at Ardfert and Claregalway or were rebuilt and subsequently destroyed as at Buttevant. Fragments of a thirteenth-century cloister arcade may survive in Claregalway. Many early friaries were located in urban areas and therefore the cloister areas, if not the churches themselves, were often immediately subject to exploitation for other uses following the dissolution of monasteries in the sixteenth century. There is also a possibility that many of the earliest cloisters and ancillary buildings were initially built in wood and only later rebuilt in stone.[9] Whether the Franciscans simply followed Augustinian building practices in constructing long narrow churches is a question that needs further exploration. The rows of lancets, 'long enfilades of lancets' (a phrase coined by Leask[10]) lighting the choirs of Ardfert, Buttevant, Cashel, Castledermot, Clane, Claregalway, Kildare, Kilkenny, Kildare, Nenagh and Waterford appear to have been borrowed from Augustinian prototypes. They can be compared, for example, with the Augustinian priories of Athassel, Co. Tipperary and Ballyboggan, Co. Meath. The more substantial surviving evidence of Augustinian cloisters with thirteenth-century features suggests that the mendicants sometimes eschewed elaborate ancillary stone buildings, at least in the early stages.[11]

By analyzing the plans of the earlier friaries and ignoring the later additions of crossing towers, transepts and nave aisles, three major groupings can be identified, based on the overall length of the church. The *Kildare group* includes Kildare, Killeigh and Monasteroris friaries, which have an internal width of

---

9 Stalley observed the lack of evidence for early cloisters at Cistercian monasteries and also suggested that early cloisters might have been constructed in wood. R. Stalley, *The Cistercian monasteries of Ireland* (1987), p. 160. **10** Leask, *Irish churches and monastic buildings*, ii, p. 90. **11** Evidence for a thirteenth-century cloister arcade at Kells Priory, Co. Kilkenny is discussed by J. Montague, 'The cloister arcade' (2007). The elaborate thirteenth-century doorway to the chapter house at Athassel would imply that an earlier cloister arcade was replaced by the fifteenth-century range in-situ. See M. O'Neill, 'Christ Church Cathedral as a blueprint for other Augustinian buildings in Ireland' (2009).

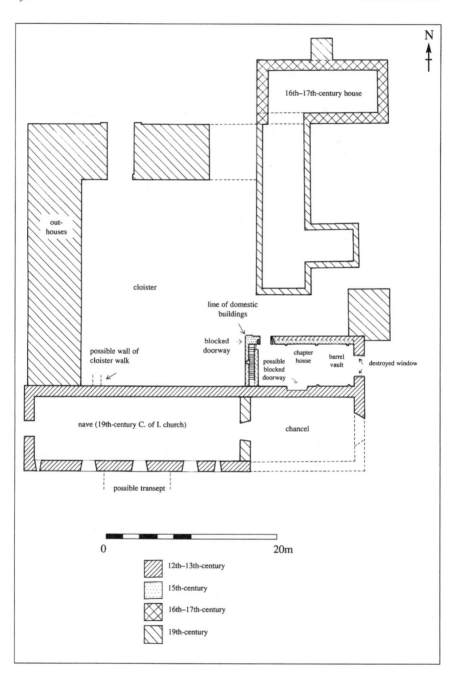

11 Plan of Killeigh friary (FitzPatrick & O'Brien).

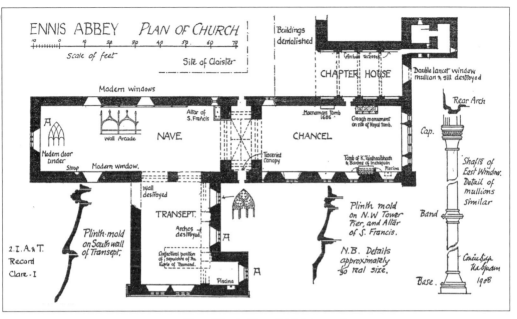

12 Plan of Ennis friary (Ui Briain 1908).

7 metres and a length of *c.*36 metres (Figure 11). A second group, the *Castledermot group*, includes Castledermot, Ardfert, Ennis, Waterford and Kilkenny (before its choir extension) (Figure 12). These have an internal width of 7 metres and are *c.*38.5 metres long. A third group, the *Claregalway group*, includes Claregalway, Kilconnell, Multyfarnham and Nenagh friaries (Figure 13). These are somewhat wider, *c.*7.4m and longer at 41 metres. The difference in length between all these groups is between *c.*2 and *c.*5 metres. An underlying proportional system for the first two groups seems to be based on a square with sides of *c.*5 metres – the medieval perch (16 feet 6 inches). Doubling a square with sides 5 metres long creates a square with sides *c.*7 metres long. This is the starting point determining the internal width and lengths of the *Kildare* and *Castledermot groups*. Manipulating the square with sides 7 metres long to create root-2 and golden section rectangles, creates rectangles some 7 by 9.9 metres and 7 by 11.3 metres respectively.[12] Combinations of these shapes can be seen to dictate the underlying lengths of the buildings. Similarly, for the third group, the *Claregalway group*, derived rectangles from a square with sides of 7.4 metres, can be used to generate the internal length. It would appear then that very clear and consistent principles for laying

---

12 For a discussion of proportional systems see M. O'Neill, 'The medieval parish churches in County Meath' (2002), pp 35–42 and R. Stalley, 'Gaelic friars and Gothic design' (1990).

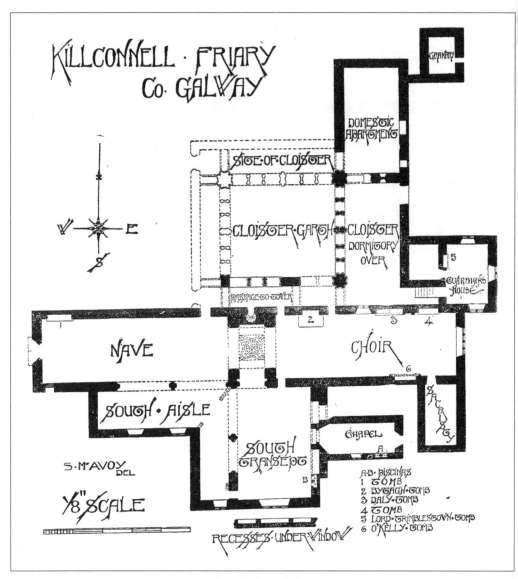

13 Plan of Kilconnell friary.

out new sites were employed by the masons of these friaries and that a level of under-lying uniformity exists which has not heretofore been discussed in any detail.

Regional variations may also be a factor in relation to the layout of friaries, particularly in the south east and south west, but the loss of such key buildings as Cashel, Cork, Limerick and Youghal makes it difficult to be dogmatic. Again in the case of the midlands, the loss of the friaries at Galway and Athlone does not

14 Buttevant. Antiquarian drawing records crossing tower, fourteenth century in appearance. The tower fell in the late nineteenth century.

allow for any certainty regarding regionality. The massive and massively shattered and robbed remains at Clane, measuring some 8 metres by 49 metres, which is close to Armagh in dimensions, suggests that there may have been large friaries at Carrickfergus, Dublin and Drogheda, long since demolished.

Adaptations to the church: transepts, cloisters, naves and crossing towers
Later thirteenth and early fourteenth-century adaptations to these long rectangular churches were threefold: single transepts, aisled naves and crossing towers were added to them. Transepts were added at Buttevant, Castledermot, Clane, Kilkenny, and Multyfarnham. Those at Ardfert, Claregalway and Ennis are fifteenth century. The transept is aisled at Castledermot and also, apparently, at Kilkenny. In addition, Castledermot has three eastern chapels in the transept and a similar plan obtained in Kilkenny. A single nave aisle could be added, on the same side as the transept, thus widening the nave and providing additional circulation space and access to the transept chapels. This occurred at Armagh, Castledermot, Clane and Waterford and later at Ardfert and Claregalway. A very clear masonry break on the exterior of the west front of Castledermot demonstrates that the aisle is a later addition. A series of crossing towers dating to the mid-fourteenth century are to be found at Cavan, Dundalk, Kilkenny and Multyfarnham and, based on antiquarian sketches, also at Buttevant and Killeigh (Figure 14 and Plate 34).[13]

13 A sketch by Rosemary Tarleton (1896) reproduced in E. FitzPatrick & C. O'Brien, *The medieval churches of County Offaly* (1998), fig. 89 on p. 91. The tower at Buttevant is recorded in R.R. Brash, 'The local

Cloisters

In these early foundations there appears to be no definite rule as to the location of the transept and the consequent concomitant position of the cloister on the other side of the church. The available evidence suggests that the cloister was located to the north of the church at Ardfert, Armagh, Buttevant, Carrickfergus, Cashel, Clane, Ennis, Killeigh, Multyfarnham, Roscrea, Timoleague, Waterford and Wicklow, and to the south at Castledermot, Claregalway, Kildare, Kilkenny and Nenagh. In the case of fifteenth-century foundations, only Askeaton has the cloister located to the south of the church, and where evidence is available, fifteen were located to the north (Adare, Creevelea, Donegal, Galbally, Kilconnell, Kilcrea, Kilcullen, Kinaleghin, Lislaughtin, Meelick, Moyne, Muckross, Quin, Ross, Sherkin). Overall, six have or had cloisters on the south and twenty-eight on the north side of the church (Map 6). By comparison, of the twenty-one Augustinian plans published by O'Keeffe, only two (Inisfallen, Co. Kerry and Inchcleraun, Co. Longford) have the cloister on the north side.[14] Of the thirty-four major Cistercian monasteries only one, Hore Abbey, Co. Tipperary, had the cloister located to the north of the church. Based on Hogan's list of Dominican friaries, available evidence suggests eight had the cloister to the north, and seven to the south of the church.[15] In contrast to the Franciscans, there is no obvious bias for north cloisters among the late medieval Dominican foundations where evidence exists. Thus while some friaries (both Dominican and Franciscan) had cloisters located to the south, the large number of convents with cloisters to the north is a phenomenon worthy of further study.[16]

Choirs and tracery

The early series of choirs, though generally unaltered – Kilkenny was extended to the east – were often remodelled with new styles of tracery in the late thirteenth and into the fourteenth century. The seven-light graduated east window at Kilkenny, dated to either 1321 or 1347 is wonderfully confident compared to the earlier five-light compositions at Ennis and at the Dominican priory of Kilmallock, Co. Limerick founded in 1291 (Plate 35).[17] More obviously Decorated style windows are found at Buttevant, Castledermot and Multyfarnham, and on the crossing towers listed above as at Dundalk and Kilkenny. Antiquarian sketches

antiquities of Buttevant' (1852–3) (opposite), p. 85.   **14** T. O'Keeffe, *An Anglo-Norman monastery* (1999), plans on pp 111–14.   **15** A. Hogan, *Kilmallock Dominican Priory* (1991), p. 53; P. Conlan, 'Irish Dominican medieval architecture' (2002).   **16** It should be borne in mind that this analysis of cloister location is based on small samples: 17% of Augustinian priories, and 30% of Dominican friaries. For Franciscan friaries the sample rises to 60%, with a 4 to 1 bias in favour of northern cloisters.   **17** R. Butler (ed.), *The annals of Ireland of Friar John Clyn and Thady Dowling* (1849), pp 15, 34. For Kilmallock see Hogan, *Kilmallock Dominican Priory*.

record that other Decorated style windows once also existed at Castledermot, Killeigh, Kildare and Multyfarnham.[18]

A number of inter-related issues are raised by the evidence presented above. What caused the demand for additional congregational space or circulation implied by adding nave aisles and the additional altars provided by transepts? Was this a reflection of either a demand by the friars for individual altars or by patrons demanding votive masses? And what of the rise in popularity of belfry towers? The introduction of new architectural styles, such as Decorated window forms, implied an active and informed workforce. How much of this activity continued into the period immediately following the Black Death, or indeed how much was prompted by that event is an issue that needs further exploration. The east window at Kilkenny, however well-wrought, might be considered unremarkable by 1321 but was certainly old-fashioned if executed as part of the choir extension in 1347. A fraternity was set up in the friary in 1347 to build a new bell tower and repair the church (Plate 34).[19] Was the tower completed at Kilkenny before the outbreak of the Black Death in 1348 or does it, and many more bell-towers, post-date that calamitous event? There is some documentary evidence for building activity soon afterwards elsewhere. At Ennis, the refectory and sacristy were constructed by Matha Caoch MacNamara in 1349, and in the same year a 'certain good room' was constructed at Nenagh by Robert Fynian.[20] Before 1359, Joan de Burgo, countess of Kildare, built a 'beautiful chapel' in which she herself was buried (*capellam pulchram ubi sepulta est*) and she also provided other buildings for the friars at Kildare.[21] Presumably this was a (north) transept chapel and thereby a link was established in that friary between votive masses and transepts. A careful study of friary cloister buildings and crossing towers might answer questions raised by architectural historians mainly concerned with secular buildings, as to how much building activity continued more or less unabated throughout the fourteenth century.

THE LAYOUT OF LATER FRIARIES

When the plans of the late medieval friaries are examined, it is apparent that the same dimensions employed in the earlier series were also used. The *Adare group*, including Ross and Lislaughtin (with a truncated nave), follows the proportions of the earlier *Castledermot group*. A second major group, the *Askeaton group*,

18 Recorded in Grose, *The antiquities of Ireland*, i, pl. 121 (Multyfarnham); ii, p. 123; and at Killeigh by Tarleton, as noted above fn 13. **19** B. Williams (ed.), *The annals of Ireland by Friar John Clyn* (2007), pp 242–3. **20** D.F. Gleeson (ed.), 'The annals of Nenagh' (1943), p. 161. **21** Ibid., p. 162.

includes Askeaton, Sherkin, Muckross, Quin, Moyne and Creevelea. These follow the proportions of the earlier *Kildare group*. It is evident that, in these new buildings, rather than re-thinking the relationship between aisled nave and aisled transept, the formula of adding features inherited from the fourteenth century was continued. This includes blank areas of wall at the west end of the nave acting as an arcade respond, and a particularly awkward joining of nave and transept arcades. Even at Askeaton, in every other way the work of a highly competent master mason, this architectural curiosity is utilized. At Kilconnell (in the *Claregalway group*) on the other hand, the master mason overcame this tendency. There, a pier respond receives both the transept arcade and arcade opening into the nave, all integrated with the south-west pier of the crossing tower. The crisply-cut limestone detailing of the architecture in both these buildings is exquisite and the contrast between the cloisters is hugely informative. At Askeaton the Perpendicular detailing of the arcade arches suggests an early fifteenth-century date and a Pale or even an English provenance for the architect and masons (Plate 36). At Kilconnell, the cloister is considerably later than the church and transept, possibly by some fifty years. Here the latest forms of Irish medieval architecture are found. Although still highly competent, the cloister is in a stripped down abbreviated Gothic style in which the capitals of the cloister arcade are left in block form and are supporting elliptical arches of huge voussoirs (Plate 29). A less abridged form of the cloister arcade pier is found at nearby Rosserrilly friary (Plate 40). The contrast between Askeaton and Kilconnell underlines the key role of patronage and the model used for additions to friary architecture which continued in the later fifteenth century and into the sixteenth century.

Cloisters

Another aspect of earlier paradigms underlying the proportions of fifteenth-century churches is that it dictated the size of the cloister. At Claregalway, a thirteenth-century foundation, demand for increased accommodation in the late medieval period is reflected by the addition of a three-storey dormitory. It may be that the integrated cloister evolved as one solution to the demand for additional accommodation. Instead of the lean-to cloister alleys of the thirteenth century, here the walks are vaulted and the upper floor of the ranges is extended out over the cloisters. This solution maximized accommodation, but made for narrow (and dark) ground-floor rooms behind the cloister alleys (Plates 31, 36, 38, 39). This solution may have been devised in the east of the country where expansion of the friaries in urban locations was difficult, but it is much more likely that the idea was imported. Martin cites evidence for integrated cloisters in English friaries at Ware, Walsingham and Dunwich, and also suggested that there was

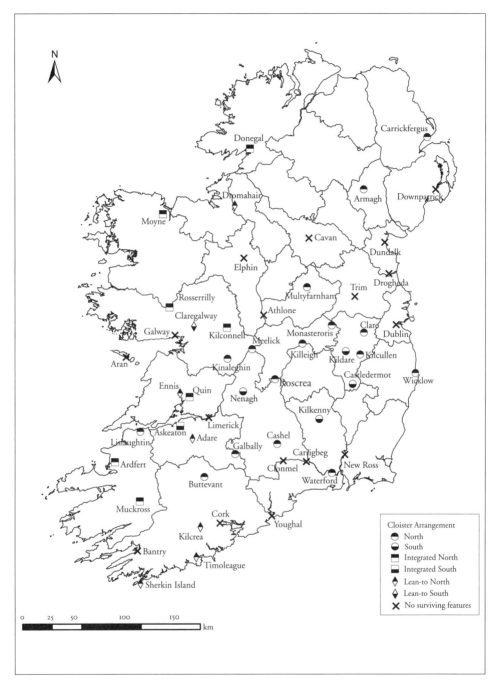

6 Irish friaries. Depicts location of cloister to north or south of church where evidence survives. Also indicates whether cloister is lean-to or integrated. Drawn by Anthony Corns.

evidence for them also at London, Bedford and Yarmouth.[22] Askeaton has an integrated cloister and Perpendicular detailing to the cloister, suggesting an early fifteenth-century date. The endowments of wealthy patrons here, however. allowed for a bright refectory to be built beyond the south-side cloister. Integrated cloisters are found at some of the most spectacularly preserved later sites, Askeaton, Kilconnell, Moyne, Muckross, Quin and Rosserrilly and as an addition at Ardfert, but these were by no means universal. Lean-to cloister arcades were built in the late medieval period at Adare, Creevelea, Kilcrea, Sherkin and added or rebuilt at Buttevant, Claregalway, Ennis and Timoleague (Plates 36–41).

Friary churches are not cruciform in plan, the east range of the cloister is never anchored to a north or a south transept, and can almost drift to the east or the west on the church flank. There is usually a doorway under the crossing tower, the walking place under the tower or crossing leading to the cloister. In several cases, at Claregalway, Kilcrea, Kilkenny, Muckross, Multyfarnham, Quin, and Sherkin, the doorway is aligned with the east alley of the cloister, but often the visitor has to orientate themselves as best they can when venturing into the cloister area, often located counter-intuitively with the church to the south.

The cloister arcades, either as part of lean-to or integrated alleys, generally employed what are called 'dumb-bell piers': an articulated base, a shaft composed of a web joining notionally separate colonettes, and a capital similar to the base. It is likely that this type of pier was, like the integrated cloister, initially imported from the west of England or Wales (for example, Furness in England, Basingwerk and Valle Crucis in Wales are possible Cistercian sources),[23] but was seized on with gusto by Irish masons. The arcades were often arranged within segmental arches containing three sub-arches with dumb-bell piers, and attenuated versions of this motif could be employed in the choir in sedilia and piscina surrounds.

Additional buildings and tombs
Demand for more space in the later period is reflected in the further ranges of buildings around the cloister at Adare, Claregalway, Creevelea, Moyne, Quin, Rosserrilly (a second cloister) and Timoleague (Plate 43). Tall narrow sacristies, or occasionally a chapter house (Ennis and Killeigh), flank the east end of the choir on the same side as the cloister (Figures 11 & 12). In such cases, the east front then has a characteristic double gable as at Askeaton, Ennis, Kilcrea, Quin and Sherkin.

The sepulchral function of the friaries which, as will be discussed below, accounts for their high, albeit ruined, survival rate, is reflected on a smaller register in the amount of surviving tomb sculpture. In the choir of Adare friary

22 A.R. Martin, *Franciscan architecture in England* (1937), p. 30. **23** S. Harrison & D.M. Robinson, 'Cistercian cloisters in England and Wales. Part II: Gazetteer' (2006).

there is a wonderful example of the coalescence of patronage and burial. The triple sedilia on the south wall of the choir is flanked by wall tombs, the eastern recess even doubling as a piscina. There is perhaps a sameness to some of these wall tombs, suggesting both the existence of distinct late medieval workshops and also the likelihood that polychromic decoration helped differentiate these memorials within a building, as documented in the early twentieth-century for Adare (Plate 42).[24] It is clear that a regional workshop operated in the south-west: tomb sculpture at Adare, Ardfert, Askeaton, Ennis and Lislaughtin share many similarities. This tomb style consists of a somewhat elliptical arch over the tomb niche decorated with shallow roll mouldings. The separate hood mould over the arch has sweeping ogee curves, again with shallow roll mouldings, rising to an elaborately carved finial. Pilaster buttresses flank the tomb, rising from bases at floor level and terminating in crocketed finials. Workshops can also be identified in the production of sediliae and piscinae, the former at Adare, Askeaton, Lislaughtin and Muckross, and the latter at Quin and Ross. In these sites the so-called 'dumb-bell pier' is also employed. It seems that the late medieval Irish mason made full use of any mastered motif.

DISSOULTION AND DONATUS MOONEY'S EVIDENCE

Donatus Mooney's visitation

The high quality of the masonry, the internal wooden architecture and the striking form of the crossing towers were all emphasized in the visitation undertaken by Donatus Mooney as provincial of the Irish Franciscan province in 1616.[25] Though writing some seventy years after the Dissolution of the monasteries, he is an important witness to the state of the friaries when compared to the sometimes tendentious accounts of the 1540–1 Royal Commission on extents of monastic possessions.[26] He described the then surviving crossing tower at Drogheda as composed of 'elegantly cut marble blocks' (*ex lapide marmoreo secto optimo artificio constructa*)[27], the buildings of Moyne (Plate 32) as almost entirely constructed of marble (by which he presumably meant limestone), Kilconnell as built of excellent stone, 'a great part of which is elegantly chiselled', and of Quin he said that all the walls were of polished marble. He described the cut stone of Creevelea cloister as being a greyish marble, well chiselled and polished (Plates 30 and 31). By way of contrast he observed that the building materials of Limerick were inferior and except for the church, that Cashel friary was not well built (Plates 30

24 T.J. Westropp, 'Paintings at Adare "Abbey", Co. Limerick' (1916).   **25** 'Brussels MS. 3947'.   **26** White, *Extents of Irish monastic possessions* (1943), passim.   **27** 'Brussels MS. 3947'.

and 31). He also had a keen awareness of spatial planning and massing. He described the friary at Quin, built on the site of an earlier De Clare castle, as 'a singularly beautiful pile of building, such as is seldom met with in monastic establishments'. The buildings of Moyne were described as spacious, in contrast to Buttevant, which retained its thirteenth-century un-aisled nave, and later un-aisled north transept, which he described as 'though ample in size, not well proportioned'.

Mooney is also an important witness to a late medieval roof construction tradition in friaries. Elaborate stone ribbed vaults sometimes survive over the piers and responds supporting the crossing towers. Cloister alleys and domestic ranges were often less elaborately vaulted, while the main liturgical spaces of nave, choir and transept retain no evidence of stone vaulting.[28] However, Mooney's comments allow the possibility of wooden vaulting in some instances. In Claregalway, he reported that in the recent past 'the roofs, the ceilings, and other parts in which wood was used, were of excellent workmanship'. He added that at Kilconnell, the 'ceiling of the church is exceedingly beautiful' and in Kilcullen the church and side chapels 'ceilings and paintings are somewhat discoloured by the damp and other destructive agencies'. Alternatively, he may have been describing an elaborate open roof construction, of coupled, braced collar or perhaps hammer-beam construction. At Timoleague, for example, he reported that the ceiling over the chapter room and refectory was supported on beams of carved oak. Buttevant, Kilconnell and Kilcrea friaries were roofed with shingles, a lighter, and possibly more readily available, roofing material than either slates or lead. Slate was used at Quin and lead on the roof at Wexford.

There were seven altars in Kilconnell. The extensive list of vestments at Adare, which surprised Mooney, would suggest that a large number of altars once existed there also, possibly in the transept chapels and presumably altars existed at the east end of the nave. While Kilconnell remained intact in 1616, the statues, paintings and rood of Kilcrea had been destroyed some years previously, a refrain echoed by Mooney in relation to many other friaries. Even before the Dissolution, organs and stained glass were removed from Killeigh friary by Lord Deputy Grey to furnish Maynooth collegiate church.[29] At Clane in 1537, the church, chancel and part of the dormitory were destroyed by Grey to repair Maynooth castle.[30] Grey was also responsible for demolishing Dundalk friary.[31]

28 Kildare may be an exception to this to judge from the clasping buttresses between the bays. Compare, for example, the choir of Newtown Trim Cathedral, Co. Meath. **29** Lord Leonard Grey to Cromwell, 31 Dec. 1537 (*State Papers Henry VIII*, ii, p. 529). Discussed by M.A. Lyons, *Church and society in County Kildare* (2000), p. 95; FitzPatrick & O'Brien, *The medieval churches of County Offaly*, pp 88–98. **30** White, *Extents of Irish monastic possessions*, p. 164; Lyons, *Church and society in County Kildare*, p. 60. **31** White, *Extents of Irish monastic possessions*, p. 146.

The effects of Dissolution

The poor survival and the disappearance of friary buildings from the east of the country was due to a number of factors. Thirteenth-century friaries were most often located in or near urban areas.[32] Following the Dissolution, they succumbed either to urban expansion, outright demolition, being put to secular use, or were sometimes donated to municipal authorities for civic use, often as courthouses.[33] Few had extensive demesne lands requiring the buildings to be retained by the farmers of new leases.[34] A small number of friaries, among them Ennis, Killeigh and Monasteroris, became parish churches immediately or sometime later.[35] Many of the same factors account for the disappearance of English medieval friaries. Thus the student of English friary architecture is also drawn to the study of Irish friaries for evidence to interpret scant remains in England.[36]

Unlike monastic incumbents of Cistercian, Benedictine and Augustinian houses, the friars were not pensioned off at the Dissolution, rather the legal fiction of voluntary abandonment without compensation was promoted by the crown surveyors. There is some evidence that actual dissolution was gradual.[37] The friars in Dublin did not withdraw until four years after formal suppression and several more years in the case of Drogheda. Outside the crown and loyal territories and major towns, actual dissolution depended largely on the will of the local magnate. The friars at Kilcullen placed many of their goods in the hands of the local lord, Sir Thomas Eustace, and re-emerged to claim them in Queen Mary's reign.[38] As noted above, Donatus Mooney found the church and chapels there in reasonable repair in 1616, although the friars by then were not allowed to inhabit the buildings. Multyfarnham, within the ambit of the Pale, was a blatant example of survival under the protection of the Nugents. When the crown surveyors visited the house in 1540, almost a year after the suppression commissioners, they found every indication of continuing habitation: the church was still standing, the buildings well kept, and an uncluttered drainage system existed. They also found the household furniture intact, and the friars' books un-

---

32 The friaries at Clonmel, Drogheda, Kilkenny, New Ross, Trim and Waterford were located within the town walls. 33 Bradshaw, *Dissolution of the religious orders*, p. 142. 'In Cavan, Dromahaire, Ennis, Enniscorthy, Galway, Trim and Wicklow, the old convents of the Franciscans were used as courthouses and for other public uses'. Mooney, 'The golden age of the Irish Franciscans', p. 22. 34 In the case of Cistercian monasteries and Augustinian priories, the new leaseholders of former impropriated parishes were responsible for collecting the tithes and employing a curate, hence the farmers of the tithes or leases. 35 Ennis was first used as a courthouse and later became the Church of Ireland parish church of Drumcliff. A date-stone of 1644 on Killeigh church probably indicates its refurbishment as a parish church. In the case of Monasteroris it is unclear when it became parochial. 36 A.W. Clapham, 'The architectural remains of the mendicant orders in Wales' (1927); Martin, *Franciscan architecture in England*; Stalley, 'Gaelic friars', p. 192. 37 See C. Lennon, 'The dissolution to the foundation of St Anthony's College, Louvain, 1534–1607', in this volume. 38 Lyons, *Church and society in County Kildare*, pp 159–60; Bradshaw, *Dissolution of the religious orders*, p. 144.

confiscated.[39] Clearly the suppression commissioners had left Multyfarnham largely as they had found it. It was later burned to the ground by Sir Francis Sheehan in 1601, as graphically described by Donatus Mooney who witnessed the event himself, and by the time of his visitation the friars were living in a small house on the site. In most cases, however, the secularization or outright destruction of friary buildings forced the friars in the eastern half of the country to disperse. Very few sued for re-possession during Mary's reign (with the exception of Multyfarnham, Trim, Kilcullen and Enniscorthy), the only sure indication of the survival of a community.[40]

In areas outside the ever-expanding centralizing Tudor government, the friars could continue to occupy friaries by practicing tactical withdrawal in times of danger. However, by the end of Elizabeth's reign many friaries had been burned, and with growing confessionalization the friars were unable to inhabit others. By the time of Mooney's visitation less than half a dozen friaries were then genuinely inhabited (Moyne, Rosserrilly, Kilconnell, Clonmel, Multyfarnham), and several more were still in good repair. These included Galway and Ennis, which was being used as a courthouse, Kilcrea, Buttevant, which was still roofed, and Waterford, which was in use as a hospital and alms house. A slightly earlier parliamentary report of 1613 complained that even within the English Pale monasteries had been re-edified, 'where friars publicly preach and say mass'. An accompanying list enumerates Multyfarnham, Kilconnell, Buttevant, Kilcrea, Timoleague, Quin, Muckross, and in Kilkenny and Waterford cities, presumably in the friaries there.[41] During the early period between 1615–50, small communities returned to private or rented houses in Dublin, Kinaleghin, Limerick, New Ross, Wexford, Cashel and Moyne. Residences were established in the vicinity of the earlier sites at Athlone, Carrickfergus, Dundalk, Askeaton, Down, Sherkin, Youghal, Lislaughtin and Trim. There was some rebuilding at Kildare and Quin but this was the exception and there was not a wholesale re-occupation of the friaries.[42] Another factor, of course, was the use of long-lasting carboniferous limestone for the walling and cut-stone detail of so many friaries.

In general, however, it is not the relatively late occupation of the friaries that accounts for their spectacular, if ruinous, condition into the present century. Their survival was related to their important function as mausoleums for their original patrons and their descendants. Mooney, in the early seventeenth century, explicitly recognized this function of the friaries as accounting for their good condition. His repeated refrain was that 'the principal families' or 'all the nobles

39 White, *Extents of Irish monastic possessions*, pp 274–5.   **40** Bradshaw, *Dissolution of the religious orders*, pp 137–45.   **41** *Cal. S.P. Ire.* (James I, 1611–14) (HMSO 1877), p. 394.   **42** Mooney, 'The golden age of the Irish Franciscans', pp 23–4.

of that country', the 'majority of the nobility', the 'chief families of the district' were buried at Galway, Kilconnell, Ennis, Timoleague, Muckross, Kilcrea, Cashel, Clonmel, Waterford and Kilcullen friaries. Adare provides a particularly good example of a friary that remained relatively intact due to the link between its patrons and continuous use as a place of burial. As previously discussed, and although not mentioned in this context by Mooney, Adare was replete with wall-tombs, at the east end of the nave, in the transept chapels and in the choir. Some of these may be those of the founding patrons recorded by Mooney from a book that had been read in chapter each Friday to commemorate the benefactors:

> I have found the following particulars relating to this convent in the book, which, according to the constitution of the Order, as well as the Province, should be read in the presence of the Community, on each Friday of the year, that the memory of our departed benefactors should not be forgotten. This book is at present in possession of an old man, named James Hickey, who had been syndic of the convent:–

> 'The church of the Friars Minor at Adare was dedicated in honour of St Michael the Archangel, on the 19 November, 1464, the feast of St Pontianus, Martyr, and St Elizabeth, Widow, Thomas, Earl of Kildare, and his wife Johanna, daughter of James, Earl of Desmond, built the church and a fourth part of the cloister at their own expense [*south side of cloister nearest nave and the private chamber over*]. They also furnished the windows of the church with glass, and presented the bell and two silver chalices. The convent was accepted, on behalf of the Order, at the Provincial Chapter, held at Moyne, on the feast of the Apostles SS Peter & Paul, in the same year, and the brethren of the Family of Observance entered into possession on the feast of All Saints following. The church was consecrated in honour of St Michael the Archangel, on his feast, in the year 1466. The following places, outside the church, were also consecrated that they might be used for burial of the dead. The whole circuit of the cloister, inside and outside, both sacristies, and the entire cemetery, except a portion on the south, which was set aside for those who might die without the right to Christian burial.'

> 'The other parts of the edifice were built by the following:–

> 'The bell-tower, by Conor O'Sullivan, a pious and devout stranger who has settled amongst us (as the ancient book described him). He also presented us with an excellent chalice, gilt with gold. Margaret Fitzgibbon, wife of

Cuulaid O'Dea ... erected the great chapel [*?south transept or perhaps the choir*]. One of the small chapels was built by John, son of the Earl of Desmond; the other by Leogh de Tulcostyn, and Margaret, wife of Thomas Fitzmaurice [*transept chapels*]. Donough O'Brien, son of Bryan Duv, of Ara, and his wife, built the dormitory. We owe another fourth part of the cloister to a Tertiary, Rory O'Dea, who gave us a useful silver chalice. Another tertiary, Marianus O'Hickey, erected the refectory, and it was he who furnished the northern side of the choir with its beautiful panellings and stalls. Donald, the son of O'Dea, and Sabina, his wife, finished another fourth of the cloister. Edmond Thomas, Knight of the Glen, and his wife, Honore Fitzgibbon, erected the infirmary... Johanna O'Loughlin, widow of Fitzgibbon, added ten feet to the sanctuary, under which she directed a burial place to be formed for herself. Conor O'Sullivan, who built the belfry, died 16 Jan, 1492; Margaret Fitzgibbon, who built the Lady Chapel, on 23 Jan 1483, ...

'Some of the precious possessions of this convent are yet in existence. They are at present in Cork, under the custody of Thomas Geraldine, a ciborium for the Blessed Sacrament, gilt with gold and of good workmanship; a silver processional cross, and six or seven chalices, some of which are gilt with gold. The register is among the other registers of the Province. I have, also, seen a list of the sacred vestments, and was much surprised at the large number, but all of them have perished under the decaying hand of time.

'The friars were driven from Adare during the war between the Earl of Desmond and Queen Elizabeth. The convent, which up to that time had been kept in excellent repair, was allowed to go to ruin. At present the roof has fallen in, but the walls stand, and the glass even is uninjured in some of the church windows.'[43]

It would appear from Mooney's evidence that either the benefactors for one side of the cloister and the kitchen range at Adare were unrecorded or that this building work was financed by income received by the community itself (Plate 43). It is interesting that the document stressed the consecration of burial areas as well as the church on the feast of St Michael, the Archangel in 1466. At Galway, according to Mooney, there was a long tradition that burial fees in the friary provided for building maintenance. At Clonmel, before the Dissolution,

---

43 'Brussels MS. 3947', pp 63–4. Translated in Caroline Countess of Dunraven, *Memorials of Adare* (Oxford, 1865), pp 75–7 and in *The Franciscan Tertiary*, 5:12 (April, 1895), pp 354–6.

fees collected at the 'Station' were also given to acquire the building fabric. Perhaps a similar strategy was applied at Adare to complete the convent. Bequests in medieval wills to repair or maintain parish church fabrics are relatively common. Examples are found in Co. Meath at St Mary's Drogheda, at Stackallen and at Tara.[44] While no other detailed Franciscan list of benefactors survives, the Adare list suggests that where a single patron was traditionally associated with a friary, other unrecorded patrons may have contributed to the cost of specific parts of these expensive building complexes. Another corollary to be drawn from this valuable document is that high quality building and masonry work was not necessarily confined to the choir and nave of the church. Transepts, transept chapels, cloister alleys, refectories and even dormitories and infirmaries could attract specific patronage. In the case of Timoleague, according to the Book of Obits of the friary, the bell-tower, the library, the infirmary, and one of the dormitories were built by Bishop John Edmund De Courcy, between 1498 and his death in 1515.[45] In a Dominican context, the Athenry Register is a comparable, if earlier, document to the Adare list.[46]

CONCLUSION

The modern traveller to the late medieval friaries, many of which continued in use into the early modern period, has to be cognisant that they sometimes incorporate later architectural accretions. One good example is that of the west door at Moyne with its pulvinated frieze. Other late features include corner hearths (Rosserrilly, Timoleague) and inserted fireplaces blocking earlier windows in the domestic ranges (Claregalway, Kilcrea and Timoleague) – all features characteristic of seventeenth-century architecture. Crossing towers were also later adapted for residential use, as at Moyne, Creevelea and the west tower at Ardfert. In the case of the guardian's house at Rosserrilly there are balanced front and gable elevations, while an even later house was constructed at Moyne. This house, gable-ended and with a substantial chimney stack, is likely to be somewhat earlier than the early eighteenth-century house at Killeigh, where the roof is hipped and there is a larger proportion of wall to window on the front elevation. Other outbuildings and offices north of the church at Killeigh may incorporate medieval fabric though less obviously than the largely intact vaulted chapter

44 O'Neill, 'The medieval parish churches in County Meath', pp 44–5. **45** The entry is quoted by Sir James Ware in BL Add MS 4821, ff 100r–113v. **46** M.J. Blake, 'The abbey of Athenry' (1902); A. Coleman (ed.), 'Registrum monasterii fratrum praedicatorum de Athenry' (1912); see C. Ó Clabaigh, 'Patronage, prestige and politics' (2008).

house attached to the now shortened chancel. The complex at Killeigh of a church with later nineteenth-century furnishings, the early eighteenth-century house incorporating medieval windows and chimney stacks, and the outbuildings serves to underline the fact that the majority of friaries are accretions of late medieval and early modern buildings. Frozen in this state, they are more 'readable' than the cathedrals and parish churches which continue in use to this day and incorporate many later changes. These friaries also contain some of the masterpieces of Irish medieval figural tomb sculpture as witnessed at Ennis and Kilconnell (Plates 44-6).[47] In searching out or happening across the carved depictions of St Francis in the friaries, the modern traveller is following in the footsteps of a myriad of earlier post-Dissolution pilgrims.

TABLE OF FRIARIES

Friary	County	Fd. Date	Chancel	Nave	Crossing Tower	Transept	Cloister	Refectory, Dormitory etc.
Adare	Lim.	1464	x	x	x	x	x	x
Aran	Galway	1484						
Ardfert	Kerry	c.1253	x	x		x	x	
Armagh	Armagh	1263	x	x				
Askeaton	Lim.	c.1400	x	x		x	x	x
Athlone	W.Meath	c.1239						
Bantry	Cork	c.1460						
Buttevant	Cork	1276	x	x		x		
Carrickbeg	Water.	1336			x			
Carrickfergus	Antrim	1232						
Cashel	Tipp.	c.1265						
Castledermot	Kildare	c.1247	x	x		x		
Cavan	Cavan	c.1325						
Clane	Kildare	c.1258	x	x				
Claregalway	Galway	c.1252	x	x	x	x	x	x
Clonmel	Tipp.	1269						
Cork	Cork	c.1229						
Donegal	Donegal	1473	x	x		x	x	
Downpatrick	Down	1240						

47 J. Hunt, *Irish medieval figure sculpture 1200–1600* (1974), i, pp 120–7, 150; ii, plates 235–45, plates 257–9.

Friary	County	Fd. Date	Chancel	Nave	Crossing Tower	Transept	Cloister	Refectory, Dormitory etc.
Drogheda	Louth	1240						
Dromahair	Leitrim	1508	x	x	x	x	x	x
Dublin	Dublin	c.1233						
Dundalk	Louth	c.1246						
Elphin	Roscom.	1453						
Ennis	Clare	1240	x	x	x	x	x	x
Enniscorthy	Wexford	1460						
Galbally	Tipp.	1471	x	x	x	x		
Galway	Galway	1296						
Kilconnell	Galway	1414	x	x	x	x	x	x
Kilcrea	Cork	1465	x	x	x	x	x	x
Kilcullen	Kildare	1486						
Kildare	Kildare	c.1254	x	x				
Kilkenny	Kilken.	1232	x		x			
Killeigh	Offaly	c.1303	x	x				
Limerick	Lim.	1267						
Lislaughtin	Kerry	1470	x	x		x		x
Meelick	Galway	1414						
Monaghan	Mon.	1462						
Monasteroris	Offaly	1325						
Moyne	Mayo	1455	x	x	x	x	x	x
Muckross	Kerry	1440	x	x	x	x	x	x
Multyfarnham	W.Meath	c.1268			x	x		
Nenagh	Tipp.	c.1252	x	x				
Quin	Clare	1433	x	x	x	x	x	x
Roscrea	Tip.	c.1477	x		x			
Rosserrilly	Galway	1498	x	x	x	x	x	x
Sherkin Island	Cork	1460	x	x	x	x	x	x
Stradbally	Laois	c.1447						
Timoleague	Cork	c.1307	x	x	x	x	x	x
Trim	Meath	c.1282						
Waterford	Water.	1240	x	x	x	x		
Wexford	Wex.	c.1268						
Wicklow	Wicklow	c.1268		x		x		
Youghal	Cork	c.1229						

A select prosopography of some Irish Franciscans on the Continent

IGNATIUS FENNESSY OFM

By the year 1606 there were only 118 Irish Franciscans at home and abroad.[1] After the founding of St Anthony's College at Louvain in the following year, the most important development in the Irish Franciscan province was, undoubtedly, the opening of St Isidore's College in Rome in 1625. That enabled many more young Irishmen, who had to leave their dissipated province in Ireland,[2] to aspire to the religious life with the friars and to enter their novitiate and continue their studies for the priesthood in Rome. Because both the colleges were engaged in the same kind of educational activities, it was only to be expected that there would be cooperation as well as some competition between them, besides connections of other kinds.

The Irish friars on the Continent represented different ethnic and social groups and, as evidenced during the period of the Catholic Confederation, held diverse political views on the state of their native country. They became involved in ecclesiastical, intellectual and political life at home and abroad and were academically well-prepared to engage in serious research, teaching and writing on a range of topics in history, philosophy and theology. Their tireless efforts in sustaining their colleges in Louvain and Rome were remarkable and in many cases they seemed to regard themselves as citizens of both Ireland and Europe.

LUKE WADDING (1588–1657)[3]

The person who inspired the friars in Rome, and also in Louvain, was one of the most remarkable Irishmen of the first half of the seventeenth century. Born in Waterford on 16 October 1588, Luke Wadding was baptized on 18 October, the feast of St Luke the Evangelist. He was the eleventh child of fourteen born to Walter Wadding and Anastasia Lombard, who were well-to-do, with land in the county and a tomb in the Franciscan friary. He was related to Peter Lombard, archbishop of Armagh, to Thomas Walsh, archbishop of Cashel, and to four other bishops, Peter Comerford of Waterford, David Rothe of Ossory, and John

---

1 Jennings, *Louvain papers*, p. 18 no. 21, para. 1.   2 Ibid., 'pauci restabant dissipatae provinciae, oppressae nationis Hiberniae'.   3 Luke Wadding merits a biography in his own right and it is planned to publish such a volume in the future.

Roche and Nicholas French both of Ferns. He himself was offered the sees of Armagh and Waterford, which he refused. He blocked the Catholic Confederates' move to have him appointed a cardinal and he even received some votes at the papal conclave in 1644. These events demonstrate his eminence both in Ireland and in Rome.

After his parents died in 1602, his brother Matthew, a merchant, brought him to Lisbon and placed him in the new Irish College there. However, he entered the Franciscan order, and was ordained a priest in 1613. He studied at Salamanca and went to Italy in 1618, as theologian to a special embassy sent by the King of Spain in connection with the doctrine of the immaculate conception of the blessed Virgin Mary. In Rome, where he was based for the rest of his life, he quickly attracted attention as a theologian and an author. He became one of Ireland's most prolific writers, and began to publish many works including a concordance of the bible in Hebrew and one in Latin. He was the first to publish all the writings attributed to St Francis of Assisi, as well as a large edition of the works of John Duns Scotus, whom many at the time thought of as an Irishman. Before he died he produced eight large tomes on the Annals of the Friars Minor (*Annales Minorum*). About two dozen of his works were published, and six more were almost ready for the printer. He was a valued consultant to several Roman congregations, and helped in the revision of the Roman breviary and was successful in having St Patrick's feast placed in the calendar for the universal church.

As with Flaithrí Ó Maoil Chonaire, founder of St Anthony's College Louvain, Luke Wadding saw the urgent need to train friars to return on the mission to Ireland. He was offered the small church and friary of St Isidore's in Rome which originially had been owned by the Spanish Franciscans. With the assistance of wealthy benefactors, he decorated and extended the house, and collected lecturers and students there. He played an important part in founding nearby a college for the Irish diocesan clergy. He was also instrumental in establishing Irish colleges in Prague, in Poland (briefly) and at Capranica near Viterbo. There was a constant exchange of ideas, students and teachers between St Isidore's and St Anthony's in Louvain.[4] Of the eighty-one 'companions and disciples of Wadding' listed in Gregory Cleary's book, about twenty of them had some association with Louvain, with most of the movement being from Rome to Louvain rather than in the opposite direction.[5]

Wadding is often confused with two others of the same name. One, a Jesuit and his contemporary cousin who died in 1651, and like Fr Luke Wadding studied

4 For details of Wadding's life see I. Fennessy, *ODNB*, vol. 56 (2004), pp 643–9; eadem, 'Who was Luke Wadding?' (2002–3).   **5** Cleary, *Father Luke Wadding*; Jennings, *Louvain papers*, as above in fn. 1.

in Salamanca. The other Luke Wadding was bishop of Ferns (d. 1687) who published a book of religious verse.[6] He may or may not have written a short poem in English about Christmas which is still often wrongly attributed to the founder of St Isidore's. It contains two verses from a Wexford carol collected (and perhaps written) by Fr William Devereux (1771).[7] Here it may be added that it does not seem likely that Luke Wadding, founder of St Isidore's, knew Irish. He was indeed a good linguist, but he left his native town, Waterford (an English stronghold), for good when he was about fourteen years of age. Eight lines in Irish in honour of Nicolaus Peyresius published in Rome in 1638 have been attributed to him; but these could have been a translation by some other friar in St Isidore's College of a short eulogy in Latin composed by Luke Wadding.[8]

JOHN BARNEWALL (*fl.* 1620s–40s)

John Barnewall was a son of Lord Trimbleston. He received minor orders and the subdiaconate in Mechelen (Malines) in December 1617.[9] He defended theses in Scotistic theology in 1620 in Louvain, and presided over the defence of theses by others in 1627.[10] It has been suggested that he was sent as a lecturer to Germany in 1637, taught subsequently in Prague, and on his return to Ireland was the local superior in the hermitage at Slane.[11] Another contemporary claimed that he had been teaching philosophy and theology at Louvain for eight years before being elected minister provincial on 15 August 1638 at the chapter held in Quin, Co. Clare.[12] One of his pupils in Louvain was Peter Walsh, the author of the *Loyal Formulary or Irish Remonstrance* (1674), who referred to 'the learned Fr John Barnwell' as a forerunner of Cornelius Jansen. It was argued that the theses on St Augustine's teaching on grace, free will and predestination defended in 1627 by Patrick Brennan OFM written under the presidency of Barnewall were inspired by Jansen, but this was denied.[13] He was still in office as minister provincial on 1 November 1642 when he signed a letter to Luke Wadding about the state of Ireland at the time.[14] He may have been related to the Flemings of Slane, and was mentioned in the will of Patrick Fleming OFM.[15] In 1648 he was amongst those

6 P.J. Corish, *ODNB*, vol. 56 (2004).   7 J. Ranson, 'The Kilmore carols' (1949), pp 61–7.   8 C. Ó Maonaigh, 'Uaidín Gaelach' (1957).   9 B. Jennings, 'Irish names in the Malines ordination registers' (1951), p. 149.   10 I. Fennessy, 'Canon E. Reusen's list of Irish Franciscan theses in Louvain' (2006), pp 22–3.   11 Cleary, *Father Luke Wadding*, p. 132.   12 'Brussels MS. 3947', p.III, n.46.   13 A 1641 copy in Franciscan Library Killiney (FLK), shelfmark XP 115/2 (see Patrick Brennan and fn. 20 below); see Jennings, 'Malines ordination registers', p. 154, fn. 4.   14 *Merchants' Quay report*, p. 214.   15 Canice Mooney in FLK copy of Cleary, *Father Luke Wadding*, p. 132, notes in pencil, 'confer the will of Patrick Fleming in FLK mss D1'. These manuscripts are now housed in UCD Archives.

who opposed the excommunications issued by the papal nuncio Rinuccini.[16] In July 1649 at Kilkenny he joined with many other guardians in condemning Redmond Caron, the pseudo-commissary provincial appointed by Peter Marchant in the interests of the duke of Ormond. There was another John Barnewall, a Jesuit, who was ordained priest at Mechelen (Malines) on 4 April 1609.[17]

BONAVENTURE BARON (1610–96)

Bonaventure Baron was born in Clonmel, Co. Tipperary, the son of Lawrence Baron and Mary Wadding, the sister of Luke Wadding OFM. His mother died when he was only six years old and his father when he was twelve. His teachers were Robert Sall or Saul in Clonmel and John Flahy in Waterford. When he was sixteen he went to study at the friary at Timoleague, Co. Cork, and there he joined the Franciscans, exchanging his baptismal name, Bartholomew, for Bonaventure. In 1629 he was sent to Louvain to complete his course in philosophy. He studied for a short time at Augsburg and Salzburg, before proceeding to Rome to continue his studies in theology. Ordained a priest in Rome in 1634, he lectured there for most of the rest of his life, in arts, philosophy and theology. He was a renowned Scotist and humanist, as well as a writer, poet, preacher and historian. In the 1660s he travelled around the Continent undertaking research in Austria, Germany and France. During the next decade, he spent some years in Milan and Florence, and was appointed Franciscan commissary for the province in Croatia. He published twenty-two large volumes, several containing a number of different works, and many of them were printed at Lyons. A rather domineering character, he had a difference of opinion with some Roman censors, and in 1690 one volume of his literary work (prose and poetry) was placed on the index of forbidden books, twenty-one years after it was published. He died in his eighty-sixth year in St Isidore's on 18 March, 1696.[18]

BERNARDINE BARRY (*fl.* 1660s)

Bernardine Barry was a Munsterman from the diocese of Cloyne who went as a youth to St Isidore's College and was ordained in Rome. He may have been the *Frater Bernardinus à Jesu* ordained there on 17 September 1635. After his studies he

---

16 J.T. Gilbert, *History of the Irish Confederation and the war in Ireland* (1890), iv, pp 269–78.   **17** Jennings, 'Malines ordination registers', p. 155.   **18** See Baron's own 'Address to Posterity' (in Latin) in UCD-OFM B64, xii–xxii; Cleary, *Father Luke Wadding*, pp 88–100; T. Wall, 'A distinguished Irish humanist, Bonaventure Baron' (1946); Jennings, *Wadding papers* (index); B. Millett, 'Bonaventure Baron, O.F.M., *Hibernus Clonmeliensis*' (1950).

was sent in 1638 to lecture in the Franciscan friary of Santa Maria Nova in Naples, but was recalled to teach in Rome in 1639. He became vicar at St Isidore's on 26 November 1642. At the chapter of September 1647 he was appointed guardian of St Anthony's College, Louvain, and was reappointed in February 1648, remaining in that position until 1650–1. It may have been at this time that he was twice sent as an 'ambassador' to the King of France, according to the Spaniard Pedro Manero OFM, the minister general of the order (1651–5). Manero had turned against Luke Wadding, accusing him of being anti-Spanish, which was not the case. Barry arrived back in Rome on 1 June 1652, and was appointed guardian there in the following December. He was nominated on the 23 September 1653 as the temporary vicar provincial for Ireland, by Cardinal Francesco Barbarini at Wadding's instigation, despite the likely objections of the Spanish minister general. The appointment was made because on 23 June 1653 the minister provincial, Francis O'Sullivan had been killed and in the circumstances it was difficult to hold an election in Ireland. The minister general appointed Bonaventure Mellaghlin vicar provincial on 12 May 1654 without mentioning Barry, who continued as guardian in St Isidore's until 5 December 1655. He was later guardian at Louvain and provincial commissary for the colleges at Louvain and Prague. In that capacity, on 16 September 1661, while in Louvain, he gave his permission for the posthumous printing of Hugh Ward's work on St Rumold. Even though he had not been in Ireland since his youth, in July 1666 he was elected minister provincial at the first voting. This was not accepted by the Ormond party among the friars (those influenced by the powerful duke of Ormond), and a vicar provincial of their choice was elected instead. Barry would not sign the Remonstrance or Protestation of Loyalty as formulated for Ormond and disapproved of by the papal nuncio, Rinuccini. The situation was not rectified for about four years, but Barry did not succeed in becoming minister provincial. A long list of candidates proposed for Irish dioceses *c.*1665 contains the name of Bernardine Barry of the diocese of Cloyne. He died at Louvain about the beginning of May 1668. There was another P. Barry admitted to St Isidore's on 1 June 1652.[19]

19 R.L. Browne, 'History of the Franciscan Order in Ireland' (1898); B. Millett, 'Ninety candidates proposed for Irish dioceses *c.*1665' (1955), pp 113–14; Giblin, *Liber Lovaniensis* (index); *Father Luke Wadding commemorative volume* (index); with regard to the date of Barry's death, and his precedence over Francis O'Molloy confirmed in 1652, see B. Jennings, 'Some correspondence of Father Luke Wadding, O.F.M.' (1959), pp 91–2; B. Millett, 'Copies of some decisions from the missing discretorial registors of St Isidore's College, Rome, 1652–1739' (2001), pp 87–90.

EDMUND BRAY (d. 1676)

Edmund Bray was a Munster man. There were two of the name. Edmund junior was ordained at Mechelen (Malines) on 7 March 1637, and was appointed guardian at Clonmel in 1647. Edmund senior, subject of this entry, was ordained at Mechelen (Malines) on the 23 February 1630, and was guardian at Clonmel in 1641, when Bonaventure Baron wrote to him on the death of Anthony Hickey in Rome (d. 26 June 1641). He was guardian in Clonmel again in 1650. Baron related later that when he himself was 'barely an adult' (aged 16) joining the friars and sick with fever seemingly in Timoleague friary *c*.1626, Edmund Bray, who was also there then, was not afraid to nurse him and contract the fever too. He may have been with Baron in Augsburg and Salzburg for a few months before going to Louvain, where he dedicated his theses in logic (*c*.1629) to his cousin, Patrick Comerford, the bishop of Waterford and Lismore. He continued his studies in St Isidore's College, Rome, and defended theology theses in 1633. By July 1634 he was teaching in Salzburg, first philosophy and then theology. He lectured also in the friary at Augsburg. As noted above, he was guardian of Clonmel in 1641 and 1650. During the period of the Catholic Confederation he supported the papal nuncio Rinuccini and Owen Roe O'Neill, and was regarded by Ormond as hostile to his plans. He was in Louvain in June 1655, when he was proposed with three others by Luke Wadding as a possible guardian of St Isidore's College in Rome but he was not appointed. At the chapter of 1658 he was appointed the minister provincial's vicar. He was in Clonmel on 26 May 1671 when he wrote a letter to Francis Harold OFM in Rome. Before the chapter of 1672 he was placed on a list of possible provincial ministers. A jubilarian, Bray died in Louvain on 2 July 1676.[20]

PATRICK BRENNAN (*fl.* 1640s)

On 9 September 1627, in Louvain, the young Franciscan student, Patrick Brennan from Leinster, defended some theses on St Augustine's doctrine on grace, free will, and predestination. These were reprinted in 1641 by the printer James Zegers and attached to his pamphlet criticizing a booklet by a Jesuit, Pierre de Bivero, who condemned Cornelius Jansen's *Augustinus*. With the theses, Zegers printed also approbations of Jansen's work by some doctors of the Sorbonne university.

20 Jennings, 'Malines ordination registers', p. 158; Bonaventure Baron, OFM, *Opuscula prosa et metro, argumento etiam varia*, tomus I (Wurzburg, 1668), *Opusculum sextum*, pp 8–9, and ibid., tomus II (Lyons, 1669); B. Millett, 'Irish Scotists at St Isidore's College, Rome', p. 413; see also FLK MS C115 and UCD-OFM MS D5, p. 209.

In this way the Franciscan was wrongly connected with the teachings of Jansen, a connection which was strongly denied. In 1632 Brennan was appointed a lecturer in philosophy at St Isidore's, where he later taught theology. In 1639 he returned to Louvain to teach, and presided at the defence of theses there up to 1647 when he was declared a *lector jubilatus*. He was appointed guardian in Louvain in 1645. In December of that year he signed an approbation at the end of Anthony Gearnon's *Parrthas an Anma* which states that he had read it, a proof that he knew Irish. There, too, he supported John Colgan in his appeal for funds to continue the publication of the lives of Irish saints. The chapter of 1648 elected him guardian of New Ross friary, but it seems that he was then moved to Kilkenny, where the friars were divided by political efforts to split the Franciscans during the Catholic Confederation, which was based in that city. When he returned to Ireland, he supported the efforts of the papal nuncio, Rinuccini, and Owen Roe O'Neill. This stance drew the wrath of the Marquis of Ormond in 1649 on Brennan and nineteen other Irish Franciscan superiors. Brennan was imprisoned in Kilkenny for a short while. On his release from prison, Fr Brennan followed the nuncio to Galway. The provincial chapter of 1650 appointed him vicar of the minister provincial. In that year the Bishop of Ross, Boetius MacEgan OFM, was captured by a Cromwellian army and hanged. The following year, Patrick Brennan was in Rome, and as vicar made a formal petition to the Cardinal Protector of the Franciscans for the appointment of a successor to the martyred bishop, proposing another friar, Tadhg Ó Dálaigh, for the position. After that he disappears from the records.[21]

VALENTINE BROWNE (*c.*1594–1672)

Valentine Browne was a graduate of Louvain, and although he had only a tenuous link with Rome, as minister provincial during a very difficult period, he had to keep the colleges open. He was born in Galway and was related to the Burkes and Blakes, all prominent merchant families in Galway. He himself was described as 'inveterately Anglo-Irish'. After his early studies at home and then in the Irish College at Douai, in 1617 he joined the Franciscans in Louvain. He became a lecturer in theology and returned home to teach novices in his native city. In 1629

---

21 *Humilis et supplex querimonia Iacobi Zegers ... adversus libellum ... Regiae Capellae Bruxell. concionatoris, et theses PP. Societatis Lovanij, anno 1641;* and also *Sententia D. Augustini ... de gratia, lib. arbit., praedestinatione & reprobatine. Publice defensa ... Respondente F. Patricio Brinan die 9. Septembris 1627:* both editions by Iacobus Zegers (Louvain, 1641). See also fn. 12 above and Cleary, *Father Luke Wadding,* pp 87–8; Giblin, *Liber Lovaniensis* (index); *Father Luke Wadding commemorative volume,* pp 342ff, 368; Fennessy, 'Canon E. Reussen's list of Irish Franciscan theses', p. 23.

he was elected minister provincial in succession to the martyred Francis O'Mahony, and held that office until 1633. During this period the friars were persecuted and had to leave their friaries, often living with friends and relatives, and trying to send candidates and students abroad. Browne corresponded with Luke Wadding in Rome about their plight. Both of them had also to try to counteract the anti-religious propaganda of Patrick Cahill in Paris. In May 1632 Browne wrote a special letter to Mícheál Ó Cléirigh encouraging him 'by the merit of holy obedience to persevere to the end … in this laborious work of the Annals which you have already begun …'. This was an important document for Mícheál Ó Cléirigh to have in his possession as it assured people in Ireland that he was not acting on his own but had the blessing and support of the minister provincial and his religious superiors. Valentine Browne resided in Galway. He was still there as guardian in 1639, and in 1642 welcomed the Poor Clares to the city. In July 1648 he was suspended from public ministry for opposing the papal nuncio's excommunication of the supporters of a truce between the Catholic Confederates and Lord Inchiquin. He rejected the authority of the minister provincial, Thomas MacKiernan, and accepted the controversial visitator Redmond Caron. He had to retract in 1650, but remained an Ormondist and favoured the surrender of Galway to English forces. He was a follower of Peter Walsh and signed his controversial formulary of loyalty to the English king. In his seventies he held onto marginal influence in the province, and died in 1672 at the friary of Bally Clare, now Claregalway.[22]

ROBERT CHAMBERLAIN (CHAMBERLANE/MAC ARTÚIR) (*c.*1570–1636)

Robert Chamberlain's Co. Louth family had taken the Irish name Mac Artúir, and therefore Robert was considered to have belonged to a native Irish family. Before he was thirty years of age he studied theology in Salamanca and was ordained a priest there. Capable of corresponding in Irish, English, Latin and Spanish, he became a counsellor and confessor to Hugh O'Neill, earl of Tyrone, and was his emissary to Spain. In 1607 he met the exiled earls of Tyrone and Tyrconnell at Douai, and probably accompanied them to Louvain with Flaithrí Ó Maoil Chonaire. He continued in the service of Spain, and in 1610 entered the Franciscan order in Louvain. He became a respected lecturer in theology, but kept up his interest in Irish literature. In 1616–17 he contributed two poems to the poetic dialogue known as the Contention of the Bards, and was acting superior of St Anthony's College for a time. In 1622 it was reported to the English court that

---

22 I. Fennessy, 'Valentine Browne' *ODNB*, vol. 8 (2004).

Chamberlain had been to Rome, and had returned with a message from Hugh O'Neill concerning a landing of ships in Ireland. A later report recorded his return to Rome, possibly to assist in arranging a Spanish marriage for one of O'Neill's sons. On the death of Aodh Mac Aingil, he refused to be considered for the archbishopric of Armagh, despite considerable political pressure. Neither could he be persuaded at any time to become superior of St Anthony's College, Louvain, where he died on 11 June 1636.[23]

BONAVENTURE DELAHOYDE (DE LA HOIDE/HYDE) (*fl.* 1640S)

Bonaventure Delahoyde was a Munster man. It seems that his parents wanted him to be educated in Belgium. A student named Edward Delahoyd left the Irish College at Douai to join the Irish Franciscans in Louvain. This may have been Bonaventure, a name taken on his entry into religion. He received minor orders at Mechelen (Malines) in December 1621, and probably was ordained a priest there later. Having studied philosophy and some theology, it is said that he accompanied John Punch who entered St Isidore's College, Rome, on 9 September 1625. His name does not appear, however, in the diary of St Isidore's College for that year. But he continued to follow theology courses there under Anthony Hickey, and on the 2 September 1627 he was sent from Rome to Louvain. He lectured there in philosophy and theology, and at Augsburg and also Salzburg. In 1630 he was a discreet or counsellor to the guardian, and in 1636 he himself was appointed the guardian at Louvain. He was vicar of the province by 1639, and was back in Ireland. At the chapter in 1645 he was appointed guardian of Quin friary, and then of Ennis friary in 1647 and 1648, and of Galway in 1650. He was captured there, imprisoned and deported. He died in 1653 in a friary named in Latin 'Oropesa', in Castile, Spain. He left behind him a Latin manuscript compendium of popes, emperors, heretics and events, in which there is a note naming the author and saying he was a learned, religious and prudent man who never anywhere wasted his time.[24]

23 Meehan, *The fate and fortunes of Hugh O'Neill, earl of Tyrone, and Rory O'Donel, earl of Tyrconnel,* pp 158, 305ff, 315; F. O'Brien, 'Robert Chamberlain OFM' (1932); I. Fennessy, 'Robert Chamberlain', *ODNB,* vol. 10 (2004). **24** See sources in B. Jennings in Cleary, *Father Luke Wadding,* pp 123–4; Giblin, *Liber Lovaniensis* (index); Millett, *The Irish Franciscans,* pp 268–9, nn 109–11; I. Fennessy, 'The B manuscripts in the Franciscan Library Killiney' (1995), p. 190 (MS B109). The B manuscripts are now in UCD Archives.

PATRICK FLEMING (1599–1630)

Patrick Fleming, baptized Christopher Fleming, was a Co. Louth man and nephew of Thomas Fleming OFM, the archbishop of Dublin from 1623 to 1651. He was sent to Douai in Belgium to be educated by another uncle of his, Christopher Cusack, who was president of the Irish College there. He joined the Irish Franciscans in Louvain in 1617, and was professed a year later by Anthony Hickey, taking the name Patrick in religion. On 18 December 1621 he was ordained a deacon at Mechelen (Malines), and a priest in 1622. The following year he went to Rome with Aodh Mac Aingil. They met Hugh Ward OFM and Thomas Messingham, the rector of the Irish College in Paris, and as a result it was agreed to research and publish the lives of the Irish saints. He visited libraries on the Continent, and sent material back to Messingham. In Rome he sent what he could find to Hugh Ward. In 1624 he was chosen to defend publicly theses at the general chapter of the Franciscans and the following year he became the first lecturer in philosophy in Luke Wadding's new foundation, St Isidore's College, where he himself continued to study. He searched for more Irish material in libraries in Italy, France, Germany and the Spanish Netherlands, and was back teaching in Louvain in 1627. There he worked on his collected lives of St Columban, but this work was interrupted when the Irish Franciscans obtained permission to establish a college in Prague in Bohemia. In December 1630 he was sent there as superior and lecturer in theology. Despite some opposition, the friars made progress in Prague, when the Thirty Years War intervened. When the army of the elector of Saxony was drawing near Prague, the Irish friars decided to leave for safer quarters. On their way to the friary at Votice, Patrick Fleming and his travelling companion, Matthew Hoare, a young deacon originally from Dungarvan, Co. Waterford, were killed by some Hussites. Their tomb is in the chapel of the friary at Votice. Fleming's collection of documents on the life of St Columban was published later by Thomas Sheeran.[25]

ANTHONY HICKEY (O'HICKEY/O hICEADHA) (1586–1641)

Anthony Hickey was a Munsterman, baptized Diarmuid, and a member of a medical family, the hereditary physicians to the O'Briens of Thomond. He was born in 1586 and had seven brothers and one sister. He studied in Paris and in the Irish College at Douai, before joining the Franciscans, aged twenty-one, on 1

---

25 M. O'Reilly & R. Brennan, *Lives of the Irish martyrs and confessors* (1882), pp 661ff; B. Jennings, 'The Irish Franciscans in Prague' (1939); I. Fennessy, 'Christospher Fleming', *ODNB*, vol. 20 (2004).

November 1607, one of the first novices in the newly founded St Anthony's College at Louvain, where he was given the name Anthony in religion. He was ordained a priest on the 6 March 1610 at Mechelen (Malines). He taught theology in Louvain and was acting superior there in 1617. In February 1618 he signed an approbation for Aodh Mac Aingil's *Sgáthán Shacramainte na hAithridhe*, which suggests a knowledge of Irish. In 1619 he was chosen to assist Luke Wadding in his literary and historical work in Rome, and his defence of the Franciscans against the accusation published by the Dominican Abraham Bzowski (Bzovius) in 1616–17, and later against the attacks on religious in Ireland by the secular priests Paul Harris and Patrick Cahill. In June 1625, Hickey became the first lecturer in theology appointed to the new St Isidore's College. He became a consultor for Roman congregations, an agent for some Irish ecclesiastics, a definitor general of the Franciscan order, and a most valuable assistant to Wadding in his voluminous publications. An author himself, he was a kind-hearted man, a conciliator, and admired by Pope Urban VIII, who lamented his death on 26 June 1641 at the early age of fifty-five.[26]

PAUL KING (*c.*1610–55)

Paul King a native of Kilkenny was born about 1610, and baptized David, the son of Cornelius King, a follower of Brian Fitzpatrick, baron of Upper Ossory. His uncle was Murtagh King, a convert to Protestantism, who translated the Old Testament into Irish for the bishop of Kilmore, William Bedell. David King remained staunchly Catholic and entered the Franciscan order in Rome, receiving the name Paul of the Holy Spirit. He studied under Bonaventure Baron, and revered him, although he later became an enemy of Baron's uncle, Luke Wadding, despite the fact that Wadding paid a ransom for him when, on one journey, he was captured by pirates who then patrolled the seas south of Ireland. For example, the infamous Sack of Baltimore in West Cork took place in 1631. It is curious that King mentioned that another Franciscan, Denis O'Driscoll, archbishop of Brindisi (1640–50), had been 'redeemed from the hands of the Turks at Madrid' *c.*1635, a year before King met him. In 1641 King was sent to teach theology in the friary at Brindisi on the heel of Italy, probably at Archbishop O'Driscoll's request. King was later recalled to act as a secretary at the Franciscan curia, Aracoeli, in Rome. He returned to Ireland in 1646 or early 1647.

26 Luke Wadding, *Scriptores* (1906), pp 26–7; Jennings, *Louvain papers*, no. 11 and no. 66, section III; J. Brady, 'The Irish Colleges in the Low Countries' (1949), p. 79; I. Fennessy, 'Hickey, Diarmuid', *ODNB*, vol. 27 (2004).

At the provincial chapter held in September 1647, he was appointed one of the lecturers in theology at the Kilkenny friary, and guardian there at the middle chapter of February 1648. The city was at the centre of the Catholic Confederation's struggle to obtain freedom of religion. A letter of his urging Owen Roe O'Neill to seize Kilkenny was intercepted, and he fled to Louvain, where he wrote another controversial letter about the nuncio's opponents dated 4 May 1649, which led to a debate in his favour and against him in print. He was sent to Rome as agent for the pro-nuncio friars, and was made guardian there in November 1649. In 1652 he was succeeded by Bernardine Barry and died in Rome before 4 August 1655. He planned to write a history of the Franciscan order in ten volumes (perhaps in opposition to Luke Wadding), but produced only a prospectus of forty pages entitled *Idea Cosmographiae Seraphicae* (Rome, 1654).[27]

AODH MAC AINGIL (HUGH MACCAGHWELL/HUGO CAVELLUS) (1571–1626)

Aodh Mac Aingil was born in Downpatrick, Co. Down.[28] Nothing is known about his parents or his early education, apart from the fact that he attended a famous school on the Isle of Man. On his return to Ireland he was chosen by Hugh O'Neill as a tutor for his sons, and on an invitation from King Philip III of Spain, was sent by him to accompany the young Henry O'Neill to Salamanca to continue his studies. In Salamanca they studied at the university until Henry became a soldier. About 1603–4, Mac Aingil studied law and joined the Franciscans with whom he had been lodging. He was thirty-three years of age, and became a member of the Spanish province of St James, as did Luke Wadding some ten years later. His teachers imbued him with a love for the theology of John Duns Scotus, whom he mistakenly considered to be a fellow Irishman from Downpatrick. He was ordained a priest before the end of 1605 when he was a preacher to the army. His influence at the royal court in Spain probably played a part in the founding of St Anthony's College at Louvain. He went there himself in June 1607 and was appointed a lecturer in theology in the following

27 *Vindiciarum Catholicorum Hiberniae. Auctore Philopatro Irenaeo ad Alithophylum* (Paris, 1650), ii, 1ff. The author was John Callaghan. See also J.T. Gilbert (ed.), *A contemporary history of affairs in Ireland from 1641 to 1652* (1880), ii: 2, pp 73ff, 211ff; P.J. Corish, 'John Callaghan and the controversies among the Irish in Paris' (1954); Jennings, 'Some correspondence of Father Luke Wadding, O.F.M.' (anti-Wadding); C. Giblin, 'The *Processus Datariae* for Denis O'Driscoll, 1640' (1965), p. 42 (his age); R. Bagwell's article on Paul King, revised by S. Kelsey, *ODNB*, vol. 31 (2004); for the pirates see D. Eakin, *The stolen village. Baltimore and the Barbary pirates* (2006). **28** Not at Saul; see C. Giblin, 'Hugh MacCaghwell O.F.M. and Scotism', p. 375, n.2.

November.[29] His influence on the development of the college was so great that Wadding regarded him as one of its founders. He was acting superior there in 1607 and guardian in 1610. When he journeyed on foot to Rome to attend the general chapter of the order in 1612, he brought Anthony Hickey with him. He was guardian in Louvain again in 1613 and 1617. He was used as a go-between by an agent of King James I of England in a vain effort to discover the intentions of Hugh O'Neill in Rome.[30] He initiated the defence of Scotistic theology even before Wadding and Anthony Hickey in Rome, and Wadding drew largely on his work for his own edition of Scotus. Several of the Louvain friar's Franciscan students defended both Scotus and Mac Aingil in print. He wrote poetry in Irish,[31] and a work on the sacrament of confession published in Louvain in 1618.[32] As a definitor general he was a member of the highest council of the order and in 1623 he was teaching in their house at Araceoli in Rome. He had made the journey to Rome this time with another student of his, Patrick Fleming, who wrote an account of his master. Mac Aingil also taught in the newly-opened St Isidore's College. He was appointed to the see of Armagh in April 1626 and was consecrated archbishop in St Isidore's the following June. Sadly, before he could depart for Ireland, he died in Rome on 22 September 1626 and was buried in St Isidore's.[33]

BERNARD MEDE (MEADE/MEDUS/MIACHE) (*fl.* 1620s)

Bernard Mede was baptized Nicholas, a nephew of Robert Myagh, the vicar general for Cork diocese. He studied in the Irish College at Douai, and then joined the Franciscans at St Anthony's College, Louvain. On 18 May 1610, when a young student in Louvain, he wrote a long letter in Latin to his uncle. His letter was intercepted and is preserved among the Irish State Papers.[34] He returned to Ireland about 1614 and was captured by soldiers on a raid on the Drogheda friary. Some merchants claimed he was one of their party having just returned from the Continent and when the soldiers were off guard he managed to escape. A friar of that name, who was known as a theologian and preacher, made a copy of the Office or Breviary Life of St Finbarr, in Cork in April 1624, which was intended

29 Jennings, *Louvain Papers*, no. 21, pp 19–20 paras 3–4. **30** M.K. Walsh, *Destruction by Peace. Hugh O'Neill after Kinsale* (1986) and 2nd edition re-named *An exile of Ireland. Hugh O'Neill, prince of Ulster* (1996). **31** Mhág Craith, *Dán na mBráthar Mionúr*, i, pp 157–78, ii, pp 189–98, nn 30–6. **32** Ó Maonaigh (ed.), *Scáthán Shacramuinte*. **33** Nicolaus Vernulaeus, 'Oratio II Panegyricus … Domino F. Hugoni Cavello …', *Rhetorum Collegii Porcensis inclitae Academiae Lovaniensis Orationum Pars Tertia* (Cologne, 1657), pp 811–27; L.F. Renehan, *Collections on Irish church history* (ed. D. McCarthy), (Dublin, 1861), i, pp 24–7; G. Cleary, 'MacCaghwell (Cavellus), Hugh' (1913); Terry Clavin, 'MacCaghwell, Hugh', *ODNB*, vol. 35 (2004).

for the scholars in Louvain. The manuscript is preserved now in the Bibliothèque des Bollandistes, Brussels. A Bernardine Meade was elected guardian of Youghal friary in 1627 and of Cork in August 1629. He is listed here because there was another friar of the same name with whom he is confused, and who was in Rome. The latter defended theses in theology in St Isidore's in 1643, and became a lecturer in philosophy at Stronconi in Umbria in 1645. It is recorded that in 1654 the former assisted an Italian Franciscan from Calabria in writing on vellum a very large choir book for St Isidore's containing antiphons and Masses. This Fr Bernardine helped to prepare the vellum and to delineate the ornamental capital letters. For the record, there was a third friar named Meade, but called Bonaventure, who was guardian in Cork friary in 1645–7.[35]

FRANCIS PORTER (*c*.1631–1702)

There is no direct evidence that Francis Porter ever visited Louvain, but his writings against Jansenism were well known there;[36] and his activities in favour of the exiled Stuart monarch, James II, brought him from Rome as far as Paris at least. Born in Kingstown, Co. Meath in 1631–2, he was the first son of Simon Porter, and was given the name Walter at baptism. The only thing known about his early education is that he attended the Irish College at Lille in France, and on the completion of his studies in the humanities in 1653, he received a certificate from the Jesuits there. This is an interesting connection, in the light of his later anti-Jansenist labours. He may have entered the Franciscans in Rome in October that year, for in September 1654 he wrote a testament renouncing his right of primogeniture in favour of his brother Patrick. He was a priest at St Isidore's College in 1663, and was appointed a lecturer in philosophy there in the following year, and of theology in 1668. In 1674 he was acting superior of St Isidore's. He was interested in becoming the bishop of Meath after the death of Patrick Plunkett in 1679. He succeeded in having the anti-religious diocesan statutes of that diocese corrected by the Holy See in 1686. He published seven works in Latin, including *Securis evangelica ad haeresis radices posita* ('The axe of the gospels put to the roots of heresy') in 1674. An expanded second edition appeared in Rome in 1687 and later in Bohemia. In this, and in another work, his intention

34 Jennings, *Louvain papers*, no. 26, pp 23–5; the date is Louvain, 4 Ides of May. The Ides is the 15 May; the 4 Ides is counted inclusively from that, which is 18 May.   **35** Giblin, *Liber Lovaniensis*, p. 72, n.1; C. Mooney, 'The mirror of all Ireland' (1949), pp 13–14; P. Ó Riain (ed.), *Beatha Bharra. Saint Finbarr of Cork* (1994), pp 3–4 & index; Cleary, *Father Luke Wadding*, p. 140; Fennessy, 'The B manuscripts', p. 208 (UCD-OFM MS B166).   **36** See a reference in a letter from Bernardine Gavan OFM in Louvain to Patrick Duffy OFM in Rome dated 6 December 1695, in Jennings, *Louvain papers*, pp 295–6.

was to convict all heretics of atheism using their own principles and the infallible teaching of the Catholic Church. He published a collection of ecclesiastical definitions and decrees, which was placed on the index of prohibited books. A further edition was published at Avignon. This was a very useful source of canon law long before the official collection of the *Codex Iuris Canonici* was published in 1917. Patrick Porter, the brother of Francis, had been at Avignon, and was since 1688 the tutor to Henry Fitzjames, the son of James II and Arabella Churchill. In 1690 Francis was appointed theologian and historian to the exiled Stuart king, and in that year produced a brief account of Ireland and its history from 1532, which was written in the Stuart cause and translated into French. Later it was used in the contentious chapter 7 of Thomas Burke's famous *Hibernia Dominicana*. Porter published a translation in Latin (with additions) of a work by the French Jesuit, Menestrier, against the invention of the prophecies of St Malachy concerning the popes. Francis Porter died at St Isidore's College, Rome on 6 April 1702. On the monument erected in 1736 to his memory, it is stated that he was eighty years of age, but he himself said in 1696 that he was then sixty-four, which gives his age at death as seventy.[37]

JOHN PUNCH (PONCE/PONCIUS) (*c*.1599–1661)

John Punch was born in Cork. He joined the Franciscans in Louvain, studied philosophy at Cologne, and theology first in Louvain and then in Rome, where he was one of the first students at St Isidore's College in 1625. He was rector of the Irish College near St Isidore's for a time in 1630, and taught philosophy and theology at St Isidore's for many years. His method departed from the age-old practice of commenting systematically on the famous work on Christian doctrine, the *Book of the Sentences* of Peter the Lombard (d. 1160), and he developed a more modern course. With others, he assisted Luke Wadding in publishing the works of John Duns Scotus. In 1648 he left Rome for France, taught at the friary in Lyons for short while, and then stayed in Paris, where he died. He published his philosophy tracts in Lyons and his theology works in Paris. Punch was an anti-Ormondist and defender of Rinuccini, which led him into controversy in print. He defended also the good name of Wadding against false rumours that the latter was opposed to the nuncio for reasons of self-aggrandisement. He defended the Irish Franciscans who had been forced to flee from persecution and to join continental friaries, where their presence sometimes caused problems.[38]

37 I. Fennessy, 'Porter, Walter', *ODNB*, vol. 44 (2004) with sources.   **38** Cleary, *Father Luke Wadding*, pp 83–6; M. Grajewski, 'John Ponce, Franciscan Scotist of the seventeenth century' (1946); *Father Luke*

THOMAS STRANGE (STRONGE) (d. 1645)

Thomas Strange was a Waterfordman and an alumnus of Louvain. He was a cousin of Luke Wadding's, and corresponded with him with regard to historical sources. Archbishop James Ussher extended an invitation to him to make use of his library. A subdeacon from the Spanish province of St James, he entered Louvain in June 1607. Before that he was a student at the Irish College in Douai. He became a lecturer in theology, a notable preacher, and he attained high positions in the Irish province. He was an agent in the English court for Irish clergy, and was proposed for the episcopal see of Waterford. Falsely accused of heresy by secular priests in Dublin, he cleared his name with the assistance of Luke Wadding at home and in Rome. He died in Waterford in 1645.[39]

FRANCIS TARPY

Little is known about Francis Tarpy. It is recorded that, after completing his studies, he left St Isidore's College, Rome, on 15 March 1627 to return to Ireland. A year later, the archbishop of Cashel, Thomas Walshe, met him in Antwerp in August, and gave him letters to be forwarded to Luke Wadding in Rome. At the chapter held on 15 August 1629, he was appointed as a lecturer in philosophy in Galway, and given faculties to preach and hear confessions of the laity. The following year he was asked to teach philosophy in Louvain, and later to teach theology in Prague.[40]

AODH MAC AN BHAIRD (HUGH WARD) (c.1593–1635)

Aodh Mac an Bhaird was the son of Eoghan Ward and Mary O'Cleary from Tirhugh, Co. Donegal. He entered the Irish College in Salamanca in January 1612. Encouraged by Luke Wadding, he joined the Franciscans there in 1616. He was officially attached to the friary in Donegal. By 1622 he was in Paris with the Spanish confessor to the Queen of France, and teaching in the Franciscan friary

Wadding commemorative volume (index); Mooney, *Irish Franciscans and France*; Millett, *The Irish Franciscans*. **39** A. Coleman, 'An Irish friar and an Irish Protestant theory' (1906), for a twentieth-century controversy arising from a letter he wrote in 1629; B. Millett, 'Guide to material for a biography of Father Luke Wadding', in *Father Luke Wadding commemorative volume*, p. 233; also other references to Strange (pronounced Strang) in the same volume; Jennings, *Louvain papers*, no. 21, para. 3 and no. 89 para. 1; Jennings, *Wadding papers* (index), including his letters to Wadding; *Merchants' Quay report* (index); and Luke Wadding, *Scriptores* (1906), p. 217. **40** Cleary, *Father Luke Wadding*, p. 124; B. Jennings, 'Miscellaneous documents II, 1625–1640' (1949), p. 2.

there. He was appointed to teach theology in St Anthony's College, Louvain, and arrived there in 1623. From 1626 to 1629 he was guardian in Louvain, and in 1633 an official visitor of friaries in Lille. During these years he was able to visit many libraries in Germany and France. Never very robust, he died at an early age in 1635. Fluent in Irish and versed in history, he collected the lives of Irish saints in libraries on the Continent, and corresponded with the famous Jesuits hagiographers, the Bollandists. He was one of the originators of the movement to document the lives of Irish saints and his dedication and work was highly praised in print by John Colgan in Louvain and Luke Wadding in Rome. Wadding corresponded with him regularly, claiming that Mac an Bhaird left behind many pieces of histories and martyrologies. He was interested in the secular history of Ireland, too, and appreciated the abilities of Mícheál Ó Cléirigh, sending him to Ireland in search of material in old manuscripts. His only book, published posthumously in 1662, was on St Rumold, the apostle of Mechelen (Malines), who was thought to have been an Irishman and archbishop of Dublin, but was probably an Anglo-Saxon martyred missionary.[41]

CONCLUSION

This survey deals with a select number of Irish friars who were formed in either St Anthony's College, Louvain or in St Isidore's College, Rome or who had important connections with both colleges. There were many more, some of whom such as Flaithrí Ó Maoil Chonaire[42] or Bonaventure Ó hEodhasa were very eminent, others who are yet to be identified. As is clear, however, even from this brief prosopography, the friars were deeply embedded in the ecclesiastical, intellectual and political life of their native land and of Europe and their influence was considerable in both places. What can be said of this whole volume can also be stated in relation to this prosopographical work. It builds on the research of earlier Franciscan scholars and also points the way to many new topics of research for future scholars in the field.

---

41 M. O'Reilly & R. Brennan, *Lives of the Irish martyrs and confessors*, pp 688–711; F. O'Brien, 'Irish Franciscan historians of St Anthony's College, Louvain'; P.A. Breatnach, 'An Irish Bollandist: Fr Hugh Ward and the Louvain hagiographical enterprise' (1999).   **42** See B. Hazard, *Faith and patronage: Flaithrí Ó Maoil Chonaire, c.1560–1629* (forthcoming).

Abbreviations

ACSI	Archivio del Collegio di Sant'Isidoro, Rome.
AFH	*Archivum Franciscanum Historicum.*
AFM	J. O'Donovan (ed.), *Annala rioghachta Eireann. Annals of the Kingdom of Ireland, by the Four Masters from the earliest period to the year 1616* (7 vols, Dublin, 1851, repr. Dublin, 1998).
AGFM	Material relating to the Irish Province (*Australia* 1, *Consultationes, Hibernia* 1–5) has been short-title calendared by Patrick Conlan in various volumes of *Collectanea Hibernica*, 1976 to 1993. See bibliography.
AGFM, *Irlanda*	A loose box of Irish documents in AGFM.
APF	Archivio della S. Congregazione de Propaganda Fide, Rome.
APF, *Acta*	*Acta congregationum generalium.*
APF, *SC Irlanda*	*Scritture riferite nei Congressi (Irlanda).*
APF, *SOGC*	*Scritture originali riferite nelle Congregazione Generali.*
BL	British Library.
BL Cat. Ir. MSS	R. Flower, *Catalogue of Irish manuscripts in the British Library* (2 vols, London, 1926).
BL, Add. MS	British Library, Additional MS.
BR	Bibliothèque Royale de Belgique, Brussels
'Brevis synopsis'	B. Jennings (ed.), 'Brevis synopsis provinciae Hiberniae FF. minorum', *Analecta Hibernica* 6 (1934), pp 139–91.
'Brussels MS. 3410'	J. Moloney (ed.), 'Brussels MS. 3410', 'Micheál Ó Cléirigh, A chronological list of the foundations of the Irish Franciscan province', *Analecta Hibernica* 6 (1934), pp 192–202.
'Brussels MS. 3947'	B. Jennings (ed.), 'Brussels MS. 3947', '*Donatus Moneyus, De Provincia Hiberniae S. Francisci*', *Analecta Hibernica* 6 (1934), pp 12–138. Translated in *The Franciscan Tertiary* 4 (1894) – 9 (1899).
Cal. S.P. Ire.	Calendar of State Papers relating to Ireland, 24 vols (London, 1860–1912).
Cat. Ir. MSS FLK	M. Dillon, C. Mooney and P. de Brún, *Catalogue of Irish manuscripts in the Franciscan Library Killiney* (Dublin, 1969).
Cat. Ir. MSS RIA	*Catalogue of Irish manuscripts in the Royal Irish Academy*, 28 fasc. (Dublin, 1926–70)
Colgan, *AS*	J. Colgan, *Acta sanctorum veteris et maioris Scotiae, seu Hiberniae, sanctorum insulae* ... tomus primus (Louvain, 1645; repr. Dublin, 1948).
Colgan, *TT*	J. Colgan, *Triadis thaumaturgae seu divorum Patricii, Columbae et Brigidae, trium veteris et maioris Scotiae seu Hiberniae, sanctorum insulae, communium patronorum acta* (Louvain, 1647; repr. Dublin, 1997).
Comment. Rinucc.	R. O'Ferrall and R. O'Connell, *Commentarius Rinuccinianus de sedis apostolicae legatione ad foederatos Hiberniae catholicos per annos 1645–9.* Edited S. Kavanagh, 6 vols (IMC, Dublin, 1932–49).
Conlan, *FI*	P. Conlan, *Franciscan Ireland* (Mullingar, 1988).
CPL	*Calendar of Papal Letters*
DAA	Dublin Diocesan Archives.
DIB	*Dictionary of Irish biography.*
DIFP	Fanning, R., et al. (eds), *Documents on Irish foreign policy* (Dublin, 1998–).
DPA	Dominican Provincial Archives, Tallaght.

FLK	Franciscan Library Killiney (Dún Mhuire).
GRSH	P. Walsh (ed.), *Genealogiae regum et sanctorum Hiberniae* (Dublin, 1918).
Heist, *Vitae SS Hib.*	W.W. Heist (ed.), *Vitae sanctorum Hiberniae ex codice olim Salmanticensi nunc Bruxellensi* (Subsidia hagiographica 28, Société des Bollandistes, Brussels, 1965).
HMC	Historical Manuscripts Commission.
IMC	Irish Manuscripts Commission.
Jennings, *Michael O Cleirigh*	B. Jennings, *Michael O Cleirigh and his associates* (Dublin & Cork, 1936). Reprinted N. Ó Muraíle (ed.), *Mícheál Ó Cléirigh, his associates and St Anthony's College, Louvain* (Dublin, 2008).
Jennings, *Wild Geese*	B. Jennings (ed.), *Wild Geese in Spanish Flanders 1582–1700* (IMC, Dublin, 1944).
Jennings, *Wadding papers*	B. Jennings (ed.), *Wadding papers 1614–38* (IMC, Dublin, 1953).
Jennings, *Louvain papers*	B. Jennings (ed.), *Louvain papers 1606–1827* (IMC, Dublin, 1968).
Liber Dubliniensis	A. Faulkner (ed.), *Liber Dubliniensis. Chapter documents of the Irish Franciscans, 1719–1875* (Killiney, 1978).
Liber Killiniensis	I. Fennessy (ed.), *Liber Killiniensis. Irish Franciscan chapter bills, 1876–1999* (Killiney 2003).
Liber Lovaniensis	C. Giblin (ed.), *Liber Lovaniensis. A collection of Irish Franciscan documents, 1629–1717* (IMC, Dublin, 1956).
MartD	J. Henthorn Todd and W. Reeves (eds), *The martyrology of Donegal. A calendar of the saints of Ireland* (Irish Archaeological & Celtic Society, Dublin, 1864).
MartO	W. Stokes (ed.), *Félire Óengusso Céli Dé. The martyrology of Óengus the Culdee* (Henry Bradshaw Society 29, London, 1905).
MartT	R.I. Best and H.J. Lawlor (eds), *The martyrology of Tallaght from the Book of Leinster and MS 5100–4 in the Royal Library, Brussels* (Henry Bradshaw Society 68, London, 1931).
Measgra	S. O'Brien (ed.), *Measgra i gcuimhne Mhichíl Uí Chléirigh. Miscellany of historical and linguistic studies in honour of Brother Michael Ó Cléirigh, O.F.M., chief of the Four Masters, 1643–1943* (Dublin, 1944).
Merchants' Quay Report	G.D. Burtchaell and J.M. Rigg, *Report on Franciscan manuscripts preserved at the convent, Merchants' Quay, Dublin* (Dublin, 1906).
Millett, *Irish Franciscans*	B. Millett, *The Irish Franciscans 1651–1665* (Rome, 1964).
Millett & Lynch,	B. Millett & A. Lynch (eds), *Dún Mhuire, Killiney, 1945–95: Dún Mhuire. Léann agus seanchas* (Dublin, 1995).
MRH	A. Gwynn & R.N. Hadcock, *Medieval religious houses Ireland* (Dublin, 1970).
NHI	*A new history of Ireland.*
NLI	National Library of Ireland, Dublin.
ODNB	*Oxford dictionary of national biography.*
PRO SP	Public Records Office, London, State Papers.
RIA	Royal Irish Academy, Dublin.
TCD	Trinity College Dublin.
UCD	University College Dublin.
UCD-OFM	Catalogue reference for manuscripts and papers transferred from FLK to UCD Archives.
Wadding, *Annales*	L. Wadding, *Annales Minorum* 32 vols, 3rd ed., (Quarrachi, 1931–64).
Wadding, *Scriptores*	L. Wadding, *Scriptores Ordinis Minorum* (Rome, 1650. Reprinted *Scriptores* Rome, 1906).

Bibliography

MANUSCRIPTS

Belfast
Public Record Office of Northern Ireland
MS T1461.

Brussels
Bibliothèque Royale
MS 3947.   MS 5095–6.
MS 4639.

Cambridge
University Library
Add MS 4205.

Dublin
Franciscan Library Killiney

FLK MS C12–14.   FLK MS E13.
FLK MS C26 *Statuta domestica* (Prague).   FLK MS E16.
FLK MS C26 *Ex libro memorabilium, Statuta* FLK MS E18.
   domestica.   FLK MS E26.
FLK MS C30.   FLK MSS E37–9.
FLK MS C42.   FLK MSS E41–4.
FLK MSS C85–7.   FLK MSS E46–7.
FLK MS C105.   FLK MS E54.
FLK MS C115.   FLK MS E58.
FLK, MS C118.   FLK MS E64.
FLK MS C120.   FLK MS E66.
FLK MSS C177–9.   FLK MS E88.
FLK C220 (Clonmel).   FLK MS J/1/29.
FLK MS C345.   FLK MS L16.
FLK MS C426.   FLK MS M–F1 (Mullock diary).
FLK C669/2 (Dardis diary).   FLK MS M (notebook 1 of E.B. Fitzmaurice).
FLK MS C841 (*Chronicle I*).   FLK MSS P44–6 (old enumeration).
Mooney, C., *Chronicle of the Irish Province of* FLK XB58 (brochure).
   the Friars Minor 1939–63 (*Chronicle II*). FLK XB 360 (brochure).
FLK MS E2.   FLK XB530 (brochure).
FLK MS E3.   FLK XP115/2.
FLK MS E4.   FLKXV14
FLK MS E11.

Prague Transcripts, vol. x (1662–1702).
'Other Mission Box': St Anthony's Education Centre (Boksburg, 1982 & 1985).
Hoade, E., *Chinese mission memories* (typescript, Athlone, 1985, copy in FLK (China)).

Jesuit Provincial Archive, Leeson Street
John Polanco, S.J., to Richard Creagh, 2 Dec. 1565 (Germ. 106, ff 44–5 in MacErlean Papers).

Marsh's Library
MS Z3.5.3.

Poor Clare Convent, Harold's Cross
Extract from letter from Dr Concannon to Dr Troy, 25 Aug 1808, Harold's Cross Convent, Document no 11 (Photostat in NLI MS 8402).
Harold's Cross 'Annals of the Poor Clares to 1901' (NLI microfilm P3500).
Dublin, Poor Clare Convent, Harold's Cross 'Register 3' (NLI microfilm P3500).

Royal Irish Academy

MS B iv 2.	MS 23 L 19.
MS C iii 3.	MS 24 L 28.
MS C iv 1.	MS 23 M 70.
MS D i 2.	MS 23 P 6.
MS 23 I 9.	MS 23 P 7.

Trinity College Dublin

TCD MS 567.	TCD MS 883/1–2.
TCD MS 813–17.	TCD MS 1375.
TCD MS 830–17.	TCD MS 1431.

University College Dublin

UCD–OFM MS A16.	UCD–OFM MS B116.
UCD–OFM MS A34.	UCD–OFM D1.
UCD–OFM MS B64.	UCD–OFM MS D5.
UCD–OFM MSS B110–1.	

Galway
Poor Clare Convent

Chronicle of Mother Mary Bonaventure Browne (bound volume).	MS A11.
	MS A12.
Chronicle, Galway, Poor Clare Convent (second bound volume).	MS A14.
	MS A15.
(Files A, 1–18: seventeenth-century documents)	MS A18.
MS A1	(Files B, 1–16: eighteenth-century documents)
MS A2.	MS B1.
MS A3.	MS B4.
MS A4.	MS B7.
MS A6.	MS B14.
MS A7.	Unpublished inventory of ecclesiastical silver plate, prepared by R.J. Lattimore, 1997.
MS A9.	

Provincial Offive archives 'La Verna', Gormanston
Acta Definitorii Provinciae Hiberniae, 1963–1990.
Acts of the Extraordinary Provincial Chapter 1968.

Chronicle of the Province of Ireland of the Friars Minor, 24 November 1963–8 July 1985.
Proceedings of the Provincial Chapters of 1969 – 1990 with accompanying documentation.

London

British Library	Egerton MS 196.
Add. MS 4821.	Egerton MS 198.
Add. MS 19,865.	Sloane MS 3567.

National Archives (formerly Public Record Office)

PRO SP 63/60/25.	PRO SP 63/166/59.

Oxford

Bodleian Library

Carte MS 60.	Rawlinson MS C439.
Carte MS 118.	

Rome

Archives of the Conventual Franciscans
Regestis Ordinis, f. 51; H. Sbaralea, *Minoritanea Ecclesiae Synopsis*, MS C. 188.
St Isidore's College
Visitation book
Liber Discretorialis Coll. S. Isidori, 1741–1878.
Libro maestro dell intrate ed uscite del convento de S. Isidoro delli religiosi Franciscani Irlandesi a Roma, 1787–1860.

Sheffield

Sheffield Archives
Wentworth Wodehouse Muniments, Strafford Letter Books, vol. 20, no. 175.

MATERIAL (CONSTITUTIONS, NEWSLETTERS, STATUTES ETC.) RELATING TO THE FRANCISCAN ORDER. SOME WORKS ARE ANONYMOUS, IN MANUSCRIPT OR TRANSCRIPT FORM OR FOR INTERNAL CIRCULATION.

Analecta Franciscana Hibernica, Antonianum 5 (1930), pp 396–400.
Assisi.
Begley, P., *Puncta Disciplinae pro Provincia Hiberniae S. Patritii O.F.M.* (Dublin, 1899).
Carey, L., *Epistola circa instaurationem Collegii S. Isidori de Urbe ad Rev. P. Lucam Carey, O.F.M., eiusdem Collegii quondam guardianum et huius responsio* (1909).
Carmody, M., 'Pius IX and the reform of religious life: an Irish Franciscan response, 1852–54' (draft article in FLK).
Collegium S. Isidori de Urbe et S. Mariae de Plano Capranicae, FF Minorum recollectorum Hiberniae fundatio a P. Luca Waddingo; cum appendicibus in quibus de statu recenti utriusque collegii fit mentio (Rome, 1892).
Communications, 1967–1990.
Definitory news, 1981–1990.
Dillon, N., *The mirror of discipline.* (A translation of Bernard of Besse's *Mirror of religious instruction* [original in Latin]).

Franciscan news, 1988–1990.

Gannon, B., *Epistola de quibusdam abusibus eliminandis* (Cork, 1910).

General Chapter documents Madrid 1973 (Cincinnati, 1974).

Historia Missionum, I Asia centro-orientale et Oceania (Rome, 1967).

Hoade, E., *Chinese mission memories* (Athlone, 1985: typescript in FLK).

Irish Definatory News

Janknecht, G., *Memoria initii et progressus reformationis almae Provinciae Hiberniae O.S.F., 1883–1893*.

—, *Memoria initii et progressus reformationis almae Provinciae Hiberniae O.S.F., 1883–1893*.

Kazenberger, Kilian, *Liber Vitae, seu compendium expositio litteralis in sacram regulam S. P. Francisci Seraphici* (1733; Irish ed., Dublin, 1881).

Life of Saint Francis and rule of the confraternity of the cord (Limerick, 1820).

Ordinationes a visitatore et commissario generali ac definitorii Provinciae Minoriticae Hibernensis Patribus infrascriptis statutae (Dublin, 1867).

Ordinationes factae in capitulo die 24 Aug. 1908 habito quae ab omnibus observari debent.

Ordinationes et Liber Usualis P[rovinciae] Hib[erniae] S[ancti] F[rancisci] (Ennis, 1913).

Ordinationes pro Conventibus Missionariorum Pr[ovinciae] Hib[erniae] O.F.M. S[ancti] F[rancisc]i (Dublin, 1857).

Planning and renewal process, 1988.

Proceedings of the Provincial Chapter 1972.

Proceedings of the Provincial Chapter 1978.

Puncta disciplinae in choro servanda (Ennis, 1904).

Regula Bullata [Rule of 1223], iii.

Regula non Bullata, viii.

Rhodesia Franciscans 1958–1972 (Salisbury, 1972); *The Rhodesian Franciscans* (Salisbury, 1975).

Rule and general constitutions of the Franciscan brothers (Dublin, 1910).

Schematismus totius ordinis fratrum minorum (1st. ed. Assisi, 1903; 2nd ed. Assisi 1909)

Seanchas na mBráithre, 1961–1990.

Statuta Fratrum Minorum Strictioris Observantiae Provinciae Hiberniae exerata, examinata et approbata in comitis provincialis legitime celebratis Dublinii mense Novembris a.d. 1873, Adm. Rev. P. Pamphilus a Malleano commissario generale visitatione (Dublin, 1873).

Staututa Provincialia almae provinciae S. Patricii Fratrum Minorum Hiberniae, condita in capitulo provinciali eiusdem Provinciae habito Dublinii in nostro conventu ad Immaculata Conceptionem B. V. M. die 7a Augusti a.d. 1895 (Dublin, 1895).

The Franciscan Almanac (Dublin, 1930).

The Franciscan brothers of the west of Ireland – historic notes on their monastic foundations and their works (Galway, 1934).

The Franciscan Directory … in Ireland for 1882 (Dublin, 1881).

The Franciscan people.

The Seraphic Directory (Dublin, 1863).

Stewart, R.M., '*De illis qui faciunt penitentia*' – *the rule of the secular Franciscan order, origins, development, interpretation* (Rome, 1991).

van den Kerckhove, G., *Commentarii in generalia statuta Ordinis S. Francisci Minorum provinciis nationis Germano-Belgicae* (Ghent, 1700).

Vatican II, *Dogmatic constitution on the church* (*Lumen gentium*).

Vatican II, *Decree on the appropriate renewal of the religious life* (*Perfectae caritatis*).

PRINTED SOURCES
Primary printed sources are indicated by an asterisk.

Anon., 'Over half a century', *Franciscan College Annual* (1956), pp 5–15.

Anon., 'Franciscan altar plate', *Franciscan College Annual* (1952), pp 53–60.

Anon., *Sisters of St Clare: a brief history* (1985).

a Sancto Antonio, Joannes, *Bibliotheca universa franciscana* 3 vols (Matriti, 1732–3).*

Aigrain, R., *L'hagiographie, ses sources, ses méthodes, son histoire* (Paris, 1953), repr. with bibliographical supplement by R. Godding (*Subsidia hagiographica* 80, Brussels, 2000).

Anderson, A.O. & M.O. (eds and trans.), *Adomnan's life of Columba* (Edinburgh, 1961; revised ed. Oxford, 1991).*

Ariew, R., *Descartes and the last scholastics* (New York, 1999).

Bagwell, R. [revised by S. Kelsey], 'Paul King', *ODNB*, vol. 31 (2004), pp 654–5.

Bak, F., '"Scoti schola numerosior est omnibus aliis simul sumptis"', *Franciscan Studies* 16 (1956), pp 143–65.

Balič, C., 'Wadding, the Scotist' in *Father Luke Wadding commemorative volume*, pp 463–507.

—, 'The medieval controversy over the Immaculate Conception up to the death of Scotus' in E. O'Connor (ed.), *The dogma of the Immaculate Conception: history and significance* (Notre Dame, 1958), pp 161–212.

—, 'The life and work of John Duns Scotus' in J. Ryan & B. Bonansea (eds), *John Duns Scotus, 1265–1965* (Washington, DC, 1965), pp 1–28.

Barnewall, John, *Universa theologia iuxta mentem Doctoris Subtilis* (Louvain, 1620).*

Baron, Bonaventure, *Prolusiones philosophicae, logicis et physicis materiis bipartitae* (Rome, 1651).*

—, *Divus Anitius Manlius Boctius absolutus: sive De consolatione theologiae, libri quatuor* (Rome, 1653).*

—, *Orationes panegyrici sacra-prophani, nec non controversiae et stratagemata* (Rome, 1643, Lyons, 1656).*

—, *Fr. Ioannes Duns Scoti per universam philosophiam, logicam, physicam, metaphysicam, ethicam contra adversantes defensus, quaestionum novitate amplificatus*, 3 vols (Cologne, 1664; Lyons, 1668).*

—, *Fr. Joannes Duns Scotus Ordinis Minorum Doctor Subtilis per universam philosophicam, logicam, physicam, metaphysicam, ethicam, contra adversantes defensus, quaestionum novitate amplicatus, tribus tomis distinctus* […] (Cologne, 1664).*

—, *Ioannes Duns Scotus* […] *de Deo trino, contra adversantes quosque defensus* (Lyons, 1668).*

—, *Opuscula prosa et metro, argumento etiam varia*, tomus I (Wurzburg, 1668).*

—, *Opuscula prosa et metro*, tomus II (Lyons, 1669).*

—, *Ioannes Duns Scotus defensus et amplificatus de Angelis* (Florence, 1676).*

Barry, J., 'Richard Stanihurst's *De rebus in Hibernia gestis*', *Renaissance Studies* 18:1 (2004), pp 1–18.*

Bartlett, T. (ed.), *Revolutionary Dublin, 1795–1801: the letters of Francis Higgins to Dublin Castle* (Dublin, 2004).*

Begley, J., *The diocese of Limerick from 1691 to the present time* (Dublin, 1938).

Berman, D., 'Enlightenment and counter-enlightenment in Irish philosophy', *Archiv für Geschichte der Philosophie* 64 (1982), pp 148–65.

—, 'The culmination and causation of Irish philosophy', *Archiv für Geschichte der Philosophie* 64 (1982), pp 257–79.

— & A. Carpenter (eds), 'Eighteenth-century Irish philosophy' in S. Deane (ed.), *The Field Day anthology of Irish writing*, 3 vols (Derry, 1991), i, pp 760–806.

—, 'Disclaimers as offence mechanisms in Charles Blount and John Toland' in M. Hunter & D. Wooton (eds), *Atheism from the Reformation to the Enlightenment* (Oxford, 1992), pp 255–74.

Bernard, G.W., *The king's reformation: Henry VIII and the remaking of the English church* (Yale, 2005).

Bérubé, C., 'La première école scotiste' in Z. Kaluza and P. Vignaux (eds), *Preuve et raisons à l'université de Paris. Logique, ontologie et théologie au XIVe siècle* (Paris, 1984), pp 9–24.

Beschin, I., *Vita del servo di Dio P. Bernardino dal Vago da Portogruaro, ministro generale dei Frati Minori, arcivescovo titolare di Sardica (1822–1895)* 2 vols (Treviso, 1927).

Best, R.I. & H.J. Lawlor (eds), *The martyrology of Tallaght* (Henry Bradshaw Society 68, London, 1931).*

Beuchot, M., *Historia de la filosofía en el México colonial* (Barcelona, 1996).

Bhreathnach, E. & B. Cunningham, *Writing Irish history: the Four Masters and their world* (Dublin, 2007).

Bigger, F.J., 'The Franciscan friary of Killconnell in the County Galway and its ruins', *Journal of the Galway Archaeological and Historical Society* 1 (1900–1), pp 145–67; 2 (1902), pp 3–20; 3 (1903–4), pp 11–15, 167.

Bieler, L., 'Trias thaumaturga, 1647' in O Donnell, *Father John Colgan O.F.M.*, pp 41–9.

Blake, M.J., 'The abbey of Athenry', *Journal of the Galway Archaeological and Historical Society* 2 (1902), pp 65–90.

Blake, M.J., 'The obituary book of the Franciscan monastery at Galway', *Journal of the Galway Historical and Archaeological Society* 6 (1910), pp 222–35.*

Bland, D., *A history of book illustration. The illuminated manuscript and the printed book* (London, 1969).

Bossy, J., 'Catholicity and nationality in the north European Counter-Reformation' in S. Mews (ed.), *Religion and national identity: studies in church history* (Oxford, 1982), pp 285–96.

Bottin, F., 'Bartolomeo Mastri: dalla "subtilitas" scotiana all'eremeneutica "generalis"' in Forlivesi, *Rem in Seipsa Cernere. Saggi sul pensiero filosofico di Bartolomeo Mastri (1602–1673)*, pp 189–204.

Bradshaw, B., *The dissolution of the religious orders in Ireland under Henry VIII* (Cambridge, 1974).

—, 'The English reformation and identity formation in Ireland and Wales' in B. Bradshaw & P. Roberts (eds), *British consciousness and identity. The making of Britain, 1533–1707* (Cambridge, 1998), pp 43–111.

Brady, J. (ed.), 'The Irish colleges in the Low Countries', *Archivium Hibernicum* 14 (1949), pp 66–91.*

Brady, J., 'Keeping the faith at Gormanston, 1569–1929' in *Father Luke Wadding: commemorative volume* (Dublin, 1957), pp 405–13.

Brady, J. (ed.), *Catholics and catholicism in the eighteenth-century press* (Maynooth, 1965).

Brain, J.J., *St John Vianney seminary* (Pietermaritzburg, 2002).

Brash, R.R., 'The local antiquities of Buttevant', *Journal of the Royal Society of Antiquaries of Ireland* 2 (1852–3), pp 83–96.

Breatnach, P.A., 'An Irish Bollandus: Fr Hugh Ward and the Louvain hagiographical enterprise', *Éigse* 31 (1999), pp 1–30.

—, 'Repertoria manuscriptorum Collegii S. Antoni' in P.A. Breatnach et al. (eds), *The Louvain manuscript heritage* (Dublin, 2007), pp 3–20.

Brenan, M.J., *An ecclesiastical history of Ireland*, 2 vols (Dublin, 1840–64).

Brown, K.D., *The Franciscan Observants in England, 1482–1559* (University of Oxford D. Phil. thesis, 1986).

Browne, P.W., 'Talav an Eask', *Irish Ecclesiastical Record* 6 (1915), pp 126–38.

Browne, R.L. (trans.), 'History of the Franciscan order in Ireland', *The Franciscan Tertiary* 4 (1894)–9 (1899).*

Buchalter, Don M., *Hibernian specialized catalogue of the postage stamps of Ireland, 1922–1972* (Dublin, 1972).

Buckley, J.J., *Some Irish altar plate. A descriptive list of chalices and patens, dating from the fourteenth to the end of the seventeenth century, now preserved in the National Museum and in certain churches* (Dublin, 1943).

Burke, W.P., *The Irish priests in the penal times, 1660–1760. From the State Papers in H.M. Record Offices, Dublin and London, the Bodleian Library, and the British Museum* (Waterford, 1914; repr. Shannon, 1969).*

Butler, R. (ed.), *The annals of Ireland of Friar John Clyn and Thady Dowling, together with the annals of Ross* (Dublin, 1849).*

Byrne, C.J. (ed.), *Gentlemen-bishops and faction fighters. The letters of bishops O Donel, Lambert, Scallan and other Irish missionaries* (St John's, 1984).*

Bzovius, A., *Annales ecclesiastici, XIII* (Antwerp, 1617).*

—, *In quatuor libros Sententiarum* (Antwerp, 1620).*

Caball, M., *Poets and politics: continuity and reaction in Irish poetry, 1558–1625* (Cork, 1998).

—, 'Faith, culture and sovereignty: Irish nationality and its development, 1558–1625' in B. Bradshaw & P. Roberts (eds), *British consciousness and identity. The making of Britain, 1533–1707* (Cambridge, 1998), pp 112–39.

—, 'Innovation and tradition: Irish Gaelic responses to early modern conquest and colonization' in H. Morgan (ed.), *Political ideology in Ireland* (Dublin, 1999), pp 62–82.

Callaghan, John, *Vindiciarum Catholicorum Hiberniae. Auctore Philopatro Irenaeo ad Alithophylum*, vol 2 (Paris, 1650).*

Campbell, P.J., 'The Franciscan petition lists: diocese of Armagh, 1670–71', *Seanchas Ardmhacha* 15 (1992–3), pp 186–216.*

Camps, A. & P. McCloskey, *The Friars Minor in China 1294–1955, especially the years 1925–55* (Rome, 1995).

Caramuel y Lebokowitz, Juan, *Theologia moralis fundamentalis* (Lyon, 1657).*

—, *Haplotes*, in *Trismegistus theologicus*, tome III (Viglevani, 1679).*

Carey, V., '"Neither good English nor good Irish": bi-lingualism and identity formation in sixteenth-century Ireland' in H. Morgan (ed.), *Political ideology in Ireland, 1541–1641* (Dublin, 1999), pp 45–61.

Carmody, M., 'Peter Francis O'Farrell, O.F.M.' (MA thesis, James Cook University, Queensland, 1982).

—, *The Leonine Union of the order of Friars Minor 1897* (New York, 1994).

Carney, M., 'Agreement between Ó Domhnaill and Tadhg Ó Conchobhair concerning Sligo castle', *Irish Historical Studies* 3 (1942–3), pp 282–96.*

Carpenter, A. & A. Harrison (eds), 'Luke Wadding (1558–1657)' in S. Deane (ed.), *The Field Day anthology of Irish writing* (Derry, 1991), i, pp 262–3.

Carretero, E.D., 'Tradicion Immaculista agustiniana a través de Egidio de la Presentación', *La Ciudad de Dios* 66 (1954), pp 343–86.

Casey, William, *Vindicationes apologeticae Doctoris Subtilis* (n.p., 1638).*

Casway, J.I., 'Owen Roe O'Neill's return to Ireland in 1642: the diplomatic background', *Studia Hibernica* 9 (1969), pp 48–64.

—, *Owen Roe O'Neill and the struggle for Catholic Ireland* (Philadelphia, 1984).

Ceyssens, L., 'P. Patrice Duffy O.F.M., et sa mission antijanséniste', *Catholic Survey* 1 (1952), pp 228–66.

—, 'Florence Conry, Hugh de Burgo, Luke Wadding and Jansenism' in *Father Luke Wadding commemorative volume*, pp 295–404.

—, 'François Porter, franciscain irlandais à Rome (1632–1702)' in I. Villapadierna (ed.), *Miscellanea Melchor de Pobladura: studia franciscana historica P. Melchiori a Pobladura dedicata, LX aetatis annum et XXV a suscepto regimine Instituti historici O.F.* (Rome, 1964), pp 387–419.

Chadwick, O., *The Popes and European revolution* (Oxford, 1981).

Chambers, L., *Michael Moore c.1639–1726: provost of Trinity, rector of Paris* (Dublin, 2005).

Chambers, M.C.E., *The life of Mary Ward (1585–1645)* ed. H.J. Coleridge, 2 vols (London, 1882–7).

Claessens-Peré, A.M., *Silver for Sir Anthony* (Ghent & Antwerp, 1999).

Clapham, A.W., 'The architectural remains of the mendicant orders in Wales', *Archaeological Journal* 84 (1927), pp 88–103.

Clark, R., *Strangers and sojourners at Port-Royal: being an account of the connections between the British Isles and the Jansenists of France and Holland* (Cambridge, 1932; repr. 1952).

Clarke, A. with R. Dudley Edwards, 'Pacification, plantation and the Catholic question, 1603–23' in Moody, Martin & Byrne, *NHI* iii, pp 187–232.

Clarke, A., *The Old English in Ireland, 1625–42* (London, 1966; repr. Dublin, 2000).

Clarke, H. (ed.), *Dublin, part I: to 1610* (Irish Historic Towns Atlas, Dublin, 2002).

Clavin, T., 'Baron, Bartholomew', *ODNB*, vol. 4 (2004), pp 13–14.

—, 'Conry, Florence', *ODNB*, vol. 12 (2004), pp 996–8.

—, 'MacCaghwell, Hugh', *ODNB*, vol. 35 (2004), pp 82–3.

—, 'Punch, John', *ODNB*, vol. 45 (2004), pp 561–2.

Cleary, G., 'MacCaghwell (Cavellus), Hugh', *The Catholic Encyclopedia*, vol. 9 (New York, 1913), p. 484.

—, *Father Luke Wadding and St Isidore's College Rome: biographical and historical notes and documents. A contribution to the tercentenary celebrations 1625–1925* (Rome, 1925).

— (ed.), *Ireland's tribute to St Francis seven lectures on Franciscan subjects* (Dublin, 1928).

Coburn Walshe, H., 'The rebellion of William Nugent, 1581' in R.V. Comerford, M. Cullen, J.R. Hill & C. Lennon (eds), *Religion, conflict and coexistence in Ireland: essays presented to Monsignor Patrick Corish* (Dublin, 1990), pp 26–52.

Coen, M., *The wardenship of Galway* (Galway, 1984).

Cogan, A., *The diocese of Meath: ancient and modern* 3 vols (Dublin, 1862–70 repr. Dublin, 1993).

Coleman, A., 'An Irish friar and an Irish Protestant theory', *Irish Ecclesiastical Record* 20 (1906), pp 193–206.

— (ed.), 'Registrum monasterii fratrum praedicatorum de Athenry', *Archivium Hibernicum* 1 (1912), pp 201–21.*

Colgan, John, *Acta sanctorum veteris et maioris Scotiae, seu Hiberniae, sanctorum insulae … tomus primus* (Louvain, 1645; repr. Dublin, 1948).*

—, *Triadis thaumaturgae seu divorum Patricii, Columbae et Brigidae, trium veteris et maioris Scotiae seu Hiberniae, sanctorum insulae, communium patronorum acta* (Louvain, 1647; repr. Dublin, 1997).*

—, *Tractatus de Ioannis Scoti, Doctoris Subtilis theologorumque principis, vita, patria, elogiis encomiasticis, scriptis* (Antwerp, 1655).*

Comóradh i n-onóir Mhichíl Uí Chléirigh: bráthar bocht, ceann na gCeithre Máistrí (Dublin, 1944).*

Concannon, H., *The Poor Clares in Ireland, c.1629–c.1929* (Dublin, 1929).

Conlan, P., 'A short-title calendar of *Hibernia*, vol. 1 (1706–1869), in the General Archives of the Friars Minor, Rome', *Collectanea Hibernica* 18–19 (1976–7), pp 132–83.*

—, *St Anthony's College of the Irish Franciscans, Louvain: 1927–1977, 1607–1977* (Dublin, 1977).

—, 'The Franciscan friary, Killarney, 1860–1902', *Journal of the Kerry Archaeological and Historical Society* 10 (1977), pp 77–110.

—, 'A short-title calendar of material of Irish interest in five volumes in the General Archives of the Friars Minor, Rome', *Collectanea Hibernica* 20 (1978), pp 104–46 (including Australia 1 (1852–98), pp 130–46).*

—, *A true Franciscan, Br Paschal* (Gormanston, 1978).

—, 'The outlaw friars of Athlone 1916', *Journal of the Old Athlone Society* 2:5 (1978), pp 39–44.

—, 'John Benedict Daly, O.F.M.', *Journal of the Old Athlone Society* 2:5 (1978), p. 55.

—, 'A short-title calendar of *Hibernia*, vol. 2 (1870–6), in the General Archives of the Friars Minor, Rome', *Collectanea Hibernica* 21–2 (1979–80), pp 160–204.*

—, 'The Irish Franciscans in Australia in the nineteenth century: connections with the early pioneer priests', *Footprints* 4:4 (1981), pp 23–5.

—, 'The Irish Franciscans in Australia: Patrick Bonaventure Geoghegan', *Footprints* 4:5 (1981), pp 24–9; 4:7 (1982), pp 19–24.

—, *St Isidore's College Rome.* (Rome, 1982).

—, 'A short-title calendar of *Hibernia*, vol. 3 (1877–88), in the General Archives of the Friars Minor, Rome: Part 1, ff.1–400', *Collectanea Hibernica* 23 (1982), pp 86–115; 'A short-title calendar of *Hibernia*, vol. 3 (1877–88), in the General Archives of the Friars Minor, Rome: Part 1, ff. 401–809', *Collectanea Hibernica* 25 (1983), pp 178–208.*

—, 'The Irish Franciscans in Australia: Daniel MacEvey, James Platt, Nicholas Coffey', *Footprints* 4:8 (1982), pp 13–17.

—, 'The Irish Franciscans in Australia: Lawrence Bonaventure Sheil', *Footprints* 4:9 (1982), pp 17–23.

—, 'The Irish Franciscans in Australia: William Cunningham, John Cronin, Thomas Barry, Joseph Clampett, Charles Hugh Horan, Patrick Keating, Patrick O'Keeffe', *Footprints* 4:10 (1983), pp 4–11.

—, 'The Irish Franciscans in Australia: Fr Peter Francis O'Farrell, O.F.M.', *Footprints* 5:3 (1984), pp 28–36.

—, 'A short-title calendar of *Hibernia*, vol. 4 (1889–93), in the General Archives of the Friars Minor, Rome', *Collectanea Hibernica* 26 (1984), pp 95–128.*

—, *Franciscan Ennis* (Ennis, 1984).

—, 'The Irish Franciscans in Newfoundland', *The Past* 15 (1984), pp 69–76.

—, 'A short-title calendar of Irish material in the *Consultationes generales*, vols 1, 2 and 3 in the General Archives of the Friars Minor, Rome', *Collectanea Hibernica* 27–8 (1985–6), pp 189–95.*

—, 'A short-title calendar of *Hibernia* vol. 5 (1894–9), and of Irish material in *Saxonia S. Crucis*, vol. 3 (1890–1900) in the General Archives, Rome', *Collectanea Hibernica* 27–8 (1985–6), pp 196–231.*

—, 'The Irish Franciscans in Sydney', *Footprints* 6:1 (1986), pp 8–14; 6:2 (1987), pp 17–20; 6:3 (1987), pp 11–15; 6:4 (1987), pp 32–7.

—, 'Vocations to the Irish Franciscans 1800–1980', *Archivium Hibernicum* 42 (1987), pp 29–37.

—, *The Franciscans in Drogheda* (Drogheda, 1987).

—, *Franciscan Ireland* (Mullingar, 1988).

—, *The Irish Franciscans in the prefecture of Suihsien* (Athlone, 1988).

—, 'The Franciscan house in Thurles' in W. Corbett & W. Nolan (eds) *Thurles: the cathedral town. Essays in honour of Archbishop Thomas Morris* (Dublin, 1989) pp 177–86.

—, 'A short-title calendar of *Hibernia* 6 (1888–92), in the General Archives of the Friars Minor, Rome', *Collectanea Hibernica* 34–5 (1992–3), pp 190–209.*

—, 'Declaration of Emperor Joseph II on the Irish and English Franciscans and Dominicans in the Low Countries, 1782', *Collectanea Hibernica* 34–5 (1992–3), pp 116–38.*

—, 'Berkeley Hall – St Anthony's Hall – Honan Hostel (UCC)', *Journal of the Cork Historical and Archaeological Society* 100 (1995), pp 16–28.

—, *Secular Franciscans down the ages* (2nd ed. Dublin, 1996).

—, *The missionary work of the Irish Franciscans* (Dublin, 1996).

—, 'The Franciscans in Clonmel: 1269–1998', *Tipperary Historical Journal* (1999) pp 98–100.

—, 'Irish Dominican medieval architecture' in M.A. Timoney (ed.), *A celebration of Sligo: first essays for Sligo Field Club* (Sligo, 2002), pp 215–28.

—, 'The Franciscans at Buttevant', *Journal of the Cork Historical and Archaeological Society* 107 (2002), pp 195–8.

—, 'Will they ever stop fighting? – the bishop of Cork and the regulars in 1915', *Journal of the Cork Historical and Archaeological Society* (forthcoming).

Connaughton, J.M., 'Pendant reliquaries in Ireland: an overlooked tradition?' (Ph.D. thesis, Trinity College, Dublin, 2005).

Connolly, S.J. (ed.), *The Oxford companion to Irish history* (Oxford, 1998; repr. 2002).

Coombs, J., 'The possibility of created entities in seventeenth-century Scotism', *Philosophical Quarterly* 43 (1993), pp 447–59.

Corish, P.J., 'John Callaghan and the controversies among the Irish in Paris, 1648–54', *Irish Theological Quarterly* 21 (1954), pp 32–50.

— (ed.), 'Bishop Caulfield's '*Relatio status*' 1796', *Archivium Hibernicum* 28 (1966), pp 103–13.*

—, *The Irish Catholic experience. A historical survey* (Dublin, 1985; 1986 repr.).

—, 'Wadding, Luke', *ODNB*, vol. 56 (2004), pp 649–50.

—, 'Dún Mhuire: fifty years' in Millett & Lynch, *Dún Mhuire*, pp 1–7.

— & B. Millett (eds), *The Irish martyrs* (Dublin, 2005).

Cotter, F.J., *The Friars Minor in Ireland from their arrival to 1400* (New York, 1994).

Cox, L., 'The Dillons, lords of Kilkenny West: part one' *Ríocht na Mídhe* 11 (2000), pp 71–87.

Craig, M., *The architecture of Ireland. From the earliest times to 1800* (Dublin, 1982).

Cregan, D., 'The social and cultural background of a counter-reformation episcopate 1618–60' in A. Cosgrave & D. McCartney (eds), *Studies in Irish history presented to R. Dudley Edwards* (Dublin, 1979), pp 85–117.

Creighton, A., 'The Remonstrance of December 1661 and Catholic politics in restoration Ireland', *Irish Historical Studies* 34 (2004), pp 16–41.

Crowley, W., 'Gleanings of past years: our library', *Franciscan College of Agriculture, College Annual* (1985), pp 31–9.

Cullen, M., J.R. Hill & C. Lennon (eds), *Religion, conflict and coexistence in Ireland: essays presented to Monsignor Patrick Corish* (Dublin, 1990), pp 26–52.

Cunningham, B., 'Theobald Dillon: a newcomer in sixteenth-century Mayo', *Cathair na Mart: Journal of the Westport Historical Society* 6:1 (1986), pp 24–32.

—, 'The culture and ideology of Irish Franciscan historians at Louvain, 1607–1650' in C. Brady (ed.), *Ideology and the historians* (Dublin, 1991), pp 11–30.

— & R. Gillespie, '"The most adaptable of saints": the cult of St Patrick in the seventeenth century', *Archivium Hibernicum* 49 (1995), pp 82–104.

— & R. Gillespie, 'The cult of St David in Ireland before 1700' in J.R. Guy & W.G. Neely (eds), *Contrasts and comparisons: studies in Irish and Welsh church history* (Welshpool, 1999) pp 27–42.

—, *The world of Geoffrey Keating: history, myth and religion in seventeenth-century Ireland* (Dublin, 2000).

—, '"Zeal for God and for souls"': counter-reformation preaching in early seventeenth-century Ireland' in A.J. Fletcher & R. Gillespie (eds), *Irish preaching 700–1700* (Dublin, 2001), pp 108–26.

— & R. Gillespie, *Stories from Gaelic Ireland. Microhistories from the sixteenth-century Irish annals* (Dublin, 2003).

—, 'The making of the Annals of the Four Masters' (University College Dublin, PhD thesis, 2005).

—, 'Illustrations of the Passion of Christ in the *Seanchas Búrcach* manuscript' in Moss et al. (eds), *Art and devotion in late medieval Ireland*, pp 16–32.

—, '"An honour to the nation", publishing John O'Donovan's edition of the Annals of the Four Masters, 1848–56', in M. Fanning & R. Gillespie (eds), *Print culture and intellectual life in Ireland, 1660–1941* (Dublin, 2006), pp 116–42.

—, *O'Donnell histories: Donegal and the Annals of the Four Masters* (Rathmullan, 2007).

—, 'John Colgan as historian' in R. Gillespie & R. Ó hUiginn, *Ireland and Europe* (forthcoming).

Curran, O.C., *History of the diocese of Meath, 1860–1993* (Mullingar, 1995).

d'Alençon, P.E., 'Hickey, Anthony', *Dictionnaire de théologie catholique*, vol. 6 (1920), cols 2358–9.

D'Altari, M., *Aetas poenitentialis; l'antico Ordine Francescano della Penitenza* (Rome, 1993).

Dalton, J.P., 'The abbey of Kilnalahan – III', *Journal of the Galway Historical and Archaeological Society* 6 (1909–10), pp 187–221.

Dandalet, T. J., *The Spanish in Rome, 1500–1700* (Yale, 2001).

Darcy, J.D., *Fire upon the earth Bishop M.A. Fleming* (St Johns, Newfoundland, 2003).

Dawson, J.E.A., *The politics of religion in the age of Mary, Queen Of Scots: the Earl of Argyll and the struggle for Britain and Ireland* (Cambridge, 2002).

De Buck, V., 'L'archéologie irlandaise au couvent de saint Antoine de Padoue à Louvain', *Études religieuses, historiques et littéraires de la Compagnie de Jésus*, 4th ser., 3 (1869).

de Castro, M., 'Wadding and the Iberian Peninsula' in *Father Luke Wadding commemorative volume*, pp 119–70.

de Caylus, D., 'Merveilleux épanouisseement de l'école scotiste au XVIIe siècle', *Études franciscaines* 24 (1910), pp 5–12, 493–502; 25 (1911), pp 35–47, 306–17, 327–645; 26 (1911) pp 276–28.

de Clercq, J. & P. Swiggers, 'The Hibernian connection: Irish grammatcography in Louvain' in A. Ahlquist (ed.), *Diversion of Galway: papers on the history of linguistics from ICHoLS 5* (Amsterdam, 1990), pp 85–102.

de Herrera, Francisco, *Disputationes theologicae et commentaria in primum librum Sententiarum doct. Subtilis a 28 usque ad 48* (Salamanca, 1589).*

—, *In Secundum* (Salamanca, 1600).*

—, *Manuale theologicum et resolutissima dilucidatio principalium quaestionum quae communiter in quatuor libris Sententiarum disputantur* (Rome, 1607, Paris, 1616, & Venice, 1644).*

Delehaye, H. et al. (eds), *Propylaeum ad Acta Sanctorum Decembris* (Brussels, 1940).*

—, *L'œuvre des Bollandistes à travers trois siècles: 1615–1915* (Subsidia hagiographica 13a, Brussels, 1920).

de Molina, Luis, *Concordia liberi arbitrii cum gratiae donis, divina praescientia, providentia, praedestinatione et reprobatione concordia* (Lisbon, 1588).*

de Ovando, F., *Breviloquium scholasticae theologiae in quatuor libros Magistri Sententiarum* (Salamanca, 1584, Madrid, 1587).*

de Paredes, Juan Ovando, *Commentarii in tertium librum Sententiarum Ioannis* (Valencia, 1597).*

de Rada, Juan, *Controversiae theologicae inter S. Thomam et Scotam super quatuor libros Sententiarum* (Salamanca, 1586, Venice, 1601, 1604, 1617, & Cologne, 1620).*

de Sosa, Mateus, *Optata diu articulatio et illustratio libri primi Sententiarum Doctoris Subtilissimi I.D. Scoti, cum fidelissima integritate et puritate Thomae modum redactae […] nec non et controversiis, quae circa textum Scoti cum excitantur*, 2 vols (Salamanca, 1629).*

De Wulf, M., *Histoire de la philosophie médiévale* 3 vols (Paris-Louvain, 1925, 5th edition).

Di Fonzo, L., 'Sisto IV. Carriera scolastica e integrazioni biografiche (1414–1484)', *Miscellanea Francescana* 86 (1986), pp 1–491.

—, 'Il minorita inglese Giovanni Foxholes. Maestro scotista e arcivescovo (ca. 1415–1475)', *Miscellanea Francescana* 99 (1999), pp 320–46.

Di Giovanni, V., *Storia della filosofia in Sicilia dai tempi antichi al secolo XIX* (Palerme, 1872).

Dillon, C. (ed.), 'Cín lae Uí Mhealláin: friar O Meallan journal' in C. Dillon, H.A. Jefferies & W. Nolan (eds), *Tyrone: history and society* (Dublin, 2000), pp 327–402.*

Dillon, M., C. Mooney, & P. de Brún (eds), *Catalogue of Irish manuscripts in the Franciscan Library Killiney* (Dublin, 1969).

Dirks, S., *Histoire litteraire et bibliographique des Frères Mineurs de l'Obervance de St François en Belgique* (Antwerp, 1885).

Dischl, M., *Transkei for Christ. A history of the Catholic Church in the Transkeian territories* (Umtata, 1982).

Donnelly, N., *Roman Catholics. State and condition of Roman Catholic chapels in Dublin, both secular and regular, A.D. 1749* (Dublin, 1904).

—, *Short histories of Dublin parishes*, vol. 15 (Dublin, 1915).

Downey, D., 'Augustinians and Scotists. The Irish contribution to Counter-Reformation theology' in B. Bradshaw & D. Keogh (eds), *Christianity in Ireland. Revisiting the story* (Dublin, 2002), pp 96–108.

—, 'Archbishop Florence Conry of Tuam' in Duddy (ed.), *Dictionary of Irish philosophers*, pp 86–90.

Doyle, B., *The Irish contribution to the church in South Africa 1820–1900* (MA thesis, University of Pretoria, 1963; copy in FLK MS XV 14).

Doyle, J.P., 'Mastri and some Jesuits on possible and impossible objects of God's knowledge and power' in Forlivesi (ed.), *Rem in Seipsa Cernere*, pp 440–68.

Duddy, T., *A history of Irish thought* (London, 2002).

— (ed.), *Dictionary of Irish philosophers* (Bristol, 2004).

Duffy, E., *The stripping of the altars. Traditional religion in England, c.1400–1580* (New Haven & London, 1992).

Dunne, M., 'Nicholaus Vernulaeus, Aodh MacAingil and the anonymous author from the *Collegium Pastorale*', *Léachtaí Cholm Cille* 38 (2008), pp 151–71.

—, 'Hugo Cavellus (Aodh Mac Aingil, 1571–1626) on certitude' in Stone & Roegiers, *From Ireland to Louvain.*

Dunraven, C., *Memorials of Adare* (Oxford, 1865).

Duns Scotus, Johannes, *Opera omnia,* 10 vols (Lyons, 1639).*

—, *Quaestiones super libros Metaphysicorum Aristotelis*, libri I–V (*Opera philosophica*, iii) (Washington, DC, 1997).*

Eager, I.F., *The Nun of Kenmare* (Cork, 1970).

Eakin, D., *The stolen village. Baltimore and the Barbary pirates* (Dublin, 2006).

Edwards, D., *The Ormond lordship in County Kilkenny, 1515–1642: the rise and fall of the Butler family* (Dublin, 2003).

Egan, Anthony, *The Franciscan convert; or, A recantation-sermon of Anthony Egan...preached in London on April 6, 1673* (London, 1673).*

Egan, B. (ed.), 'Inventory of articles belonging to the friary of Donegal, 1698' in O Donnell, *Franciscan Donegal,* pp 113–17.*

—, *Franciscan Limerick: the order of St Franics in the city of Limerick* (Limerick, 1971).

—, 'An eminent Franciscan of the emancipation era', *Journal of the Cork Hisorical and Archaeological Society* 76 (1971), pp 21–4.

—, 'An annotated calendar of the O'Meara papers', *Archivium Franciscanum Historicum* 68 (1975), pp 78–110, 366–420.

—, *The friars of Broad Lane: the story of a Franciscan friary in Cork, 1229–1977* (Cork, 1977).

—, 'The Friars Minor and the Honan Hostel, University College, Cork', *Archivium Franciscanum Historicum* 73 (1980), pp 641–78.

—, 'A West Limerick chaplain of World War I', *Limerick Association Year Book* (1982), pp 33–7.

Etzkorn, G.J., 'John Foxal, O.F.M.: his life and writings' *Franciscan Studies* 49 (1989), pp 17–24.

Fagan, P., *Dublin's turbulent priest: Cornelius Nary, 1658–1738* (Dublin, 1991).

—, *An Irish bishop in penal times. The chequered career of Sylvester Lloyd OFM, 1680–1747* (Dublin, 1993).

— (ed.), *Ireland in the Stuart papers. Correspondence and documents of Irish interest from the Stuart papers in the Royal Archives, Windsor Castle* 2 vols (Dublin, 1996).*

Fanning, R., M. Kennedy, D. Keogh, & E. Halpin (eds), *Documents on Irish foreign policy*, vol. I, 1912–22 (Dublin, 1998).*

— (eds), *Documents on Irish foreign policy*, vol. III, 1926–32 (Dublin, 2002).

Fastiggi, R., 'Mary's Coredemption according to Francisco Suarez, S.J. (1548–1617)' in *Mary at the Foot of the Cross – IV: Mater Viventium. Acts of the Fourth International Symposium on Marian Coredemption* (New Bedford, MA, 2004), pp 338–51.

Faulkner, A., 'Thomas Magauran, O.F.M. (*c.*1640–1715)', *Breifne* 4 (1970–5), pp 87–91.

—, 'Tóruidheacht na bhfíreun air lorg Chríosda (1762): the translator', *Éigse* 15 (1973–4), pp 303–11.

—, *Liber Dubliniensis. Chapter documents of the Irish Franciscans 1719–1875* (Killiney, 1978).*

—, 'Letters of Charles Bonaventure Maguire, O.F.M. (1768–1833)', *Clogher Record* 10 (1979–81), pp 284–303; 11 (1982–3), pp 77–101; 187–213.*

Fenning, H., 'Some problems of the Irish mission, 1733–1774: documents from Roman archives', *Collectanea Hibernica* 8 (1965), pp 58–109.*

—, *The undoing of the friars of Ireland: a study of the novitiate question in the eighteenth century* (Louvain, 1972).

—, The *Irish Dominican province, 1698–1797* (Dublin, 1990).

—, 'Documents of Irish interest in the *Fondo Missioni* of the Vatican archives', *Archivium Hibernicum* 49 (1995), pp 3–47.*

—, 'Dublin imprints of Catholic interest, 1701–1739', *Collectanea Hibernica* 39–40 (1997–8), pp 106–54.*

—, 'Dublin imprints of Catholic interest, 1790–1795', *Collectanea Hibernica* 46–7 (2004–5), pp 72–141*

Fennessy, I., 'The B manuscripts in the Franciscan library, Killiney' in Millett & Lynch, *Dún Mhuire*, pp 150–215.

— (ed.), 'Printed books in St Anthony's College, Louvain, 1673', *Collectanea Hibernica* 38 (1996), pp 82–117.*

—, 'Richard Brady OFM, bishop of Kilmore, 1580–1607', *Breifne* 9 (2000), pp 225–42.

—, 'Guardians and staff of St Anthony's College, Louvain, 1607–1999', *Collectanea Hibernica* 42 (2000), pp 215–41.*

—, 'Alphabetical indexes for Irish Franciscan incunabula in Rome and Dublin', *Collectanea Hibernica* 43 (2001), pp 34–49.

—, 'An alphabetical index for some manuscripts in St Isidore's College, Rome', *Collectanea Hibernica* 43 (2001), pp 50–85.

—, 'Books listed in Wexford friary shortly before 1798', *Collectanea Hibernica* 44–5 (2002–3), pp 127–72.*

—, 'Who was Luke Wadding?', *Franciscan College Annual* 53 (2002–3), pp 23–5.

—, *Liber Killiniensis. Irish Franciscan chapter bills 1876–1999 and other lists, including a catalogue of friars on lists already published* (Killiney, 2003).*

—, 'Father Peter B. Bradley and Irish Franciscan chaplains in World Wars I and II', *The Irish Sword* 94 (2003), pp 448–61.

—, 'Browne, Valentine', *ODNB*, vol. 8 (2004), pp 221–2.

—, 'Chamberlain, Robert', *ODNB*, vol. 10 (2004), pp 958–9.

—, 'Fleming, Christopher', *ODNB*, vol. 20 (2004), pp 46–7.

—, 'Hickey, Diarmuid', *ODNB*, vol. 27 (2004), pp 13–4.

—, 'Porter, Walter', *ODNB*, vol. 44 (2004), pp 975–6.

—, 'Wadding, Luke', *ODNB*, vol. 56 (2004), pp 643–9.

—, 'Books in the Franciscan friary, Cork, in the days of the French Revolution and Jansenism', *Collectanea Hibernica* 46–7 (2004–5), pp 16–71.

—, 'Repercussions of reform – some papers concerning Brother Jarlath Prendergast, OFM, and also St Anthony's Hostel, Cork', *Collectanea Hibernica* 46–7 (2004–5) pp 275–86.*

— (ed.), 'Canon E. Reussen's list of Irish Franciscan theses in Louvain, 1620–1738', *Collectanea Hibernica* 48 (2006), pp 21–66.*

— (ed.), 'The Meelick obituary and chronicle (1623–1873)', *Archivium Hibernicum* 60 (2006–7), pp 326–435.*

Fitzgerald, J., *Sowers of the seed. Irish Franciscans in Victoria during the 19th century* (Box Hill, Victoria, 1976).

FitzPatrick, E. & C. O'Brien, *The medieval churches of County Offaly* (Dublin, 1998).

Fitzpatrick, W.J., *The life, times and correspondence of the Right Reverend Dr Doyle, bishop of Kildare.* 2 vols (Dublin, 1861).

Fitzsimon, Henry, *Catalogus praecipuorum sanctorum Hiberniae* (Liège, 1619).*

—, *A catholic confutation of M. Iohn Rider's clayme of antiquitie* (Rouen, 1608).*

Fleming, Christopher, *Meditations and prayers adapted to the stations of the holy way of the cross. With additional instructions, extracted from the sermon delivered by the late Rev. Father Fleming* (Dublin, 1795).*

—, *Sermons on different subjects, both of faith and morals* 2 vols (Dublin, 1822–3).*

Flower, R., *The Irish tradition* (Oxford, 1947).

Ford, A. & J. McCafferty (eds), *The origins of sectarianism in early modern Ireland* (Dublin, 2005).

Forlivesi. M., *Scotistarum princeps: Bartolomeo Mastri (1602–1673) e il suo tempo* (Padua, 2002).

— (ed.), *Rem in Seipsa Cernere. Saggi sul pensiero filosofico di Bartolomeo Mastri (1602–1673)* (Padua, 2006).

—, 'The nature of transcendental being and its contraction to its inferiors in the thought of Mastri and Belluto' (2006), pp 261–338.

—, '"*Ut ex etymologia nominis patet*". The nature and object of metaphysics according to John Punch' in Stone & Roegiers, *From Ireland to Louvain* (forthcoming).

Foster, J.W. (ed.), *Nature in Ireland: a scientific and cultural history* (Dublin, 1997).

Franciscan Fathers (eds), *Father Luke Wadding: commemorative volume* (Dublin, 1957).

Franchini, G., *Bibliosofia e memorie letterarie di scrittori francescani Conventuali* (Modena, 1693).

Fraser, A., *Six wives of Henry VIII* (London, 1992).

Fuhring, P., *Ornament prints in the Rijksmuseum II. The seventeenth century*, trans. J. Kilian & K. Kist, 3 vols (Rotterdam 2004).

Gairdner, J., *Letters and papers, foreign and domestic, of the reign of Henry VIII* (London, 1892; Kraus Reprints, 1965).*

García Hernán, E., 'Irish clerics in Madrid, 1598–1665' in T. O'Connor & M.A. Lyons (eds), *Irish communities in early modern Europe* (Dublin, 2006), pp 267–93.

Gerberon, Gabriel, *Histoire générale du jansénisme* 3 vols (Amsterdam, 1700).*

Giblin, C., 'Franciscan teachers in Ireland during the seventeenth and eighteenth centuries', *Franciscan College Annual* (1947), pp 35–40.

—, 'Daniel O'Connell and the Irish Franciscans', *Franciscan College Annual* (1950), pp 69–78, 80.

—, 'A seventeenth-century idea: two Franciscan provinces in Ireland', *Franciscan College Annual* (1951), pp 55–67.

—, 'The Irish mission to Scotland in the 17th century (till 1647)', *Franciscan College Annual* (1952), pp 7–24.

— (ed.), *Liber Lovanensis: a collection of Irish Franciscan documents, 1629–1717* (Dublin, 1956).*

— (ed.), 'Catalogue of material of Irish interest in the collection Nunziatura di Fiandra, Vatican archives', *Collectanea Hibernica* 1 (1958), pp 7–134; 4 (1961), pp 7–137; 5 (1962), pp 7–130; 5 (1962), 7–130; 9 (1966), pp 7–70; 13 (1970), pp 6–99; 14 (1971), pp 36–81.*

— (ed.), *Irish Franciscan mission to Scotland, 1619–1646: documents from Roman archives* (Dublin, 1964).*

—, 'The *Processus Datarie* for Denis O'Driscoll, 1640', *Collectanea Hibernia* 8 (1965), 38–42.

—, 'A list of the personnel of the Franciscan province of Ireland, 1700', *Collectanea Hibernica* 8 (1965), pp 47–57.*

—, 'Hugh MacCaghwell, O.F.M. and Scotism at St Anthony's College Louvain' in *De doctrina Ioannis Duns Scoti*, 4: *Acta congressus scotistici internationalis Oxonii et Edinburgi 11–17 sept. 1966 celebrati* 4 vols (Rome, 1968), pp 375–97.

—, 'The Franciscan ministry in the diocese of Clogher', *Clogher Record* 7 (1970), pp 149–203.

—, *Irish exiles in Catholic Europe* in P.J. Corish (ed.), *A history of Irish Catholicism*, 4:3 (Dublin, 1971).

—, 'Papers relating to Meelick friary, 1644–1731', *Collectanea Hibernica* 16 (1973), pp 48–88.*

—, 'Vatican archives: Lettere di Particolari: material relating to Ireland', *Archivium Hibernicum* 31 (1973), pp 112–23.*

—, 'Ten documents relating to Irish diocesan affairs, 1740–84, from Franciscan Library, Killiney', *Collectanea Hibernica* 20 (1978), pp 58–88.*

—, 'Papers of Richard Joachim Hayes, O.F.M., 1810–24, in Franciscan Library Killiney: Part 1, 1810–15', *Collectanea Hibernica* 21–2 (1979–80), pp 82–148.*

— (ed.), *The diocese of Raphoe (1773–1805): documents illustrating the history of the diocese from the 'Congressi' volumes in the archives of 'Propaganda Fide', Rome* (Killiney, 1980).*

—, 'The contribution of Irish Franciscans on the Continent in the seventeenth century' in M. Maher (ed.), *Irish spirituality* (Dublin, 1981), pp 88–103.

—, 'James Dixon and Jeremiah O'Flynn, two prefects apostolic in Australia', *Collectanea Hibernica* 25 (1983), pp 63–85.

—, 'Papers of Richard Joachim Hayes, O.F.M., 1810–24, in Franciscan Library Killiney: Part 4, May-Dec 1816', *Collectanea Hibernica* 25 (1983), pp 86–177.*

—, 'Hugh McCaghwell, O.F.M., archbishop of Armagh (+1626): aspects of his life', *Seanchas Ardmhacha* 11 (1983–5), pp 259–90. Reprinted in Millett & Lynch, *Dún Mhuire*, pp 63–94.

—, 'The Franciscans in Elphin', *Roscommon Historical and Archaeological Journal* 2 (1988), pp 23–9.

—, 'Papers of Richard Joachim Hayes, O.F.M., 1810–24, in Franciscan Library Killiney: Part 8, August-December 1817', *Collectanea Hibernica* 30 (1988), pp 55–119.*

Gilbert, J.T. (ed.), *A contemporary history of affairs in Ireland,* 3 vols (Dublin, 1879–80).*

—, *History of the Irish Confederation and the war in Ireland,* 7 vols (Dublin, 1882–91. repr. New York, 1973).

Gillespie, R., *Reading Ireland: print, reading and social change in early modern Ireland* (Manchester, 2005).

Gilson, E., *Jean Duns Scot. Introduction a ses positions fondamentales* (Paris, 1952).

Glanville, P., *Silver in Tudor and early Stuart England. A social history and catalogue of the national collection, 1480–1660* (London, 1990).

Gleeson, D.F. (ed.), 'The annals of Nenagh', *Analecta Hibernica* 12 (1943), pp 157–64.*

Glynn, J.A., *Life of Matt Talbot 1856–1925* (4th ed., Dublin, 1932).

Godding, R., 'Irish hagiography in the Acta sanctorum (1643–1794)', in J. Carey, M. Herbert & P. Ó Riain (eds), *Studies in Irish hagiography: saints and scholars* (Dublin, 2001), pp 289–316.

Gordon, J.F.S., *The Catholic church in Scotland from the suppression of the hierarchy to the present time: being memorabilia of the bishops, missionaries, and Scotch Jesuits* (Aberdeen, 1869).

Grajewski, M., 'John Ponce, Franciscan Scotist of the seventeenth century', *Franciscan Studies* 6 (1946), pp 54–92.

Grannell, F., *The Franciscans in Athlone* (Athlone, 1978).

Griffin, M.I.J., *History of the Rt. Rev. Dr. Michael Egan D.D.: first bishop of Philadelphia* (Philadelphia, 1893).

Grosart, A.B. (ed.), *The Lismore Papers. Autobiographical notes, remembrances and diaries of Sir Richard Boyle, first and 'great' earl of Cork* (London, 1886).*

Grose, F., *The antiquities of Ireland* 2 vols (London, 1791–7).*

Grosjean, P., 'Édition du *Catalogus Praecipuorum Sanctorum Hiberniae* de Henri Fitzsimon' in J. Ryan (ed.), *Féil-sgríbhinn Eóin Mhic Néill* (Dublin, 1940), pp 335–93.*

Guilday, P., *The English Catholic refugees on the Continent, 1558–1795* (London, 1914).

Gwynn, A., & R.N. Hadcock, *Medieval religious houses Ireland* (Dublin, 1970).

Habig, M.A., *St Francis of Assisi. Writings and early biographies,* trans. R. Brown et al. (Chicago, 1973).

Hagan, J., 'Miscellanea Vaticano-Hibernica, 1580–1631', *Archivum Hibernicum* 3 (1914), pp 227–365.*

Hall, D., *Women and the church in medieval Ireland, c.1140–1540* (Dublin, 2003).

Hammerstein, H., 'Aspects of the continental education of Irish students in the reign of Elizabeth I' in T.D. Williams (ed.), *Historical Studies* 8 (Dublin, 1971), pp 137–54.

Hanly, J. (ed.), *The letters of Oliver Plunkett, 1625–81, archbishop of Armagh and primate of all Ireland* (Dublin, 1979).*

Harbison, P., *The crucifixion in Irish art: fifty selected examples from the ninth to the twentieth century* (Dublin, 2000).

—, *Cooper's Ireland. Drawings and notes from an eighteenth century gentleman* (Dublin, 2000).

Hardiman, J., *The history of the town and county of the town of Galway. From the earliest period to the present time* (Dublin, 1820).*

Harold, Francis, *Vita fratris Lucae Waddingi* (modern editon, Rome, 1932).*

Harris, Paul, *The excommunication published by the L. archbishop of Dublin, Thomas Fleming alias Barnwall* (Dublin, 1633).*

Harrison, A., *Ag cruinniú meala. Anthony Raymond (1675–1726), ministéir Protastúnach, agus léann na Gaeilge i mBaile Átha Cliath* (Baile Átha Cliath, 1988).

Harrison, S. & D.M. Robinson, 'Cistercian cloisters in England and Wales. Part II: Gazeteer' in M. Hennig & J. McNeill (eds), *The medieval cloister in England and Wales. Journal of the British Archaeological Association* 159 (2006), pp 167–207.

Hartnett, M., *Haicéad. Translations from the Irish* (Oldcastle, Co. Meath 1993).

Harvey, J., *The perpendicular style, 1300–1485* (London, 1978).

Hayes, R., 'Priests in the independence movement of '98', *Irish Ecclesiastical Record* 66 (1945), pp 258–70.

Hazard, B., 'Political strategy in the service of religious and cultural modernization: the public career of Florence Conry, c.1560–1629' (PhD thesis NUI Maynooth, 2008), pp 115–18.

—, *Faith and patronage: Flaithrí Ó Maoil Chonaire, c.1560–1629* (forthcoming).

Heal, F., *Reformation in Britain and Ireland* (Oxford, 2003).

Heaney, C., *The theology of Florence Conry* (Drogheda, 1935).

Heist, W.W. (ed.), *Vitae sanctorum Hiberniae e codice olim Salmanticensi* (Subsidia Hagiographica 28, Brussels, 1965).*

Hennessy, W.M., *The annals of Loch Cé. A chronicle of Irish affairs from A.D. 1014 to A.D. 1590*, 2 vols (London, 1871, repr., 1939).*

Henry, G., *The Irish military community in Spanish Flanders, 1586–1621* (Dublin, 1992).

—, 'Ulster exiles in Europe, 1605–1641' in B. Mac Cuarta (ed.), *Ulster 1641. Aspects of the rising* (Belfast, 1993), pp 37–60; 195–200.

Hernmarck, C., *The art of the European silversmith 1430–1830*, 2 vols (London & New York, 1977).

HMC, *Eighth report* (London, 1881).*

HMC, *Tenth report, Appendix. Part 5. The manuscripts of the Marquis of Ormond, the earl of Fingall, the Corporations of Waterford, Galway etc* (London, 1885).*

HMC, *Report on the Franciscan manuscripts* (London, 1906).* See *Merchants' Quay Report*.

HMC, *Report on the manuscripts of R.R. Hastings* 4 vols (London 1928–47).*

Hoade, E. & C. Mooney, 'Ireland and the Holy Land', *Franciscan College Annual* (1952), pp 69–77.

Hoenen, Maarten J.F.M., 'Scotus and the Scotist school. The tradition of Scotist thought in the medieval and early modern period' in E.P. Bos (ed.), *John Duns Scotus (1265/6–1308): Renewal of Philosophy* (Amsterdam, 1998), pp 197–210.

Hoffmann, T., '*Creatura intellecta*'. Die Ideen und Possibilien bei Duns Scotus mit Ausblick auf Franz von Mayronis, Poncius und Mastrius* (Münster, 2002), pp 263–76.

Hogan, A., *Kilmallock Dominican priory: an architectural perspective, 1291–1991* (Limerick, 1991).

Hogan, E., 'Irish historical studies in the seventeenth century, III: Patrick Fleming OSF', *Irish Ecclesiastical Record*, 2nd ser., 7 (1870–1), pp 193–216.

—, *Distinguished Irishmen of the sixteenth century* (London, 1894).

—, 'Life of Father Stephen White, S.J., theologian and polyhistor', *Journal of the Waterford and south-east of Ireland Archaeological Society* 3 (1897), pp 55–71, 119–34.

Holzapfel, H., *Manuale Historiae Ordinis Fratrum Minorum* (Friburg, 1909).

Honnefelder, L., 'Scotus und der Scotismus. Ein Beitrag zur Bedeutung der Schulbildung in der mittelalterlichen Philosophie' in J.F.M. Hoenen Maarten et al. (eds), *Philosophy and learning. Universities in the Middle Ages* (Leiden, 1995), pp 249–462.

Howley, M.F., *Ecclesiastical history of Newfoundland* (Boston, 1888; repr. 1979).

Howley, R., 'Irish missionary types – II. The Right Rev. Dr. Mullock O.S.F.', *Irish Ecclesiastical Record* 10 (1889), pp 12–26.

Hughes, P., *The Catholic question, 1688–1829 – a study in political history* (London, 1929).

Hunnybun, W.M. (ed.), 'Registers of the English Poor Clares at Gravelines, including those who founded filiations at Aire, Dunkirk, and Rouen, 1608–1837', *Micellanea* 9 (Catholic Record Society Publications, 14 (1914)).*

Hunt, J., 'The Arthur cross', *Journal of the Royal Society of Antiquaries of Ireland* 85 (1955), pp 84–7.

—, *Irish medieval figure sculpture 1200–1600: a study on Irish tombs with notes on costume and armour* 2 vols (Dublin, 1974).

Hunter, R.J., 'Catholicism in Meath, *c*.1622', *Collectanea Hibernica* 14 (1971), pp 7–12.

Hyde, D., *A literary history of Ireland from earliest times to the present day* (London, 1899, revised edition, 1967).

In memoriam Mary O'Hagan, abbess and foundress of the Convent of Poor Clares, Kenmare (London, 1876).*

Irish Catholic Directory.

Iriarte de Aspurz, L., *Franciscan history: the three orders of St Francis of Assisi* (transl. P. Ross) (Chicago 1983).

Jackson, B., 'Sectarianism: division and dissent in Irish Catholicism' in A. Ford & J. McCafferty (eds), *The origins of sectarianism in early modern Ireland* (Cambridge, 2005), pp 203–15.

Janeiro, I. Vázquez, 'El arzobispo Juan de Rada y el molinismo', *Verdad y vida* 20 (1962), pp 351–96.

—, 'Fr. Francisco de Herrera, OFM, y sus votos controversia de auxiliis,' *Verdad y vida* 23 (1965), pp 271–318.

—, 'Los Juan de Ovando. Dos teologos homonimos del Siglo XVI', *Revista Española de Teologia* 38 (1978), pp 273–310.

Jansen, B., 'Zur Philosophie der Skotisten im 17. Jahrhunderts', *Franziskanische studien* 23 (1936), pp 28–58.

Jefferies, H.A., *Cork: historical perspectives* (Dublin, 2004).

Jennings, B., *The Irish Franciscan College of St Anthony at Louvain* (Dublin, 1925).

— (ed.), 'Brussels MS. 3947: Donatus Moneyus, De provincia Hiberniae S. Francisci', *Analecta Hibernica* 6 (1934), pp 12–138.*

— (ed.), 'Brevis synopsis provinciae Hiberniae FF. Minorum', *Analecta Hibernica* 6 (1934), pp 139–91.*

— (ed.), 'Documents from the archives of St Isidore's College, Rome', *Analecta Hibernica* 6 (1934), pp 203–47.*

—, *Michael O Cleirigh, chief of the Four Masters and his associates* (Dublin, 1936). Reprinted in N. Ó Muraíle (ed.), *Mícheál Ó Cléirigh, his associates and St Anthony's College, Louvain. Brendan Jennings OFM, Paul Walsh, Felim O Brien OFM and Canice Mooney OFM* (Dublin, 2008).

—, 'The religious orders in Ireland in the seventeenth century' in *Blessed Oliver Plunkett: historical studies* (Dublin, 1937), pp 75–81.

—, 'The Irish Franciscans in Prague', *Studies* 28 (1939), pp 210–22.

—, 'The chalices and books of Kilconnell Abbey', *Journal of the Galway Archaeological and Historical Society* 21 (1944–5), pp 63–70.

— (ed.), 'Miscellaneous documents – I 1588–1634', *Archivium Hibernicum* 12 (1946), pp 70–200.*

—, 'The Irish Franciscans at Boulay', *Archivium Hibernicum* 11 (1944), pp 118–53.

—, 'The abbey of St Francis, Galway', *Journal of the Galway Archaeological and Historical Society* 22 (1946), pp 101–19.

—, 'Miscellaneous documents – II 1625–1640', *Archivium Hibernicum* 14 (1949), pp 1–49.*

—, 'Irish names in the Malines ordination registers, 1602–1749', *Irish Ecclesiastical Record* 75 (1951), pp 149–62, 76 (1951), 44–8, 128–40, 222–3, 314–18, 399–408, 483–7: 77 (1952), 202–7, 366–9.

— (ed.), *Wadding Papers, 1614–38* (IMC, Dublin, 1953).*

—, 'An appeal of the Ulster Franciscans against Blessed Oliver Plunkett', *Seanchas Ardmhacha* 2 (1956), pp 114–16.*

—, 'The Irish Franciscans in Poland', *Archivium Hibernicum* 20 (1957), pp 38–56.

— (ed.), 'Some correspondence of Father Luke Wadding, O.F.M.', *Collectanea Hibernica* 2 (1959), pp 66–94.*

—, 'Sint-Truiden: Irish Franciscan documents', *Archivium Hibernicum* 25 (1962), pp 1–74.*

—, *Wild Geese in Spanish Flanders 1582–1700. Documents relating chiefly to Irish regiments, from the Archives Générales du Royaume, Brussels, and other sources* (IMC, Dublin, 1964).*

— (ed.), *Louvain papers 1606–1827* (Dublin, 1968).*

Johnstone T. & J. Hagerty, *The cross on the sword. Catholic chaplains in the forces* (London, 1966).

Kauffmann, C.M., *Biblical imagery in medieval England 700–1550* (London & Turnhout, 2003).

Keane, J.E., *Striving for the stars: a historical review of the Franciscan province of the Holy Spirit Australia-New Zealand and in Singapore* (Franciscan Archives Historical Series No. 1, Waverley, 1990).

Kearney, R. (ed.), *The Irish mind: exploring intellectual traditions* (Dublin, 1985).

—, 'John Toland: an Irish philosopher?' in P. McGuinness, A. Harrison & R. Kearney (eds), *John Toland's Christianity not mysterious: texts, associated works and critical essays* (Dublin, 1997), pp 207–22.

Kelly, C., 'Calendar of source material … Franciscan community in Australia 1879–1905', *The Provincial Chronicle of the Holy Spirit Province, Australia-New Zealand* 7 (1953), pp 1–98.*

Kelly, M. (ed.), Stephen White, *Apologia pro Hibernia adversus Cambri calumnies. Nias sive fabularum et famosorum libellorum Silvestri Giraldi Cambrensis sub vocabulis topographiae, sive de mirabilibus Hiberniae, et historiae vaticinalis, sive expugnationis eiusdem insulae … refutatio auctore Stephano Vito* (Dublin 1849).*

— (ed.), Philip O'Sullivan Beare, *Historiae Catholicae Iberniae compendium … a D. Philippo O'Sullevano Bearro, Iberno* (Dublin, 1850).*

— (ed.), John Lynch, *Cambrensis eversus* 3 vols (Dublin, 1850).*

Keogh, D., *Ireland and the Vatican. The politics and diplomacy of church-state relations, 1922–1960* (Cork, 1995).

King, H.A., 'Late medieval crosses in County Meath c.1470–1635', *Proceedings of the Royal Irish Academy* 84 (1984), pp 79–115.

Kirby, P., 'Forging links: the Irish church in Latin America' in Kirby (ed.), *Ireland and Latin America: links and lessons* (Dublin, 1992), pp 133–48.

Knebel, S., *Wille, Würfel und Wahrscheinlichkeit: Das System der moralischen Notwendigkeit in der Jesuitscholastik 1550–1700* (Hamburg, 2000).

Knowles, M.D., *Great historical enterprises* (London, 1962).

Knott, E. (ed.), 'An Irish seventeenth-century translation of the rule of St Clare', *Ériu* 15 (1948), pp 1–187.*

Kogler, T., *Das philosophisch-theologische Studium der Bayrischen Franziskaner. Ein Beitrag zur Studien und Schulgeschichte des 17. und 18 Jahrhunderts* (Munster, 1925).

Leask, H.G., *Irish churches and monastic buildings*, 3 vols (Dundalk, 1955–60).

Le Bachelet, X., 'L'Immaculée Conception', *Dictionnaire de théologie catholique* 15 vols (Paris, 1903–72), vol. 7 (1922), cols 845–1218.

Lee, E., *Sixtus IV and men of letters* (Rome, 1978).

Lennon, C., *Richard Stanihurst the Dubliner 1547–1618. A biography with a Stanihurst text on Ireland's past* (Dublin, 1981).

—, *An Irish prisoner of conscience of the Tudor era: Archbishop Richard Creagh of Armagh, 1523–86* (Dublin, 2000).

—, 'The Nugent family and the diocese of Kilmore in the sixteenth and early seventeenth centuries', *Breifne* 9 (2001), pp 360–74.

—, 'Taking sides: the emergence of Irish Catholic ideology' in V.P. Carey & U. Lotz-Heumann (eds), *Taking sides? Colonial and confessional mentalités in early modern Ireland* (Dublin, 2003), pp 78–94.

Lilly, W.S. & J. Wallis, *A manual of law specially affecting Catholics* (London, 1893).

Lloyd, S., *The Doway catechism in Irish and English. For the use of children and ignorant people* (Dublin, 1738).*

Lodge, J., *The peerage of Ireland*, revised by M. Archdall, 7 vols (London, 1789).

Lynam, E.W., *The Irish character in print 1571–1923* (Shannon, 1968).

Lyne, G., 'Rev. Daniel A. Beaufort's tour of Kerry, 1788', *Journal of the Kerry Archaeological and Historical Society* 18 (1985), pp 183–214.*

Lyons, M.A., 'Foreign language books, 1550–1700' in Gillespie & Hadfield (eds), *The Oxford history of the Irish book,* vol. 3, pp 349–67.

—, *Church and society in County Kildare c.1470–1547* (Dublin, 2000).

— & T. O'Connor, *Irish communities in early modern Europe* (Dublin, 2006).

Mac Aingil, Aodh [Cavellus], *In quatuor libros sententiarum*, 2 vols (Antwerp, 1620).*

Macalister, R.A.S. & J. MacNeill (eds), *Leabhar gabhála, the book of conquests of Ireland: the recension of Micheál Ó Cléirigh, part 1* (Dublin, 1916).*

Mac Aogáin, P. (ed.), *Graiméir ghaeilge na mBráthar Mionúr* (Dublin, 1968).*

Macardle, D., *The Irish Republic* (London, 1968 edition).

Mac Cana, P., *Collège des Irlandais Paris and Irish studies* (Dublin, 2001).

McCarthy, M., *Marsh's Library, Dublin: all graduates and gentlemen* (Dublin, 2003).

Mac Conmara, M., 'Aodh Mac Aingil (1571–1626) agus Scotachas Éireannach' in MacConmara (eag.), *An léann eaglasta in Éirinn 1200–1900* (Dublin 1988), pp 61–101.

Mac Craith, M. & D. Worthington 'Aspects of the literary activity of the Irish Franciscans in Prague, 1620–1786' in O'Connor & Lyons (eds), *Irish migrants in Europe after Kinsale*, pp 118–34.

—, 'Creideamh agus athartha: idéolaíocht agus aos léinn na Gaeilge i dtús an seachtú haois déag' in M. Ní Dhonnchadha (ed.), *Nua-léamha: gnéithe de chultúr, stair agus polaitíocht na hÉireann, c.1600–c.1900* (Dublin, 1996), pp 7–19.

—, 'The political thought of Florence Conry and Hugh MacCaughwell' in Ford & McCafferty, *The origins of sectarianism in early modern Ireland*, pp 183–202.

Mac Cuarta, B., *Catholic revival in the north of Ireland, 1603–41* (Dublin, 2007).

MacCulloch, D., *Reformation: Europe's house divided, 1490–1700* (London, 2004).

McDonnell, H., *The Wild Geese of the Antrim MacDonnells* (Dublin, 1996).

—, 'Responses of the MacDonnell clan to change in early seventeenth-century Ulster' in O'Connor & Lyons (eds), *Irish migrants in Europe after Kinsale*, pp 64–87.

McErlean, J., 'Notes on the pictorial map of Galway: the index to the map', *Journal of the Galway Archaeological and Historical Society* 4 (1905–6), pp 133–60.

MacErlean, J.C. (ed.), *Duanaire Dháibhidh Uí Bhruadair. The poems of David Ó Bruadair* (Irish Texts Society, 3 vols (London, 1910–17).*

McEvoy, J., 'Aodh MacCawell OFM and the Scotist theology of the Immaculate Conception of Mary' in Stone & Roegiers, *From Ireland to Louvain*.

MacFhinn, P., *Mílic* (Baile Átha Cliath, 1943).

Mac Giolla Comhaill, A., *Bráithrín Bocht ó Dhún* Aodh MacAingil (An Clóchomhar Teo., 1985).

K.M.G. [Kevin MacGrath], 'Multyfarnham in '98'', *Franciscan College Annual* (1948), pp 101–2.

MacGrath, K., 'John Garzia, a noted priest-catcher and his activities, 1717–23', *Irish Ecclesiastical Record* 72 (1949), pp 494–514.

—, 'Some Donegal Franciscan chalices' in O Donnell (ed.), *Franciscan Donegal,* pp 73–8.

—, 'The Irish Franciscan Library at Prague' *Franciscan College Annual* (1951), 29–33.

—, 'Sidelights on the Irish Franciscans 1798–1850', *Franciscan College Annual* (1952), pp 81–8.

McGrath, T., *Religious renewal and reform in the pastoral ministry of Bishop James Doyle of Kildare and Leighlin, 1786–1834* (Dublin, 1999).

McGuinne, D., *Irish type design. A history of printing types in the Irish character* (Dublin, 1992).

McKenna, A. et al., 'Florent Conry' in J. Lesaulnier & A. McKenna (eds), *Dictionnaire de Port Royal* (Paris, 2004), p. 293.

McKenna, J.E., *Diocese of Clogher: parochial records,* 2 vols (Enniskillen, 1920).

McKenna, L. (ed.), *Philip Bocht O Huiginn* (Dublin, 1931).*

MacLysaght, E., 'Report on documents relating to the wardenship of Galway', *Analecta Hibernica* 14 (1944), pp 1–249.*

MacNamee, J.J., *History of the diocese of Ardagh* (Dublin, 1954).

McNeill, C., 'Report on recent acquisitions in the Bodleian Library, Oxford: Rawlinson manuscripts class B', *Analecta Hibernica* 1 (1930), pp 118–78.

Mac Raghnaill, F. (eag.), *Bonabhentura Ó hhEodhasa, An Teagasg Críosduidhe* (Baile Átha Cliath, 1976).*

Mac Suibhne, P., *Paul Cullen and his contemporaries, with their letters from 1820–1902* 5 vols (Naas, 1961–77).

Mhág Craith, C. (ed.), *Dán na nBráthar Mionúr* 2 vols (Dublin, 1967–80).*

Mahoney, E.P., 'Duns Scotus and the school of Padua around 1500' in C. Bérubé (ed.), *La tradizione scotista veneto-padovana* (Padua, 1979), pp 215–27.

Maracci, H., *Biblioteca Mariana* (Rome, 1648).*

Marshall, P., 'Papist as heretic: the burning of John Forest, 1538', *Historical Journal* 41 (1998), pp 351–74.

— & A. Walsham (eds), *Angels in the early modern world* (Cambridge, 2006).

Marthalet, B.L., *The catechism yesterday and today. The evolution of a genre* (Collegeville, MN, 1995).

Martin, A.R., *Franciscan architecture in England* (Manchester, 1937).

Martin, F.X., 'The Irish friars and the Observant movement of the fifteenth century', *Proceedings of the Catholic Historical Committee* 6 (1960), pp 10–16.

Mason, Francisco, *Tractatus,* with his *Apologia pro Scoto Anglo* (Douai, 1656).*

Massari, M., 'My Irish campaign', *Catholic Bulletin* 7 (1917).

Mattingly, G., *Catherine of Aragon* (London, 1942).

Mayer, T.F. (ed.), *The correspondence of Reginald Pole: volume 2. A calendar, 1547 – 1554: a power in Rome* (Aldershot, 2003).*

Meehan, C.P., *The fate and fortunes of Hugh O'Neill, earl of Tyrone and Rory O'Donel, earl of Tyrconnel* (Dublin, 1886), ['Remonstrance by Florence Conry to the Catholic members of the Parliament held in Dublin, 1613 [Valladolid, 1614], pp 395–97.

Meek, D.E., 'The Reformation and Gaelic culture: perspectives on patronage, language and literature in John Carswell's translation of "The Book of Common Order"' in J. Kirk (ed.), *The church in the Highlands* (Edinburgh, 1998), pp 37–62.

Meersseman, G.G., *Dossier de l'Ordre de la Pénitence au xiii siécle* (Fribourg, 1961).

Messingham, Thomas, *Officia s.s. Patricii, Columbae, Brigidae, et aliorum quorundam Hiberniae sanctorum* (Paris, 1620).*

Miller, D.W., *Church, state and nation in Ireland, 1898–1921* (Dublin, 1973).

Millett, B., 'Bonaventure Baron, O.F.M., *Hibernus Clonmeliensis*' in P. O'Connell & W.C. Darmody (eds), *Siege of Clonmel commemoration: tercentenary of the siege of Clonmel souvenir record* (Clonmel, 1950), pp 41–6.

—, 'Guide to material for a biography of Father Luke Wadding' in *Father Luke Wadding commemorative volume*, pp 229–62.

—, 'Ninety candidates proposed for Irish dioceses *c.*1665', *Catholic Survey. Irish Franciscan Review* 2 (1955), pp 91–125.*

—, *The Irish Franciscans 1651–1665* (Rome, 1964).

—, 'Calendar of volume 1 of the *Scritture riferite nei congressi, Irlanda* in Propaganda archives', *Collectanea Hibernica* 6 & 7 (1963–4), pp 18–211.*

—, 'Statues of the provincial synod of Cashel, 1661', *Archivium Hibernicum* 28 (1966), pp 45–52.*

—, 'Survival and reorganization 1650–95' in P. Corish (ed.), *A history of Irish Catholicism*, vol. 3, no. 7 (Dublin, 1968), pp 1–63.

—, 'Irish Scotists at St Isidore's College, Rome, in the seventeenth century' in *De doctrina Ioannis Duns Scoti. Acta Congressus Scotistici Internationalis Oxonii et Edinburgi 11–17 sept. 1966 celebrati*, 4 vols (Rome, 1968), vol. 4, pp 399–419.

—, 'Conor O'Devany, O.F.M., and Patrick O'Loughran', in *Diocese of Dublin cause for the beatification and canonisation of the servants of God Dermot O'Hurley and companions*, ii (Rome, 1988), pp 473–571.

—, 'Irish literature in Latin, 1550–1700' in Moody, Martin & Byrne (eds), *A new history of Ireland*, iii, pp 561–86.

— & A. Lynch, *Dún Mhuire Killiney 1945–95. Léann agus seanchas* (Dublin, 1995).

—, 'The translation work of the Irish Franciscans', *Seanchas Ardmhacha* 17 (1996–7), pp 1–25.

—, 'The beatified martyrs of Ireland (1): Patrick O'Healy, O.F.M., and Conn O'Rourke, O.F.M.', *Irish Theological Quarterly* 64 (1999), pp 55–78.

—, 'The Irish Franciscans and education in late medieval times and the early Counter Reformation, 1230–1630', *Seanchas Ardmhacha* 18 (2001), pp 1–30.

— (ed.), 'Copies of some decisions from the missing discretorial registers of St Isidore's College, Rome, 1652–1739', *Collectanea Hibernica* 43 (2001), pp 86–111.*

—, 'Patrick O' Healy, O.F.M., and Conn O'Rourke, O.F.M.' in P.J. Corish & B. Millett (eds), *The Irish martyrs* (Dublin, 2005), pp 32–56.

—, 'Appendix: The historiography of the martyrs', in Corish & Millett, *The Irish martyrs*, pp 184–201.

Mitchell, M., *The man with the long hair* (Cork, 1993).

Moloney, J. (ed.), 'Brussels MS 3410: a chronological list of the foundations of the Irish Franciscan province', *Analecta Hibernica* 6 (1934), pp 192–202.*

Montague, J., 'The cloister arcade' in M. Clyne, *Kells Priory, Co. Kilkenny: archaeological excavations by T. Fanning & M. Clyne* (Dublin, 2007), pp 187–206.

Mooney, C., 'The golden age of the Irish Franciscans, 1615–50' in *Measgra*, pp 21–33.

—, 'The mirror of all Ireland: the story of the Franciscan friary of Cork, 1229–1900' in J. O'Callaghan (ed.), *Franciscan Cork* (Cork, 1949), pp 5–26, 97–100.

—, 'The Irish sword and the Franciscan cowl', *The Irish Sword* 1 (1949–53), pp 80–7.

—, 'Colgan's inquiries about Irish place-names', *Celtica* 1 (1950), pp 294–6.

—, *Irish Franciscan relations with France, 1224–1850* (Dublin, 1951).

—, 'The friars and friary of Donegal, 1474–1840' in O Donnell (ed.), *Franciscan Donegal*, pp 3–49.

—, *Devotional writings of the Irish Franciscans 1224–1950* (Killiney, 1952).

—, 'Bishop Boetius MacEgan of Elphin', *Franciscan College Annual* (1952), pp 142–5.

—, 'The founding of the friary of Donegal', *Donegal Annual* 3:1 (1954–5), pp 15–23.

—, 'Franciscan architecture in pre-reformation Ireland', *Journal of the Royal Society of Ireland* 85 (1955), pp 133–73; 86 (1956), pp 125–69; 87 (1957), pp 1–38, 103–24.

—, 'Accusations against Oliver Plunkett', *Seanchas Ardmhacha* 2 (1956–7), pp 119–40.

—, 'The writings of Father Luke Wadding, O.F.M.', *Franciscan Studies* 18 (1958), pp 225–39.

—, 'Father John Colgan, O.F.M., his work and times and literary milieu' in O Donnell (ed.), *Father John Colgan, O.F.M.*, pp 7–40.

—, *Irish Franciscans and France* (Dublin & London, 1964).

—, 'A Leitrim victim of the French Revolution', *Breifne* 2 (1964), pp 332–52.

—, *The first impact of the Reformation. A history of Irish Catholicism*, vol. 3:2 (Dublin, 1967).

—, 'St Anthony's College Louvain', *Donegal Annual* 8 (1969), pp 18–48.

—, 'Scríbhneoirí Gaeilge Oird San Froinsias' in Millett & Lynch, *Dún Mhuire* (1995), pp 37–56.

Moorman, J.R.H., *A history of the Franciscan order from its origins to the year 1517* (Oxford, 1968).

Moran, P.F., *History of the Catholic archbishops of Dublin since the reformation* (Dublin, 1864).

— (ed.), *Spicilegium Ossoriense* 3 vols (Dublin, 1874–84).*

Moriarty, C., 'A corner of memory', *Franciscan College Annual* (1949), pp 99–100.

Moss, R., C. Ó Clabaigh, & S. Ryan (eds), *Art and devotion in late medieval Ireland* (Dublin, 2006).

Murphy, I., *The diocese of Killaloe in the eighteenth century* (Dublin, 1991).

—, *The diocese of Killaloe, 1800–1850* (Dublin, 1992).

Murray, J.J., *Flanders and England. A cultural bridge. The influence of the Low Countries on Tudor-Stuart England* (Antwerp, 1985).

Murray, L.P., 'The will of James Hussey of Smarmore, Co. Louth, "Priest" (AD 1635)', *Journal of the County Louth Archaeological Society* 8:4 (1936), pp 303–21.

—, 'The Franciscan monasteries after the dissolution', *Journal of the County Louth Archaeological and Historical Society* 8:3 (1935), pp 275–82.

Murray, P., *Oracles of God. The Roman Catholic church and Irish politics, 1922–1937* (Dublin, 2000).

Neary, J., 'Maurice O'Fihelly "Flos Mundi" and his times', *Irish Ecclesiastical Record* 25 (1925), pp 176–81.

Ní Mhurchadha, M., *Early modern Dubliners* (Dublin, 2008).

Ní Mhuirgheasa, M. (eag.), *Stair an Bhíobla ó láimhsgríbhinn do sgríobh Uáitéar Ua Ceallaigh tuairm na bliadhna 1726* 4 iml (Baile Átha Cliath, 1941–5).

Noonan, P., *They're burning the churches. The final dramatic events that scuttled apartheid* (Bellvue, South Africa, 2003).

Novak, L., 'Scoti de conceptu entis doctrina a Mastrio retractata et contra Poncium propugnata' in Forlivesi, *Rem in Seipsa Cernere*, pp 237–58.

Oberman, H.A., *The dawn of the reformation. Essays in late medieval and early reformation thought* (Edinburgh, 1986), repr. 1992.

Ó hAnnracháin, T., 'Catholicism in early modern Ireland and Britain', *History Compass* 3 (2005).

O'Boyle, J., *The Irish colleges on the Continent. Their origin and history* (Dublin, 1935).

O'Brien, C., *Poor Clares, Galway, 1642–1992* (Galway, 1992).

— (ed.), *Recollections of an Irish Poor Clare in the seventeenth century: Mother Mary Bonaventure Browne, third abbess of Galway, 1647–1650* (Galway, 1993).*

O'Brien, F., 'Irish Franciscan historians of St Anthony's College, Louvain. Father Hugh Ward', *Irish Ecclesiastical Record* 32 (1928), pp 113–29.

—, 'Robert Chamberlain, O.F.M.', *Irish Ecclesiastical Record* 40 (1932), pp 264–80.

O'Brien, S. (ed.), *Poor Clare tercentenary record 1629–1929* (Galway, 1929).

— (ed.), *Measgra i gcuimhne Mhichíl Uí Chléirigh: miscellany of historical and linguistic studies in honour of Brother Michael Ó Cléirigh, OFM, chief of the Four Masters, 1643–1943* (Dublin, 1944).

—, *John McGuinness. God's civil servant* (Dublin, 1948).

Ó Buachalla, B., '*Annála Ríoghachta Éireann* agus *Foras Feasa ar Éirinn:* an comhthéacs comhaimseartha', *Studia Hibernica* 22–3 (1982–3), pp 59–105.

O'Byrne, F., 'Florence Conry, archbishop of Tuam', *Irish Rosary* 31:2 (1927), pp 845–7, 896–902; 32:1 (1928), pp 346–51, 454–60.

O'Byrne, S., *The personality of Venerable Matt Talbot (1856–1925)* (Dublin, 1999).

O'Callaghan, J., 'The Letter of Most Rev. Fr Leonard Bello, O.F.M., minister general, to the National Congress of the Franciscan Tertiaries', *Assisi* 10 (1938), pp 484–5.

—, 'The Pope and the congress', *Assisi* 10 (1938), pp 513–15.

—, 'The first national congress of Franciscan Tertiaries', *Assisi* 10 (1938), pp 595–623.

O'Callaghan, M., 'Language, nationality and cultural identity in the Irish Free State, 1922–7', *Irish Historical Studies* 24 (1984), pp 226–45.

Ó Clabaigh, C.N., 'Preaching in late medieval Ireland: the Franciscan contribution' in A.J. Fletcher & R. Gillespie (eds), *Irish preaching, 700–1700* (Dublin, 2001), pp 81–93.

—, *The Franciscans in Ireland, 1400–1534. From reform to reformation* (Dublin, 2002).

—, 'The other Christ: the cult of St Francis of Assisi in late medieval Ireland' in Moss et al. (ed.), *Art and devotion in late medieval Ireland*, pp 142–62.

—, 'Patronage, prestige and politics: the Observant Franciscans at Adare' in J. Burton & K. Stöber (eds), *Monasteries and society in the British Isles in the later Middle Ages* (Woodbridge, 2008), pp 71–82.

—, 'O'Fihily, Maurice', in Duddy (ed.), *Dictionary of Irish philosophers*, pp 263–4 and *DIB* (forthcoming).

Ó Cléirigh, T., *Aodh Mac Aingil agus an scoil Nua-Ghaedhilge i Lobháin* (Baile Átha Cliath, 1936, repr. 1985).

O'Connell, P., 'Dr. James Louis O'Donnell (1737–1811), first bishop of Newfoundland', *Irish Ecclesiastical Record* 103 (1965), pp 308–24.

O'Connell, W.D., 'Cork Franciscan Records, 1764–1831' in Seán Ó Ríordáin (ed.), *Historical and archaeological papers* (Cork, 1942).

O'Connor, D., *Lough Derg and its pilgrimages* (Dublin, 1879).

O'Connor, T. (ed.), *The Irish in Europe, 1580–1815* (Dublin, 2001).

—, '"Perfidious Machiavellian friar": Florence Conry's campaign for a Catholic restoration in Ireland, 1592–1616', *Seanchas Ardmhacha* 19 (2002), pp 91–105.

—, 'The Irish College, Rome in the age of religious renewal' in *The Irish College, Rome 1628–1678. An early manuscript account of the foundation and development of the Ludovisian College of the Irish in Rome* (Rome, 2003).

— & M.A. Lyons (eds), *Irish migrants in Europe after Kinsale, 1602–1820* (Dublin, 2003).

—, 'Religious change, 1550–1800' in Gillespie & Hadfield (eds), *The Oxford history of the Irish book, III. The Irish book in English 1550–1800* (Oxford, 2006), pp 169–93.

—, *Irish Jansenists, 1600–70. Religion and politics in Flanders, France, Ireland and Rome* (Dublin, 2008).

Ó Cuív, B., 'Flaithrí Ó Maolchonaire's catechism of Christian doctrine', *Celtica* I (1950), pp 161–206.

O'Curry, E., *Lectures on the manuscript materials of ancient Irish history* (Dublin 1861).*

O'Doherty, D.J., 'Students of the Irish College, Salamanca (1595–1619)', *Archivium Hibernicum* 2 (1913), pp 1–36; 3 (1914), pp 87–112.

Ó Doibhlin, D., 'Penal days' in H.A. Jefferies & K. Devlin (eds), *History of the diocese of Derry from earliest times* (Dublin, 2000), pp 167–86.

O Donnell, T., *Franciscan abbey of Multyfarnham* (Multyfarnham, 1951).

—, 'A Gaelic grammarian', *Franciscan College Annual* (1952), pp 159–62.

— (ed.), *Franciscan Donegal* (Ros Nuala, 1952).

— (ed.), *Father John Colgan, O.F.M., 1592–1658. Essays in commemoration of the tercentenary of his death* (Dublin, 1959).

O'Donovan, J. (ed.), *Annala rioghachta Eireann. Annals of the kingdom of Ireland by the Four Masters from earliest times to the year 1616.* 7 vols (Dublin, 1851; repr. 1990).*

O'Dwyer, P., *Mary: a history of devotion in Ireland* (Dublin, 1988).

Ó Fachtna, A. [Faulkner, A.] (ed.), *Antoin Gearnon, Parrthas an Anma* (Baile Átha Cliath, 1953).*

Ó Fiaich, T. (ed.),'From Creggan to Louvain', *Seanchas Ardmhacha* 2 (1956), pp 90–113.

—, 'The fall and return of John Mac Moyer', *Seanchas Ardmhacha* 3 (1958–9), pp 51–86.

O'Fihely, Maurice (Mauritius Hibernicus de Portu), *Epitomata castigationum, conformitatum atque elucidationum in questiones metaphysice, de primo principio tractatum, atque theoremata doctoris subtilis fratris Ioannis Duns Scoti.* This work was published for the first time as an appendix to *Ioannes Duns Scotus Questiones subtilissime in Metaphysicam* (Venice, 1497). The most recent reprint of Mauritius's work is Wadding's edition of the *Opera omnia* (Lyons, 1639) iv.*

Ó Huallacháin, M., 'Some papers of Henry Hughes, O.F.M., vicar apostolic of Gibraltar, 1839–56', *Collectanea Hibernica* 39 & 40 (1997–8), pp 210–71.*

O'Keeffe, T., *An Anglo-Norman monastery. Bridgetown Priory and the architecture of the Augustinian Canons regular in Ireland* (Cork, 1999).

Ó Lochlainn, C., *Tobar fíorghlan Gaedhilge* (Dublin, 1939).

O'Mahony, C. & C. Giblin, 'St Francis's Academy, Clonmel', *Franciscan College Annual* (1951), pp 93–6.

Ó Maoil Chonaire, F. [Conrius], *De Augustini sensu circa B. Mariae Virginis Conceptionem* (Antwerp, 1619).*

—, *Tractatus de statu parvulorum sine baptismo decedentium ex hac vita juxta sensum B. Augustini* (Louvain, 1623).*

Oman, C., *English church plate 597–1830* (London, 1957).

—, *English engraved silver 1150 to 1900* (London, 1978).

Ó Maonaigh, C. [Mooney, C.] (eag.), *Smaointe beatha Chríost* (Baile Átha Cliath, 1944).*

— (eag.), *Aodh Mac Aingil, Sgáthán Shacramuinte na hAithridhe* (Baile Átha Cliath, 1952).*

—, 'Uaidín Gaelach', *Feasta* 10:6 (1957), pp 2–4.

— (eag.), 'Agalladh Iosa agus Mhuire aige triall chum na páise, réir mar innseas Bonaventura naomhtha duinn' in Ó Maonaigh (eag.), *Seanmónta chúige Uladh* (Baile Átha Cliath, 1965), pp 29–30.*

Ó Mearáin, L., 'The apostasy of Miler MacGrath', *Clogher Record* 2 (1958), pp 244–56.

Ó Muraíle, N., 'The autograph manuscripts of the Annals of the Four Masters', *Celtica* 19 (1987), pp 75–95.

— (ed.), Paul Walsh, *Irish leaders and learning through the ages.* (Dublin, 2003).

— (ed.), *From Ráth Maoláin to Rome. Turas na dtaoiseach nUltach as Éirinn* (Rome, 2007).*

— (ed.), *Mícheál Ó Cléirigh, his associates and St Anthony's College, Louvain. Brendan Jennings OFM, Paul Walsh, Felim O Brien OFM and Canice Mooney OFM* (Dublin, 2008).

O'Neill, M., 'The medieval parish churches in county Meath', *Journal of the Royal Society of Antiquaries of Ireland* 132 (2002), pp 1–56.

—, 'Christ Church Cathedral as a blueprint for other Augustinian buildings in Ireland' in J. Bradley, A.J. Fletcher & A. Simms, *Dublin in the medieval world* (Dublin, 2009), pp 168–87.

O'Rahilly, T.F. (ed.), *Flaithrí Ó Maolchonaire, Desiderius* otherwise called *Sgáthán an chrábhaidh* (Dublin, 1955).*

O'Reilly, M. & R. Brennan, *Lives of the Irish martyrs and confessors* (New York, 1882).

O'Reilly, M., 'Seventeenth-century Irish catechisms – European or not?' *Archivium Hibernicum* 50 (1996), pp 102–12.

Ó Riain, P. (ed.), *Beatha Bharra: Saint Finbarr of Cork. The complete life* (Irish Texts Society 57; London, 1994).*

—, 'John Colgan's Trias thaumaturga' in the 1997 reprint of J. Colgan, *Triadis thaumaturgae seu divorum Patricii, Columbae et Brigidae, trium veteris et maioris Scotiae seu Hiberniae, sanctorum insulae, communium patronorum acta* (Louvain, 1647; repr. Dublin, 1997).

—, 'The *Catalogus praecipuorum sanctorum Hiberniae*, sixty years on' in A.P. Smyth (ed.), *Seanchas: studies in early and medieval Irish archaeology, history and literature in honour of Francis J. Bryne* (Dublin, 2000), pp 396–430.*

—, 'Irish hagiography of the late sixteenth and early seventeenth centuries' in S.B. Gajano & R. Michetti (eds), *Europa Sacra: raccolte agiografiche e identità politiche in Europa fra medioevo ed età moderna* (Roma, 2002), pp 45–56.

— (ed.), *Four Irish martyrologies: Drummond, Turin, Cashel, York* (Henry Bradshaw Society 115; London, 2003).*

—, *Feastdays of the saints: a history of Irish martyrologies* (Subsidia Hagiographica 86, Brussels, 2006).

Ó Riain-Raedel, D., 'Das Nekrolog der irischen Schottenklöster', *Beiträge zur Geschichte des Bistums Regensburg* 26 (1992), pp 7–119.

Oromi, B., *Los Franciscanos españoles en el Concilio de Trento* (Madrid, 1947).

Ossanna, F., 'La teologia morale e i maestri francescani conventuali' in Fr Costa (ed.), *Impegno ecclesiale dei Frati minori conventuali nella cultura ieri e oggi (1209–1997)* (Rome, 1998), pp 311–57.

Ó Súilleabháin, P. (eag.), *Rialachas San Froinsias* (Baile Átha Cliath, 1952).*

— (eag.), *Tadhg Ó Neachtain, Beatha Naoimh Antoine ó Phadua* (Cill Iníon Léinín, 1957).*

— (eag.), *Froinsias Ó Maolmhuaidh, Lucerna fidelium* (Baile Átha Cliath, 1962).*

—, 'The library of a priest of the penal days: introduction', *Collectanea Hibernica* 6–7 (1963–4), pp 234–44.

—, 'Roinnt caiticeasmaí Gaeilge', *Éigse* 11 (1964–5), pp 113–15.*

—, 'Documents relating to Wexford friary and parish, 1733–98', *Collectanea Hibernica* 8 (1965), pp 110–28.*

—, 'A celebrated eighteenth-century preacher in Dublin' *Irish Ecclesiastical Record* 106 (1966), pp 104–8.

O'Sullivan Beare, Philip, *Historiae Catholicae Iberniae compendium* (Lisbon, 1621).*

O'Sullivan, W., 'The Slane manuscript of the *Annals of the Four Masters*', *Ríocht na Mídhe* 10 (1999), pp 78–85.

'Ovando, François d'', *Dictionnaire théologie Catholique*, vol. 11 (1931), col. 1674.

Pařez J., & H. Kuchařová, *Hiberni v Praze – Éireannaigh i Prág: Dějiny františkánské koleje Neposkvrněného početí Panny Marie v Praze, 1629–1786* (Prague, 2001).

Pařez, J., 'The Irish Franciscans in seventeenth- and eighteenth-century Prague' in O'Connor & Lyons (eds), *Irish migrants in Europe after Kinsale, 1602–1820*, pp 104–17.

Pazzelli, R., *St Francis and the Third Order* (Chicago, 1991).

Pazas, M.R., 'Religiosos irelandeses de la Provincia de Santiago', *El Eco Franciscanco* 62 (1945), pp 168–211.

Pérez, A. Goyena, 'Teólogos extranjeros formados en España: D. Fr. Hugo Cavello (Mac Aingil) Francisco, Arzobispo de Armagh (1571–1626)', *Estudios eclesiásticos* 6 (1927), pp 38–53, 281–336.

Phelan, M.M., 'Irish sculpture portraying the five wounds of our Saviour' in E. Rynne (ed.), *Figures from the past: studies on figurative art in Christian Ireland in honour of Helen M. Roe* (Dun Laoghaire, 1987), pp 242–8.

Pim, H.M., *A short history of Celtic philosophy* (Dundalk, 1920).

Plummer, C. (ed.), *Miscellanea hagiographica Hibernica* (Subsidia Hagiographica 15, Brussels, 1925).*

Poppi, A., 'Il contributo dei formalisti padovani al problema delle distinzioni' in *Problemi e figure della scuola scotista del Santo* (Publicazioni della Provincia patavina dei frati minori conventuali, 5) (Padova, 1966), pp 601–790.

—, *Ricerche sulla teologia e la scienza nella Scuola padovana del Cinque e Seicento* (Venice, 2001).

Poulenc, J., 'Deux registers de religieux décédes au grand couvent de Paris au XVIIe siècle', *Archivum Franciscanum Historicum* 59 (1966), pp 323–84.

Power, P. (ed.), *A bishop of the penal times* (Cork, 1932).

Punch, John, *Scotus Hiberniae restitutus*, in his *Commentarii theologici quibus Ioannis Duns Scoti quaestiones in libros Sententiarum elucidantur et illustrantur* (Paris, 1661).*

—, *Integer cursus ad mentem Scoti*, i (*Logica*) (Rome, 1642); iii (*Libri de generatione et corruptione, meteoris, anima, parvis naturalibus, et metaphysica*) (Rome, 1643). Republished as the *Integer philosophiae cursus ad mentem Scoti, primum editius in Collegio Romano fratrum minorum Hibernorum. Nunc vero ab authore, in conventu magno Parisiensi recognitus, mendis quibus scatebat, expurgatus; Moralis insuper Philosophia, varijsque additionibus locupletatus* (Paris, 1649; Lyons, 1659, 1672).*

Quantin, J.-L., *Le Catholicisme classique et les pères de l'Église. Un retour aux sources (1669–1713)* (Paris, 1999).

Ranson, J., 'The Kilmore carols', *The Past* 5 (1949), pp 61–102.

Recio Morales, O., 'Irish émigré group strategies of survival, adaptation and integration in seventeenth- and eighteenth-century Spain' in O' Connor & Lyons (eds), *Irish communities in early modern Europe* (Dublin, 2006), pp 240–66.

Reinhold, J., 'Zum Streit um die Moralsysteme des Probabilismus bei den Sächischen Franziskanern', *Franziskanische studien* 21 (1934), pp 107–24.

Renehan, L.F., *Collections on Irish church history from the MSS of the late Laurence F. Renehan*, ed. D. McCarthy, 2 vols (Dublin, 1861–73).*

'Report on the state of popery, Ireland, 1731', *Archivium Hibernicum* 2 (1913), pp 108–56; 3 (1914), pp 124–59; 4 (1915), pp 131–77*

Reusens, E., *Documents relatifs a l'histoire de l'université de Louvain (1425–1797)*, tome v. *Collèges et pedagogies*, iii (Louvain, 1889–92).*

Richardson, John, *The great folly, superstition and idolatry of pilgrimage in Ireland* (Dublin, 1724).

Roberts D. (ed.), *Essays on the Scottish reformation 1513–1625* (Glasgow, 1962).

Robertson, J., 'Notes referring to the Archer chalice', *Journal of the Royal Society of Antiquaries of Ireland* 29 (1899), pp 28–31.

Robson, M., *The Franciscans in the Middle Ages* (Woodbridge, 2006).

Rochford, Robert, *The life of the glorious bishop S. Patrick apostle and primate of Ireland* (St Omer, 1625).*

Roe, H.M., 'Illustrations of the Holy Trinity in Ireland, 13th to 17th centuries', *Journal of the Royal Society of Antiquaries of Ireland* 109 (1979), pp 101–50.

—, 'Illustrations of the Holy Trinity in Ireland: additamenta', *Journal of the Royal Society of Antiquaries of Ireland* 110 (1980), pp 155–7.

Roest, B., *A history of Franciscan education (c.1210–1517)* (Leiden, 2000).

Rogers, P., 'The Irish Franciscan Observants and the royal supremacy', *Capuchin Annual* 6 (1935), pp 203–14.

Ronan, M.V., *The Reformation in Ireland under Elizabeth, 1558–80* (London, 1930).

—, *An apostle of catholic Dublin: Father Henry Young* (Dublin, 1944).

—, 'Priests in the independence movement, 1796–8', *Irish Ecclesiastical Record* 68 (1946), pp 95–103, 404.

Ross, A., 'Some notes on the religious orders in pre-reformation Scotland' in Roberts, *Essays on Scottish reformation*, pp 185–233.

Rosweyde, Heribert, *Martyrologium Romanum … accedit Vetus Romanum martyrologium hactenus a Cardinale Baronio desideratum, una cum martyrologio Adonis ad mss. exemplaria recensito opera et studio* (Antwerp, 1613).*

Rothe, David, *De processu martyriali quorundam fidei pugilum in Hibernia, pro complemento Sacrorum Analectorum* (Cologne, 1619).*

Rourke (Ruerk), A., *Cursus theologiae scholasticae in via venerab. P. Subt. que doct. Joannis Duns Scoti, decursus per quatuor eiusdem sententiarum libros* 6 vols (Valladolid, 1746–64).*

Russell, C.W., and J.P. Prendergast (eds), *Cal. S.P. Ire., James I, 1606–1608* (London, 1874, Kraus reprint, 1944).*

Ryan, S., 'Popular religion in Gaelic Ireland, 1445–1645', 2 vols (PhD thesis, National University of Ireland, Maynooth, 2002).

—, '"Reign of blood": aspects of devotion to the wounds of Christ in late medieval Ireland' in J. Augusteijn & M.A. Lyons (eds), *Irish history: a research yearbook* (Dublin, 2002), pp 137–49.

—, 'Bonaventura Ó hEoghusa's *An Teagasg Críosdaidhe* (1611/1614): a reassessment of its audience and use', *Archivium Hibernicum* 58 (2004), pp 259–67.

—, 'Steadfast saints or malleable models? Seventeenth-century Irish hagiography revisted', *The Catholic Historical Review* 91 (2005), pp 251–77.

—, 'From late medieval piety to Tridentine pietism? The case of seventeenth-century Ireland' in F. Van Lieburg (ed.), *Confessionalism and pietism: religious reform in early modern Europe* (Mainz, 2006), pp 51–6.

—, '"New wine in old bottles": implanting Trent in early modern Ireland' in T. Herron & M. Potterton (eds), *Ireland in the Renaissance* (Dublin, 2007), pp 122–37.

—, 'Weapons of redemption: piety, poetry and the instruments of the passion in late medieval Ireland' in H. Laugerud & L. Skinnebach (eds), *Instruments of Devotion* (Aarhus, 2007), pp 113–23.

—, 'Fixing the eschatological scales: judgment of the soul in late medieval and early modern Irish tradition' in P. Clarke & T. Claydon (eds), *The church, the afterlife and the fate of the soul. Studies in Church History* 45 (Woodbridge, 2009), pp 184–95.

Savall, D., 'La interpretacíon escotista en la provincia de Santiago. Fr. Francesco de Herrea ye el pecado de los angeles', *El Eco franciscano* 56 (1939), pp 48–59.

Scapin, P., 'Maurizio O'Fihely editore e commentatore di Duns Scoto' in A. Poppi (ed.), *Storia e cultura al Santo* (Vicenza, 1976) pp 289–301.

Scaramuzzi, D., *Il pensiero di Scoto nel Mezzogiorno d'Italia* (Rome, 1927).

—, 'La prima edizione dell'*Opera Omnia* di D. Duns Scoto (1639)', *Studi Francescani* 27 (1930), pp 381–412.

Schabel, C., *Theology at Paris, 1316–1345: Peter Auriol and the problem of divine foreknowledge and future contingents* (Aldershot, 2000).

Schiller, G., *Iconography of Christian art*, trans. J. Seligman, 2 vols (London, 1969).

Schmutz, J., 'Bulletin de scolastique moderne (I)', *Revue thomiste* 100 (2000), pp 270–341.

—, 'L'héritage des Subtils. Cartographie du Scotisme de l'âge classique', *Études Philosophiques* 57 (2002), pp 51–81.

Schneeman G., *Controversiarum de diviniae gratiae liberique arbitrii concordia initia et progressus* (Freiburg, 1881).*

Scott, G., 'The education of James III' in Edward Corp et al. (eds), *A court in exile: the Stuarts in France 1689–1718* (Cambridge, 2004).

Sebastian, W., 'The controversy after Scotus to 1900' in E. O'Connor (ed.), *The dogma of the Immaculate Conception: history and significance* (Notre Dame, 1958), pp 213–70.

Servais, D., *Histoire litteraire et bibliographique des Frères Mineurs de l'Obervance de St François en Belgique* (Antwerp, 1885).

Sharp, J., *Reapers of the harvest: the Redemptorists in Great Britain and Ireland 1843–1898* (Dublin, 1989).

Sharpe, R., *Medieval Irish saints' lives. An introduction to Vitae sanctorum Hiberniae* (Oxford, 1991).

Short, W.J., *The Franciscans* (Wilmington, 1989).

Silke, J.J., *Kinsale. The Spanish intervention in Ireland at the end of the Elizabethan wars* (New York, 1970; repr. Dublin 2000).

—, 'Irish scholarship in the Renaissance', *Studies in the Renaissance* 20 (1973), pp 169–206.

—, 'The Irish abroad, 1534–1691' in T.W. Moody, F.X. Martin & F.J. Byrne (eds), *NHI* iii, pp 587–633.

—, 'The last will of Red Hugh O'Donnell', *Studia Hibernica* 24 (1984–8), pp 51–60.

—, 'Raphoe and the reformation' in W. Nolan et al. (eds), *Donegal: history and society* (Dublin, 1995), pp 267–82.

Smeets, P.U., *Lineamenta bibliographiae Scotisticae* (Rome, 1942).

Smith, A. (ed.), 'Journey to Connaught. – April, 1709 [by Dr. Thomas Molyneux]', *The Miscellany of the Irish Archaeological Society* I (Dublin, 1846), pp 161–78.*

Sousedik, S., 'Der Streit um den wahren Sinn der scotischen Possibilienlehre' in L. Honnefelder, R.Wood & M. Dreyer (eds), *John Duns Scotus. Metaphysics and ethics* (Leiden, 1996), pp 191–204.

Spruit, L., *"Species Intelligibilis": from perception to knowledge*, 2 vols (Leiden, 1994–5).

Stalley, R., 'Irish Gothic and English fashion' in J. Lydon (ed.), *The English in medieval Ireland* (Dublin, 1984), pp 65–86.

—, *The Cistercian monasteries of Ireland. An account of the history, art and architecture of the White Monks in Ireland from 1142 to 1540* (New Haven, 1987).

—, 'Gaelic friars and Gothic design' in E. Fernie & P. Crossley (eds), *Medieval architecture and its intellectual context. Studies in honour of Peter Kidson* (London, 1990), pp 191–202.

Stanihurst, Richard, *De rebus in Hibernia gestis* (Antwerp, 1584).*

—, *De vita S. Patricii Hiberniae apostoli libri II* (Antwerp, 1587).

Steele, R. (ed.), *Tudor and Stuart Proclamations, 1485–1714*, 2 vols (Oxford, 1910), ii, Ireland.*

Steppler, F., 'A college is founded', *Franciscan College Annual* (1947), pp 93–6.

Stewart, R.M., *De illis qui faciunt penitentiam: the Rules of the secular Franciscan Order* (1991).

Stokes, W. (ed.), *The tripartite life of St Patrick with other documents relating to that saint*, 2 vols (Rolls Series 89, London, 1887).*

Stokes, W. (ed.), *Féilire Oengusso céli Dé. The martyrology of Oengus the Culdee* (Henry Bradshaw Society 29. London, 1905, repr. Dublin, 1984).*

Stone, M.W.F., 'Scholastic schools and early modern philosophy' in D. Rutherford (ed.), *The Cambridge companion to early modern philosophy* (Cambridge, 2006), pp 299–327.

—, 'Punch's riposte: the Irish contribution to early modern Scotism from Maurice O'Fihely OFM Conv. to Anthony Rourke OFM Obs.' in J. McEvoy & M. Dunne (eds), *The Irish contribution to European Scholastic thought* (Dublin, 2009), pp 137–91.

—, 'Early modern Catholic theology: scholasticism and its discontents' in S. Coakley & R. Cross (eds), *The Oxford handbook to the reception of Christian theology* (Oxford, forthcoming).

—, 'Florence Conry on the *limbus infantium*. Tradition and innovation in Early Modern Augustinianism' in M.W.F. Stone & J. Roegiers (eds), *From Ireland to Louvain: A study of the philosophical and theological achievements of the Irish Franciscans to commemorate the 400th anniversary of the foundation of the College of St Anthony of Padua* (Leuven, forthcoming).

Stradling, R.A., *The Spanish monarchy and Irish mercenaries. The Wild Geese in Spain, 1618–68* (Dublin, 1994).

Stratton, S.L., *The Immaculate Conception in Spanish art* (Cambridge, 1994).

Strieder, P., *Dürer. Paintings. Prints. Drawings* (London, 1982).

Sweeney, T., *Irish Stuart silver: a short descriptive catalogue of surviving Irish church, civic, ceremonial & domestic plate dating from the reigns of James I, Charles I, the Commonwealth, Charles II, James II, William & Mary, William III & Queen Anne, 1603–1714* (Dublin, 1995).

—, *Ireland and the printed word: a short descriptive catalogue … 1475–1700* (Dublin, 1997).*

Tait, C.,'Irish images of Jesus 1550–1650', *Church monuments* 16 (2001), pp 44–57.

—, 'Art and cult of the Virgin Mary in Ireland, *c.*1500–1660' in Moss et al. (eds), *Art and devotion in late medieval Ireland*, pp 163–83.

Teetaert, A., 'Ponce, Jean', *Dictionnaire théologie catholique*, vol. 12 (1933), cols 2546–8.

The manner of receiving the poor Sisters of St Clare to clothing: and the ceremonies of their professing in that religious order (Dublin, 1795).*

The Westmeath Independent.

Thomson, R.L. (ed.), *Foirm na n-Urrnuidheadh: John Carswell's Gaelic translation of the Book of Common Order* (Scottish Gaelic Texts Society 11. Edinburgh, 1970).*

Todd J.H., & W. Reeves (eds), *The martyrology of Donegal. A calendar of the saints of Ireland* (Irish Archaeological Society, Dublin, 1864).*

Ua Súilleabháin, S., 'Údar sgáthán an chrábhaidh', *Maynooth Review* 14 (1989), pp 42–50.

—, 'The lost has been found: the earliest surviving bilingual Irish dictionary' in J. Carey, M. Herbert & K. Murray (eds), *Cín Chille Cúile: texts, saints and places. Essays in honour of Pádraig Ó Riain* (Aberystwyth, 2004), pp 392–405.

van Os, H. (ed.), *The art of devotion in the late middle ages in Europe, 1300–1500* (London & Amsterdam, 1994).

Varesco, R., 'I Frati Minori al Concilio di Trento', *Archivum franciscanum historicum* 41 (1948), pp 88–160.

Vernulaeus, Nicholas, *Rhetoricum Collegi Porcensis inclitae academiae Lovaniensis Orationum* (Louvain, 1657).*

—, 'Oratio II Panegyricus … Domino F. Hugoni Cavello …', in *Rhetorum Collegii Porcensis inclitae Academiae Lovaniensis Orationum Pars Tertia* (Cologne, 1657), 811–27.*

Vorreaux, D. & A. Pembleton, *A short history of the Franciscan family* (Chicago, 1989).

Wadding, Luke, *Vita R.P.F. Ioannis Duns Scoti* (in *Ioannes Duns Scoti, Opera omnia*, i, cols. 1–34; later published as a self-standing tome, Mons, 1644).*

—, *Immaculatae Conceptioni B. Mariae Virginis non adversari eius mortem corporalem. Opusculum primum* (Rome, 1655).*

—, *De redemptione B. Mariae Virginis. Opusculum secundum* (Rome, 1656).*

—, *De baptismo B. Mariae Virginis. Opusculum tertium* (Rome, 1656).*

—, *Scriptores Ordinis Minorum* (Rome, 1906).*

Wall, T., 'A distinguished Irish humanist: Bonaventure Baron, O.F.M. of Clonmel (1610–96)', *Irish Ecclesiastical Record* 67 (1946), pp 92–102, 317–27.

—, 'Parnassus in Waterford (apropos of Latin proses)', *Irish Ecclesiastical Record* 69 (1947), pp 708–21.

—, 'Days of reading and a sermon to the books at Multyfarnham', *Franciscan College Annual* (1949), pp 13–21.

—, 'Some Franciscan "ex libris" from Multyfarnham library', *Franciscan College Annual* (1951), pp 83–5.

Walsh, K., *A fourteenth-century scholar and primate: Richard FitzRalph in Oxford, Avignon and Armagh* (Oxford, 1981).

Walsh, M.K., 'Irish books printed abroad, 1475–1700', *Irish Book* 2 (1963), pp 1–36.

—, 'The last years of Hugh O'Neill: Rome, 1608–16', *Irish Sword* 7 (1965–6), pp 2–14, 136–46, 327–37.

—, '*Destruction by peace'. Hugh O'Neill after Kinsale* (Armagh, 1986) (2nd edition, *An exile of Ireland. Hugh O'Neill, prince of Ulster* (Dublin, 1996)).

Walsh, P. (ed.), *Tadhg Ó Cianáin. The flight of the earls* (Dublin, 1916).

— (ed.), *Genealogiae regum et sanctorum Hiberniae, by the Four Masters* (Maynooth, 1918).*

—, *Gleanings from Irish manuscripts* (Dublin, 1933).

—, 'Travels of an Irish scholar: Michael Ó Cléirigh', *Catholic Bulletin* 27 (1937), pp 123–32.

— (ed.), *Beatha Aodha Ruaidh Uí Dhomhnaill* (Irish Texts Society, 2 vols, London, 1948–67).*

Walsh, Peter, *History and vindication of the Loyal Formulary or Irish Remonstrance* (London, 1674).*

Walsh, R., 'A list of ecclesiastics that took the oath of allegiance', *Archivium Hibernicum* 1 (1912), pp 46–76.*

—, 'A list of the regulars registered in Ireland, pursuant to the Catholic Relief Act of 1829', *Archivium Hibernicum* 3 (1914), pp 34–86.*

Walsh, T.J., *Nano Nagle and the Presentation Sisters* (Dublin, 1959).

—, *The Irish continental college movement: the colleges at Bordeaux, Toulouse and Lille* (Cork, 1974).

Werner, K., *Die Scholastik des späteren Mittelalter*, 5 vols (Vienna, 1881–7).

Westropp, T.J., 'Paintings at Adare "Abbey", Co. Limerick', *Journal of the Royal Society of Antiquaries of Ireland* 45 (1916), pp 151–2.

Whelan, K., 'The role of the Catholic priest in the 1798 rebellion in county Wexford' in K. Whelan (ed.), *Wexford: history and society. Interdisciplinary essays on the history of an Irish county* (Dublin, 1987), pp 296–315.

White, N.B., *Extents of Irish monastic possessions, 1540–1541, from manuscripts in the Public Record Office, London* (Dublin, 1943).*

Wijffels, A.A., 'Calendar of documents relating to St Anthony's College, Louvain, 1782–5, in Brussels, general archives of the realm, Privy Council, 713A', *Collectanea Hibernica* 24 (1982), pp 81–93.*

Williams, B. (ed.), *The annals of Ireland by Friar John Clyn* (Dublin, 2007).

Williams, N., *I bprionta i leabhar: na Protastúin agus prós na Gaeilge, 1567–1724* (Dublin, 1986).

Wogan, A., 'Recollections of the early days of Multyfarnham College', *Franciscan College Annual* (1948), pp 13–15.

Yates, P., *Recollect Franciscan poverty. History and legislation of a stricter observance reform* (Rome, 2005).

Young, H., 'The Catholic Directory for 1821', *Reportorium Novum* ii:2 (1959), pp 324–63.

Zegers, Jacobus (ed.), *Humilis et supplex querimonia Iacobi Zegers ... adversus libellum ... Regiae Capellae Bruxell. concionatoris, et theses PP. Societatis* (Louvain, 1641).*

— (ed.), *Sententia D. Augustini ... de gratia, lib. arbit., praedestinatione & reprobatine. Publice defensa ... Respondente F. Patricio Brinan die 9. Septembris 1627* (Louvain, 1641).*

Glossary

Capuchins A branch of the Franciscan order founded by Matteo da Basci of Urbino (d. 1552), an Observant. The rule, drawn up in 1529, urged a return to primitive simplicity. Its members wear a pointed cowl (capuche). The first Capuchin friar, Stephen Daly, came to Ireland in 1615. The Capuchins remained separate after the incorporation of various branches of the order into the Friars Minor in 1897.

Chapter A meeting of the representatives of the friars, normally superiors of communities and members of the definitory (council of the province) every three years, to discuss the state of the province, pass necessary legislation and elect superiors.

Commissary General A representative of the minister who governed a number of provinces belonging to a specific branch of the order, such as the German-Belgian nation of the Recollects to which the Irish province belonged from *c.*1630. Commissariate refers to the territory over which he rules.

Conventual A branch of the Franciscan order which followed a mitigated form of the rule allowing it to hold property in common. This branch died out in Ireland after the Reformation but has since returned in recent years.

Cordeliers A name used especially in France for members of the Observant movement because of the knotted cord they wore around their waist. The name was also used by a political faction during the French Revolution.

Council of Trent Met at Trent in Italy spanning the period 1545–63. The council, originally summoned by Pope Paul III in 1537, had three phases: 1545–7, 1551–2, 1562–3. It was both an internal reforming council and one propelled forward by the impact of Protestantism. Its spiritual, disciplinary and administrative reforms encompassed all aspects of church life from basic doctrine to the organisation and management of dioceses.

Definitory The council of friars that advises the minister general or minister provincial in the running of the order or the province.

Discreets The council of friars that advises the local superior or guardian in the running of the community.

First Order A label used to delineate one part of the Franciscan movement. The First Order consists of members of the Capuchin, Conventual and Franciscan orders who live the rule of St Francis in community and in accordance with vows of chastity, poverty and obedience. The Second Order is female and contemplative – the Poor Clares.

Friars Minor All members of the First Order are Friars Minor, though ever since the four families, Observant, Reform, Recollect and Discalced (also known as Alcantarines) were unified by Pope Leo XIII in 1897 in a single order, the title 'Order of Friars Minor' (OFM) without qualification has been reserved to this body. Franciscans were occasionally referred to as 'minorites' in the past.

Gallicanism A body of doctrine, especially strong in France, which advocated almost complete autonomy of national churches from the authority of the papacy. French Jansenists who opposed papal condemnations of their teaching were, on occasion, especial advocates of Gallican principles.

Guardian The superior of a local community of friars.

Jansenism Cornelius Jansen (1585–1638) was bishop of Ypres. A book entitled *Augustinus* was published posthumously and in his name in 1640. Five propositions in *Augustinus* pertaining to the action of divine grace were condemned as heretical by Pope Innocent X. The Jansenists, as they became known, disputed that the propositions as condemned by the Pope were those contained in the book. The controversy, which was particularly strong in France, persisted until the mid-eighteenth century. Jansenism was characterized by considerable moral rigour and is often used, incorrectly, as a synonym for puritan.

Minister General The superior of the whole order.

Minister Provincial The superior of a province of the order. Since at least the fifteenth century his term of office has normally been three years and it was only in the 1920s that it was extended to six years.

Novitiate Refers to the probationary members of a religious community who are under obedience to a superior. The term can refer to the building in which novices live or to their probationary term itself usually consisting of one to three years. At the close of probation novices take vows but are free to depart at anytime during the novitiate.

Observant Members of the Franciscan order who considered themselves adherents of the 'primitive' rule of St Francis confirmed in 1223. The movement started in Italy in the first half of the fourteenth century and was formally separated from the 'conventual' branch of the order in 1517. In Ireland, Observants were very quickly in the majority and remained so from the sixteenth century onwards.

Placet Literally means 'it pleases me (or us)'. A formula used in ecclesiastical or university assemblies to signify assent to a proposal or measure.

Pontificalia All insignia – dress, vestments, and other items – worn or used by bishops alone.

Portiuncula Refers to both the little chapel repaired by St Francis and now contained in the Basilica of St Mary of the Angels in Assisi and regarded as the cradle of the order, and the plenary indulgence granted annually on 2 August, the feast of St Mary of the Angels, in all Franciscan churches.

Province The order is divided into provinces with each one enjoying quasi-automous powers. Ireland has been a province since the thirteenth century. The seat of residence is known as the Provincialate.

Questing The seeking of alms from benefactors.

Recollect The Recollect family grew out of one of the many reforms of the order. It began in France in the sixteenth century and lasted there until the French Revolution. It survived in Belgium, Germany, England, Ireland and spread to the US.

Regulars Members of religious orders or congregations who follow a rule, and live the vows in a community.

Seculars Clergy who live outside of religious communities. This term is frequently used to denote the ordinary clergy of a diocese.

Scholastic A philosophical method that aimed at trying to understand revealed truth by applying natural reason. From the thirteenth century it was the dominant intellectual tradition for several centuries and enjoyed a revival in Catholic circles beginning in the late nineteenth century.

Scotism The intellectual system based on the writings of the Scottish Franciscan, John Duns Scotus (*c.*1265–1308). The system was accepted by the Franciscans and was enormously influential throughout the later middle ages and into the early modern period. The Irish Franciscans of the seventeenth century were particularly assiduous in promoting it urged on by the fact that they believed Scotus was Irish.

Seraphic College A Franciscan minor seminary established mainly for the purpose of training potential candidates to the order.

Third Order This embraces both lay people, formerly known as Tertiaries but now officially called Secular Franciscans, who follow a rule adapted to secular life, and regulars belonging to diverse congregations who are inspired to live the

Franciscan charism. Communities of regular Tertiaries existed in the medieval period in Ireland and, after a lapse of centuries, do so once again.

Vicar Provincial The assistant to the minister provincial. 'Custos' was also used in the past to designate the title holder.

Visitation Periodic inspection of the temporal and spiritual affairs of religious houses or of parishes by an authorised individual such as a provincial, delegate or bishop. This individual is known as a visitator or visitor.

Index

Compiled by Julitta Clancy

Numbers in **bold** type refer to illustrated plates